OUTGROWING DEMOCRACY:

A History of the United States in the Twentieth Century

Books by John Lukacs

THE GREAT POWERS AND EASTERN EUROPE

TOCQUEVILLE: THE EUROPEAN REVOLUTION AND CORRESPONDENCE WITH GOBINEAU (ED.)

A HISTORY OF THE COLD WAR

DECLINE AND RISE OF EUROPE

A NEW HISTORY OF THE COLD WAR

HISTORICAL CONSCIOUSNESS

THE PASSING OF THE MODERN AGE

THE LAST EUROPEAN WAR, 1939–1941

1945: YEAR ZERO

PHILADELPHIA: PATRICIANS AND PHILISTINES, 1900–1950

OUTGROWING DEMOCRACY: A HISTORY OF THE UNITED STATES IN THE TWENTIETH CENTURY

OUTGROWING DEMOCRACY:

A History of the United States in the Twentieth Century

by JOHN LUKACS

DOUBLEDAY & COMPANY, INC.
GARDEN CITY, NEW YORK 1984

Library of Congress Cataloging in Publication Data

Lukacs, John, 1924–
Outgrowing democracy.

Includes index.
1. United States—Civilization—20th century. 2. United States—Civilization—1865–1918. 3. United States—Politics and society—20th century. 4. United States—Politics and government—1865–1900. I. Title.
E169.1.L855 1984 973.91
ISBN 0-385-17538-8
Library of Congress Catalog Card Number 81–43553

Printed in the United States of America
First Edition

TO GEORGE F. KENNAN

"Integer vitae scelerisque purus"

CONTENTS

PART I
A HISTORY OF AMERICAN DEMOCRACY 1

1. THE SECOND CENTURY 3

2. TOCQUEVILLE REVERSED 59

PART II
A HISTORICAL INTERPRETATION 89

3. THE AUTOMOBILE CENTURY: The Material Development of American Life 91

How the Americanization of the world preceded, and how it shows every sign of succeeding, the rise and the decline of American prosperity and power.

4. THE LEAP ACROSS THE SEA: The Development of an American Nation 123

How the Americanization of millions of immigrants, which succeeded beyond all fears and expectations, consequently resulted in a, perhaps temporary, decrystallization of the national character.

5. THE BOURGEOIS INTERLUDE: The Half-Century When American Civilization Was Urban and Urbane 159

How the United States, born in the eighteenth—the central—century of the Modern Age, eventually became a nation which is neither bourgeois nor urban.

6. THE TWO EMPIRES: The Passing of the Anglo-American Age in the History of the World 201

How the United States inherited much of the British Empire at a time when the characters and the interests of the British and of the American peoples became more and more different.

7. THE ELECTIVE MONARCHY: The Degeneration of Popular Democracy to a Publicity Contest 256

How the propagation of popular democracy resulted in an American political system that is monarchical and bureaucratic at the same time.

8. MUTATIONS OF MINDS AND MORALS: The Transformations of American Thinking 289

How, contrary to the lamentations of intellectuals, vast portions of American life became intellectualized.

9. INHERITANCES AND PROSPECTS: The Passage from a Democratic Order to a Bureaucratic State 368

How and why a new science of politics, a new economics, and a new kind of history are necessary for a new world.

REFERENCES 405

ACKNOWLEDGMENTS 409

INDEX 410

PART I

A HISTORY OF AMERICAN DEMOCRACY

1

THE SECOND CENTURY

(1)

In 1876 Americans celebrated their first centennial—more precisely, the one hundredth anniversary of their Declaration of Independence. An idea current during the twentieth century is that we now live in the posthistoric age, that our fathers and grandfathers were the last generations who had an interest in history. Yet in 1876 Americans were hardly interested in history at all. What pleased and inspired them were the newest exhibits of industry. The buildings of the Centennial Exhibition in Philadelphia were filled with machinery. What pleased and inspired their imagination in 1976 was a parade of old-fashioned sailing ships. In 1976, the year of the second centennial, the interest of Americans was consumed by history—on all kinds of levels, to be sure, but by history nonetheless. Whether this interest rose from mere curiosity or from nostalgia we cannot tell. What we can see are evidences of the evolving interest of Americans in their past, all other evidences to the contrary notwithstanding, including that of the thoughtless gradual elimination of most history teaching from their schools.

This is but one example of how often public movements of ideas on the surface of a democratic nation do not correspond to movements immediately beneath. That is one of the reasons why a truthful history of a democracy—all of the vaunted "openness" of its politics and all of the openness of its archives notwithstanding—is, and will be, more difficult to write than the history of aristocratic states: a problem that Tocqueville described summarily, in forty-eight sentences comprising one of his shortest, most brilliant, profound, and overlooked chapters ("Some Characteristics of Historians in Democratic Times"), in the second volume of his *Democracy in America.*

Unlike *Democracy in America,* this book is a history. Like Tocqueville, its author is a foreigner; unlike Tocqueville, he has lived in the United States for thirty-seven years. *Democracy in America* was an interpretation of American institutions and of the democratic character. This book is an interpretation too, but an interpretation of the historical development of the second century of the nation, of a certain American period, of certain American institutions, of certain American characteristics. There is another difference. The subject of Tocqueville's book was democracy, even more than it was America. This emphasis was especially true of the second volume, which in 1840 received less critical acclaim than had the first, but which a century later read even more tellingly than the first. Tocqueville's mind was as precise as it was honest, whence the exactitude of his title: *De la Démocratie en Amérique* (About Democracy in America). He came to America because he wanted to study democracy, not the reverse. At the time of his journey, one hundred and fifty years ago, the United States was a prototype of a democratic state and of a democratic society, perhaps their sole exemplar in the world.

This condition did not prevail for long. During the second century of its existence the United States ceased to be the unique prototype of a democratic nation. Yet—another example of the often paradoxical nature of historical development—it was only during this second century that the emulation and the imitation of the United States became worldwide. With all respect due to the poetic hyperbole, the famous shot in 1775 was not heard around the world. For at least a century America was too remote, her example too extreme and perhaps even bizarre to be taken up by the politically conscious classes. The democrats and liberals of Europe were fired by the example of France, or stimulated by their admiration for England. Except for the short-lived 1848 constitution of the Second Republic in France (Tocqueville was one of its drafters) few American institutions were adopted by constitution-makers in Europe. Even in South America the ideology of French republicanism generally prevailed over the North American example. The Mother of Parliaments was the British one in Westminster, not the American Congress in Washington. A century after 1776 this began to change. It was then that the Americanization of the world began—a process that was social, cultural, political, and which goes on in full force even now. In the history of mankind the twentieth century has been the American century. Tocqueville was one of the few who one hundred and fifty years ago foresaw that the United States and Russia would become the two main powers of the world sooner or later; but even he did not foresee how American habits, institutions, and forms, ranging from American techniques to Americanized speech and manners, would be adopted, sometimes thoughtlessly but always eagerly, in the strangest places and by the strangest people all around the world, including Russians, Asians, Africans.

In 1776—indeed, for a long time thereafter—Americans believed that their Declaration of Independence was a unique fact in the history of mankind. Two centuries later we have more than one reason to disbelieve this. The federal constitution and the consequent creation of the United States was a greater achievement than was the Declaration of Independence and perhaps even than the winning of the war for independence, which the colonies could not have achieved without the help of foreign powers. The United States was established in 1789, not in 1776. In this respect alone the comparison with France is telling. The small but sturdy North American ship of state was launched at the very moment when the French began to dismantle their ancient monarchical structure. The result of that dismantling had all kinds of disastrous consequences for the French, whereas the seaworthiness of the American ship of state proved to be adequate soon after its launching, when the Atlantic storms of the last great war between the British and the French empires blew up.

Americans were the first colonial people who declared their independence from a European country, but very soon afterward that kind of achievement was no longer unique. Fifty years after 1776 most of the states in the western hemisphere were former colonial countries; two hundred years after 1776 most of the states of the world were former colonial countries, more than a hundred of them, and their numbers are still growing. All of them celebrate their declarations of independence. Few have achieved the prosperity and the lawful order which the framers of the American Constitution secured for the American nation.

The Founders foresaw that the North American Republic would be prosperous and powerful. They did not foresee—indeed, they did not wish to contemplate the prospect—that their nation would become the mightiest power in the world, involving itself in the affairs of seven seas and of six continents. Jefferson's phrase of "a decent respect for the opinions of mankind," Washington's wish to see the United States as "a respectable nation," John Adams's statement that the United States "does not go abroad in search of monsters to destroy" show their moderation and good sense. Yet the old Puritan idea of "A City Upon a Hill," illuminating the destiny of the rest of the world by its example alone, lived on in their minds. In the same speech (in Washington, on the Fourth of July, 1821) John Adams spoke of the United States as "a beacon on the summit of mountains to which all the inhabitants of the earth may turn their eyes for a genial and saving light till time shall be lost in eternity, and this globe itself dissolves, nor leave a wreck behind." There is an odd duality, something curiously unhistorical and profoundly pessimistic, within that otherwise proud and wise peroration. It suggests the end of time. If the creation of the United

States was the culmination of the history of mankind, this also means the opening of the last—and not merely the most recent—phase of the very existence of mankind, indeed, of the great globe itself. If the United States were to decline, the entire world would decline with it; and after the passing of the United States nothing would follow. Something of this sentiment was repeated by Lincoln forty years later: "The last, best hope of earth." Whether Americans still think this is a moot question, but by no means a theoretical one: for the fate of mankind indeed seems catastrophic if Americans do not liberate themselves from the thought that they *are* the last hope of earth—from the vision of an American *Götterdämmerung,* especially in the nuclear age.

Let me repeat: the generation of patriots who established the Republic did not think that it would become the greatest imperial power of the world. Many of them also thought (as Adams said in the above-cited speech) that 1776 could not be repeated. But a century later there came a change. By that time many Americans thought that 1776 could, indeed, that it must be, repeated; that the destiny of their country was more than that of being an example, that it was its destiny to extend its example through much of the world. Global American imperialism did not develop until the late 1890s but there was a subtle and profound transformation of American attitudes which led up to it. When the Chicago Columbian Exposition opened in 1893, Chauncey M. Depew gave the speech of dedication. "This day," he said, "belongs not to America but the world. . . . We celebrate the emancipation of man." The century of American world power, the American century in the history of the world, was about to begin.

The generation of the founders knew many things that we no longer know, or that we have forgotten to the extent that we know them very badly. (As the fine and tragic American poet Randall Jarrell wrote hardly more than thirty years ago, "I think that George Washington would be extremely afraid of the traffic on the Merritt Parkway, but I think that we would be afraid of George Washington.")*[1] There is, however, one important thing that we ought to know and that they could not know. This is that we are near the end of the Modern Age, of the age that began about five hundred years ago and in the very middle of which—during its century of the so-called Enlightenment, in the so-called Age of Reason—the North American Republic was born. Two hundred years ago, and for a long time afterward, this was an advantage to Americans, not a handicap.

* All numbered footnotes will be found under *References,* on pages 405ff.

Even in the beginning of the twentieth century two of the leading American historians took that as a matter of course. "It was the eighteenth century," James Harvey Robinson and Charles A. Beard wrote in 1907, "which set the problems of progress and suggested their solutions, leaving to its successor the comparatively simple task of working them out in detail and making fuller application of them." Yet we, near the end of the twentieth century, ought to recognize that the ideology of the so-called Enlightenment has proven largely outdated, that it has little to teach us. Much of the mechanical and of the educational philosophy, many of the institutions of the eighteenth century are now hopelessly antiquated, which is why so many of the institutions of the United States have become arteriosclerotic. Two hundred years after its birth the United States has been unable to avoid the degeneration of many of the vital vessels of its political and legal and administrative and educational institutions, the kind of degeneration that brought many states of Europe to their decay. In Adams's time, in Tocqueville's time, the United States was ahead of Europe—paradoxically because it was behind Europe. Bureaucratization and centralization had not yet affected its vitals, at least not during the first hundred years of its existence. During the last hundred years America and Europe became more alike; in many ways Americans caught up with the worst habits of Europeans. Within this devolution lies the portent of the dreary possibility which even Tocqueville did not state in the following terms, though he did recognize its meaning on occasion: for it is quite possible that in the history of mankind the democratic period may have been an episode, in some cases so brief as to be nearly illusory, and that the age of aristocracy is followed not by the age of democracy but by the age of bureaucracy.

This is a universal phenomenon. The danger for the American resides in the historical condition that he has fewer defenses during the passing of the Modern Age than many Europeans have. Nothing in history passes away completely. The European man, as Ortega y Gasset once wrote, "has been 'democratic,' 'liberal,' 'absolutist,' 'feudal,' but he no longer is. This does not mean . . . that he does not in some way continue being all these things; he does so in the 'form of having been them.' "[2] Most Americans, on the other hand, have been *only* democratic, their country and their society having been born in the eighteenth century—I repeat, in the middle of the Modern Age. Therein lies the danger: for the most painful and violent troubles of society are wont to occur near the end of an age, because it is then that masses of people are constrained to change their minds about essentials; and—all of the prevalent materialist conceptions of human life to the contrary—people will a thousand times more easily discard their material goods than change their essential beliefs, not to speak of their ways of thinking.

There was another matter which the founders of the United States had not foreseen. They believed in the essential possibility and in the essential virtue of a prosperous Republic; but they believed in the moderation of prosperity as they believed in the moderation of power. They did not think that "American" would become synonymous with "richest" in the eyes of the peoples of the world, nor that in the very imagination of many Americans themselves the potential of being "rich" would become a virtue, something inseparable or even identical with that of being "free." But during the second century of the Republic, at the latest after 1870, there occurred a tremendous rise in the material standards of American life, something probably unprecedented in the history of the world. Even the Depression of the early 1930s did not make a dent in this kind of progress; it merely slowed its growth for a few years. The average life expectancy of Americans, for example, increased from about forty-six to seventy-six years within a century. There were a few individual observers who had certain doubts about the benefit of this kind of progress: "Inventions and organizations," wrote Santayana around 1920, "which ought to have increased leisure, by producing the necessaries with little labour, have only increased the population, degraded labour, and diffused luxury." But after 1970 another change came about. The very material benefits of American life began to decline. This development now coincided with developments in other nations. In 1979 a remarkable book by the French Jean Fourastié, *Les trente glorieuses,* described the facts of the most astonishing increases in the material benefits of life for Frenchmen and Frenchwomen in their entire history within the thirty years from 1946 to 1975. In the United States we may speak of the *cent glorieuses,* of the hundred "glorious" years, from about 1870 to 1970. Countries such as France had begun to catch up with the United States after the Second World War. Their material progress was facilitated, at least in part, by the American example as well as by American munificence. That, as Fourastié also wrote, these thirty glorious years meant little or no intellectual and spiritual growth, that they were years of widespread moroseness and breakdowns of personal relationships among the French, is beside the point here: the point is that by 1976 France had to face *la fin des temps faciles* (the end of Easy Street), and not merely because of shortages of "energy." The subsequent rise of unemployment and of a recession were but the first signs that the period of seemingly unlimited material and economic expansion was over. This was, *mutatis mutandis,* true of the United States as well. Whether this will lead to unforeseen social, material, economic troubles is not certain.

Whether it will lead to an eventual end of inflation is even less certain. Perhaps these conditions may lead to a resurgence of an appreciation for stability and security. But in that event this must involve the recognition that the unquestioning and unquestioned pursuit of quantitative growth has become near-madness—as if growth were not only the mark of inflation but also of the most dreaded and widespread disease of the twentieth century, secreted in most cases from within the human organism, that is, of cancer. In the English of the King James Bible "increase" meant benefit, and "abundance" happiness: they did not mean quantitative growth.

Such a recognition will require a rethinking—a rethinking that will have to issue from experience—of human nature and its relationship to the universe. For here we meet a grave problem and a deep symptom of the approaching end of the Modern Age, which is the increasing insubstantialization of matter. Contrary to the now outdated nineteenth-century mode of thought (from which Darwin and Marx and Freud and even Einstein could not liberate themselves), mind is not merely the evolving result of matter; matter itself has been influenced and created by mind. From the beginning of history the influence of mind over matter has been—to be sure, unevenly—increasing. This, and the recognition thereof, is perhaps the only meaningful evolution there is: the evolution of our consciousness (of which the now badly leaking theory of Darwinism was but part), with our attendant recognition of the inevitable limitations of the human mind but also of its participation in the universe (a recognition eventually superseding not only Darwin and Marx, thinkers of the nineteenth century, but also Descartes and Newton of the seventeenth century, formulators of the mind-set of the Modern Age).

In the history of the United States (history being something quite different from "evolution") evidences of the increasing mental intrusion in the structure of events have now begun to accumulate, even though their meaning has been obscured by the vested interests of vast administrative and intellectual establishments clinging, more and more desperately, and less and less honestly, to the ideals of a "scientific" materialism. Unlike in Jefferson's time, happiness and unhappiness are now less dependent on external factors. Two hundred years ago the external material forces of nature—an ice storm or a drought or a disease due to infection—produced miseries against which we have become protected to a large extent. But an unhappy person is unhappy when he thinks he is unhappy—whether he has reasonable causes for that kind of thinking or not; and during the twentieth century this kind of unhappiness is created less and less by material conditions. His physical well-being, too, has been affected more and more by ailments which are produced from within himself, not from without—ailments that are not subject to immunization and physical prevention and which, therefore, are always to some extent psychosomatic. In 1970, unlike in 1870, most of his problems were secreted from the inside, they were not really the direct results of the outside material world, which is why he could actually *feel* nausea, depression, loneliness, or boredom either in more acute or in more complex ways than had his ancestors. On another level it is surely arguable that the increasing pollution of the material world (the "environment") has been consequence, rather than cause, of the pollution of minds: of increasing carelessness, a weakening of moral convictions, civic responsibilities, sense of community, among other things. On yet another level, the progress of biological and medical science (which is nothing but the progress of biological and medical scientists), while resulting in all kinds of benefices, including alleviations of illness and pain, also led to things such as abortion and genetic engineering, that is, to the indifferent destruction or the conscious manipulation of human matter from a refusal to admit the existence of human soul—less because of a dedication to "scientific" truth than because of a bureaucratic and professional dedication to materialism: to the avowal of a largely outdated, though professionally still predominant and profitable, idea.

Though intangible, spirit *is* a substance: and the better we recognize this, the better off we are, as we liberate ourselves from the superficially sophisticated but essentially primitive materialism of the late Modern Age. The recognition of the existence of spirit enriches our reason; but the insubstantialization of matter leads to abstraction, inflation, unreality, at times spilling over into madness. Examples of this tendency include the increasing transformation of tangible money into automatic and abstract accounting figures; the computation of non-products within the figure of the gross national product, including advertising and promotion as if they were realities of production; the mistaking of images for realities; the categorization of human characteristics, capacities, and motives through definitions; the tendency to prepare for war through abstract technological and ballistic calculations, replacing considerations of geography, history, and national character in the relations of states: in sum, the increasing preference for the abstract, a fatal tendency to which the otherwise pragmatic American people have become less and less immune.

During the twentieth century—and especially in recent decades—an American had become much less subject to his natural environment than had his ancestors one hundred years before. That central heating or hot water or automobiles or telephones made his life materially easier is obvious. Yet at the same time he had also become less self-sufficient, dependent on the services of all kinds of people when his engines or appliances broke down, and on all kinds of institutions and corporations (ranging from electric power companies to municipal offices and hospitals) over which he had little or no control. This was only partly the outcome of technology; it had even more to do with the development of a bureaucratic state, a society in which most people are employed in administration and service—that is, not materially productive—occupations. The development of such a society in itself illustrates the insubstantialization of matter, with the remoteness of real matter increasing apace with the abstractness of patterns of thought, of expressions, of communications, of all kinds of exchanges, ranging from financial transactions to language, and with the increasing (and often inhuman) impersonality of definitions, rules, and decisions affecting all kinds of things in the life of the individual.

This insubstantialization of matter is, however, but one variety—though perhaps the most deplorable and dangerous one—of the mental intrusion in the structure of events, something that may be phrased as the progressing spiritualization of matter: admittedly an ambiguous and difficult phrase. This progressing spiritualization of matter is a dual development: full of promises, full of dangers. One of its outcomes is that of nuclear energy. Since about 1925 we know (or, rather, we ought to know), mostly from Heisenberg, that the ideal of objectivity—dependent on the Cartesian separation of subject from object—has proven imperfect even in the very study of matter, where the human act of observation cannot be separated from, because it interferes with, the object. (In our mass communications we have had an increasing variety of examples of such interferences, whereby the "observers" of the "media" create the "news"; or whereby the "popularity polls" create the "popularity," and "publicity" given to "public opinion" creates "opinion.") At the same time the inventive abilities of the human mind have been able to transform matter into energy, which is what nuclear power is all about. To list its promises and its dangers is not my task here, except to say that radiation—invisible and impalpable to the senses—is also a form of the spiritualization of matter, achieved by a manipulation of materials but originating in the human spirit and with all kinds of material consequences in the end (consider only the relationships of radiation and cancer).

Allow me to cite Jakob Burckhardt's words of more than a century ago, ignorant as he was of nuclear physics but percipient of history and human nature: "The sudden change from democracy," he said, "will no longer result in the rule of an individual—but in the rule of a military corporation. And by it, methods will perhaps be used for which even the most terrible despot would not have the heart."

The spiritualization of matter thus requires a recognition, not so much of the tremendous potentialities of matter, but of the tremendous potentialities of the human mind—and therefore a conscious realization, not only of the sinful nature of man, but the already overdue necessity to rethink the entire meaning of progress.

Such themes—what the end-phase of the Modern Age means for the institutions of the United States and for the evolving character of its people; the bureaucratization of American life, the mutations of American thinking, the inflation of words and of ideas, of institutions and of money, the insubstantialization of matter with its dangers, the spiritualization of matter with its evident dangers and potential promises—are not merely the speculations of a philosophical historian. They are now undeniably evident: and to a historical description of such developments this book is devoted.

(2)

A foreigner approaching the United States in 1883, one hundred years ago, saw no skyscrapers, no Statue of Liberty. As his ship entered New York Harbor and drew near to the brown mass of houses there spread out before him a very large uniform city, "teeming with life, humming with trade, muttering with the thunder of passage": iron wharves, an immense traffic of ships going to and fro, broad-beamed barges and scows, an enormous, flattened city spread to an inland horizon so vast as to suggest an endless world beyond, a port city bigger than anything such a traveler would have seen in Europe but a recognizable city nonetheless. This did not differ much from the first impressions of someone arriving in New York in our time. There would be, too, that first impression of space: an immense pattern of uniform suburban housing spread out before the visitor during those minutes when the plane breaks out from under the clouds, and that feeling, uneasy for a European, of an unknown vastness of a world beyond. His plane would sweep down on an airport that would soon appear bigger, more crowded, more monstrous than the great modern airports of Europe or of Asia, but a recognizable airport nonetheless.

For about three generations, from about 1890 to 1955, the first impressions were different.† During the 1890s the skyline of New York began

† Lord Acton in 1853: "The city cannot be seen, for it is very flat and quite surrounded by shipping." Walt Whitman in the 1880s: ". . . the solid-planted spires tall shooting to the stars."

to acquire the first marks of its characteristic shape, in which the forms of modernity and of American energy were crystallized: a startling apparition of steel and stone, the first modern city of the world, a wondrous and electrifying phenomenon, no matter how often the traveler might have seen it in pictures. After about 1955 the experience of this first impression became rare, except for the fewer and fewer passengers who arrived by sea and for that fortunate handful in the great airplanes who, seated at the right windows, could glimpse for a moment the Manhattan skyscrapers as the plane was descending on the then greatest airport of the world, the name of which in 1955 was Idlewild.

One hundred years ago there were few foreign visitors to the United States of America. Most of the people who first glimpsed the new continent did so as immigrants. Great waves of mass immigration had begun splashing ashore. The immigrants traveled third- or fourth-class in the steamships; they were relieved that the long ocean journey was ending, while their hearts were gripped and their minds befuddled with insecurity. Even before landing they found that the severe barriers of class which had kept them apart from other passengers and other places on the ship were still in existence. They were examined and vetted on shipboard and then herded into vast iron halls before they were permitted to tread the broad stony avenues and streets of the New World. Those who had sailed first-class or cabin-class had it easier: they were inspected, too, but most of them could land without having to wait in Castle Garden or later on Ellis Island. Money spoke its own language, even in the United States of America. But money was there to be made, in different ways than in the Old World.

Two hundred years ago the very word "America" may have been unknown to the majority of the peoples of the earth. One hundred years ago the image of the New World had spread over Europe, Russia, and the Far East; it was recognizable to millions for the first time in the history of mankind. A letter would come from America, or about America—a letter from a relative or from an agent of a shipping company to people who had never before received a letter from abroad. Many of these recipients were of the first generation in their families who could read. They would on occasion read more than letters about America: books, fairy tales, adventure stories, newspaper articles. One hundred years ago most of this suddenly increased literature about the United States was composed on the popular level. There was, as yet, no increase in the quantity of serious literature, political or travel books about America. Hack journalists and adventure writers, many of whom had never been in America, wrote most of the literature about the United States. They were read avidly by all kinds of people, among them the young Adolf Hitler. In the 1880s hacks concocted American wonder tales for their newspapers in many European cities, cock-and-bull stories for the most part.

There was an interesting condition of this kind of literature and of the image it produced (or, rather, of the image to which it corresponded). It was the image of a world that was interesting and desirable, for it was both ahead of and behind Europe. The United States was a world of great wealth and great machines; but it was also a world of bountiful land, on the edges of which lived herds of wild animals and Indians, a land of opportunities and of a spaciousness that had vanished in Europe long before: for it was in Europe, where the cramped living space and the constrictions of bureaucracy, where the decrease of land and the increase of government made life more complicated and difficult. This combination of elements of a promising future and of an idyllic past is recognizable in the image of the United States one hundred years ago. Apart from the masses of immigrants, a few adventurous Europeans who came to the United States—they had to be rich, since travel to and in the United States was very dear—were enchanted less with the steam-heated and electric hotels of Fifth Avenue in New York than with the hunting life of the American West, with its peculiar combination of wildness and comfort. It was something out of past centuries, this nomadic and virile life, only a few days' travel away from the railroads and electricity. That there was a dark side of this world they did not know, except for a few among them who chose to stay and were then swallowed up by the deeper currents of the American mainstream in which they had to learn to swim anew. The "Far West" and the "Wild West" had become household words in the Old World. For Americans the West was the frontier, for Englishmen and for Europeans it was a mountainous garden of their imagination. One hundred years ago much of the West was in that wondrous, half-mystic phase when the marriage of civilization to virgin land had just occurred: English and European travelers were enraptured by the virginal beauty of the landscape, describing it in flowery terms, looking forward to its settlement, in which prospect they saw nothing but good, all of the amusing roughness of American pioneer manners notwithstanding. In that passing prospect there was no room for dust storms or for trolley lines—or for the American inclination to maintain an image of the West as forever fresh, manly, and wild.

While the immigrants were crowding into the swelling cities of America, the American physical presence in the world increased. The American sewing-machine became a standard presence in millions of homes in Russia, England, Austria-Hungary, Italy, Japan; soon the American typewriter and the American telephone would follow. In the 1880s the Americanization of the world began in earnest. We know something about how people in the Old World, from Birmingham manufacturers to Russian Jews, responded to this. About Japan and China we know less. But the image was there, too: after about 1870 unsung hundreds of thousands of their peoples chose to allow themselves to be transported across the Pacific, in conditions of foulness and mortal danger that were even worse than those of the Irish ship-bottom people a generation before. In the 1880s that oriental stream was reduced. The elected representatives of the American people passed the first law to restrict immigration, the Oriental Exclusion Act. They did so in the same year that the first boatloads of Russian Jews bumped against the pilings of the piers of Philadelphia, Boston, and New York. The native people of the United States were beginning to recognize that space in their country was not unbounded and endless, that there was not room for everyone in what they still thought was the New World.

The people of the United States: how to describe them? I began with a description of the New World through the eyes of foreign visitors and immigrants because this is something I know about; but this is a rhetorical device, too, postponing the difficult task that immediately rises ahead, the description of a people in this vast country one hundred years ago. This is more difficult than to describe the state of England or of the German people at that time, in spite of the then fast-increasing standardization of American life, because of the vastness of the country, including places where groups of people lived lives wholly different from the rest: Cajuns in Louisiana, recently freed Negroes in the South, Scandinavian immigrants in the wind-battered huts of the Dakotas, Irish immigrants in the stifling tenements of the cities, a list that is potentially endless. The distance was often mental, not physical, the distance of the mental lives of, say, Chinese laborers in California towns from those of the emigrant Yankee merchant families there; of the first swarms of Russian Jewish immigrants on the Lower East Side of New York from the stiff and proper American gentile bourgeoisie often only a few squares away; of the Magyar or Slovak miners in Pennsylvania from that of their Welsh or Irish supervisors—a distance, in each case, of less than one-half mile, but with the original casts of their mental lives not merely two continents but two historical ages, apart.

Because of the vastness of the country and of the indefinite power of the American democratic dogma there were not many bloody struggles among these different peoples. The vastness of the country and the vagueness of the dogma allowed for the existence of all kinds of aspirations, provided only that they flowed in one direction, one way. There could be, and there would be, no criticism of that direction: the direction of American progress. Thus the vagueness of the dogma corresponded to the swelling of the nation as well as to a certain rigidification of the American mind.

One hundred years ago this rigidification, perhaps for the first time in their history, began to afflict millions of Americans, including millions of the older American families. The conditions of American blacks reflected this: by 1900 their status—legal as well as social—was less promising than it had been in 1870. In the 1880s there was a hardly noticeable but instinctive stiffening of American manners, and perhaps even of morals. Much of this stiffening was defensive: a growing self-consciousness of being American, *established* American. This was a similar, though not identical, phenomenon to that cult of respectability that had ushered in the Victorian Age in England. This late-blooming American version of Victorianism may have included cramped habits of mind but it did not mean that Americans would not trust their hearts. The world of Howells' Silas Lapham differed from the world of Dickens' Josiah Bounderby because their hearts were different, no matter how heartily their minds would have agreed with the accepted materialist ideas that they would have exchanged (or, rather, repeated) in order to feel good in the smoking-lounge of a transatlantic steamer had they met there.

There was, therefore, a duality in American life one hundred years ago, a problematic quality different from that espied by Hawthorne or Melville or Poe, who wrestled with the darkness of the soul like so many Jacobs and angels in the gaslit democracy of an earlier age. Much of American life, including small-town life, was idyllic one hundred years ago —unbelievably innocent, spacious, sustained by inexpensive land and cheap food, benevolent to the extent of near-absurdity. Underneath that superficial orderliness of human relations there were fearful passions. Rudyard Kipling recognized this in an instant. In 1889 he was suddenly, and utterly, charmed by the villages of Pennsylvania (the genuineness of his attraction to this kind of life was proved by the fact that a few years later he tried to settle in the United States), but he also saw "the terrifying intimacy" of life in American small towns, "disturbed by the hatreds and troubles and jealousies that vex the minds of all but the gods." A coming generation of American naturalist writers and progressive thinkers would be aware of this later, just when the small-town era of the American democracy was coming to an end.

They missed an essential condition, even though they were participants and beneficiaries of it. This was that the tendencies of human life, that is of the human heart and human mind, do not correspond to the "laws" of "natural science"; that, for instance, compression and decompression, depression and expression may develop together, out of the same source. The sometimes hardly conscious stiffening of the mind-set of older Americans occurred together with the increasingly conscious broadening of their aspirations to respectability. For the first time in the history of the United States an American bourgeois world was beginning to appear that was not very different from the high bourgeois worlds of England and of Europe. Those people of the American upper classes who, beforehand, had given tone and direction to social and cultural life in the Republic—certain Quakers in Philadelphia or Unitarian Bostonians, for example—were quaint and isolated versions of an American bourgeoisie whom sympathetic Europeans could regard with something akin to anthropological interest. But around 1890 the lives of a significant portion of the American people now included book reading, theatergoing, sight-seeing-traveling, art collecting—cultural activities that corresponded to those of their European counterparts. The bourgeois phase of American civilization had begun.

After a century of self-conscious separation the shapes of American and European lives were becoming more similar. As late as 1870 city life in Boston or New York or Philadelphia (not to speak of Chicago) was very different from city life in London or Paris or Hamburg. Twenty-five years later these differences had diminished, though of course they had not vanished entirely. By the 1890s there were estates in the American suburbs where the American upper-middle class led a kind of aspiring-gentry existence that, at least in its outward forms, resembled that of its counterparts in England and even of certain villas on the outskirts of the cities of the Continent. There were now, for the first time in American history, metropolitan operas, metropolitan museums, metropolitan concert halls, metropolitan orchestras, metropolitan transportation systems, metropolitan financial institutions, metropolitan bankers, and even certain cosmopolitan writers, such as Henry James, attempting to describe the exact proportions of the compound of cosmopolitanism and of Americanism in the hearts and minds of some of his subjects.

For one generation now (the trend had set in around 1867–68) the size of native American families had been decreasing. This decline of the birthrate was most pronounced among the middle and upper classes at the very time when the proportion of their children going on to college increased. The English (and Scots) influence on the American college model was still considerable. Yet there was a rising German influence on American pedagogy, and the first graduate schools on European models had come into being. A great, though gradual, change in the situation of American women was developing: after about 1895, the majority of American women, including the majority of farmers' wives, did not have to work outside of their own households. At the same time—and in this respect American society differed from the European bourgeois—the patronage of culture was carried on by American women. This feminization of the arts had mixed results. The recognition that women, all kinds of women, possessed an innate taste for refinement wherefore they had to play the principal part in the progression of culture was all to the good; the accepted idea that culture was essentially decorative, secondary to material progress, was not. Yet materially, too, the situation of American women was nearly unique in the world. By 1900 they possessed a very large portion of tangible financial assets (in part because their life expectancy was longer than that of their husbands).

The Republic was rich, and its currency solid enough, so that an American kind of capitalism had arrived with a vengeance; but all of its outward and often rude manifestations notwithstanding, this was not an ungenerous kind of capitalism, demanding little more than a single-minded acceptance of the American mode of progress. Consequently many Americans thought they had a vested interest in the maintenance of the social and financial and political system in the midst of which they were living. It was thus that many Americans, perhaps even a majority of American families, became temperamentally conservative—even though they were loath to identify themselves with that adjective, except perhaps when it came to their financial investments. This widespread conservatism (in this the history of the United States is a refutation of Marx, again and again) explains the failure of the Populists in the 1890s—and also the continued existence of municipal corruption in the democratic institutions of the Republic. This phenomenon of endemic municipal corruption was strangely similar to other ex-colonial and now democratic parts of the British Empire, such as Canada or Australia; the phenomenon of populism was not. The American Populist movement—it was a movement even more than a party—rose in the Midwest, in the West, and in the South, gaining strength from the troubles and the dissatisfactions of American farmers in the midst of an agricultural depression, even though their troubles were often of their own making (the American farmer had become a mechanic and a businessman, evident not only in his special aspirations but in his very clothing; but he was often not very good at being an incipient and marginal capitalist). The Populists were a folkish movement, early examples of the American version of national socialism, to which I shall return. Agitated by a folkish suspicion of a cosmopolitan and internationalized, Anglophile, and city-ridden capitalist East, the fanaticism of the Populists was, in a characteristic American way, not unmixed with generosity: they believed that democracy in America was being thwarted by not being democratic enough, corrupted as it was by bankers, goldbugs, capitalists, alien elements. Their ideal was government by "the people." They were defeated not by the capitalists but by the condition that "the people" were more conservative than they, the Populists, had expected; indeed, many of "the people" were becoming bourgeois.

(3)

In the 1890s the structure of the republican society of the United States was changing, together with the texture of American life. One of the consequences thereof was another turning point: the beginning of the American world empire. Throughout the world, modern imperialism had an appeal to the democratic masses. In the history of the American Republic, imperialism had been originally a territorial phenomenon, not a seaborne and global one. Its purpose had been the acquisition of land. For nearly thirty years after the Civil War the American Merchant Marine and the Navy declined. In the 1890s this changed. The purpose was now the assertion of the American presence on the seas, or at least in the western Pacific and the Caribbean; the aim was the appearance of the United States among the world powers of the age, then at the zenith of their imperial effulgence and colonial possessions. The realization of the importance of sea power, allied with the conviction that in the history of the world the primacy had now passed to the Anglo-Saxon (or Nordic or Teutonic) races, was strong and clear in the minds of only a handful of intelligent Americans, most of them Republican Progressives. The Populists had no foreign policy beside their domestic dislike and fear of foreigners. Imperialism was not, however, an idea perpetrated by a minority upon the consciences of a dullard or indifferent population. By 1894 the politicians—especially those within the Republican Party—began to appreciate its political potential. The desire for prestige and for expansion was widespread among the American people at large—which is why the war against Spain in 1898 was popular.

Even before that war it appeared that the prestige and the respect for the power of the American giant republic was very great. Indeed, it was almost universal. There was not one European government, whether of old-fashioned Austria or of democratic Britain, which showed the slightest inclination of siding, or even openly sympathizing, with Spain. It was the last time that Americans feared that their great sea-girt cities could be bombarded by the warships of a European power. One English battleship, Lodge said in 1890, could reduce New York to ruins. (This was one of the arguments of the Republicans' Big Navy program which had begun as early as 1891.) The cities and the plains of the Republic were now safe, safe from everything except from the internal danger of conspiracies perpetrated by anarchists. "[Admiral] Dewey's victory transformed the narrow, intellectual movement—expansionism—into a broad and popular crusade —imperialism."[3] The great majority of the American people took satisfaction from the pictures of the Stars and Stripes solidly planted on faraway islands and floating over the oceans, just as their ears took satisfaction from the originally somewhat odd, but soon intensely familiar, martial band music of Sousa, with some of its Central European strains, but no matter, for it was at that time that American popular music, indeed, that the tuning of American ears was changing, too, from their simpler Anglo-Celtic strains to newer rhythms and melodies. Thus the American Dominion Over Palm and Pine came into being at the very time when Kipling warned their English cousins that *their* dominion over palm and pine might be short-lived: "Lest We Forget!"

This was the era of sea power and of democracy. As Jakob Burckhardt wrote of ancient Greece, "Sea power appeared above all to be intrinsically linked to democracy, and people in the Piraeus were even more democratically minded than those of Athens"—and people in America more than in England. This was the era of Theodore Roosevelt, too—one of the few American presidents whose stamp on an era preceded his presidency and continued for some time after it. He became President by accident, when McKinley was killed by an anarchist in 1901. He was not a prototypical representative of the American people; he was, however, a prototypical delegate of their aspirations. The war with Spain was not of his making; but the consequences of that war, including later the acquisition of the Panama Canal Zone, the building of the great Navy, and the appearance of the United States as the arbiter of the Russo-Japanese War, were. Politically speaking, the world did not become round until about 1900, centuries after Copernicus. In 1900, for the first time in history, world powers had arisen whose motherland was not in Europe. They were the United States and Japan. Their movements and their very presence would instantly involve and influence the relationships of that complicated web of states which formed the substance of the European system of powers.

The new spirit of nationalism of which Theodore Roosevelt was the prime representative differed from the older American nationalism in certain ways. Roosevelt was not an ideologue, but he was sufficiently concerned with the growing influx of millions of immigrants from the strangest and farthest corners of the Old World to promote a "new nationalism" that would succeed the older, often regional, patriotism of the older American stock, leading to fusions in the "melting pot" (that, too, was a relatively recent phrase at the time, from the title of a play by Israel Zangwill). This "new nationalism" was not internationalist, and certainly not cosmopolitan, as indeed Theodore Roosevelt was not, all of his wide learning and acquaintance with European history notwithstanding. In one sense it was seagoing and imperial: in another sense it represented—or, more accurately, it wished to represent—a new version of the ideal American self-image: that of the young male hero of the West. Theodore Roosevelt was only one of many young Americans of the upper classes who, often for reasons of health, had been sent by their families to the American West in the 1880s. Coming from the brown coal-laden air of the smoky, swelling cities of the East, their lungs and minds and hearts were instantly invigorated by the clear air of the West. Subsequently they were inclined to idealize the open-air life in the West, seeing in the western American a renewed, and the most recent, exemplar of the healthy Anglo-Saxon male—which Roosevelt as well as his friend Owen Wister would recognize, and proclaim, as a national, and not at all a cosmopolitan, type. All of this appears very definitely in the writings and letters of Owen Wister: but this idealization of the new western man was not confined to men of Roosevelt's or Wister's background. The willingness of the American people to accept, indeed, to be inspired by, this kind of idealization was evident in the enormous and lasting success of Wister's *The Virginian,* published in 1902, which made the cowboy a central figure of the American legend: and the conception, the publication, and the success of *The Virginian* belongs less to the history of American literature than to the history of American imagination.

There was, however, a great difference between Roosevelt and Wister. During the last thirty years of his life, Wister brooded about the inevitable decline of the Republic (and of Western civilization). He was even more pessimistic than Henry Adams; Roosevelt was not. Many of Roosevelt's pronouncements and his actions were impulsive, peremptory, aggressive, flamboyant. There was a determined youthfulness in Theodore Roosevelt's character, reflecting, at its worst, a kind of myopic boyishness of which some of his thoughtful contemporaries, such as Wister or Adams, were exempt. Still, unlike the case of many Americans who otherwise shared his ideas, in Roosevelt's life this was not a case of arrested adolescence: his durable boyishness was not puerile, it was annealed to his strenuous striving for an American maturity.

Roosevelt was a step ahead of his countrymen, whose imagination and whose ideas, all of the superficial acceleration of dynamos, of industry, of mass communications notwithstanding, were slowing down. There were many reasons for this: foremost, perhaps, the decreasing biological vitality of the older American stock whose life-span was extending but who had fewer children, certainly fewer than those of the recent immigrants; and while the reasons for this may be arguable, the evidences are not. For one thing, *The Virginian,* with its idealization of the cowboy hero, was published at the very time when the era of the open West was already gone. On a theoretical-intellectual level, too, the famous thesis of Frederick Jackson Turner, to the effect that the American frontier made the character of American history, was also outdated (not to speak of the fact that Turner had lifted his idea from certain European geographers and pursued it thereafter with what Oscar Wilde would call the enthusiasm of a short-sighted detective). The American frontier was closing, even though the West was still largely empty. It was not only that with the admission of Oklahoma, Arizona, and New Mexico to statehood in the first dozen years of the twentieth century there was now an unbroken block of forty-eight states, from sea to sea and from frontier to frontier. It was that for every prospector or roustabout in Seattle or San Francisco there were now a hundred dentists and another hundred self-conscious bohemians, American "progressives." The daughters of Methodist pioneers of 1900 in the Pomona Valley in California were flappers as early as 1915 (and perhaps divorcées by 1925). The most cynical and bitter of American writers and social observers, Ambrose Bierce, was a San Francisco journalist. Here is the paradox: the first fifteen years of the twentieth century were marked by widespread social changes and by the swift and impressive rise of the United States in the world; yet at that very time sensitive observers saw that certain things and certain people in America looked preternaturally old. A few English writers, Thomas Hardy and Arnold Bennett, saw this: they were not alone.‡ In 1915 Van Wyck Brooks contemplated the decaying old houses on Long Island: "How overwhelmingly they seem to betray a losing fight against the wilderness!" Americans, wrote D. H. Lawrence in 1916, "are *not* younger than we, but older: a second childhood.

‡ Knut Hamsun as early as the 1880s: "Americans are fundamentally a *conservative* people who in many fields still cling to positions that even Norway, as behind the times as it is, has long abandoned." Hamsun, *The Cultural Life of Modern America* (Morgridge, ed., Cambridge, Mass., 1969), p. 18.

But being so old, in senile decay and second childishness, perhaps they are nearer to the end, and the new beginning." American buildings were aging more rapidly than buildings elsewhere in the world, save for the tropics. Around 1910 the very shapes of certain high buildings and of certain gigantic American machines were Gothic, mastodonlike, outdated monsters with steely teeth: skyscrapers, yes, but with Renaissance plastering and reminiscent of high-button shoes; mastodon machines, yes, but reminiscent of stovepipe hats, as if American imagination had been congealed and frozen within the ideas and ideals of the nineteenth century. One could detect from American comportments and countenances, from American forms and faces, this dual and paradoxical condition at the time: the youthfulness of the American smile and the loose modern movements of American limbs but also the impression that certain American faces had become prematurely old: waitresses with the faces of old trolley cars, small-town businessmen with the faces of typewriters. And to conclude with yet another paradox: all of the publisher's success of *The Virginian* notwithstanding, the cowboy and the Western scenario became a central element in American imagination through their representations in the movies, a new kind of American popular entertainment which was produced by Jewish immigrant entrepreneurs who often knew little English, the very people whom Wister, the creator of *The Virginian,* hated from the bottom of his soul.

By 1912 the Wurlitzer era was in full swing. Throughout the Republic jangled the music of the movies, of the nickelodeons, of the mechanical cash register (a then typically American sound), of the trolley cars.* The movies had their initial impact on the very forms of American behavior: the jerky movements of people in the first movies coincided with a noticeable quickening of the American stride, a change from the long-legged careful Yankee stepping to the nervy strutting of George M. Cohan (whereof the urban shuffling of Charlie Chaplin may have developed in the form of a pantomimic exaggeration). In the memoir of an American writer I once read that when he first rode in a trolley he knew exactly how to grasp an overhead strap because he had seen how it was done in a movie. The year 1912 was, of course, an important milestone in the history of the Republic. Theodore Roosevelt could have won the presidency again, but the politicians of the Republican Party denied him the nomination. This was the last time that the American people had to choose among three important candidates. Wilson won with 6.2 million votes, Roosevelt had

* "The fiddles are tuning up all over America," said John Butler Yeats (the poet's father): but it was not ragtime that he meant.

4.1 million, and Taft 3.4 million. It is thus not a hypothesis to state that had the Republican vote not been split, Roosevelt would have won. Less than two years later the First World War broke out in Europe. It is well-nigh impossible to calculate what would have happened in Europe, in the United States, indeed, in the history of the world, had Theodore Roosevelt been the President of the United States in 1914. It was the politicians who denied Theodore Roosevelt the nomination; however, the American people could still have voted him into the presidency. Because of their essential cautionary conservatism, they didn't. This is why 1912 was a milestone but not a turning point. Among other things, the experience of 1912 consolidated, indeed, rigidified, the two-party system for the rest of the century. No serious candidate would ever bolt his party again; and in the minds of many Americans the conventions of the two mammoth parties were part and parcel of the Constitution. Also, by 1912 the victory of the progressive ideology was complete. Theodore Roosevelt was a Progressive; so was Woodrow Wilson. The federal income tax and the popular election of senators were constitutional amendments that passed rapidly, all of the cumbrous constitutional procedure for amendments notwithstanding.† Progressive education, progressive hygiene, progressive medicine, progressive manufacturing, progressive labor, progressive engineering, progressive capitalism, progressive citizenship, progressive Americanism, progressive social science—an entire and wholesale progressive ideology of human nature and of history, too, were becoming, indeed, they had become, the main element in the American civic religion, and a not inconsiderable element in the ideas professed by churchmen of many of the established religions. The very notion of "Americanism"—a vague term but widely current at the time, into which the earlier "new nationalism" was funneling—was a progressive notion. It was through his progressive adaptation that the immigrant would become more and more American, Americanism meaning something becoming and not merely being.

Yet this progressivism was, in many ways, outdated—perhaps more outdated than many other developments in American life. With very few exceptions the ideas of the Progressives were nineteenth-century ideas: utilitarian, liberal, meliorist, positivist, largely dependent on certain British forms of thought that had been prevalent before 1890. This was certainly true of Wilson, who was even more a typical Progressive than Roosevelt; and we shall see the abiding influence of the framework of his mind. The

† Burckhardt: "Athens had no lack of wise laws and cited them with praise. The Athenians did not rescind the old laws, but kept on adding new ones and thus let the chips of contradiction fall where they would."

dominant idea that the improvement of democracy was principally a matter of education (this was perhaps one of the significant differences between the Progressives and the Populists, the latter tending to believe that the extension of democracy leads to the improvement of education) was an old American idea. Leaving aside a consideration of the underside of fatalism within the American progressive mentality—for beneath the optimistic belief in the perfectability of society we may detect a much less hopeful trust in the improvability of man—let us merely note that in 1912 few Americans were aware of the reaction to this kind of nineteenth-century thinking, of the rumblings of the first postscientific revolutions of minds. That in 1912 not only Darwin, Gladstone, Mill, Zola, Tolstoy but also Dostoevski, Nietzsche, Bergson, and Freud were known to intelligent Americans mattered little; the latter still saw in these people essential heralds of progress simply because they were avant-garde. For by 1912 avant-gardism and modernism had arrived in America, too. Indeed, modernism was not only lodged in certain American minds but it was there in certain American forms—in the modern skyline of New York, for instance, and in the sudden outburst of Surrealism in American expressions, including poetry, in the breaking away from what Santayana had called "the genteel tradition," largely Anglo-Saxon, which had lingered on in American letters and learning and art until about 1912, around what Professor Henry F. May would call "the end of American innocence." There was now, for the first time in the history of the United States, a class of people who were conscious cultivators and consumers of modernism: a coagulation of an American intelligentsia (which, unlike a few decades later, was composed of amateur intellectuals rather than professional ones).

Much more important than what was revolving in the minds of American intellectuals was the revolutionary transformation of the United States effected by the automobile. Neither the internal-combustion engine nor the automobile were American inventions; but the mass production and the popular possession of automobiles was. While the greatest catastrophe of European history descended on its peoples in 1914, American engineers achieved the opening of the Panama Canal and the mass production of automobiles. The prophet and the leading producer of popular automobilization was Henry Ford, an exemplar of the paradox of being ahead of as well as behind his time. Ford was a determined believer in progress who pronounced his contempt for history and for tradition, but who had a profound distrust of alien and modernist influences; a thoroughgoing materialist who was, however, deeply imbued with a populist idealism; a nationalist *and* a pacifist; a salesman whose product destroyed vast areas of traditional American small-town life and who, at the same time, devoted a large part of his fortune and spiritual energies to rebuilding models of old-fashioned American villages and promoting old-fashioned square dancing. What was more important, the automobilization of the United States, beginning to unfold in the second decade of this century, created new aspirations and influenced the very forms of American living. In Europe the automobile was, as yet, the possession of rich people who lived mostly in the cities. In America, too, the first crowds of automobiles appeared on the avenues of Chicago and New York; but the automobile was even more a small-town phenomenon. It was the midwestern American who took to the automobile with the enthusiasm of a believer. Ford was a Midwesterner and the gigantic American automobile factories took root in the cities of the Midwest; until this day the American automobile is the characteristic American object in Indianapolis rather than Boston, or in Gary rather than Los Angeles, all of the dependence of the latter on automobile movement notwithstanding. The automobilization of the United States meant a movement away from the East, and from the sea-borne to a land-borne expansion of movement. That the internal-combustion engine would change not only the face of continents but the very conditions of war after five hundred years was not, of course, known to Ford, though it was to be recognized by Hitler. For the first time in five hundred years land power was becoming more important than sea power, though this was not evident until the Second World War, and to many people not even then.

It is in the nature of democratic and progressive minds to believe that wars belong to the crude and reactionary past, and that the age of wars has been followed by the age of revolutions—something that has been part and parcel of the American civic religion, too, since most Americans think of the birth of their nation as the result of a revolution rather than what it was, a war of independence. The progressive and sociological view, according to which the struggles of societies and classes had replaced the wars of states and nations was, of course, the fundamental belief of Marx, too, as well as of other materialists and utilitarians; many millions of people, including many intellectuals, profess to believe this even now. Yet they were, and still are, wrong. For one thing, in Europe the era of democratic and liberal revolutions that had begun even before the American one, about 1760, ended with the revolutions of 1848; what followed that era was a century of wars. Statesmen such as Bismarck and even Disraeli recognized this condition; theorists such as Mill, Marx, and Lenin did not. The two greatest events of the last one hundred years were the two world wars. They stand athwart the history of modern mankind as two immense dark mountain ranges, dividing the landscape of an entire century. It is in the shadow of these enormous mountain ranges that we still live; they have formed our lives and the entire order, or disorder, of the world in which we live. That relatively few American families lost members in these world wars was a fortunate condition. Still the two world wars were the principal events of their century, too, because of their consequences. The consequences of other developments, such as the Depression, that affected the lives of so many Americans, do not compare with the consequences of the two world wars in the long run.

The year 1914, the beginning of the great European tragedy, was a halcyon year for many Americans. In 1914 many of the sporadic symptoms of a social crisis that had been accumulating two years earlier in the United States were abating; the political excitement was largely gone. The Republic baked in the summer; alternating currents of somnolence and of activity simmered in American minds. The outbreak of the European war filled many Americans with a kind of inner satisfaction, a satisfaction of something well-earned; what was happening in Europe was typical of the antiquated, corrupt, autocratic, reactionary institutions of the Old World, something that Americans had left behind for good. As the European war went on, Americans became interested in the spectacle, including its atrocities. They thought that they were out of it not so much by good luck, or even by geographical distance, as by virtue of their Americanness. In about two years this national sentiment became transformed—or, rather, it transformed itself. In 1914 there was not one American in a thousand who thought that the United States would, or should, take a part in this European war. In the spring of 1917, less than three years later, the majority of Americans became convinced—or, rather, they had convinced themselves—that the United States was destined to take part. This was one of the greatest and swiftest revolutions of public opinion and popular sentiment in the history of the nation—in itself an unusual phenomenon, since in the history of the American democracy such great changes are usually cumbrous and slow. The component factors of this revolution were numerous and complicated. Public opinion played its part in mobilizing and crystallizing popular sentiment. The most important element in the transformation of public opinion was the conclusion which many respectable Americans had reached—a conclusion in which the influence of British propaganda played the lesser, and the tactlessness of German behavior the larger, part—to the effect that a victory of Germany over Britain would pose a deadly danger to America's security. But this kind of opinion, no matter how reasoned (the fact that the American upper classes in 1914–18 were still predominately of Anglo-Saxon stock played a part in it) would not have had its way without a corresponding surge of popular sentiment.

By 1917 many Americans were willing to enter the war because of their national sentiment of pride. Indeed, a general aspiration for American *intervention* preceded the actual *participation* in the war. The sentiment (and, on occasion, the conviction) that the United States could, or should, teach a lesson to Europeans as an arbitrating world power, tossing the weight of her resources—moral and material resources—into the scale began to be manifest at least two years before the declaration of war actually came about. This was the element that such otherwise very different men as Henry Ford and Theodore Roosevelt and Woodrow Wilson, and that such different endeavors as Ford's Peace Ship, the Rooseveltian Plattsburg training encampment, and Wilson's Fourteen Points had in common.‡

Wilson was an unusually complex person—probably the only President in the history of the Republic whose place in that history is uncertain, since his posthumous reputation may still be subject to a drastic revaluation. This revaluation will not depend on newly found valuable documents but on the inevitable condition of historical, indeed, of all human, thinking: we see the past with the eyes of the ever-unfolding present (as well as the reverse). At the time of this writing there is reason to believe that the opinions of an increasing number of thoughtful Americans have entered a postliberal and postprogressive (something which is not the same as an antiliberal and antiprogressive) phase, by which I mean that more and more people are compelled to recognize the essential insufficiency of many of the progressive ideas about the world. By 1917 it was Wilson, not Roosevelt, who was the quintessential Progressive, almost to the point of caricature. Wilson failed because of many things, among which the Republican politicians' refusal of his single-minded advocacy of the League of Nations was but a part. Twenty-five years later he seemed to have been vindicated. In 1944 the movie *Wilson* showed him as one of the great prophetic American martyrs of world history. The concerted support of American opinion for the United Nations was another vindication of Wilson; it was to be a League of Nations on a greater and grander scale. Another thirty years passed before a growing number of Americans became disillusioned not only with the United Nations but—whether consciously or not—with the institutionalization of many of the ideas that progressives such as Wilson had espoused fifty years before. This is the

‡ It was reflected, too—ostensibly as preventive moves against eventual German expansion—in the quickening of American intervention in the Caribbean before 1917: in the dispatch of American marines to Haiti in 1915 and to Santo Domingo in 1916, and in the insistence that Denmark sell the Virgin Islands to the United States in 1916–17.

main reason why Wilson's reputation may yet change, perhaps even drastically so.*

But in one very important sense Wilsonianism lived on. He was the first President who led the United States into a war in Europe. He was the first presidential proponent of an American internationalism. Had Theodore Roosevelt been President in 1914 the rhetoric and probably the very substance of American internationalism would have been different. Subsequently generations of Americans were educated along a Wilsonian kind of internationalism. This has been his legacy for more than sixty years now. It was not altogether his creation: we have seen, and we shall see, that Wilson's view of foreign policies corresponded, alas, with the insubstantial ideology professed by other leading Americans. A few months before the Bolshevik revolution, Elihu Root, returning from a mission to Russia, recommended "a program to strengthen the morale of the Russian army, mainly through the introduction of recreational activities under the guidance of the Young Men's Christian Association."[4]

In any event, Wilsonianism transcended political parties and even selective ideologies. Opponents of Wilson were plentiful during his Administration and his lifetime; in 1919 and afterward they carried the day. Yet anti-Wilsonianism—that is, a determined and historical-minded opposition to the progressive moralistic and legalistic "internationalist" philosophy of Woodrow Wilson—has had few successful representatives in American public life during the last six decades. Whether this unfortunate legacy of a Wilsonian kind of internationalism will fade together with the overall fading of the Progressives' ideals is still too early to tell.

(4)

The year 1917 was the greatest turning point in the history of the Republic since the Civil War—indeed, in some ways since 1776, in some ways since Jamestown and Christopher Columbus. For more than three hundred years the human movement across the Atlantic was westward, from the Old World to the New: the ships, the soldiers, and the masses of migrants moved in that direction. In 1917, for the first time, this mass movement was reversed. Soon more than a million American soldiers were

* Another reason is that of his racial and ethnic prejudices, which have not yet received the attention they deserve.

to be shipped to Europe. Their presence would decide the world war. Soon after their return they and their relatives and political representatives would put an end to the mass migration of people from the Old World to the New. Conversely, the influence of the New World on the Old would continue even after the return of the American Army from Europe: the Americanization of Europe (and of much else besides) would go on and on.

Americans have not yet recognized the full significance of that turning point. They saw the American participation in World War I as an episode in their national history, mostly because of the shortness of its duration and the short span of the national enthusiasm that had created and accompanied it. Fifty years after 1917 the fiftieth anniversary of the Russian Revolution was celebrated and commemorated everywhere in the world, including the United States. For every fifty articles or books or academic symposia commemorating the Russian Revolution perhaps one commemorated the American entry into World War I. In 1967 the fiftieth anniversary of the American declaration of war passed almost unnoticed. Yet that American entry into the war was a more important—by which I mean far more consequential—event than was the Russian Revolution, in the long run as well as in the short run. In the long run: because what has happened since has been the Americanization of the world and not its Russification. In the short run: because the Russian Revolution was one of the by-products of the war. It had no effect on the outcome of that war, while the American entry into the war decided that outcome. The Russian Revolution meant that after two hundred years Russia was withdrawing from Europe, militarily, politically, culturally; the American declaration of war meant that after three hundred years America was entering Europe. In 1917 the Germans were unable to win the war even after Russia had dropped out of the ranks of their enemies. For the first and the last time in history the United States and Britain and France could defeat Germany even without Russia—a condition that would not repeat itself during the Second World War, which is why it is at least arguable that the zenith of American power in the world may have been 1918 even more than 1945. But, as Chesterton once said, the best things are lost in victory and not in defeat.

It was not a costly victory. An entire year passed before the American divisions were enrolled, formed, equipped, and shipped to France. More than a year passed until they were sent into the field of battle. By that time the Germans knew that their last offensive had failed, they could not break through the British and French lines to Paris. Still the American presence in France helped to tilt the balance in the end. After the Americans took part in their first battles, victory came swiftly. The angel of peace, clad in the gray robe of armistice, stood in the wings. The Germans were ready to surrender their conquests on Wilsonian terms: they saw in Wilson's Fourteen Points a more hopeful prospect than the punitive terms that their French and British enemies would inflict upon them. As also during and after the Second World War, the Germans thought that they had relatively little to fear from the Americans. They were right; but then they were wrong again. Wilson, who saw the war in ideological and even in messianic terms,† wanted more than an armistice or even a peace with Germany; he wanted the demolition of the German monarchy. He was also acutely aware of his domestic enemies, the Republicans, who—unlike in the Second World War—were agitating for unconditional surrender.

Like every surrender, the German surrender in 1918 looked as if it were unconditional; in reality it wasn't. This did not matter then. What mattered was what Americans would, or would not, do. The United States was now not only the most powerful but also the richest and most modern country in the world. The global supremacy of the English pound sterling was gone; Wall Street had become the capital of world finance, and the dollar the symbol of the Creditor Nation. The long-limbed American doughboys in Europe may have been unsophisticated but they were also modern: modern in their movements, habits, needs, entertainments, language. Their grinning faces and the laughing smiles of the American girls whom they had pulled up to themselves and kissed good-bye were modern. They shuffled and danced and marched to war to the tunes of Irving Berlin, compared to which "Auprès de ma Blonde" or "Tipperary" were survivals from the style of the nineties, floating out from the music halls.

Wilson was the first President who left the White House to sail for Europe; he did so hardly a month after the armistice. Like many of his successors (especially Nixon comes to mind) this man who, as he himself avowed, had not at all been attuned to think in terms of foreign affairs, now enjoyed his respectful reception, indeed, adulation, abroad—especially after he heard the ominous rumblings of political opposition and disaffection at home. He would preside over the peace conference in Paris,

† In March 1917 he had greeted the Russian Revolution as the most promising event in the history of the world since 1776. His message to the Congress, 2 April 1917: "No autocratic government could be trusted to keep faith or observe its covenants." Lansing in the cabinet meeting of 20 March 1917, representing Wilson: "The revolution in Russia, which appeared to be successful, had removed the one objection to affirming that the European war was a war between Democracy and Absolutism; that the only hope of a permanent peace between all nations depended upon the establishment of democratic institutions throughout the world."

creating a peace that would end all wars, and establish, among other things, a League of Nations, the first step toward a parliament of the world—a step, albeit indirect, toward the political Americanization of the globe. His four months in Europe were a disaster—for Europe and, in the long run, for the United States as well. With all of his then tremendous prestige Wilson could not effectively influence Lloyd George and Clemenceau and Orlando, his gnarled partners. His methods and his rhetoric were largely useless. His prestige melted like a cold pat of margarine when removed from the icebox. He exemplified a frequent American paradox: the generosity of his ideas failed because of the absence of magnanimity in his mind. The results were the badly botched peace treaties, a messed-up map of Europe, and the instant rise of national sentiments of revenge that would culminate in a second world war.

For all of this Wilson was not more—but also not less—responsible than were his European counterparts, even though his responsibility (or lack of it) issued from different habits of mind. A century earlier, at the Congress of Vienna, Talleyrand and Castlereagh and Metternich were different men, with different purposes, but they spoke the same kind of language. At the Congress of Paris, Lloyd George and Clemenceau and Wilson, all men from the middle classes, all representatives of democratic states and of parliamentary constitutions, understood each other hardly at all.

(5)

Wilson returned to a powerful and self-righteous nation, in the bosom of which this self-righteousness was not unmixed with anxiety. In 1919, as also after the Second World War, the country was less united than it seemed. On the surface "Americanization" had been enormously successful; the twenty or more million Americans born in the lands of the Central Powers had caused no trouble, they manifested no disloyalties. Yet the alliance with Britain and France was not very popular among many Americans. That there was hardly any sentiment to continue such an alliance after the war was soon apparent. German-Americans, Scandinavian-Americans, Irish-Americans had become isolationists, and the Democratic Party was losing the allegiance of many people of the two former groups. Most Progressives and Populists in the Midwest and in the West were now bitter opponents of further American involvements in Europe, as were many American radicals and socialists. The numerical and political importance of the latter was nugatory, except in one sense. During and after the war, many people of the older American stock tended to see any sign of nonconformity with the then accepted American political and social ideas as suggesting at least potential treason. This explains the often extreme, and ludicrous, attempts to suppress the presence of anything associable with German culture during the war, a suppression that ranged from the elimination of Wagner from opera programs to the elimination of dachshunds from the list of recognized breeds by American kennel clubs. Soon after 1918 this anti-German campaign transmuted itself into an Americanism campaign which was anti-Bolshevik, antiradical, at times anti-Semitic, anti-immigrant, and generally anti-European. Many of the formerly suppressed anxieties of the older American stock, lest further immigration lead to the eventual overpowering of their beliefs and ways of life, had come to the surface. Amid all of the clanging, dynamic, loud, music-ridden, boosterish America of 1920 the desire for respectability ran rampant. One of the strangest books ever published in the history of the Republic was the "autobiography" of Edward W. Bok, an immigrant, and by 1920 a respected and influential public figure and millionaire, entitled *The Americanization of Edward W. Bok,* who saw himself as a monument of respectability. His book was a collection of self-righteous fictions, a book that had to be believed to be read. Yet in 1920 this book was an instant best seller because of Bok's shrewd comprehension of what Americans wanted to believe: the story not merely of the honest immigrant who made good, but of the honest immigrants who had made America better, and who regarded the United States, he would later write, as "the only first-rate civilization in the world."[5]

"The only first-rate civilization in the world": this was something different from the racial pride that had separated Victorian Englishmen from the rest of mankind. It was also different from that more innocent sense of American exceptionalism and of American uniqueness that had marked many American attitudes during the nineteenth century. It was not a statement of promise;‡ it was a proclamation of achievement. Of course not all Americans shared this sense of unique achievement. When, later in the twenties, Sinclair Lewis made his protagonists, successful

‡ It was a statement of promise for the isolationist and populist Senator La Follette, who as late as 1923 expressed the very sentiments uttered by John Adams a century earlier (see above, p. 5): "The greatest contribution that America can make to Europe and to the world is to restore and perfect her democratic institutions and traditions, so that they will stand as a beacon pointing the way to all peoples."

American businessmen such as Babbitt and Dodsworth, talk in a similar vein, proclaiming that a city such as Zenith in the American Midwest was the zenith of the world, thousands of American readers understood the ironical purposes of the author. Still these readers were in a minority. The twenties was the last decade when the differences between the United States and Europe were so great that they suggested differences of kind, not merely differences of degree. The people of the United States were optimists; the peoples of Europe were not. This was partly the result of two different traditions; of their different civic education, of the great differences in their respective experiences during the last great war, and of the fact that the material standards of American life were so much higher than those of the peoples of Europe. In his last (December 1928) State of the Union address President Coolidge said, "No Congress of the United States, ever assembled, on surveying the state of the Union has met with a more pleasing prospect than that which appears at the present time. . . . The great wealth created by our enterprise and industry and saved by our economy has had the widest distribution among our own people and has gone out in a steady stream to serve the charity and the business of the world. The requirements of existence have gone beyond the standard of necessity into the region of luxury. . . . The country can regard the present with satisfaction and anticipate the future with optimism."

The twenties was the "isolationist" decade—though not in every sense of that term. The twenties was not a very political decade: in 1920 and in 1924 the number of voters dropped and, for the first time in the history of the nation, it became fashionable for some Americans to be cynical about politics and perhaps even about democracy. But isolationism signified a deep division—not only among the people but often within the minds of the same people. A minority of Americans were conscious internationalists who deplored the provincial self-righteousness of the isolationists, their narrow-minded rejection of European culture, as well as the fact that the United States did not participate in international institutions such as the League of Nations. Yet the internationalists did not see that their very concept of internationalism was an American one—the wish to see American institutions and ideas prevail all over the world. The majority of Americans believed—not only for political reasons, and not only because of the disillusioning memories of the war—that the United States should never again be involved in a European conflict. This kind of a pacific belief coexisted, often within the minds of the same people, with an assertive kind of civic militarism. This took place after the Army and Navy had been deflated to their peacetime size. During the twenties, veterans' organizations such as the American Legion grew faster than before. The cult of the flag and the pledge of allegiance to the flag at the beginning of every school day, as well as on other occasions, the (belated) promotion and final pronouncement of "The Star-Spangled Banner" for the official national anthem, habits such as putting one's right hand on one's heart during the rendition of the national anthem, American oddities such as drum majorettes, the military bedecking and panoply of high school parades, perhaps even the militarization of the spectacle of American football became national customs during the 1920s. Some of these practices had begun in the 1890s. Often they were propagated for the purpose of "Americanizing" the immigrant children. The pledge of allegiance to the flag was invented by Populists and Republicans in Kansas in 1892. By 1920 these practices had become national, "Americanism" in itself having gradually changed its connotation from an ideology of becoming into an ideology of being. The transformation of an older patriotism to a newer nationalism was completed. This strident nationalism was represented in many midwestern and western state assemblies. Just as in Europe the radical and folkish nationalism of people like Hitler was profoundly different from the nationalism of a Bismarck, in the United States, too, the main proponents of Americanism in the 1920s were different from those of the "new nationalism" a generation earlier. In 1894 the Regents of the University of Wisconsin, admonished by a populist legislature, had refused to dismiss a pro-Socialist professor; in 1924 the same legislature passed a law that forbade "the teaching of any historical facts considered unpatriotic by politicians and the people." A New Jersey law in 1921 prohibited textbooks which "belittle, falsify, misrepresent, distort, doubt or deny the events leading up to the Declaration of Independence or to any war in which this country has been engaged." The state assembly of Illinois in 1923 declared that the official language of Illinois was not English but American; in at least three other states the legislatures were authorized to supervise textbooks; Oregon (a characteristically progressive state) in 1925 ordered that all children had to attend the public schools in order to assure their Americanism. Anti-Semitism and anti-Catholicism (the Oregon law, struck down by the Supreme Court in 1925, was aimed at schools run by Catholic nuns) were prevalent. Between 1919 and 1925 the Ku Klux Klan reached its greatest strength in certain midwestern states; it was no longer restricted to the South.

During the twenties church memberships and church assets rose by leaps and bounds—a fact that should at least balance the accepted image of the Jazz Age, with all of its attendant cosmopolitanism. As the thoughtful historian Paul A. Carter wrote, ". . . gazing away from Manhattan's Great White Way any night during the decade following 1920, one could have seen wide, dark stretches of the continent where the roar of the twenties was muted indeed; where life was lived by a rhythm in which there was not the faintest echo of jazz."[6] The isolationism of the twenties, too, was inconsistent as well as incomplete. The demand and the desire for isolation from Europe was often strongest among the same Americans who were in favor of American expansion—at least of American missionary and business expansion—in the Pacific and in the Far East. (But, then, for some Americans Asia has always been the Farthest West, not the Far East.) That there was more to this than mere regionalism was evident in some of the pronouncements of the otherwise isolationist and Republican political leaders. Coolidge sent the Marines into Nicaragua; he kept them in San Domingo and in Haiti at the same time that he proclaimed the policy of Inter-American Solidarity and the absolute unwillingness of the United States "to intervene or govern" any Latin American republic.* In his inaugural address Coolidge had said that "the legions that the United States sends forth are armed, not with the sword but with the cross"; yet he later explained American intervention in the Caribbean as the benevolent action of an "International Policeman" (in the 1920s this term did not yet have unpleasant connotations). One of Coolidge's friends, the Republican Congressman Charles A. Eaton, proclaimed that the United States had to help "solve the problems" of neighboring nations, "not for our gain, not for our glory, not because we are militaristic or imperialistic, but because our Nation is the big brother in the family." It took a lone American poet and seer to detect a different meaning. In *Shine, Perishing Republic* Robinson Jeffers wrote in 1925, "While this America settles in the mold of its vulgarity, heavily thickening to empire . . ."

The incompleteness and the inconsistence of isolationism appeared on other levels too. During the 1920s American investments abroad were greater than they had been before, even though the economy of the Republic was still self-sufficient. The nation depended surprisingly little on foreign trade; the overwhelming mass of American production was consumed by the American people themselves. But on the financial level the United States and much of Western and Central Europe had become interdependent, as the consequences of the 1929 stock-exchange crash would reveal. And while the flood of immigrant masses from Europe was now reduced by stringent American laws to a trickle, the transatlantic migration of civilizational and cultural luxuries increased faster and faster. Boatloads of

* Wilson, too, had proclaimed that "America does not want any additional territories" at the same time that his Administration was pressing Denmark to sell the Virgin Islands to the United States.

paintings, sculptures, entire medieval castles, famous canvases by European painters were unloaded in New York every week. During the twenties the often incredibly rich American private collections and the collections of the great public museums came of age. The importation of their contents was accompanied by the importation of European artists, musicians, conductors, theater and movie actors and actresses. Many of them now took up permanent residence in the United States, the new immigration laws notwithstanding. American literature, too, was losing its earlier dependence on English traditions and on English models. H. L. Mencken, the most celebrated (and therefore the most influential) American critic of the decade, devoted his main efforts to the demolition of these remnant English influences on the American mind—indeed, on the American literary language. The favorite place of the self-conscious American "exiles" was Paris. A tour of Europe was no longer the monopoly of the American upper classes. Continental writers such as Mann, Hamsun, Keyserling were now occasional American best sellers. In sum, during this isolationist decade Europe was closer to America than it had been before . . . in some ways.

Yet the climate of the two continents was entirely different. The atmosphere of the twenties in England and in Europe was a mottled gray, with a few vivid streaks, but gray nonetheless. The atmosphere of the twenties in America was that of relentless yellow sunshine, the shimmering heat on Constitution Avenue, on the courthouse square of Dayton, Tennessee, as well as sparkling on Gatsby's cream-colored automobile, "terraced with a labyrinth of windshields that mirrored a dozen suns." Most Americans believed not only that the character of their civilization was different from that of the European nations but that it was destined to be increasingly different. That the First World War had been a catastrophe for Europe and a triumph for the United States was rather obvious. That it had been a catastrophe for an entire civilization of which, after all, the United States was a part was thought (or, rather, thought through) by few Americans during the twenties. Their isolationist ideology was the very opposite of reactionary, wedded as it was to the American ideology of progress. The brilliant cars of Gatsby's people moved to and from New York on modern Long Island highways between, as Fitzgerald saw and described it, a landscape of cinders and ashes: but "the past," Carl Sandburg wrote, "is a bucket of ashes"—this populist and progressive poet's words corresponding exactly with those of the prophet and producer of the automobile civilization. "History," said Henry Ford in an often-misquoted statement, "is more or less bunk. It's tradition. We don't want tradition. We want to live in the present and the only history worth a tinker's dam is the history we make today." Edison "has done more toward abolishing poverty than have all the reformers and statesmen since the beginning of the world." "I don't know anything about history," he said on another occasion. "I wouldn't give a nickel for all the history in the world. . . . I don't want to live in the past. I want to live in the Now." (Doesn't this sound like the "Now" generation of the 1960s and 1970s?) He also said, "Books muddle me." Ford was the most popular American in 1923; he was seriously proposed as a presidential candidate.

At the end of the decade Julius Klein, Hoover's Assistant Secretary of Commerce, said, "Tradition is the enemy of progress."[7] In the United States the belief in progress was still unbroken; in Europe it was not. There was another difference. The twenties was the modern decade—perhaps the last, perhaps the only modern decade—in America as well as in Europe. Yet while in America modernism and the cult of progress were nearly synonymous, in Europe they were not. The very word "modern" in German, French, even in English usage meant a break with prevailing customs and ideas, suggesting something that was radical and perhaps also amoral; in America it did not. A modern girl was an all-American girl, a modern automobile was an all-American automobile. The cult of modernity was not merely the jealous possession of a few thousand self-conscious American intellectuals. In popular culture, too, modernity had arrived with a vengeance: movies were modern, cellophane and celluloid were modern, jazz was modern. Yet a characteristic American duality prevailed throughout the twenties. Millions of Americans who believed in the virtues of Prohibition also believed in the virtues of Sex Education. Prohibition was not a step backward: like many other American things, it meant Progress. Ford himself said that "booze had to go out when modern industry and the motor car came in." Popular pastors were often permissive about divorce. The frequent divorcings of movie actors and actresses did not bother people; indeed, people followed the reports of high life in Hollywood with fascination; but divorces *had* to be followed by remarriages (some of the contracts specified that the actor or actress, if divorced, would have to remarry within a specified time, the costs of the proceedings to be covered by the motion-picture company). The movies brought whole sets of glamorized eroticism into the—increasingly pictorial—element of Americans' imagination until their minds were stuffed with them; yet the movies were governed by groups of patriots and politicians who established codes, defining on occasion how many square inches of skin could be shown on the screen or for how many seconds a kiss was allowed to last.

In some ways the United States was ahead of Europe; in other ways it was not. An example of this was the Scopes trial—it would be called a "media event" now—and, even more, its interpretation. The state of Tennessee had proscribed the teaching of Darwinian evolution. In 1925 a test case was made out of this. Clarence Darrow, a Chicago lawyer and a prototypical progressive figure, represented the high school teacher Scopes; William Jennings Bryan, the grand old man of populism, three times a presidential candidate, represented the state of Tennessee. That "trial" was seen (and still is seen today) as the contest between the two sides of the American mind: the rural, backward, fundamentalist Bryan pitted against Darrow, representing the contest between conservatism and liberalism, reaction and progress, religion and science, the nineteenth century and the twentieth century. These juxtapositions were false. What Bryan represented were ideas not of the nineteenth but of the seventeenth century, gnarled puritan and biblical and anti-aristocratic survivals in the American mind; what Darrow represented was the principal belief not of the twentieth but the nineteenth century, the belief in the absolute and definite and exclusive validity of Science, a belief that was already outdated in 1925, even though few people knew it at the time. The Bryan–Darrow clash also marked the final divorce of populism and progressivism. Thereafter most populists moved toward the Right, in a national socialist direction; most progressives toward the Left, in an international socialist direction.

Capitalism, too, was something much more typical of the nineteenth century than of the twentieth. In Europe it was shot full of holes during and after the First World War; in the United States it was not. None of the economists understood (not that they do even now) that the economic life of a people is not merely conditioned by mental habits but that national economics itself is a fiction, surely in the original Latin meaning of *fictio*—"mental construction" or, in other words, beliefs. In Europe capitalism was in trouble not merely because of the debts that the states of Europe had accumulated during the war but because the trust of peoples in the social order of liberal democracy and in the honesty and efficiency of parliamentary government were vanishing; in America they were not. It is amazing how in the United States the extraordinary growth of popular prosperity, of the volume of all kinds of purchases, and of personal consumption—in short, how the inflation of society during the twenties—left the value of the national currency largely unaffected. The prices of stocks rose by leaps and bounds but the general price level rose hardly at all. The first condition reflected the unbroken American belief in the future of progress; the second reflected the strength of the belief in the unchanging solidity of the American system. Progressive practice and unchanging idealism: a duality that was typical of the Victorian mind during the nineteenth century and that was typical of America in the twenties, indeed, for some time thereafter. This is why the stock-market crash of 1929 and the Depression that followed was a curious development: a nineteenth-century event in the midst of a twentieth-century society, the last occurrence of deflation in a world which was, in almost every sense, inflationary. This was, too, why the Crash and the Depression, while involving much of the rest of the world had different consequences in America and in Europe. In Europe it contributed to a near-fatal weakening of political democracy; in the United States it eventually led to a solidification of political and of social democracy, through the New Deal.

(6)

All through the Depression years the American people were surprisingly docile. It was almost as if they had felt faintly guilty for the excessive prodigality of the twenties. In any event, their resentments were short-range and fairly parochial; their faith in the American system—and, more important, in American ideals—remained largely unbroken. At the deepest phase of the economic crisis, in 1932, in Germany nearly half of the electorate voted for extremist parties, Nazis and Communists; in the United States the Communist vote in 1932 was one fourth of 1 percent. Perhaps the history of the Depression years is yet another indication of the slowness of American reactions. In the United States the effects of the stock-market collapse accumulated more slowly than in other countries; so did the resentments and the impatience of the people. The Depression, besides, strengthened American family life; it brought families closer together. It may even be argued that both in the rhetoric and in the expectations of people there was less cynicism and more naïveté in 1932 than, say, in 1924. This naïveté—lapsing at times into political puerilism—is detectable beneath, and sometimes within, the blackest and bleakest description of the American scene by radical and leftist writers in the thirties. It was represented in a movie, *Gabriel Over the White House,* made shortly before the 1932 presidential election and enthusiastically supported by William Randolph Hearst. A youngish American President, originally a typical selfish politician, suffers a shock due to an automobile accident after which he undergoes a character change or, rather, a change in his principal political convictions. He personally leads the fight against gangsters, capitalists, and corrupt politicians; he is supported by an army of unemployed workers; he puts an end to Prohibition ruled by gangsters and institutes national liquor stores; he strong-arms Congress to follow his dictates; shortly before his death he establishes an era of universal peace and disarmament as he demonstrates to an assembly of foreign statesmen the invincibility of American air power. The screenwriters of 1932 obviously believed that the American people were eager for such a President—in effect, for a benevolent dictator. The political tone of the film demonstrated, too, the inclinations to socialism that lay beneath the professions of free enterprise and to the nationalism that lay beneath the peculiarly American ideas of an international world order.

The Depression, at its worst, amounted to a crisis of confidence in the financial institutions of the nation. It did not amount to a crisis of confidence in the political institutions of the Republic. Yet the strain on the social fabric of the American people was becoming considerable. The selection of Franklin Roosevelt was a blessing for them at the time. "A second-rate mind with a first-rate temperament" Oliver Wendell Holmes was supposed to have said about Roosevelt. Whatever the qualities of the mind, the temperament now counted foremost. Roosevelt invigorated the confidence of the people, including their financial institutions. The recognition that Roosevelt with his New Deal—which, in many ways, amounted to the definite establishment of the American Provider (or Welfare) State—was, in reality, the rescuer of American capitalism is not a perverse or a paradoxical statement. At any rate, American socialism will always have a strong capitalistic element within it, just as American capitalism is often socialistic in its methods and even in some of its aims. This meant that the kind of social reforms and the kind of government intervention that the New Deal brought about were American and national, not international.

It is at this point that—at least to my mind—a world political (or, rather, historical) excursion is in order. In the 1920s the destinies of America and Europe seemed to be separated, in more than one way. In the 1930s the political effects of the Depression in Germany and in America were very different—but not in every way. In a very important sense what was happening in Europe was happening in the United States, too: the rise of a new Right—radical, populist, and nationalist. Looking back after nearly forty years of cold war when the principal adversaries, the two superpowers of the world, have been the United States and the Soviet Union, it is tempting to historicize their antagonism and to point out that communism represented by the latter and capitalism represented by the former were the two main competing ideologies in the world already in 1917, and to show that more than a hundred and fifty years ago intelligent men such as Tocqueville and Napoleon foresaw the rise of America and

Russia, each ruling half of the world. Yet during the second quarter of the twentieth century—more precisely, from 1920 to 1945—a new force arose in the world which—inadequately and imprecisely—has been called fascism. Whatever its name, this new force was most powerfully incarnated by Germany; and it took the combination of Western democracy and communism, incarnated by the United States, Great Britain, and the Soviet Union, to defeat Germany and fascism. Neither the democratic powers nor the communist Soviet Union could have done it alone.

In the United States, as in Germany too, the crisis of capitalism during the Depression increased the mass appeal of radical nationalists rather than of international Socialists or Communists. After 1933 Roosevelt's main rivals were people on the radical Right, not on the radical Left.† His erstwhile allies Huey Long and the Reverend Charles Coughlin were breaking away from him. The career of the former was cut short by assassination; around the latter a mass following began to gather. In Coughlin's radio talks a preaching of social justice and of a respectable American nationalism included anti-communism as well as anti-capitalism, with recognizable symptoms of anti-Semitism. The roots of this kind of ideology were populist, isolationist, midwestern, folkish—no matter how American, they corresponded to much of the national socialist programs of many European nations in the thirties. But in 1937 a single archiepiscopal admonition was sufficient to stop Father Coughlin's national radio hour; and the challenge to Roosevelt from the nationalistic Right abated, at least for a while.

There can be no question but that the great majority of Americans in the 1930s wanted strong centralized government, less to oversee their lives than to correct the wrongs and inequities in the life of the nation. The head of a national police is never popular; but in the United States in the 1930s J. Edgar Hoover and his G-men were popular heroes perhaps second only to Roosevelt himself. Yet the organization, regulations, and institutions of the New Deal would not have succeeded without the personal imprint of the President. He was a leader, which is what most (though not all) believers in the merits of strong centralized government also wanted. For whatever reasons, confidence came naturally to Roosevelt. His grin was not the often-appalling grin that politicians wear as if it were a mask. Even when we consider the shallowness of some of the ideas that Roosevelt entertained, they do not amount to much beside the patrician self-confidence

† On the level of popular sentiment. On the level of public opinion the influence of progressives and even of Communists remained considerable; about the essential difference between popular sentiment and public opinion see Chapter 7, pp. 263ff.

with which he presided over the destinies of the Republic at a complicated and difficult time. His empiricism was the empiricism of a patrician, not of a bureaucrat. This was one of the reasons why the optimism of America asserted itself even before the ravages of the Depression were to disappear. In 1937 there were still nine million unemployed in the United States; but somehow the overall impression of the Republic was not that of a depressed nation. The rest of the world saw in the United States a bright and youthful and perhaps even a happy-go-lucky country, blessed with riches and opportunities, emanating gold and silver dust across the Atlantic in the afternoon sunshine, burdened with none of the darkening clouds that hung over the skies of the great cities of Europe and England. Seldom in the history of the twentieth century was this impression of American youthfulness—of youthfulness even more than of good fortune—so much in contrast with Europe. This was important, because the second great involvement of the United States in the destinies of Europe was about to begin. In this respect, too, Roosevelt's presence was a blessing, though perhaps only in the short run. Had someone like Hoover been the President of the United States in 1939 there might not have been a second world war; but Adolf Hitler would have won his European war.

(7)

We have seen that the movements of public opinion and of popular sentiment in the history of the American democracy are often very slow. The subsequent time lag is often a formidable handicap for American foreign policy, in addition to the other formidable handicap that Tocqueville saw: ". . . it is in the nature of democracies to have, for the most part, most confused or erroneous ideas on external affairs, and to decide questions of foreign policy on purely domestic [political] considerations." The first four or five years of the Roosevelt administration caused few problems in this respect. When it came to world affairs, Roosevelt was better equipped than Wilson had been. However, like Wilson, Roosevelt thought for some time that his main, and perhaps only, business consisted of domestic concerns. His foreign policy ideas in 1932 were not very different from Hoover's. A mixture of benevolent isolationism and of internationalism marked the few foreign policy decisions of Roosevelt's first administration: the overdue decision to establish diplomatic relations with Soviet Russia, the reduction of the states of the American military protectorate in Cuba, the commitment to the eventual independence of the Philippines. By 1937, however, a large undertow was obstructing the course of the American ship of state: the aforementioned time lag. During the thirties the ideas, the reactions, and the arguments that, fifteen or more years earlier, disaffected Progressives and intellectuals had raised against the then recent memory of American intervention in World War I had filtered down to the popular level. Not only most of the Republicans but many of the Democratic senators and congressmen who had supported Roosevelt were now more or less convinced isolationists. In 1937 Congress passed a Neutrality Act, prohibiting American shipping and trading with any nation at war. A Republican congressman proposed a constitutional amendment calling for a national referendum before an American declaration of war, thus taking the matter out of the hands of Congress as well as of the President; it was defeated but not without some difficulty. A division among the American people had opened at the very time when Roosevelt became aware of the darkening of the international horizon, with its ominous prospects of a second world war.

The First World War was almost entirely fought in Europe; the Second World War would be fought in Asia as well as in Europe. About the existence of American responsibilities and interests in Europe (and England) the American people were evidently divided. About the existence of American interests in the western Pacific such a division was less evident. Fifty years before the 1930s, Americans had been overwhelmingly in favor of halting immigration from across the Pacific; their decision to restrict immigration from across the Atlantic was more difficult, but it finally came decades later. On the conscious level of statecraft, too, American decisions about the Far East were usually made more swiftly than decisions involving the relations of the United States with European states. This difference in the frequency and the relative swiftness in which corrections and changes in the course of the American ship of state were made was perhaps due to the condition that Americans were habitually more self-confident in regard to Asia than Europe. The presence and the influence of the United States in the Far East had a long history. Russia was a close neighbor of Japan; yet it was the United States, coming from the faraway eastern shores of the Pacific, that opened up Japan in 1853. Fifty years later the tangible influence of the United States in China as well as in Japan was greater than that of Russia and even of Britain. In 1900 the mere enunciation of the American Open Door principle (not backed up by any kind of American resolution to enforce it) temporarily halted the division of China. By that time the Americanization of many Japanese institutions had already begun. Five years later the Japanese were pleased to accept Theodore Roosevelt as the arbitrator in their war with Russia during which the Japanese went from triumph to triumph—only to be disappointed in finding that Roosevelt was not partial to them in the drafting of the peace treaty of Portsmouth. During the First World War Japan built a formidable navy. She was about to establish a kind of protectorate over eastern China, reducing the central Chinese Government to the status of a satellite, when the United States intervened again, and the Japanese had to desist—temporarily. After the First World War a mere American frown was sufficient to deter the British from renewing their propitious naval alliance with Japan when that was due in 1921. The following year Charles Evans Hughes, one of the few first-rate secretaries of state in the twentieth century, presiding in Washington over an international conference, put through a general naval disarmament plan which reduced the preponderance of the Japanese Navy in the Pacific as well as another international declaration against the further dismemberment of China. Whatever the long-range consequences of these acts of American statesmanship in the Far East, they were more successful than the attempts to implement some of the Wilsonian ideals in Europe had been. At any rate, few Americans knew or cared enough to object to this kind of American statesmanship in the Orient, while American involvement in Europe was another matter.

What Americans did not realize was that the principal reality in the Far East was the continuing dissolution of China. More than a hundred years before the Washington Conference of 1922, Napoleon, on St. Helena, said that the future belonged to America and to Russia, after which the "sleeping giant" of China was bound to awake. Yet for most of the twentieth century China was less a sleeping giant than a prostrate and shivering monster. The Japanese recognized this better than had others. About 1930 they also recognized that the British and the Russians and even the Americans had plenty of domestic troubles; consequently none of them would go to war against the Japanese if and when the latter moved ahead in China. The Japanese had taken all of Korea twenty or twenty-five years earlier; now (in 1931) they would take all of Manchuria; after that, Peking. Their calculations were right, at least in the short run. Apart from a doctrinal condemnation by the Secretary of State, Stimson, there was not the slightest sign of American, and of course not of British or French, naval or military movements. The long run was another matter. In 1933 Stalin responded eagerly to the American proposal of formal diplomatic relations in part because he feared a Japanese movement against the Far Eastern provinces of the Soviet Union. During the next eight years American–Soviet relations had their ups and downs, but eventually 1933 would lead to 1945, to the short-lived but decisive American–Russian military alliance against Japan. The other matter that the Japanese failed to recognize was the rising American sentiment in China's favor. In 1937 the Japanese resumed their advances in China. They occupied Peking; within a year they occupied all of the great coastal cities of China. The Chinese military resistance against Japan was desultory; the American indignation at Japanese aggressiveness was not. Whether the Japanese involvement in China really threatened American interests may be a moot point in retrospect; it was not a moot point at the time. The naval restrictions of the decade before were gone too. The Japanese were building a big modern navy. The prospect of a war in the Pacific was now considered possible by both sides; their clandestine intelligence operations were stepped up.

Yet it was the rise of Germany, even more than that of Japan, that began to command Roosevelt's attention by 1937—a rise that was even more spectacular than that of Japan, even though Central Europe was far removed from the imperial sphere of the United States. Hitler wanted to achieve German domination in Europe, and at least the uncontested rule of Germany over Central and Eastern Europe. Unlike his predecessor, the Kaiser, he was not much interested in colonies. He hoped against hope that the British would allow such a German preponderance in Europe, in exchange for a respectful German noninterference in the continued existence of the worldwide British Empire. He did not recognize that by the 1930s the existence of the British Empire depended on the goodwill of the United States. He did not realize that his fond dream of a British alliance with Germany was impossible for many reasons, the principal one being that this would necessitate a British choice between Germany and the United States—which, for the British, would be no choice at all. Hitler eventually came to understand that the British resolve to oppose him was powerfully activated, if not principally motivated, by the knowledge of the British that they could count on American sympathy and eventual support, and that Roosevelt was the principal factor in the latter.

Roosevelt and Hitler could not have been more different, in upbringing, ideals, temperament, and character; yet their public careers had a chronological correspondence. Both assumed power in early 1933; both died in April 1945. The spectacular domestic achievements of both took place during the first six years of their respective reigns; during the second six years they became the leaders of giant states at war. Hitler underestimated the primitive powers of Stalin's Russia; Roosevelt underestimated Stalin's appetite for territorial power. In 1937 these matters still lay in the future. In October 1937 in Chicago, Roosevelt, speaking in near-Wilsonian terms, declared the desirability to "quarantine" the aggressor states of the world, by which he meant Japan, Hitler's Germany, perhaps Mussolini's Italy. Whatever the reactions of the American people to that speech (they are still debated by historians) it marked a turning point in Roosevelt's interests. Exactly a month after that speech Hitler delivered an important secret speech to his generals, the meaning of which has been debated by historians, but the chronological purport of which was rather clear: time was working against Germany, whose armed forces must be ready to translate her opportunities into actual conquest before it was too late.

Thereafter the rhythm of Hitler's and Roosevelt's progress diverged. The year 1938 Hitler's, not Roosevelt's. Hitler conquered Austria, dismembered Czechoslovakia, forcing Britain and France to agree to the dominance of the Third Reich on the Continent. Many Americans watched this German progress with horrified interest. When Hitler's brutal persecution of German Jews was stepped up in the autumn of 1938 this had an impact on many Americans, including Roosevelt. During the winter of 1938–39 Roosevelt, confidently and secretly, began to suggest the possibility of American support to certain politicians in London and Paris who preferred to resist, rather than appease, the Third Reich. Hitler was aware of this. By January 1939 he concluded that Roosevelt was his archenemy, a condition that Hitler attributed to the influence of Jews.

In 1939 there were still millions unemployed in the United States. Critics of Roosevelt have often claimed that he counted on the coming of the war to put an end to this considerable remnant of the Depression. They are confusing cause and effect. The domestic condition of unemployment had nothing to do with Roosevelt's crystallizing resolve to arm against Hitler. It was the other way around: the ending of the unemployment was one of the results of the American armament program that began in 1939–40. Indeed, no matter how fast the American armament program proceeded (in retrospect, remarkably fast), Roosevelt's inclination to war against Hitler developed gradually, because of his awareness of the domestic persistence of isolationism.

When Hitler invaded Poland in 1939 Roosevelt declared the neutrality of the United States; but, unlike 1914, the President of the United States said that he could not ask his countrymen to remain neutral in their sentiments. The entire world now watched the United States, whose prestige and power were enormous. Unlike the Kaiser, Hitler carefully kept the United States in mind. He gave definite orders not to interfere with American ships—that is, not to give Roosevelt a pretext for an American declaration of war. Unlike in 1914, virtually every diplomatic and military move of the French and British governments was made with its effects on American opinion in mind—even before Roosevelt's confidant, Churchill, the incarnation of the Western resistance to Hitler, became the leader of Britain in May 1940, when the dramatic phase of the Second World War suddenly opened. The German armies poured into Western Europe, rushing to the Channel. At first Roosevelt thought that, if worse came to worst, the British fleet would come over to America. Churchill told him that he could not commit a future British government to that: if Britain were to be defeated, the existence of the fleet would be the only card held by a government seeking an armistice. Yet apart from their disagreement about such a lugubrious eventuality Roosevelt and Churchill fairly saw eye to eye about Hitler. Even the tragic collapse of the French armies—which surprised many Americans even more than it surprised the British—did not shake their resolution. Six weeks after the fall of France, Roosevelt made his first practical commitment on the British side. He declared that as commander in chief of the American armed forces it was within his province to offer fifty old American destroyers to Britain in exchange for the American occupancy of certain British bases in the western Atlantic and in the Caribbean. During the following sixteen months, Roosevelt's departures from neutrality developed in succession. His Lend-Lease program offered arms and ships to the British (and to all of their allies, including later the Russians) without limit and on credit; American marines, sailors, and soldiers were sent forward into Greenland and Iceland; American warships were ordered to extend their patrols to the middle of the Atlantic and fire at German naval craft at sight; American diplomacy and intelligence operations now included the stirring up of opposition and resistance against Germany in every corner of the world. Yet Hitler would not be baited: he ordered German naval forces not to respond to any American provocation, not even in self-defense.

During this time—that is, before Pearl Harbor—many Americans, perhaps even the majority of the nation, were perplexed and divided. In 1939, unlike in 1914, many Americans thought and feared that sooner or later they would be sucked into this European war. Between 1939 and 1941, unlike between 1914 and 1917, there was no real revolution in American opinion and sentiment; there was, instead, a decrease in the national reluctance to commit the United States to the cause of defeating Hitler, though not necessarily at the cost of American lives. The decrease of this massive reluctance was, however, agonizingly slow. As a matter of fact, the presence of opponents to an American commitment on the side of Britain (and a year later on the side of Russia) was not noticeably decreasing. Around the sincere and attractive personality of Colonel Charles Lindbergh gathered millions of Americans whose opposition to Roosevelt's foreign policy was much more deep-seated than was their opposition to the social and financial reform of the New Deal. They ranged from Coughlinites and German-Americans to former Populists and western Progressives, from old Republican isolationists to even a few socialist pacifists. Roosevelt was aware of this public opposition in which he saw the visible tip of the iceberg of American isolationist sentiment. He may have overestimated the size of the iceberg; in any event, he moved cautiously both before and after his unprecedented third-term election in November 1940. He could have taken satisfaction from the circumstance that in June 1940 the Republicans nominated a candidate, Wendell Willkie, who was, like Roosevelt, an internationalist who favored the support of Britain. Yet Roosevelt in 1940 was less swift and daring in his means of summoning popular support for his foreign policy than he had been in domestic affairs during the New Deal.

When in September 1940 Hitler abandoned his plan to invade Britain directly, he suddenly offered Japan an alliance, aimed against the United States, which the Japanese, rather thoughtlessly, accepted at once. Thereafter American opposition to Japanese expansion (which was considerable, since in Southeast Asia the Japanese were taking advantage of the collapse of France and of the Netherlands, and of the difficulties of the British at bay) increased swiftly. In early 1941 the American chiefs of staff made a very important decision. If it came to a double war against Germany as well as Japan, the defeat of Germany—that is, the European theater of war—would have the priority. This strategic decision, which proved to be reasonable and effective, nonetheless did not quite accord with the preferences of American popular sentiment. Ideally speaking, Roosevelt and his administration should have striven for peace in the Pacific in order to enable the United States to concentrate its efforts on the Atlantic side, in support of Britain. This was not what happened. Probably Roosevelt knew that it would be easier to maneuver the Japanese than to maneuver Hitler into an incident, attacking American ships or bases; more probably he knew that fighting the Japanese would be even more popular, especially in the Midwest and in the West, than fighting the Germans.‡ It was thus that Pearl Harbor put an end to conscious American isolationism. It united the nation in more than one way, though some of the elements of the bitter divisions before Pearl Harbor now became submerged, to reappear, in somewhat altered forms, after the war. The record of the negotiations and relations between Japan and the United States before Pearl Harbor is com-

‡ A strange nemesis: most of the warships sunk at Pearl Harbor were named after the states of the Far West, including three of the four last states that had joined the Union: the *Arizona*, the *Oklahoma*, the *Utah*, the *California*.

plex. Misunderstandings, including sometimes willful ones, coagulated and congealed on both sides until the Japanese—somewhat reluctantly—came to the conclusion that time was working against them, and that what the Americans wanted was a Japanese abandonment of nearly all of their latter-day conquests, including those in China. That during the ten days before Pearl Harbor Roosevelt knew of the imminence of a Japanese attack seems certain; there is, however, no incontestable evidence that he or his principal commanders knew of a Japanese assault coming as far east as Hawaii.

(8)

Pearl Harbor was not the only catastrophe. It was followed by six months of American defeats on land and at sea. Within days American outposts in the western Pacific were surrendering. General MacArthur in the Philippines was no more prepared for the Japanese attack than the commanders in Hawaii had been, and with less excuse. His retreat from the Philippines was inglorious; like the weakling British commanders in Singapore, MacArthur vastly overestimated the size of the Japanese army that was pressing down on him. On the Atlantic side, packs of German submarines were roaming to and fro, sinking American ships freely, their sightings at night made easy by the halos of light around the coastal towns and cities. There were moments of irresolution and near-panic—when, for example, MacArthur proposed that in order to save his troops the independence and neutrality of the Philippines should be promptly proclaimed; when the Japanese–American citizenry of the West Coast were herded into concentration camps, with the assent of the President and of Francis Biddle, the doctrinaire liberal Attorney General of the United States; when crews of American merchant ships refused to sign up for transatlantic convoys and even for the coastal runs from New York to ports in the Caribbean. Yet all of this mattered little. It was counterweighted by American confidence from the beginning. There was virtually no one who thought that the United States and her allies could not win the war. There were people who entertained doubts about America's allies and about the ultimate outcome of the war, but their criticisms were fragmentary. The monstrous reputation of Hitler was of great help to Roosevelt, not to speak of the fact that after Pearl Harbor it was Hitler who declared war on the United States without waiting for Roosevelt to act.

The resolution of the American people was soon manifest in the very waging of the war. Less than five months after Pearl Harbor, and hardly two months after the fall of Singapore, American planes dropped bombs on a surprised Tokyo. In the battles of the Coral Sea and Midway (the latter the first sea battle in history where the opposing fleets did not see each other, the battle being fought mainly by airplanes from their respective carriers) the American Navy and its Air Corps showed that they were equal to or better than the hardiest of their Japanese counterparts, and not only because of superior American equipment, and the American reading of important Japanese signals. Six months after Pearl Harbor the British found that the problem was no longer American slowness but the prospect of American recklessness. Roosevelt and his generals were seriously contemplating an invasion of France in November 1942, something that Churchill (rightly) thought would debouch in disaster. He succeeded, instead, in convincing Roosevelt that the Allies should land in French North Africa instead. When this landing took place, in November, the fortunes of the whole world war were turning. Within a month the Russians had surrounded a German army at Stalingrad, the British had turned back the Germans in the Western Desert, the Americans had forced the Japanese on the retreat in Guadalcanal, and, with the landings in North Africa the Mediterranean offensive against Germany and Italy had begun. That the appointed American commander of the entire European theater, Eisenhower, was a cautious strategist mattered little. What mattered was that a year after Pearl Harbor the war was as good as won.

The American people doubted that not for a moment. They also saw that this world war, like the first, would cost them relatively little in blood, sweat, and tears. Their cities and their land were unvexed by foreign attacks; most of their sons and their husbands were not likely to lose their lives in such holocausts as Verdun during the First World War or Stalingrad during this one; most of them would return to families that were suffering few hardships during the war years and whose prosperity was indeed increasing. The industrialist Henry J. Kaiser in 1943 estimated (and the government agreed with him) that ten million new houses would be needed after the war—a war by which not a single house in the United States was destroyed. Half of all the workers in American aircraft factories were women; by 1942 more than one of every three American workers was a woman. The factories and the shipyards were turning out nearly three hundred airplanes and launching more than four ships each day for the country and for its allies. More than two thirds of the gold stock of the world was deposited in Fort Knox. There were shortages of meat, sugar, and gasoline, here and there; but price controls worked, generally speaking; prices rose less than 22 percent during the entire four years of the war, and savings rose even higher—by more than 24 percent. Thus the impression on the world of American prosperity and power was no illusion; the prosperity and the power were sustained by the confidence of the American people.

In 1943 the march to victory was slowing down. Roosevelt and the American commanders refused Churchill's urging to exploit the Mediterranean campaign after Mussolini's fall. The invasion of France was postponed until the late spring of 1944. Roosevelt and his advisers chose to postpone, too, considerations of the political state of Europe after the war. One of the sources of this kind of procrastination was the President's tiredness. He had aged suddenly, he was less and less able to concentrate, a fact kept from the American people for many years, indeed for decades afterward. Yet another source, on the more conscious level of Roosevelt's own thinking, was his persistent concern with isolationism, his anxiety that the American people would not support a protracted American presence in Europe after the war. (This anxiety was, to some extent, justified: the war against Japan remained more popular than the war against Germany; many of Roosevelt's Republican opponents were plumping for an "Asia First" strategy.) Another source, connected with the first two, was Roosevelt's mental investment in the prospects of a promising relationship with Stalin. The Russians were chewing up the German Army (and perhaps they would take a big bite at the Japanese, too)—even before American boys would have to get into fierce and bloody battles with the Germans on the European continent. When Roosevelt and Churchill and Stalin met, first at Teheran in 1943, then fourteen months later at Yalta, Roosevelt took very great care to avoid the impression that he and Churchill were in cahoots. He wished to impress Stalin of the contrary. On several occasions he sided with Stalin rather than with Churchill. This positioning of himself between Churchill and Stalin was not merely symbolic. It issued from Roosevelt's belief that in the progressive evolution of the world the United States occupied a middle position, between the sometimes admirable but essentially antiquated virtues of the British as incarnated in the Old Tory Churchill and the sometimes admirable pioneer egalitarian society of the Soviet Union as incarnated in the rough-and-ready Stalin. This belief was not Franklin Roosevelt's brainchild, nor was it his monopoly. It was exactly what most enlightened Americans, including their intellectual and military establishments, believed at the time. Wendell Willkie and Henry Wallace visited the Soviet Union and returned to write glowing best sellers about their experiences. In 1943 there was hardly any difference between the ideology of Willkie's *One World* and *The*

American Century, the dominant presence of which Henry Luce had announced two years earlier. *Time* and *Life* and *Fortune,* the opinion-making magazines such as *The Atlantic* or *Saturday Review,* the editorials of the principal newspapers were in accord. They represented the American ideology at the time.

By the time of the Yalta Conference the American and the British and the Russian armies were moving forward on German soil. In the Pacific the American Navy had destroyed the Japanese fleet, and the fires of war were burning closer and closer to Japan. It was now demonstrably true that the United States, perhaps alone among the great powers of the world, could fight a world war on two fronts, triumphantly so. This was not lost on Stalin, who, nonetheless, was surprised to see how easily Roosevelt let him get what he wanted, if not more. He would get an uncontested Russian zone of influence over the eastern half of Europe, over eastern Germany, and a restoration of the dominant position imperial Russia had had in the Far East before the Russo–Japanese War of 1904–5 in exchange for his going along with Roosevelt in two matters: promising to take Russia into the war against Japan, and to take Russia into the United Nations. At Yalta he also helped Roosevelt in muffling some of the political problems of Europe in verbiage. The Yalta declarations were hailed by Americans (including some who were beginning to be anxious about problems that might arise with Russia after the war) and by such different people as General MacArthur, ex-President Herbert Hoover, and Miss Elsa Maxwell, as The New Dispensation for the World, a revelation of internationalism surpassing even the Fourteen Points.* Soon it appeared that imprecise grandiloquent statements such as "The Declaration for Liberated Europe" meant but one thing for Stalin: American acquiescence in Russian rule in Eastern Europe in exchange for his noninterference with American rule in Western Europe—indeed, with American rule almost anywhere else in the world. That Yalta amounted to such a division of the globe was obvious to a few people such as General de Gaulle. To the American people it was not obvious at all.

* Elsa Maxwell in a column about Yalta: "This is it! The model for permanent peace! A new method of life!"

(9)

When Roosevelt suddenly died, on 12 April 1945, the American sun stood at its zenith. American power seemed irresistible. It was as if the United States could rule the world. The Japanese were cracking under the hail of American bombs; in Europe, American troops could have swept into Berlin and Prague had their commander, Eisenhower, wanted them there, which he didn't. In Moscow the Soviet newspapers ran black-bordered first pages with Roosevelt's photograph; even in Tokyo the Japanese press spoke respectfully of this American President whose world renown at this moment was perhaps greater than that of any American President in history. Hardly anyone knew how feeble and ill this President had been for some time. The American people were uneasy at the prospect of the new president, Harry S Truman, an unknown quantity to them. They ought to have been uneasy with something else, with the duality in the American national mind. In one way they wanted to rule the world; in another way they did not.† These contradictory reactions corresponded with certain domestic political currents that began to appear on the surface almost immediately after Roosevelt's demise—undercurrents which may have been strategically and logically contradictory while their emotional source was a kind of xenophobia: a distrust of the British (who might involve the Americans in European "power politics") as well as a growing distrust of the Russians (whose immoral ideology of "atheistic communism" had insidious supporters within the United States).

About the Pacific there was no such division. There was no need for the United States to share its victory with others. Victory after victory crowned the record of the Navy and of the Army. A sense of American self-confidence was not only wholly warranted, it was represented by the wise moderation of certain American political decisions, foremost the decision (in contrast to Wilson's in 1918) to keep and to respect the institution of monarchy in Japan. At Yalta, and even later in 1945, Roosevelt and his commanders were willing to pay a considerable price (considerable espe-

† See about this Chapter 6, pp. 242ff. The New York *Times* on 11 June 1945: "General Eisenhower declared that the European war had been a holy war—more than any war in history. 'Speaking for the Allied forces,' he added, 'I say we are going to have peace even if we have to fight for it.' "

cially at the expense of China) for Stalin's promise to enter the war against Japan three months after the end of the war against Germany—mostly because of the bloody prospect of an American invasion of the Japanese homeland. As the summer progressed, the necessity for such a Russian participation lessened. Stalin kept his word and declared war on Japan on 9 August; but this merely speeded up the resolution of the Japanese Emperor and of his conservative chamberlains to accept the American terms for surrender, a resolution that had been forming earlier, and to the final crystallization of which the two American atomic bombs cast on Hiroshima and Nagasaki contributed as much as the Russian declaration of war. Three weeks later the formal surrender of the Japanese in Tokyo Bay was a great event. That shining scene reflected the apogee of American power. A giant American fleet sparkled in the sun. The American airplanes came out of the clouds, roaring over the bay and laying their celestial stripes over Japan. The American commanders had a sense of occasion. The battleship *Missouri* flew the thirty-one-star flag of Commodore Perry together with the flag that had flown over the Capitol in Washington on Pearl Harbor Day. The words of General MacArthur to the Japanese delegation shone with American self-confidence and with a certain magnanimity. The Japanese bowed courteously; they accepted the dominant presence of the American victors in their midst.

The United States was not only the greatest power on earth—she had the monopoly of a new weapon, the atom bomb. Truman told Stalin of its existence during the summit conference in Potsdam in July, the last summit and an inconclusive one. Stalin pretended not to be greatly impressed, and perhaps he was not. Soon it was evident that the American Government would not share the secret of the manufacturing of the bomb with the Russians; but it was also evident that the American Government would not use its monopoly of the bomb in order to revise or to correct the division of the world agreed upon at Yalta. The majority of the American people saw in the bomb yet another manifestation of the superiority of American technology, even though the bomb had been thought up by scientist refugees from Europe. A minority of Americans were disturbed by the specter of the bomb, convincing themselves that what was now urgently needed were universal disarmament, world government, and the sharing of everything, including atomic secrets, with the Russians. This kind of harebrained ideology was, however, not less American than that of the American nationalists (another minority then), who were at least tempted to think that with the possession of the bomb the United States could lay down the law of the world to the Russians.

The majority, though beginning to manifest some uneasiness about communism, accepted (even though without much enthusiasm) the new dispensation of internationalism, including the United Nations. The United Nations seemed to be a grandiose and novel idea; we have seen that President Roosevelt made many concessions to Stalin for the sake of assuring the participation of the Soviet Union in the United Nations. Yet the United Nations was perhaps the most evident example of an idea and of an institution which seemed supermodern and broad-minded whereas, in reality, it was outdated and narrow. Outdated: because the United Nations was nothing more than a "streamlined," that is, a superficially redesigned, version of Wilson's League of Nations, which had issued from nineteenth-century ideas of British utilitarian liberalism, including the pipe-dreams of a Parliament of Man. Narrow: because the internationalist concept of the United Nations was but the result of a specifically *American* concept of internationalism, again of a Wilsonian kind, legalistic and institutional instead of realistic and historical. The pedigree of its idea, the formulation of its concept, the propagation of its institutionalization, the place of its founding assembly (San Francisco), the location of its headquarters (Manhattan; situated on land donated by the Rockefellers), the very appearance, the architecture, the procedures, the entire atmosphere of its bureaucratic skyscraper were specifically American. That the United Nations, during the nearly four decades of its existence, has served a few (very few) practical purposes on occasion is undeniable; what is, alas, even less deniable is the rapid degeneration of its functions. Less than two decades after its establishment it became, often, a theater for anti-American rhetoric, and an obstacle, instead of an instrument, for the promotion of American interests. In sum, its very degeneration has been a clear and manifest example of the shortcomings of the dominant philosophy of American internationalism, dominant in the minds of people such as Wilson and Roosevelt and the Rockefellers, indeed, in the minds of what could be called, with pardonable imprecision, the entire American internationalist Establishment at the time.

The source of these simplistic assumptions was not American naïveté—it was the shortcoming of American thinking about human nature. In a best seller about the age of Jackson, published in 1945, the young historian Arthur M. Schlesinger, Jr., proclaimed that men are neither beasts nor angels—a typically moderate and liberal article of faith. To the contrary, the history of the Second World War alone should have demonstrated that men, as Pascal had said, are both beasts and angels. That the moral range of "normal" humanity was far greater than the generally accepted (and acceptable) progressive view was something Americans had yet to learn.

That kind of experience with human nature—within the nation even more than outside it—was perhaps the essence of the mental and spiritual experience of many Americans during the difficult and sometimes painful times that followed the last world war. In 1945 the American people took it for granted that they were the greatest nation in the entire history of the world, and that their relatively easy victory in World War II merely confirmed this. Yet this sun-baked American zenith had its dark side, like the moon.‡ The very achievement of the atom bomb was a triumph of technology over reason. There were many Americans who uneasily sensed this. Other Americans, perhaps the majority, found it difficult to admit that the United States had not won the war alone, that it had to share the victory with the Soviet Union, particularly in Europe, and along a definite geographical frontier. The cold war—that imprecise term did not become current until about 1948—with Russia had been forming even before the war had ended. It was greatly, though not exclusively, the result of a reciprocal misunderstanding. Stalin feared that the Americans, now well established in Western Europe, were about to challenge his overlordship of Eastern Europe, something that they had at least tacitly allowed him at Yalta. The American Government feared that after the establishment of Communist governments in Eastern Europe the Russians were about to provoke and sustain Communist revolutions in Western Europe. This was a mutual misreading of intentions. Yet perhaps they only shaped the beginning of the cold war without causing it. As late as 1944 the American Government wished to limit both the duration and the geographical extent of the American occupation in middle Europe. Its main concern then had been to assure that the Russians remain the principal allies of the United States and that they participate in the final assaults on Germany and Japan. Three years later its main concern was the presence of Russians and Communists in the middle of Europe and in the Far East.

This revolution in the expectations and in the position of the United States Government in regard to the Soviet Union corresponded with a revolution of American popular sentiment. American public opinion and popular sentiment had not really been in harmony toward the end of the war. Public opinion was more interested in Europe than was popular sentiment; public opinion rationalized certain illusions about Russia and the postwar order that American popular sentiment had not entertained: but

‡ In November 1945, a few months after the first successful detonation of an atom bomb in the Indian desert of New Mexico an American gangster, "Bugsy" Siegel, laid down the foundations of another monument of a nocturnal desert civilization in the Far West, the first casino-hotel in Las Vegas. Alamogordo 1945, Las Vegas 1945: the conjunction of these dates and places contains a meaning, at least to this historian's mind.

two or three years after the war the equation of anti-communism with the American national interest was accepted by Washington as well as by the American people at large. The roots of this revolution, however, went deeper than rationalization about foreign policy. People who had been isolationists were now interventionists—and also the reverse. That many Americans now had second thoughts not only about the nation's wartime foreign alliances but about the entire Roosevelt ideology was evident in the 1946 congressional elections when the Republicans picked up more than the usual gain of midterm seats, their slogan having been a clever one: HAD ENOUGH?*

This was the time in the political history of the United States when the ideology and the distinctions of the two American political parties ceased to be an exclusively and peculiarly American phenomenon, uninterpretable to foreigners. The combination of nationalism and socialism, the worldwide pattern of the political development of the twentieth century (of which Hitler's Nazism was a totalitarian and extremist German version) survived the war and the demise of Hitler. Since the Second World War practically all governments of the world, and every political party in the world, have espoused, or at least have been forced to practice, variants of the mix of nationalism and socialism, whether they have admitted this or not. In the United States, too, nationalism proved more powerful than internationalism—while after the New Deal and the war a return to unbridled capitalism in the United States was practically out of the question. The principal difference between the Republicans and the Democrats was now mainly the difference of the compounds of their nationalism and socialism. The Republicans, true to their past, were almost always more nationalistic than socialistic; the Democrats were often (though not always) less nationalistic and more socialistic than the Republicans.

* Proposed to the Republican National Committee by the Harry M. Frost Advertising Agency in Boston.

2

TOCQUEVILLE REVERSED

(1)

After World War II most Americans still believed not only that they were living in the most prosperous nation in the world but that they led the best lives among the peoples of the world: the freest people in the freest country, the most Christian of peoples in the most Christian of countries. Their behavior did not necessarily confirm these beliefs. The characteristic American duality remained. Between 1944 and 1948 the marriage rate of Americans was the second highest in the entire world.* The marriage age also dropped to the lowest level in the history of the nation. The cult of the family was asserted more strenuously in the United States than in many other countries. Yet in 1946 alone more than 18 percent of American marriages were dissolved, a percentage that would not be reached again until the 1970s, after the children of so many immature early marriages had grown up to marry and divorce in turn.

For many reasons the national disillusionment with the memories of the war and with the wartime alliances was less strong and less durable than the disillusionment after 1918. One of these was the character of Harry Truman. His command of the American ship of state was steady from the beginning, much steadier than many people, including the remnants of the crowd around Roosevelt, had thought it would be. Truman's view of the world differed as much from that of people such as Senator Taft, who feared communism and thought (and said) consequently that fighting Hitler's Germany may have been a mistake, as from people such as Henry Wallace, who thought (and said) that American opposition to Russia was wrong. Truman's strength of character was such that he represented not only a middle Americanism between such ideological and political extremes but was often superior to both. Perhaps this was why he won

* The first was Egypt, where child marriages were very common at the time.

the election in 1948, when otherwise the national reaction against the foreign policy of the war had risen. Moreover, most of the nationalist voters who had now come to equate anti-communism with American patriotism were not willing to risk their social benefits accumulated through the New Deal. Their traditional distrust of the businessman-Republican mentality was still strong, even though the differences between the social philosophies of the two national parties had diminished.

In global strategy, too, the government of the United States took a relatively moderate course between the extremes of isolationism and of global interventionism. The Soviet Union and the spread of communism would be "contained" along the "iron curtain." Stalin would be told: this far and no farther. "Containment" was a phrase coined by George F. Kennan in 1947; "iron curtain" was a phrase made popular by Churchill when he visited the United States the year before. It is ironic that neither Churchill nor Kennan saw the world in the way Washington and the American Establishment were to see it. Churchill as well as Kennan thought that the existing division of Europe was wrong; eventually they tried to suggest its partial dissolution or at least its revision, but in vain. Washington was not unhappy with the division of Europe and of the Far East, provided only that the Russians and Communists would not break the line and penetrate farther; meanwhile, on this side of the iron curtain, the organization of the Free World under American leadership, and with its main instruments of American financial and economic aid, would be set up. It was thus that in 1947 the Truman Doctrine, the Marshall Plan, and the first steps toward a North Atlantic Alliance came about. The first committed the United States to underwrite the defense of Greece and Turkey—a commitment that the threadbare British Labour government had pressed on its rich American ally; the Marshall Plan underwrote the economic reconstruction of Western Europe, partly because of the erroneous assumption that communism thrives on economic distress. No matter: while it did little or nothing to reduce the kind of anti-Americanism that issues from ignorance and envy, the Marshall Plan was yet another example of American generosity. Its eventual cost ($12 billion) was about the same as the cost of the war materials shipped from the United States to the Soviet Union during the war. The Marshall Plan did not deliver Western Europe from succumbing to communism, just as Lend-Lease had not been the deliverer of the Soviet Union from the assault of Nazism; yet the important contributions of Lend-Lease to the Russian war effort, and of the Marshall Plan to the reconstruction of Western Europe, are not to be gainsaid. In 1948 Stalin forced the last feeble Eastern European pseudodemocratic government (of Czechoslovakia) to accept full-scale

Communist rule; he also tried to blackmail and starve West Berlin by way of a blockade, a clumsy attempt that he gave up a year later. By that time the North Atlantic Treaty Organization was in existence. For the first time the United States and Canada were committing themselves not only to the defense of Western Europe but to the stationing of some of their armed forces there in peacetime.

This kind of a moderate internationalism—moderate in its conception, yet ultimately far from modest in its consequences—was supported by all that was enlightened and broad-minded in American opinion at a time when this kind of opinion was still principally represented by the educated Anglo-Saxon elite of the nation. It did not, however, correspond to the changes that had already taken place in the national composition of the American people or with certain powerful ideological currents among them. The main element in these currents was the unquestioning and unquestioned identification of anti-communism with American patriotism and the reciprocal identification of every kind of national or global evil with Communist conspiracy or inspiration. These currents were fed by the uneasy resentments of millions of Americans against certain representative specimens of leadership who were more liberal, cosmopolitan, eastern, educated, and established than the "average" American—whoever the latter might be. There was, alas, ample (though sometimes confusing) evidence that some intellectual bureaucrats had given themselves some importance by engaging in conspiracies with Communists during the Roosevelt years. The record of the American intelligentsia, too, had not been very inspiring, many of its members having espoused double standards, including their granting the broadest possible benefit of doubt to pro-Communist causes. The result was the overwhelming popularity of anti-communism by the end of the decade, a second Red Scare, less ludicrous but in some ways more insidious than the first one had been, and the consequent emergence of various demagogues and opportunists who would make political profit from this national mood. When in 1949 the Chinese Communists succeeded in forcing Chiang Kai-shek to abandon the Chinese mainland, the Republicans claimed that the Democrats had now lost China, and that this was yet another enormous step in the march of world communism toward the conquest of the globe.

Truman and his advisers were wise enough not to get the United States involved in the civil war of China. They also succeeded in writing a peace treaty with Japan, practically excluding Russia from the drafting of it, with surprisingly little opposition from Stalin. Unfortunately, Dean Acheson, the Secretary of State, gave insufficient attention to Korea, a country that, not unlike Germany, was divided into Communist and non-

Communist halves after 1945. Having consequently concluded (after an Acheson policy speech that had failed to mention South Korea within the American defense perimeter in the Far East) that they had little or nothing to fear from the Americans, the North Korean Communists invaded South Korea in June 1950. Truman's reaction was admirably swift. American troops went into action immediately as representatives of the United Nations, whose Security Council condemned the North Korean aggression. At first the American and allied troops were pushed back to the southern tip of Korea, but then the naval superiority of the United States asserted itself, as its troops were supported without fail across the Korean Straits from Japan. In a brilliant amphibious operation in September, General MacArthur landed behind the lines of the North Koreans, whose resistance was collapsing. An American army was nearing the Chinese frontier, behind which the Chinese showed signs of extreme agitation. President Truman, who had been told of the possibility of Chinese intervention, flew out to the Pacific to meet General MacArthur midway. The imperious commander of the Far East assured his commander in chief (as a matter of fact, somewhat contemptuously) that there was no danger of Chinese or Russian intervention. He was wrong. In less than a month hordes of Chinese troops crossed into Korea and drove the Americans back. MacArthur thought, and said, that a few bombs, possibly atomic ones, thrown on Manchuria would win the war against international communism. Truman, to his great credit, refused to believe this. Subsequently MacArthur went so far as to criticize his commander in chief in interviews freely granted to Republican politicians. In April 1951 Truman fired MacArthur, a courageous act, though its immediate repercussions were great and harmful to Truman's own reputation and to that of his party. MacArthur was now the darling of every American who had doubts about the Roosevelt or Truman policies and who was convinced of the global and conspiratorial power of communism. It was not wealthy dowagers but the stevedores of New York who demonstrated loudly against Truman upon the news of MacArthur's dismissal. In the summer of 1951 the Korean front line solidified again in the middle of the peninsula and the war died down. The man who would profit from the ensuing armistice as well as from the recent memory of the war was, however, not Truman but Eisenhower.

Eisenhower won the election in 1952, and again in 1956, hands down. This was the last time that the mainly eastern, though already diluted, financial and social powers in the Republican Party could nominate their choice against candidates from the Midwest or the West. Eisenhower presided over the destiny of much of the world at a time when the chief adversary of the United States was in considerable disarray. Stalin died a few weeks after Eisenhower's inauguration. The new Russian leaders were deeply unsure of themselves. Their acquired empire was shaken by riots and revolutions, in East Berlin, Poland, and Hungary. They were eager to improve their relations with the United States; they even indicated their willingness to explore the possibility of a reciprocal disengagement from the center of Europe, provided that this would not mean a unilateral retreat by the Soviet Union. Yet Eisenhower, the same man who in 1945 had gone out of his way to favor the Russians, now responded to this new situation not at all. He who in 1945 had embraced Marshal Zhukov and who had grasped Stalin's hand with all of the sentimental fervor of an American politician was now sour and distrustful when he had to meet Khrushchev in Geneva and then in Washington, having consented to these meetings after considerable reluctance (to the first one only after the Russians had agreed on the reciprocal evacuation of Austria in 1955). Toward the end of his administration Eisenhower refused to receive the Cuban Castro (confirming the latter's hostility to the United States); and in 1960, in Paris, Eisenhower was forced to admit that all of his peace propaganda notwithstanding he had ordered (or at least had allowed) American spy planes to crisscross the Soviet Union for years until one of them was finally shot down.

The 1950s, the Eisenhower Era, was a decade of missed opportunities. This was not uncharacteristic of this bureaucratic general and President who, despite his acquired experience with European affairs, directed American foreign policy largely along the lines drawn by the Dulles brothers, John Foster Dulles, the Secretary of State, and Allen Dulles, the head of the Central Intelligence Agency. During the 1950s the CIA grew into the principal instrument of American foreign policy, at times superseding the Department of State. It is true that during the Eisenhower presidency the general development of the nation was unvexed by crises, that Eisenhower—all of the Republican propaganda of the "liberation" of Eastern Europe notwithstanding—did not really challenge the division of Europe and of Germany, that in 1954 Eisenhower scotched the plans of American military intervention in what was then still French Indochina, that eventually he and his advisers put an end to the demagogic career of Senator Joseph McCarthy, and that at the very end of his presidential tenure Eisenhower made an unexpected speech against the dangers of a military-industrial "complex" that dominated the destinies of the nation—a warning whose original inspiration remains obscure to this day. But it was Eisenhower whose political opportunism and procrastination allowed Joseph McCarthy to become a national figure with a mass following and with an effect on the very course of the American ship of state for two years at least; and it was the same Eisenhower during whose presidency the military institutions and the imperial responsibilities of the United States grew to monstrous proportions. In 1960 military spending was three times that in 1950, the year of the Korean War. Military expenditures for scientific research and development alone jumped from an annual average of $245 million during World War II to $1.5 billion in 1956—the year before the Russians' success with their first orbital Sputnik accelerated these American expenditures even more rapidly. The foreign policy platform of the Republican Party in 1956 called for "the establishment of American bases all around the world"—the party that was still called "isolationist" by some of the public commentators, evidence of the outdated character of their political thinking. By 1958 the United States had alliances and military arrangements with nearly sixty countries: Eisenhower himself could not have listed them.

(2)

During the 1950s most of the American people went along with this development without thinking much about it. One of the reasons was the now nearly universal acceptance of anti-communism with its attendant American responsibilities and opportunities, something that even American intellectuals had come around to share; the other was the large general swelling of American popular prosperity. The general tone and temper of the Eisenhower era was, in truth, inflationary; but incomes rose faster than prices, and ownership of all kinds of things (at least on paper) was made available to all kinds of Americans through consumer credits of every possible kind, which were now offered to the vast majority of the population for the first time in their history or, indeed, in any history. Sixty percent of the people owned their houses in 1961, at least on paper. I write "at least on paper" because the actual ownership of houses or even of cars was seldom completed; before most people paid off their mortgages or debts they moved on, possibly to a more expensive automobile or house. The very sense of possession and of permanence had changed; and the efforts of American industry and business, encouraged by increasingly complex tax laws that allowed the deduction of all kinds of promotions, as if they were expenses of production, were now directed to the production of consumption even more than to the consumption of production.

For many Americans—perhaps especially for those who were too young to remember the twenties—the Eisenhower era of the fifties were halcyon years in retrospect. There were no wars, few crises, a low rate of inflation, the mass availability of all kinds of goods and pleasures, all of this accompanied by a prevalent national respectability of standards of thinking and of behavior which would seem old-fashioned enough to evoke a kind of nostalgia, especially after the dissolution of many of these standards during the late sixties. These impressions are not without some substance; yet I believe that they are essentially misleading. The apparent uniformity of the bland years of the fifties obscured the occurrence of changes that were profound and enduring in their consequences. We shall see—this being the main chronological thesis of this book—how many of these changes came to pass at the very same time, about 1955–56, by a curious, or perhaps not so curious, coincidence. We have seen how in 1956 the so-called conservative Republican Party proclaimed the desirability of an American military presence "all around the world"; yet it was in 1956 that the decline of the United States from its position as the first superpower began, since it was then (during the crisis of the Hungarian Revolution) that the Eisenhower administration proved demonstrably unwilling to consider any alteration of the division of Europe with the Russians. It was in 1956, too, that the United States helped to force the British out of Suez, speeding up the termination of the British Empire, whereby Churchill's lifelong design for an Anglo-American union or confederation of some kind finally disappeared. It was during the mid-fifties that the competitive quality of American manufactures began to decrease. It was then that the cities of the nation began to deteriorate and actually to lose population. It was then that the relatively short efflorescence of an urban and bourgeois culture in the history of American civilization came to its end. It was in 1955–56 that for the first time in American (and in world) history the majority of a working population were no longer engaged in any kind of production but in "administration" and in "services," leading to a posturban, postindustrial, posturbane, bureaucratic society. It was then that the often senseless cult of "growth" became an unquestioned American shibboleth, without any thought given to the affinity of the two matters: growth and inflation. The year 1955 was the last in which the consumer price index actually dropped by a fraction of a percentage. There was a mild recession later in the decade, but prices kept rising nonetheless. In 1956 gold began to flow out of the United States; within the next fourteen years half of the nation's gold stock was gone.

This was, then, the duality of the Eisenhower years: the grandiose increase in American consumption at the time when the inflation of prices finally caught up with the inflation of society; the bureaucratization of

American life at the time when American productivity (except in agriculture) began to decline; the enormous swelling of the American military establishment and of its expenditures at the time when the primacy of American power in the world was beginning to pass (and when the Russians, too, under Khrushchev, were searching for certain accommodations with the United States); the rapid decline, indeed, the partial disappearance, of public transportation, including railroads, at the very time when the rapidly swelling suburbs needed public transportation more than ever; the automobilization of the country growing at its fastest, promoted by the government, including the interstate highway system, at the time when the American primacy of automobile production began to erode; the establishment of the American nuclear power industry at the time when the portents of domestic as well as foreign nuclear proliferation were becoming dubious, to say the least; the great extension of all kinds of communications, including television, at a time when breakdowns of personal and family communications began to involve the private lives of all kinds of Americans. In the mid-1950s the birthrates and the marriage rates were very high; yet there were many indications that the cult of suburban "togetherness," no matter how widespread, was very superficial, since the cohesion of American family life as well as the strength of American religious beliefs were less substantial than they had been two generations, or even one generation, before. Eisenhower himself, albeit unwittingly, expressed this kind of duality. "Our government," he said, "makes no sense unless it is founded in a deeply felt religious faith—and I don't care what it is." He himself did not find it necessary to attend church—that is, to be publicly seen in church—until shortly before his election. In 1954, 96 percent of Americans polled said that they believed in God. That this quantitative statistic was largely meaningless is obvious; what was not meaningless was the compulsion of people to construct such a "poll" and to publicize its results.†

Yet, at the very time when we can, alas, detect the accumulating evidence of the beginning of a general decline in the solidity of American prosperity and of American power, the prestige of the United States and the impact of the American image on the world were more widespread than ever before. The Americanization of the world—by which I mean the imitation of American forms and patterns of life—was growing by leaps

† See Chapter 8, p. 351. Also: "New church constructions approached $1 billion in 1958, over twice the funds devoted to construction of public hospitals . . . in 1953 five of six nonfiction bestsellers had a religious theme." James Gilbert, *Another Chance: Postwar America 1945–1968* (New York, 1981), p. 238.

and bounds in five continents; even the Soviet Union and some of the Communist states were not exempt from some of its influences.

The most important effect of these influences was the emergence of democratic consumer societies, especially in Western Europe, where an American type of social democracy was finally catching up with often antiquated and merely politically democratic systems, with the consequent willingness to grant consumer credit to the masses, with its results of mass automobilization but also of the greatest increase in material standards and incomes that the populations of many countries experienced in their entire histories. These social transformations occurred mostly during the quarter century from 1948 to 1973, spurred by the American example as well as by American moneys (as in the instance of the Marshall Plan). What this meant was that by 1960, at the end of the Eisenhower years, the kind of democratic prosperity for which the United States had been famous for nearly two centuries was no longer unique. The material, and often the cultural, standards of the English, French, Italian, West German, Scandinavian, Japanese, etc., peoples, very much including their working classes, now approximated—and in some instances bypassed—those of the American masses. Nor was the American political system any longer unique. Not only had two-party systems emerged in a number of countries, but their very political rhetoric and political practices, ranging from party convention to pollsters, began to resemble those of the United States. Some of the symptoms suggesting the development of certain endemic crises within the private lives of people, mostly because of breakdowns of personal communications, had now their recognizable counterparts in the lives of millions of people in other nations. What this meant was that, for the first time, *Democracy in America* no longer referred to a unique historical situation. When Tocqueville wrote his great classic the United States was perhaps the only actual and working democracy in the world. One hundred and twenty-five years later there was a British, Irish, Dutch, Belgian, Swiss, French, Italian, Swedish, Norwegian, Finnish, West German, and a Japanese democracy; in many other countries, too, the developments of social as well as of political democracy were advancing rapidly. Now a new Tocqueville was needed who would reverse the order of the title: *American* democracy, instead of *Democracy* in America. What has remained, what is still typically *American* in American democracy? How does American democracy differ from the other democracies of the globe now? Such a book is yet to be written. Its value will have to depend on the proper recognition of the priority of national (and cultural) elements over those of the social (and institutional) ones; and its conception will have to include a comparison of the different compounds of nationalism and socialism within the states and the peoples of the globe during the second half of the twentieth century.

(3)

It was Tocqueville, too, who wrote more than a hundred and fifty years ago that "a new science of politics was necessary for a new world." This was not forthcoming. The political terminology of the nineteenth century continued to dominate American political thought, which was evident not only in the names of the two political parties but in the attribution of ideological camps: liberals and conservatives. During the 1950s a significant change occurred in this regard. As late as 1950 the word "conservative" was eschewed even by right-wing Republicans. By 1960 the adjective had become respectable, not merely among the conservative minority (then still a small minority among American intellectuals) but also in public usage. This was but the beginning of a gradual change whereby in the 1970s, for the first time in their history, the majority of Americans so questioned would designate themselves as "conservatives" rather than "liberals." It was then that the monopoly of liberalism in American intellectual life, too, was finally broken. Near the end of the 1950s certain American intellectuals proclaimed "the end of ideology" as a result of the great general consensus within a prosperous mass society. The revolutionary play-acting of the sixties, the mass ideological thirst of a spoiled generation, ready to be quenched by the weirdest kinds of potions, was just around the corner, proving these intellectuals wrong. But before the collapse of the assumptions about the deep general consensus and the perennial growth of mass prosperity came the episode of the Kennedy years.

In 1960 the handsome and telegenic and rich John Fitzgerald Kennedy narrowly won over the much less handsome, telegenic, and munificent Richard Nixon in the race for the presidency. Many people saw in this event a resurgent triumph of American liberalism over conservatism. They were wrong. The contest was between two nationalists, the main difference in their programs being that Kennedy, perhaps because of his wealth, was less inclined to oppose the further development of the American welfare state than was Nixon. In this sense, as also in others, Kennedy was the less narrow-minded of the two. During his public career John Kennedy, as did his brothers, became more and more liberal, characteristic examples as they were of the American tendency which (as are most

American political and social phenomena) is yet another refutation of Marx: the higher people rise on the American social (social, rather than financial) scale the more liberal they can afford to (indeed, they often think they must) become—a tendency which, however, may have run its course at the time this history is being written.

To many people the presidency of John Kennedy meant the beginning of something, a new era, with this youthful President inaugurating a fresh age after the bland and middle-aged Eisenhower years. Twenty years later we have become bedeviled (if that is the right word) with sordid revelations about his private life. This at least suggests that the dissolution which, with all of its degenerating symptoms, began to surface in the mid-sixties, one or two years after Kennedy's death, had, in reality, begun at the top a few years earlier—even though the vast majority of Americans were unaware of this. They saw in the Kennedys a renewed and fashionable ideal of American togetherness, represented by the admirable lives of such successful and self-confident leaders. But, apart from what some of his private doings may or may not reveal about Kennedy's character, we may detect some of the insubstantialities of his thinking from phrases that had sounded so promising at the time. John Kennedy, born in 1917, had in his inaugural address "served notice to the world," as he put it, that "the torch has been passed to a new generation." Hordes of this generation would soon demonstrate their pyromaniacal inclinations on both sides of the Atlantic. "We will get America moving again," Kennedy said—and move it did, but in what direction?‡ He spoke of the "meteoric rise" of the United States: but, truly, a meteor cannot rise, it is a meteor by virtue of its fall.

The presidency of John Kennedy marked the end, rather than the beginning, of another important matter: the upsurge of American Catholics and of American Catholicism. Protestant and anti-Catholic prejudices had marked the very foundation of the United States. Throughout the history of the Republic, Catholics were a minority. Even in the twentieth century their influence in the cultural and social life of the nation was quite limited; as late as the 1950s, as the sensitive poet-historian Peter Viereck wrote, anti-Catholicism was "the anti-Semitism of intellectuals." Yet Franklin Roosevelt was already very much aware of the great political

‡ Bernanos in 1946: "The world believes it is moving ahead, because it holds a most materialistic idea of moving ahead. A world in motion is a world that clambers up slopes, not one that tumbles down. No matter how fast you fall down a hill, all you are doing is falling down. Between those who think that civilization is a victory for man in the struggle against the determinism of things . . . and those who want to make man a thing among things, there is no possible scheme of reconciliation."

power latent in the Catholic hierarchy; many of his domestic and foreign political choices were evidences of this. Then, after 1945 and during the cold war, a situation arose which in the history of the nation had no precedent: being a Catholic was no longer a handicap, it was an advantage in all kinds of employment, particularly in federal service and in politics, especially because a practicing Catholic was regarded as a natural anti-Communist. This increase in the respectability, prosperity, and power of American Catholics seemed to have culminated in the election of the first Catholic President. Yet the developments of the 1960s—as well as those later revelations about the private life of this President—showed that the outwardly rigid and conservative and dogmatic structure of belief among American Catholics withstood the temptations of worldliness and of modernization hardly better than the structure of beliefs among other American religions or among Catholic populations abroad. American Catholics, including John Fitzgerald Kennedy, were, after all, *American* Catholics, adherents of a faith which, for them, was rooted more in a national ethos, in national customs, and in national habits of thought than in a supranational morality with its traditional philosophy. In a questionnaire circulated among Catholic college students (by this teacher, among others) one of the questions read, "Are you an American who happens to be a Catholic, or are you a Catholic who happens to be an American?" Ninety-eight percent chose the former.

The nationalism of John F. Kennedy was evident in the very first hours after his election. Before everything else, he announced the reappointment of Allen Dulles and of J. Edgar Hoover, the two chiefs of the national secret police organizations. Soon after his inauguration Kennedy, and the nation, suffered a serious defeat in Cuba. On that island, for whose liberation the United States had gone to war with Spain sixty years before, on that island which had profited so much from American commerce and industry that it became the third richest state in Latin America in 1958, there arose, in defiance of all of the "laws" of economics as well as of the United States, a revolutionary leader whose hatred of America led him to proclaim himself a Communist—not the other way around. The CIA had already convinced Eisenhower to prepare clandestine operations against Cuba, through the arming of Cuban patriots in exile. Under Kennedy these plans went ahead; but the patriots' landing in April 1961—they had become the client mercenaries of a clandestine American agency—in the Bay of Pigs failed. This was one of the first evidences of the novel powerlessness of the gigantic Republic, armed with weapons that could destroy half of the world and with spy planes that could photograph all of it. A generation before, the report of a single intelligent American diplomat would have been sufficient to enlighten his government about the realities within Cuba. In 1961 an entire secretive bureaucracy of agents, technicians, analysts, and mercenaries armed with the most modern of instruments proved incapable of ascertaining what was going on within that island. A generation before, the presence of a lone American warship would have sufficed to cow a recalcitrant Cuban tyrant into submission; now the mightiest power on earth was constrained to accept the presence of a savage inimical dictatorship a mere ninety miles from the Florida shores. In this respect, too, the Kennedy era marked the end rather than the beginning of something: the decline of real American power, obscured though that was by the enormous increase of military bureaucracy and technology.

After the fiasco of the Bay of Pigs, Kennedy was determined to get back at Castro. The latter was acutely aware of this; most Americans were not. To the Russians the establishment of a Communist (or at least of a pretended Communist) government in Cuba was an unexpected tropical fruit that had fallen into their laps. They were unwilling to extend a binding alliance to that peculiar island half a world away from their territorial empire; but after increasing evidence of American clandestine attempts against Castro, accompanied by increasingly strident requests by the latter, the Russians agreed to supply certain medium-range rockets to Cuba, provided that these be guarded by Russians, lest the itchy fingers of Cubans handle them at their own pleasure. In October 1962, when some of these rockets were being openly shipped to Cuba, Kennedy acted firmly; he declared a blockade of the island. The Russians relented. They withdrew their missiles from Cuba in exchange for Kennedy's secret promise not to invade that island (something that Castro had wanted from the beginning, disappointed though he was with the unwillingness of his Russian allies to support him to the hilt) as well as for the removal of American rockets from Turkey.

In November 1962 John Kennedy's popularity stood at its zenith, mostly because of his victory in the Cuban missile crisis, even though Castro's rule in Cuba was not changed thereby. One year later Kennedy was assassinated by a shadowy character who, in turn, was to be assassinated three days later by another man whose death in prison another year or so later made it forever impossible to disentangle the record of their past relationships, including clandestine connections with Cubans, mobsters, and the CIA.

(4)

This was in November 1963 when certain changes in American life were becoming apparent. The influence of the intelligentsia, perhaps for the first time in the history of the Republic, was now considerable. Federal moneys given to universities and colleges rose tenfold from 1955 to 1970. The ranks of professional intellectuals were inflated because of the massive grant incomes on which the universities came to depend. Often this swelling of the faculties meant a deterioration in the quality of the professorate. "Knowledge without integrity," Dr. Johnson had said, "is a dreadful thing." Now not only the integrity but often the very knowledge of the new breed of ambitious and professionalized intellectuals was wanting. Perhaps as a belated reaction against the Eisenhower years, a renewed and, in many ways, fashionable radicalism was publicly espoused by many intellectuals and by groups of vociferous students. A renewed cult of youth—assisted perhaps by the Kennedy phenomenon—was evident in the new forms of clothes, behavior, music, and entertainment that spread across the American scene, much of which was raucous, raunchy, primitive, and often maddening. This was accompanied by a rising national preoccupation with sex, promoted and encouraged by publicity. A magazine such as *Playboy,* which had begun publishing in 1953, ten years later became a national feature, bought by millions of men who were no longer shamefaced in buying it, even though by that time virtually all verbal and pictorial restraints in its contents had been eliminated. Its publisher had become a national celebrity, proclaiming his imbecile "Playboy Philosophy"; the most celebrated writers of the nation sent articles for publication in *Playboy,* while the most celebrated public figures (including, in 1976, Jimmy Carter, the presidential candidate) were pleased with the opportunity of publicity that their interviews in *Playboy,* involving at times the most intimate matters of their private lives, provided. Beginning about 1963 an unprecedented wave of pornography flooded the country. Pornographic descriptions and ruminations now comprised considerable portions of the novels written by celebrated authors such as Norman Mailer and John Updike. In the 1920s and 1930s iron-faced American customs agents had rummaged through suitcases of their countrymen returning from abroad in search of forbidden books and prurient pictures. Beginning in the 1960s it was American pornographic books and magazines and pictorial material that flooded much of the rest of the world, the United States having become a principal producer, purveyor, and exporter of this kind of stuff. The courts, including the Supreme Court, abolished most legal obstacles against this transnational flood of filth. The carnal gluttonies and the sexual perversions of many of the most admired, envied, and opulent members of New York society called for a new Suetonius, the task that the once talented Truman Capote set for himself. Halfway through his chronicle (a portion of which appeared in a national magazine in the early 1970s) he halted in his labors; whether because of accumulating threats of libel or because of the accumulating deadweight of his own indulgences, this author cannot tell.

Soon this kind of dissolution affected a large number of American families, the private lives of Americans, disturbing and often disrupting the always tenuous and difficult relationships of the sexes. After 1950 in some of the western European nations an increasing number of married women took jobs outside of their homes. We have seen that in the United States a superficially conservative tendency to family "togetherness" was still dominant throughout the 1950s. The change came after 1965, one of its evidences being the increasing number of married women seeking employment outside the home. Contrary to accepted opinions, the source of this upsurge was seldom economic necessity, surely not at the time. It was the collapse of the already much weakened appeal and prestige of the earlier, bourgeois ideals of domesticity among American women. Of the ideals of being happily married, of the contentments inherent in bringing up well-protected and well-bred children, of keeping a well-furnished home and a well-bedecked table, of reaching thereby a well-deserved social approbation together with the opportunities of a well-filled social and cultural calendar, only the first one—the ideal of marriage—remained strong, because of its biological and atavistic nature. The rest had to be attained—if attained at all—without the kind of domesticity secured by a husband and, if need be, without the marriage bond at all.

Lyndon B. Johnson, the next President, was largely unaware of the meaning of these developments. His entire political upbringing had occurred during the Depression years; whatever his crude manners, his political ideas were formed by memories of those years. He believed in the beneficial virtues of the New Deal and of the American provider state. He also remembered the narrow provincialism of many of the isolationists. Consequently he pronounced the creation of what he called "The Great Society": a brummagem term, the aims of which were hazy, and yet to some of whose accomplishments we may pay respect, for this Texan President did much to extend the civil and electoral rights of blacks and of many others as well. What he did not understand—coming from a state in which the inflation of values, riches, society, and rhetoric had been a way of life for some time—was that his social and economic programs were thoroughly inflationary and therefore eventually ruinous for the nation at large. Besides the financial health of the Republic (it was after 1965 that the erosion of the value of the dollar began to accelerate), American productivity went on declining. During the 1960s the American share of world steel production fell by half. The further extension of the welfare state led to the rise, and not to the decline, of social problems and racial crises. In the 1960s fights and riots and lootings broke out in the cities of the nation, often in the North, provoked by blacks and not whites for the first time. (During the tragic riots in Houston and Brownsville in 1917 or in Detroit in 1943, dozens of people had died: but in these riots whites had fought Negroes, the latter having been provoked by the former.) A century after Lincoln and after the emancipation of American blacks, millions of blacks ceased to emulate whites. The former, perhaps for the first time in the history of the American people, felt contempt, rather than fear, of the latter. For one thing, the cult of primitiveness and of carnality, assiduously perpetrated by publicity and accepted by whites, convinced many blacks that they were physically and sexually stronger than whites, and that in the increasingly junglelike deterioration of the cities there were opportunities to be reaped from this kind of power. All over the nation the rate of crime rose enormously during these very last of the superficially prosperous years of the nation when more and more people had more and more money to spend, and spend they did.

Some of these matters were evident by 1964; yet in 1964 Johnson won the election easily against Goldwater, who seemed to represent a half-baked kind of superpatriotism which most Americans were not ready to trust. Four years later it was the war in Indochina that brought Johnson down, having destroyed much of his self-confidence. His single-minded memory of past isolationism (the same thing was true of his Secretary of State, the foundation bureaucrat Dean Rusk) and his unquestioning faith in the American military prevented Johnson from questioning the projections of his bureaucrats and of his bureaucratic generals. Thus he involved the nation more and more deeply in that jungle war. We have seen that in 1954 Eisenhower himself halted the development of American involvement on the side of the remnant French army in Indochina. Yet thereafter, with the thoughtless momentum so characteristic of the bureaucratized military and political departments in the Washington of that time, American political, financial, and even military involvement in Vietnam increased bit by bit. The rate of the military increase was relatively slow during the Kennedy years, but it was then that the political involvement of the United States grew; it was with the support of the CIA that Diem, the patriotic dictator of South, that is, free, Vietnam, was murdered in Saigon a mere three weeks before the bullets of another assassin cut Kennedy down. This Vietnam War was different from the Korean War. It was a guerrilla war, not a clear-cut invasion across a frontier line. It was also something new: an undeclared war into which the mighty North American Republic slid deeper and deeper, week by week, through the accumulating reams of paper churned out by a military and political bureaucracy in Washington. In 1965 its momentum moved forward in a lurch.* President Johnson, failing to recall the inefficiency of strategic air bombardment during the Second World War (and during the Korean War) ordered the American bombing of the battle zones and eventually of certain places in North Vietnam. He also consented to the request of General Westmoreland to increase the number of American soldiers in Vietnam to half a million. Against this growing American presence the North Vietnamese could muster neither Chinese nor Russian volunteers. Yet they did not lose the war. The United States was to lose it, for a number of reasons, including its unwillingness to wage war in the way wars had been fought in the past. Johnson and the generals were unwilling to invade North Vietnam. He and they thought that they could win by half measures, securing South Vietnam abroad and the Great Society at home at the same time. They should have recalled the words of Wellington: "A great country can have no such thing as a little war."

Johnson's untimely division of purposes developed apace with the division among the American people. The longer the war went on the less popular it became. After 1965, opposition to the war, some of it on respectable moral and political grounds, became inextricably mixed with opposition to the draft by millions of young people, many of whom were well-to-do. The dissatisfaction with the war proceeded apace with the dissolution of decency and order in the country. In 1968 television and the newspapers interpreted a crazed "Tet" offensive by the North Vietnamese as the victory of the latter instead of what it was, a series of desperate attacks ending in failure. During the same year the public commentators proclaimed the lemminglike automobile migration of half a million half-naked and half-drugged young Americans to a "festival" in Woodstock, New York, as a revolutionary revelation of a new culture instead of what it

* In the same year one third of the nation's youth were found to be physically and/or mentally unfit for military service.

was, yet another example of the crowd conformism of young people in a mass.

Yet despite the wider-ranging presence of self-serving and dishonest elements within that opposition, the opposition to the war did represent, in many places and among many Americans, the survival of traditional American decency and of idealism. The politicians knew that. As early as 1966 Johnson offered peace to the North Vietnamese, but in vain. By 1968 all of the political leaders, including Richard Nixon, committed themselves to seeking an end to the war. The war, and the popular opposition to the war, had broken Lyndon Johnson's spirit; his wife, whose beneficent influence was considerable throughout his career, convinced him not to seek the presidency again. He died soon afterward. Richard Nixon won the election against Hubert Humphrey, one of the last leftover politicians from the New Deal years. Had Robert Kennedy not been killed by a crazed Arab during the campaign, Nixon might not have become President. As things happened, he presided over the Republic for five and a half turbulent years. Eventually he wound up the Vietnam War, because he had to. Interminable "conferences" between the Vietnamese and the Americans were started in Paris. At Christmas 1972 Nixon and his adviser Kissinger decided to bomb Hanoi so that the North Vietnamese would return to the conference table. It was the only successful strategic bombing of the entire war. The armistice, signed six weeks later, and greeted with a sigh of relief across the United States, included the provision of the piecemeal American military evacuation of South Vietnam. That evacuation broke the spirit of the South Vietnam Government and its military. In April 1975 the North Vietnamese took Saigon amid scenes of a shameful American withdrawal that had few precedents in the history of the nation; but this happened at a time when the American people were too exhausted to care deeply.

From the beginning of the Nixon presidency the national spirit showed signs of exhaustion. In 1969 the management of the American space program achieved a fantastic feat: their technicians shot a capsule to the moon, to the surface of which two American astronauts, Armstrong and Aldrin, descended. Their short walk on the moon could be seen on the television screens in every American home, indeed, everywhere in the world. Yet a few years later not one in ten Americans could remember the names of the two astronauts. In New York fewer than one third as many people turned out at their triumphant reception than had greeted national heroes such as, say, Lindbergh more than forty years before. Of course television had something to do with this, as did perhaps also the fact that these astronauts, unlike a lone flyer such as Lindbergh, were largely passive passengers within their spacecraft. Still the relatively muted and largely ephemeral duration of this national reaction suggested the existence of an apathetic strain within the national psyche. In any event, by late 1970 even the anarchic upsurge of the 1960s was largely spent. The President and the Vice-President spoke of a "Silent Majority," suggesting that the great mass of the people, mostly those of the white working classes, were not less patriotic and loyal than they had been before, even though they did not make their opinions known. There was some truth in this assessment, but not enough. Opposition to the Vietnam War gradually spread even among the working class, whose menfolk, unlike the college-exempted and frequently draft-dodging sons of the better-situated classes, were carrying an unjust share of the dangers and burdens of the war.

Now, in the 1970s, the end of the hitherto nearly unique material prosperity of American lives had come. For the first time the per capita income of the average American was no longer the highest in the world. It slipped to second, third, fifth, sixth place behind that of the citizens of comparable industrial democracies (not to speak of those of Middle Eastern statelets, such as Kuwait, awash with oil money). Gold was flowing out of the United States in such quantities that in 1971 Nixon stopped the redemption of American international obligations in gold. Prices rose again with the rapidly declining value of the dollar; in 1974 the latter bought less than half the number of Swiss francs or West German marks than it had bought three years before. More important was the declining quality of American life: the breakdown of normal security in the cities and even the suburbs of the nation, the stunning decline in the standards of American schools (largely consequent to the inflation of their staffs and to their thoughtless abandonment of standard requirements) and the decrease in the quality and character of public service. The Vice-President, Spiro Agnew, figurehead of a suburban and well-heeled Republicanism, who in 1970 assumed the position of the chief spokesman of some of those American elements that stood for decency and for order, in 1973 was forced to resign the vice-presidency because of the accumulated evidences of thievery which he went on practicing even while in his office.

Amid these disturbing symptoms of national unease, the President pursued his fascination with world affairs. In 1969 he had proclaimed the American landing on the moon as the greatest event since the Creation, promptly putting Jesus Christ in his place. In 1972 he chose to give the traditional State of the Union address in two installments: one dealt with the State of the Union, the other one Nixon called, simply and squarely, the State of the World. In spite (or perhaps because) of the difficult predicament of the United States in Vietnam, Nixon kept proclaiming that America was "Number One"—whatever that meant. It is not difficult to detect how this kind of grandiloquence issued from a certain kind of unsureness, something that was, alas, typical of Richard Nixon's character. He kept proclaiming that America was "Number One" at the very time when his advisers had convinced him that the United States had to share its superpower status with the Soviet Union and perhaps even with China. In 1971 Nixon, who had made his career as a protagonist of the struggle against communism, announced to the world that he was going to Communist China. The sensation of this announcement, and of the eventual visit, obscured the condition that, as her conduct of domestic and foreign policies was to reveal, China was far from being a superpower and that the Russians had not much to fear from the Chinese for the time being.

Nixon's reputation was not particularly damaged by the superficiality of his view of world politics (and by that of his advisers), about which Americans cared relatively little, even after the Vietnam armistice. The domestic scandal and intrigue of the Watergate episode brought him down, forcing him to resign the presidency in ignominy hardly a year and a half after he had won an overwhelming victory against his Democratic opponent. Yet in one important sense Nixon's domestic and foreign policies were entangled together in the Watergate business. The episode itself was not very important, amounting to petty criminality: a gang of hired adventurers, Republican ideologues, and dogmatic anti-Communists were caught as they were trying to break into the Democratic Party offices situated in the bizarre Watergate apartment complex in Washington in search of confidential political papers there—papers which in the electoral climate of 1972 should have been of ridiculously little worth for an incumbent President facing a thoroughly unpopular opponent. What destroyed Nixon's reputation and his credibility were the consequences of this unsavory episode: the successive revelations of his lying, of secret recordings, and of the destruction of some of these—and, most important, the underlying evidence that he was inclined to justify, and to explain, not only to himself but to his cronies and eventually to the American people that these petty illegalities were justifiable in the name of "national interest" and of "national security." The relentless attacks of the press and of what was now called "the media" wore Nixon down; and the unpleasant side of his character was now revealed before more and more people. His resignation, in August 1974, was therefore in accord with the then sentiments of the great majority of Americans, including those of the Congress of the United States, Republicans as well as Democrats.

When less than a year earlier the resignation of his Vice-President, Agnew, had become inevitable, Nixon appointed Gerald Ford as his Vice-President, knowing that this was a man who would not (or could not) overshadow his own reputation. The arrival of Ford in the White House in August 1974 was greeted by the nation with great relief. It took some time for people to recognize that this amiable man, who found himself happiest on the golf course with Hollywood personalities, was bumbling, ignorant, and incompetent. Even more than his predecessor he depended on the global advice of the globular Kissinger, whose rise to this kind of eminence, including his Secretaryship of State, was in itself symptomatic of the transformation of American society and of the decline of those traditional reservoirs wherefrom public servants of the highest ranks had been customarily tapped. During the 1970s Presidents Nixon and Ford and Carter found it necessary to appoint foreign-born academics from the dubious and recent "field" of International Relations to explain the world to them. The results were not reassuring. We have seen that the last chapter of the American retreat from Indochina was disgraceful. In 1973 a sudden flare-up of war between Israel and her Arab and Egyptian neighbors led to the—in reality, long overdue—decision of the Arab states to increase drastically the price of oil. This meant not only the end of cheap gasoline, of cheap heat and cheap oil-fired power for Americans but the virtual termination of whatever control American oil companies may have exercised in those countries, and another great lurch forward in the relentless growth of inflation. The so-called China Opening by Nixon and Ford came to little more than the willingness of the Chinese to ingest large quantities of Coca-Cola (the Soviet Union having opted for Pepsi-Cola the year before). In Cuba, Fidel Castro's rule as well as his reliance on Russia remained constant. The dangerous presence of nuclear armaments across the world grew beyond any kind of conceivable reason. In 1979 the populace, the politicians, and the mullahs of Iran, degenerate and gypsified descendants of the rotting ancient state of Persia, mounted a revolution, discarding their Shah and blaming all of their numerous frustrations and tribulations on the United States. A horde of louts stormed the American Embassy compound in Teheran, imprisoning more than fifty Americans—"hostages" according to their captors' terms, shamefully accepted by the rest of the world—for more than a year. The puerile President of the United States (who preferred Jimmy to James for his official name) proved unable to rescue the hostages, or even to threaten the Iranians effectively, all of the might of the United States notwithstanding. Eventually the captives were released, but not before the very hour when the former Hollywood actor Ronald Reagan was inaugurated as President of the United States.

(5)

In the domestic history of the American people the 1970s provided an obvious, but to some extent misleading, contrast to the upheaval of the late 1960s. The people involved in the upheavals of the 1960s were, after all, a minority of the population: mostly young people, and unevenly distributed across the nation at large. In the 1970s many a rebellious young man turned, at least superficially, conservative, shedding his rebel garments and long hair apace with his ideology.† Yet many of the new ideas and patterns of behavior current among what was still a minority in the 1960s began to be accepted by large numbers of people in the 1970s. The widespread use of the very word "lifestyle" (or "life-style") was in itself a symptom of the dissolution of traditional family life. Adultery, abortion, illegitimacy, homosexuality, the purchase and the consumption of certain drugs were now familiar matters, especially since stories of such matters were included in popular movies and television shows, as if these had now become standard practices among the majority of the American people. The typical reader of a pornographic magazine such as *Playboy* in 1960 was a college boy in a dormitory or a lonely salesman in his motel room; ten years later such a magazine would be openly read and left on the seats of airplanes by all kinds of businessmen; another ten years later and the average reader of *Playboy* may have voted for Reagan, he may even have been a self-styled "conservative." Only sixteen years after the American birthrate had been the highest among the "developed" industrial democracies of the world and twenty-five years after the American marriage rate had been the second highest in the entire world, the birthrate fell to an unprecedented low in the nation's history and stood for a while among the lowest in the world. When we consider that even this figure included a very high proportion of illegitimate births we cannot but conclude that the domestic aspirations of many Americans had fundamentally changed—and so had their confidence in the future of children. In 1976–77 the number of divorces granted was one half that of all marriages performed. In 1973 the Supreme Court, presided over by a Republican (and "conservative") law-

† Except for his sneakers. A nation whose millions of young people wore sneakers, day in and day out: this transformation of rebellious youth to sneaky youth says something about the spirit of the seventies, though exactly what this writer cannot tell.

yer appointed by Nixon, declared that the right of a woman to have an abortion performed on herself in a public hospital was a right guaranteed by the Constitution. Thereafter each year more than one million embryos —some of them five or even six months old—were burned in electric ovens, or in some cases packed away in formaldehyde.‡ By 1979 there were more abortions in New York City than there were live births; and nearly twice as many abortions than there were live births in Washington.

The number of Americans afflicted (or thought to be afflicted) by psychological disorders rose higher in the 1970s than in the 1960s. Riots were now fewer, but the crime rate continued to rise. This had little to do with economics. In 1920 nearly half of all American families were below the poverty line. In 1979 only 12 percent were. Yet crime rates were much higher in 1979 than in 1920, and very much higher than during the Depression. Another disturbing phenomenon was the increasing presence of "amateur" criminals. Until about 1920 a considerable portion of crimes were committed by a more-or-less recognizable class of criminals. Two generations later the line between professional and amateur (or between compulsive and occasional) criminals, was largely washed away. Throughout the history of the United States violent crimes have been astonishingly frequent, but the number of Americans killed by handguns in the 1970s was often one hundred times higher than the murder rate in comparable nations such as West Germany or Britain. Even more astonishing was the increasing frequency of senseless murders—murders committed by impulse, out of rage, for no evident purpose. Even more horrifying was the recurrent phenomenon of awful crimes involving dozens of young people and children killed after or during their sexual abuse. On one occasion, the so-called Jonestown massacre of 1978, more than seven hundred Americans were killed, or induced to kill themselves, by their self-proclaimed "leader," a man whose "philanthropic" activities in California had been praised by public figures but a year or so before. In the 1920s a scandalous or otherwise sensational murder case preoccupied the nation for weeks, sometimes for months, and the trial was headlined and covered by the newspapers for days in a row. Fifty years later many of the horrible mass murders mentioned above were seldom followed up by the media; they

‡ In February 1982 hundreds of fetuses were found in Los Angeles in repossessed crates by a storage company. The owner of the laboratory storing them had not paid the storage money due. What he intended to do with the embryos we do not know. Three days later a district attorney in New York ruled that a man who had raped a woman who was six months pregnant and stabbed her in the stomach afterward could not be charged with murder because of the existing abortion laws.

disappeared from the first pages of newspapers, and from the television news after the first day, if indeed they had appeared there at all.

In the meantime the immense damages perpetrated by the education and university bureaucracies in the 1960s spread, to such an extent that by 1980 a considerable portion of the American population (including even college students) was functionally illiterate. The presence of illiterate literates—people who had little inclination to read because they had had little experience of it—was now apparent at the highest levels of the government.

Attempts to control (which in many cases amounted to not much more than to explain) many of these distressing developments were still made by institutions and by a liberal-progressive rhetoric that had become increasingly corroded and inefficient, often to the extent of intellectual dishonesty. That was true of many of the courts, of much of the legal profession, of the educational and academic bureaucracy as well as of the administrative machinery of the welfare state,* whether on the federal or on the local levels. Popular reaction against this coagulated slowly and unevenly, but coagulate it did. The majority of the American people, including the majority of their youth, now chose the word "conservative" and not "liberal" in identifying their political philosophies or predilections. Whatever the inaccuracy of the term, the tendency was real: the United States, by 1980, had entered the postliberal era, at least politically so. The sweep of the victory of Ronald Reagan in 1980 was an evident consequence of this. He got a decisive mandate from the American people to correct the course of the American ship of state as well as to change those structures within the great vessel that had become infested with vermin. Two years after Reagan's election this historian is compelled to state that Reagan's "conservatism," while not devoid of certain merits, had proved to be lamentably shortsighted and shallow. The redecoration of the captain's quarters, an easing of some of the restrictions of first-class, and the overloading of the decks with new kinds of armaments, whether necessary or not, did not amount to the kind of overhaul of which the structures and institutions of the American ship of state were in great and dire need. Concerning the course of the ship of state, the anti-Communist rhetoric and the mammoth armament program of the Reagan administration merely repeated the 1950s, even though in the 1980s the situation in the world as well as the financial capacities of the United States had become

* Senator Daniel P. Moynihan: ". . . one-third of all children born in America during the 1980s will likely spend some portion of his time on welfare before reaching the age of 18." *The New Republic,* 9 June 1982.

quite different. At the same time Reagan's nationalist, Republican, and so-called conservative administration seemed hardly aware of and not at all willing to face the evident danger to the nation: the mounting flood of all kinds of people who have been entering the gaping portals of the nation from the south.

Much of this was due to the Californian tastes and to the Californian provenance of this President, conditions that corresponded with shifts of preponderance within the nation at large. The population center of the United States has moved steadily westward from the beginning, even though it crossed the Mississippi only recently. In 1940 California was the fifth most populous state of the Union; twenty-three years later it was the first. Its influence on the rest of the nation increased accordingly, and not only because of the evident size of its population and of its wealth. (We shall see, for example, how the majority of the nation moved from predominantly rural to predominantly urban and then to predominantly suburban dwelling, in a shift that entailed civilizational and cultural mutations. In suburbanization, as in some other things, California was ahead of the rest of the nation.) The population movements did have obvious political consequences. The importance of most southwestern and western states grew rapidly after 1960, though the fashionable pronouncements of the so-called Sunbelt having become the new central region of American prosperity and civilization may have been premature or perhaps even insubstantial. The Republican Party certainly gained from this kind of shift: its main strength was now in the Southwest and the West, something quite different from the political geography of the nation even a generation ago. It was not only that Hoover, Ford, Nixon, and Reagan were western Presidents, the latter two Californians; Reagan was only a transplanted Californian, but this did not matter; somewhat like the originally midwestern Ford, he was thoroughly at home in California. Yet—and this is the crux of the problem—the Californian way of life, and the Californian mode of thinking, often represented but a caricature, meaning a distorted image, of some of the characteristics of modern American civilization. The pursuit of happiness, Jefferson's unfortunate phrase tacked to the end of the Declaration of Independence, led millions of people to California, where the cult of this very pursuit had often led to the degeneration of the ideals of personal liberty, and sometimes of life itself. In this respect the influence of California has been a solvent rather than a consolidant factor in American civilization and in the national resolution of priorities.

In a seldom-read Appendix ("A Fortnight in the Wilderness") in *Democracy in America,* Tocqueville foresaw this too. After the migratory race of Americans will have reached the Pacific Ocean, he wrote, it "will retrace its steps to disturb and to destroy the social communities which it will have formed and left behind." It was in the so-called ascetic centuries, Chesterton said, that "the love of life was evident and enormous, so that it had to be restrained. In our hedonist age pleasure has always sunk low, so that it has to be encouraged." The economic lucubrations of certain California economists rested on the belief that the pursuit of happiness ought to be encouraged, that spending by the wealthier Americans would be a sufficient stimulant to the economy, "trickling down" sooner or later to the masses. Had Ronald Reagan told the American people that things were indeed difficult, and that the time had come for all Americans to tighten their belts, the nation would have hearkened to such an admonition and followed it: for such were, and such are still, reactions expectable from the yet unexhausted sources of American patriotic idealism. This did not occur to this President, it was not within his character. It was not the first time that the willingness of the American people to sacrifice was underestimated by its leaders.

(6)

Two hundred years after the founding of the American state the essentially Anglo-Saxon and Anglo-Celtic character of the national community declined, its remnants surviving here and there, within what were once the best and most enduring institutions of the Republic. It is true that the stream of mass immigration, while disrupting the then crystallization of a specifically American national character, did not (contrary to the then anxious and ominous predictions) lead to a fatal decomposition of national unity; but the end of this matter is still in the future, especially now when the thoughtless inclinations of recent governments have permitted the flooding of the nation by large crowds of migrants from the tropical South. It is at least arguable that the main danger to the United States may not even be the Soviet Union but the so-called Third World, whose savagery had already penetrated large areas of the United States and the presence of which within the United States has become widespread and evident.

The founders of the Republic were aware of the burden of race, of the fact that there was a large minority of black slaves in the southern states of the Union.† This burden eventually grew into an accursed condition, with the result of the disruption of the Republic and a murderous civil war. Whether the motives of the North were principally those of enlightened and moral generosity we do not really know; in any event, this is immaterial for the historian, proceed as he must from Dr. Johnson's maxim that intentions must be gathered from acts.‡ The act is what counts: the act of putting an end to slavery, which is what the North did and what most of the American people wanted. But after the Civil War the institutionalization of Negro political and civic equality in the South became corrupted, while in the North the majority of people had grown indifferent, if not hostile, to the cause of the equality of the blacks. Much of that equality was fictitious: it was legal not moral, a discrepancy which was perhaps even worse in the North than in the South, where everyday life had brought whites and blacks to know each other. As late as seventy years ago 90 percent of blacks still lived in the South. Thereafter some of the worst riots occurred in the North, where a sharp and acrid hatred for Negroes appeared among populations living close to blacks. During the two world wars a mass migration of blacks to the North began. Yet during the first half of the twentieth century in the United States, whose people saw themselves as citizens of the freest and most advanced democracy in the world, social, civil, educational, occupational, and legal restrictions of Negroes existed that were unequaled in most civilized nations. During the 1920s the educational opportunities of black Americans rose; but it was not until after the Second World War that many of the above-mentioned barriers were removed, beginning mostly in the fields of entertainment and in sports. The civil rights of blacks were extended and secured; remarkably, most of them by Democratic presidents who had come from southern or

† The founders of the Republic knew that slavery was wrong (it had few intellectual defenders at the time), but they considered it somehow bound to the natural order of things and to old customs, the breaking of which would be unduly dangerous. Whatever its consequences, this kind of thinking was different from modern (or populist) racism. It was also an early example of the old-fashioned elements in the thinking of these eighteenth-century Anglo-Americans, placing them behind the French—to the advantage of the former.

‡ James C. Malin: "Where is one to look for sincerity and integrity in connection with this controversy over human slavery, and the subsequent controversy over the status of the free negro, over the questions for immigrants, and over religious freedom? The natural predisposition of all who believe in human freedom is to assume that those advocating freedom were themselves decent people. After careful study of the horrors, the danger is that one may swing to the opposite and indefensible extreme and question whether there was any downright human integrity present." Malin, *The Contriving Brain and the Skillful Hand* (Lawrence, Kansas, 1955), p. 167. The Free State Party and the Republican Party in Ohio and Kansas were anti-Negro as well as antislavery. "Bloody" Republican Kansas in 1861 and after denied Negro suffrage (by popular vote).

pro-southern states. In 1954 the Supreme Court of the United States—alas, on the basis of arguments drawn from the abstractions of sociology—declared that segregation, the same thing that less than fifty years earlier had been declared constitutional by the Supreme Court, was contrary to the Constitution in both letter and in spirit. The result was twofold: a massive demolition of the remnant disabilities of blacks especially in the South (where in many states as late as 1960 few blacks were allowed to register and to vote), a demolition which occurred with remarkably little violence and bloodshed. Yet the legal abolition of segregation led to a *de facto* segregation in the North, often with the worst kind of portents. Ten years after 1954 the presence of whites in black neighborhoods vanished almost entirely; whites entering black neighborhoods were taking their lives in their hands, while the rate of criminality involving blacks (the perpetrators as well as the victims of crimes) rose to enormous proportions. Thus the two separate societies of white and black Americans continued to exist, albeit distributed differently than before. That the association of whites and blacks in many occupations and on certain levels of society increased was encouraging; that a cruel and crude kind of savagery was now the everyday way of life in large portions of American cities, reminiscent of the Third World, was not.

(7)

In 1983, at the time of this writing, the momentum of American decline seemed to be gradual, not dramatic; at times it has seemed to halt; often it has seemed that it was not irreversible. The prestige of the United States was still very great. One of the reasons for this was the contrast with the deteriorating prestige of the Soviet Union. Despite their vast armament program (marking the last phase of the transformation of that so-called Communist state into a nationalist military imperium) the Russians were losing their influence among the various Communist parties and states of the world. Their influence—again, apart from their military presence—was waning even in their East European sphere.* The condition that the

* It should be noticed, however, that for the first time in history Americans had taken to certain Russian habits and practices. Very few Americans drank vodka as late as in 1950; by 1974 vodka replaced scotch as the favorite hard liquor consumed by Americans. In the 1970s the fur caps of state troopers, the padded shapeless quilt coats favored by many Americans, even certain spellings and acronyms (Amtrak, Alyeska) suggested a, probably unconscious,

cultural and civilizational influence of the Russians outside of the primitive native population within the U.S.S.R. proper was nearly nonexistent, contributed to the continuing influence of American civilization and of American popular culture virtually everywhere on the globe, including many dishonest people who professed to hate the very country whose products and habits and expressions they were imitating. American techniques, American modes, American forms had become increasingly ubiquitous, ranging from the contents of television programs to their very formats, from juvenile clothing to all kinds of uniforms, from the international language of air transportation to the linguistic habits of managerial bureaucrats, from popular forms of entertainment to the very shapes of computer figurations. Mass democracy and mass communication imitated and repeated American forms everywhere in the world. Whether the manifestations of mass civilization were symptoms of senility or of adolescence during what may be but the beginning of the democratic epoch in the lives of many nations was not yet clear.

In the history of the United States the 1980s were not the beginning of the democratic age. While some of the ancient nations of Europe were turning to puerility, within the United States there were evidences of growing maturity too. One evidence of national maturity was that of the reactions of Americans to the decline of their national power in the 1970s and to the decline of their very personal fortunes in the early 1980s. These declines produced little or no demagoguery but, to the contrary, a rather impressive and responsible willingness on the part of many Americans to adjust their lives to their new and more restricted material conditions.† The belief of the American people in American democratic ideals was still strong. Whether the prevalence of this belief rested on such human qualities that could withstand a radical change in their accustomed institutions and in their accepted ideas was yet to be seen.

American emulation of certain things Russian. (They amounted to little when compared to the massive emulation and adaptation of American things and of American expressions by the peoples of the Russias.)

† This willingness amounted on occasion to something near enthusiasm: consider the interest of many Americans in energy-saving devices and instruments, and not merely because of financial motives.

PART II

A HISTORICAL INTERPRETATION

3

THE AUTOMOBILE CENTURY

The Material Development of American Life

How the Americanization of the world preceded, and how it shows every sign of succeeding, the rise and the decline of American prosperity and power.

(1)

From the beginning of their history Americans believed that they were better off than the rest of the world. This ungainly phrase "better off" must do, since Americans had not always believed that they were richer, though they believed that they were freer than any other people in the world. Probably more Americans believed that they were free because their country was unique than believed they were unique because they were free; but we must postpone our inquiry into the structure of their beliefs here. First in order, though not necessarily in importance, comes the material development of American life. The difficulty of this subject is inherent in the contradictory condition: even though what happens is not identical with what people think happens, for a long time what happens and what people think happens is inseparable. Americans are not a materialistic people, even though many of them, and the rest of the world, are accustomed to think that they are.

The land and sea and forest and mineral resources of the United States were very rich, but then so were those of many other sparsely peopled countries. During the nineteenth century in the United States the notion of democracy became synonymous with popular prosperity. Much of this was the result of the solidity of the American constitution as well as the result of the rapidly growing population, the conditions of whose Americanness were inseparable from their willingness to work. The source of these conditions included the surviving strength of belief in the old American Puritan dispensation as well as the newer American belief, held by the vast majority of the people, that success and money, that social position and wealth, were synonymous. The American phrase "making money" reflected this. In the United States you made money, while in England you earned it, in Germany you deserved it *(verdienen),* in countries with Latinate languages you won it *(gagner, ganar, gagnare).* "To make good" was an old English phrase which was revived in the United States in the 1880s, with a change in its meaning. It no longer meant only restitution: it had everything to do with respectability, and with the material awards that were connected with respectability.

Americans, even one hundred years ago, did not think that they were remote from the rest of the world. They thought—and with many reasons—that they hardly depended on the rest of the world. They made their money in their own country, for their own purposes, according to their own rules. Around 1890 this began to change. Americans who recognized that the conditions of American money could not be entirely separated from the exchangeability of money in the rest of the world were few: they were often called reactionaries by their opponents, even though they were the most intelligent people of the Republic. In reality it was the silverites and the Populists of the 1890s who were the reactionaries, all of the common belief in their "progressiveness" notwithstanding. Just as the religious beliefs of someone like William Jennings Bryan harked back to a lollarding puritanism of the seventeenth century, so did his simplistic biblical views of the American economy. When the United States became a world power in 1898, this meant that the great American Republic had caught up with the rest of the other world powers, that it began to be involved in the web of the world. It also meant that the financial and material conditions of American life were no longer separable from the financial and material conditions of Europe.

Ever since then there have been historians and theorists who argued that the roots of American imperial expansion were economic. Other historians, more sensibly, argued that trade merely followed the flag, that American economic involvement in the world followed American imperialism, the extension of the American military and political presence across the oceans. Of course the two developments were related to each other, but not on the level of simplistic causality. Their parallel development was existential, not causal. That it makes little sense to attribute causal motivations to this change in American history may be illustrated by the endurance of the national belief in American uniqueness and in American innocence decades after these changes had taken place. In 1900 the American empire was established in the Philippines and in the Caribbean at a time when most Americans not only professed to believe that their domains were fundamentally different from the empires of all other nations but when many of them believed that the United States was not imperialist at all. The beliefs in the virtues and in the practicality of American isolationism were most pervasive and widespread among the people of the Middle West, in the very states whose farming populations began by 1890 to depend on foreign trade, among that portion of the American people whose prosperity depended on exports more than did any other portion of the nation.

Here are a few telling figures about the beginning of change in the 1890s. They are telling only in retrospect, since the recognition of their meaning was long nonexistent. Until the middle of the nineteenth century foreign trade was not an essential factor in the national lives of most peoples, including Americans. Before 1850 the American people sold very little to foreigners; they bought a little more. Before 1850 American imports almost always exceeded exports. For sixty years after 1873, with one exception (1898), each year Americans sold more than they bought from abroad; their exports exceeded their imports. Some of this was due to protection: the majority of American industrialists wanted, and got, high tariffs which limited competitive imports, thus protecting their profits and the high wages of their workers. But the volume of American involvement with the rest of the world was increasing. Before 1892 there was no single year in which American exports amounted to $1 billion. After 1896 there was no single year in which American exports were less than $1 billion. By 1914 American exports were up to nearly $3 billion, and this was before the export volume would double, treble, quadruple because of the world war. Imports reached the $1 billion mark only in 1903; as late as 1914 they were still under $2 billion.

In 1860 American food exports amounted to about one fifth of the total volume of exports. By 1900, when the export total had grown fourfold; the farm exports had increased ten times in forty years. During the 1890s the farm exports were more than 10 percent of American farm income—this at a time when American production and population were still predominantly agricultural and rural. Most of this was due to the phenomenal success of American agriculture as it became mechanized. In his best seller *The Americanization of the World,* published in 1902, the famous English journalist W. T. Stead tried to drive this home to his readers. He quoted a pamphlet by another journalist, Mackenzie:

> In the domestic life we have got to this: The average [English]man rises in the morning from his New England sheets, he shaves with "Williams" soap and a Yankee safety razor, pulls on his Boston boots over his socks from North Carolina, fastens his Connecticut braces, slips his Waltham or Waterbury watch in his pocket, and sits down to breakfast. There he congratulates his wife on the way her Illinois straight-front corset sets off her Massachusetts blouse, and he tackles his breakfast, where he eats bread made from prairie flour (possibly doctored at the special establishments on the lakes), tinned oysters from Baltimore and a little Kansas City bacon, while his wife plays with a slice of Chicago ox-tongue. The children are given 'Quaker' oats. At the same time he reads his morning paper printed by American machines, on American paper, with American ink, and, possibly, edited by a smart journalist from New York city. . . .
>
> At his office, of course, everything is American. He sits on a Nebraskan swivel chair, before a Michigan roll-top desk, writes his letters on a Syracuse typewriter, signing them with a New York fountain pen, and drying them with a blotting-sheet from New England. The letter copies are put away in files manufactured in Grand Rapids.
>
> At lunch-time he hastily swallows some cold roast beef that comes from the Mid-West cow, and flavors it with Pittsburg pickles, followed by a few Delaware tinned peaches, and then soothes his mind with a couple of Virginia cigarettes. . . .[1]

Yet this was a "color piece," an article of journalistic exaggeration: true, but not true enough. Or: even if true, it made not much difference to America. The phenomenal prosperity of the United States in 1900, and for a long time thereafter, had little or nothing to do with foreign trade. Until the middle of the Second World War (except for the years of the First World War) American agriculture and American industry depended on foreign trade less than did almost any other great nation of the world. More than 90 percent of America's production was bought or used by the American people themselves. Unlike the other democracies of the world, the United States remained an essentially autarchic country—a paradox, when we consider that during the Second World War the United States fought the two imperial states of Germany and Japan which had made autarchy into a national ideal.

In sum, what Americans produced Americans consumed. Yet about 1900 the publicity industry began to contribute something new. It involved itself in the production of consumption, which is not the same thing as the consumption of production. And here we arrive at the main tendency of the twentieth century, which is inflation. The American people were for a long time exempt from its ravages but not forever. Nothing is inevitable in history: and yet it seems as if inflation were the natural consequence of democracy, especially of modern democracy—a monetary condition which even Tocqueville may have ignored, since he, quite properly, paid little attention to theories of economics. But then he may have been right after all: because inflation is not just a monetary, or even a merely "economic" condition. For what are the elements that make the development of inflation inseparable from the development of democracy, especially in the twentieth century? On one level the development of government in the direction of a welfare (or, more accurately, of a provider) state—and Tocqueville had foreseen this*—leads to increasing public spending and to increasing bureaucracy. On another level there is the simple and inescapable condition: when there is more and more of something, it is worth less and less—a condition which is as true of the currency as it is of jewelry, of social status, as of carnal opportunities—and, of course, of words, the latter condition first and admirably stated in Aesop's fable about the boy who shouted "wolf" so often that after a while the value of *his* word "wolf" fell to nothing.

This is the essence of the inflationary condition, the sources of which are not economic or monetary—there being no such thing as a "purely" economic condition, or of an isolated economic motive. During and after the Second World War economists concluded that the coming danger was that of another deflation after the war. As usual, they were wrong. So were the leading businessmen. In a *Fortune* survey in 1946 they predicted that a major depression and unemployment would occur during the next ten

* In a famous passage in "What Sort of Despotism Democratic Nations Have to Fear" in *Democracy in America:* ". . . An innumerable multitude of men, all equal and alike, incessantly endeavoring to procure the petty and paltry pleasures with which they glut their lives. Above this race of men stands an immense and tutelary power, which takes upon itself alone to secure their gratifications and to watch over their fate. It covers the surface of society with a network of small complicated rules, minute and uniform, through which the most original minds and energetic characters cannot penetrate. . . . The will of man is not shattered, but softened, bent, and guided; men are seldom forced by it to act, but they are constantly restrained from acting. . . . I have always thought that servitude of the regular, quiet, and gentle kind which I have just described might be combined more easily than is commonly believed with some of the outward forms of freedom, and that it might establish itself under the wing of the sovereignty of the people. . . ."

years. The very opposite happened. After the war inflation began to accelerate; by the 1950s it had become irreversible, a seemingly natural condition of life; by 1970 it had become endemic, and dangerous.

Its first evidences were, however, there at the beginning of the century, much earlier than we have been accustomed to think. For a long time (in many ways this is true even now) the fundamental difference between a country such as the United States and the countries of Europe was that in America land was plentiful and cheap, whereas in Europe it was expensive and scarce. Yet the United States was not only different from Europe, it was also different from other sparsely inhabited and land-rich nations, such as those of Latin America or even Australia. The growth of wealth was more decisive than was the availability of land. Around 1880 the United States was entering the urban phase of its history. Not until the second decade of the twentieth century had the United States—second among the nations of the world, following Great Britain—become predominantly urban—meaning, among other things, that the majority of its productive population were no longer engaged in agriculture. Yet well before 1920 American ambitions became city-bound. City rents had risen at the very time when agricultural rents decreased. The prices of rents began to grow immediately after the Civil War: they rose 51 percent from 1860 to 1880. After 1890 other inflationary symptoms followed. Neither the industrial unrest and agricultural depression of the mid-nineties nor the financial near-panic of 1907 affected them very much. Until 1900 wholesale prices were relatively stable, but from 1900 to 1910 they increased more than 25 percent. The cost of living, too, rose from an index of 75 in 1891 to 100 in 1900, another 25 percent increase.

This may be significant in retrospect, but at the time it made little difference, for two reasons at least. The prosperity of the United States was such that the disposable personal income nearly doubled from 1897 to 1911. The total national wealth almost doubled in twelve years, from $88 billion in 1900 to $165 billion in 1912. The total of national saving was calculated at less than $1 billion in 1897; it passed $5 billion in 1912, a rise corresponding to the increase in personal savings. What was more important, the national currency remained solid; it was exchangeable into gold or silver, and its value remained unchanged in relation to other currencies of the world. What is amazing is that this kind of stability was unaffected by the otherwise inflationary condition of its circulation. The total dollars in circulation passed $1 billion in 1879, $2 billion in 1898, $3 billion eight years later; it passed the $4 billion mark in 1914–15. The circulation of money increased apace with the circulation of people. Sociologically, the decades before World War I were decades of democratization, that is, of the inflation of society.

The inflation of society meant not only (sometimes not at all) an increase of population, but the rapid movement of large numbers of people upward, spending more and more money—a vertical as well as a horizontal movement. That movement reveals—or, rather, it ought to reveal—something about the aspirations of modern peoples, and perhaps especially of Americans: aspirations of respectability and of social vanity; aspirations that are immaterial rather than material; aspirations that are different from greed, more complex and also less prone to self-discipline. All of the makings of inflation were there before World War I. As Agnes Repplier wrote in 1910, "Every class resents the extravagance of every other class; but none will practice denial. . . . A universal reluctance to practice economy indicates a weakness in the moral fiber of a nation, a dangerous absence of pride. There is no power of the soul strong enough to induce thrift but pride." Yet the social order remained stable because of the belief of the overwhelming majority of people in the American system and in American ways. The sense of stability was such that during this time interest rates remained largely unchanged, as did the volume of the sales of stocks. The value of the dollar, too, remained relatively stable at the very time when its very circulation and the inflation of society were accelerating: an extraordinary phenomenon, which would probably not have lasted long. Sooner or later the inflation of money would have caught up with the inflation of society, that is, with the inflation of wants. For the increase of money is the consequence, not the cause, of the movement of minds: a simple truism which would not be worth repeating were it not that it runs counter to the most widespread idiocy of the twentieth century, to the belief in economic determinism, and in Economic Man.

The principal characteristic of the twentieth century is inflation: inflation of money, of wealth, of production, of people, of society, of communications, of words. Every state and every people on earth have been subject to it in one way or another. At times a crisis of confidence in the authority of a national government led to a runaway inflation: this happened in Central Europe after World War I, and in a number of other countries after World War II. For a while the United States, alone among the great powers of the world, escaped this fate. After World War I she was not only the most productive but the richest state of the world; she changed from a relative debtor to a creditor among nations. Before 1914 the most renowned international currency was the British pound, and the financial capital city of the world was London; by 1918 the dollar replaced the pound, and New York, London.

During the 1920s the dollar was still as good as gold, in some places even better. Yet during the 1920s the inflation of American society grew by leaps and bounds. Perhaps for the first time in the history of the world the distribution of wealth within a society did not resemble the shape of a pyramid or of a tree. The American middle class became so large that American society bulged out in the middle; it inflated itself into something like a balloon. Again the inflation of society ran ahead of the inflation of money.† The international value of the dollar remained high and solid, and within the United States prices increased hardly at all. There were a few exceptions: the prices paid for movie actors and actresses, for Florida real (and also for unreal) estate, and for stocks and bonds had risen beyond the dreams of avarice. The last were more important, because a respectable portion of the population was involved with them. In late 1929 the stock-exchange boom caved in. Such stock-exchange panics had occurred periodically in the European and in the American capital markets before 1914 with few important effects in the long run. The panic of 1929, too, would have been no great loss for the United States and the world had it not been for two new elements: the speculation now included at least one million people, not merely a few thousand financiers and fast-money men; and international finance was now entangled with the finances of the United States, otherwise a self-proclaimed isolationist power. The result of the American people's sudden deflation of confidence in their own speculations was the international depression that engulfed the Western world for five or six years.

This Depression, no matter how widespread and unpleasant were its effects—and in the United States the Depression, not the two world wars, was the traumatic experience of an entire generation of Americans—was an anomaly, hardly qualifying even for the proverbial exception that proves the rule. The rule of the twentieth century was inflation, not depression. The year 1929 was a nineteenth-century event in the midst of a twentieth-century society. One illustration of this is that the drop in prices was temporary and undramatic. At the lowest point of the Depression, in 1932–33, stock prices had fallen by 70 percent and farm prices close to 50 percent; but the drop in the average prices for essentials was only 30 percent, including the prices of automobiles, which were reduced by 20

† Dwight Morrow on inflation, 1927: "It is the social effect which is so dangerous. It transfers the habit of spending from those who have long experience of spending to those who have had no experience." On the other hand, as Ronald Berman pointed out in 1980, "The remarkable thing about the American middle class is not its standard of living but its extent. . . . Mass culture may be vulgar, but mass society has not become authoritarian."

percent, not more. The prices for United States government bonds dropped hardly at all, which shows that all of the considerable social tensions notwithstanding, the confidence of the people in the American system remained solid.

This is an important consideration because of what was to follow. It was in the 1930s that the American provider state came into existence, and it was then that the line separating public from private enterprise in the United States began to erode. This development, too, had its origins earlier than we have been accustomed to think. It is true that during the nineteenth century private property and public property were two different things, both of them protected by strict laws. It is also true that for a long time the value of money was as permanent as was the possession of goods, and that the state did not interfere (not much, at any rate) with private ownership. So far as the latter went, the more one paid for some things, the more lasting they were. The most expensive suit or automobile was the longest-lasting, all of the whirligig of fashion notwithstanding. The richest people built the solidest of houses, with foundations twenty feet deep and walls two feet thick. Yet in the United States they would often abandon these houses within one generation. Americans were, and still are, a restless people, moving from one place to another, and exchanging their possessions at a rate which to most Europeans seemed, and still seems, incredibly fast. People who are exchanging their material possessions that fast (while their ideas change at a very much slower rate) are not materialists, far from it. Americans were not self-centered individualists either: the primacy of their social considerations dominated their individual ambitions. By 1900, in the western part of the United States, superficially the openest and freest portion of the country, legal limitations of private property existed (for example, the right of public domain governing the use of bodies of water) to an extent that a Western European bourgeois would have regarded intolerable, whereas to Americans these were matters of course. Unlike Europeans, jealous of their possessions and of their privacy, Americans did not build walls around their houses. They still don't. These are matters that seldom figure in the statistics, and not in the limited imaginations of economists. They mean that even a century ago the sense of ownership, and of possession, among the American people was different from that, say, of the French. They also meant that the American people trusted their system of government, while the French did not.

In 1933 the American Government discovered that its prime duty was to provide to its people something like full employment, not only at the cost of balanced budgets, national debts, and other fictitious bookkeeping figures but eventually at the cost of productive efficiency and of solid money. After 1934 Americans were no longer allowed to exchange their money for gold. Their money was now worth what the government said it was. The American people did not mind this. Their belief in their government and their belief in the wealth of their country remained unshaken. Yet the enormous wealth of the United States was not merely attributable to its great natural assets or to its prodigious production. That production was the consequence of the first mass market in history, not the cause of it. It was made possible, among other things, by giving credit—in more than one sense—to the masses. "*On ne prête qu'aux riches* [One has to be rich to be able to borrow]" was a common European witticism of the world before 1914, indeed, before 1945. This had no meaning in America, certainly not after 1920, when the shape of American society was beginning to bulge out, from the shape of the traditional pyramid to that of the superdemocratic balloon.

The Depression changed the development of this tendency toward mass ownership not at all. True, stocks and bonds could no longer be bought for small marginal payments (not many people wanted to buy them in the thirties anyway). More important was the change in the ownership of industries. During the thirties the line separating public from private property was beginning to be washed away. Factories and industries were no longer owned by capitalists and their families, they were governed by managers. Huge amounts of stocks and bonds, too, were no longer owned by individual investors and speculators: they were managed by financial bureaucrats for impersonal institutions and pension funds. During World War II the government became the single largest purchaser of American production. This practice continued after the war. Whether General Electric under Eisenhower was nationalized or not made as little difference as whether Krupp under Hitler was nationalized or not. Both depended on government orders, on government regulations; their employees had to be screened and supervised by the government. By 1960 perhaps as much as 30 percent of American industry depended upon government orders, certain industries more than 90 percent. Their leaders would make speeches on occasion, extolling the virtues of the American private enterprise system—a tribute to the national habit of self-deception perhaps. Others would call this "people's capitalism" instead of recognizing what this was —and still is: a peculiarly American form of state socialism, corresponding to American bureaucracy.

Until the middle of the twentieth century the material conditions of American life—vast resources, much empty land, a minimal dependence on foreign trade, prodigious mass production allied to prodigious mass consumption, the highest wages and a solid and most prestigious currency

—were inimitable. The results of the Second World War ended this uniqueness. The United States divided Europe with the Soviet Union; she did not have to divide the financial leadership of the world. This meant added and novel responsibilities, including the American financing of the rebuilding of Western and Southern Europe. More important, the prestige of the American system led to its emulation. This impression with American things was not new: already during the 1920s there were millions of people in Europe who knew the names of American movie stars but who did not know the names of their own prime ministers. Yet the large-scale Americanization of democracy in Europe had to wait until after the Second World War. The victory of the United States led to the restoration of parliamentary democracy in Western Europe, and to its establishment in Western Germany and in Japan; more important, in many countries it led to the Americanization of their political process, including the development of two-party systems; even more important, it led to the Americanization of entire societies. Governments followed the American example: they were giving credit, material and financial credit, to their masses. By 1960 even some of the Communist states in Eastern Europe were moving in this direction. It is both paradoxical and ironic that the Americanization of the world began in earnest at the very time when the unique conditions of American democracy as well as the uniquely powerful status of the United States had begun to wane; but that is another story, to which we must return.

(2)

Let us now contemplate the automobile, a primal element in the Americanization of the world, for the American century has been the automobile century: the automobile has been symbol as well as symptom, cause as well as effect, of its development.

The nineteenth century was the century of steam. The twentieth century has been the century of oil and of the internal-combustion engine. The railroad and the steamship changed the face of the world, and of the United States in particular, with tracks laid to tie entire continents together and ship canals dug to connect entire seas. Between 1880 and 1897 alone the American railroad mileage doubled. The railroad and the steamship brought people closer together. Without them mass immigration, the largest single development in the history of the American people, would have been a trickle, not an oceanic stream. (It may be argued that the automobile and the airplane, while bringing people together on occasion, effectually make them move away from one another—but that is another matter.) We know who built the first locomotive. In 1900, seventy-five years after George Stephenson's first regular steam train in Lancashire in England, there were about one hundred thousand locomotives hauling people and freight throughout the world. We do not know who built the first automobile (around 1885 French and German engineers put together certain working models). In 1980, ninety-five years later, the total of automobiles in the world was literally innumerable, probably more than one-half billion. In the United States there were about 37,000 locomotives in 1900. Their number reached its peak, 67,000, in 1928, after which it began to decline to the level of 1890. The total number of American automobiles in 1900 was eight thousand; in 1978 it was nearly 150 million—seven cars and trucks for every ten Americans, infants and cripples included.

The automobile was (and it still is) the most wonderful of conveniences—not so much because of its comfort (which is limited in even the most luxurious of cars) and not even because of its reduction of distances, but because it allows its owner to be the master of his time rather than of space; he can leave whenever he wants, and return whenever he chooses; he does not depend on schedules of public transport. The inconveniences and the powerlessness which affect him when his car does not function well or when he is caught in a traffic jam, when his powerful motor pulsates uselessly, and when his free choice is reduced to switching his car radio on or off, are considerable. But trains are halted in the middle of their tracks, too, and these inconveniences do not compare to the relative freedom which his use of his car still provides, and which has become an inevitable part of his everyday life. The automobile was (and still is) an invention particularly attractive to Americans for many reasons: their mechanical inclinations, the peculiar character of their individualism, their tendency to be wasteful about space while being avaricious about time. Yet in one important sense the automobilization of the United States, and of the world, was as illogical as the discovery of America had been. (America was a continent which was discovered through error, and its colonization should have followed and not been preceded by three centuries the colonization of Africa, that vast continent close to and visible from Spain.) The automobile was made for individual use (and for individual ownership); and the century of individual enterprise was the nineteenth century, not the twentieth. If history were governed by logic, the automobile should have belonged to the nineteenth century, after which people would have recognized that thousands of people, in large steel cars, sped forth on rails, could travel faster, cheaper, and more effectively than in thousands of individual vehicles clogging up their cities and their roads. In the age of mass democracy public transportation should have replaced private transportation; railroads should have replaced automobiles, not the reverse. But history is not governed by logic—or, rather, it has a logic of its own. Had the automobile not been invented and put into mass production, the cities of the early twentieth century would have experienced even worse traffic jams of horse-drawn carriages, with entire armies of poor sweepers required to clean the streets of mountains of horse droppings at night. Traffic jams in the great cities of the world preceded automobile traffic jams by half a century at least. Traffic counts taken at a fashionable thoroughfare in Paris at the beginning and at the end of the grossly inflated era of the Second Empire showed a nearly threefold increase of carriages in twenty years. Around 1900 many of the main thoroughfares of American cities were as crowded as they are now, by horse-drawn carriages and trolley cars.

The inflation of society led to this, just as the inflation of society led to the mass manufacture of automobiles. Henry Ford was not an especially brilliant inventor; his talent lay in mass production and in mass salesmanship, not in invention. In 1914 he put together the equipment needed for the mass production of automobiles, and he chose to pay his workers the then inflationary wage of five dollars a day (while he reduced their lunch time to fifteen minutes). This was a famous event in the history of the United States. After the Second World War certain European writers would go into raptures about it, comparing this wondrous American achievement in 1914 with the catastrophe that Europe had brought upon herself in that most fateful year.‡ Yet this event was predictable. Even more than in his mass production of automobiles the genius of Henry Ford lay in his very American vision of their mass consumption. He had the

‡ In the 1950s the French Father Raymond Bruckberger reproduced the dialogue of the lawsuit when Ford (in 1915), who had cut dividends, was questioned by the attorney of the Dodge brothers. Ford said that he did not want "awful" profits, just enough "to do as much as possible for everyone concerned . . . and incidentally to make money. . . . If you give all that, the money will fall into your hands; you can't get out of it." Father Bruckberger: "In all the world's universities all young people seeking some knowledge of political economy should be required to learn this remarkable dialogue by heart. It is as important in economics as the Declaration of Independence is in politics . . . it marks a kind of Copernican revolution. . . . Indeed, this fantastic dialogue should be looked upon as the businessman's Hippocratic oath." To a Frenchman, perhaps; to an American, no. "Ford's world is the world of the hired man," Ezra Pound wrote in the 1920s. "Ford himself is the hired man raised to the thousandth degree . . . a revolutionist to such a degree that the bickering of the impotent reds about him is almost comic. . . . But where does this get us? For everything above comfortable brute existence there is a vacuum."

compounded soul of a Populist, a salesman, and a preacher—a peculiarly American combination. He noticed, well before 1914, that the automobile was on its way to becoming an all-American item, not merely a sporting gadget for the rich. Across America, in small towns in the Middle West and elsewhere, the owner of the first car was often the owner of the drugstore or the hardware merchant, not the banker or the lawyer, the aristocracy of the town. Ford saw what other American advertising geniuses, in other fields, had noticed before him: a vast potential market, a large reservoir ready to be tapped. Ford began tapping it with all of the clanking, booming noise of a steam shovel. Soon other manufacturers joined in—after, not before, they had assured themselves that this reservoir was eternally renewing itself, that it seemed bottomless.

This was "private enterprise," so to say; but, just as a half century earlier with the railroads, the government responded to the popular desiderata. It built the roads, eventually assisting the automobile industry to a far greater extent than it had the railways. As late as 1880 the maintenance of the roads was the business of local municipalities. (They would often allow delinquent taxpayers to work on road repairs, "working off the road tax.") In 1916 the Federal Aid Road Act made national funds available for highways. By 1917 every one of the states had its highways department. In 1921 the Federal Highway Act was passed.

By 1920 the automobile was in the middle of the American scene. It was the inevitable central phenomenon of the American town—more, of the American imagination. The physiognomy of American towns, of American cities (especially in the West), and even of the land (where tractors were replacing the horses very fast) conformed to it. In 1926 a working-class wife said to the Lynds, the authors of *Middletown,* "We'd rather go without clothes than give up the car." In 1927, 30 percent of American families had radios, 40 percent had phonographs, 67 percent had cars. It is true that between 1910 and 1920 the price of the average automobile fell by 38 percent. But in 1912 there was one car for every 114 Americans; by 1920 for every 13. In 1921 the New York *Times* ("The use in the near future of anything like twice the present number of cars seems most unlikely"), and in 1926 *The New Republic,* proclaimed that the automobile market had become saturated. They were wrong. In 1928 only seven million Americans had incomes over $2,000 a year; but there were 17.5 million cars on the roads. In October 1929, during the trial of the striking textile workers of Gastonia, the prosecutor of the state of North Carolina addressed the jury with this patriotic question: "Do you believe in the flag, do you believe in North Carolina, do you believe in good roads?"* The kind of life described in *The Great Gatsby* was unimaginable without automobiles—and not only in a practical sense (its heroes and heroines forever careening in their cars between Long Island and New York) but because they were automobile people, their automobiles were as important expressions of their personalities as were their clothes and manners; they were self-propelled, automobile Americans. In Sinclair Lewis's *Dodsworth* the Innocent American was the president of a large automobile company who believed that his factory and office and city and country formed the new Rome, that they were the center of the world, which was not altogether an illusion. During the 1920s the automobilization of the world moved apace with its Americanization. In 1928 Walter P. Chrysler said, "It devolves upon the United States to motorize the world." (Hoover followed him in 1929: "two cars in every garage.") The pictorial and the musical impressions of America were replacing its verbal and literary images through the movies, magazines, and picture supplements of newspapers; they brought the United States closer to Europe. American life was now the ideal of millions. This happened more than a decade before the shiny global magazines produced by Henry Luce spoke of "The American Century" and before Pan American Airways became the first airline to cross entire oceans, signaling the panamericanization of the world.

There was a great difference nevertheless. The ideal was unreachable, in more than one way. For one thing, mass immigration to the United States was drastically restricted after 1921. For another, during the twenties automobiles in the United States were produced for the masses; elsewhere they were not. In 1920 there were eight million automobiles in the United States, in 1929, 18.5 million. In some European countries their numbers rose at an even higher rate—but there were thousands or tens of thousands of them, not millions. The mass production of automobiles had begun in Britain, France, Germany, Italy: yet in the peak year of the Depression, 1933, there was one automobile for every five inhabitants of the United States, but only one for every twenty-three in Britain, for every twenty in France, for every fifty-eight in Germany, for every 108 in Italy, for every 555 in Hungary, for every 5,000 in the Soviet Union.† In the

* Jules Abels, *In the Time of Silent Cal* (New York, 1969), p. 77. As late as 1955 American liberals would, on occasion, say similar things. Bernard De Voto: "A highway is not only a measure of progress, but a true index of our culture." The new highways would unbind "the giant" American nation. Cited by James Gilbert, *Another Chance* (New York, 1981), p. 112.

† After the United States came New Zealand: one automobile for every nine inhabitants —perhaps significantly, the most egalitarian welfare state in the world.

years before the Second World War, Mussolini and Hitler began the mass automobilization of their countries. These adversaries of democracy admired many things about the United States. The North Italian *autostrade* built under Mussolini preceded the first American limited-access superhighway (the Pennsylvania Turnpike) by nearly fifteen years. One of the few photographs that show Hitler smiling dates from 1938, as he is contemplating a table model of the Volkswagen.‡ During the Second World War in Europe the knowledge of how to drive a car was the most valuable qualification that would elevate a recruit in the ranks; it was much more of an advantage than the knowledge of how to ride a horse had been in previous wars. Still, until at least the middle of the century, automobiles, even in the most democratic nations of Europe, were the property of the upper classes, by and large. In the United States they were not. The *Andy Hardy* series of movies, made in the 1930s and distributed worldwide, had as their hero a fifteen-year-old American middle-class boy (Mickey Rooney) in a small town, not yet out of high school, having his own car, the instrument of his swift progress across town and with the girls. This was a dream to which no fifteen- or sixteen-year-old boy elsewhere in the world could reasonably aspire. It reflected the inimitable nature of the United States.

The Americanization of the world (or, more precisely, the Americanization of the imagery and of the aspirations of millions across the world) was not affected by the so-called Depression. People in Europe read about the American financial crisis, they looked at certain photographs, which made very little difference to them: their images of a shiny, wealthy, automobile America, the belief in the inimitable richness of the United States were as pervasive as they had been before. That they were not altogether wrong was to be proven not only by the ascent of the United States to the status of superpower after 1940; it was proven by the automobile lives of Americans during the very Depression years. Whatever the hardships and painful experiences of Americans during the Depression years, they did not give up their automobiles, probably because they did not have to. From 1929, the peak year of the affluent twenties, to 1933, the low year of the Depression, the sales of new automobiles declined, but the number of private automobiles in the United States dropped less than 10 percent. By

‡ Ford in 1924: "When the automobile becomes as common in Europe and Asia as it is in the U.S. the nations will understand each other. Rulers won't be able to make war. . . . This is the biggest thing the automobile will accomplish—the elimination of war." Norman Beasley, "Henry Ford Says," *Motor,* January 1924. (This was the same Ford who at that time gave some support to Hitler—the Hitler who knew what the motor would do for war.)

1935 their number reached the level of 1929 and grew thereafter every year. (The number of trucks dropped hardly at all.) In 1936 D. W. Brogan, the Scots student of the American character, was in the Middle West. On Main Street, he wrote, "There were endless cars; it was possible that here, as in other American towns like this, it was thought more important to have a car which is a public asset than a bathroom which is private." *The Grapes of Wrath,* that saga of the Depression, celebrated in literature as well as in the movies, showed some of the poorest of Americans, the Okies, moving westward across the desert in old automobiles but in automobiles nevertheless, driving from the dust storms onto the surface of superb dustless highways (highways built with federal aid increased during the decade from 194,000 miles in 1930 to 236,000 miles in 1940). For a Russian or Ukrainian peasant in the thirties the scenes and the people of *The Grapes of Wrath* would have evoked not pity but wonderment: to them these indigent Americans would have seemed super-*kulaks,* perhaps even *amerikanski* millionaires.

During the Second World War the American Army took to motorization more easily than any other army in the world. The change which the internal-combustion engine brought to war was a revolutionary revelation, brilliantly recognized (in vain) by the young Charles de Gaulle in France; to a polo-playing cavalry officer like George Patton it came as a matter of course. In the 1890s, and for a long time thereafter, the planners and the prophets of American world power rested their case on the Anglo-Saxon belief that sea power was the key of history. "Naval power in world affairs still governs history," cabled Franklin Roosevelt to the French Premier Reynaud in June 1940 in answer to the Frenchman's desperate plea for instant American help. Roosevelt was wrong: while it was true that Hitler could not cross the Channel without a navy, and that the Anglo-American armies could land in France principally because of their naval superiority, four years later the invasion and liberation of Western Europe were feasible because nearly four fifths of the German Army were fighting in Russia. Had he had a large reserve army, Hitler could have sped it to Normandy and driven the invaders into the sea. For the first time in centuries, troops could be moved faster on land than on the seas, because of the automobile engine.

After the Second World War the momentum of automobilization increased. There was (for the first and only time during the automobile century) no production of private cars in the United States between 1941 and 1946; yet the number of private automobiles grew by 50 percent during the 1940s, and the number of trucks nearly doubled. There were 151 million Americans in 1950 and 228 million in 1980, an increase of 50 percent; but from 1950 to 1980 the number of their automobiles increased threefold, and the number of their trucks nearly fourfold. In 1949, 48 percent of all Americans owned one car, and only 3 percent more than one; by 1976, 30 percent had two or more. In 1950 there were few American wives who had their own car; in 1970 the wife's car was standard even for the lower middle class. High school boys who had their own jalopies in 1950 were not rare, but they still constituted an enviable class among their peers; the same thing was true among American Negroes or among Spanish-Americans.* By 1970 the planners and administrators of public high schools in the smallest and least prosperous towns had to make provisions for huge parking areas for hundreds of the students' cars. The national habit of automobilization was, of course, encouraged by the production of consumption, from the practice of extending all kinds of credit to all kinds of people, a national financial habit that followed the Second World War, after which consumer credit, in all kinds of ways, and from an increasing variety of sources, became an American institution. In 1948 three out of ten American buyers of new cars bought them on installment; in 1975 nearly seven out of ten did, in spite of much higher interest rates and costs. (Installment buying of used cars did not rise; it showed a slight decline during the 1950s and 1960s.) The government willingly and mightily contributed to automobilization. Under the Eisenhower administration the enormous interstate highway system came into existence. The construction of superhighways and expressways became the principal expenditure of state governments, too. They, and the American military, worked hand in hand with the monstrous and corrupt truck lobby, involved with construction companies and with that most monstrous and corrupt of unions, the Teamsters. One of the results was the increasing allowance of giant trucks, tractor-trailers sometimes weighing more than eighty or ninety tons. Their numbers nearly doubled during each decade after 1955.†

Automobilization changed not only the imagery, it changed entire

* In 1901 New York and Connecticut were the first states requiring drivers' licenses; South Carolina and South Dakota were the last (the latter in 1954). The lowest minimum age at which one is able to obtain such a license is fifteen, in Mississippi, one of the least prosperous of the states of the Union; this may be correlated with the fact that in the neighboring state of Alabama the number of cars nearly doubled from 1960 to 1975, while the population rose by less than 3 percent.

† Highway construction destroyed large portions of the American land, and of American city neighborhoods (in 1970 more than 50 percent of Los Angeles consisted of highways, streets, and parking lots). The large trucks often destroyed the surface of the roads soon after they had been built, and on occasion they would destroy all kinds of involuntary obstacles, including smaller cars, on their way. As late as 1950 American drivers of trucks had to undergo stringent training and examination; by 1970 this was no longer the case. The truck-

patterns of American life. But what is interesting to notice is that during the swiftest and most expansive phase of American automobilization the mobility of the owners of private cars had actually slowed down. I am not only referring to traffic jams, the particular problem in large cities before 1940,‡ which after 1950 became a standard condition even in small American towns. Between 1950 and 1970 the share of private cars in intercity traffic remained the same. Meanwhile the share of air travel increased fivefold, while that of the railroads fell to less than 1 percent—but, then, so did that of buses, to 2.1 percent, probably because of their association with the lower class in the minds of many people. The original and practical blessing of the automobile, that of providing unexpected horizons of mobility for men and women, was declining. Until about 1950 a spin in the family car on Sunday afternoon was a widespread American practice. After 1960 driving for pleasure, except occasionally for the youngest drivers, largely ceased to exist. Since 1940 the average yearly mileage of American privately owned automobiles has remained about the same. More and more people depended on their automobiles for the practical purposes of transportation, the main reason why the number of private cars increased while public transportation, in spite of federal and other subsidies, deteriorated.

The "love affair" of Americans with the automobile is a cheap journalistic cliché, used over and over again during the last twenty years by amateur experts on the national psyche who kept returning to the question: was this love affair coming to an end? The question was wrongly stated. States of amorousness notwithstanding, by the middle of the century the nation was *married* to the automobile, and the question which remains for our descendants is whether this marriage will remain indissoluble or not. It surely seems indissoluble even now, even though it is beset with plenty of troubles, troubles which began earlier than we have accustomed ourselves to think, that is, before the rise of gasoline prices in the 1970s. As early as 1950 the design and the quality of American automobiles were no longer exemplary. Until about 1950 American cars were

---

ing lobby did its best (or, rather, its worst) to keep the proportion of traffic deaths resulting from trucks out of official statistics—up to this day they are difficult to ascertain. This is especially heartrending since the average American driver of the average car (excluding youths under twenty-one) is still among the best drivers in the world. The total of American motor vehicles (automobiles and trucks) was about 32 million in 1940 and 108 million in 1970, an increase more than threefold; the number of motor-vehicle accidents increased at a slower pace, however, while the number of deaths in car accidents actually declined.

‡ There were 596,000 private cars in New York City in 1930 and 1,325,000 in 1956, a nearly 250 percent increase during a period when the population of the city declined and when traffic jams were getting much worse.

bigger, better, with more advanced features than automobiles built elsewhere, and usually more durable than the latter. They were the luxury cars of the world: a Cadillac, a Lincoln, a La Salle were the coveted automobiles of millionaires and of statesmen, symbols of status and monuments of solidity, not much beneath the reputation of a Rolls-Royce. Before the Second World War the world car was the Ford. After 1950 it was the German Volkswagen. Before 1955 the number of Americans who bought foreign cars was infinitesimal, less than a handful of Hollywood stars and millionaires. After 1955 imported cars began to dot American highways everywhere. Unlike in the 1920s, in the 1950s there were relatively few improvements in the technical features of American cars. More important, due to high labor costs as well as to the bureaucratization of the mass automobile manufacturing companies, American automobiles were no longer competitive. In 1950 Americans produced four million automobiles, when all the rest of the world produced hardly more than half a million. In 1963, for the first time in history, less than half of the automobiles built in the world were made in the United States. By 1967 more than 10 percent of American cars were imported from abroad; their portion of the American market continued to rise, to nearly 30 percent in 1980.

Few Americans noticed the significance of this until 1973, when—subsequent to the short burst of war between Israel and Egypt and to the American association with the fortunes of the former—the Arab countries decided that they might as well raise the price of their oil. Now the expense of their marriage with the automobile stared Americans in their faces. Between 1950 and 1970 the American consumption of oil more than doubled, while imports rose threefold, and Americans had become dependent on foreign oil; by 1973 this dependence amounted to 40 percent at least. In 1980 the price of gasoline (not to speak of the increased cost of cars and the soaring rates of their insurance) was six times what it had been in 1954. Many people (and, of course, experts) predicted that the American dependence on private automobiles would be drastically reduced. This did not happen, since problems of expense are seldom sources, they are consequences of marriages in trouble—and a marriage is not in trouble until the people involved think so. In 1980 there were more cars on the road than ever before. More American teen-agers had cars than before.* Despite huge governmental subsidies, public transportation was getting steadily worse, and increasingly neglected; most people would not use it, an entire generation having grown up who had not known trains. In the

* Had the government raised the minimum driving age, this single sensible regulation would have reduced the national gasoline deficit by half.

cities public transport was not only dirty and inefficient and no longer cheap; it had become dangerous to life and limb, as gangs of young savages were raiding the cars and the stations. In 1980, 88 percent of Americans traveled to and from work in their automobiles; more than one third of American families owned more than one automobile; three fourths of the nation's freight and more than 90 percent of its perishable food was hauled in trucks. Chrysler, one of the three large American automobile companies remaining, perched itself on the edge of bankruptcy, but the government elected to bail it out, with the support of most Republicans, their preachings about the American free-enterprise system notwithstanding. The year 1980 was a statistical milestone: Japan alone produced more cars than the United States. No matter: the fervency of the American love affair with the automobile may have been a thing of the past, yet Americans proceeded along on the assumption that their marriage with the automobile was indissoluble.

(3)

People who are married often tend to look alike after a while. The automobile changed the face of America in more than one way. National characteristics appear even in the standardized products of mass manufacture. American automobiles tended to look American, and I am not referring only to their size or to some of their features that reflected American conditions. The automobile conformed to the national physiognomy while the national physiognomy, too, was affected by the automobile. For one thing, Americans in this century are not used to walking, which shows in their gait. For another, there was a resemblance in the faces and the frames of Henry Ford and Calvin Coolidge to the gaunt Ford Model T;† thirty years later there was a correspondence between the physiognomies of the corpulent Buicks and Oldsmobiles of the 1950s and that of Charles Wilson, Eisenhower's statesman from General Motors. Mechanization affected the very imagery of Americans, not only their external imagery but

† A poetic eye recognized this. Hilaire Belloc in *The Garden Party (circa* 1930): "The Poor arrived in Fords / Whose features they resembled . . ." the end of which cautionary verse also suggests his view of the inflation of society: "For the hoary social curse / Gets hoarier and hoarier, / And it stinks a trifle worse / *Than in* / The days of Queen Victoria, / *when* / They married and gave in marriage, / They danced at the County Ball / And some of them kept a carriage. / AND THE FLOOD DESTROYED THEM ALL."

the way in which their imaginations worked, in the ways they thought about human nature. "Your automobile," said an advertisement in 1910, "should receive the care you regularly devote to yourself." Thirty years later an advertisement by an insurance company advocating annual medical examinations for people began, "How Long Would You Run *Your* Car Without a Check-Up?" One hundred and fifty years ago the metaphor coined for the locomotive, "the Iron Horse," conveyed an image from the living world with which people were familiar. In the 1920s "he is the spark plug of the organization" conveyed an—much more abstract—image from mechanics with which Americans *thought* they were familiar.

This seemed to be very modern and up-to-date; yet it derived straight from the eighteenth century when the French encyclopedists for the first time wrote of Man As a Machine, a view toward which certain Americans such as Franklin, too, had tended, even though he was judicious enough to trim his phraseology to the moral breezes of his day. Certain European visitors to the United States noted this surprising condition, that the most "modern" American ideas and their representatives seemed very old. Among them were the Dutch historian Huizinga and the arrogant and stentorian but not unintelligent Count Keyserling, who met Ford and Rockefeller in the 1920s. Keyserling wrote that he seldom met one of these field marshals of business and industry "who did not look centuries old; the kind of parchment-face I mean is the face of a mummy. And what does this type of man talk about? Never a new idea—a perpetual rehearsal of slogans which have their roots in the eighteenth century; chewing the cud of higher standards of living, better institutions, a sound community-life, and so forth and so on. If such talk is not a sign of senility, I have never seen one. . . . This inherent childishness also explains the fact that one rarely hears of any other standard of value but of that of quantitative achievement."‡

Mobility, after all, is not identical with progress. The old prototypical village American, eternally rocking back and forth on his porch rocker was moving but he was not advancing. The prototypical young American,

‡ Hermann A. Keyserling, *America Set Free* (New York, 1929), p. 188 and *passim.* Also: "[America is socialist,] but it expresses its socialism in the form of general prosperity, and Russia in the form of general poverty." In the same year Douglas Woodruff in *Plato's American Republic* (London, 1926): "Americans will often talk as if ideas were less real than facts, instead of more real. . . . What are facts? . . . They may be anything. Lists of names, and long technical words are accepted as fact. The biggest fact is the Divine Fact, Progress, which they worship. . . . Might not that be called an idea? . . . You might say so . . . but I would advise you not to do so, for the Americans dearly love progress and will not tolerate your insults."

eternally chewing gum, shows a face that is as auto-mobile as it is mechanical, frozen in motion while it is devoid of expression. Whether the automobile changed the faces of Americans, it surely changed the face of America. Seen from the air, the gigantic highways soon become the principal features of the landscape. Compared to them the railroad tracks are but thin strands of wire, difficult to espy. The automobilization of the United States was consequence as well as cause: it corresponded not only to American ambitions, but to certain conditions of the American psyche. Americans, I repeat, tend to be wasteful with their space while they are avaricious with their time; but there were ample evidences of these tendencies long before the automobile appeared. The automobile, its critics have been telling us,* destroyed much of the American city; but then, Americans have not been much of an urban people. Their movement to the suburbs developed before their automobiles. In certain places (such as Philadelphia) the upper class was beginning to abandon the city and set up in country estates as early as 1875; elsewhere (this was the more usual pattern) the younger married couples of the middle classes moved out of the cities in search of a neighborhood where they could afford family houses of their own. The American ideal of people owning their houses was an admirable and healthy one, achievable in the United States with its large spaces for far more people than in overcrowded Europe. Yet the desire for this ideal form of dwelling, motivated though it was by the purposes of solidity and of respectability, did not lead to permanence of residence. Americans moved more often than any other civilized people in the world. Suburban life, besides its cultural disadvantages, divided people rather than bringing them together; suburban people knew few people and few features beyond their immediate neighborhoods. Ever since 1890 Americans have moved farther and farther away from where they worked. Until about 1920 public transportation, especially the electric streetcars, made this possible for millions. After that the automobile began to com-

* A fine and telling summary of what it did to one city in Walter Muir Whitehill's *Boston in the Age of John F. Kennedy* (Oklahoma University Press, 1966), pp. 44–45: "The automobile, with its attendant acolytes of traffic engineers and real estate speculators, in the single decade of the nineteen fifties all but accomplished the ruination of both city and country in eastern Massachusetts. A monstrous overhead highway, named in honor of former Mayor John F. Fitzgerald, cut ruthlessly through the center of Boston. The Storrow Drive, which separated the Back Bay from the Charles River Basin by six lanes of fast-moving traffic, hopelessly destroyed a great human amenity. No sooner was the circumferential Route 128—originally conceived to get traffic around the city—completed than the fields through which it passed became the sites of new factories that created urban traffic problems outside the limits of Boston. . . . Suburban shopping centers began to siphon off retail trade from Boston as well. . . . Year by year the city was progressively coming apart at the seams. . . ."

promise not only life in the cities, it destroyed most of the public transport, with the odd result that it was in the mass democracy of the United States that cities eventually became the least safe of places and that public transportation became one of the worst systems, if not *the* worst, of the civilized world. That prototypical postmodern and posturban city (in reality a conglomeration of suburbs), Los Angeles, had the world's best streetcar service in 1915. Thirty years later its public transportation was the worst in the world.† That urban life was the ideal of the nineteenth century and that suburban life that of the twentieth century is obvious. What is less obvious is that the American dream of the suburban house, like the American ideal of mechanization, harked back to the eighteenth century: wasn't it Voltaire who said that the serene ideal of human existence is to cultivate one's garden? During the twentieth century this ideal became translatable to the lives of millions; indeed, the provider state would entitle millions to it.

And here we return to the starting point of our argument: the inflation of society grew before the inflation of money, the inflation of circulation before the inflation of traffic, the inflation of verbal communications before the inflation of physical communications. The inflation of money was a consequence rather than a cause. After the 1930s most prices would never drop again. Between 1940 and 1960 prices more than doubled; but disposable personal income rose more than threefold.‡ A new generation of Americans became accustomed to this kind of prosperous inflation as a fact of life. This American kind of national socialism made for an unprecedented prosperity. Standardized mass production and standardized mass credit, helped along by the inflation of wages, made it possible for millions to acquire and to consume things that they themselves had not thought of but a few years before. Around 1905 the millionaire J. P. Morgan, with a somewhat wooden witticism, said that the kind of person who had to think what a yacht would cost him couldn't afford it. Fifty years later the reverse was true: the kind of person who was thinking of having one would go ahead and afford it. In this new and increasingly classless society thousands of truck drivers had power boats if not yachts, the wives and daugh-

† In one instance the automobile industry contributed to this: General Motors and other automobile-related industries (Standard Oil Ohio, General Electric, Goodyear) bought out the Los Angeles Electric Tramway Company in 1927.

‡ During World War II prices rose remarkably little, as we have seen, but not only because of wage and price controls; principally because the confidence of the American people in the value of their currency was strong, and because the habit of instant spending was not yet widespread. In 1944 they saved 22.2 percent of their personal incomes (25.1 percent after taxes); in 1980, a mere 3.7 percent.

ters of plumbers would go on winter cruises in the Caribbean. Millionaires now counted much less than before, not only because of inflation and taxation but because, in this credit economy, earning capacity—which for the great majority meant regular employability—counted much more than the possession of wealth. Within four years—between 1952 and 1956—consumer debt increased by 55 percent. Through the influence of the publicity industry the production of consumption became more important than the consumption of production, one of the consequences of which was that entertainment, vacation, recreation became the principal elements in the economies of entire states.

This transformation of society meant a transformation in the character of goods and in the character of money. They became less permanent and less durable. Unlike in the past, the high cost of a certain item was now due to its relative rarity rather than to its durability. This was true of clothes as well as of machines and houses. It had something to do with the decline, and sometimes with the virtual disappearance, of individual craftsmanship. It had much more to do with a subtle transmutation of the sense of ownership. On paper more Americans owned cars and houses in the 1960s than ever before. In reality they were renting and discarding them.* Most people still found it more satisfactory to buy houses than to rent them: but since they were moving every few years, their sense of ownership was less than that of people, whether owners or renters, who had been living in the same place for a long time. In sum, the previously clear distinction between the ownership and the rental of properties began to blur. The social thinker Thorstein Veblen, who had castigated the materialism of the wealthier class of Americans for their "conspicuous consumption" sixty years before, was not too far wide of the mark, though he was a little premature. At that time the principal instrument of keeping up with the Joneses was the conspicuous possession of things: their conspicuous consumption came only later. By the 1960s the meaning of the adjective "conspicuous" paled. Consumption remained the overwhelming reality: but this was different from materialism, since the very act of consumption involves the disappearance of matter. Eventually it came to mean the narrowing of choice too. The number of Americans who could buy a house during the accelerating inflation of the late 1970s, with their increasing mortgage rates, declined: but it is, as yet, doubtful whether the increase in town houses and the thin trickle of middle-class people returning to the

* The New York *Times,* Finance Section, Sunday, 25 August 1957: "Times have changed. Owning a house is no longer so important as being able to use it while paying for it."

cities would lead to a revival of urban life in America, or whether the increasing financial obstacles to moving "up" would lead to an increase in the permanence of residence—something that is, after all, one of the principal marks of a stable civilization.

The terms of an "acquisitive" or of an "affluent" society, intellectually fashionable in the 1960s, were way off the mark. "Acquisitive" means an eagerness to possess, to maintain, to keep. "Affluent" means a kind of prosperous ease that flows from the possession of considerable personal reserves. Neither of these adjectives fits the millions of buyers and consumers and renters who discarded things almost as fast as they bought them. Their personal savings were low. In the past, when money was scarce, people who earned some of it may not have been well educated, but they certainly knew what to do with it. A principal problem of the American provider state was not only its bloated bureaucracy, it was that a large number of people did not know what to do with their money. One source of this kind of improvidence was the habit of instant gratification, especially among younger people. This condition was related to another: many Americans were not only chronically unemployed, they were chronically unemployable. This was not merely the result of insufficient education. Nor was it only the problem of the poor on the bottom of the economic jar. The deficient interest in durable possessions and the consequent—though less conscious—frustration with the pleasures of possessions (leading not only to the rapid abandonment but to the rapid deterioration of possessions because of their nonmaintenance) were characteristic of the "new poor": men and women and children whose poverty was less material than it was social and psychic and spiritual.

We have seen that installment buying became widespread after the Second World War; but thereafter consumer debt rose phenomenally; in 1968 it was nearly ten times what it had been twenty years before. The transformation of the character of money was of course involved with this credit-card economy, with its transactions consisting of mere paper. Revolving credit began in 1955. In 1966, for the first time in American history, the dollar was no longer exchangeable into silver equivalents. Silver disappeared from American coinage that was struck or, in some cases, pasted together of cheaper and baser materials. The American people were told that all of this meant nothing, which they no doubt believed, though they did not act accordingly. The relatively moderate inflation now began to accelerate. In the 1970s subsequent American governments blamed this inflation on the increasing price of oil. Yet the acceleration of inflation had preceded the latter. Well before 1973 the value of the dollar had begun to erode not only within the country but also abroad. In the mid-sixties—

corresponding to the soiled character of so many other matters: soiled cities, filthy images, ugly lettering, the increasing raggedness and sloppiness of clothes, of manners, of speech—dollar bills, too, became dirty, soiled, and torn, since they were passing from hand to hand with increasing rapidity. They were no longer folded and handled and kept with a kind of anxious respect; they began to resemble the soiled and ragged and inflated money of European countries after the war. When the finances of a state are sound her money is crisp and clean. So was the money of the old-fashioned democracy of Switzerland and that of the new Americanized democracy of West Germany. During the 1970s the value of the dollar, when offered in exchange for Swiss or German money, had fallen by more than half. By 1980 the per capita income of the Swiss and of the West Germans was, for the first time in history, higher than that of Americans.

Thus the United States, after a century, ceased to be the richest country of the world. But the turning point in this development, too, occurred earlier than we have been accustomed to think. It was in 1956—remembered, if remembered at all, as one of the dull, prosperous, powerful Eisenhower years—that for the first time Americans imported more automobiles than they sold abroad. This was not an isolated event. It was then that the Treasury of the United States possessed more gold than ever before or after. After 1957 the American gold stock began to decline; gold began to flow out of the United States in increasing quantities each year (except for 1969), and fourteen years later the gold stock was less than half what it had been in 1956. Around 1956, too, American production, on the whole, began to stagnate: the production of certain Western European nations grew faster than that of the United States; Japan was soon to follow. For the first time certain European mass products surpassed their American counterparts in quantity as well as in quality. Thirty years after the first industrial revolution, after the thirty years of relative European peace following Napoleon, the first signs of the end of Britain's industrial leadership on the Continent began to appear. Something like this was happening to the United States twelve years after the demise of Hitler, and after a decade of the cold war. The trade balance of the United States now became adverse. Something else, too, happened in 1956, an event of greater significance. For the first time in the history of the world the majority of the working population of a country—the United States—was no longer engaged in production. In 1956, for the first time, more Americans were employed in administration than in agricultural and industrial production together. This meant that the industrial and urban phase of American history was now over: the United States, having passed from the predominantly agricultural to the predominantly industrial age during the second decade of the twentieth century, now entered the postindustrial age. The bureaucratization of its society was now proceeding fast.

Few people, at the time, noticed the importance of this. In 1957 the Soviet Union preceded the United States in launching the first space satellite. Yet twelve years later the United States preceded the Russians in shooting astronauts to the moon; and the technological superiority of the United States over Russia continued even when the previously incontrovertible primacy of American power in the world was decreasing. During the last twenty-five years the prestige of the American way of life survived the decline of American power. There were many disturbing elements in this overall picture of decline, but the general impression was still very high. The value of American money, though eroded, was still considerable, and the confidence of the American people in their form of government remained solid. And so—all superficial statements to the contrary—was the envy and the desire of the rest of the world for American ways of life.

(4)

The sixteenth century was marked by the predominance of Spain in the world; the seventeenth by that of France; the eighteenth by the world wars between France and England; the nineteenth century by that of Britain; the twentieth century by that of the United States. These statements do not refer only to military or to political or economic predominance: they involve prestige as well as power. During the eighteenth century the influence of French manners, of French forms of expression, of the French language was wider than was the presence of French armies or of French political alliances. During the nineteenth century it was the British who were imitated: not only their objects of manufacture but their clothes, manners, sports, parliament, clubs. The twentieth century has been the American century. To describe the evidences of this American influence throughout the world—this must now include Asia and Africa, since, let me repeat, in many ways the world did not become round until about 1900—does not belong in this book, for reasons of space alone: it would fill an encyclopedia; it is a chronicle which has not yet been compiled and written and perhaps never will. We should, in any event, note that the enemies of the United States were as impressed with American ways as its admirers. As early as 1914, Lenin, exiled in Switzerland, called for "the transformation of all the separate states of Europe into a Republican United States."

Lenin, Stalin, Khrushchev, Brezhnev, Andropov, these successive rulers of the Soviet Union were different people, but one of the things they had in common was their respect and envy for the United States. "Fordism," assembly-line production, electrification, Americanization were approbatory terms in Soviet usage as early as the 1920s. One of the common features of the Germany of the Weimar Republic and of the Germany of the Third Reich was the popularity and the emulation of certain American ways.† Sun Yat-sen, the founder of "modern" revolutionary China, admired and respected the United States; his two successors, the anti-Communist Chiang and the Communist Mao, would turn to America in the hour of their need, greedy for American succor and for American things. The Americanization of Japan had, of course, long preceded Pearl Harbor and the viceroyalty of General MacArthur in Tokyo. The frenetic anti-American rhetoric of the "leaders" of the so-called Third World during the last quarter century was often false, obscuring their envy and desire for American things. The president of the "nation" that kept innocent Americans in prison and screamed its hatred of America to the skies, the Iranian Bani-Sadr, would often draw reporters' attention to his proudest intellectual achievement, his book bearing the title *Economics of Divine Unity,* in his own words "a theory of synthesis of Koranic codes and of American macroeconomics," whatever that was.

More significant than these schizophrenic tendencies of political figures were the inclinations of the masses. Their Americanization was different from the Anglicization or from the Gallicization of earlier centuries, which were phenomena among the upper classes. Here and there fastidious men and women would write ironically about this: "It is perhaps pardonable to point out," Philip Guedalla wrote in the 1920s, "that barbarian invaders have come always from the East, because there was, prior to the discovery of America, nowhere else for them to come from." Yet a resolute kind of anti-Americanism was as rare among them as among others: English snobs such as Nancy Mitford or Evelyn Waugh might decry Americanisms and American influences while they accepted American emoluments and the power and protection of the United States. This dualism was evident among the masses, too: anti-Americanism could be popular, but beneath it bubbled the rage of envy. The same Iranians who shouted that America was "the Great Satan" sported blue jeans, played American

† An interesting footnote of the intellectual history of this century was the pro-Americanism of many Fascist or pro-Fascist intellectuals in Europe: Bardèche, Brasillach, Drieu la Rochelle, Wyndham Lewis; many of them admired American movies, as did Goebbels.

rock records, coveted American gadgets, and sex magazines; they lined up for American movies and at American fast-food emporia.

Much of that American influence was pictorial. As early as 1915 Pancho Villa's guerrillas in Mexico paraded before an American movie director, staging attacks and, in one instance, an actual execution before the Americans' movie cameras. (The movie was never completed.) In 1979 an American television reporter of PBS network succeeded in getting an interview with leaders of the Teheran mob imprisoning the American hostages. When the Iranians found out that CBS was available, they canceled the arrangement with PBS. Whatever the contents—which are often American television films bought for replay—of their television programs, the style, the format, the background music, and the editing of television in Europe and elsewhere followed American styles and American patterns, including even those of movement and acting. This was not true of literature. Few Europeans tried to write like, say, Twain or Hemingway. But there are clichés in pictorial representation: photography, stance, pose, movement, and background noises, just as in speech and writing.

During the 1950s "Coca-Colonization" was a cheap anti-American cliché. The phenomenon which it (mis)represented was an example of the split mind as well as of the palate, worth contemplating for the psychology (or, rather, for the epistemology) of taste alone. Coca-Cola, this southern and gothic potion, sweet and dark-colored, is among the least thirst-quenching of soft drinks because of its sugar content, inferior in this respect to many of the nonalcoholic bottled beverages of native origins in different countries; yet in the 1950s it became a worldwide status symbol.‡ Moneyed Arabs as well as Iraqi revolutionaries, anti-Communists as well as Communists, took pride, and pleasure, in its consumption. (In an Eastern European capital in the 1970s, I saw families ordering Pepsi-Cola on ceremonial occasions, ostentatiously, as if it were champagne. The barman in my hotel was both surprised and disappointed when on a hot afternoon I asked for a glass of freshly squeezed lemonade instead of a—more expensive—Pepsi-Cola.) In the 1970s the division among the Communist superpowers deepened. The Russian Government, after profound deliberations,

‡ So were American chocolates and other munchables inferior in taste to Swiss or other European ones: but no matter. In 1955 Mary McCarthy wrote about Lisbon, "In the delicacy shops, Tootsie Rolls and Ritz crackers rested on beds of red velvet, like holy images." From my European travel diary, 1958: "Milan. Two smart shops on the Via Montenapoleone. (1) An antique shop named Old America—Antichità: careful Milanese imitations of Shaker chairs and tables, very much in fashion now; (2) in the window of a smart grocery shop, a kind of Milanese Vendôme, packages of Rice Krispies and Corn Flakes prominent up front (with their space-satellite toy coupons)."

chose the franchise to produce and to distribute Pepsi-Cola to their thirsty millions, whereas the Chinese chose Coca-Cola. People spoke about the enormous powers of American multinational corporations, of which the above could serve as examples; but the reality was different. We have seen that until the Second World War more than 90 percent of American production was consumed by the American people themselves. From the consequences of this most American corporations have not recovered till this day: in the world markets American conditions of salesmanship, tailored as these were to Americans, to their habits and circumstances, were not advantages, they were handicaps. The supernational corporations were soon dependent on the locals. Throughout the Middle East Americans had prospected for and found oil; they drilled for it and refined it, but when the local rulers chose to expropriate the results and the profits at an increasing rate, these multinational corporations found that they could and would do little or nothing. So much for the myth of the gigantic power of American multinational corporations—or, at that, of the international imperialism of the American economy. They were subjects of nationalization, in one form or another. By the 1970s it was evident that the control (and sometimes even the profits) that American corporations exercised or collected abroad were largely matters of paper. By the late 1970s Arabs as well as certain Europeans and the Japanese reversed the trend: they began to appear in the United States, buying up American properties and corporations themselves.

Yet in the most important sense Americanization continued. Whether blue jeans or automobiles were manufactured in the United States or not mattered little. What mattered was the presence of these symbols of American civilization throughout the world.* When Nikita Khrushchev visited the United States in 1959 he was stunned by the enormous masses of American automobiles on the roads and in the parking lots. After his return to Russia he proclaimed that this was not what the people of the Soviet Union needed: instead of such masses of private cars the Soviet Union would devise new methods of public transportation in its cities, including large fleets of taxis. This was one of the sources, perhaps even a principal source, of Khrushchev's unpopularity and of his demise. He could no more halt automobilization than King Canute could sweep back the ocean waves. His resignation was followed by the first construction of a

* Automobiles in Europe (excluding the U.S.S.R.): 1946: 6.6 million; 1976: 118 million. Yet the automobilization of the world was still well behind that of the United States. In 1977 the three most automobilized countries were West Germany, France, and Japan, with a total population about equal to that of the U.S.; the total of their motor vehicles was 51 million.

modern giant automobile plant in the Soviet Union. His successor, Brezhnev, was an addict of automobiles, collecting them with the enthusiasm and the greed of a Hollywood mogul of the thirties.

During the nineteenth century the prestige of Britain, the admiration and the emulation of things British, was involved with the condition that the British gentleman was a cultural prototype. This was a relatively new development in the relations of nations. It included the image that one nation inspires in others. To a large extent this was due to such developments as popular literacy, tourism, and pictorial representation, since as late as 1850 the great majority of Europeans had not *seen* an Englishman. Conversely, in 1917 and after, communism to most people in Eastern Europe was repulsive because it was associated with Russia and the Russians. But when it came to the image of Americans in the eyes of other peoples, this was different again. When Americans produced the atom bomb or when they sent men to the moon, people throughout the world were not really surprised: America was the land of wonders, America where perhaps everything was possible. Yet the same people had only vague notions about American people. The men and women who in the eighteenth century admired someone like Voltaire saw in him a representative Frenchman, with his Gallic wit, piercing eyes, sardonic sharp face; the men and women who adored the Prince of Wales in the 1920s saw in him a royal nobleman of the Anglo-Saxon race, Prince Charming. The people who admired certain famous Americans admired them because of their achievements: Lindbergh was an American, Kennedy was an American, Kissinger was an American. Beyond this Americanness, and beyond certain items of gossip purveyed by the so-called media, about the national characteristics of such Americans they knew little. During the nineteenth century a knowledgeable European waiter could tell the difference between an upper-class Englishman and a middle-class one, sometimes even between an Englishman and a Scot. During the twentieth century few Europeans could tell the difference between a New Englander and a Southerner, between a patrician American and an American of the middle classes, often not even between a native American and an English-speaking immigrant. In spite of the ubiquitous American tourist or of the representative American official or businessman, most Europeans had but a vague and confused mental picture of Americans themselves. This was, at least partly, due to the circumstance that during the twentieth century the very physiognomy of Americans had temporarily decrystallized—an important condition, to the discussion of which we shall now turn.

4

THE LEAP ACROSS THE SEA

The Development of an American Nation

How the Americanization of millions of immigrants, which succeeded beyond all fears and expectations, consequently resulted in a, perhaps temporary, decrystallization of the national character.

(1)

The greatest event in the history of the United States was the immigration of masses of people from Europe. It made the country populous, it changed the nature of its society and the character of the nation. These transformations are not yet completed, and the end result is obscure, even though sixty years ago the representatives of the American people passed laws which reduced immigration from an oceanic tide to an irregular stream.

We do not know the numbers, even approximately. During the century before 1920 the total of immigrants to the United States was perhaps 32 to 36 million; 1825 was the first year when more than 10,000 immigrants entered the country. In 1842 for the first time more than 100,000 came, in 1881 more than 600,000, in 1905 more than one million. Between 1925 and 1975 there was only one year (1968) when the total reached 400,000, according to government records, but there is plenty of trouble with these government records, a point to which I must return.

The main characteristics of this transatlantic and transcontinental migration are beyond dispute. From Europe it was the steamship, and within Europe the railroads leading to the ports from the interior of the continental states that made the transportation of the masses possible. For more than two centuries most immigrants to North America came from the British Isles, including Ireland. (From 1820 to 1890 the total of immigrants from the two islands was about the same, 4.7 million from England, Wales, Scotland, and 4.7 million from John Bull's Other Island. Since 1960 immigrants from the former have been more numerous than those from the latter—a reversal to the pattern of the seventeenth century.) The Irish immigrants began to surpass the number of English immigrants in the 1830s; they came in large numbers during their tragic famine-ridden decade of the 1840s; they were the largest single group until the 1870s; after 1890 their numbers were fewer. Large numbers of immigrants from the Germanies appeared around 1840; in the 1870s they surpassed the Irish; after 1900 their numbers began to decline. Scandinavians came in large numbers after 1850. Orientals, peoples from the Austro-Hungarian and the Russian empires, Italians came in streams after 1880; Greeks after 1900. By that time the numbers of Slavs, Italians, Greeks, Germans, and Jews from the then Russian Empire surpassed those of immigrants from Scandinavia and from the English-speaking countries. The national sentiment turned against immigration, and in 1921 the restrictive law was passed.

During the last sixty years the evolution of immigration to the United States has been irregular. Its successive stages were often consequent to the inclinations of the American people and government to alleviate the hardships of people whose dislocations were sometimes the results of American foreign policy, or of the lacking application of it. Before and during the Second World War some people in the Roosevelt administration stretched the law to admit potential victims of Hitler's tyranny. Unwilling to contest the domination of Eastern Europe by the Soviet Union, after the Second World War the United States enacted the Displaced Persons' Act, admitting more than 300,000 refugees from portions of Central and Eastern Europe then ruled by Russia and by other Communist governments. After the Hungarian Rising of 1956 the Eisenhower administration passed a law admitting tens of thousands of Hungarians. To accept large numbers of refugees from Cuba was preferable to going to war with Cuba. The American abandonment of Indochina in 1975 was followed by the admission of Vietnamese and Cambodian refugees. These successive variations of the immigration laws soothed the national conscience. They were not devoid of the universalist inclinations of American generosity: in 1980, as in 1880, the great majority of Americans believed that to become an American citizen is the greatest secular blessing that can be bestowed on a human being.

However, 1980, like 1880, was an important turning point, the beginning of something new and worrisome. In 1980, for the first time, the government came close to admitting that there was a new kind of invasion of the United States from the south, which it could hardly control. In May and June 1980 thousands of Cubans, including political prisoners as well as the criminal dregs of the population, arrived in Florida in small boats. Meanwhile, in the southwestern states of the Union, the number of illegal aliens had grown to be unascertainable and innumerable, perhaps as high as 12 million. Most of these were Mexicans, but there was a steady stream of Central Americans, Caribbeans, and South Americans of every kind. For the first time in North American history the mass migration came not from across the Atlantic but from the south. For the first time in more than a century the control, the registration, and the actual enumeration of these new migrants had broken down, with consequences that are literally incalculable.

(2)

There are all kinds of problems with the statistics of immigration. The compilation of figures of the different agencies, reproduced and presented in *Statistical Abstracts* or in *Historical Statistics of the United States* are stonily precise (example: in 1882 the numbers of immigrants entering the United States from the Orient were 39,579 Chinese; 5 Japanese; 10 Indians; 35 from the rest of Asia). There are reasons to believe that these figures may be inaccurate arithmetical representations of reality, often 20 or 30 percent off the mark, and almost always in the direction of underestimation. The main source of this uncertainty is that of the many illegal entries, a statistical and governmental problem for every modern state but perhaps especially for the United States because of its long unguarded frontiers, because of the absence of a national police authority requiring the registration and identification of residences, and because of the relative ease (and the manifold opportunities of bribery) through which illegal aliens can find employment and eventually citizenship in the United States.

There are other hindrances in the way of obtaining reliable statistics. Until 1867 the government made no distinction between aliens who landed in American ports as immigrants and others who were temporary visitors. (Perhaps this suggested the American belief that everyone who landed in the United States came here to stay.) The detailed record-keeping of the Bureau of Immigration began only in 1892, nearly half a century after mass immigration had begun. Until 1908 there was no record kept of immigrants who came in not through the ports but who crossed into the United States over the land frontiers. More surprisingly, since 1957 no data exist of emigrants, that is, of immigrants who chose to return to their native countries. There was the added problem of defining the provenance of immigrants. What counted for the American immigration authorities was the birthplace of the immigrant, not his previous citizenship or his residence: a man born in Rumania was counted as Rumanian, even if his parents were English or his citizenship French. Add to this the problems of changing frontiers and states. During the century of American mass immigration, from 1830 to 1920, more than a dozen new states came into existence in Europe, while other states and empires broke up; and the American authorities did not wish to be bothered with complex and fluctuating identifications of nationality. Poland, for example, figures as a separate entry for immigrants' birthplaces only from 1820 to 1898 and then again after 1920. In 1900, *98 percent* of immigrants classified as "Russian" were actually non-Russian; the 1910 census recorded that among "Russian" foreign-born citizens Yiddish and Hebrew were the native languages of 52 percent and Polish of 26 percent. Since the immigration records seldom categorized religion, in the mountains of statistics compiled with ever-increasing assiduity by the government and by the census there exist but the vaguest and most contradictory data about the number of Jewish immigrants. Yet after 1950, for the first time in the history of the world, the majority of Jews in the world lived in the western hemisphere, a historical turning point. In 1825 only 0.3 percent of the Jews of the world lived in the Americas; in 1925, 30 percent; in 1950, 51.5 percent.

Still, with all of their inaccuracies, there are all kinds of surprising matters latent within the enormous mass of immigration statistics—surprising, because they often run counter to accepted ideas. The first of these is that, no matter what its consequences, this kind of mass immigration for the United States was a necessity. Not only had the masses of immigrants furnished the principal element of labor that made the United States the richest state of the world; without them the increase in the American population would have slowed down two or three generations before the drastic decrease around 1970. Without the immigrants the population of the United States would be barely more than half of its main competitor in the world, the Soviet Union. The decline in the fertility of the American native stock had begun to develop before the peak of mass immigration occurred. For a long time the United States was exceptional; the willingness of its people to have children was greater than that of any comparable industrial democracy of the world. Between 1850 and 1860 (this after the last large territorial accretion) the population of the United States rose at the phenomenal rate of 35.6 percent (and this at a time when infant mortality was still very high). Thereafter it gradually declined. During the decade of the greatest immigration, 1900 to 1910, the population increased by 21 percent, an increase that was still higher than that of any comparable nation but less than before.

Before 1850 the census gave no statistics of the numbers of foreign-born Americans. The most reasonable estimates suggest that they amounted to less than 10 percent of the American population even around that time, after the first large wave of Irish immigrants of the famine years. There is no evidence that at that time the foreign-born produced more children than did the native-born Americans. Thereafter this began to change. In 1920 foreign-born women bore four babies to every three born to native mothers. (This was, to some extent, balanced by the condition that mortality among the foreign-born was higher; as late as 1920 the Irish in New York had the highest rate of mortality and the lowest rate of life expectancy.) Until the 1960s the families of second- and third-generation immigrants were larger than those of the older Anglo-Saxon and Anglo-Celtic native stock. Religion was one factor in this development (Catholics had more children than Protestants and Jews), nationalism was another: the faith in America of the children of immigrants remained fervent and unbroken. Another contributory factor was the preponderance of young males among the immigrants. During the century of mass immigration 60 to 65 percent of all immigrants were males, among Italian immigrants from 1870 to 1900 78 percent. (The exception were the Irish, with a slight preponderance of females among them.) Eventually and consequently there were more marriages between immigrant men and native women than between native men and immigrant women. The immigrant men contributed to the general population increase, to the childbearing of native women, and to the confused and confusing nature of demographic statistics.

In 1850, 2.5 million of the population were foreign-born, in 1910 over 14 million (a total that equaled the number of natives in twenty-two states of the Union). In 1850 English was the native language of 97 percent of citizens who were foreign-born (this includes, of course, the great mass of the Irish), in 1910 it was 58 percent and decreasing fast, since by then the overwhelming majority of immigrants were coming from southern and eastern Europe and Russia. These immigrants were more visible than many of the older ones. Their appearance and their expressions made them immediately recognizable, an alien element in the midst or on the edges of the American mass. Their visibility contributed to the increasing national sentiment in favor of immigration restriction. The immigrants were unevenly distributed. In 1900 more than 30 percent of the people in Massachusetts were foreign-born, in North Carolina one hundredth of this ratio, 0.3 percent. They congregated in the cities: in 1900 in American cities of more than 100,000 people nearly 40 percent were foreign-born. Less than one third of the people in New York City were of native parents. Among the great cities in the East only in Philadelphia and Baltimore did natives of native parents still constitute a majority.

This filled many people with anxiety, sometimes even second-generation immigrants who feared that the immigrant tide would produce uncontrollable and perhaps violent reactions against most people of recognizably foreign origin. In 1905 the United Garment Workers of America, mostly Jewish in membership, passed this resolution: "RESOLVED: That we warn the poor of the earth against coming to America with false hopes . . ." The resolution included a request to the Congress to suspend, or at least restrict, immigration for a definite number of years. It also stated that "the overstocking of the labour market has become a menace to many trade-unions, especially those of the less skilled workers. Little or no benefit can possibly accrue to an increasing proportion of the great numbers yet coming; they are unfitted to battle intelligently for their rights in this Republic, to whose present burdens they but add others greater. The fate of the majority of the foreign wage-workers now here has served to demonstrate on the largest possible scale that immigration is no solution of the world-wide problem of poverty"[1]—language surely different from the famous sentimental lines composed by Emma Lazarus less than twenty years earlier, and forever associated with the Statue of Liberty. In 1906 an association of eminent Jews in New York, anxious about the potential threat of anti-Semitism, offered free transportation and a large cash payment for every Jewish immigrant who would oblige himself (and his donors) to settle west of the Mississippi, removing himself from New York and the East. These warnings took place shortly before 1907, the largest single year of the immigrant influx; yet we shall see that these anxieties about the immediate dangers were exaggerated.

There was another factor that has not received the attention it deserves. Many of the immigrants did not stay in the United States. This was another difference between the immigrants who came before 1880 and those who came after. The masses of the misery-ridden Irish who had arrived before 1850 had no intention of returning to Ireland. Many of the Italians and the Greeks who came half a century later came with the intention of saving enough so that they could return to their native places with some money. (The Jews were an exception: few intended to return, few did.) But here we face the murky and complex matter of the immigrants' motives. "The short and simple annals of the poor": Thomas Gray's elegiac phrase is, at least in their case, a half-truth. The "simple" people, perhaps especially in the age of mass democracy, were not so simple. The personal records of the millions of unlettered, or barely lettered, immigrants are scarce and short: but the purposes of their decision to brave the leap across the sea, the great leap in their lives, were complex. What makes the matter even more difficult, the recollections of their motives became transformed, obscured, often unduly simplified—for public as well as for private purposes—as their lives went on. The purposes of most immigrants to America included, originally and naturally, the prospect of their returning to their native places, enriched materially (and perhaps even mentally) after their hard but remunerative American years. In the end most of them, perhaps except for visits, stayed in the new country, but not all of them, by any means.

The purposes and the motives of the immigrants were complex. Here is an example: as late as 1887 (the year of Emma Lazarus' famous poem) there were hardly any immigrants who arrived in the United States from Greece; in 1900 their number was 9,000; in 1910 they were more than 100,000. It was, as one American consul reported, "a radical, violent exodus of all the strong young men." And why? There was no essential change in the political and in the economic state of Greece during that quarter century: no famine, no foreign occupation, no particular depression, no sudden increase in the duties and in the extent of military service (except for a short war with Turkey in 1897)—to escape the latter was a frequent motive of emigration during those decades. All that we can say (and see) is that increased possibilities of transportation (ships carrying immigrants from ports in Greece) and increased communications (letters from immigrants describing their lives in the United States—here again we encounter the essential phenomenon of an inflation of words)—made the idea of the leap across the sea current and popular. The exodus gathered around the idea of material gain: but, still, that was an idea, no matter what its imagined object. Contrary to Emma Lazarus' phrase, America beckoned not as a haven for the poor and for the huddled masses yearning to breathe free but as a prospective place for material enrichment; these young Greeks, as other immigrants, probably knew that life in America, at least in the beginning, would be less free than life in the sun-baked villages of Greece. Before 1876 direct passage from Italian ports to America already existed; yet less than 1 percent of all emigrant Italians came to the United States (80 percent went to Switzerland and France). In 1890, 46 percent sailed for the United States. That the financial purpose was dominant (though never exclusive) may be glimpsed from the fact that before

1850 the relative ebb and flow of mass immigration did not correspond to economic conditions in the United States where, for example, the financial panic and the depression of 1837–38 coincided with the first large wave of immigrants from Central Europe, probably because few of the latter were aware of that economic condition. But the financial crises and the depressions of 1873–75, of 1893–94, of 1907–8, and of 1930–34 coincided with a temporary drop in the number of immigrants during those years.

In any event, the number of immigrants returning to their homelands was increasing. During the last decade of the nineteenth century almost half of the immigrants departed again. During the first decade of the twentieth century 57 percent of Italian immigrants returned to Italy, during the second decade 82 percent. Italians were a special case at one extreme, Jews from the Russian Empire at the other; but this phenomenon of a large number of departing immigrants was universal. In 1900 for every 100 steerage passengers arriving in American ports there were 37 steerage departures. These ratios remained approximately the same during the entire peak immigration period, from 1890 to 1920. Between 1908 and 1910 there were more Belgian emigrants than immigrants. The First World War had an obvious effect: between 1911 and 1920 the total of French emigration exceeded that of French immigration by 20 percent, but this also included women and children and men of nonmilitary age. During the same time the number of English and Welsh immigrants and emigrants was about the same; the number of emigrants to Austria-Hungary was slightly less than half of their immigrants; relatively few Irish chose to return. From 1918 to 1920 there were 78 departures for every 100 arrivals.

There is, however, an additional factor to be considered: many immigrants who had returned to their homelands came back to the United States again. The numbers of these reimmigrants are not easily ascertainable, but they may have amounted to nearly one third of all emigrants. What we can ascertain is that a large portion of the emigrants were people who had come to the United States for a short term. Of all emigrants in 1908 nearly 95 percent "had not been here over five years."[2] These figures also cast a doubt on the declaration of American employers in quest of cheap labor (it was American capital, not American labor, which favored and expedited the transport and the packaging of large masses of foreign labor from beyond the seas), to the effect that the immigrants were enriching the nation automatically. In 1910 an American association of manufacturers argued that the profits which immigrants created in this country were about $100 million a year, including the $25 million that the immigrants brought with themselves (an average of $25 to $30 per person); yet during the same year, 1910, the immigrants sent $250 million out of the United States, back to their families across the sea.

Immigration changed the religious and the racial composition of the Republic. The United States was founded as a Protestant country, all of the Enlightenment language about the separation of church and state notwithstanding. (This constitutional guarantee arose even more from the radical English and Scottish Protestant tradition than from that of the Enlightenment: it was disestablishmentarian, principally directed against the possible establishment and privileges of a state church such as the Church of England.) In 1785 there were about 23,000 white Catholics in the thirteen colonies, less than 1 percent of the entire population. In 1920 there were approximately 20 million Catholics, about 20 percent of the population. They were not a majority, but the Roman Catholic Church was already the largest single church in the nation. The number of Catholic priests in 1920 alone was nearly as large as the entire Catholic population in 1785. This did not mean that the Republic was priest-ridden: the ratio of priests to the Catholic population remained about the same, a little less than one priest to one thousand Catholics. It meant that about one half of all immigrants during the century of mass immigration were Catholics. The number of Jews in 1790 was infinitesimal: before 1880 their numbers were still minimal, but about 1920 there were at least three million and perhaps more than five million, that is, anywhere between 3 and 5 percent of the national population. The figures on religion reported by the United States Census are not only fragmentary, they are also incomplete and unreliable; they do not accord with the most elementary rules of statistics. In addition, American Jewish organizations tended to play down the number of Jews in the United States, probably because of their cautious concern with potential anti-Jewish sentiments.* It was not until 1899 that statistics of immigrants coming from Europe were recorded by race (that year 39.8 percent of all immigrants from "Russia" were reported as "Hebrews").[3] It is at least arguable that Jews do not constitute a characteristic race; it is hardly arguable that many immigrants from the Caribbean

* As the *Historical Statistics of the United States* (1976) puts it ("Religious Affiliation," Series II 788–805): "All denominations make their own definitions of membership or affiliation and, accordingly, there are also variations in the basis of compilation. . . . The Jewish Congregations report on the number of Jews in communities having congregations. The Roman Catholic Church, the Lutheran bodies, and the Protestant Episcopal Church report as members the total number of baptized persons, including infants. . . ." Until 1916 the Jewish Congregations "reported only 'heads of families, seat holders, and other contributors.' The figures for Jews were admittedly incomplete." A glance at the statistics in vol. I, p. 391 shows the incompleteness of the guesswork, so incomplete as to be hardly worth recording.

do; but during recent decades statistics about the presence of the latter in the United States have been as uncontrollable as their influx has been.

(3)

We may—on humanistic as well as on scientific grounds—deny definitions of race. We cannot deny the existence of racial sentiments. It was because of such sentiments that after the First World War the great majority of the American people chose to restrict immigration drastically. In 1882 the Congress yielded to popular sentiment in the West and excluded Chinese from entry into the United States for ten years; in 1902 this exclusion was made permanent; five years later a cumbrous treaty with Japan excluded Japanese immigrants (including Japanese and Chinese holders of passports valid for Hawaii, Canada, and Mexico)—all of this at a time when in certain western states immigrants from Europe were allowed to vote even when they were not American citizens. (This was not merely the practice of most ward leaders. It reflected the old American populist inclination: the sense of sovereignty of the people was stronger than that of the sovereignty of the state. Alien suffrage was abolished in midwestern states between 1894 and 1918, last in Arkansas in 1926.)

The radical restriction of immigration from the Old World followed the First World War. Because of its time—1921—historical interpretation customarily regards this as part and parcel of the then American revulsion from Europe, including the Red Scare, the Return to Normalcy, to Isolationism. This was so: but there was more to it. Popular sentiment against immigration had become important as early as the 1890s. After 1900 respectable public opinion joined with it; indeed, gave it a lead. Respectable American public figures and serious American scholars spoke and wrote about the eugenic and political dangers of unrestricted immigration. The fact that not until 1921 did Congress enact the first drastic immigration bill was due to the peculiar conditions of American political arithmetic and to the consequent slowness of legislation. In the large populous industrial states of the Union there were many first- and second-generation immigrants who would vote against party politicians who favored immigration restriction. For a long time neither of the two large parties could afford to lose this kind of bloc vote. But by 1921 the national sentiment against immigration had become so overwhelming that the millions of proimmigration voters no longer counted as much. The bill passed both the House and the Senate with large majorities, the latter voting for it 78 to 1.

This bill, the so-called Johnson Act of May 1921, had been preceded by various bills whose purpose was to weed out "undesirables," including criminals, prostitutes, anarchists, and illiterate immigrants; but those restrictions, no matter how stringently applied, never affected more than 1 or 2 percent of the total of immigrants who, since 1892, were coming in through the crude and humiliating sieve of Ellis Island. As usual with difficult bills, it was a complicated piece of legislation, with all kinds of special categories and loopholes fabricated into it. Essentially it limited immigration from Europe to 3 percent of the number of foreign-born of each nationality group among American citizens in the census year of 1910. In May 1924 Coolidge (who harbored a considerable amount of nativist and racist sentiments) signed a newer bill, the Johnson-Reed Act, which, among other features, reduced the quota to 2 percent and set its base back to foreign-born Americans of 1890, discriminating thereby against southern and eastern Europeans, including Italians, Greeks, Slavs, and Jews. For once the President and the politicians were in accord with popular sentiment as well as with public opinion. These two acts were probably the most decisive pieces of legislation ever passed by an American Congress: they did not merely mark, they established the end of an era.

Thirty years later Professor John Higham, the historian of nativism and immigration, wrote, "Above all, the policy now adopted meant that in a generation the foreign-born would cease to be a major factor in American history."[4] He was wrong. As so often in American political history, the legislation had come too late. For the purposes of the nativists the acts of 1921 and 1924 proved to be a palliative and not a preservative, a dietary restriction and not a cure. The fears of the American people were myopic and short-range: they feared radical agitators, unkempt Jews, Italian anarchists, Bolsheviks who would overturn the American order. "Rats" and not "beavers," "tearers-down" and not "builders-up" said Coolidge's Secretary of Labor at the time, not very elegantly or even humanely. Yet he, and the majority of Americans, were as wrong about the inclinations of the immigrant rats as about the habits of the native beavers. The former were more orderly (and the latter less orderly) than people then imagined. And the effects of immigration were long-range. The children and the grandchildren of the foreign-born have been a major factor in American history: but in ways very different, indeed often the very opposite of what their advocates and their detractors visualized sixty years ago. During the last sixty years the behavior of Americans, beavers included, has changed, sometimes beyond recognition. And now we come to the main theme of this chapter: *how,* rather than *why,* the masses of immigrants became Americanized.

(4)

During the first decades of the twentieth century the opposition of the great majority of Americans to mass immigration from Europe was widespread and deeply rooted. Its roots were old, older than the generally accepted version, according to which the opposition began to rise only when the new unkempt masses were beginning to be visible, after 1880. Nativist politicians and political parties enjoyed much popular support as early as the 1830s. In 1856 the Committee of Foreign Affairs of the House of Representatives opined, "Crime and pauperism are the bane of the republic. . . . Our country has been converted into a sort of penal colony to which foreign governments ship their criminals"—an extraordinary statement for a committee of congressmen. By 1900 opposition to immigration was widespread. The American working classes and most of their unions disliked the immigrants, and not for the material considerations of the competition of cheap labor alone: they distrusted foreigners and did not wish either to understand or to mingle with them. The ascription of racial and national categories were a standard portion of the workingmen's mental and psychological equipment. Around 1900 the Irish stevedores on the New York and Boston waterfronts (themselves often foreign-born Americans) would say of the Italian stevedores, newly arrived, "It takes two or three of them to do the job of a white man."

On a more educated level this xenophobia of the democratic masses was shared by the cultured and intelligent men and women of the Republic who otherwise have often proven more liberal than the working class. In Owen Wister's *The Virginian* (1902), a minor figure introduces himself, " 'Scipio Le Moyne, from Gallipolis, Ohio,' he said. 'The eldest of us always gets called Scipio. It's French. But us folks have been white for a hundred years.' " The reader of *The Virginian* can hear Wister chuckle as he writes this. But then Wister, this melancholy Philadelphian, referred to the immigrants in his diary as "alien vermin, that turn our cities to Babels and our citizenship to a hybrid farce . . . the invasion of the Hun, the Vandal, the Croat and all the rest of the steerage." Even more interesting, and sadder than Wister's case, is that of his friend John Jay Chapman, the profound idealist and American aristocrat of the spirit. In 1912 Chapman, stirred to the depths of his heart by the news that a Negro had been burned alive by the jeering people of Coatesville, Pennsylvania, left his library and drawing-room world in New York for Coatesville to act as a witness in the true Christian sense of the word. He hired a hall where he stood up alone and chose to speak in deeply moving phrases against the horror that Americans had visited upon another human being in their midst. Ten years later Chapman was the bitterest opponent of immigrants, particularly of Jews and Catholics.

Wister and Chapman were extreme pessimists and individualists, but in their fear of immigration they were not alone. On more measured levels of discourse their concerns were shared by many of the most thoughtful Americans of their period, including professors, educators, and even some of the Progressives. In 1913 the moderate and intelligent Frank Julian Warne wrote, in his *The Immigrant Invasion,* "By continuing our present policy we choose that which is producing a plutocratic class of idle nobodies resting upon the industrial slavery of a great mass of ignorant and low standard of living toilers. By restricting immigration we influence the bringing about a condition that will give to a large body of citizens a decent and comfortable standard of living." Among the many people he cited in this work was the Socialist Englishman H. G. Wells, who wrote around 1910, "The older American population is being floated up on the top of this influx, a sterile aristocracy above a racially different and astonishingly fecund proletariat." Wells had "a foreboding that in this mixed flood of workers† that pours into America by the millions to-day, in this torrent of ignorance, against which that heroic being, the schoolmarm, battles at present all unaided by men, there is to be found the possibility of another dreadful separation of class and kind. . . . One sees the possibility of a rich industrial and mercantile aristocracy of western European origin, dominating a darker-haired, darker-eyed, uneducated proletariat from central and eastern Europe. . . . That is the quality of the danger as I [Wells] see it."

Such sentiments were a national preoccupation. They had many manifestations and many facets. Their principal element was the fear that the new immigrants would neither be willing nor able to become good—meaning: reliable and patriotic—Americans. At a time (before the First World War) when portions of American cities were peopled by men and women who hardly spoke English, or not at all, Theodore Roosevelt wondered

† Curiously (or perhaps not so curiously) Wells, on occasion, called them "coloured." (They were all Europeans.)

aloud whether "we are becoming a polyglot boardinghouse." Yet the detached fine philosopher Santayana wrote, around the same time, of "the unkempt polyglot peoples that turn to the new world with the pathetic but manly purpose of beginning life on a new principle." He was right. The fears of the American people concerning the newcomers soon proved to be unwarranted—or, rather, they failed to materialize. Instead of a mass of irresponsible, Godless, cosmopolitan, anarchist foreigners, the immigrants, and their children, became reliable, churchgoing, conformist, nationalist citizens very fast.

During the First World War there were at least four million people in the United States who were natives of the then enemy nations of the Central Powers (even omitting the non-German and non-Magyar immigrants from the German and Austro-Hungarian empires), and perhaps twice as many second-generation immigrants from those stocks: yet among them evidences of disloyalty to the United States were so few as to be hardly worth noting. The same phenomenon occurred, *mutatis mutandis,* during the Second World War. It is true that immigrants formed a large portion of American radical movements during the first half of the twentieth century;‡ yet both the extent and the influence of these radical parties and movements was sporadic and limited; they did not attract the great majority of immigrants.

The immigrants conformed to America (or, rather, to what they thought was America) because they had little else to conform to. Grave troubles, sufferings seared in their hearts, branding humiliations, and superficial injustices were often their share. Yet living among themselves, and among their Americanized compatriots, they became Americanized, too, because they thought that was the only avenue of their advancement. This was different from the—relatively rare—instances when in the Old World a man of one nationality had gone to live in another state. The immigrants, and their children, became Americans of a sort, but Americans nonetheless. Most of them worked hard, and not only because of their original aspirations for a bit of capital which often faded in the heat of daily American living; they worked hard because Americanness meant—at least superficially—working hard. They joined their immigrant churches in droves, including millions who had seldom, if ever, darkened the doors of the

‡ During the first decade of its existence many of the meetings of the Communist Party of the United States were conducted in Yiddish. Presidents who feared anarchists had reason to feel that way: the Pole who shot McKinley in 1901, the Italian who attempted to kill Franklin Roosevelt in 1933 (and shot the mayor of Chicago instead) where anarchists; the men who attempted to kill Truman in 1950 were Puerto Ricans. (The assassin of John Kennedy was a native-born, but a previously denationalized and Sovietized American.)

churches in their old countries—again, because churchgoing and church membership were American, and respectable. This element of respectability to which the working class aspired was one of the things that Marx had completely failed to recognize. The conformism and the essential conservatism of the working classes has been a worldwide phenomenon, but perhaps in few places as much as in the United States. The immigrants conformed to the requirements of American life, and to what to them seemed American respectability.

Here was the essential phenomenon: to become American was (and still is) easier (or, at any rate, different) from becoming a Frenchman or a Swiss or an Englishman. It was easier, legally speaking: the requirements of naturalization in the United States have been less difficult and lengthy than in most other countries (we have seen that in many states immigrants could actually vote before having become citizens). *Being* an American has always been something different from being a national of a European country; it carries with it a sense that is universal and social as well as national and particular; consequently *becoming* an American was something different too. Its requirements were (and still are) not so much an increasing rootedness in this country, not so much the evidences of identification with its traditions and with its history, as a certain kind of conformity with the prevalent patterns of behavior and speech and thought, that is, with the popular or public or intellectual culture of the day.* To exchange one set of conformities with another is easier than to substitute one set of traditions with another, especially for younger people: and the Americanization of the immigrants' children was amazingly successful. I write "amazingly" because some of its evidences have gone counter to the "laws" of biology and heredity. In many instances the development of young immigrants—ironically, during the very period when social Darwinism was dominant—suggest that Lamarck may have been right and Darwin wrong. The acquisition of American characteristics altered the very physiognomy of many an immigrant, within one generation, indeed, within a few years—something that could not be attributed merely to change of the climate or of the diet. This was what the great anthropologist Franz Boas found around 1910 in his study entitled "Changes in Bodily Form of Descendants of Immigrants" and then submitted the documentation thereof to the con-

* This may be one of the reasons of the (seldom observed) condition that a European may, on occasion, learn to speak a perfect and nearly unaccented English in England but a perfectly unaccented American English almost never. This is especially true of educated people who tend to concentrate on the pronunciation of certain words rather than on the intonation of certain phrases.

gressional committee studying immigration. The very physical characteristics of certain immigrants had changed. The precise cranial and physiological measurements of this serious anthropologist recognized this; but it was noticed by visiting Europeans too. In a study entitled "The Mechanization and Standardization of American Life," the German scholar Richard Mueller-Freienfels wrote that surprisingly enough, after a few years as a rule, and certainly after a few generations "the immigrant, whether he be English, German, Russian, Syrian, or Greek, has become 'an American.' And this transformation affects even his features! . . . And if this transformation affects the features which would seem to be independent of the will, it is naturally far more perceptible in the bearing and behavior, in speech and accent, and in social manners."[5]

The Americanization of immigrants' names could be the subject of an interesting study. There were occasions when Slavic immigrants in the mining districts of Pennsylvania changed their names to Kelly or Costello, emulating the Irish foreman, unaware that these names were not Anglo-Saxon. (A classic example of a melting-pot name: Alvin O'Konski, a second-generation American who was a congressman, rabid isolationist and nationalist from the Middle West in the 1940s.) American Jews had a predilection for bestowing Scottish surnames on their children: Milton, Sidney, Mortimer, Irving. (In his short novel *A Cool Million,* the gloomy and thoughtful Nathanael West constructed a splendid category of Puritan-Jewish names: Ezra Silverblatt, Asa Goldstein, etc.) By the 1950s the oddness of the Norman-Jewish or Gaelic-Jewish configurations of such names as Norman Podhoretz, Norman Mailer, Paddy Chayefsky, the names of well-known Jewish American writers, was no longer noticeable. In the early 1960s the first Italian governor of Massachusetts, Foster Furcolo (another melting-pot name) chose to list his name as Furcolowe in the Yale Alumni Directory—this at a time when Italians had replaced the Irish (who two generations before had replaced the Anglo-Saxons) as the most numerous group in Boston and in Massachusetts.†

Hyphenated-Americans: this is how people referred to the descendants of immigrants, Italian-Americans, Polish-Americans, etc., at least during the first half of the twentieth century. Later this usage faded, except for Mexican-Americans and Hispanic-Americans. An Italian-American or a Swedish-American may have been different from an older American; but he was different from an Italian or from a Swede, too; and if he did not

† This crossover occurred in 1960, when in the urban area of Boston 255,000 people were of Italian stock, 254,000 of Irish; in 1964 both candidates for the governorship of Massachusetts (Bellotti and Volpe) were Italian-Americans.

have his full share of Americanness, he had his full share of Americanism. The roots of "Americanism," of this peculiar and unique word, went far back in American history; it was first employed by John Witherspoon two hundred years ago. In the beginning of this century it was a very widely used and prevalent term, a kind of popular and public desideratum.‡ Its currency had been inflated by the problem of the presence of masses of immigrants: they were required to be educated in loyalty, citizenship, Americanism. Americanism meant allegiance to the United States and to American standards—to all kinds of standards. It was a vague but strong term. On occasion it carried a menacing tone: hence the peculiar American usage of "un-American" (consider the House Un-American Activities Committee), something which has no European equivalent, "un-French" or "un-English."

The immigrants' Americanization was successful, much more successful than their opponents had thought—yet not without cost to the immigrants themselves. Beneath their Americanization there lurked, ever so often, a traumatic condition. By wanting to become and to be regarded fully American they would often suppress the memories—memories, and not merely the fragmented traditions—of their parents and their grandparents. Often the children of the immigrants were ashamed of their parentage, and sometimes even of their parents—a trauma more conscious, but certainly not less strong, than the childhood traumas attributed by Freudians to the subconscious. Often it was not until the third generation that the descendants of immigrants came to terms with the dual element in their parental histories, and often not even then. Curious dualities seemed to exist in their minds, expressed in their everyday language. Third- or fourth-generation Americans will often say, "My mother was German." "My grandfather was Polish." They meant, of course, German-Americans, Polish-Americans, not first-generation immigrants. This kind of usage seldom, if ever, occurs in Europe, though it occurs in other ex-colonial countries: Australia, New Zealand, Canada, and throughout Latin America. (One of my students, Italian-American by name and looks, a third-generation American, argued forcefully in her "family history" paper and in conversation with her teacher that she knew and wished to know little or nothing about her ancestors from Italy. "We have always regarded our-

‡ The crafty and wise Senator Boies Penrose in 1919 said that the keynote of the Republican Party in the coming presidential campaign would be "Americanism." His friend Talcott Williams, a knowledgeable journalist: "Senator, you are the man I have been looking for. What is Americanism?" Penrose: "Dam'f I know, but I tell you, Talcott, it is going to be a damn good word with which to carry an election." So it was.

selves as Americans, nothing more or less.") A few sentences later she referred to one of her American aunts with the phrase "She is a full-blooded Italian.") Often the immigrants from Europe did not bring the Old World and the New World closer together. The Atlantic was a vast psychic chasm, rather than a bridge connecting two civilizations.

The leap across the sea . . . The acknowledged memories of first- or second- and sometimes of third-generation Americans have not only been disharmonious, they have been often self-laden with myths. Of course human beings have a natural inclination to embellish the character of their ancestry, but the inclinations of many immigrants, including those who became famous and successful, have been more complex. When Admiral Rickover visited his native Poland in the 1960s a reporter asked him, "Will you visit the town where you were born?" The admiral answered, "What for?" In 1980 the famous director of the Philadelphia Orchestra received the Medal of Freedom from President Carter. To a group of reporters, Eugene Ormandy said, "People always ask me where I was born. I was born at the age of twenty-one, when I arrived in the United States." Perhaps these are untypical examples. But the American tendency (or, rather, wish) to believe that a man was newly born when he arrived in America, the land of freedom, became a piece of furniture in the minds of millions of immigrants.*

It is not, however, a settled and comfortable piece of furniture. I sometimes require that my history students (the majority of them could hardly be more American, they are third- or fourth-generation) write a family history paper. Many of them know something about the provenance of the grandfather or the grandmother who came to this country from Ireland or Italy or Slovakia. Some know a fair amount, too, about the difficulties and the humiliations that this or that ancestor had withstood during the first years in the United States. Yet all of them will write about this grandfather or grandmother as if his or her life really began in America, not earlier. They are often able to give facts about the original village and the province and the occupation of the family of the immigrant ancestor; yet all of these facts notwithstanding, the tone and the direction of their writing demonstrates that these facts are mythical, insubstantial, irrelevant. Of course some of these young Americans do not know much about the Europe of two or three generations ago. But this is not really

* And it corresponds curiously with the native and fundamentalist American inclination to believe that a human being can be "Born Again"—the opposite of original sin and of the kind of salvation that depends not on conversion but on repentance. About this see Chapter 8, p. 358.

where the problem lies. The vacuum involves not only missing facts but an uneasy confusion of motives. Why did that ancestor choose to come to America? About this their family reminiscences are sometimes either nonexistent or wrapped around absurdities. They will say that this ancestor came in order to avoid war, or persecution, or a forced military service, even when these conditions did not prevail in those countries at the time. In sum, in the retrospective vision of many descendants of immigrants the Old World is shrouded in a dense fog of myth, while the image of the New World is suffused with pearly illumination from the beginning; and the leap across the sea has all the darkness of a memory hole, often self-made and self-completed.

The self-made man with the self-made memory . . . this is, after all, a frequent American phenomenon, and not the property of immigrants from Europe alone. (It has been the property of millions of native-born American emigrants to the West.) But, then, the immigrants themselves were unsure of their motives. They made the leap across the sea: and when other, native-born Americans would ask them why they came, eventually they would say what their hearers, *and what they themselves,* wanted to hear.

Superficially speaking, the Americanization of immigrants was often surprisingly easy; but the psychic process was much more complex, and difficult, than people—including writers and historians—have been accustomed to believe. Immigration was the greatest event in the evolving history of the American people. Yet the literature and the histories of immigration have been, with very few exceptions, insubstantial and shallow. There is no really first-rate history (by which I mean not only something that is encyclopedic and well researched but that is judiciously written and sensitively thought through) of American immigration. It is consequent to the nature of American history, of American society, of its texture and to its complex and democratic structure of events, that in this nation, more perhaps than in most other nations, certain novelists may tell us many things that professional historians either overlook or render colorless; but I believe there is no first-rate novel about the immigrant in America either. There is a reason for this paucity of immigrant novels. The new and the old Americans did not know each other well enough.† Those novels that exist were written either by Americanized immigrant writers who knew

† This remains true of many second-generation immigrants. One example: in E. L. Doctorow's movie-historical confection *Ragtime,* his description of the Jewish immigrant family is fairly telling, while his description of the older American family consists of cardboard figures. (See my essay in *Salmagundi,* Fall–Winter 1976.)

their kind of people but who did not know native-born Americans well enough, or by native-born Americans who knew immigrants but not enough about where they had come from. Even the best were not exempt from this condition: Abraham Cahan's *The Rise of David Levinsky* is an example of the first; Willa Cather's *My Ántonia* of the second.

The autobiographies of immigrants—especially of successfully Americanized ones—have suffered (aesthetically, not commercially) from the same condition. *The Americanization of Edward W. Bok* was a period piece. The few carping critics who regretted what Bok had written and wrought called his book "The Bokization of the United States of America." There was more to this than a cheap verbal switch. It contained an element of truth, and not merely about Bok but about the United States itself. For now we have to look at the other side, passing from how America changed the immigrants to how the immigrants changed America: its institutions, its ideas, and its very character.

(5)

This side of the coin is easier to trace; but to evaluate its meaning is more difficult.

One of the results was the transformation of American patriotism into nationalism of a newer kind. This is not the place to discuss definitions of these two words, except to note that "patriotism" is the older word and the older phenomenon (when, in the eighteenth century, Dr. Johnson uttered his famous phrase about "patriotism" being "the last refuge of scoundrels," he meant what we mean by nationalism in the twentieth). The old American Republic was federal, not centralized or national. The words "national" or "nation" are not to be found in the Constitution, and they were seldom used by the generation of the Founding Fathers. During the century of mass immigration, from 1820 to 1920, the currency of this word increased. As late as 1920, the judicious historian Charles A. Beard said that "national" was less of an American than a European word. In 1957 the conservative Felix Morley noticed the change: "The current Washington telephone directory takes ten full columns merely to list the national associations with headquarters there, running from the National Academy of Broadcasting to the National Wrecking Company."‡

‡ Felix Morley in *Modern Age*, Summer 1957. Twenty-four years later (1981) the list has grown to twenty-six columns, from National Abortional Rights to National Women's Political Caucus.

This was one of the indirect results of immigration. The Irish writer Patrick Ford wrote in 1881 that life in America lifted the Irishman out of "the littleness of countyism into the broad feeling of nationalism." The Irish were a somewhat special case; yet their easy identification with Americanism may have differed from that of other immigrant groups in degree, not in kind. We have seen that this identification was relatively easy, easier for immigrants in America than for other migrants in the countries of the Old World, since Americanization meant less conformity to old and complicated traditions than to the standards of behavior, of speech, and to the public ideas of the day. Its main instrument was the American school, which was the breeding ground of American nationalism. The result was often a nationalism which was as strident as it was shallow. During and after the First World War, including the first Red Scare, the fears and the anger of American nationalists were directed mainly against the potential disloyalty of immigrants. During the second Red Scare, thirty years later, many of the most strident nationalists *were* second-generation immigrants. There was Joseph R. McCarthy, the son of an Irish-American father and a German-American mother, from the progressive and populist state of Wisconsin, whose equation of anti-communism with American nationalism was widely accepted and popular at the time, but whose purpose was not merely the nailing down of disloyal Communists but the humiliation of Americans of an older, Anglo-Saxon stock, of people of more mellow and liberal persuasions.* In 1949 I was amused to read that an American Legion post in Philadelphia accused the directors of the Philadelphia chapter of United World Federalists (an innocuous group of liberals) of un-Americanism. The names of the accused were, without exception, English, Welsh, or Scottish; their accusers' names were Ukrainian, Italian, and Slovak. In 1958 the senior class of Notre Dame University voted to give its Patriot of the Year award to Wernher von Braun, the rocket enginer, who thirteen years before had directed the fire of Hitler's rockets at London. (Von Braun may have deserved the award of Engineer of the Year, but Patriot of the Year?)

The decline of the older kind of American patriotism and the rise of a newer, ideological kind of American nationalism was not entirely due to immigration. Much of it was the result of the mechanical standardization

* This was not an uncommon phenomenon. In Germany many of the leading Nazis were not Prussian (and Protestants) but Austrians, South Germans (and ex-Catholics), Hitler included: they wanted to demonstrate the strength of their German nationalism. (Hitler wrote in *Mein Kampf* that he was a nationalist and not a patriot.) But, unlike in America, the hatred of these Nazis was not directed primarily at the older patriotic and patrician classes; it was directed at the Jews.

of American schooling, of the machinery of publicity, of the increasing rootlessness and impermanence of American habits of residence. Yet immigration had something to do with it. The foreign-born, and especially their children, did not cease to be factors after the era of mass immigration had closed. During the nineteenth century the influence of immigrants on American statecraft was generally slight. (This was true even of the influence of Irish-Americans who were very successful in American politics, but usually on the local and state levels. The occasional anti-English outbursts of American public or congressional figures during the nineteenth century were at least partly due to the then still patriotic inclination for Twisting—at least rhetorically—the Lion's Tail.) But during the twentieth century the influence of immigrants, and of their descendants, on American foreign policy, too, was increasing; in this respect 1920 was not a turning point. Foreign governments were aware of this. The Balfour Declaration, that is, the public decision of the British Government in 1917 to offer Palestine as a homeland for Jews was made to evoke sympathy and support among American Jews for Britain. During the last sixty years the influence of Irish-American, or Greek-American, or Italian-American organizations was often considerable.†

More important—and certainly more widespread—than their influence on American nationalism was the influence of the immigrants on American life and culture, indeed, on the American character. "We are a young Nation," George Washington wrote in 1783, "and have a Character to establish." Within the next century the American national character began to crystallize. "When I first came here"—1831: the year of Tocqueville's journey to North America—"the whole country was like some remote part of England that I had never seen before, the people were like *queer* English people" wrote the sensitive and intelligent Fanny Kemble to a friend. "Now," she wrote thirty-five years later, "there is not a trace of their British origin, except their speech, and they are becoming a real nation." This was evident in the national physiognomy of Americans. There was something like an American face by 1860. Consider Lincoln, with his very American features, all of his English-Scottish-Irish ancestry notwithstanding (or, at that, of Uncle Sam, a symbol whose expressive countenance was at least as representative of his people as that of John Bull of the English people at the time). During the next one hundred years

† On occasion their influences were exaggerated, as in the case of Polish-Americans in the mind of President Roosevelt in 1944; this President went so far as to ask Stalin for certain concessions in order to soothe the opposition of Polish-Americans to his own party at home. Stalin was—properly—skeptical.

immigration disrupted and delayed this crystallization of the American character. It became easy to recognize an American by his clothes, by his speech, his gestures, his attitudes, bearing, haircut, glasses—but not by his face. One hundred years after Lincoln there was hardly such a thing as an American face: because of the effects of mass immigration the very physiognomy of the American people had changed.

The most celebrated American soldier-hero of the First World War was Sergeant Alvin York, a Tennessee American from old Anglo-Saxon stock. The popular heroes (and martyrs) of the Second World War were the five Sullivan brothers, Irish-Americans. When the novelist James Michener wrote a popular novel about the Korean War, he gave his pilot-hero the German-American name of Brubaker. In 1981 President Reagan decorated a hero of the Vietnam War, a Sergeant Benavides.

The contribution of the immigrants to American life has been immense, ranging from the American physical to the American intellectual diet, from food and drink to music. Hot dogs, spaghetti, pizza, German-type beer, and wine-making (and lately oriental food) were all immigrant contributions which became standard-American soon. In these, as in many other instances, the adaptation of new tastes and habits by the native population came even more swiftly than the adaptation of American tastes and habits by the immigrants. If the Americanization of the immigrants was at once simple and complex, involving transformations of form and thought on various levels, so was the immigrant influence on American tastes, habits, thoughts, rhythm, music, speech. Immigrants created most of the American movie industry, accelerating thereby the development of American popular imagination from a predominantly verbal to a predominantly pictorial form. The contribution of immigrants (mostly of Jewish immigrants) to the emerging formula of American musical comedy was very great. This included the kind of popular music that, even more than the movies, was America's unique art form during the first half of the twentieth century. While the best of the verses and refrains were often written by native-born Americans, the music composed by second- (and at times first-) generation Americans such as Gershwin, Kern, Rodgers, and Arlen created a new and sophisticated musical idiom, the essence of which (contrary to popular belief) was only partially dependent on the original Negro element in jazz.‡ Here is the ultimate example: the zenith of American elegance in motion was expressed by Fred Astaire, a seeming quintes-

‡ "Syncopated music is the tonal expression of the . . . English language to monosyllabism. It does not represent negro encroachment on alien musical territory. No negro ideology inspired 'The Last Rose of Summer.' That is wholly English, and it owes its invincible effect to the syncopation of the second bar.

sence of Anglo-Americanness in his looks, movements, and even his voice, who was born F. Austerlitz, of Jewish immigrant parents.

After 1890 American education became increasingly subject to Germanic influences, while the first generation of an American intelligentsia was akin to a Russian one. This meant that the older, Anglo-Saxon and Anglo-Celtic, Protestant and biblical traditions of American education were progressively weakening. These developments included the transformations of American speech. Of course the American language became more and more different from the English one: the desire for an American national language was expressed by Noah Webster two hundred years ago. In the 1920s H. L. Mencken could propose that the American language was in full growth, more manly, vital, direct, and clear than the English literary language at the time. Some of this was due to immigrant influences. In his encyclopedic *The American Language and Its Supplements* Mencken attempted to establish the list and the pedigree of all of those American words and phrases that had become part of everyday language, many of them immigrant imports. Yet by 1960 it could also be argued that Mencken's argument had been at least one-sided, if not altogether wrong. The vitality of American slang had weakened (often a kind of aphasic slurring took its place), while the everyday language became more and more encumbered, psychologized, bureaucratic, artificial, and inorganic. To this devolution England was not immune; the Americanization of language in England proceeded by leaps and bounds; but the kind of vitality and direct strength that during the 1920s seemed to mark the advancement of American over that of English writing became largely lost.* The changing composition of the American people played a role in the changing character of their language, albeit indirectly. Its intellectualization and its bureaucratization corresponded with—if they were not altogether the results of—certain mental inclinations to which the educated descendants of non-English-speaking immigrants were not immune.

Significant changes, in any event, occurred in the composition of

---

"The negroes with their pronounced sense of rhythm must have become susceptible to the syncopating tendencies in the English language at a very early date. They had their own drum music which was rhythm pure and simple. In America they learnt choral music. . . . Syncopation, lacking in English hymns, was the basis of the new type. It is the syncopation in the third bar that raises 'Swanee River' so far above the level of the ordinary street songs turned out by the million in the nineteenth century. There was no trace of mockery in the syncopated popular songs of black and white America. . . ." H. E. Jacob, *Johann Strauss, Father and Son: A Century of Light Music* (New York, 1940), pp. 367–68.

* Around 1920 English writers such as Chesterton delighted in American slang: "He can take it." "I am nuts about him." (His examples.) Compare this with the slang of fifty years later: "Far out." "No way." "Beautiful." "Pig out."

American culture and of American intellectuality. As late as 1945 the major portion of the established professorate in the leading universities was still Anglo-Saxon in origin; so were the directors, the editors, and the staffs of the principal publishing houses, the editors of the main literary and intellectual journals, and most of the recognized novelists, poets, and writers in the United States. By 1970 this was far from being the case. On the lower level of popular culture similar transformations took place. The fact that a New York comic-intellectual type such as Woody Allen (his assumed name as well as his choices of women were obviously Anglo-Saxon) could portray himself in his movies as a protagonist of a—recognizably and successfully—typical *American*† scenario may have been as significant as the fact that the very tones and the lilt of his New York intellectual accent was typical of many other intellectuals across the Republic. But whether such an ephemeral phenomenon illustrates the future crystallization of a new and more cosmopolitan American nationality or the decrystallization of what remains of its ineluctable essence is something that our descendants, not we, will be able to tell.‡

(6)

What is the greatest difference between the America seen by Tocqueville and the America of the late twentieth century? It is the difference between the characteristics of two populations. Even before mass immigration began, Tocqueville foresaw that eventually the United States would consist of more than one hundred million people, and become one of the two greatest powers of the earth. He foresaw many things, including the Civil War; but he died in 1859, before the transformation, and the decrystallization, of the American national character was about to begin.* In

† The difference between Woody Allen and Groucho Marx was the difference of the historical condition of two generations—as was the difference between, say, George Gershwin and Leonard Bernstein. Groucho's humor was wonderfully American: intelligent, without being intellectual; he was a supremely American entertainer, not a prototypical American intellectual.

‡ Robert Lilienfeld in *The New American Review,* 1982: the Americans of the eighteenth and early nineteenth century were "a brave and frugal people who would not recognize their descendants."

* Yet in a letter, to Beaumont, from Bonn, 6 August 1854, about German immigration: "My old [!] opinion, that the rapid introduction into the U.S. of men not of Anglo-Saxon race

Democracy in America he employed the term "Anglo-Americans" throughout. With every reason: one hundred and fifty years ago the white population of the United States consisted predominantly of people whose ancestors had come to America from the two British Isles.† Tocqueville was aware of the fact—seldom noted by his commentators, then and now—that while democracy was becoming a universal phenomenon, the United States was a society with characteristics peculiarly its own. He did not live long enough to contemplate the effects of mass immigration; but there is ample evidence in *Democracy in America* to suggest that, for Tocqueville, the happy mediocrity of American lives and the stability of American institutions were due not only to the conditions that they were founded on democratic principles; they were even more due to the condition that they were Anglo-American.

The American people (and perhaps especially the children and grandchildren of the immigrants) have long believed that the United States has been unique because of its democracy. Yet while the United States was the first ex-colonial country, the first nation which declared and achieved its independence from a mother country in the Old World, this condition soon ceased to be unique. Even by Tocqueville's time more than a dozen republics in Central and South America had proclaimed and achieved their independence from old Spain and from Portugal (the first instance was the Haitian revolution from France)—countries and peoples in whom Tocqueville had scant, if any, interest. Two hundred years after the Declaration of Independence the great majority of the "independent" states of the world are ex-colonial countries while most of the states of the world are "democratic" in one way or another. In one way or another: the United States is obviously different from a "people's democracy" such as Bulgaria or from an ex-colonial democracy such as Ecuador not merely because of its size or because of its material resources. During the first one hundred years of its existence the United States became powerful and prosperous, and generally capable of maintaining within its democracy a respectable amount of private freedoms anchored in what were essentially Anglo-Saxon laws and institutions, to the forms and to the rhetoric of which the majority of the American people were accustomed. This was the main difference between the United States and, say, Argentina. The United

is a great danger to be feared in America—a danger which renders the final success of democratic institutions a problem as yet unsolved."

† The somewhat imprecise term "Anglo-American" should not disturb us: more than almost any other European of his age, Tocqueville knew and understood the Irish as well as the English, as his voluminous correspondence and his important travel notes about England and Ireland attest.

States became great, wealthy, and thriving because it was principally—in the literal sense of that adverb—Anglo-Saxon: an imprecise term, but no matter. This happened not only because the institutions and laws and structures inherited from England had served the American people in the eighteenth century to better purposes than the governing ideas of that century had served the French people. It was true because of the national character of the American people. Had they been composed mainly of Spanish or French or German settlers, the institutions—and not merely the culture—of the United States of America would have been very different.

During the nineteenth century the strength of the English inheritance weakened but slowly. Mass immigration affected American institutions as well as the crystallization of the American character; but the United States remained basically Anglo-Saxon, and it was so regarded by Europeans. As late as the Second World War Europeans spoke of the British *and* of the Americans as "Anglo-Saxons." The term was imprecise but there was substance in it, and not only because of the Anglo-American military and political alliance of those few years. During the first half of the twentieth century the relationship of the British and the American empires was closer than ever before, a relationship of vast importance which is the subject of Chapter 6 of this book. Yet during the same time the relationship of the American people to the English people was no longer what it had been. The elements of the original Englishness of the United States had been weakening, within its institutions as well as within the character of its people.

Immigration had of course contributed to this devolution, though it was not alone in bringing it about. In 1900, when the oceanic tide of immigration was in full flow, the men and women of Anglo-Saxon or Anglo-Celtic and Protestant stock still ruled the nation. The elite of American society, whether in the cities or in the small towns, the representative authorities, the American judiciary, the presidents of nearly all of the prominent cultural and educational institutions, the owners and the chairmen of the industries and banks and corporations—in sum, the American upper class, the men and women who gave the direction to and the tone of public opinion—were predominantly, indeed, overwhelmingly, Americans of that stock, even though numerically they were no longer a majority. After 1950 the decline of their position of leadership set in. The Anglo-American element in American life was being overwhelmed: a tremendous event, with enormous consequences, the end of which is not yet.

One of the elements of this decline was biological. We have seen that during the second half of the nineteenth century Americans of the older stock began to produce fewer children. As their numerical predominance was lessening, it was inevitable that in the age of egalitarianism and of mass democracy this should have political consequences sooner or later. These began on the local level. In Boston, where the conspicuous animosities between the older population and the newer immigrants were especially sharp, the first Irish mayor was elected in 1884; by 1900 first- and second-generation Americans amounted to almost half of the population of the city, and the traditional Bostonians of New England origin were probably down to 10 percent. More significant, and by no means inevitable, was the decline of certain convictions in the minds of the "best people" among the latter. The inclination of the New England intellect toward an abstract kind of idealism had probably something to do with this devitalization, a certain anemia of the spirit. Attempting to rise beyond the clannishness and the rigid convictions of their class, they embraced the abstract notion that the uniqueness of the United States resided in its democratic nature. As early as 1844 Emerson said that the United States was "the country of the Future, a heterogeneous population crowding on all ships from all corners of the world to the great gates of North America, and quickly contributing their private thought to the public opinion, their toll to the treasury, and their vote to the election." Two generations later Barrett Wendell, one of the last of the intellectual and Anglophile Old Puritans, who had been an opponent of immigration, changed his views. He was, he said, deeply touched by the writing of Mary Antin (a Russian-Jewish immigrant who wrote about her Americanization in ways that were both sentimental and false). "To Wendell, the Antins, who lived in a section of the city once inhabited by Wendells, were a 'miracle.' This attitude, with its almost intolerable generosity, was that of Wendell's kind in its last days of confidence."‡ That was around 1910, when a political Brahmin such as Henry Cabot Lodge would still proclaim his opposition to unrestricted immigration. Yet at the same time (1912) Bliss Perry, of Harvard, wrote in his *The American Mind,* "From the beginning, the American people have been characterized by idealism. It was the inner light of Pilgrim and Quaker colonists; it gleams no less in the faces of the children of Russian Jew immigrants today."[6] Two generations later, in the 1960s, the two principal historians of the city of Boston, Samuel Eliot Morison and Walter Muir Whitehill, patrician eminences in their own right, de-

‡ Mary Antin wrote in 1912, "The descendants of the people who made America are not numerous enough to swing a presidential election." Agnes Repplier: "And if a negligible factor now, what depths of insignificance will be their portion in the future?" "The Modest Immigrant" in *Counter-Currents* (Boston, 1916).

clared John Fitzgerald Kennedy to have been one of the finest presidents of the United States and one of the finest male flowers of American civilization, a youthful Washington and Pericles rolled into one. How much of this attitude sprang from generosity, how much of it grew from a gracious wish to bow to the inevitable is difficult to tell. The element of generosity was there, and the attitudes were not hypocritical: but it may not be presumptuous to detect in them the dying out of former convictions, and not merely of crude and racial ones.

In the 1920s the older nativist strain in the United States asserted itself self-consciously for the last time, its elected representatives closing the main gate of immigration with a loud bang. At that time the Anglo-Saxon element was not only predominant at the upper reaches of society but still widespread and influential among the middle classes: Babbitt as well as the members of the Ku Klux Klan were Anglo-Saxons, and the entire cast of Dreiser's *American Tragedy* had Anglo-Saxon names. (It may be significant that in the most sensitive gem-novel of the twenties, *The Great Gatsby,* the real name of Gatsby is Gatz, a German name from the Dakotas. He is desperately in love with the bright promise of the rich and youthful Anglo-Americans of his age; compared to Gatz/Gatsby, these bright, sun-kissed young people are for the most part rotten, selfish, and cowardly.) Yet the assertiveness and the self-congratulation of these Americans rested on fatally shallow grounds. Their vitality had weakened. Their assertions of the primacy of America in the world because of the primacy of the business "spirit" within the American mentality marked a degeneration. In January 1924 Coolidge proclaimed, "After all, the chief business of the American people is business." In the same year the author of *This American Ascendancy* wrote that "the finest achievement of mankind is the very tangible thing which we call AMERICAN BUSINESS." Upon the inauguration of the School of Business, which would grant degrees in Masters of Business Administration from Harvard, the president of Harvard (Abbott Lawrence Lowell) said that the graduates were entering "upon one of the oldest of the arts and the latest of the professions." The dean of the Divinity School of the University of Chicago wrote, "Business is the maker of morals. What else but business can make morality?" In the most popular nonfiction book in 1925 and 1926, *The Man Nobody Knows,* by Bruce Barton, Christ was "a virile go-getting he-man of business, the first great advertiser, a premier group organizer, master executive, a champion publicity-grabber." The president of the Federal Council of Churches of Christ of America said, "Moses was one of the greatest salesmen and real estate promoters that ever lived." Another president of what, in the 1920s, was one of the largest American real estate firms: "Jesus Christ was the best salesman of his time." Church billboards read, "Come to Christian worship and increase your business efficiency." These mock-prophets of Americanism were predominantly of Anglo-Saxon and of New England descent.

During the 1920s this kind of brummagem business-Americanism existed side by side with another kind of Americanness, with the rising Americanism of the movies, which was produced and put together by people whose origins and backgrounds and aspirations were worlds apart from those of the older Anglo-Americans. Or were they? The tremendous success of the movie industry in the 1920s was more than the success of a new kind of mass entertainment, appealing to the increasingly pictorial element of American imagination. It suggested the deep-set duality of the twenties, of that decade when extremes of conformity and of licentiousness coexisted not only within the oddest places in the nation but within so many American minds. It suggests that the Americanness of Hollywood was more successful, because it was stronger, than the Americanness of New England, or what had survived of the latter. During the Depression, during the Second World War and after, the world and the aspirations fashioned by Louis B. Mayer and by the cult of American celebrity outlived the aspirations represented by Calvin Coolidge and the cult of the American salesman. The former had the greater influence on the lives of Americans of successive generations. The recent, and most conclusive, evidence of this rise of the California American and of the decline of the Massachusetts one was there in the presidential election of 1980 in the overwhelming mandate that the American people gave to Ronald Reagan, whose belief in American capitalism and whose public espousal of certain conservative American values was genuine, but whose ways of thinking and speaking, whose personality and whose ways of life (he was, after all, a divorced movie actor) had been created and fashioned by Hollywood.

Eventually the devolution of the older Anglo-American convictions became apparent not only on the cultural but also on the social plane. One of the significant elements in the social heaving and molting and moldering of the 1960s was the visible change in the physiognomy of the national ideal. Around 1900, when the Anglo-Saxon element in the national population was already a numerical minority, its influence in American life and on American aspirations was still predominant: the Gibson girl was a thoroughly Anglo-Saxon type, with touches that were Amazonian as well as American. The pictorial ideal of the American male (shown by Charles Dana Gibson in his serial drawings of the man who conquers the heart and the mind of the Gibson girl) as well as in the features of the most admired American actors of that period) corresponded to this. The movie culture of the 1920s reflected certain changes but, as yet, not very many, all of the passing craze for tangoing "sheiks" and Rudolph Valentino notwithstanding. Exceptions, of course, existed: but as late as the 1950s the features of the most famous actors and actresses, as well as those of the models in the advertisements, did not differ much from the national physiognomic ideals of fifty years earlier. In the 1960s, however, the male models were dark, hairy-chested, black-mustachioed, suggesting explicitly a kind of male sexuality that was very different from that latent in Anglo-Saxon types. A generation earlier the appearance of this newer type—often a mix: an Italian-American with a crease in his face, southwestern or Californized, half-Italian, half-cowboy—was the exception. The designers and the publicity managers and the producers of these newer models knew what they were doing. They were in accord with a national development* which appeared now in innumerable instances in the sixties, when millions of women of the American upper classes chose the sexual companionship of darker men, the descendants of immigrants. This was significant because, all of the openness of American society notwithstanding, during the first half of the twentieth century there remained considerable inbreeding among the American upper classes. They consorted with each other, they went to the same schools, they married each other. What this change in these women's sexual preferences suggested was not necessarily the desire for more sexual satisfaction but a desire for male strength—as if the recognition of the dying out of the fire in the old Anglo-American male stock was swimming up to the surface of consciousness.

(7)

During the 1960s the trend against the older Anglo-American memories ran at full tide. It was then that the silly and imprecise word WASP—faintly derogatory of the Anglo-American remnant, even though it was not unmixed with deep-running currents and with aspirations of desire and

* In the 1950s a name such as the one given to the actress Kim Novak (another mix: the tomboyish Anglo-American and suburban Kim and the Slovak Novak) no longer carried a low-class immigrant connotation, it was prototypically American and popular. In the 1970s the national television hero was given the name of Kojak (in reality a bald and stocky Greek-American by the name of Savalas)—"Kojak," which is neither Greek nor Slavic: an artificially compounded immigrant name which was, therefore, "typically" American.

envy—was made up.† By 1960 in the United States there were hardly more Anglo-Americans than there were non-whites. In 1965 the immigration laws were revised. The national-origins quota system was abolished. (The categorical restrictions of immigration from Asia had been terminated in another revision in 1952, but the Asian quotas were minimal.) In 1965 the annual limitation was set at 170,000, and immigration from Asia, Africa, and Central and South America made easier. Relatives of American citizens were given preference over others. There followed an increase of immigration, mostly from the Caribbean and from the poorer states of South America (including also increases of Greeks, Italians, and Soviet Jews). Additional and special legislation followed, allowing the entry of considerable numbers of Indo-Chinese and Cubans. Much of this was liberal, myopic, and thoughtless, with results that were soon apparent.

From 1820 to 1960 more than 80 percent of the immigrants had come from Europe (between 1930 and 1960 more than 90 percent); from 1970 to 1980 less than 18 percent came from Europe. During the 1940s most immigrants had come from Germany, Canada, the United Kingdom, Mexico, and Italy, in that order. During the 1960s the list and the order changed entirely: Mexico, Canada, Cuba, the United Kingdom, Italy. During the 1960s Latin American legal immigration rose to 39 percent. During the 1970s there was not one European or English-speaking country among the top five: Mexico, the Philippines, Cuba, Korea, China. In that decade about 4.4 million immigrants arrived legally, and at least twice as many illegally. Hence the 1970s were the largest single decade of immigration in the entire history of the United States (at least five times the immigration of the 1930s and 1940s). The legal immigrants included more than 310,000 Filipinos, more than 205,000 Chinese, more than 9,000 Haitians, more than 140,000 Indo-Chinese, more than 240,000 Koreans. (Between 1975 and 1981 another 570,000 immigrants came from Indochina.) I am not even mentioning the millions of Mexicans, other Central Americans, and Cubans. All of this happened before 1980, the largest single year of

† The desire for the sexual possession of (preferably blond) Anglo-Saxon women (preferably from the upper strata of society) was the principal and underlying element in many of the writings (and presumably in the aspirations) of such Jewish-American writers and celebrities as Norman Mailer, Philip Roth, Woody Allen. Among them Roth was the most honest. He recognized this aspiration (in *Portnoy's Complaint),* one of the sad themes of which is Portnoy's disappointment with the lack of pride among Anglo-Saxons, including the blond Anglo-Saxon females bedding down with him. In the late 1970s a kind of social reaction arose: the obsession with what was, or is, "preppy" (another silly and imprecise term) suggested a faint revival of admiration for the manners of the older American stock. (It may be significant that the author of the *Preppy Handbook,* which sold like wildfire around 1980, was a young Jewish woman.)

immigration, when, on one occasion, 8,000 immigrants were naturalized in Los Angeles at a mass ceremony. In 1980 alone more than 800,000 immigrants arrived—at least 125,000 from Cuba and 15,000 from Haiti. Since 1968 nearly two thirds of all immigrants came from Asia and Latin America. In that peak immigration year of 1980, 85 percent of immigrants arrived from Asia and Latin America, and only 6 percent from Europe. One of President Carter's Central American specialists wrote an article in *The Atlantic Monthly,* pleased with the prospect that the United States was becoming "a Caribbean nation."[7]

After one hundred and sixty years of American possession, Florida was being Hispanized—or, rather, Caribized—again, and at an alarming rate. By 1980 the population of Miami had become half Cuban. Most of these Cubans were refugees from Castro's Communist regime; but with the passsage of time it was evident that few of them would ever return to Cuba. Whether this Caribization of Florida was in the interest of the United States did not disturb the minds of the congressmen and senators and of the bureaucracy for a long time. The people who were disturbed were the older residents of Miami, themselves refugees from a colder Anglo-Saxon North one or two or three generations before.

The Cuban story consisted of a short jump across the Florida Straits, that of the Indo-Chinese a cramped flight across the Pacific, from one half of the world to another. The third migration, which had the characteristics of a landslide, was the flooding of the American Southwest with millions of Mexicans and other Central and South American illegal migrants, a flood that during the 1970s the Immigration Service and the Border Patrol could not control. In 1975 the commissioner of the Immigration and Naturalization Service spoke of an "invasion" that was "out of control"; six years later the Attorney General of the United States raised the prospect of an annual influx of 1.5 to 2 million illegal immigrants alone. As these lines are being written, a proposal for a new immigration act represents a much-belated, and not very efficient, attempt to control the tide let loose, among other things, by the act of 1965. Since that time 10 percent of the total population of El Salvador and Nicaragua may have moved to the United States. Ninety percent of the illegal immigrants have been Mexicans. Less than 15 percent of these were actually apprehended, and less than 1 percent were actually prosecuted. One out of every five persons of Hispanic origin in Texas was there illegally. In 1981 alone there were 320 million border crossings in the Southwest (Mexicans are allowed to cross into the United States for a day of shopping or for visiting their relatives). Such an oceanic movement could have been controlled only through a determined policy requiring stringent and perhaps unpopular practices.‡

The government and the politicians were not ready for this. Yet the very essence of American nationality was being diluted—culturally, and not merely racially.* Large portions of the Republic were beginning to resemble the Third World. For two centuries North America was largely, though not entirely, immune to what happened to the peoples south of the border: the land reverting to its ancestral people, the Indian curse on the conqueror. This Mexican and Caribbean (and South American, and Asian) invasion may be the most important event in the history of the United States during the last decades of the twentieth century, just as mass immigration from Europe had been the most important event before the First World War—like the latter, a development with unforeseeable consequences; unlike the latter, a migration of peoples comparable to that which had overwhelmed the Roman Empire when another great age was coming to its end. The danger was—perhaps—no longer the overflowing of the melting pot: the pot itself was melting, with the largest holes appearing in the South and the West.

Since the Immigration Act of 1965, four of the five presidents of the United States—Johnson, Nixon, Carter, Reagan† came from the South or

‡ I write "perhaps" because such practices would not be unpopular with the majority of the American people; they would be unpopular with minorities and—more important for the politicians and the bureaucrats—with the "image" of the United States in Mexico and in the Third World. The 1965 Immigration Act was part and parcel of the surge of the last corrupt chapter of political liberalism in the United States, true; but the indifference (and, on occasion, the political cowardice) of politicians to this new, clear and present, danger to the Republic has not at all been a monopoly of liberals. The Reaganite, right-wing, anti-Soviet, militant Republicans of the Southwest tried to avoid facing it. "Senator John Tower [a right-wing militarist and so-called conservative] is regularly a featured player in a well-known amateur satirical skit staged each year in Dallas; when the 1980 skit was to be based on the Alamo, Tower refused to participate, his staff explaining that the Senator did not want to risk offending Mexican-Americans. This is not an unrevealing episode; the force of the 'ethnic mosaic' idea has become so strong that Texans' own history has become an embarrassment." (From a personal letter by a serious student of the new immigration who is now preparing an important work on the subject.)

* In 1980 a poll showed that only 12 percent of all Hispanics and Caribbeans in the Southwest (including American citizens) considered themselves Americans first and Hispanics second. In at least four states of the Southwest bilingualism led to biculturalism: in some textbooks Juárez assumes a role comparable to that of Lincoln. But this is not only a phenomenon in the Southwest, California, and Florida. The examples of such a cultural transformation are myriad. (I am told, for example, that in 1982 the only remaining downtown movie theater in St. Paul, Minnesota, advertised "Chinese Films Three Days a Week.")

† The California Professor Julian Nava: "America is not a country. The *United States* is a country, America is a continent. A *brown* continent." Carter named Nava Ambassador to Mexico. Reagan named a movie actor Ambassador to Mexico.

from the Southwest or from the West. They paid little attention to these developments. During the 1970s the number of Asians in California increased 140 percent, of Central and South Americans 93 percent (and of American Indians 118 percent). The shift of the American population (and consequently the political deadweight) continued in a southwestern direction. Despite their asseverations of conservatism, Californians such as Nixon and Reagan had a view of the globe which was Pacific rather than Atlantic—at the time when the Atlantic ports of the United States were sinking into decay, and when the Atlantic had become empty of passenger ships. During the last thirty years the relationship of the United States with the nations of Western Europe was largely untroubled; the relationship with England was smoother than ever; but the instinctive ties of the American people with the Old World, including England, were growing feebler each year. Shortly after the Second World War Herbert Agar would still write: "We are all the descendants of people who fled from Europe. A few of our ancestors may have come out of curiosity, but most of them came out of poverty or despair or because the police were on their tracks. Our instinctive wish is to be let alone by Europe, to stop fretting about Europe, to turn our eyes toward the Pacific. 'Eastward I go only by force,' wrote Thoreau, 'but westward I go free. . . . I must walk toward Oregon and not toward Europe.' That was harmless enough while we were growing up. The adolescent can turn against his family with impunity, because his family is still protecting him—but not so the grown man. We could walk as far as Oregon, but then we had to face about and accept our heritage. We belong to the West, without which we must perish. We do not belong to Asia."[8] Agar knew that at the bottom of the hearts of the surviving American isolationists lay a distrust of Europe, even when the security of the Old and of the New World were linked more closely than ever before. Security, however, is one thing, destiny another. Whether the destinies of Americans and Europeans will grow closer or further apart is difficult to tell. It will depend on their minds and hearts, on their consciousness rather than on communications. And the evolution of consciousness has little or nothing to do with the evolution of technology. The refusal to consider the reality of their ancestral connection with the Old World, which has been so typical of all kinds of immigrants, including their descendants who passed through a superficial Americanization to their final Americanness, may or may not be passing now when more and more Americans are no longer indifferent to their roots; but whether the consciousness of these roots will eventually grow beyond the leap across the sea is difficult to tell. But the United States is no longer a New Country, peopled with new men and women, and the word "roots" is more than a metaphor. As a sensitive woman writer from New England wrote about her native land: the modern American landscape "has far more bright flowers than there were in the primitive wilderness. Few of our native plants will flourish in open fields and along sunny roadsides where the soil is neither very wet nor very dry, and the flowers that grow there are nearly all immigrants. Botanizing in these places with the help of a manual, one comes time and again on the phrase 'naturalized from Europe.' A short list exhausts the native New Englanders that are both common and conspicuous among the field flowers: milkweed, cranesbill, robin's plantain, steeplebush, asters, goldenrod. . . . The rest—daisies, most buttercups, bouncing Bet, clover, Queen Anne's lace, the common dandelion, and all the others have followed in the wake of European man."[9]

5

THE BOURGEOIS INTERLUDE

The Half-Century When American Civilization Was Urban and Urbane

How the United States, born in the eighteenth—the central—century of the Modern Age, eventually became a nation which is neither bourgeois nor urban.

(1)

We are nearing the end of the twentieth century as well as the end of an age which began about five hundred years ago, the age which people three hundred years ago began to name the Modern Age, to distinguish it from the Ancient and Medieval centuries. (During the Middle Ages no one thought that he was living in the Middle Ages; that term did not take hold until the Middle Ages had passed.) When the American Revolution took place the notion of the Modern Age had become an accepted idea. The eighteenth century was the central century of the Modern Age—chronologically and, in many ways, intellectually. It was the century of the Enlightenment—like "Modern Age," an inaccurate and unduly optimistic term, but no matter. The United States was the first modern state in the world. This idea was represented in the symbols and in the statements of its founders, including its Great Seal: *"Novus Ordo Seclorum,"* a New Order of the Ages, of the secular world. This categorical statement was also imprecise and unduly revolutionary in tone: again, no matter, since this was what the great majority of Americans thought, at least for a long time.

During the nineteenth century the ideas of the eighteenth century were put to work, they were translated into practical matters, and they reached their full fruition. Whatever was wrong or insubstantial in those ideas need not concern us. In the history of Europe and North America the nineteenth century was the greatest and most prosperous of centuries. It was the century of the rising middle classes: they were in the presence of rising standards of comfort, of security, and of power, visible and palpable and part of their lives.

It is now possible for us to designate this period with greater accuracy, on material grounds alone. The greatest advance in the material standards of American life took place between 1895 and 1955; this corresponded with the zenith of American power and prestige in the world. During the last third of the nineteenth century the greatest surge of material progress began. From the Civil War to the First World War, infant mortality was reduced by more than two thirds. Life expectancy increased by nearly one third. The progress of medicine alone was such that by the early twentieth century it was possible for an American to live a lifetime, and to undergo severe operations on his body, without ever experiencing protracted or unbearable pain. Central heating, indoor plumbing, running hot and cold water, elevators, electric light and power, the telegraph, the telephone, the locomotive, the steamship, the airship, the automobile, the airplane, radio, transcontinental railroads and transcontinental canals—these were all achievements of the century preceding the First World War. Thereafter the rhythm of invention slowed down. During the last fifty years the only inventions that have made the everyday lives of people easier are air conditioning, television, and Scotch tape, of which perhaps only the last one has been an unmixed blessing. There have been impressive advances in medicine, but not in the availability of medical attention. After 1970 the very conditions of material comforts became difficult, costly, and in some instances they deteriorated. But what is important here is that the inventions of the nineteenth century were available to the masses of the American people fairly soon after they appeared. Whether we speak of infant mortality or of automobile mortality, on the average Europe was fifty years behind the United States. The material acme of American living standards was reached in the 1950s. Here is an example: in 1902, 8 percent of American houses had electricity, in 1925 more than half (53.2 percent), in 1955 nearly 99 percent. What was happening within the lives, and within the heads and hearts, of the people in these houses is, of course, another question.

(2)

The sixty years from 1895 to 1955 were not only the zenith of American power and prestige and prosperity. This was the urban period in the history of the American people. The founders of the Republic had not, with few exceptions, looked forward to an urban society: but a century after American independence had been won, urban America had arisen. In 1790 less than one thirtieth of the American population lived in towns with more than 8,000 inhabitants; by 1880, 24 percent lived in cities; by 1920 the majority of the American population was urban. The rise of New York City was, of course, the most spectacular example. Still, as late as 1880 New York was the only American city with a population over one million, in the same league as London, Paris, Berlin, Vienna, St. Petersburg. Thereafter urban growth was rapid. By 1890 Chicago and Philadelphia had passed the one-million mark. During the First World War, New York surpassed London as the largest city in the world, corresponding to the rise of the American empire over that of the British Empire, in financial and industrial and political power. But by the middle of the twentieth century the urban phase of American history was passing. Cities in China, Mexico, South America, Japan, and Russia were now larger than those of Europe and of America. Even more significantly, after 1950 New York, Philadelphia, Boston, and Chicago ceased to grow. Of the two most urbane cities of the early Republic, Boston began to lose population after 1930—from 1950 to 1960 Boston decreased by 13 percent. The population of Philadelphia after 1930 hardly grew at all. New York City after 1950 was losing population. Other cities in the United States, especially in the South and in the Southwest, went on increasing: but it is arguable that Los Angeles or Phoenix or Houston or Dallas were no longer cities in the traditional sense of the term. Whatever their municipal boundaries, the overwhelming majority of their populations (and this was the trend in the now increasingly stagnant eastern cities, too) were living in the suburbs.*

This corresponded to the turning point in the history of the country after 1955. When the census of the United States in 1920 showed that, for the first time in American history, the majority of the population was no

* Between 1958 and 1968 the volume of sales in Chicago increased by 5 percent, in its suburbs by 86 percent.

longer rural but urban,† the same census also showed that for the first time the majority of the working population were no longer engaged in agriculture but in industry. The majority of the population were abandoning the cities, moving to the suburbs. From 1950 to 1970 the suburban population doubled, from 36 to 72 million; 83 percent of the total population growth took place in the suburbs. The census in 1970 confirmed this: for the first time in the history of the world the majority of a nation lived neither in its cities nor in its countryside but in its suburbs. Thus the urban (and the industrial) age of American civilization was passing. It was shorter—much shorter—than people have been accustomed to think.

So was the bourgeois period of American history. That, too, was an interlude, a chapter in the development of the American people, corresponding to much of the urban and the industrial phase: an important period which is not altogether dead and which, because of its amplitude and richness, has had all kinds of consequences, but it was a period nonetheless. Its relative brevity had much to do with the rise and the decline of the American city, and with certain peculiar characteristics of the latter that had preceded its rise. The American city, from its beginnings, was different from its contemporary European cities, just as the medieval European city was something quite different from the Roman *urbs* or from the Greek *polis,* just as Russian or Chinese cities were (and still are) different from European ones. These differences were not only physical—even though their principal element emerged from the physical condition that the European city had walls, walls providing a definite separation of city from the surrounding country and its inhabitants—whence the words *bourgeois* and *citizen.* Since the Middle Ages in Europe it had been a privilege for certain people to live within a city. Life in the city was safer than life outside it. After 1950 this was no longer true, even less true in the United States than in Europe.

This deterioration in the safety of cities had much to do with the preference of millions of Americans for the suburbs; but it was not the only factor in their choice. We must keep in mind, too, that in the history of Western civilization we have not yet seen a highly developed culture that was not predominately urban. The adjective "urbane" suggests this, as does the word "citizen" (in Russian and in many oriental languages its equivalents do *not* derive from the word for "city"). It is still an open question whether a suburban people can develop something resembling a high level of culture.

† We must, however, keep in mind that the census-takers of 1920 took the rigid rule of counting as "urban" any community with a population over 2,500.

What were the characteristics of the urban and bourgeois period of American history? Without resorting to statistics, it is hardly possible to illustrate this otherwise than by describing peoples' aspirations and recording general impressions. In the 1880s the charming diarist "Maud" wrote about Cairo, Illinois, "We've the most magnificent hotel (run on the grandest scale) in this part of the country, telephone system, new Opera House, elegant one, going up, street-cars soon to be running, and we are altogether citified."[1] Before 1895 and increasingly again after 1955 the general impression of the United States was that of a country that was *less* urban than the countries of northwestern Europe—while in 1915 or in 1925 the impression was different: America and American life were *more* urban than Europe. I am not only thinking of New York, with its skyscrapers and its coruscating lights; and I am not only referring to the standard pictorialization in the movies where, until about 1960, the brilliant richness and the sumptuosity of an American apartment, usually photographed high above a city, through the picture windows of which glistened a luminous sea of lights, gave (and on occasion still gives) a powerful impression of the kind of urbanity which was beyond most Europeans' dreams of avarice. Look at a photograph of Chicago or Seattle around 1915. Typical and impressive—impressive in the pictorial and in the civilizational sense—are the streets dominated by buildings whose size, decorations, entrances, storefronts, and stonework are more majestic and monumental than those of the cities of Europe. Unlike many of the large American buildings fifty years before them, these impressive buildings are more than facades: they suggest the interior riches of a bourgeois society. Or consider Fifth Avenue or Park Avenue in New York around 1925. Again I am referring not merely to their monumental exterior aspect but to the kind of life in their interiors, in those apartment houses or in the lobbies of the smart American hotels, to their decorations and furnishings, to the clothes of the people who frequented them, to much of their talk, and to the American cocktail music, the brief melodies of which were sustained by the intricate, melancholy, and sophisticated harmonic structures of Gershwin or Kern or Porter to which American ears by then had become fully accustomed. These were no longer effete urban excrescences on the eastern edge of the United States. They were typically American.

"The Englishman is essentially territorial. The American to-day is urban," wrote Harold Nicolson in 1927. This was not an altogether superficial development. Most American writers were representatives of as well as contributors to an American bourgeois culture, and not only because of their subject matter. It was not only that America had "caught up" with Western European bourgeois culture, or that New York had caught up with London or Paris. Writers such as Henry James or Edith Wharton, painters such as Thomas Eakins or Winslow Homer reflected the interior plenitude of American lives; their work was representative of solid and high standards of craftsmanship as well as of a rapidly developing civilization which, with all of its faults, was evidently progressing fast. Unlike the case of most of the self-conscious "moderns," there was a correspondence —not always harmonious, but a correspondence nevertheless—between these representatives of an American bourgeois culture and the lives of an increasing number of American people. Between 1895 and 1955 the standards of a large number of American people—of their material comforts, their families and their manners, their social civilities as well as their cultural and educational aspirations—came to resemble (and even, on occasion, to supersede) in many ways, though not in all, the standards of the lives of European and English bourgeois families. By the early twentieth century important strata of the American people were living interior lives that, while admittedly not identical with those of Europe, marked a civilization which may be called urban and urbane and bourgeois.‡ Bourgeois, and not merely middle-class: to this crucial distinction we must now turn.

(3)

In the 1920s, Charles A. Beard, one of the most original and independent historians of the United States, wrote that the United States had only one large class, "the petty bourgeoisie. . . . The American ideal most widely expressed is the *embourgeoisement* of the whole society—a universality of comfort, convenience, security, leisure, standard possessions of food, clothing and shelter." Yet standard possessions of food, clothing, and shelter are middle-class aspirations, not bourgeois ones. Beard's virtual equation of bourgeois and middle-class was wrong. They were not, and are not, the same thing. Every society, every group (including animal populations) has a recognizable segment, situated in the middle, between the upper and the lower classes. Not every society had, or has, a bourgeoisie. The existence of a middle class is a universal, a sociological phenomenon. The existence of the bourgeois has been a particular phenomenon, a histor-

‡ In a novel such as Evan Connell's *Mrs. Bridge* (1960) the protagonist-heroine was wholly American-bourgeois; but the American-bourgeois phase of her life lasted less than one generation in Kansas City, from 1915 to 1945.

ical reality. I wrote earlier that the notion of the bourgeois, of Western European origin, had little to do with capital or with income, while it had very much to do with the city. *Bourgeois, Bürger, burgher, borghese* meant city dweller. *("Stadtluft macht frei,"* some Germans said: the city air makes you free.) The essence of the meaning was that of a free man, possessing full municipal rights. (Consider the House of Burgesses in the constitution of Virginia.) This kind of freedom became a matter of spirit, and not merely of status; of aspirations and standards rather than of wealth or income. It embodied notions of urbanity and culture. Because of this, and in spite of the original differences between American and European cities, there was such a thing as an American bourgeoisie and there was a chapter of American history when this bourgeoisie—and not merely on financial grounds—was very important.

But in writing this I must break through two large intellectual obstacles. "Bourgeois" and "bourgeoisie" are not English words. (Most of the three hundred million people whose native language is English cannot spell them without one mistake or two.) The reason for this is that, even though the origins of the two words are the same, *bourgeois,* unlike *citizen,* was imported into England and the United States from France, where it had acquired a bad reputation. During the nineteenth century, and during most of the twentieth, "bourgeois" suggested not only "middle-class," but also "unimaginative," "pedestrian," "selfish," "materialist," "philistine." The origins of this kind of vilification had come from aristocrats and snobs; but during the nineteenth century it was propagated enthusiastically by bohemians, artists, dandies, aesthetes, Marxists, and all kinds of radicals. Yet this usage of the term was narrow and inaccurate.* Not only was the equation of bourgeois and middle-class wrong; so was the equation of the bourgeois with the capitalist spirit. One could be a bourgeois without being a capitalist, which was true of many people in the professions; conversely, one could be a capitalist without being a bourgeois. (The new rich were often excluded not only from the aristocracy but also from the patrician bourgeoisie.)

So much for the distinction between middle-class and bourgeois. How does this apply to the history and to the development of the American people? The principal ideas of the Modern Age, in the middle of which during the eighteenth century the United States was created, *were* bour-

* Leading American intellectuals were wrong about this. Edmund Wilson in *The New Republic,* 4 May 1932: "The writer who has made me feel most overwhelmingly that bourgeois society was ripe for burial was none of our American Marxist journalists but Proust"—a sure indication not only of Wilson's inadequate terminology but of his intellectual blinders.

geois, to a considerable extent. More important: as the nineteenth century progressed, certain ways of life as well as certain aspirations of the American middle classes became more and more bourgeois. Consider, for example, Mark Twain's description of small towns on the Mississippi in the 1830s, Dawson's Landing in *Puddinhead Wilson,* to wit. At first this description of those peaceable American villages, with their rambling-rose cottages, seems unduly sentimental. But soon it becomes apparent that the writer knows what he is writing about. The children are, of course, American children, that is, noble savages, but there is an efficient cause beneath all of that relative stability and peace: it is the remoteness from the greater world. Unlike in Europe, land is plentiful and cheap; the circulation of money is limited; vanities are limited. It is not a bourgeois world. But by 1850, or at the latest by 1865, the world of Dawson's Landing had disappeared. By 1900, another generation later, the cult of the bourgeois family had arisen, including the bringing up of children who must rise higher than, or at least as high as, their parents on the social and educational scale. The aspiration for certain standards of culture, for solidity and for security, the increasing urbanity and interiority in the lives of Americans were in full development. In 1800 these aspirations were rare, all of the happy mediocrity of American lives in the early Republic notwithstanding. The characters of Hawthorne, Melville, Poe were not bourgeois; a century later the characters of Sinclair Lewis as well as of F. Scott Fitzgerald were. (And those of Hemingway, too, no matter how he would deny that: like his protagonists, he did, after all, take a great deal of pride in being at home in the Paris Ritz as well as with a 30.06 in the bush.) In the 1920s such disparate fictional characters as Tom Buchanan and George Babbitt were American bourgeois, just as in real life such disparate people as Andrew Mellon and Clarence Darrow were—even though each of them would, more or less uneasily, deny the epithet.

The American upper classes were largely bourgeois. The word "aristocracy" confused this issue. During the nineteenth century in England and Europe the aristocracies still consisted largely of the nobility, of people with titles; in America they did not. (Perhaps it is significant that the name applied to old families in Boston was Brahmins, a name of a caste in India, and not a European term.) In America, ever since the zenith of the bourgeois interlude, the word "aristocracy" has been flung about with abandon; social maniacs like the prissy bachelor who administered the society lists in New York as well as enraged Populists in the hinterlands were obsessed with it; yet "aristocracy" in America was largely a fiction. People thought that "aristocracy" consisted, simply and squarely, of the very rich; that the financial and the social pyramids were one and the same; that distinctions of birth were like distinctions of wealth. In reality, the American social order, especially in the older cities of the East, with its unwritten laws, had little in common with the aristocracies of Europe and of England, while it had much in common with the old patrician societies of early modern Europe, nearer to the middle of the Continent, with a social and civic order represented by the great merchant families in cities such as Basel, Geneva, Amsterdam, Hamburg, or with the *grands bourgeois* (often Protestant) families of France. It had little in common with Proust's world of the Guermantes; it had many things in common with the world of Thomas Mann's Buddenbrooks. In sum, its components were patrician rather than aristocratic; bourgeois rather than feudal; resting, in the older cities and places, on distinctions derived from the consanguinity of families with high civic reputations and not from noble ancestors; on breeding even more than on blood; on the preeminence of the family, among other matters.

The bourgeois were conformists—not more nor less than were other people, not more nor less than before 1895 or after 1955. But during that interlude they conformed to civilized values. During the Bourgeois Interlude they began to devote a fair portion of their interests, and a more than fair portion of their money, to the collection and the propagation of art. It was thus that the Metropolitan Opera, Carnegie Hall, the great American private collections, the great museums, and the great symphony orchestras came into being. Again the dates 1895 and 1955 are good approximations. During the six decades between these years the great transatlantic migration of paintings, sculptures, libraries, artists, musicians, scientists, and on occasion of entire buildings took place. During the first half of the twentieth century the United States was the greatest and most prosperous power in the world; 1895–1955 coincides with the beginning and with the end of the rise of the American empire. Yet it would be simplistic and crude to explain this great movement of art and culture in materialistic terms alone. The 1890s were the end of the beginning. Many of the American collectors had sophisticated tastes by then; their enthusiasm and generous purchases and donations often sprang from a tangible and vitalizing element of American idealism. The development was so rapid that in 1902 Ralph Adams Cram, Henry Adams's friend, speculated that the top of American society may have reached the verge of aristocracy, that some of the rich bourgeois of the United States were on the verge of becoming the Medicis and the Borgias of the Modern Age (as had happened in Italy four hundred and fifty years earlier), that an American Renaissance was in the making. More recently certain art historians referred to the years from 1876 to 1917 as the American Renaissance (and to the years 1912–13 as the Little Renaissance, which was very little indeed). They were wrong—

but only in the long run. The greatest migration and transportation and translation of art and artists from one continent to another in the entire history of mankind did take place, after all. Compared to it the previous last great intellectual migration, that of the Byzantine Greek scholars to Italy at the time of the fall of Byzantium, was a puny affair. But there the comparison ceases. Fifty, one hundred, one hundred and fifty years after that migration the Italian Renaissance was in full development. Fifty years after 1900 the American Renaissance was passing. The 1950s were the beginning of the end: the degeneration of the collections, and of the tastes and of the purposes of the collectors, had begun.

The zenith of the bourgeois period in American history—again, chronologically as well as existentially—was the 1920s. (One of the reasons for this was the then still extant time lag between America and Europe: in Europe the First World War had knocked the stuffing out of the bourgeoisie; in America it had not.) But by 1920, at the latest, a new social phenomenon had arisen in the United States. This was the appearance of the intelligentsia: a new class which, despite its self-consciousness, was not easily definable, since it was a class composed not of wealth or birth or even formal education but a class of opinion. Like many (though not all) of the European intellectuals, the American intelligentsia regarded (or at least it thought that it regarded) anything bourgeois as a kind of pest, to be shunned and avoided at all (verbal) costs—a kind of self-conscious snobbery that was only to be expected. It is significant that, for the first time, there was a certain coincidence in the aspirations (and in the snobbery) of many Americans of the upper classes and of the intelligentsia in this regard. By the 1920s their self-conscious urbanity had developed to an extent that they would proclaim their distinctions from the rest of the middle class as sharply as possible. Between 1915 and 1925 appeared the first issues of such successful magazines as *The Smart Set, Vanity Fair, The New Yorker.* Their very names and subtitles were telling. The subtitle of the first was "A Magazine for Cleverness," and, again, "A Magazine for Minds That Are Not Primitive"; *The New Yorker* announced that it was not a magazine for the old lady in Dubuque (incidentally, a place not far from "Dawson's Landing"); its first modern cover showed an imaginary New York aristocrat of refinement, a Beau Brummel from the (nonexistent) American Regency days, contemplating a butterfly through his eyeglass. By 1925 "modern," in America, meant sophisticated, urban, and urbane. "The most horrendous enemy of the superior man," Mencken wrote, "is the 'husbandman,' the farmer. No more grasping, selfish and dishonest mammal indeed is known to students of the anthropoidea. . . . The intelligentsia are beleaguered in a few walled towns by these Fundamentalists armed with dung forks"—a word picture that was a forerunner of "American Gothic" (1930), a picture to which we shall return. Even fifty years later (1980), the American social historian Richard Lingeman referred to "American Gothic" as a caustic portrait "that outraged the bourgeoisie."[2] Not at all: in 1930, and ever since, the reactions of the American bourgeois to "American Gothic" were similar to those of the American intelligentsia.

In any event Mencken's description of the American farmer as the lowest kind of fundamentalist peasant was written (and thought) at the very time when the American farmer wished to become—indeed, when he was becoming—a businessman, yet another component of that American middle class which Charles A. Beard had wrongly defined as bourgeois. During the 1920s *Middletown* and other sociological surveys showed that the vast majority of Americans considered themselves middle-class. By 1939 this figure had risen to 88 percent in a Gallup poll; in 1940 a poll by *Fortune* magazine got the figure of 79.2 percent.† These percentages of self-ascription were unreal in the sense that they went at least 20 or 25 percent beyond what could be defined as "middle class" on grounds of income or of occupation; yet they were real in the sense that this was how the people sampled saw, or at least how they wished to see, themselves. In an important sense, however, this social phenomenon was becoming less and less meaningful. As we have seen in Chapter 3, this was the result of the inflation of society, whereby the shape of modern democratic American society came to resemble something like an enormous onion, or a balloon. But the homogeneity of this balloon was superficial. The sense of personal authenticity and liberty, the desire for privacy, the cult of the family, permanence of residence, the durability of possessions, the sense of security, and the urbanity of the standards of civilized life—all of them bourgeois qualities—were weakening. In the September 1955 issue of *The Ladies' Home Journal,* its male columnist wrote, "Only 10 percent of the families in this country earn over $10,000, whereas more than half the families earn $5,000. We are becoming one vast middle class, which to the American way of thinking is good and wholesome and sort of cozy." In reality, and especially in view of what was to follow, this kind of self-satisfied chuckling was altogether wrong: it was wholesome and cozy not at all. In reality, by 1955 the bourgeois interlude in the history of the American people was closing. During the next quarter century the dissolu-

† In 1948 a similar poll in Canada numbered those who considered themselves "middle-class" 65 percent, another one in the same year in Britain 48 percent. But the latter figure included all of the otherwise significant English variations of upper-middle, middle, lower-middle; also, the responses depended whether the alternative was "lower" or "working" class.

tion of the bourgeois and urban standards became more and more obvious. The inflation of communications, of pictures, of words, of money, of education was involved with the inchoate development of a new kind of society that was bureaucratic and not bourgeois, suburban and not urban.

A few people recognized this earlier than most. A few years before 1955 the thoughtful and modest poet Phyllis McGinley wrote, "But I think that some day people will look back on our little interval here, on our Spruce Manor way of life, as we now look back on the Currier and Ives kind of living, with nostalgia and respect."[3] "Some day . . ." she mused in 1948; well, less than a generation, thirty years later, the respect and nostalgia for the bourgeois civilization—marked, among other things, by the rise of the reputation of the word "bourgeois,"‡—suggest that this day may have already arrived. The bourgeois interlude did not vanish entirely; many of its elements are with us still—in part because of the solidity and the durability of its goods. Consider even now, near the end of the twentieth century, the interior of many an American house. Technically as well as aesthetically, from heating and plumbing facilities to the furniture and decorations, the interiors of these houses are not very different from what they were fifty years ago. Now contrast those interiors, and the lives of their inhabitants of, say, 1930 with those of 1880. The two scenes are so different as to be unrecognizable. Not only was the world of 1930 very different from the world in 1880: it *looked* entirely different, and this included the ways in which most people dressed, undressed, danced, moved, listened, read, thought. Not only the images but many of the material realities of the Bourgeois Age have remained with us, at least for some time.

But while the *embourgeoisement* of the American people has developed faster than that of many of the peoples of Europe, so has its dissolution.

‡ "Our languages are beginning to reflect this [I wrote in 1970]. In the United States, too, the reputation of 'bourgeois' has lately begun to rise, at least among cultivated people. Thus the stock of words rises and falls through the years. Their histories are our histories, they both reflect and create the prevailing tendencies of consciousness which are the deepest matters in the histories of nations. In the stock exchange of words and minds 'modern' has been falling, 'bourgeois' has been rising: a small trend, probably not without some significance."

(4)

What were the reasons for the relative shortness of this American bourgeois period? When in 1815, after the French revolutionary and Napoleonic wars, Great Britain emerged as the greatest world power, a British revolution—all of the disruptive and radical changes of industrialization notwithstanding—did not occur; what followed was the Age of Respectability, the Victorian Age, corresponding to the zenith of the bourgeoisie in Europe. There are many similarities between the situation of Great Britain after 1815 and the situation of the United States after 1945, after the revolutionary German world wars. (In 1945 the United States, like Britain in 1815, was the richest power of the world; like Britain in 1815, the United States in 1945 was, excluding Eurasian Russia, the only substantial world empire; after 1945 the United States, like Britain in 1815, became an essentially conservative power, upholding the status quo in the West; soon after 1815 the British chose their war hero Wellington for their Prime Minister; in 1952 Americans chose General Eisenhower for President.) Yet, all superficial appearances notwithstanding, after 1945 the bourgeois element in American life was weakening, not strengthening. Some of the reasons for this were more obvious than were others. Most of them were rooted in the American character.

The main, and the most obvious, element was restlessness. Restlessness is one of the components of the American character. The origins of this American restlessness, which had nothing to do with English or European habits or inheritances but with certain subterranean inheritances and territorial conditions of this great and open continent, go back well before the Revolution.

By the early twentieth century the American frontier era had closed, but the restlessness remained. This was as true of urban America as it was of the West. Americans moved from one part of the country to another; and in their cities from one neighborhood to another. Permanence of residence, that essential element of civilization, and especially of bourgeois civilization, was relatively rare, even at the height of the American bourgeois interlude. This had something to do with the peculiar characteristic of American cities, whose business portions and residential portions were separate and increasingly distant from each other. It had much to do with the relative cheapness and availability (even after 1900) of real estate in

America; and with social ambitions, whereby even in a work- and job-oriented society the status of a person was represented not by where he worked but by where he lived. The rise of real estate prices after World War II affected this movement not at all; suburbanization and the increasing number of Americans employed by corporations kept contributing to it. In 1956 the average American family moved every four years, an incomparable statistic which tells us more about Americans than many other figures, and which has no near equivalent in the otherwise democratic and Americanized societies of Western Europe.* During the 1970s the inflation of real estate prices, the diminution of available suburban land, and transportation difficulties and costs made the acquisition of private houses for most Americans more difficult. There was a small trickle of certain people back into the cities. Interestingly enough, this happened when crime in the cities was rising, when city services and amenities were deteriorating, and when the traditional American family was dissolving. We have reasons to be skeptical about the reurbanization of America, in 1980 and after.

It should be obvious that the moving of people from one house to another and their rise in society—what sociologists call their "horizontal" and "vertical" mobility—amounts to much the same thing. In 1869 a successful American, Charles O'Connor, "an ornament of the New York Bar," proclaimed that in America "a man is accounted a failure, *and certainly ought to be* [my italics] who has not risen above his father's station in life." This ornament of the New York bar did not see how this attitude suggested the rejection of one's parents—and the rejection of the Old World whence many of them had come—something that was one of the weakest elements of the American psyche, for to be ashamed of one's parents is the deepest of psychic wounds. Eighty years later, after World War II, the antibourgeois Wyndham Lewis wrote that "pious attachment to the soil" or "historical tradition" scarcely existed in America, and that this was a good thing, because the American was attached "to the absence of these things. It is attachment . . . to a slightly happy-go-lucky vacuum, in which the ego feels itself free. It is . . . something like the refreshing anonymity of a great city, compared with the oppressive opposite of that, invariably to be found in the village. Everything that is obnoxious in the Family is encountered in the latter: all that man gains by escape from the Family is offered by the former."[4] But this preference of "the free

* Here, too, 1955–56 was a turning point. Expenditures on new residential and private housing units increased from $3,222 million in 1941 to $3,300 million in 1946 and to . . . $18,774 million in 1955! Thereafter they declined; they reached the 1955 level again only in 1962, climbing to $24,272 million in 1970—and that in inflated dollars.

ego" in the "refreshing anonymity of a great city" has become a deadly—and not merely deadening—untruth.

"The United States is full of people who have escaped from their families, figuratively," Wyndham Lewis wrote in 1948. No: literally, and not merely figuratively. In 1913, in the same year that Mother's Day became a nationally observable holiday,† the American people passed another milestone: for the first time in American history more than one person in one thousand was divorced. In that year Margaret Sanger coined the term "birth control." This chronological coincidence of Mother's Day with divorce and birth control is at least telling. By 1930 the American divorce rate rose by another 56 percent, by 1970 more than 350 percent. By 1980 nearly one out of two new marriages was bound to terminate by divorce. The American fertility rate was extraordinary: 3.5 children in the 1950s; this had fallen by one half two decades later. In 1978 alone there were more than a million abortions; in the same year nearly half of American women under the age of twenty-four were childless. The number of unmarried women increased by one third from 1970 to 1980; the number of unmarried couples living together doubled, while the number of children decreased drastically. In 1980, for the first time in the history of the United States, nearly two thirds of American homes (63 percent) did not contain a child.

These radical changes occurred mostly during the 1970s, that is after the fashionable radicalism of the 1960s and the so-called youth revolution was largely spent. Except for illegitimacy, the most drastic changes involved the white middle-class population.‡ This was a phenomenon whose elements are more complicated than they might seem at first sight. The immature tendency toward instant self-gratification, which was a prime factor of inflation, remained a prime element in these developments too. But I am not only referring to the kind of thoughtlessness and irresponsibility that marks the impulse for instant self-gratification in casual sexual connections, usually on the part of the young male. Even more important was the immaturity of people entering the marriage bond, whereof the

† Mother's Day, in 1913, was promoted by the florists of the United States, "and is still a source of profit for them, has its whole point in . . . a society in which parents and children lose touch with one another." Cited by Robert A. Nisbet from Margaret Redfield's article in the *American Journal of Sociology,* November 1946.

‡ In 1965, 22 percent of black families were without a father and headed by females; in 1980 nearly 40 percent were in this category. In 1975 nearly 50 percent of all black children were illegitimate. In 1980 two thirds of the households headed by women with children received welfare payments, and half of all American children were likely to live in households headed by women before they reached the age of eighteen.

divorce rate was often the result. This national tendency preceded the 1960s and the 1970s. Early marriages (and the so-called baby boom) were a unique, and overwhelming, American phenomenon between 1945 and 1960. In these decisions the female was often deadlier than the male, attracted as she was by the ephemeral glories of her wedding ceremony. One would think that early marriages belonged to the rural and Victorian Age. The opposite was true. In 1890, when the life expectancy of American women was barely 45 years, and when the median age of American females was 21.6 years, the median age of their marriage was 22. Thereafter they chose to marry earlier and earlier. In 1956, at the peak of the cult of suburban togetherness, and amid the inflated prosperity of the Eisenhower years, their life expectancy and their median age was 50 percent higher than in 1890; yet the average American bride in 1956 got herself married less than a month after her twentieth birthday*—another important difference between the United States and the other, superficially similar, democratic societies of Western and Northern Europe. In 1979 the divorce rate in the so-called Sunbelt (Republican and "conservative"!) was the highest in the nation: 8.2 per 1,000 people in Dallas, Fort Worth, Houston (3.7 in New York, 3.4 in Philadelphia). But Dallas, Fort Worth, and Houston also had the highest marriage rates in the nation: (12.7 per 1,000 in 1979). This suggests the Western-American coexistence of "conservatism" and progressivism (or, rather, the superficiality of the former) as well as the continued coexistence of the ideals of married togetherness with the broad acceptance of divorce.

The American religion of progress had much to do with this. From Franklin's cheerful vulgarities we may catch more than a glimpse of American attitudes toward sex: it is not difficult to imagine Franklin as a forerunner of the advocates of sex education, public as well as private. Contrary to the general assumption, the Puritans were not opposed to progress. It was Cotton Mather who wrote (in 1723) that Americans must "Cultivate well projected Inventions," for they would put "the World in much better circumstances than it is. We try for Machines to render the Wind as well as the Water serviceable to us; and extend our Empire into all the Elements." The Puritans, and their successors, did not see that the worship of progress—if only in its mechanical forms—could not but lead to a loosening, instead of a tightening, of sexual mores and of family

* In 1957 one out of two American girls married before they were twenty. During the 1960s and 1970s the median age of marriage rose (but, then, so did the practice of cohabitation). It must be added that the drop in the American fertility rate in the 1970s was connected with this fact: women were marrying later than before.

bonds; and Americans were a people who worshiped progress in every form. There was a difference between British and American attitudes during the nineteenth century in this respect. The Victorians in England, as Harold Nicolson wrote, "believed, with excruciating conviction, in the value of individual endeavor; they were obsessed with the tremendous responsibility of their own future; and as they watched *uneasily* [my italics] the monster civilization which they fathered getting more and more beyond their control, they clung *despairingly* [my italics, again] to the pretense that they were a serene generation of happy and enlightened people who knew exactly why and whither it was all progressing, who were delighted to observe that it was progressing so fast."[5] Americans watched progress not at all uneasily; their belief in it, except for a scatteration of their earliest intellectuals, was untroubled by the slightest premonitions of skepticism, let alone despair. Americans believed not only in the progressive improvability of the world; they believed in the progressive improvability of human society, including their own.

One of the results of this belief was sex education. During the nineteenth century, prophets and advocates of radically new relationships between the sexes, appropriate for a New People of the New World, cropped up in the oddest places in America: Shakers, Mormons, utopian communitarians, Free Love advocates, the Women's Party. But after 1890 the cause of sexual progress ceased to be the monopoly of the radicals.† It was taken up by some of the most respectable, and established, American men and women and organizations, by judges, editors, preachers, and scholars. One of the most persistent advocates of sex education was Edward W. Bok, the editor of *The Ladies' Home Journal,* the most successful magazine not only in the United States but in the world during the first quarter of the twentieth century—yet Bok, on his own admission, never understood, and never cared to understand, women.‡ His fabulous career, and that of his magazine, was nonetheless due to his conviction that the time had arrived for him to address himself to the profitable reformation of American women. In 1913 he wrote in *The Ladies' Home Journal* that "today sex knowledge and sex hygiene form a discussable topic in the American home." This was what the radical advocates of Free Love in the

† Not that the Shakers, Mormons, etc., were typical nineteenth-century radicals; in many ways they were deeply conservative; their vision of the world and their religion had seventeenth-century and pre-Renaissance elements.

‡ In *The Americanization of Edward W. Bok* he wrote about himself in the third person singular: "Edward Bok's instinctive attitude toward women was that of avoidance. He did not dislike women, but it could not be said that he liked them. They had never interested him." (New York, 1920), p. 168.

first American Bohemian enclaves, in San Francisco or in Greenwich Village, and staid people such as Bostonian hygienists or the Colorado judge who proposed the salutary innovation of trial marriage, had in common. They were, all, progressives who believed that sex "hygiene" and sex "knowledge" were the same thing, that sex education was an American duty, that it belonged to the realm of American public education and to the public school system as a matter of course, to the great and enduring benefit of the nation. About such matters the radical intelligentsia and the *Reader's Digest* often saw eye to eye. In August 1957, when a temporary decline in the national divorce rate had occurred, Albert Q. Maisel composed an optimistic survey for the *Reader's Digest:* "Divorce Is Going Out of Style."

> The girl of 19 and the boy of 21 who walk down the aisle today . . . often are far different from the wild, eloping kinds of a generation ago. Usually they have tested their affection and loyalty for each other during three or four years—and often more—of "going steady." . . . They've acquired an intimate knowledge and a deep tolerance of each other's habits, reactions and attitudes. Thus, marriage poses no overwhelming problem of adjustment. . . . Almost all of today's young couples enter marriage with a far better understanding of the physical and physiological aspects of sex than their parents ever had a chance to obtain. Until 1924, for example, when Professor Ernest Groves started this country's first course in Marriage and Family Living at Boston University, authoritative sex education was virtually unobtainable for most young people. Today nearly 70 percent of all colleges and more than 1000 high schools offer such courses. There are also at least a half dozen highly competent books on marriage from which much can be learned.

What followed, of course, was a quadrupling of compulsory sex education courses, an astronomical increase of marriage and sex manuals, and the doubling of the divorce rate to boot.

The proponents of sex education and of sex "hygiene," the "researchers" of American sex habits were, implicitly or explicitly,* prophets and

* Kinsey was an entomologist who in the 1940s turned his attention to human sexual practices after having studied the mating processes of bees; he crowned his career by assembling a vast pornographic archive for the University of Indiana. There was a difference between his statistical "researches" in the 1940s and the "researches" by Masters and Johnson a quarter of a century later, however: a difference reflecting a further change in attitudes. Kinsey's avowed object was the statistical study of sexual practices; Masters and Johnson's

advocates of increasing sexual "freedom." All of these "studies" were inhuman, in spite of their "humanistic" purposes; they refused to see that the relations of the sexes are essentially matters of the mind and of the heart. People whose minds contain an unquestioning belief in progress will not understand that "progress" cannot make men and women freer than they are; and that the essence of human liberty consists of the capacity and the freedom—yes, the freedom—of human beings to establish their own personal restraints.

"All greatness of character," wrote Tocqueville's fine American contemporary, James Fenimore Cooper, in *The American Democrat* in 1838, "is dependent on individuality," and he deplored that individuality did not really flourish in the soil of the American democracy. Individualism was a specifically bourgeois trait; it was not a specifically American one. The successful bourgeois, the entrepreneur, did not only attempt to rise in the world; he wished to rise beyond his original social class or stratum. This kind of aspiration in the United States was relatively rare. The pressure to conform, in possessions, consumption, habits (including sexual habits), appearances, clothing, speech, and in thought allowed relatively little room for genuine privacy, including private aspirations. Most Americans wished to rise in the world: but they wished to rise within their communities, within their neighborhoods, within their groups—within them, not outside them. Surely it was this—and not some kind of capitalist or materialist crudeness—that Veblen's "conspicuous consumption" or "keeping up with the Joneses" or Bryce's "mass fatalism" meant. Even in the 1890s, during what Henry Seidel Canby called "The Age of Confidence," the "plain people," the masses of old Americans, were "content with their place. . . ."[6] This was at the beginning of the bourgeois interlude in the history of this country, at the end of which, in the 1950s, Margaret Mead noted the curiously American "absence of any ideal beyond the imputed norm of behavior for one's own class, age, sex and level of education. . . . There has always been in the United States a curious paradox between the belief in a world in which any man could be President and the actual narrow range of competition in which most people compete only with those very close to them . . . and very seldom hope to get out of their own league."[7] The explanation of this phenomenon could not be sought merely in a lack of broad-minded education, in a wanting knowledge of the world. It was not difficult to detect in it a lack of imagination and self-confidence—a condition which applied, and which still applies, especially

---

was to measure the element of "pleasure" in these practices. The "results" of the latter were even more ludicrous than were those of the former.

to American youth, all of the clichés about their ambitiousness and their appetite for freedom notwithstanding.

When Dr. Johnson said that "it is better that some should be unhappy than that none should be happy, which would be the case in a general state of equality," he expressed a profound truth which, for once, is as Christian as it is bourgeois, but not very American at that, in spite of Jefferson's windy phrase about the right to the pursuit of happiness. The American belief, at least for a long time, has been that equality and liberty are not only related but that they are nearly identical matters, and that their progress is reciprocal, mutual, and parallel. It was Tocqueville who argued most clearly that the relationship between equality and liberty was more complicated than what many people were accustomed to think; they *were* related, one could not exist without the other, but their progress was not necessarily parallel. To this we may add that while equality may be bestowed on people from the outside, the sense of liberty comes from the inside of a person; it is after you have been granted equality that the real problem of what to do with your liberty begins.† The desire for equality may be elevated and inspiring, but often its source is a lack of self-respect; the desire for liberty may not be always elevated and inspiring, but its source is almost always self-respect. The greatest achievement of the Bourgeois Age, and of the bourgeois interlude in the history of the United States, was the enrichment of interior life, rather than that of exterior possessions and appearances; it was the advance of personal liberty even more than that of social equality. This liberty was a reality, not an abstraction. Its sources were largely English, as Santayana wrote: "The best heritage of America, richer than its virgin continents. . . . Absolute liberty and English liberty are incompatible, and mankind must make a painful and a brave choice between them." "England," as Burke expressed it, "is a nation which still, I hope, respects, and formerly adored, her freedom. The colonists . . . took this bias and direction the moment they parted from your hands. They are, therefore, not only devoted to liberty, but to liberty according to English ideas and on English principles." By the middle of the twentieth century it was obvious that most Americans did not recognize the necessity for such a choice. American democracy was being pushed to its extreme through the instruments of a political process that had become the servant of the machinery of publicity. The result was cultural and not merely political equality, and the diminution of personal

† This corresponds to the material condition suggested in Chapter 3: the test of character is not so much how much money a person "makes" but how he is spending it.

security, of liberty, of individualism, of privacy, and of many other, earlier achievements of English law and of the bourgeois spirit.

(5)

Restlessness and the cult of progress and the promotion of equality were obvious features of American life and thought that inhibited the full development of the American bourgeois era and shortened its duration. Less obvious than these were other obstacles to the American bourgeois spirit. These were the German and the medieval and the Indian strains in the American people, coursing beneath the mainstream of events, occasionally breaking through to the surface.

The principal sources and the principal institutions of the Modern, or Bourgeois, Age derived from Western Europe, including the British Isles. In the history of Europe, until very recently, Germany occupied an ambiguous position. Geographically, socially, culturally in the middle of the Continent, between East and West, the German people entered the Modern Age later, more reluctantly, and with more difficulty than had other nations of northwestern Europe. Medieval and feudal elements survived in German institutions and in German life and thought even in the nineteenth century. Individualism, capitalism, the cult of reason, and political democracy for a long time grew poorly in the otherwise rich soil of German culture. For a long time they did not seem to fit the then still formless German character. This was bound to affect the development of the American people—even though German immigrants became assimilated in the United States very fast, acquiring their American and losing many of their German characteristics within one or two generations. As with immigration at large, this transformation affected not only the immigrants but the host people as well. In sheer numbers, the German-American presence in the United States was very considerable during the bourgeois period. In 1920 about 18 percent of the native white population was of German origin. Soon afterward the American people elected their first President whose ancestry was German, Herbert Hoover.‡ The second American President of German stock was Eisenhower. Hoover and Eisenhower were

‡ The ancestors of every previous President had come from the British Isles, except for Theodore Roosevelt, whose Dutch ancestors had, however, preceded even the English in America.

also the first presidents born west of the Mississippi. Hoover was somewhat of an Anglophobe, he had certain sympathies for Germany; Eisenhower had not.

Between 1820 and 1970 immigrants from Germany were the largest single group, 44 percent more than immigrants from Britain. In 1982 the Census Bureau reported that more Americans could trace their ancestry to Germany than to any other country: 28.8 percent (Irish: 24.4; English: 22.3).

The affinity of certain Americans for German culture preceded the physical presence of large numbers of German immigrants. The New England mind maintained, from the beginning, a sentimental idealization of Germans and Saxons, a preference which had been propounded by the English Puritans of the seventeenth century, and which lingered on long afterward. John Adams believed in the thesis that the Germanic tribes had been the originators of Anglo-Saxon freedom, maintaining the latter against the influence of Roman law and against a Norman aristocracy. George Bancroft, the first successful national historian, was an ardent Germanophile; as American minister to Prussia he was sufficiently undiplomatic to rejoice publicly at the Prussian victory over France in 1870. (So did the author of *Little Women* in Boston: "Hooray for old Pruss!" wrote Louisa M. Alcott.) By 1890 a German Ph.D. degree "or at least a residence in Germany for study, was almost indispensible to a young American teacher, wishing a post of college grade. In all the range of higher study—in philosophy, philology, physical science—German authorities were quoted, German methods adopted, German approbation courted. The word 'seminar' came over with the thing, and studies became known as 'disciplines.' German governesses were placed in many American nurseries, and 'made in Germany' was as true of our education as of our children's toys and the cutlery of our kitchens. The real excellence of German microscopes and chronographs justified the state of mind which gave so uncritical a reception to German 'Idealismusse' and German 'Weltanschauungen' in general. . . ."[8] "In 1908 a group of professional people, in rating the traits of various immigrant nationalities, ranked the Germans above the English and in some respects judged them superior to the native whites. In 1903 a Boston sociologist pronounced the Germans the best ethnic type in the city."[9] As late as 1910, when still nearly half of American high school students took Latin, "a quarter took German, the most popular foreign language."[10]

Apart from the East, the deepest and most widespread German influences existed in the Middle West, where they lasted longer than in New England. Partly because of their Anglophobia, partly because of certain

American political and tribal traditions, the Populists and the isolationists (in the Midwest, not in the South) for about two long generations—from about 1880 to 1960, again corresponding to the entire span of the American bourgeois interlude—were pro-German. The German word and idea of the *Volk* and *völkisch* (which have no equivalents in French; in England, too, a folk culture was long gone) harmonized with the ideas of American populism, and with the concept of the "folk," especially among Germans and Scandinavians in the Midwest. But in the midwestern and eastern cities, too, large numbers of non-German immigrants were more closely attuned to German mental habits and popular culture than to English ones. (This was especially true of the Jews, including their German-Yiddish language.) On various levels this partial Germanization of the United States brought salutary improvements, as in the case of the adoption of German models of higher learning by American graduate schools, in the inclusion of several German dishes in the American diet, in the changing American preference for German-type beer, in the definite German influence in enriching and elevating the standards of American classical and popular music and the musical theater, from Victor Herbert through Hammerstein and Fiedler to Kern. The anti-German hysteria during World War I was short-lived. During the twenties the German strain in the United States was evident. Thoughtful Englishmen such as Harold Nicolson, who had spent considerable time in both Germany and the United States in the twenties, noticed it. "There are moments even when I feel," he wrote, "that a German visitor to America might find himself more at home than any Englishman. He would find again that lack of individual self-confidence, that preference for corporate action, which are so marked a feature of his own gregarious countrymen. He would welcome the frequent notice-boards and public injunctions; he would share the love of speed and size, he would appreciate the graphs, the statistics and the belief in knowledge as opposed to learning. . . ."[11]

A perceptive American noticed much the same thing: ". . . the German with whom, I regret to say, we Americans have more in common than we have with the English."[12] This was written in 1930, the same year in which Grant Wood created his famous pictorial pronouncement in which the faces, the glasses, the stance, the countenances of the grim couple are German, not Anglo-Saxon (consider only the faded blond Gretchen hairdo of the farmer's wife); yet his title for the picture was "*American* Gothic."

During the Second World War the reputation of Germany in the United States again declined; but there was little or no repetition of the anti-German hysteria of World War I. Like the anti-Germanism of World

War I, that of World War II did not last. The masses of American soldiers entering Germany in 1945 found the country and its people much more congenial than they had found the English or the French. In the autumn of 1945 a Gallup poll revealed that more than half of American servicemen thought that Hitler had done much good, at least before the war. By 1948 the astute Populist Joseph McCarthy realized that a pro-German stand was actually a political asset surely in Wisconsin. By the early 1950s Germany was the European country most respected by most Americans. Under the administration of John Foster Dulles, West Germany replaced Britain as the prime American ally in Europe. The natural affinity for things German appeared on various levels of American life. The Anglo-American presence in various American institutions and organizations, including the Republican Party, was declining. Other examples, on other levels, abounded.* One of them was the German influence in the American space program. In 1958, twenty-five years after Hitler had come to power and less than thirteen years after his demise, the most congratulated man in the United States was Wernher von Braun (we saw that the students of the University of Notre Dame voted him to be the recipient of the Patriot of the Year award). That year, and for some time thereafter, the German Iron Cross was the favorite emblem of hordes of American youths; they wore it around their necks and pasted it on their motorcycle helmets.

After 1960 this kind of Germanophilia declined. At the same time the assimilation of German-Americans was so complete that a German name was the near-social equivalent of an English or Irish one. Meanwhile German influences in American culture† continued to spread, often through

* E.g., a full-page advertisement by a midwestern machinery company *(U.S. News and World Report,* 25 August 1953): "A country in Europe (let's call it 'X') isn't doing as well as its harder working, more self-denying neighbors, the Germans. A woman in 'X', jealous of the Germans' prosperity and her own country's lack of it, said, 'We'd be all right if the Germans would only sleep an hour later every morning.' But she is wrong. Even borders, treaties, foreign aid and international plans cannot change for long the rule that the more you produce, the more you will have; the less you produce the less you will have—whether you are a nation, an industry or an individual worker at a machine."

† The bureaucratization of the American language involved many German influences. I am dealing with the bureaucratic practice of abstractness, impersonality, and the increasing use of the—largely non-English—passive tense in Chapter 9; here let me draw attention to the increasing preference for nouns at the expense of verbs, and to the other, German, tendency to add unnecessary prepositions to verbs ("check out" for "check," "face up to" for "face," "meet up with" for "meet," etc.). There was, too, the curiously unimaginative surrealism of "young" American slang (the older American slang had been terse, rough, and pragmatic in its descriptiveness): "laid back," "freak out," "put-down," "hung-up," "way-out," etc., in which the noun depends entirely on the preposition and which are neither pragmatic nor descriptive.

the influence of German-Jewish immigrants and their progeny, until recently anti-German Germans. Many of these people reached the top levels of the American educational and cultural establishment, including universities, movies, the world of design and of fashion. (Their names were sometimes Anglicized, sometimes not: Kissinger, Preminger, Wilder, Nichols, Max, Weitz, etc., were but a few noteworthy examples.)

So much about the German strain. But let us return, for the last time, to "American Gothic." Grant Wood's picture was a statement against the medieval presence in America. Millions of immigrants to the United States, including Germans, had a strong medieval—that is, pre-bourgeois—strain in their lives and in their thinking. They had come to America from backward, pre-bourgeois and sub-bourgeois portions of the Old World. They became American before becoming modern, enlightened, bourgeois. This was also true of some of the earliest migrants from the British Isles,‡ perhaps especially of the Scotch-Irish, many of the Irish, and the Puritans. The latter, all of their middle-classness and incipient capitalism notwithstanding, were not a bourgeois people. In many ways the minds of the Puritans were medieval. They hankered after many of the patterns of thought of the Middle Ages, and even for some of the institutions of the Middle Ages. Their revolt was one against the spirit of the Latin and of the Catholic and the humanist Renaissance, not against the fundamentalist Middle Ages. These medieval habits of thought were lodged in one portion of the minds of the early American settlers, in the other half of which they were progressives and not reactionaries. In 1705 the city fathers in Philadelphia outlawed fornication, simply and squarely, which was a rather medieval thing to do, and added a clause that the innocent spouses of the guilty parties had the right to sue for divorce, something that was very modern, very American, by no means typically European or bourgeois. This kind of dualism has marked many American aspirations and institutions from the beginning.

American religiousness had a medieval strain throughout its history. This appeared in the fundamentalism of many American Protestant sects. It showed in the arguments of William Jennings Bryan at the Tennessee "monkey trial" in 1925. His mind was a compound of the medieval and of the supermodern American, stuffed with the radical convictions of a Lilburne and of a Henry Ford. Two hundred years before Bryan, the English Leveler Lilburne called himself "a spiritual warrior enlisted under

‡ And of the Canadian French. Tocqueville noted this. "Old France is in Canada; the new is with us." He compared their language to the puritanical Vaudois French of Switzerland.

the banners of Christ"; Bryan announced that the trial in Dayton, Tennessee, he would be engaged in would be "a duel to the death" for the cause of Christianity. The few European observers were fascinated with this kind of thing, in the midst of the modern America of the twenties. The correspondent of *Le Matin* wrote about Bryan that "he gave the impression of one returned to earth from the wars of religion." Many of the attitudes of American Catholicism, too, reflected medieval and even Byzantine habits of thought. In 1955 one of my freshmen students wrote, "America is closer to the middle ages because we kept our religion while the Europeans are not really religious"—a not untypical assertion by a generation of students among whom I found another freshman who thought that "Western civilization" meant civilization west of the Mississippi. In 1957, when the first American space rocket was launched, priests blessed a St. Christopher medal that was inserted in its tip; and the newspapers reported that some of the mechanics said rosaries in order to stop "gremlins" from causing trouble with the engines. Elements of medieval populism that had not been seen in Europe for centuries lived on in the United States. Consider, for instance, the American emphasis on first names, at the expense of family names, something which is not merely a result of democratic gregariousness. It strongly suggests the weakness of the kind of personal pride that derives from a distinct family: of the kind of family attachment that was emphatically bourgeois and not at all medieval. And where else in the world would people speak with such familiar ease of "St. Pete" and "St. Joe"; where else could one see, as I once saw in the yearbook of a Catholic high school, the pictures of a basketball player stopping in the chapel on his way to the game with the caption ". . . saying a reverent hello to Christ"?*

This tendency to the popularization of the sacred was something very different from the somber calculations of bourgeois religiosity; it was different, too, from the childishness that appears sometimes in the religious processions of, say, southern Italy; it was primitive and complicated at the same time. There is a Byzantine streak in the modern American character. The Byzantines had summarized the classics and the New Testament to make them easier reading; a thousand years later Bok, the super-Ameri-

* 1945. The eight-column banner headline of the Christmas number of the Catholic diocesan newspaper in Cleveland:

IT'S A BOY IN BETHLEHEM
CONGRATULATIONS GOD—CONGRATULATIONS MARY—
CONGRATULATIONS JOSEPH

(*Time,* 31 December 1945)

canized magazine editor, asked Lyman Abbott for a "short and snappy life of Christ." Horace Greeley spoke of our "Gothic race," with its "resistless tendency . . . toward the sand of the mighty Pacific sea." He meant the northern masses, but there was a Gothic facet to the American South, too, evident in the shapes of their superstitions and their steamboats, in the dark sweetness of their potions as well as in their ceremonies, including those of the Byzantine-medieval Klan, with its penitential oaths and hoods (the latter identical to those of the penitents marching in the *feria* of Seville) and its Gothic cult of the letter "K": Klans, Kilglapps, Klaverns, Kleagles. Even more Gothic than the neo-Gothic cathedrals financed by American businessmen in the nineteenth century were their cathedrals of commerce, their Gothic iron factory halls, the cupolas of their mansions, their fascination with the mastodon and the spirit of Barnum. There is a medieval element in American politics, in the practices of the Congress, in many ways more like a medieval assembly than a bourgeois parliament, the speeches and the debates on its floor being less important than the practices of its committees and of their investigations, judicial bodies, as in the Middle Ages, having the power of hauling people before them to "testify." Or consider the Breughelesque spirit of the nominating conventions, with their overwhelming imperative to proclaim unanimity with a shout. There is a medieval strain in the American presidency: for the President, perhaps especially in the twentieth century, was something like an elected monarch; and there was ample evidence for the inclinations of millions of Americans toward an elective monarchy of a particular family or a clan. The American popular imagery was full of medieval symbols. Consider the names of American gangs in one single city, where these were recorded in 1958: Chaplains, Bishops, Dukes, Templars, Scorpions, Crusaders, Lords, Demons, Dragons. Demons and Dragons had a powerful hold on the American popular imagination. Weren't Superman and Batman and the figures of *Star Wars* supermodern versions of medieval archangels, after all?

Like the German strain, these medieval tendencies existed on many levels, not only on those of popular culture. Henry Adams repeatedly and self-consciously argued that he was a belated survival from the eighteenth century, from the American Englightenment: yet, as his writings after 1900 increasingly showed, he hankered for a medieval synthesis. His contemporary, the patrician Owen Wister, saw in the cowboy a revival of a specimen of the Middle Ages. The Knight of the Round Table was the ancestor of the cowpuncher: "From the tournament to the round-up! Deprive the Saxon of his horse, and put him to forest-clearing or in a counting-house for a couple of generations and you may pass him without even seeing that his legs are designed for the gripping of saddles. . . . So upon land had the horseman his foster-brother, his ally, his playfellow, from the tournament of Camelot to the round-up of Abilene, where he learned quickly what the Mexican vaquero had to teach him." This was "the gist of the matter," Wister wrote, and it was the gist of his vision at that time of his life. The Cowboy was the Last Cavalier. In 1894 Frederic Remington drew the picture that Wister had put into words. The hope, the new American national type, was "no product of the frontier, but just the original kernel of the nut with the shell broken,"[13] a reversion to the Middle Ages. Yet there was a contradiction here: the hero of *The Virginian* (the first and enduring prototype of the American "Western") acted and spoke more like a Puritan than like a rumbustious cavalier. And the contradiction went deeper: Wister, like Adams in "The Virgin and the Dynamo" had little or no optimism left: both of them believed in the determinism of history, in the inevitable catastrophe that the accelerated advance of technology and of immigration would bring. Adams and Wister were clear examples; but we can, on occasion, find this split-mindedness even among such American intellectuals whose inclinations, unlike Wister's or Adams's, were urban and bourgeois. In 1925–26, the year of Bryan's Last Crusade in Tennessee, Lewis Mumford, whose entire career was devoted to making American life urban and urbane, deplored "the breakdown of the medieval synthesis." A generation later this kind of split-mindedness lived on within the ranks of the American conservative movement, whose proponents would often extol the merits of the medieval hierarchical order as well as the prospects of nuclear energy. Russell Kirk, one of the most thoughtful American conservative thinkers, would propagate the restoration of medieval and bourgeois virtues sometimes within the same essay or article or even paragraph: his writings reflected both the Royalist and the Puritan aspects of his persona, of the Cavalier and of the Covenanter at the same time.

In one very important way these medieval tendencies of the American spirit were but the results of what happens to extremes: when people draw the extreme consequences of an idea they are bound to arrive at its very opposite. There were many Americans who, having drawn some of the extreme consequences of the materialistic categories of the Age of Reason, arrived at their cultivation of a faith. There was a kind of unrestrained spiritualism at the base of the American mind from the beginning. This did not mean that America "remained" medieval from its beginnings. It meant that this peculiar coexistence of medieval with supermodern habits of mind has been typically American. For Americans have been often unable as well as unwilling to recognize the peculiar coexistence of their, often evidently contradictory, mental categories—and this kind of inability was in itself a medieval habit of mind. The Middle Ages were the era of the split mind, after all; as C. Delisle Burns wrote in *The First Europe,* the medieval world was unwilling to face the condition "that contradictory statements could be found in equally authoritative sources."[14] "A too systematic idealism," Johan Huizinga wrote in *The Waning of the Middle Ages,* "gives a certain rigidity to the conception of the world. . . . Men disregarded the individual qualities and the fine distinctions of things, deliberately and of set purpose, in order always to bring them under some general principle. . . . What is important is the impersonal. The mind is not in search of individual realities, but of models, examples, norms. . . . There is in the Middle Ages a tendency to ascribe a sort of substantiality to abstract concepts."[15] All of this was as true of the Puritan divine as it is of the Professor of Sociology, of Disneyland as well as of the State Department, of Superman as of the Public Relations man. It has been true, too, of the American ideology of anti-communism in most of its manifestations.

Impersonality as well as the unquestioning acceptance of the substantiality of abstract concepts is an element of primitive societies, including those of American Indians. What Huizinga explained on the intellectual level, Salvador de Madariaga expressed in cultural-racial terms about the Americas: "But men cannot take possession of a land without that land taking possession of them. And this come-back of the continent, whereby the conquerors were conquered by their conquest, is the chief process that during three centuries controls the evolution of the Spanish Empire. . . ." This Indian element has remained recognizable, and palpable, not only in countries where the physical presence of Indian people has dwindled to a minimum, such as Argentina or the United States. As late as the 1920s and 1930s very different Europeans and Englishmen recognized, indeed, they *felt,* that Indian presence: D. H. Lawrence as well as Salvador de Madariaga, Hermann Keyserling as well as Wyndham Lewis, Claud Cockburn as well as Noel Coward. "Even now," Wyndham Lewis wrote in 1948, "something Indian remains: Mexico is peopled by aboriginal Americans, and when the Indian culture of Mexico melts into the great American mass to the north, the Indian will probably give it its art, as the Negro has its music. . . . The new involvement of the United States in Asia will have for its result the Asiatic element numerically competing with the Negro in the States." In spite of the enormous migration of masses of people from the American East to the Far West, especially California, the Indian and oriental features have not weakened, rather the contrary. I am not writing merely of the actual presence of such influences on the newer occupants, or on the shapes of the land itself. Whether we consider the more-or-less conscious oriental influences on California horticulture or on the architecture of Frank Lloyd Wright; or the perhaps slight but perceptible Indian element in the countenances of such different Americans as Eleanor Roosevelt, Robert Kennedy, Ronald Reagan—of men and women probably without any Indian blood in their veins—or the general restlessness of much of modern American life, we must recognize the presence of influences, and even of preferences, that are the opposites of those prevalent in Europe. They are influences of a very old continent on a young people who came to occupy it.

(6)

The Indians did not discipline their children in the European sense. American parents disciplined their children little, even during the bourgeois decades. Many parents emancipated themselves from the rigors and duties of authority often before they emancipated their own offspring. Much of this was involved with the cult of youth, beneath which one could, on occasion, detect the preternatural fear of getting old, and even the fear of growing up: to postpone maturity, to postpone the end of a wonderful kind of freewheeling existence, has been typically American. For a long time young Americans *knew* that their youth was the equivalent of the golden, of the best years of their lives. F. Scott Fitzgerald wrote of his last days in Princeton, "Some of us wept because we knew we'd never be quite as young any more." This was the opposite of European bourgeois youth who—often prematurely, and at best precociously—looked forward to the mature enjoyments of adulthood. Americans, at least for a long time, had not. This condition was both cause and consequence of that peculiar characteristic of American youth which many foreigners have noticed: the weakness of their imagination—in spite (or, rather, because) of their extensive freedoms. A young Englishman, teaching in an American school, said to Agnes Repplier in 1930, "What struck him most sharply about American boys was their docility. He did not mean by this their readiness to do what they were told, but their readiness to think as they were told, in other words, to permit him to do their thinking for them."

We have seen that the "togetherness" of the 1950s was a complex phenomenon. From 1946 to 1964, 77 million American babies were born—amounting to one third of the entire population. Yet not only did the tremendous increase of marriages develop together with the increase of divorces; the average size of the American family hardly increased in the 1950s. In 1956 and 1957 more children were born than at any other time in the history of the nation; yet we have seen that 1956–57 was a turning point downward, in more ways than one, the end of the American bourgeois interlude. The "Generation Gap," that fashionable shibboleth of the sixties, was in full swing much earlier. The word "teen-ager" had come into existence in the 1930s; and in many ways the 1950s were marked less by the solidity of families than by the prevalence of teen-age mentalities and tastes and habits which many young marrieds carried into their adulthood. When in 1967 the editors of *Time* chose the "Under-25-Generation" for their "Man of the Year" they were, as so often, out of date. As early as 1954–55 the majority of buyers of records and majority of moviegoers in the United States were teen-agers.

The teen-agers' imaginations were weakened, among other things, by the increase of pictorialization. While the Middle Ages were predominantly pictorial, the Modern Age began to develop at the time of the invention of the printed word: "the Gutenberg Age," as Marshall McLuhan put it, perhaps drawing exaggerated conclusions therefrom. There is a fundamental difference in the mental operations of reading and looking. The first requires a more active participation of imagination than the latter: instead of looking at ready-made pictures, the reader must create his own picture from black squiggles on white paper symbolizing and forming words. When in the United States in the 1880s the newspaper entrepreneurs realized that here was a reservoir of new millions of potential newspaper readers ready to be tapped, they brought forth the penny newspaper and the yellow press on whose pages, from the very beginning, a strident, vivid, and primitive variant of texts was complemented by the increasing reproduction of all kinds of pictures, and eventually of photographs. Thus the Golden Age of the Press, lasting approximately from 1880 to 1940 (again a time span corresponding largely to the bourgeois chapter of American history) when, before the full development of radio and television, the newspaper had a near-monopoly of public information, when it was not yet wholly dependent on advertising, and when newspaper magnates were more powerful than ever before or after, carried within itself the seeds of its demise. In the United States the mass readership of newspapers was more extensive than anywhere else in the world. Add to this the fact that in the United States their material base, paper, was astonishingly cheap. In the 1920s the New York *Times,* probably the bulkiest newspaper in the world, cost two cents; the Sunday editions of newspapers, weighing several pounds, cost five cents; *The Saturday Evening Post,* weighing nearly a pound, consisting often of more than 270 pages, cost five cents. But the public was no longer reading much. Between 1893 and 1923 in the one hundred leading American newspapers the space devoted to editorials and to letters to the editors decreased by 79 percent; and while news about crime increased by 58 percent, illustrated matter increased by more than 84 percent. There were the comics: a particularly American form of popular entertainment, which most people read, especially in their Sunday papers. Whatever their content, the comics accorded with the needs, and formed the habits, of a nation of slow readers. The movies followed the comics—they were, in many ways, adaptations of the comics, a form of public entertainment which, again, was tapped by aggressive entrepreneurs.† By the 1920s American youth learned more from the movies than from all the reading matter they encountered. After 1930 the talking movies and the picture magazines meant the decline of the Golden Age of the Press. The relatively short-lived Golden Age of the American newsmagazine (1935–55), where opinion was disguised as information, administered to the needs of a population to know something about the increasing complexities of the entire world; and, as in the case of *Life,* where the newsmagazine and the picture magazine were one and the same, they contributed further to the pictorialization of American imagination. After World War II, then, came television, which eventually put an end to the Golden Age of the newspaper as well as that of the American newsmagazine, with consequences that are too obvious to detail.

In any event, television was both cause and consequence of the decline of the verbal culture that had been part of the Bourgeois Age in the Western world. Its technological complexities notwithstanding, this development was again reminiscent of the Middle Ages when the imaginations of most people were strongly pictorial. It certainly had its effect on the alarming decline of the standards of American education. In 1978, 50 percent of the students entering colleges in New Jersey and in California had to take a course in "remedial" English. In 1979 a standard 1928 reading test showed that the intelligence quotients and the reading ability of American college students in the better colleges of the nation were beneath those of 1928. The most significant of these figures revealed that the American college student in 1979 read 80 percent more slowly than his predecessor fifty years before. This happened in a decade when 40 percent of American

† Those who recognized the pantomime quality of this form of popular entertainment were wrong. Chaplin in 1920: "Movies need dialogue as much as Beethoven symphonies need lyrics."

youth had entered college in one way or another, and when Americans spent more years in schools than ever before.

By 1970 there were many American high school students who could go through their high school years without ever reading a book. The number of American bookstores and of book readers declined. The material living conditions of Americans in 1980 were not very different from the conditions of forty years before. It was in the operations of their minds that the passing of the Modern Age, and of the American bourgeois interlude, was most evident.

(7)

Yet it did not pass altogether. American history is full of paradox: but the contradictory elements often exist on different levels. They are not unduly difficult to detect, but it is difficult to direct attention to them because of the deadening ubiquitousness of publicity, because of the unceasing national preoccupation of what *seems* to be happening on the mere surface of American life. During most of the publicized 1960s and the early 1970s it seemed that radical and revolutionary changes were overwhelming the nation. As so often, public spokesmen and intellectuals described their essence wrongly. ("The worst, the most corrupting lies," Georges Bernanos wrote at the end of the Second World War, "are problems poorly stated.") They proclaimed that the worst American characteristic, violence, was rampant. Yet what had emerged was not violence but savagery. Violence, at its worst, suggests a sharp and brutal assertion of life, whereas savagery is permeated by despair. Blocked by a stuck door in a fire, or by a bent piece of metal in an accident, we may use violent force to save life, a kind of action enforced not only by our emotions but dictated by our intelligence—very different from savagery, which is principally, and impurely, emotional. Violence may be life-giving; savagery smells of death. The desire to inflict pain is the result of savagery not of violence; the desire to inflict humiliation, too: savage humiliation involves the reduction of another person to something nonhuman. Violence has been part and parcel of American history; but violence is, curiously enough, often the result of a kind of superficial optimism not pessimism: violence is, after all, a consequence of impatience; it has a purpose, even if a bad one, whereas behind savagery lurk purposelessness and fatalism.

During the last twenty years the crime rate in the United States rose to heights unequalled in the history of any civilized nation. The majority of American crimes were committed by juveniles. The new Vandals were not invaders from the outside, they came up from the midst of the people everywhere. When the fashionable "revolutionary" wave of the 1960s declined, crime and vandalism went on rising. During the first four years of the 1970s more Americans were murdered within the United States than were killed during the entire war in Vietnam. After the fall of Rome wolf packs roamed the abandoned cities of Italy; in some American cities wolf packs of young people roamed the streets. One of every two people arrested were under twenty-five: the offspring of "togetherness" and the "Baby Boom." Outside the cities, too, American civilization was succumbing to the temptations of a motorized and drugged witches' sabbath at the edges of which reappeared the impassive savage ghost of the Indian.

But at the same time something else was happening too: the increasing respect of all kinds of Americans for what was old and tried and solid. The generation gap, too, was declining. By 1970, for the first time in the history of this country, large numbers of American children, certainly those of the middle and upper classes, could no longer expect to rise above their fathers' stations in life. Doctors or lawyers and bankers could no longer count on their children becoming doctors or dentists or lawyers. This slowing down of vertical mobility meant that, after having come of age, these children would respect their parents, at least because they were not passing beyond them in American society. Thirty years before George Orwell had written how socialism "found its warmest adherents in the middle class. Its methods, if not its theories, obviously conflict with what is called 'bourgeois morality' (i.e. common decency), and in moral matters it is the proletarians who are bourgeois." By 1970 the American working class were not proletarians; they were adherents of bourgeois—or, at least, middle-class—morality, in more senses than one. The reputation of the word "bourgeois" began to rise, while the reputation of "modern" and "progressive" began to decline.

This was the paradoxical condition: the disrespect for law, order, marriage, the decline of literacy, possessions, education, occurring together with the rising respect for whatever was old, solid, durable, familiar, and bourgeois. Such contradictory conditions existed in American history before, too, but in a different way. While the "radical" and "revolutionary" changes in thought and in the "life-style" of the 1960s were, in reality, little more than extreme adaptations of ideas that had been new in the 1920s, the situation in the 1960s was the opposite of what had prevailed forty years earlier. The twenties were progressive and conformist at the same time. In spite of the clichés about the Jazz Age, during most of the twenties the national divorce rate actually declined. During the twenties the Americanism of young people was at least as orthodox, if not more, than that of the older generations. Forty years later the opposite was true. After 1970 the ubiquitous and persistent American restlessness was lessening. There were the beginnings of reurbanization. In 1976 a survey of the Harvard Class of 1968 (a vintage year of idiocy among the youth of the Republic) showed that more than 60 percent of them were engaged in restoring old houses.‡ Because of economic conditions similar to those of the United States in the 1970s, and because of the shoddiness of much of modern housing, something of this pattern existed in European countries, too; but in the United States this was not a particular avocation of the upper classes. In 1968, 28 percent of all prospective owners of American houses were building their houses themselves. "The contempt for permanence," about which Van Wyck Brooks had written in 1918, in his important and melancholy essay "Old America," ". . . so familiar, so intensely American," was receding. This was probably not the result of mere nostalgia: for it affected millions of Americans who knew the old life not at all.

The most contradictory, and probably the most significant, of these paradoxical dualities was the development of the status—social as well as self-ascribed status—of American women. The gradual advance of the Western world toward the democratic age brought a gradual rise in the status of women and in the respect paid to them. As early as one hundred and fifty years ago the status of American women was already extraordinary. Observers of the American scene, such as Tocqueville, noted this and liked it. Their opinion of American women was high: the spirit, the freedom, the self-assurance, and the virtuousness of American women impressed them favorably. These virtues included more than domesticity. In 1838 James Fenimore Cooper wrote, "[women] are the natural agents in maintaining the refinement of a people." By 1850 the very physical appearance of American women began to impress people in Europe. This, and not merely money, was a factor in the increasing number of transatlantic marriages between American women and foreigners of the upper classes (the converse of this, marriages between American men and European women were few). In her transatlantic novel, *The Shuttle,* Frances Hodgson Burnett wrote about an old American family of philistines around

‡ After reading this survey I asked my students: how many would choose to live in an old house, how many in a new house, all other things (comforts, neighborhood, price, etc.) being equal? Without exception they chose old houses. I found this interesting: twenty-five years before, when my wife and I, newly married, were restoring an old house, my students thought this very eccentric.

1850. "After the second generation the meager and mercantile physical type of the Vanderpoels improved upon itself. Feminine good looks appeared and were made the most of."[16] In his unpublished and unfinished novel about Philadelphia, Owen Wister wrote about the women of his city and society before 1900, "In a few generations they surpassed the men." In my study of Philadelphia, that relatively most bourgeois of American cities, I wrote that well before 1900, "when Victorian women were thought to be subservient, when families were paternalistic, when masculinity was unchallenged and dominant, when not only the orderly hierarchies of domestic and social life but the very appearances and countenances of men were meant to reflect the virile hegemony of the male . . . all these appearances notwithstanding, the feminine gender . . . was the stronger one." If in America old age meant nothing but decay and ugliness, if Americans, as Van Wyck Brooks wrote in the 1910s, did not know how to grow old, women were often the exceptions to this. Sarah Orne Jewett's *The Country of the Pointed Firs,* a book about Maine in the 1870s and 1880s, is a book about women, mostly middle-aged and old, small triumphs of character, compounds of gentleness and of maturity in a sea-girt, hard and rocky land. And this specifically American gentleness, this thoughtful willingness, these civilities of the American heart were best expressed around the turn of the century by American women who wrote about it because they knew it and felt it: Sarah Orne Jewett, Willa Cather, Ellen Glasgow, Edith Wharton. In sum, the women even more than the men of America were the pillars of American civilization. During the bourgeois interlude their husbands made money while these husbands remained, in many instances, overgrown boys. Their women were the true conservatives. Women took it upon themselves to patronize the arts. The opera, the theater, the ballet, certain of the great art collections, at times even the literary magazines, were inspired, supported, and sustained by American women of the upper classes. On another level, influencing all classes athwart the vast spaces of the Republic, the cause of feminism, including female suffrage, advanced more rapidly in the United States than anywhere else in the world, except for Scandinavia.

There were disadvantages to this predominance of women. The domination of the female element in American enterprises of culture led to lopsidedness, to the occasional feminization of this culture. During the bourgeois interlude the United States became a matriarchy. As Agnes Repplier put it, "We are a nation of husbands, not of men." Mrs. "Jack" Gardner and Carry Nation were not only contemporaries; both were components of the American scene. The Prohibition and the Women's Suffrage amendments of the Constitution were closely connected, and not only in time. The first woman was elected to the United States Congress in 1918, the first woman governor was installed in 1924. Yet, together with the extensions of women's rights and of their social privileges, the respect, sometimes muted and dumb and fearful, that the American male had for women was beginning to erode—an inevitable consequence of what went under the name of "sexual freedom."

During the nineteenth and the early twentieth centuries large numbers of women were liberated from their need to work. This was one of the most important achievements of the Bourgeois Age. The peak of power and prosperity in the histories of great nations has almost always corresponded with increasing opportunities for leisure. After 1920 the opportunities of American women for leisure began to decrease, while their domestic duties increased. This happened because of the diminishing availability of domestic servants. For a long time, until about 1960, American women consoled themselves to the effect that they were better off than any other womenfolk throughout the world and in the history of the world, in part because of their household appliances and cars. Yet their lives had become more constrained and more difficult than those of many of their upper-class and middle-class counterparts in Europe. By the 1960s they no longer believed in their singular good fortune. Many of them went to work outside, often dozens of miles away from their homes. The reasons for such decisions *en masse*—they included, for the first time, large numbers of women of the upper segments of society—were complex. In many instances, during the increasing inflation of wants, the reasons were financial. What was more important, many women found that domestic work, with all of the machines at their disposal, was drudgery, after all. Perhaps even more important was their realization not only of the relatively easy amenities but the satisfactions which had accompanied the social style of a former age amid an urbane existence: on one social level, patronage of the arts, volunteer work, formal entertainment, the day filled with various social duties, the accouterments of a bourgeois existence; on another, more widespread level, the respectability of domesticity, of demonstrably good motherhood, and of good housekeeping were largely gone. Meanwhile the dependence of children on their parents had diminished. So had women's dependence on their husbands. Women chose to work because their employment seemed to offer, oddly enough, more freedom. Surely it meant less isolation than their existence in a house in the suburbs—less isolation, and also less boredom. The so-called women's movement of the 1960s and 1970s represented genuine aspirations, even though they were often poorly expressed and understood, especially when going to extremes. On one level the aspirations of the women liberationists of the 1960s and 1970s and those of fifty years before were depressingly repetitious (especially for those who knew or remembered something of the former): many of the ideas and the slogans of the 1960s were hardly more than vulgarized and exaggerated repetitions of ideas current forty or fifty years earlier. On another level the differences were profound, even as few people noticed this. In the 1960s American women found the predominance of the male fettering not because it was real but because it was unreal. They could not stomach those prerogatives of the male—including not only professional or intellectual prerogatives but also the protection habitually offered by the latter—that dated back to earlier centuries, when men were indeed strong.* Now they saw—or, rather, felt—that the men were weak. Just as the "revolt" of youth in the 1960s was, in reality, often a reaction not against "authoritarian" but against permissive fathers whom they could no longer respect, women, too, despite all of the silly slogans of "male chauvinism," reacted against the assumption of strength and power on the part of their male counterparts, who were often weak. To be queen of a house in the times of a constitutional (that is, bourgeois) monarchy was one thing; but who would want to keep up the formal duties and the manifold responsibilities of a queen when the man of the household was but a chairman of a committee?

By the late 1970s a large portion, nearly half, of the American working force consisted of women. Yet the cause of female liberation was losing its strength. Many of the women recognized that the new paganism, including sexual license, held nothing good in store for them. (Compared to the "New Morality," the Old Immorality often seemed positively attractive—certainly aesthetically so.) This gradual reaction corresponded to the rediscovery, or to the newly acquired respect, for bourgeois virtues and standards on the part of many Americans who had hardly known these before. One of the interesting evidences of this was the attractiveness of life in certain American small towns—the very opposite of the atmosphere of small towns fifty or more years ago, wherefrom sensitive young people had been escaping. Another of the positive elements of this development was the increasing American attention given to good food and good cooking. That, too, had excrescences: undue gourmandise, the flaunting of a new kind of snobbery, hordes of people who knew everything about restaurants but little about food. But there was more to this development. James Fenimore Cooper, our native Tocqueville, wrote in *The American Demo-*

* As, for example, all of the manners and practices surrounding courtship and marriage that have come down to us from the feudal centuries and that had eventually become adopted by all classes.

crat in 1838, "There is a familiar and too much despised branch of civilization, of which the population of this country is singularly and unhappily ignorant: that of cookery. . . . The Americans are the grossest feeders of any civilized nation known. . . . [Yet] the voice of the table extends far beyond the indulgence of our appetites, as the school of manners includes health and morals, as well as that which is agreeable." The increased American interest in cooking (which is, alas, not altogether identical with improvements in the American diet) may have been part of the renewed respect for the manners and standards and virtues of domesticity, of that interior life which was the principal heritage of the Bourgeois Age and of the bourgeois spirit, in the United States as well as in the history of Europe, and which was reappearing, here and there, in the last fifteen years or so. This revival and respect for bourgeois values—has it been but a flurry? Will it endure? Our descendants, not we, will be able to answer this question.

(8)

This question, at the end of the Modern Age, relates to the prospect of civilization in its entirety, and not only in that of the United States. What Tocqueville saw in the United States was but part and parcel of his greater vision, of the passage of the civilized world from the aristocratic to the democratic age. He knew (and in his later works he especially emphasized) that this passage had begun earlier than people were accustomed to think, earlier than the French and than the American revolutions. The aristocracies may have kept their social, and in certain places their political, leadership, but by the time of the American Revolution the prevailing ways of thought were bourgeois. A list of principal thinkers, writers, artists, poets, philosophers of the last three hundred years will show that the vast majority came from a bourgeois background—no matter how many of them may have flailed away at the bourgeoisie. The mathematical logic of the world, the cult of reason, free trade, liberalism, the abolition of slavery, of censorship, the cult of the family, the contractual idea of the state, constitutionalism, individualism, socialism, nationalism, internationalism—these were not aristocratic ideas. This is why the Modern Age may be called the Bourgeois Age; it is at least possible that it will be so called one hundred years from now. But one hundred years after *Democracy in America,* the bourgeois world was passing. Something like a technological and bureaucratic world loomed ahead. As early as before World War II, nearly fifty years ago, and one hundred years after Tocqueville, John Buchan—a quiet, reserved, supremely responsible specimen of the high bourgeois virtues extant in Scotland and England, not a congenital pessimist but a fine writer with a sense of humor—admitted his "nightmare" in his otherwise serene and beautiful memoirs. Would the triumph of technology "be the perfecting of civilization? Would it not rather mean de-civilization, a loss of the supreme values of life?

> In my nightmare I could picture such a world. I assumed—no doubt an impossible assumption—that mankind was as amply provided for as the inmates of a well-managed orphanage. New inventions and a perfecting of transport had caused the whole earth to huddle together. There was no corner of the globe left unexplored and unexploited, no geographical mysteries to fire the imagination. Broad highways crowded with automobiles threaded the remotest lands, and overhead great airliners carried week-end tourists to the wilds of Africa and Asia. Everywhere there were guest-houses and luxury hotels and wayside camps and filling stations. What once were the savage tribes of Equatoria and Polynesia were now in reserves as an attraction to trippers, who bought from them curios and holiday mementoes. The globe, too, was full of pleasure-cities where people could escape the rigour of their own climate and enjoy perpetual holiday.
>
> In such a world everyone would have leisure. But everyone would be restless, for there would be no spiritual discipline in life. Some kind of mechanical philosophy of politics would have triumphed, and everybody would have his neat little part in the state machine. Everybody would be comfortable, but since there could be no great demand for intellectual exertion everybody would be also slightly idiotic. Their shallow minds would be easily bored, and therefore unstable. Their life would be largely a quest for amusement. The raffish existence led today by certain groups would have become the normal existence of large sections of society.
>
> Some kind of intellectual life no doubt would remain, though the old political disputes would have cancelled each other out, and the world would not have the stimulus of a contest of political ideals, which is, after all, a spiritual thing. Scientists and philosophers would still spin theories about the universe. Art would be in the hands of coteries, and literature dominated by *petites chapelles.* There would be religion, too, of a kind, in glossy upholstered churches with elaborate music. It

> would be a feverish, bustling world, self-satisfied and yet malcontent, and under the mask of a riotous life there would be death at the heart. The soil of human nature, which in the Dark Ages lay fallow, would now be worked out. Men would go everywhere and live nowhere; know everything and understand nothing. In the perpetual hurry of life there would be no chance of quiet for the soul. In the tumult of a jazz existence what hope would there be for the still small voices of the prophets and philosophers and poets? A world which claimed to be a triumph of the human personality would in truth have killed that personality. In such a bagman's paradise, where life would be rationalised and added with every material comfort, there would be little satisfaction for the immortal part of man. It would be a new Vanity Fair, with Mr. Talkative as the chief figure on the town council. The essence of civilization lies in man's defiance of an impersonal universe. It makes no difference that a mechanised universe may be his own creation if he allows his handiwork to enslave him. Not for the first time in history have the idols that humanity has shaped for its own ends become its master.[17]

"There may soon come a day," George Gissing wrote around 1890, "when, though the word 'comfort' continues to be used in many languages, the thing it signifies will be discoverable nowhere at all." As late as 1930 Ortega y Gasset, a critic of modern mass civilization, insisted in *The Revolt of the Masses* that, while admitting the faults of the bourgeois nineteenth century, its tremendous contributions will have to be recognized; that, "unless we prefer not to use our reason" we must "draw these conclusions: first, that liberal democracy . . . is the highest type of public life hitherto known; secondly, that that type may not be the best imaginable, but the one we imagine as superior to it must preserve the essence of (it); and thirdly, that to return to any forms of existence inferior to that of the nineteenth century is suicidal."[18] In other words: bourgeois civilization is the *only* civilization that accords to the notion of civilization as we know it.

In his *Study of History,* Arnold Toynbee—a very different thinker from Ortega—spoke of an abortive Far Western civilization in Ireland, on the far western edge of Europe, which existed during the Dark Ages but never developed into a full civilization. Will America be an integral continuation of the civilization of Europe, as happened to the Romans after the Greeks; or will the civilization of the United States, too, be a Far Western and abortive one? Was the American bourgeois interlude but a short version of the European Bourgeois Age, after which the democratic dissolution will lead to an end to civilization as we know it? These questions, I repeat, are not yet answerable—as indeed they were not in Tocqueville's time, one hundred and fifty years ago. Since that time the bourgeois period in the history of the United States has come and gone; but it has not vanished entirely.

6

THE TWO EMPIRES

The Passing of the Anglo-American Age in the History of the World

How the United States inherited much of the British Empire at a time when the characters and the interests of the British and of the American peoples became more and more different.

(1)

In the year 1897 Queen Victoria celebrated her Diamond Jubilee. She had ruled England for sixty years. Writers better than this one have described that day of magnificence—22 June 1897—illustrating its meaning with splendidly colorful details. Those who wrote about that day during the last eighty-five years have been largely in agreement about its significance—that is, about the situation of its date in the history of the British Empire and of the world. The year 1897 marked the pinnacle of the British Empire. It was then the largest empire in the history of the world. It included a quarter of the population of the globe, more than one fifth of all of the land of the globe; the British Navy ruled most of the seas. This corresponded with what the peoples of the globe were thinking. They saw the British Empire as the greatest power on earth. They admired the British people, not only because of their institutions and their power, but also because of their manly virtues, their habits, their very physical appearance. Much of this respect was unquestioning and enthusiastic, some of it was envious and perhaps even resentful, but no matter. Its extent was amply evident in the ways in which the British—their parliament as well as their navy, their industry as well as their sports, their clothes, and their language—were imitated in the strangest and most far-flung places. In sum,

1897 was not only the zenith of British power; it was, even more, the zenith of British prestige.

I write "even more" because, in one very important instance, in 1897 the decline of British power had already begun. Contrary to the prevalent materialist assumptions of our times, power is no less an intangible and fictitious matter than is prestige. It cannot be measured by the numbers of divisions or of warships, of budgets or of the gross national income. Its very function and existence are bound up intimately with prestige and with the will to make it prevail. At the very time of the Diamond Jubilee the willingness of the British—of their government as well as of the people themselves—to prevail against a certain nation disappeared. That nation was the United States. They were ready to defer to American power; they were ready and willing to share their domination of the world with the United States.

Between the years 1895 and 1898 there occurred a revolution in the relationship of Great Britain and the United States—involving a change in the course of the British ship of state, a small and undramatic change but one which eventually had momentous consequences. During most of the nineteenth century the balance of power between the United States and Great Britain was bilateral, reciprocal, largely even. They feared each other on occasion and respected each other to great measure, indeed, increasingly so. Their last war, the War of 1812, ended with a draw. So did most of their disputes during the rest of the century. A few such perspicacious foreign observers as Napoleon predicted that the United States would eventually rise to become the most powerful adversary of England and force her to retreat: but their opinions mattered little. A war between Britain and the United States was out of the question, though there were occasional conflicts of varying acuteness. As the century advanced, these conflicts became more and more rhetorical and less and less substantial, even though in the history of a democracy it is difficult to distinguish between these two elements. In 1895 the government of the United States sent grandiloquent, and in some ways threatening, notes to London about a conflict involving the boundaries of Venezuela. After a few exchanges of notes both sides climbed down. When, less than three years later, the United States provoked a war with Spain over Cuba, the British Government sided with the United States without reservations. What is significant is that by early 1898 not only the British Government but the people and the press had taken the side of the United States.

There were certain calculations behind this change of the British course. Few historians have made a full study of its global implications. The British, for the first time in their history, were beginning to be anxious about Germany. In order to be able to respond to the German challenge they had to secure the friendship of the United States, at almost any price. In 1898 the British Government wanted to assure the United States of its goodwill before Germany would do so. This American factor was one of the elements behind the British decision to make an *entente* with France in 1904.* Eventually this policy bore fruit: in both world wars of the twentieth century the United States stood by Britain. Eventually their alliance brought them victory as well as the gradual abdication of the British Empire and the continuing rise of an American one.

In October 1823 Thomas Jefferson wrote to President James Monroe, "Great Britain is the nation which can do us most harm of any one . . . and, with her on our side, we need not fear the whole world." Seventy-five years later this relationship was reversed. In October 1900 a Russian correspondent in *Novoya Vremya* wrote, "The British have lost all pride in their relation to the United States. They admit that they cannot resist the republic. They no longer trust to their strength, but place their trust in the racial, literary and social ties which attract the American to England."[1] There was, in this respect, a parallel between the relationships of the American and British empires with that of the German and Austrian ones. During the last four decades of their empire the Austrians sought security in their alliance with the new German Empire of their blood brothers, just as the British sought security in their evolving alliance with their American cousins. In both cases the alliance cost them their empire, and changed the course of world history, perhaps for the worse.

Within a year of the Diamond Jubilee the United States rose to the status of a world power, and not only that of the Big Brother of the western hemisphere. She defeated Spain in what one of her statesmen was to call a splendid little war; she acquired Cuba, Puerto Rico, Hawaii, an entire Pacific empire, reaching into the Philippines and the China Sea. This new kind of an American imperialism has had many competent historians; we need not detail its development. What we must note is that this development was a complex one, and not merely a response to the crisis in 1898. The building of a new and powerful American Navy had begun more than ten years earlier. In 1891 Benjamin F. Tracy, the Secretary of the Navy in Benjamin Harrison's Republican administration, asked for a navy with offensive capacities: "The nation that is ready to strike the first blow will gain an advantage which its antagonist can never offset. [In a typically

* This corresponded to one of Henry Adams's insights in 1905. If Germany would defeat Great Britain or France, "she becomes the centre of a military world and we are lost." Cited in Cushing Strout, *The American Image of the Old World* (New York, 1961), p. 105.

split-minded proposition he argued that this fleet would be one 'not for conquest, but defense.'] The sea will be the future seat of empire," he said. "And we shall rule it as certainly as the sun doth rise."[2] In 1891 James G. Blaine wrote Harrison that there were "three places that are of value enough to be taken. . . . One is Hawaii and the others are Cuba and Puerto Rico." The dates of these statements show that the imperialism of the Spanish-American War was not a sudden unexpected surge of national sentiment, and that the "new" imperialism had really little to do with the social and economic troubles of the 1890s, a thesis that many neo-Marxist and economic historians have suggested. It belonged to the American ideology of the period, reflected by public opinion as well as by popular sentiment. On the level of public opinion Republican nationalists, including Theodore Roosevelt, propagated it; Democratic politicians supported it as well. In March 1898, at Harvard, Richard Olney, the former Secretary of State, the same Olney who had threatened war with Britain less than three years earlier, spoke about "Patriotism of Race," suggesting the partnership of America and Britain. He said that the popular notion about Washington's Farewell Address ought to be revised. "It behooves us to accept the commanding position of the United States among the Powers of the earth. . . . This country was once the pioneer and is now the millionaire."[3] About American popular sentiment the Washington *Post* wrote in June 1896, one year before the Diamond Jubilee, two years before the appearance of the Rough Riders on San Juan Hill: "A new consciousness seems to have come upon us—the consciousness of strength—and with it a new appetite, the yearning to show our strength. . . . Ambition, interest, land hunger, pride, the mere joy of fighting, whatever it may be, we are animated by a new sensation. We are face to face with a strange destiny. The taste of Empire is in the mouth of the people even as the taste of blood in the jungle. It means an Imperial policy, the Republic, renascent, taking her place with the armed nations."[4]

Such evidences of the rising spirit of American imperialism were manifold: the above are but a few examples. On the important level of public opinion this spirit was not altogether ungenerous, and it was not necessarily anti-British. On the day of the Diamond Jubilee the New York *Times* wrote, "We are a part, and a great part, of the Greater Britain which seems so plainly destined to dominate the planet."[5] The owner of the New York *Times* was an American conservative Democrat of German-Jewish origin; yet the tone of this editorial was in accord with the convictions of the still predominantly Anglo-Saxon American upper class, especially in the East. At the Republican Convention of 1900, the Secretary of State, John Hay, dissuaded the party from an anti-English declaration in favor of the Boers and for the annexation of Canada. The British realized this instinctively, and not only intellectually. They believed that blood was thicker than water; that the Channel was wider than the Atlantic; that the multitudinous ties of race and tradition and culture and language that connected the British with the American people could eventually develop into more definite relationships and perhaps even into institutions and alliances and confederations that would secure the progress and the prosperity of the entire world through the instrument of Anglo-American domination. Kipling wrote his, often misunderstood, famous phrase of the White Man's Burden to help the Americans make up their minds about accepting responsibility for ruling the Philippines. In short, by 1900 the idea of a Pax Britannica was being replaced in the minds of some very acute people by the image of a Pax Anglo-Americana. This was the governing idea of Winston Churchill throughout his entire public life. His mother was American but he was no less a quintessential Englishman for that. His public career began in 1895 and ended in 1955—two dates that, as we have seen before and as we shall see again, are milestones and turning points of multiple significance.

(2)

What were the elements of this idea, both grandiose and obvious? It was more than a political idea, or a reckoning of global naval strategy; its elements were social as well as cultural, and racial as well as religious. Behind the idea of an even closer alliance of Great Britain and the United States lay the belief in the essential similarity, and eventual unity, of the English-speaking peoples of the world.

The British decision to avoid challenging the United States rested on more than diplomatic calculations. There was the lengthening historical perspective: after a century or more, British irritability and dissatisfaction with the American revolutionists had faded into nothing. As the English Liberal John Morley wrote during the year of the Diamond Jubilee: "The War of Independence was virtually a second English civil war."[6] There came, in its place, the idea of racial unity, running at full tide in the 1890s, the elements of which were Darwinist as well as Kiplingesque, a belief in the proper triumph of the fittest and in the proper burden of the English-speaking peoples of the earth. As early as 1868 Sir Charles Dilke wrote *Greater Britain:* "A Record of Travel in English-Speaking Countries." This book had at least eight editions, including American ones. The Preface read:

> In 1866 and 1867, I followed England round the world; everywhere I was in English-speaking, or in English-governed lands. If I remarked that climate, soil, manners of life, that mixture with other peoples had modified the blood, I saw, too, that in essentials the race was always one.
>
> The idea which in all the length of my travels has been at once my fellow and my guide—a key wherewith to unlock the hidden things of strange new lands—is a conception, however imperfect, of the grandeur of our race, already girdling the earth, which it is destined, perhaps, eventually to overspread.
>
> In America, the peoples of the world are being fused together, but they are run into an English mould: Alfred's laws and Chaucer's tongue are theirs whether they would or no. There are men who say that Britain in her age will claim the glory of having planted greater Englands across the seas. They fail to perceive that she has done more than found plantations of her own—that she has imposed her institutions upon the offshoots of Germany, of Ireland, of Scandinavia, and of Spain. Through America, England is speaking to the world.
>
> Sketches of Saxondom may be of interest even upon humbler grounds: the development of the England of Elizabeth is to be found, not in the Britain of Victoria, but in half the habitable globe. If two small islands are by courtesy styled "Great," America, Australia, India, must form a "Greater Britain."

This idea of a Greater Britain ran across the entire fabric of the British people; it was shared by conservatives such as Arthur Balfour, but also by some of the British socialists, by Keir Hardie as well as by John Burns. In 1898 Burns said in a speech, "The Latin and the other races were beginning to see that the world-wide supremacy of the Anglo-Saxon race was imminent, if it had not already arrived."† There was, too, a

† This idea, with its concomitant belief in the historical backwardness of the Latin peoples, was shared at the time by many Spanish, Italian, and French thinkers. Many of the Spanish "Generation of 1898" admired English institutions and lamented the absence of Kiplingesque virtues among their own people. In Italy brilliant historians such as Ferrero and Croce had similar ideas: the former pointed out in *The Young Europe*, in 1897, the decline of the Latin peoples. Twenty years later this liberal historian corrected his views in *Il genio latino*, as had the brilliant Spanish Ramiro de Maeztu, admirer of Kipling (but later a forerunner of fascism) who by 1920 convinced himself that England was declining and de-

religious element within this moderate kind of a philistine racism, in the belief that the present and the future belonged to the seafaring Nordic nations, and particularly to the Protestant and English-speaking peoples of the globe. Surely the swift and amazingly easy triumph of the United States over Spain confirmed this already current belief. Thus this sentiment was as cultural as it was racial: when Joseph Chamberlain, in 1899, proposed a grand alliance of the "Teutonic" peoples, very much including Germany, the reactions of the British governing class and of the people were halfhearted. Within a year the Boer War began. It shook some of the British confidence in their superiority. It was also marked by the conflict between imperialists and Little Englanders. In the end the British won the war, and the imperialists carried the day. Still it was during the war, in 1901, that the most direct and eloquent proposition of a union of the English-speaking nations was published. W. T. Stead, an energetic journalist and a Knight of Fleet Street during the Golden Age of the Press,‡ put the matter plainly and vociferously in a book whose very title was telling: *The Americanization of the World or The Trend of the Twentieth Century.* Here are some of its trenchant passages:

> The Americanization of the world is but the Anglicizing of the world at one remove.
>
> The English-speaking States, with a population of 121,000 self-governing white citizens, govern 353,000,000 of Asiatics and Africans. Under their allied flags labor one-third of the human race.
>
> The sea, which covers three-fourths of the surface of the planet, is their domain. Excepting the Euxine and the Caspian, no ship dare plough the salt seas in Eastern or Western hemisphere if they choose to forbid it. They are supreme custodians of the waterways of the world, capable by their fiat of blockading into submission any European State contemplating an appeal to the arbitrament of war. . . .
>
> The question arises whether this gigantic aggregate can be pooled. We live in the day of combinations. Is there no Morgan who will undertake to bring about the greatest combination of all—a combination of the whole English-speaking race? . . .

---

caying. Such a development of ideas was discernible among French intellectuals, too, after World War I.

‡ Lord Salisbury in 1901: "The diplomacy of nations is now conducted as much in the letters of special correspondents as in the dispatches of the Foreign Office." Churchill in 1902: "An age when almost the only robustly assertive institution in our society was the Press."

> The tendency of the last half century has been all in favor of the unification of peoples who speak the same language. It is not likely to slacken in the new century. The Nineteeth Century unified Germany and Italy. Will the Twentieth Century unify the English-speaking race? . . .
>
> . . . The idea of German unity seemed an idler dream in 1801 than the idea of English-speaking unity seems in 1901.[7]

This book was a great success on both sides of the Atlantic. In a strident, but by no means thoughtless, journalistic style Stead put into simple phrases what many people were thinking. Yet beneath the boosterish tone we may find even in this book certain expressions of some of those concerns that had moved Kipling in his great and stunning *Recessional.* In that poem, written for the day of the Diamond Jubilee, Kipling warned his people that the greatest of empires may pass and they must not forget that the Lord may abandon them for "frantic boast and foolish word," for putting trust with "heathen heart" in "reeking tube and iron shard." Stead was no poet, nor did he seem to particularly fear the Lord; he put *his* trust in a "great combination"; he put the matter more "pragmatically":

> What is the conclusion of the whole matter? It may be stated in a sentence. There lies before the people of Great Britain a choice of two alternatives. If they decide to merge the existence of the British Empire in the United States of the English-speaking World, they may continue for all time to be an integral part of the greatest of all World-Powers, supreme on sea and unassailable on land, permanently delivered from all fear of hostile attack, and capable of wielding irresistible influence in all parts of the planet.
>
> That is one alternative. The other is the acceptance of our supersession by the United States as the centre of gravity in the English-speaking world, the loss by one of our great colonies, and our ultimate reduction to the status of an English-speaking Belgium. One or the other it must be. Which shall it be? . . .[8]

It was to be the second. Few people foresaw this in 1901. The imperialists carried the day, even though the Little Englanders were making patriotic noises, here and there. It may have been significant—some of the Little Englanders noticed this—that many of the British imperialists during the last phase of Empire-thinking were men who had been born in the colonies (such as Beaverbrook) or others whose ancestry was not English at all (such as Milner). Yet few men and women of the British governing classes were Little Englanders. In spite of their occasional Francophilia, in spite of their acquaintance with Europe, they fully shared the sentiment of affinity with the Americans, the notion of an Anglo-Saxon Greater England. With their characteristic empiricism (a positive term for what is, alas, often hardly more than shortsightedness, or a characteristically British unwillingness to think farther ahead than what is customary) they accepted the governing idea, and the potential profits, that a closer association with the United States meant, or would mean.

With their characteristic hypocrisy, they engineered a full revolution of British public attitudes toward Americans. Hardly anything but good was written and said about Americans, including American women, American art, and American literature, in England during the fifteen years before World War I. That there were elements of hypocrisy and of snobbery within these attitudes (many of the upper-class British continued to be patronizing about Americans, whom they pretended to regard as useful and good-natured *nouveaux riches)* was sensed by few people. Anyhow, it counted little. What counted was the semblance of reciprocity: that these sentiments for an ever closer English-American association were shared by many Americans. The deepest rooted were those latent within old Americans of English stock. "Blood is thicker than water," said Josiah Tattnall, the Commodore of the U.S. Navy, when he turned his ship around to stand by a British admiral's vessel in a skirmish with the Chinese on the Peiho River in 1859. Throughout the nineteenth century officers of the American Navy regularly celebrated 22 October, Trafalgar Day. In the story "The Queen's Twin," about an American woman in Maine who had the same birthday as Queen Victoria, Sara Orne Jewett's narrator said, "I had often been struck by the quick interest and familiar allusion to certain members of the royal house which one found in distant neighborhoods of New England; whether some old instincts of personal loyalty have survived all changes of time and national vicissitudes, or whether it is only that the Queen's own character and disposition have won friends for her so far away, it is impossible to tell."[9] When Americans said the "Queen" (or the "King") they meant the monarch of England. By the 1890s these preferential values had filtered across American society. An American newspaperman explained that an accident abroad was worth reporting if it involved the death of one American or three Englishmen or ten Europeans. People who were not of Anglo-Saxon origin understood these preferences, and to some extent shared them. "Twisting the Lion's Tail" ceased to be popular rhetorical practice some time after 1895. Even American Catholics would, on occasion, share these preferences. When, in 1898,

Catholic journals in Europe pleaded for a European Catholic resistance against the barbarous and aggressive Americans, the great majority of American Catholics supported the war against Spain enthusiastically.

As in England, in the United States there was a racial and a religious belief behind these asseverations. Nearly ten years before Stead's book appeared, Andrew Carnegie had written (June 1892), "Let men say what they will, but I say that as surely as the sun in heavens once shone upon Britain and America united, so surely it is one morning to rise and shine upon and greet again the Re-united States of the British-American Union." Carnegie was born in Scotland: the imperialist Senator Albert J. Beveridge was not. "God has not been preparing the English-speaking and Teutonic peoples," he said on 9 January 1900, "for nothing but vain and idle self-contemplation and self-admiration. No! He has made us the master-organizers of the world. . . ." The Republican Progressive William Allen White wrote (20 March 1899), "Only Anglo-Saxons can govern themselves. . . . It is the Anglo-Saxons' manifest destiny to go forth as a world conqueror." A considerable portion of the American working class shared such sentiments. Their nationalism prevented most of them from paying any attention to socialism, which, to them, was of European origin, an importation by inferior stock.

The Kiplingesque and imperialist ideas of Theodore Roosevelt and Albert Thayer Mahan were knowledgeable and historically conscious crystallizations of what some Americans of the American patrician class were thinking. Yet it would be wrong to believe that their efforts were but a kind of Anglophile flummery perpetrated upon the masses of artless Americans. When the Boer War began, Theodore Roosevelt—partly because of his own Dutch ancestry, partly because he saw in the sunburned Boer pioneers and farmers something akin to the independent American frontiersmen of a century ago—expressed his sympathy for the Boers; by the time the war ended his appreciation for the British Empire had crystallized anew.* That certain Americans after 1890 began to cling, rather desperately, to their English heritage with which they attempted to reknot their ties was most evident in the life of Henry James. The same theme, on a slightly more popular level, was expressed even more clearly in Frances Hodgson Burnett's Anglo-American novel, *The Shuttle,* in 1907—her theme being that, after all that had happened and was happening, the English and American peoples had begun to reweave their joint destinies closer together, whence the title of her book. She wrote, rather finely, of a

* Yet T.R. "was not the simple symbol of the Anglo-Saxon cult that some of his critics have drawn." Strout, op. cit., p. 69.

nostalgia—a reawakening nostalgia—for England in the heart of Americans who came to visit England. The intelligent and very American girl Rosy speaks of England, "the country she was conscious she cared for most":

> "It is England we love, we Americans," she had said to her father. "What could be more natural? We belong to it—it belongs to us. I could never be convinced that the old tie of the blood does not count. All nationalities have come to us since we became a nation, but most of us in the beginning came from England. We are touching about it, too. We trifle with France and labour with Germany, we sentimentalize over Italy and ecstacise over Spain—but England we love. How it moves us when we go to it, how we gush if we are simple and effusive, how we are stirred imaginatively if we are of the perceptive class. I have heard the commonest little half-educated woman say the prettiest, clumsy, emotional things about what she has seen there. A New England schoolma'am, who has made a Cook's tour, will almost have tears in her voice as she wanders on with her commonplaces about hawthorn and thatched cottages and white or red farms. Why are we not unconsciously pathetic about German cottages and Italian villages? Because we have not, in centuries past, had the habit of being born in them. It is only an English cottage and an English lane, whether white with hawthorn blossoms or bare with winter, that wakes in us that little yearning, grovelling tenderness that is so sweet. It is only nature calling us home."[10]

And these were not merely attitudes; they were deep-seated—if often unthought—convictions held by many Anglo-Americans (and sometimes not only by Anglo-Americans; Mrs. Burnett's Vanderpoels were Holland-American by origin, like Theodore Roosevelt, on their father's side) when this century was young. And it came about: as the First World War wore on, the United States, for the first time in its history, chose to enter the war on the side of England. On one plane the shuttle was reweaving. Yet, on another plane, the threads of the shuttle were unraveling: the fabric of America, at first merely statistically, but as time went on, more and more perceptibly, became less and less Anglo-Saxon, less and less English.

(3)

Toward the end of his long life, shortly before the Diamond Jubilee, Bismarck was supposed to have said that the most important fact in the coming century was that the American people spoke English. By this he meant that the natural affinities of the American and the British peoples ought not to be disregarded, a fact that the statesmen of Europe had better keep in mind. He was right: the courses of the two empires grew gradually closer until their *de facto* alliance in 1917. Yet alliance was one thing; union, or even confederation, was another. By 1917 no one spoke such terms as Stead had enunciated and that had been current fifteen years before.

One of the reasons for this was that the conceptions of the American and of the British empires were different. The dynamism and the expansive sentiments behind the American empire were rising at the very time when the dynamism and the expansionism of the British imperial idea had begun to weaken. There was much in common in the largely Protestant, and sometimes philistine and pharisaic, sentiments with which the British and the Americans were wont to justify their imperialism; yet a closer examination of these slogans reveal significant differences. The British were justifying their imperial role to themselves; the Americans were proclaiming it to the world. The British were thinking (when they were thinking at all) in terms of their burden (which is why, all of its racial elements notwithstanding, the Kiplingian idea of race was not a forerunner of the more modern and brutal and antireligious racial ideology of the German Third Reich); the Americans were thinking in terms of their manifest destiny. The British Empire was older than the American one; yet the British imperialist ideology was relatively new, it had not surfaced until the latter part of the nineteenth century. The origins of the American idea of manifest destiny had been there at the birth of the Republic, even though the slogan was made current by an Irish-American politician and journalist around 1845. Lincoln's Secretary of State, Seward, the same man who succeeded in avoiding war with Britain in 1861, had written earlier that after thousands of years of westward expansion of the white man's civilization the United States would complete it, "until the tides of the renewed and of the decaying civilization of the world meet on the shores of the Pacific Ocean."

In 1895, during the Venezuelan dispute with Britain, the Democratic Secretary of State, Olney, proclaimed in a note to Britain that "the people of the United States have a vital interest in the cause of popular self-government." The American note to Spain on 17 January 1898, that is, before the catastrophe of the *Maine,* stated that "our American idea is that Governments derive their just authority from the consent of the governed . . . [and that the United States cannot sympathize with keeping] a people under monarchical rule, who are seeking to establish a republic."[11] In November 1897 the Cincinnati *Commercial Tribune,* filing this direct dispatch from the Almighty, declared, "A power higher than that of thrones and ministries has decreed that Europe shall play second fiddle to Uncle Sam in the commerce of the world, and you fight against fate when you try to prevent it." In 1900 Senator Albert J. Beveridge proclaimed that it was God who took "the American people as His chosen nation to finally lead in the regeneration of the world." The regeneration of the world: this was not only an order larger than the White Man's Burden; in phrases such as these there was not a trace of Kipling's warning about "frantic boast and foolish word." Indeed, many Americans, unlike the British, believed in speed: that the course of history was speeding up, with something like the Unity of the World (on American terms) in sight. Already Seward thought (and so had Henry and Brooks Adams) that imperial expansion now moved faster than in the past, that the course of history was accelerating. So did the Congregationalist minister Josiah Strong: "[The] western world in its progress is gathering momentum like a falling body; . . . [we were on the verge of] a new era, for which the nineteenth century had been John the Baptist." The main elements in this acceleration were steam and electricity and the distribution of Bibles, with the "resulting unity" of the peoples of the world.

Not all Americans were imbued with the spirit of a missionary and messianic role.† This was the time of the American bourgeois interlude,

† The role of missionaries in propagating American imperialism was not very different from the role of American imperialists in propagating the missionaries. By 1890 the number of American missionaries in the Far East was greater than that of all other missionaries combined. The slogan of the Student Volunteers for Foreign Missions (of which Henry Luce, the future president of Time-Life-Fortune and the proponent of the American Century forty years later, was a member) was "The Evangelization of the World in this Generation." By "evangelization" they ususally meant Americanization. A vulgar element in their propagations was their alliance with corporate capitalism. *The Congregationalist* stated that "Commerce follows the missionary," which was all to the good. A related example cited by Professor LaFeber (op. cit., p. 307) is this passage by the Reverend Isaac Taylor Headland, who was a missionary in China in the 1890s, in *Some By-Products of Missions* (Cincinnati, 1921, pp. 33–34): "If I were asked to state what would be the best form of advertising for the great American Steel Trust or Standard Oil or the Baldwin Locomotive Works . . . or the Singer

when more and more practices of American life and more and more American ideas were coming closer to those of the older civilizations of Europe, and when Theodore Roosevelt was beginning to mold an American internationalism in which many elements were realistic rather than sentimental. In 1910 he told his friend, the German ambassador to Washington, "In fact, we ourselves are becoming, owing to our strength and geographical situation, more and more the balance of power of the whole world." Still, the very Progressive Era, to which Theodore Roosevelt belonged, tended to share the idea of American exceptionalism. Even American intellectuals, more and more critical of some of the seemingly vulgar elements of American life, shared the essence of this belief. "Culture to most Americans in 1912 did not mean what it was beginning to mean to anthropologists. . . . It was not so much a way of describing how people behaved as an idea of how they ought to behave and did not." In American letters the standards of culture were still largely British. "This was part of the trouble: Americans for a long time had wanted to construct their own tradition . . . [yet] America, the custodians of culture hoped, might reproduce all that was good in English civilization without its grossness and cruelty."[12] This kind of "exceptionalism" did not exist among the English Liberal and Fabianist intellectuals who—uneasily and often against their own subconscious convictions—reacted against manifestations of English racial, or even patriotic, pride.

This belief in American uniqueness marked the American attitudes in 1914 as well as in 1917. When in 1914 Americans congratulated themselves that they were not like the old corrupt nations of Europe rushing at each other, and when in 1917 they assured themselves that their entry into the war meant the transformation of this last of the old corrupt wars into a crusade for something higher, for the benefit of all mankind, the substance of this self-righteous belief in their uniqueness was the same. The British, at least in 1914, entered the war for the sake of defending the balance of power in Europe, threatened as it was by Germany; their war aims were less high-flown than those of the Americans. The response of their people was no less patriotic for that.

The patriotism of the English people in 1914 must still arouse our admiration and wonder: for otherwise things had changed for them, and very much indeed. Between the Diamond Jubilee and the First World War the role of the British changed profoundly. Their imperial victory over the

---

Sewing Machine . . . I would say, take up the support of one or two or a dozen mission stations. . . . Everyone thus helped would be, consciously or unconsciously, a drummer for your goods, and the great church they represent at home would be your advertising agents."

Boers, their European alliances, their building of great dreadnoughts notwithstanding, the transformation of their empire had begun. They—Conservatives as well as Liberals—began to recognize not only that they needed the Americans behind them: they recognized, too, that their empire had become too costly, that there were responsibilities they could no longer afford. They recognized, at least they were beginning to recognize—and this could not have been more different from American beliefs—that democracy was not consistent with empire. That it was not consistent with their traditional role in Europe few of them recognized at all.

One of the chief proponents (if not creators) of the imperialist idea had been Disraeli. Yet it was Disraeli who even before 1871 mused about the meaning of a rising Germany: the unification of Germany, he said, was a revolution probably even greater than the French Revolution had been. He was entirely right, even though he and his successors did little about it. The greater her imperial tasks, the less attention Britain would pay to Europe. As a matter of fact, the imperial idea strengthened the anti-European inclinations of her people. As early as 1853 Tocqueville noticed this: "England is retiring from the interim struggle of the Continent and extending herself far and wide, as you yourself say," he wrote in a letter to one of his English friends, Henry Reeve. "This is what I call quitting the greatest theater of human affairs: for, after all, this theater is not in Sydney, not even in Washington, it is still in our old Europe." "Our great Empire," Lord Rosebery, the Liberal imperialist, mused in 1892, "has pulled us, so to speak, by the coattails out of the European system." The decision to seek the friendship of the United States at almost any cost was, I repeat, not merely the result of foreign policy calculations. It accorded with the natural inclinations and preferences of the British people, very much including that of a new, or renewed, governing class that was no longer composed of, or even led by, aristocrats with a cosmopolitan orientation and a European tradition.

The rise of this new group of people, as usual in the history of England, was gradual. The social, and at times even the political, power of the old aristocracy was still extant. The decision to make an *entente* with France in 1904, a milestone in the history of British foreign relations, was, again, not only the result of diplomatic or even strategic reckonings; cultural elements as well as the inclinations of a monarch (Edward VII, the last King of England who played an observant and active role in the foreign relations of his country) contributed to it in important ways. But between 1905 and 1908 there occurred another deep-going change. In January 1906 the Liberals won an election whose importance was at least twofold. By 1906 the last resemblance of the Liberals and the old Whigs ceased to exist; the Liberal program was no longer very different from that of Labour; both Liberals and Labourites were now partisans of democracy and of progress. This was one of the differences between this election and that of earlier Liberal triumphs; the other was that by 1906 the English aristocracy was losing its control of the government of Britain. It withdrew before the advance of democracy, abandoning its positions one by one. The Liberal budget of 1909 was the result of a typically British compromise. On the one hand Lloyd George's tax provisions of this "People's Budget" were the first step toward the development of a welfare state in Britain. On the other hand the British democracy was still nationalist: the British people wanted to have a navy superior to that of Germany. Yet a navy that would rule the seas of the world, a navy superior to both that of Germany and the United States, they no longer wanted to afford. It is interesting to note that the young Churchill, then a Liberal, gave his full support to Lloyd George, who wanted to cut the number of new dreadnought battleships to four. The Tories wanted at least six; the Navy and Lord Fisher wanted eight. It was Churchill's great and lasting merit that after he became First Lord of the Admiralty in 1911 he increased naval building to the extent that in 1914 the British Navy was well prepared. Yet its margin of superiority over the German High Sea Fleet was relatively narrow.

The inconsistency of empire with democracy was apparent elsewhere too. The transformation of the empire into a loose commonwealth had begun. The invention of dominion status was a liberal idea. By 1910 Canada, Australia, New Zealand, and South Africa were self-governing. When their loyalty to the mother country was put to the test in 1914, their patriotism and their contribution were unexceptionable; but as time went on these dominions were becoming Americanized rather than Anglicized. During the Second World War they were more dependent on the United States than on England.

During the first decade of the new century England herself became more and more American. On the level of popular culture, including journalism, the tastes and habits of many people were becoming Americanized. More important was the increasing similarity of the social distribution of power in the two nations. The United States had no aristocracy,‡ but it

‡ Perhaps for the first time in American history many of the American rich had nobilitarian aspirations. In Cussans's *Handbook of Heraldry* (London, 1893), p. 31, I found this passage: "Many people imagine—and none are more loud in the assertion than Americans themselves—that in the great Western Republic the species of gentilitial registration denominated Heraldry is uncared for. This, however, is far from being the fact. Even amongst the partisans of political equality there is a large majority anxious to exhibit their individual superiority. In proof of which, I may mention that a gentleman connected with the College of

had something akin to a governing class, which at the time was largely Anglo-Saxon, Protestant, a kind of middle upper class. In 1909 Arnold Bennett described the upper middle class as the ruling class of England: "Their assured, curt voices, their proud carriage, their clothes, the similarity of their manners, all show that they belong to a caste and that caste has been successful in the struggle for life. It is called the middle class, but it ought to be called the upper class, for nearly everything is below it." Successful in the struggle for life, the domination of such a class now depended on wealth more than on birth, in England as well as in the United States. It is not within the compass of this book, or even of this chapter, to examine the differences and the similarities between the American and the British upper classes of that period. Superficially speaking, they were similar. The term "Anglo-Saxon," referring to both Englishmen and Americans, became current in Europe even before the First World War. This corresponded with the larger, the Kiplingesque (or at least pseudo-Kiplingesque) vision of the world. Kipling had no particular affection—and, what is more important for a poet, no particular feeling—for the aristocracy of England. His dream—and in this he was not alone—was the vision of the Anglo-Saxon race as one large family, responsible for law and order across vast portions of the globe: *the* patrician people of the earth, their privileges being the outcome of their responsibilities. Yet, as is the wont of many a ruling class, very soon these people, or at least Bennett's people, were acting and thinking in terms of their privileges at the cost of their responsibilities. (An Edwardian writer such as Saki would see this: he would have few illusions about that class which Bennett admired and to which Bennett indeed wished to belong.) Perhaps even more important was the fact that the Victorian and Protestant ideals of their upbringing were no longer sufficient, except for standards of superficial deportment. In the 1890s Lord Cromer, the Viceroy of Egypt, addressed the boys of Leys School, Cambridge, telling them that they must keep three things in their minds: "Love your country, tell the truth, and don't dawdle." They did love their country, but they would not tell the truth, and they went on dawdling. The motto of the Boy Scouts, a prototypical institution of the period, one of the by-products of the Boer War, was: "Be prepared." Whatever their physical conditioning, the kind of people who made up the ranks of Scoutdom in England were not prepared for the realities of the world they had to face. They made themselves subject to the great and

Heralds recently informed me that the fees received from Americans constitute one of the most important sources of revenue of that Institution."

abiding shortcoming of the Anglo-Saxon: the unwillingness to think about unpleasant matters.

The Irish were such a matter. It was in Ireland, and in Ulster, that the deepest internal problem of the great British State boiled up before the sudden thunder of the Great War drowned it under (under but not out); and two years before the Great War it was in Belfast that the *Titanic* was launched, in the black iron shipyards of Harlan & Wolff. That name *Titanic,* the titanic trust in the tremendous black-and-red steel ship, the largest ever built, out of Ulster, Belfast, was symbolic of the titanic belief in Progress and Strength in an age ruled by the Northern and Atlantic and Protestant and Anglo-Saxon Sea-faring Races, of the titanic trust in Capital and in Science; and the fatal tragedy, the fatal wound by the icy underwater jag of hostile nature, a cold flash of terror, the sinking of the titanic vessel full of men and women of the governing classes of England and of America was a symbolic premonition of the historical catastrophe of 1914 that was to come, of the end of an age.

But only in retrospect. We must keep in mind that those in 1912 knew not what was to happen in 1914 and after. A man is hale and hearty, the center of respect, the cynosure of all eyes. Some time later he falls ill. A friend (or a doctor) now remembers: during that party, a few weeks earlier, he had seen a throbbing of a vein in his temple, or a strange shadow under his friend's eyes. Yet this man looked florid and prosperous; he *was* florid and prosperous, and that was what counted. Before 1914 it *seemed* that the Anglo-Saxons were the patrician people of the globe. That semblance was more than an illusion. That was what they believed; and that was what other people believed. So they were.

(4)

Well before the United States declared war on Germany and entered the great European war the phrase "world war" had become common—even though, unlike the Second World War, the First World War was principally, and almost exclusively, a European War. "World War" was a German *("Weltkrieg")* and an American phrase, like the World Series, inaccurate and grandiloquent, but somehow logical nonetheless: the greatest that the world has ever seen. The French called it the Great War, the British the European War or the German War for a long time, but then they, too, adopted the American usage. They shared a common language and institutions and even certain ideals, after all; now, for the first time in their history, they became allies and eventually joint victors in the war. Yet the victory in 1918 for the British (and for the French) turned out to be hollow. Their principal enemies recovered from their humiliating defeat in an amazing and, indeed, frightening manner; the British and the French recovered from their victory not at all.

Because of this we must, for a moment, reconsider the meaning of the year 1917, the turning point of the war. When the United States entered the war in 1917, this event, besides being the greatest turning point in American history, was the greatest event of the war. It decided the war for the Western Allies. Russia dropped out of the war, but America had come in. The Western Allies could thus defeat Germany without Russia, unlike twenty-five years later. All of this happened without a massive outpouring of American blood. The prestige of America weighed in the scale of the war even more than her actual power—especially since the war had become a monstrous stalemate, whereafter the American entry helped to tilt the balance. The question that arises—uneasily—in retrospect is whether the Allies (the British, rather than the French) would not have been better off without this American alliance in the long run. Had the United States not entered the war in 1917 a negotiated peace, principally between the British and the German empires, would have been a distinct possibility. The British would have kept their empire; the Germans would have kept their dominant position on the continent, at least within Central and Eastern Europe. Such a compromise peace would have prevented the coming of Hitler; it would probably have prevented Lenin and Stalin; it may have prevented a second world war. Whether it would have prevented the precipitous decline of European civilization is difficult to tell. In any event, the British dilemma would have remained the same: to seek an accommodation with Germany or with the United States. It is difficult to believe that they would have chosen the former over the latter; as in 1899 and again in 1940, they gave it hardly a thought.

By "they" I am referring to the government and to the governing classes of Britain. During the First World War in important ways they did not flinch or fail; in other ways they did. Their patriotism and their willingness to sacrifice themselves, if need be, was largely unexceptionable; they offered their flesh and their blood with the same determined courage which was typical of masses of the British soldiers during the war. Yet the vast and frequently senseless bloodletting of the armies in the fields of Flanders and Picardy was often due to the stupid and sometimes selfish policies of many of their generals. On the sea—that traditional British area of mastery—their seamanship was, at best, equal to that of the German newcomers, but no better. In the matter of high statecraft, too, British mastery was weakening. By 1918 the British Government allowed itself to be convinced not only by its powerful American allies but by all kinds of ephemeral propagandists to support the cause of national self-determination across Europe, the liberal and democratic ideas of the time having gained predominance over the older, more traditional, preferences of the Foreign Office. The British chose to support, rather than prevent, the dissolution of the Austro-Hungarian Empire in the center of Europe, an event with catastrophic consequences. The British policy in regard to the civil war in Russia, where the Bolsheviks were on the edge of defeat, was half-hearted; indeed, it was hardly a policy at all. Lloyd George, that compound of opportunism and statesmanship, was personally not in favor of the cruel and humiliating peace treaty imposed on the defeated Germans; but he did not effectively oppose his allies, especially not the demagogic press magnates of his own country. Outwardly British power and prestige in 1918 stood as high as ever. A few British officers, on occasion, ruled the affairs of entire countries and roamed freely in them. Communist commissars trembled for their favors; Arab potentates sought the smallest tokens of their friendship; a handshake or a salute from a British colonel or from a British commissioner assured the reputation of their local recipient in the view of his most powerful countrymen.* On 18 November 1918 Lord Curzon spoke in the House of Lords: "The British flag has never flown over a more powerful or a more united empire. . . . Never did our voice count more in the councils of nations; or in determining the future destinies of mankind." This was more than grandiloquence; there was reality behind it; yet this reality was temporary and brittle. It did not last.

The greatest power in the world in 1918 was the United States. She won the war with ease. The financial center of the world had gone from London to New York. The President of the United States was the universally admired statesman of the world. The American Century had begun. True, the United States had to share the victory with Britain, France, Italy, Japan; but these were not allies to be feared, unlike the Soviet Union after the end of the Second World War. It is at least arguable that in the history of the world, and of the United States, the zenith of American power was 1918, even more than 1945. In any event, the pride of the American people in their uniqueness and in their power was boundless. "Pride" is not something that can be quantified or scientifically described; but it is a decisive

* In 1919 a handful of British officers and soldiers, driving north from the Caspian, drove into Tsaritsyn—the city that was to be renamed Stalingrad and which an entire German Army failed to conquer twenty-five years later.

factor in human affairs nonetheless. Whether we call it pride, or self-confidence, this was the factor, beneath all of the tergiversations of political rhetoric and the calculations of statesmanship, that had propelled the United States into the First World War.

In 1914 Americans prided themselves (often in self-righteous and sanctimonious tones) for being exceptional, untouched by yet another bloody welter of a reactionary European war. By 1917 they were itching to get into the war, to show the world what Americans could do, to offer (and impose, if need be) their enlightened American standards on the world at large. How this revolution of popular sentiment and public opinion occurred has been the subject of many histories, though perhaps it still awaits a magisterial summing-up. It is a difficult subject, because of the texture of American history, since it developed on different levels; the desire of American self-assertion, the tactlessness of German statecraft, the ability of British propaganda, the President, the press, the American social and political elite, independently and together, played parts in it. What Americans wanted from their intervention (or from their isolation) was not at all clear. This did not matter; what mattered was the overwhelming strength of the American belief in America's primacy in the world, a belief even stronger than the desire for American self-assertion. A year after the outbreak of the war in Europe the American desire of getting involved was already evident. The liberal *New Republic* wrote on 30 October 1915, "That calm moral grandeur in which we revelled a year ago, when it seemed as if we were destined to be the arbiter of nations, is no more. . . . Instead of the thankfulness that we are providentially escaping the storm, one finds on every hand the sense that we are missing something."

Yet during the First World War (as indeed in almost every American war) there was a division among the American people, a division that would prevail among them before and during the Second World War, indeed, perhaps during the entire first half of the twentieth century. This division was superficially that between isolationists and internationalists. In reality it was a division between Americans of different national and cultural inclinations. There were a fair number of American pacifists, including Henry Ford, who in 1915 chartered a ridiculous Peace Ship, and who said that anyone who chose to be a soldier was either "lazy or crazy"; but Ford believed in American uniqueness and moral superiority just the same. Truly principled pacifists or isolationists were few; most of them were pacifists because they were socialists or Germanophiles or Anglophobes or Russophobes, not the other way around. What was significant was the gradual and, in the end, irreversible rallying of the Anglo-American population to the Allied cause. This was true not only of the Anglo-

American elite but of the population of the Old South, too, who, partly because of the southern military tradition, partly because of their Anglo-Saxon origin, were unaffected by isolationism during both world wars, in spite of their suspicions of Wall Street, of international bankers, city people, and the North—suspicions and hostility which the South in domestic politics shared with the populists of the Midwest and the West.

During the second decade of the twentieth century the influence of the Anglo-American elite in the United States was still very strong. This was a cultural preference, not merely a reaction to older, racial ties. We have seen that the First World War corresponded with the zenith of the American bourgeois interlude: and American bourgeois society was, largely though not exclusively, pro-British and pro-French—because of its own cultural traditions and preferences that were in contrast with much of the Kaiser's Germany that was tactless, aggressive, vulgar. These cultural inclinations were naturally strongest in the East; and, as Professor Henry F. May wrote in his fine *The End of American Innocence,* "The country became united for war, but those who thought that the West had finally accepted Eastern views were due for a series of postwar shocks."† Opposed to American intervention were Anglophobes such as German-Americans, Irish-Americans, Scandinavian-Americans, western populists, and, until 1917, Russophobe Jews.‡ By 1917 the gigantic public emotion of American nationalism submerged that muted opposition in an oceanic wave; but that opposition was submerged without sinking far beneath the surface, and dissolved not at all.

I wrote in the beginning of this chapter that the American entry into

† P. 371. In his bibliography May judiciously states, "The fact that defenders of the older culture almost always were strong partisans of the Allied cause is well known, though it has not received much analysis [from historians]" (p. 412). Among the older New England "custodians of culture" May cites George Edward Woodberry, who, in January 1916, "rejoicing in the emergence of a firmer pro-Allied tone, was sorry that he could not call it national: 'Thank God that it is Eastern, at least—ashes, at least of the old powers of devotion and insight still warm in the old soil. . . .' " Barrett Wendell in March 1916: "I had not before quite understood . . . the degree to which, in other parts of America than this, the traditional dislike of England has prevented the vulgar from admitting to themselves the full monstrosity of Germany" (p. 366).

‡ The Balfour Declaration was connected with this. In the secret Anglo-Russian negotiations as early as March 1916—a year and a half before the Balfour Declaration—the British Foreign Secretary Lord Grey "frankly admitted that he was considering an espousal of Zionism because of the probably political consequences among which would be 'the turning to the side of the Allies of the Jewish elements in the East, in the United States and in other places, elements at the present time hostilely inclined to a significant degree to the cause of the Allies.' " C. Jay Smith, *The Russian Struggle for Power, 1914–1917* (New York, 1956), p. 419.

the war assured the victory of Britain in the short run while it contributed to the decline of the British Empire in the long run. This was involved with another long-range factor which has not yet received either the attention or the general agreement of historians. This was the influence of Woodrow Wilson: or, rather, of the ideas that he represented. Again we must distinguish between the short and the long run of events. Wilson's influence on the war and on its outcome was tremendous but short-lived: it lasted only two years, from 1917 to 1919. In the long run the influence of his ideas has proved to be enormous and enduring. He was the President who led the United States into the First World War and presided over it. He enunciated the ideas and established the American tradition of internationalism. In the short run this internationalism was opposed and defeated by the Republican Party and repudiated by the majority of the American people. In the long run this did not matter. Within the United States his influence transcended his lifetime as well as that of the political parties. Herbert Hoover (who wrote a biography of Wilson) as well as Franklin Roosevelt, John Foster Dulles (who began his "diplomatic" career under Wilson), Dean Rusk, Bernard Baruch, Jimmy Carter (like Wilson, a peculiar Southerner who wanted to be a Yankee), Eleanor Roosevelt, Richard Nixon (who, when occupying the White House in 1968, asked for Wilson's desk), Ronald Reagan (whose middle name is Wilson) have been Wilsonians. This was a tragedy for the United States, for the simple reason (the reason is simple but its components are complicated) that Wilson's ideas about the world and about the relations of nations were inadequate, insubstantial, and generally wrong. This was a tragedy for the world at large, not only because of Wilson's failure during the peacemaking in 1918 and 1919, but mainly because of the American espousal of his principal idea of national self-determination (a leftover from the British liberal storehouse of ideals in the nineteenth century), from which ultimately enemies of Western civilization such as Hitler and savage dictators in Africa and Asia were to profit. Thomas Woodrow Wilson and Vladimir Ilyich Lenin were contemporaries, who died ten days apart (the latter on 24 January, the former on 2 February 1924). It was the idea of the former, not of the latter—national self-determination and not proletarian revolution—that turned out to be the principal factor in the history of the rest of the century. It was this pale, long-toothed Princeton professor, rather than the Tartar-skulled leader of the Bolsheviks, who turned out to be the real revolutionary.

This is not the place to analyze the character of Woodrow Wilson, whose ideas were simple while his character was not simple at all. What was characteristic of Wilson was not so much hypocrisy, as his enemies were wont to state; it was his, alas, often typically American and intellectual, split-mindedness. He possessed, indeed, he took unusual pride in possessing, two sets of ideas that were contradictory, without recognizing (and, of course, without wishing to recognize) their contradictions. In some respects Wilson was a representative of a certain degeneration of the Anglo-American mind. There was a peculiar, at times almost death-like, bloodlessness in the illusory idealism of this man, as vulnerable to reality as his body was vulnerable to the first stroke that laid him low when his influence had begun to slip in September 1919 and from which he would never recover. With all of his "advanced" and progressive ideas (it was Wilson, rather than Theodore Roosevelt, who was the quintessential American Progressive) there was something in him that was preternaturally old; and so were the categories of his mind. While his knowledge and interest in European civilization were minimal, his mind was formed by nonconformist, Presbyterian, legalistic, and moralistic categories of ideas that had been held by certain Englishmen and Scotsmen and New Englanders during the Victorian Age, Gladstonian at best, and hopelessly outdated at the worst. This kind of thinking was not typical of those who were in charge of British diplomacy, which was why the British representatives did not comprehend Wilson in the beginning—as the British ambassador in Washington in his famous conversation with Wilson about Mexico. Wilson had told him that the American purpose was to teach democracy to the Mexicans. But suppose they don't want it? the Englishman asked. Then we shall force it down their throats, the President retorted. This was the same man who during that year (1913) said, convincedly and convincingly, that the United States "was the only idealist country in the world." This schoolmasterish compound of idealism and vengefulness, of narrowmindedness that could be rigid beyond belief and a broadmindedness that was so broad as to be flat, was sorrily typical of Wilson. Yet its sources are not simply attributable to his character. He was a peculiar, but not untypical, representative of American progressivism, with its mixture of idealism and scientism. In 1913 David Starr Jordan, another prototypical Progressive, then the chancellor of Stanford University, whose public convictions eventually veered from imperialism to pacifism, wrote a small book, *America's Conquest of Europe* (published, perhaps significantly, by the American Unitarian Association in Boston) in which the propositions, and at times the very wording, were identical with many of the Fourteen Points that Wilson enunciated five years later.*

* About American imperialism: "Instead of exploitation, we have brought to the Philippines education and sanitation. We have expended on them a hundred times more than we

When the War of 1914 broke out, Wilson's first reaction was that "Europe is still governed by the same reactionary forces as of old . . ."—of which the United States had been cleansed long ago. But this kind of self-righteous isolationism was already compounded with interventionism in his mind. In the same speech he declared to Europe, "I say to you that the old order is dead. It is my part . . . to aid in composing those differences . . . that the new order, which shall have its foundation on human liberty and human rights, shall prevail." He said earlier that "it would be the irony of fate, if my administration had to deal chiefly with foreign affairs." While irony was, and remained, foreign to his mind, it was not fate but Wilson who would soon present himself as something like the president of the world. In 1914 he defined all of Europe, implicitly including Britain, as typical of the old order of corrupted international morality. He exhorted Americans to stay aloof until the belligerents were worn out. Then the United States could create "an association of nations, all bound together for the protection of the integrity of each. . . . We are the mediating nation of the world. . . . We are compounded of the nations of the world. . . . We are, therefore, able to understand all nations." This from a man who knew little, and understood nothing, of the history and of the national character of the European states, and whose comprehension of the relations of nations was consequently insubstantial. Gradually the British recognized that they had little to fear from Wilson and from American progressivism. Their victory against Germany would be assured by the entry of the American crusader into the war. What they did not recognize was that the Wilsonian and progressive idea of Making The World Safe for Democracy was not altogether different from the other American nationalist idea to the effect that What Was Good for America Was Good for the World. In the fall of 1918 the Germans were ready to accept peace on the basis of Wilson's public principles (they also knew that they had less to fear from the Americans than from the British and the French), but Wilson would not respond to the Germans until they compounded their sur-

---

have received, and if ever imperialism can be respectable we have made it so" (pp. 4–5). The subchapter entitled "Open Diplomacy" (pp. 32–36): "Another lesson which the U.S. may teach is the value of open diplomacy. A secret treaty or a secret agreement of any kind on the part of our Department of State has no validity whatever. . . . The secret treaty in the interest of imperial spoilation is the bane of Europe. . . . The secret treaty, the concession to a friendly power, the artificial interference with a rival—all these belong to the days of Machiavelli . . . ; "The Control of the Sea" (pp. 37–38): "America has never claimed such control, nor has she admitted any such right for others. . . . America has stood for the open sea. . . . To make the high seas an open highway to be traversed at any time in absolute safety by any vessel whatever would go far toward doing away with international war. . . . The nation should join to make the ocean safe for their mutual use. . . . It is never good business, as Franklin once observed, 'to knock your customers on the head.' "

render with the abolition of the German monarchy. That this kind of ideological democratism was disastrous should be obvious in retrospect. Had the Kaiser abdicated in favor of his son and of a constitutional monarchy, Adolf Hitler may have remained unknown to the world, outliving Wilson, Roosevelt, Churchill, Stalin, ending his life as a retired painter somewhere in Bavaria.

The First World War, unlike the Second, was followed by three or four more years of chaos and confusion, by armed defiance of some of the peace treaties, and by civil wars, including that within Russia. All of this had a lasting and profound effect on the relations of the American and the British empires. America's withdrawal from Europe, whereof the Republicans' repudiation of Wilson was but part, meant that the British could count less and less on American support; the Republican nationalists who succeeded Wilson in power had no desire to share the American primacy in the world with the British Empire. One of the civil wars raging in the world was the one in Ireland. In March 1919 the U.S. House of Representatives passed a resolution in favor of the Sinn Fein; the Senate followed suit; the Hearst press supported the Irish vociferously; the new breed of radical isolationists, western senators such as Hiram Johnson and William Borah, Progressives to the core, opposed "imperialism" (including intervention in Russia), by which they meant particularly the British and French empires. The British watched this potential American-Irish alliance carefully, trying their best (and sometimes their worst) to suppress its existence in their own press, hoping that it would go away, ready to do almost anything to avoid trouble with the United States. Their decision not to renew their twenty-year alliance with Japan in 1921 was closely connected with their Irish anxieties and their American calculations. Japan and Great Britain had both profited from their alliance made twenty years earlier; but now the British thought that they had to choose between sharing their naval and colonial domination of the Far East with Japan or abdicating a good part of it for the sake of keeping the United States from becoming suspicious and hostile. They knew that certain American admirals were demanding a fleet big enough to fight eventually an Anglo-Japanese alliance in the Pacific.[13] In 1921 the British decided not to renew the Japanese alliance and to partition Ireland, with most of that island becoming a "Free State," connected with England but with a few remnant formalities. It was a paradoxical phase in the history of the two empires. The United States seemed to have retreated into isolation, the British Empire seemed to be as great and puissant as ever. In reality the American empire was still growing in size (soon American marines would be laying down the law in Nicaragua), while the dissolution of the British Empire moved toward its decisive stage.

(5)

Between the two world wars the Americanization of England—and, even more, of her dominions—went on. The movies and the gramophone, jazz dancing and the cocktail shaker: these things became part of English lives, including the lives of people who had been previously unaffected by them. Even American slang, for the first time, penetrated the English language, though American pronunciation not yet. (That was to come during the second half of the century, when a more-or-less classless and faintly transatlantic accent began to replace official British pronunciation, and when the Canadian and the midwestern American accents had become almost identical.) Most people of the English upper classes and most English intellectuals still maintained their anti-American prejudices,† while they were more and more dependent on American emoluments and royalties. During the gray, depressing years of the 1930s the Prince of Wales fell in love with an American divorcee. He was a small man, foppish and largely brainless, selfish to the point of irresponsibility, and weak; she was square-jawed, oddly smart-looking, determined, and stronger than he. He became King Edward VIII and wanted to marry her. In a last rally of politic puritanism the respectable authorities of the United Kingdom resisted this. He could not get his way and abdicated. This was not necessarily in accord with the sentiments of the British people. For everyone who repeated the wag about the King's signing up as the Third Mate on an American tramp there were many others who minded the prospects of this royal Anglo-American alliance not at all. In reality the romance of Edward and Wallis was one of the last degenerating examples of that glittering long series of Anglo-American marriages that bound many of the English and the American upper classes together for about two generations, sixty years. One of Winston Churchill's mistakes was his sentimental support of the King's cause during the Abdication Crisis in 1936. But,

† Those Englishmen and Englishwomen who turned sympathetic to the evangel of communism as represented by the Soviet Union did so for a number of reasons (or, rather, rationalizations); in some instances one of their reasons was their rejection of what they saw (or, rather, pretended to see) as the vulgar materialism of the United States.

then, Churchill himself was half-American: his enthusiasm for the prospect of an Anglo-American royal family prevented him from recognizing the fatal character weakness of this king.

While the Americanization of England progressed, the Anglo-American presence in American life was weakening. Again this was evident on various levels. Behind the excrescence of the anti-German hysteria during the last year of World War I, behind the Red Scare a year or two afterward, behind the wave of anti-European and nativist sentiment that led to the swift passage of the restrictive Immigration Act of 1921, we can detect a sense of anxiety felt by many Anglo-Americans. Yet the roots of the isolationism and nationalism and missionary puritanism of the postwar years, leading to things such as the Prohibition Amendment, were populist rather than progressive—meaning that they were often Anglophobe, and not shared by the American upper classes. On one level this was not directly attributable to national or ethnic origins; vocal Anglophobes such as the mayor of Chicago or leaders of the Ku Klux Klan were Anglo-American in origin, as were various demagogic politicians in Texas, Ohio, Illinois, Wisconsin, who ordered references favorable to the English expunged from American textbooks, and who passed bills declaring that the official language of their state should be known thereafter as the *American,* not *the English,* language. During the twenties many Americans regarded English phrases or English dress or English social customs as somewhat affected, effeminate, slightly ridiculous. On another political level the influence of the Anglophobe German-Americans, Irish-Americans, and Scandinavian-Americans was rising. On the intellectual level H. L. Mencken led a crusade against the old Anglo-American dependence on English linguistic habits: English diction, to him, had "a mauve, Episcopalian, and ephebian ring."‡ Yet Mencken was only a hyperbolic articulator of a process that developed during the twenties: the final emancipation (if that is the word) of American literary culture from its English traditions and forebears. T. S. Eliot was the last important American writer to become an Englishman. By the 1930s it was Hemingway who was being imitated (that his "direct" style was curiously old-fashioned, that he was influenced by French and Russian short-story writers of the late nineteenth century, was seen by few people).

During the twenties the older Anglo-American classes (they were

‡ It is, of course, true that the habit—ingrained in the English middle and upper classes during the nineteenth century—of speaking from the back of the throat with conscious restraint, without opening the mouth widely (as G. N. Routh once put it, "keeping a 'stiff upper lip' labially as well as morally"), was very different from American habits of speech.

mostly Republicans and liberal isolationists, except in the South) still felt as close to England as before; England represented to them something that was ancient and stable within themselves. The churches and the college buildings they had financed during the twenties followed, more than ever before or after, English Gothic and Tudor models. During the twenties, too—somewhat like the English public school tradition—the place where he went to college was the determining mark of a young American's social position and status and even of his values. This continued through his entire life through the American alumni spirit. Probably, Henry Seidel Canby mused in the 1930s,

> many of the traits that had made the twentieth century American in business and the professions a strongly marked national type . . . are really traits of the alumni of the old American colleges. We Americans should have become in these decades more, not less, European, for since the Civil War a vast immigration has flooded in everywhere except the South, modifying the physical type, especially in the cities. And yet the typical reactions of the country . . . have remained characteristically un-European, and better explained by the American past, than by an Italian-American or German-American present. This stabilizing of character and temperament, and also of prejudice, is probably due to the college graduate, for our alumni strengthened their bonds and gained in class consciousness just when the so-called old American was losing his grip.*

Note that Canby writes of the "old" colleges, Yale, Harvard, Princeton, which in the twenties were still predominantly, indeed, overwhelmingly, Anglo-American, though not overwhelmingly eastern. Even in the metropolises of the Midwest and the West the American upper classes were largely Anglo-American. In Evan Connell's novel *Mrs. Bridge* there is a moving passage when the protagonist, a diffident and decent and not too well-educated wife of a lawyer from Kansas City, visits England in the late thirties:

> They landed at Southampton long before dawn and took the train to London. It was a rainy morning and most of the passengers dozed, but Mrs. Bridge stayed awake and stared out the train window, a trifle

* Canby, *Alma Mater* (New York, 1936), p. 240. A much less serious repetition of this phenomenon in the 1970s was the national projection of "preppy" standards as identical with those of an American upper class.

> groggily, at the silent, stately, fogbound farmland. And as this train carried her across the English countryside, past cottages she had never seen and would never see again, where great birds nested in the chimney crook, and from the hedgerows smaller birds came fluttering in shrill desperation to circle twice and then, finding nothing, to settle as before, and where the cattle in the mist grazed unperturbed by the train which rolled on and on beneath the somnolent English sky, as though there were no destination, past the rain-drenched, redolent fields, and the trees which cast no shadow, she thought to herself how familiar it was and that once this must have been her home. Yes, she said to herself slowly, yes, I was here before.†

Meanwhile the ties that held the British Empire together were weakening. Evelyn Waugh later called the twenties "the last decade of Englishmen's grandeur," but he was wrong. The number of English intellectuals who still believed in Empire had dwindled to near-nothing.‡ More important was a shift in social attitudes. Before the First World War the idea of the Empire, and of imperial service, was held high, often as a kind of patrimony, by the upper as well as by the middle classes of Britain. After the First World War (with exceptions, of course) the ideal was still held by the middle classes here and there but by the aristocracy less and less. Even more important was the weakened conviction among the politicians and the government. Before the First World War Santayana would still write admiringly, "Anglo-Saxon imperialism is unintended; military conquests are incidental to it and often not maintained; it subsists by a mechanical equilibrium of habits and interests, in which every colony, province, or protectorate has a different status." By 1931, when the Statute of Westminster nominally changed the empire into a commonwealth, these differences

† Evan Connell, *Mrs. Bridge* (New York, 1959), p. 158. He continues, "In London the hotel was just off Piccadilly Circus; they had some difficulty understanding the hall porter and the maid; and, in fact, at the desk or on the telephone they found it necessary to listen closely. Mrs. Bridge, unpinning her hat as she stood before the mirror in their room—a black straw hat it was, with a shiny cluster of plastic cherries on the brim—replied to her husband's comment, 'I agree with you, but don't you suppose we sound funny to them too?' "

‡ The publication of E. M. Forster's *Passage to India* in 1924 was an important event: it contributed to the widespread acceptance of the idea that Empire was wrong. It took a supremely honest and intelligent Indian, Nirad Chaudhuri, to recognize this influence and to state this thirty years later. In this respect George Orwell, another anti-imperialist, was more honest than Forster. In his classic essay "Shooting an Elephant," Orwell wrote, "A white man mustn't be frightened in front of 'natives'; and so, in general he isn't frightened"—an expression of a state of mind of which Forster was hardly capable. In Orwell's *Burmese Days* (London, 1934), his anti-imperialism, even more straightforward than Forster's, is there; but so is his recognition that the Burmese were no better than the English.

of status had become sources of weakness as well as of strength. The motive elements in the decline of the British Empire—as indeed those during its rise—were quite different from those in the case of the Spanish or the French. Toward the end of his life Santayana saw this:

> England, for instance, in the eighteenth and early nineteenth centuries, acted the great power with conviction; she was independent, mistress of the sea, and sure of her right to dominion. Difficulties and even defeats, such as the loss of the American Colonies, did not in the least daunt her; her vitality at home and her liberty abroad remained untouched. But gradually, though she suffered no final military defeat, the heart seemed to fail her for so vast an enterprise. It was not the colonies she had lost that maimed her, but those she had retained or annexed. Ireland, South Africa, and India became thorns in her side. The bloated industries which helped her to dominate the world made her incapable of feeding herself; they committed her to forced expansion, in order to secure markets and to secure supplies. But she could no longer be warlike with a good conscience; the virtuous thing was to bow one's way out and say: My mistake. Her kings were half-ashamed to be kings, her liberals were half-ashamed to govern, her Church was half-ashamed to be Protestant. All became a medley of sweet reasonableness, stupidity, and confusion. Being a great power was now a great burden. It was urgent to reduce responsibility, to reduce armaments, to refer everything to conferences, to support the League of Nations, to let everyone have his own way abroad, and to let everyone have his own way at home. Had not England always been a champion of liberty? But wasn't it time now for the champion to retire? And wouldn't liberty be much freer without a champion?[14]

The Japanese had begun to sense this; so had the Chinese;* so had Gandhi; so had Mussolini. (Curiously enough, Hitler and Stalin had not. The former professed to admire the British imperial mission, he wanted to share the world with them; the latter was an imperialist at heart.) During the 1930s the instruments of British power had grown so weak that the

* K. M. Panikkar (a not altogether honest writer) in *Asia and Western Dominance* (New York, 1956), called World War I "The European Civil War." In 1926 "even the 'old China hands,' who had watched with regret the sudden [I would say "gradual"] eclipse of European prestige, though they acted the Blimps in their clubs, never seriously felt that Western authority could be re-established over China by the use of gunboats. There was no conviction left of the European's superiority or sense of vision" (p. 265). As early as 1915 Japanese marine infantry helped the British restore order in Singapore when Indian troops had mutinied there.

government and the Sea Lords thought they could not afford to threaten Italy with war when Mussolini invaded Abyssinia. Their response to Japanese aggression in the Far East was similar. These decisions—or, rather, these muddled retreats—were taken with the ominous prospect of a rising Germany in mind. Forty years before the British had advanced their overseas empire at the cost of abandoning their active role in Europe. Now the time had come to do the reverse. Yet before 1939—that is, before the time they began to have some evidence of eventual American support against Germany—they chose to acquiesce in Hitler's domination of Central and Eastern Europe, too, provided that the new Germany's conquests were done without warring and within certain limits.

Behind all of these compromises lay their relationship to the United States. This relationship gradually, and at times imperceptibly, progressed from their acquiescence in American superiority to their principal dependence on American power. During the 1920s this was not yet altogether clear. The British abdicated to American preferences with their cancellation of the Japanese alliance in 1921 and in their acceptance of American naval superiority at the 1922 Washington Conference. As late as 1927 the estimates of the United States Navy considered the possibility of an eventual war with Britain (this led to the Republicans' Big Navy program in 1928). Yet these curious facts (as well as Roosevelt's threat in 1934 to move against some British possessions in the Pacific if the British are "even suspected of playing with Japan as against playing with us") are subjects of piquant footnotes for historical researchers, nothing else. During the thirties the relations of the American and British elites and governments actually improved; and by 1939 Churchill and Roosevelt emerged as the two protagonists of determined resistance against Hitler, even though Neville Chamberlain was still the British Prime Minister.

This was all to the good, except for two miscalculations that had large effects in the long run. Churchill, whose contacts, political and social, were those with the American governing class, and whose view of the United States was both more optimistic and realistic than Chamberlain's, did not really recognize to what extent the influence of the Anglo-Saxon element had weakened in the United States, and not only numerically. Roosevelt, whose view of the world was more spacious and more informed than Wilson's, believed that sea power was still the key to history. The new German Navy, no matter how capable, was no match for the combined Anglo-American navies; American naval power would eventually conquer Japan. Yet, all of their superiority notwithstanding, the British and American empires together could not have conquered Germany had it not been for the Russians, who chewed up most of the German land army in the east.

(6)

The Second World War was the apogee of what the English since then preferred to call the "special" Anglo-American relationship. It was one of the closest alliances in the history of modern nations. It was the closest alliance in the thousand-year history of the English people. Roosevelt and Churchill were its architects and orchestrators; yet the man who brought it about was Hitler. He hoped, before the war and even in 1940, at the time of his greatest triumphs, that the British would accept his mastery of Europe while he would leave their empire intact. He did not understand that the British, and especially a man like Churchill, would rather transfer their empire to the Americans piece by piece than make such a settlement. There were evidences of this even before the war began. As early as the summer of 1939 when the King and Queen of England for the first time visited the United States, British officials accompanying them confidentially offered British naval bases to the United States, including Bermuda and two islands in the Caribbean. During the first nine months of the war, even before the fall of France, the British made no important military or diplomatic move without their consideration of American opinion. That was the other side of the coin. During the winter of 1938–39 Roosevelt decided—secretly and carefully—to support those who would resist and, if need be, fight Hitler. The British did not and could not know (neither did Roosevelt) when the United States would actually enter the war. What they knew was that, unlike in 1914, the President of the United States was wholeheartedly behind them against Germany, in one way or another.

Well before Pearl Harbor the Anglo-American alliance had become a *de facto* reality. When the war broke out in September 1939 Roosevelt told the American people that even though the Republic was neutral he did not and could not expect them to be neutral in sentiment. Thereafter he had to wend his way through the obstacles of Congress, isolationists, and Anglophobes—and the effects of the time lag whereby the popular reaction against the memories of the First World War had materialized in neutralist legislation twenty years after that war, in the 1930s when a savage and new Germany was rising again. Perhaps unduly aware of the opposition, he moved carefully and often disingenuously. Still the evolution of his support to Britain from 1939 to 1941 was impressive. His repeal of the Neutrality Act, his warnings and condemnations of Mussolini preceded the fall of France. One of the first moves of Churchill, who, by coincidence, became Prime Minister the very day Hitler's assault on France, Holland, and Belgium began, was to turn to Roosevelt, with whom he had corresponded since the beginning of the war. Churchill had to raise the possibility that a British government (another one than his) might be forced to accept terms from Hitler if American support were not swiftly forthcoming, and that during such negotiations the one card left to the British would be the existence of their fleet. Roosevelt did not like that; he preferred a British commitment that in the event of a British catastrophe the British fleet would sail to Canada and to the United States. Eventually this awful alternative disappeared. Churchill and the British showed their will to resist Hitler even after France had fallen. It was then, after two uneasy months, that Roosevelt and the American administration decided to come down on the side of Britain, at the very moment (31 July–2 August 1940) when Hitler, for the first time, considered that Russia might have to be eliminated in order to bring the British (and, indirectly, the Americans) to their senses.

He offered fifty old American destroyers to Britain, a naval move without appreciable strategic import but with great significance, an obviously unneutral act. During the next fifteen months, from the summer of 1940 until Pearl Harbor, Roosevelt proclaimed that the United States was the arsenal of democracy; he transformed large stores of material to Britain on Lend-Lease, that is, on unlimited credit; he ordered American troops into Iceland and Greenland; he extended the American operational sphere to the Middle Atlantic; in short, he engaged the United States in an undeclared war with Germany. Hitler understood this: he ordered German ships and submarines not to respond to any kind of American provocation. Eventually his Japanese allies did in the Pacific what Hitler did not want to do in the Atlantic: they attacked the Americans and propelled a largely united country into the war.

Whether Churchill thought that American supplies alone ("Give us the tools; and we shall finish the job") would be sufficient for Britain to defeat Germany is doubtful. By 1941 it was obvious that nothing short of the full and wholehearted military participation of the United States would do. It must be said for Churchill that, grateful and expectant of American support though he was, his attitude during this crucial time was never undignified or even unduly hasty. There were inspiring moments during this difficult period of partnership. In August 1941 came the First Summit: Churchill crossed the Atlantic to meet Roosevelt off Newfoundland, where they, among other things, drafted the so-called Atlantic Charter (an improvement over the Fourteen Points, it had only eight) proclaiming the war aims of Great Britain and the United States, even though the latter was not yet officially in the war.

> On Sunday morning, August 10, Mr. Roosevelt came aboard H.M.S. *Prince of Wales* and, with his Staff officers and several hundred representatives of all ranks of the U.S. Navy and Marines, attended Divine Service on the quarterdeck. This service was felt by us all to be a deeply moving expression of the unity of faith of our two peoples, and none who took part in it will forget the spectacle presented that sunlit morning on the crowded quarterdeck—the symbolism of the Union Jack and the Stars and Stripes draped side by side on the pulpit; the American and British chaplains sharing in the reading of the prayers; the highest naval, military and air officers of Britain and the United States grouped in one body behind the President and me; the close-packed ranks of British and American sailors, completely intermingled, sharing the same books and joining fervently together in the prayers and hymns familiar to both. . . . I chose the hymns myself. . . . Every word seemed to stir the heart. It was a great hour to live. Nearly half those who sang were soon to die.[15]

(The *Prince of Wales* was sunk four months later in the warm waters of the Malay Sea, the death knell of the British Empire in the East.) When the news of the Japanese attack on Pearl Harbor came to Churchill's dining room on 8 December the American ambassador, sitting there, had to restrain Churchill from rushing to declare war on Japan on the instant: the news had to be verified first. Yet, as Harold Nicolson recorded in his diary two days after Pearl Harbor, "Not an American flag flying in the whole of London. How odd we are!"

The difficulties between Roosevelt and Churchill were yet to come. These were mostly due to Roosevelt. As the war went on the two leaders met more and more often. The volumes of their written and telephonic communications increased. Yet their differences of opinion grew. These differences never endangered the essence of the Anglo-American alliance, mostly because of Churchill, who was not only fully aware of his dependence on the United States but who was also magnanimous and forgiving. Still it was because of these differences—or, rather, because of the increasing number of instances when Roosevelt's view of the world prevailed over Churchill's—that the Second World War ended, as Churchill would call it in the last volume of his war memoirs, in *Triumph and Tragedy:* tragedy, because of the brutal division of Europe and the crystallizing cold war with Russia. Various historians, including this author, have dealt with the Churchill-Roosevelt-Stalin relationship in various books. The most interesting and the most significant of the differences in this triangular relationship were those between Roosevelt and Churchill, and not between either of them and Stalin. That Stalin was an entirely different animal was only to be expected. What was not to be expected—and what Churchill had not expected, at least for some time—was how many of the Wilsonian-Progressive ideas of American internationalism lived on in Roosevelt's mind, how dominant they were within the circle on whom (also because of his advancing feebleness) Roosevelt came to depend more and more. Apart from the personal issue (Roosevelt's vanity rankled against a recognition of Churchill's intellectual superiority), and apart from the self-evident fact that as the war went on the American contribution superseded that of the British, stood the greater issue: their different views of history, and consequently of the state of the world. It was not merely strategic calculation (his recognition of the Russian contribution in the war against Germany, and the eventual American dependence on Russia coming into the war against Japan) that led to his disturbing, and eventually disastrous, attitude, which was personal as well as political: distancing himself from Churchill when in the presence of Stalin, refusing to listen to Churchill's propositions and prospects toward the end of the war. As the end of the war approached, Churchill (he, too, was getting worn and tired) could discern not only the alarming prospect of Russia extending her sphere to the very middle of Europe; he also saw that his lifetime vision of an ever close Anglo-American partnership was not getting closer to realization.

Roosevelt's mind, rather than Roosevelt's character, was responsible for much of this. This great President's mind was not very original. Most of his ideas were representative of—indeed, they were repetitions of—the intellectual categories and states of mind current in Washington and among the American governing elite during the Second World War. The better people among them were not Anglophobes: they admired Churchill for his magnificent role in 1940. But they fully shared—indeed, some of them had helped to crystallize—Roosevelt's views about the historical situation of the United States between Russia and Britain. Most of them thought that empires no longer had reason to exist. Some thought that the British were showing signs of decadence. All believed that as America went so would the world—including Russia, which, once a member of the United Nations (another reconstituted Wilsonian idea) would become progressively more democratic, international, institutionalized, Americanized. As far as Russia went, British policy was relatively simple: half of Europe (the eastern half) dominated by Russia was preferable to all of Europe (including Western Europe) dominated by Germany. What Churchill wanted to do was to establish the maximum reasonable limits of Russian domination in Eastern Europe, by agreement with Stalin and aided by an Anglo-American military presence in the middle of the Continent. Roosevelt and his advisers prevented Churchill from descending on the western Balkans, from trying to get into Berlin, Vienna, and Prague before the Russians, and from putting some kind of pressure on Stalin for the sake of avoiding the complete Sovietization of Eastern Europe at the end of the war. That Churchill could not have his way was due not only to the presence of Communists and of pseudo-Communists in Washington (whose influence, at times, was not inconsiderable). It was the result of the ideas, and of the preferences, of the entire American leadership, including Stimson, Marshall, Eisenhower, Stettinius, Frankfurter, Hopkins, of the War Department as well as of the State Department, of old New England Republicans as well as liberals, of lawyers and of generals, including some who would soon become the world leaders of anti-communism. Their minds were not in harmony with Churchill's; they were in harmony with the state of respectable American opinion. There was a deadening uniformity of American public opinion toward the end of the war in regard to Britain and Russia. A perusal of the most popular and respectable American publications of that time should demonstrate this: in 1945 editorials and articles of *The Atlantic Monthly* were American versions of the propaganda of *Pravda.*

So much for the state, and for the tendencies of American public opinion during the war. The state of American popular sentiment was somewhat different. In some ways the nation was less united than it seemed then, and than it seems in retrospect. Before Pearl Harbor, American isolationism was a strong undercurrent, sometimes breaking through the surface. As during the First World War, Anglophobia was one of its main components. Few people admitted sympathies for Hitler and Germany; but a considerable portion of the population feared communism and Russia; and the old kind of Anglophobe populism, the fear that the British might inveigle Americans into all kinds of tricky situations, was still extant. Like the declaration of war in 1917, the event of Pearl Harbor in 1941 submerged these currents of sentiment without dissolving them. Opponents of Roosevelt, including many Republicans, favored the war against Japan much more than the war against Germany. In 1944 General MacArthur said "Europe is a dying system. It is worn out and run down. . . . The lands touching the Pacific with their billions of inhabitants will determine the course of history for the next ten thousand years." Beneath these visions of the world we can see the age-old American tendency: that of looking and going plainly westward, and the belief that the main theater of American destiny lay in the Pacific, in that Far West, and away from Europe. Against this tendency Roosevelt and Churchill carried the day. As early as March 1941 the American Joint Chiefs of Staff agreed on a war plan (Rainbow 5) according to which the primary task of the Anglo-American Allies was to defeat Germany in Europe, whereafter the defeat of Japan would follow. Yet throughout the war, among the American people fighting the Japanese was more popular than the fight against the Germans, all of the propaganda and evidence about the Germans' atrocities notwithstanding. In the European theater of war, too, it soon became evident that the millions of American soldiers did not particularly like England and the English. (The presence of the well-fed and well-paid and often undisciplined American soldiers was an irritant in Britain, too, though the British were determined to keep every incident out of the press.) These submerged elements of popular sentiment came to the surface after the war. Republican politicians would recognize them and profit from them, at the expense of the then still extant Anglo-American partnership, of the Anglo-American upper classes, of the memory of Roosevelt and, indirectly, of Churchill.

In April 1945 Roosevelt died; and less than four months later the British people voted overwhelmingly against the continuation of a Churchill government. Yet Churchill still believed in the possibility of a closer union of the English-speaking peoples. When in November 1944 De Gaulle demonstrated to him the shortsightedness of American policy and strategy in Europe, Churchill said that this might be so but that he was nonetheless committed to his principal alliance with the United States; he would not pursue an independent British policy in Europe. Soon after the war he began the composition of his splendid war memoirs, still, and perhaps forever, the principal book about the Second World War. We have seen that he gave the last volume the title *Triumph and Tragedy.* In this volume Churchill, for the first time, wrote about some of his disagreements with Roosevelt and with the Americans toward the end of the war; yet he played this theme down; he did not say "I told you so." Most probably the reason for this was the one he pursued throughout his public life. To irritate his American friends and the American people was not worth the argument; he believed and hoped that the joint destiny of the English-speaking peoples was still a living possibility.

(7)

When in July 1945 the large majority of the British people voted for a Labour government, the explanation of this electoral landslide was that the people, all of their respect for Churchill notwithstanding, did not wish to return to, or even to maintain, the social order that the Conservative Party represented, that they wished for a more equitable and democratic Britain after the war. This was true but there was another element in their choice at that time. The people of Britain were tired. With every reason: they had carried the burden of the war alone for an entire year. For the first time in their history, the civilian population of the island had suffered, from German bombs during the second year of the war, from German rockets during the last year of the war, from the shortness of rations throughout the war. If they wanted more democracy at home, this was inseparable from their unwillingness to maintain more commitments abroad. We have seen that already before the First World War this incompatibility of British democracy with imperial power was a fact; but at that time this was hardly sensed or known by the British people. In 1945 the British people sensed and knew this incompatibility in the marrow of their bones. In May 1945 Churchill exhorted them against the dangers of "the craven fear of being great." Unlike five years earlier, this phrase now echoed in the void. The people did not respond. This was the underlying reason for the limitations of British foreign policy even before the British people voted Churchill out of power. This was the reason why after 1945 their surrender of the greatest parts of their empire occurred together with their unwillingness to play an active role in Europe. In 1945 the prestige of Britain, in Europe at least, was still so great that the British could have had the leadership of Western Europe for a song. They did nothing about it; indeed, they gave it not a thought. Churchill himself, who was a great European (a rarity among British statesmen in all ages) and who, in a supreme dangerous moment in 1940, had proposed a merger of the British and the French empires, in 1946 began to propose the prospects and the virtues of a united Europe. Yet it was not only that he was out of office at the time; he was by no means single-minded about it. When he was returned to office in 1951 his government, like the previous parochially-minded Labour one, would not participate in European institutions at all. He still hoped for a closer Anglo-American union—at a time when, as we shall see, a considerable crisis in Anglo-American relations was in the making.

The end of the empire was the result of the rise (if that is the word) of British democracy at home, and of pressures from the American democracy without. During the war Roosevelt (and Mrs. Roosevelt) would, on occasion, press Churchill for the transformation of the empire. The ideas of American anti-imperialism may have been insubstantial, but the reality of the pressures was not. When the Japanese were pushing toward India, whose people had no desire to fight them, Roosevelt wrote Churchill on 11 March 1942, "Perhaps the analogy of some such method to the travails and problems of the United States from 1783 to 1789 might give a new slant in India itself, and it might cause the people there to forget hard feelings, to become more loyal to the British Empire, and to stress the danger of Japanese domination, together with the advantage of peaceful evolution as against chaotic revolution. Such a move is strictly in line with the world changes of the past half-century and with the democratic processes of all who are fighting Nazism. . . ." "This document," Churchill wrote in his war memoirs, "is of high interest because it illustrates the difficulties of comparing situations in various countries and scenes where almost every material fact is totally different, and the dangers of trying to apply any superficial resemblances which may be noticed to the conduct of war." Such American pressures were not altogether coordinated. They did not amount to a definite purpose of American policy (something that Stalin failed to comprehend: during the last years of his life he speculated that eventually a struggle, perhaps even a war, between the British and the American empires would be in the making). Still these American tendencies, together with the waning resolution of the British people and with the great diminution of British prestige in the Far East, especially after the shameful fall of Singapore in 1942, led to the fast pace of the dissolution of the Empire. In 1947 India, the largest chunk, was gone; in 1948 the British abandoned Palestine; soon they would be gone from the entire East and the Middle East.

The decisive link in this chain of events involved not India or Palestine but Greece. In 1944–45 Churchill, by agreement with Stalin, and at the cost—cost, and not only risk—of serious disagreement with Roosevelt and with the State Department, sent British troops to Greece to suppress a Communist insurrection there, to keep Greece within the Western sphere of influence. Two years later the Communist rebellion flared up again in northern Greece, now with the indirect help of Stalin. The Labour government turned to the United States: Britain could not, they said, afford to support Greece in this renewed guerrilla war. When people say that they cannot afford something this usually means that they do not want to afford it: a maxim as true in the life of individuals as in the history of nations.

This British communication to Washington, in late February 1947, was a milestone. The American Government accepted the responsibility; President Truman went to the Congress to secure an American commitment to sustain Greece and Turkey against Communist aggression. This so-called Truman Doctrine, enunciated in March 1947, was followed by the Marshall Plan and by the North Atlantic Treaty, committing American troops to be stationed in western and southern Europe, including air bases in the British Isles, for the first time in American history when there was no war. It was the swift beginning of the second phase of the expansion of the American empire. Twenty years later Dean Acheson summed it up in the title of his memoirs: *Present at the Creation.* Fifty years earlier the United States had become a world power. Now the United States became a world empire, having inherited, among other things, many of the geographical responsibilities and positions of the British one. The consequences of this American primacy in the world were enormous. In 1917 the State Department employed 1,400 men and women at home and abroad. In 1956 it employed 40,000. Much of this expansion was inevitable, but not all of it (wasn't the United States nearly as powerful in 1917 as in 1956?). Soon millions of young American men and women would find themselves in air bases and in offices thousands of miles away from home; soon they and their families would regard this as part of the normal order of things. American generals and admirals would set up their headquarters in ancient cities: Paris, Naples, Bangkok, Athens. In the 1920s Paris was the transitory home of American bohemians, self-styled "exiles." In the 1950s she was the home of American bureaucrats: of the 30,000 Americans living in Paris in 1955 more than 20,000 were employees of one or another department of the American Government. The world, or at least a large portion of it, seemed to depend on the United States. When one asked an American soldier or a clerk where he was posted he would say "Paris, France" or "Izmir, Turkey"—the usage of the American form of place names extended worldwide as part and parcel of the natural order of things, of the panamericanization of the world.†

We cannot detail here the full extent of this tremendous development.

† Another, relatively new, usage was the abbreviation "U.S." for "American," i.e., "U.S. forces," "U.S. foreign policy," "U.S. literature," etc. This habit grew during the Second World War. Examples: Walter Lippmann's 1943 book *U.S. Foreign Policy,* or the pro-Republican newsmagazine *U.S. News and World Report.* After the war the Germans picked up this habit: "der US-Dichter," "der US-Historiker," etc.

The following illustrations merely suggest how it affected the American frame of mind. Its development was begun by a Democratic administration, but the Republicans furthered it with even greater enthusiasm. In 1956 Section Nine of the Republican Party platform called for "the establishment of American bases strategically dispersed all around the world," a statement that I cited earlier in this book, suggesting this was drafted by a party whom many commentators still called "isolationist" in 1956 (and "conservative" too). When in 1960 the Russians shot down an American spy plane that had been traversing their territory at regular intervals the American people and their President reacted with indignation, as if this had been a vicious interference with the natural order of things: Americans could fly over Russia, while the reverse was unthinkable.

I wrote about some of the elements of this American transformation in the first chapter of this book and I shall have to return to some of its manifestations in other chapters. At this point I must say something about its paradoxical nature, and about its split-mindedness. In 1945, as in 1918, the United States was the greatest power in the world, a force to the good. In 1945 Americans had atomic bombs, for the first time in the history of mankind. (The people on whom they, perhaps unnecessarily, had dropped two of these bombs were the most pro-American people of all: the Japanese admired their ruler MacArthur, whose character fitted their psychic needs, a square peg in a square hole.) Until 1949 the Americans had a monopoly on the bomb. They could have ruled the world and threatened Russia with it. They didn't. They still believed in some kind of a world order, an international order (on American principles, that was). In 1947 the giant skyscraper of the United Nations was erected in New York, on a piece of land donated by the Rockefellers. The United Nations was a plastic pimple on the big brute flank of New York; within its buildings everything smelled and looked American; for at least fifteen years it seemed as yet another instrument in the panamericanization of the world. The year 1947 was that of the Truman Doctrine, of the Marshall Plan, of the setting up of the UN in New York, of the establishment of the CIA, the beginning of the American global and space empire, the "Creation" whereof Acheson spoke.

But now we come to a very important condition that has accompanied the rise of this American global empire as well as its retreat a quarter of a century later. In some ways Americans wanted to rule the world; in other ways they did not. In some ways they were willing to assume the responsibilities of a world empire; in other ways they were not. This requires explanation. We have seen that in 1945 the United States divided Europe (and Germany) with the Russians, along a geographical line that was unnatural and for a long time dangerous, and which could have been drawn farther to the east, had the American leadership agreed with Churchill at the time. Americans thought that this line would be temporary; but it was hardening into permanence. Thereafter Americans believed that the Russians wanted to Communize and conquer Western Europe; the Russians believed that the Americans wanted to Americanize and to conquer Eastern Europe. Neither of these suppositions was true. Yet the cold war grew out of this division.

Having said this, we must probe a bit further. Why was this so? Why were Stalin's fears unfounded? Why did the American Government, and the American people, not really challenge the Russian domination of Eastern Europe? From 1945 to 1947 there occurred a revolution of American attitudes toward Russia. The overall friendship for Russia gave way to a popular hostility. Almost all of this was due to the increasingly brutal Russian behavior in Eastern Europe where, after a year or so of democratic window dressing, the Soviets set themselves to the transformation of these unfortunate countries into the most abject of satellite vassal states. Yet the United States had, for all practical purposes, written Eastern Europe off to the Soviet Union in 1945 and even earlier. The American people did not know this—it was not explained to them in these terms—but the political establishment and the government did. In 1945, and for some time after, Anglo-American power was such that Stalin could have been pressed to retreat from some of the advanced positions that had fallen into his lap. Yet no one in Washington (or, at that, in New York) wanted to do anything about this. The risk of a military conflict with the Soviet Union (and the domestic risk of vocal opposition) was too great to consider such a course seriously, if at all. This is why in 1947 the government and the political elite responded so single-mindedly and enthusiastically to George Kennan's formulation of the policy of containment, defined in his "X" article in the July 1947 number of *Foreign Affairs.* "Containment" meant the defense of Western Europe; but it also meant that there would be no American attempt—strategic or diplomatic, military or political—to revise the division of Europe. This was a great relief for official Washington. It led to the creation of a military and political, bureaucratic and intelligence superstructure over something that had been already created: the American overlordship in western and southern Europe and in Japan. Despite the grandiloquent title of his memoirs, Acheson was not present at the Creation. He was present at the Packaging. Let me repeat: in 1945, and for some time afterward, the United States could have ruled the world—or, to be more precise, it could have governed the development of much of it. It did not want this kind of leadership; and yet it did want it. The newly constructed role of the United States would require considerable efforts, sacrifices by the American people, including a generous outpouring of material and blood by their sons in Korea. Yet this package was also the easy way out. Fifty years earlier the British had concluded that the continued existence of their imperial role and European influence depended on their sharing of the world with American power. Now the Americans concluded that the existence of their world order depended on their division of the world with the Russians, along lines beyond which the latter would not be allowed to go. That the British and the American empires had been friends then, and that the American and the Russian empires were opponents now, made a great deal of difference, though perhaps not a decisive one. The possibility of an American-Russian war in 1950 was nearly as remote as that of an American-British war in 1895 had been. When there was a war in which Americans were involved—in Korea or in Vietnam—they were fighting Asians, not Russians. In the Korean War the loser was Stalin and the winner was Mao Tse-Tung, whose soldiers saved the North Korean government from extinction.‡ Mao replaced Chiang, whose China Roosevelt had thought to be one of the Four Great Powers of the World, something that Churchill in 1944 called "an absolute farce" and an American "obesession" when Mao's cause was being pushed by Washington fellow travelers and Oklahoma Populists alike. This American myth about China would revive again in the 1970s when Nixon and Kissinger (and later Ford and Carter) believed—wrongly—that China was in the same league with the two superpowers and that American "openings" to China would make the Russians more amenable and cooperative.

There was not a single American politician who in 1947 would tell the American people that what was happening was the placement of the mantle of the British Empire on America's shoulders. President Truman, who had an estimable knowledge of history, understood much of this but he, too, did not regard it this way. What held American popular sentiment and public opinion together was the rapidly reheating ideology—ideology, rather than philosophy—of anti-communism. Dean Acheson, a surviving

‡ After the Korean War the Russians had to relinquish those bases and privileges in China that Roosevelt had granted them in Yalta. Before the Korean War began, North Korea was a Russian satellite; when the war ended it was a Chinese satellite; eventually it remained a vicious dictatorship of its own, playing Chinese and Russians against each other. Twenty or twenty-five years later something of the same pattern repeated itself in Vietnam: the victorious North Vietnamese turned against their erstwhile Chinese supporters. Less than six years after the Korean War, Mao had to witness Khrushchev's pilgrimage to Washington, where the latter suggested that the friendship of the United States meant infinitely more to him than the friendship of China. During the Vietnam War the North Vietnamese had to witness Mao and Nixon embracing each other in Peking.

prototype of a high legal bureaucrat from the New Deal years, knew what language to use to influential members of Congress in his confidential talk on 27 February 1947, when the British request for the American support of Greece had come through. He said that "it was clear that the Soviet Union, employing the instruments of Communist infiltration and subversion, was trying to complete the encirclement of Germany. In France . . . the Russians could pull the plug any time they chose. In Italy a similar if less immediately dangerous situation existed, but it was growing worse. In Hungary and Austria the Communists were tightening the noose on democratic governments."[16] This amounted to a vast (and presumably conscious) misreading not only of Stalin's intentions but of the political situation in Europe; but it was useful for domestic political purposes. From 1947 on anti-communism became the principal American ideology, on occasion eclipsing older principles of patriotism, on other occasions the prime choice—choice, rather than refuge—of scoundrels. On one level, the simplest and most honest one, anti-communism was the inevitable reaction of people against the previous prevalence of pro-Russian illusions in Washington and elsewhere, including the presence of Communists and pseudo-Communists in certain positions of influence. On another level the idea that American democracy represented the Kingdom of Light while Soviet communism represented the Kingdom of Darkness was attractive in its simplicity; with its simple categorizations and religious undertones it fitted easily with much of what Americans preferred to believe. On yet another level this oceanic swelling of anti-Communist and anti-Russian sentiments was a belated reaction to the last war, against the memories of Roosevelt and the New Deal and his alliances with Russia and Britain: those Americans who had, openly or secretly, not liked the American "crusade" against Germany now supported an American "crusade" against Russia. There was a feeling—often but not always unspoken—at least for a few years after 1947 to the effect that the Second World War might have been a mistake, that it had been a mistake to destroy Germany and allow Russia to win the war.* This feeling had definite populist elements, from which politicians and demagogues such as Joseph R. McCarthy profited. One of its principal domestic ingredients was a revival of the populist dislike and distrust of the surviving Anglo-American elite. In foreign policy this was

* This writer heard George Sokolsky, a "conservative" columnist speak in La Salle College, Philadelphia, on 2 April 1954, at the height of the McCarthy controversy. He said that the worst mistake America ever made was to enter the Second World War. "We goaded Britain into it, when we should have let Hitler unite Western Europe against communism." The time and the speaker (Sokolsky was Jewish) makes such a statement especially significant.

what otherwise opposite forces in the late 1940s had in common: the Russophile Henry Wallace, who said that the British were pushing the United States against Russia, and the Old-Republican Robert A. Taft, who said that the British had pushed the United States into the war against Germany. The erstwhile Communist Alger Hiss had distrusted the British because they seemed not pro-Soviet enough; his Republican prosecutor, Richard Nixon, distrusted the British because they seemed not anti-Communist enough.

In March 1946 Churchill traveled to Fulton, Missouri, where he delivered his famous "Iron Curtain" speech, one of the more significant of his long career. His speech did not have much of an effect on American popular sentiment; his influence on the makers of American public opinion, too, was slipping. He knew at least two things that went counter to the accepted American opinions at the time. One was that Europe was still more important than Asia; and that it was in the middle of Europe, not in Asia, that Stalin had overreached himself. This idea found no echo among the Republicans, including MacArthur and Taft, who in 1951 proposed a massive American intervention against China while opposing American military and political commitments in Europe. The other matter was Churchill's belief that the problem was with Russia rather than with communism, since the Communist states in Eastern Europe existed not because of the appeal of that ideology but because it was forced on them by the Russian armies, and that the principal danger to Europe and to the world was the armed presence of Russia in the middle of the Continent. This principal concern with Russia, rather than with communism,† was unappealing to Americans; even Acheson would not or could not understand it. At the last meeting with Churchill during the Truman administration, in January 1952, Acheson noted that Churchill "thought the central factor in Soviet policy was fear. He said that they feared our friendship more than our enmity. He hoped that the growing strength of the West would reverse this, so that they would fear our enmity more than our friendship and would be left thereby to seek our friendship." Something like this was to happen within a year, after Stalin died. But the new Ameri-

† This recognition was mainly due to Churchill's historical and realistic frame of mind; but there was, in this respect, a difference on the popular level, too, between the American obsession with anti-communism and the British disregard of it. As George Orwell wrote in *The English People* (London, 1947), p. 18, "The English are not sufficiently interested in intellectual matters to be intolerant about them. 'Deviations' and 'dangerous thoughts' do not seen very important to them." Very well, and perhaps even admirable on occasion: but, then, this was, too, why the British Government and British intelligence disregarded the presence of Communists and of Communist sympathizers within their establishments for a long time.

can administration would neither understand nor sympathize with Churchill.

Here we arrive at the last, sad, and sometimes shameful phase of the American-British relationship of half a century, and to the last phase of Winston Churchill's public life. In 1951 Churchill became Prime Minister again. The following year his wartime ally Eisenhower became the American President. Eisenhower's nomination had a domestic (as well as an international) significance: this was the last time that the wishes and the candidate of the eastern, internationalist, and still considerably Anglo-American element within the Republican Party prevailed. The British took enormous comfort from this. They were wrong. Eisenhower would disappoint them soon. In March 1953, barely a month after Eisenhower's inauguration, Stalin died. Churchill now thought that the time had come for the renegotiation of the division of Europe with the Russians. The new Russian leadership was very unsure of itself, divided, in some ways ready to seek the friendship of the Western powers, as he had predicted. Eisenhower and his Germanophile Secretary of State refused to listen to Churchill. They kept saying (and "leaking") that Churchill had become senile, that he was befuddled, and full of illusions about the Russians. This was the same Eisenhower who seven or eight years earlier had opposed Churchill, who had seemed to him, and to most influential Americans, too anti-Russian in 1944 and 1945, when the United States put itself in the middle between the Soviets and the British. Now they thought, and said, that the British were playing the middle game, unduly optimistic about the Russians.

Eisenhower and Dulles were not alone in this. At the time—the early 1950s—this kind of ideological anti-communism was accepted by the entire American establishment, including the remnant Anglophiles of the Anglo-American elite. The evidences are there, among other things, in the then still very influential magazines, *Time-Life-Fortune.*‡ In 1944–45 *Time* and *Life* had been sharply critical of Churchill's anti-Communist intervention in Greece. Eight years later, in *Triumph and Tragedy,* Churchill wrote modestly, "If the editors of these well-meaning organs will look back at what they wrote then and compare it with what they think now they will, I am sure, be surprised." His war memoirs were serialized in the New York *Times* and in *Life.* In the *Life* publication in 1953 this sentence was omit-

‡ Their owner, Henry Luce, had proclaimed this to be the American Century earlier; his wife, Clare Boothe Luce, was one of Eisenhower's prime ambassadors; and Luce's executive, C. D. Jackson, was a prime panjandrum in the intelligence and propaganda setup of the Eisenhower administration.

ted in its entirety. (The review in *Time* said that this last volume of the war memoirs was not as good as the earlier ones.) As late as 1946 *Time* and *Life* and Eisenhower were wary of Churchill's Iron Curtain warnings at Fulton: *Time,* with its customary sly verbal habits, presented Churchill as half-potted.* Eight years later they presented him as half-doddery.† In 1942 the editors of *Life* printed a full-page picture of Lenin with the text: "This Is Perhaps the Greatest Man of the Century." In 1953 the editors of *Life* theologized that communism was "mortal sin," while McCarthyism was only "venial sin."

Such was the American consensus in 1954. It prided itself on hard realism. In reality it rode on the momentum of a belated ideological inflation. Men such as Eisenhower were never quite at ease with Churchill. They thought that Churchill had changed his principles, when Churchill's principles regarding the world and the course of its history changed hardly at all. He adjusted his ideas to his principles, not the other way around. A man such as Eisenhower had merely successive ideas, and no principles. Toward the crucial end of the Second World War and toward the end of the first—and only—decisive phase of the cold war, Churchill saw things better, and quicker, than his American counterparts. We know now that Stalin was unsure in 1945 and that the new Russian leaders were unsure in 1953 and for some time after. It is a pity that Churchill was not listened to when he was right.

But he had neither the stomach, nor the heart, to fight these matters out with the Americans. He gave in to them. Whether he was right or wrong in this we cannot tell: the power of Britain was far gone, and his arguments would have found few echoes among the American people at that time. He gave in because of his larger vision to which he clung, with a desperate effort, to the end of his waking years: the possible unity of the English-speaking peoples. In 1955, old, and full of sleep, he retired from politics and resigned his prime ministership. Yet he would complete the last volume of his *History of the English-Speaking Nations.* He wrote these magisterial books with Americans in mind; much of his last volume that he suddenly chose to end with 1900 was devoted to his sweeping and sometimes magnificent description of the American Civil War. He ended

* "Downed five Scotch highballs . . . fiddled with his speech. . . . His valet slipped him a slug of brandy to reinforce him. . . ." *Time,* 18 March 1946.

† "Flapping his thick arms for emphasis . . ."; ". . . had not absorbed the lesson of Berlin . . ."; ". . . his burst of nostalgia . . ." In a column of less than five hundred words the adjectives "old," "older," "senile," "senescent," "nostalgic," occurred nine times. *Time,* 8 March 1954.

the book with this paragraph: "Here is set out a long story of the English-Speaking Peoples. They are now [1900] to become Allies in terrible but victorious wars. And that is not the end. Another phase looms before us, in which alliance will once more be tested and in which its formidable virtues may be to preserve Peace and Freedom. The future is unknowable, but the past should give us hope. Nor should we seek to define precisely the exact terms of ultimate union." *Ultimate union:* in this, in the great vision of his life, he was wrong. He finished the book in early 1957. Another crisis in American-British relations had passed then. There would be nothing but calm waters between the two nations from now on. But the vision, and the prospect, of an Anglo-American union had passed over the horizon, sinking away forever.

(8)

And now came the turning point, 1956: the end of the British Empire and the end of the rise of the American one.

Anthony Eden succeeded Winston Churchill as Prime Minister. Eden was the kind of weakling who once in a while feels that he must assert himself. Such people will make an attempt but fail to carry it through. In 1956, two years after the last British garrisons were withdrawn from the Suez Canal, the nationalist ruler of Egypt announced the nationalization, that is, the Egyptification, of the Canal. The tired British and the feeble French governments reacted. They thought (the French had the incipient revolt of their North African colonies in mind) that this was the occasion to reassert their power and presence in the Near East. The Egyptians were no soldiers; and the British and the French could count on the tough little army of Israel. They also thought they could count on world opinion, including the tacit support of the United States, since the Egyptian leader was flirting with those archadversaries of the Americans, the Russians.

Eden was wrong. John Foster Dulles (who, with his brother, the director of the CIA, was the real master of American foreign policy through most of the 1950s) did not like the plan, he did not like the British, he did not like the French. It became more and more obvious that Dulles would obstruct any kind of energetic or military intervention. Now Eden and the French and the Israelis connived at a clandestine plan (of which the Americans were only too well aware). At the end of October the Israelis attacked the Egyptians and drove them across the Sinai. Using this as a pretext for intervention and interposition, British and French troops, coming from Cyprus, landed at Port Said and moved south toward Suez. The road to Cairo lay open. The legions of Bonaparte and Cromer had come again: the rulers and the peoples of the Near East watched with bated breath. Eisenhower gripped the telephone and spoke to Eden in no uncertain terms. The British and the French advance stopped, halfway down the Suez road. Now the Russians got into the act: they threatened the British with war; more significantly, they proposed to the Americans a joint American-Russian intervention to establish peace in the Middle East. But the British advance had already stopped: Eden did not have the courage to push it through. He flinched not before the threat of Russian rockets but before the harsh words of an American President.

For the British people these events constituted a shock of recognition, a psychological milestone. With their characteristic slow-mindedness, all of the retreats of the previous decade notwithstanding, it was not until November 1956 that the majority of them realized that the empire was definitely at its end. On this point all of the histories, including the last chronicles of the British Empire, agree. What historians have hitherto failed to see is that October–November 1956 marked a turning point—perhaps *the* decisive turning point—in the history of the American world empire too. The Russian proposal at that time, to advance from their opposition to the British to a joint Russian-American intervention in the Near East, was largely propaganda, of course; but behind it stood the Russian realization that Stalin's fears in regard to the United States had proven unfounded. The Americans did not, and would not, challenge the division of Europe and the Russians' overlordship in Eastern Europe; they and the Americans were the dividers of the world.

This realization in Moscow coincided with the events of the Suez War. In October 1956 Khrushchev avoided an anti-Russian rising in Poland; immediately thereafter came a rising in Hungary, whose people drove out the Soviet tanks from Budapest and overthrew their Communist regime. The leaders of Russia were divided. After some hesitation they acted, mainly because they saw that the Americans would do nothing. This was important, because since 1952 the American Republican administration had favored the slogan of "liberation"—as distinct from the earlier "containment"—at least rhetorically suggesting a policy aimed at the "liberation" of Eastern Europe, while the CIA had engaged in certain activities across the iron curtain. Yet during the risings in East Berlin in 1953 and in Poland and Hungary in October 1956 the American Government, except for self-righteous declarations, did nothing. Perhaps there was nothing very wrong with this. Whether East Berlin or Budapest were worth the risks of a nuclear war was at least questionable; ten, twenty years later some of the Eastern European states would gradually regain some of their freedoms anyhow. What was wrong was the disingenuousness of the American administration. Eisenhower and Dulles claimed—the former emphatically, in his memoirs—that the Hungarian events had taken them by surprise. This was utterly untrue. They had not created, or even abetted, the Rising; but they knew very well what was going on. Yet they contented themselves with passing anti-Communist resolutions, without and within the United Nations, and calling down Eden for having dared to act independently of them. Careful observers of the United Nations scene noted a certain kind of relief within the American delegation when the Hungarian revolution had failed. The Americans were let off the hook. This was significant, since in 1956 the United Nations was, in more than one way, still an American piece of real estate, and not only because of its location. In 1956, for the last time, some kind of United Nations intervention in Hungary (the sending of a delegation, perhaps including the Secretary General himself) would have put the Russians before a difficult dilemma. Since this might have provided some difficult choices for the American Government, too, Eisenhower and Dulles relieved Khrushchev of such a dilemma. They were safer with the status quo, that is, with their division of Europe with the Russians.

As far as the United Nations went, from 1945 to about 1957 the American idea of world order and the United Nations were closely connected, the entire idea of the United Nations having been an American conception. But now the American influence in the United Nations would decline fast. This happened not because of Russian machinations but because of the rapid falling apart of what was left of the European colonial empires, a development that the American Government cheered on. Five or six years after 1956 the membership of the United Nations reached one hundred, most of the delegates representing the so-called Third World nations. Another five or six years later the UN became a hubbub of anti-American, anti-European, anti-Western propaganda. By 1970 its degeneration was complete. It was an instrument for a ritual comedy, for speeches and tales by hosts of idiots, signifying nothing.

Yet neither the evident failure of the Wilsonian ideals, nor the realization that the division of Europe was to remain, affected the momentum of the American imperial bureaucracy. The Russians now saw that the Americans were not such power-hungry monsters, that they realized they had to share Europe with the Russians. Consequently Khrushchev (who was also beginning to be worried about the Chinese) invited himself to Washington where a sour Eisenhower finally consented to receive him.

Meanwhile the momentum of American empire-building went on. The American people were less power-hungry than were their ambitious bureaucrats and intellectuals. A generation of the latter had grown up, including foreign-born expert professors of international relations, some of whom would eventually reach the highest positions of American statecraft, explaining the world to American presidents. Here is an example from 1957, from a writer whose reputation would carry him to the American ambassadorship of NATO twenty years later:

> Will the coming world order be the American universal empire? It must be that—to the extent that it will bear the stamp of the American spirit. . . . The opening of new horizons which we now faintly glimpse will usher in a new stage of human history; man will have found in cosmic ventures an equivalent for war. Man may still destroy himself, but then he will do so by means other than international war. This part of the human story is still mercifully veiled to anyone now living. For the next fifty years or so the future belongs to America. The American empire and mankind will not be opposites but merely two names for the universal order under peace and happiness. *Novus Orbis Terrarum.*[17]

During that year Henry Kissinger published his first book (a pastiche about the Congress of Vienna), from which he went on to write ever thicker and more unreadable volumes, until eleven years later came the telephone call from Nixon to the suite atop the Museum of Primitive Art where Kissinger was lunching with his patron Nelson Rockefeller. On the bureaucratic and military level the expansion of the American empire continued. In 1958 the United States had alliances, military and naval and air bases in more than sixty countries. Then came nemesis, in the warm damp backyard of the United States, in the form of Castro. During the next two decades the United States could send men to the moon; but it could not get rid of that voluble dictator in Cuba; it lost a war in Vietnam; for more than a year it was powerless in face of the screaming fanatics of Iran.

By the 1960s the retreat of the American empire had begun; yet paradoxically it was then that the conversion of American politics to internationalism was completed. John Kennedy, who had been a financial supporter of America First in 1940–41, an isolationist in the late 1940s, anti-British and anti-French in the 1950s, was now President, and a fully committed internationalist at that. The imaginary adventures of James Bond, with their mix of sex and secret agentry, were John Kennedy's favorite reading matter. Under the successors of Allen Dulles, the CIA was no longer the principal instrument in the actual making of American foreign policy; but its bureaucracy was spread all over the world. It played a greater role in American statecraft than the British Secret Service had ever played in Whitehall. In Bondian fashion it tried to find political solutions through tricks that were swift and cheap; it tried to engineer the overthrow of Castro by transporting Cuban exiles to the Bay of Pigs; under Eisenhower it planned (with that President's consent) the assassination of the allegedly pro-Communist Congolese tribal leader Lumumba; and under Kennedy the assassination of Castro, failing in all three instances. Under such conditions the involvement of American statecraft with the powers of syndicated crime evolved further,‡ involving all kinds of shady figures on the edges from time to time, including the deranged fool who shot President Kennedy out of some kind of personal frustration, as well as the seedy assassin of that assassin. But more important than these ugly appearances on the edges was the continued, indeed, the increasing, presence of an immense bureaucracy in Washington, and that historic first of a war, the Vietnam one, into which this great Republic slid gradually, through the sheer momentum of bureaucratic processes.

The Vietnam War was America's Boer War, except that the British had won the Boer War, whereas the United States lost the Vietnam War. In 1965, during the first phase of that war, Winston Churchill died. The then President, Lyndon Johnson, did not fly over to the funeral; he sent his incompetent Secretary of State, the neo-Wilsonian foundation bureaucrat Dean Rusk, who on that cold day hardly moved out of his London quarters, having had the sniffles. This did not matter: the relationship between America and Britain was as good and smooth as ever. No American had anything to fear from the British anywhere anymore; the suspicion of British cleverness and the old savvy were gone. Perhaps it is significant that James Bond, conceived by an Englishman, was an English figure. Britain was now represented by James Bond and the Beatles. Yet this kind of Anglicization of the United States was faint when compared to the still increasing Americanization of Great Britain. Pro-Americanism was now the avowed conviction of all British conservatives. Toward the end of his life even the anti-American Evelyn Waugh had turned pro-American, at least politically speaking. Henry Fairlie, a British journalist, who would eventually translate himself to Washington, recounted that, when during the early sixties he had run into some trouble in a Balkan city where there

‡ Already in 1943 American secret services, with Roosevelt's approval, used criminal connections in Sicily to facilitate the American landings there; these included the services of "Lucky" Luciano.

was no British consulate, he marched straight to the American Consul, who fixed him up. *Civis Americanus sum*—or, rather, *erit.** During the 1960s the British approached Europe; in 1973 they became members of the Common Market, sending well-dressed delegates and overpaid bureaucrats to Brussels and Strasbourg. It really made no difference. By becoming more European the British were not becoming less American. As a matter of fact they were not becoming more European at all.

Amid all of its travails, and even after the loss of the war in Vietnam, the United States was still the greatest power in the world. The Russian Navy was now, for the first time in history, several times the size of the British, but the Russians had plenty of troubles of their own. The vulgar slogan of Richard Nixon, "America Is Number One!" was not devoid of substance, though it was surely devoid of taste. It was what the American people liked to hear, which was one of the reasons (if not the principal one) they chose Ronald Reagan for their President. During the Falklands War of 1982, Reagan sided with Britain—but only in some ways, and with considerable reluctance. This Californian President, and most of his Californian advisers, had not much in common with the British, while they had some things in common—and often felt more comfortable—with South Americans.

George Santayana once called the British the only conquerors comparable to the Greeks: "sweet, boyish masters" who brought law and order and maintained it in wild tribal regions of the globe. After a while the British no longer wanted this kind of mastery, because of a kind of self-doubt whose sources were complicated and probably less enlightening than we are accustomed to think. There was, however, another source of their failure. They believed in their superiority but they did not believe enough, because they did not know enough, of the superiority of the Western civilization of which they themselves formed a part.† Their minds were often

* "An American I am"—or, rather, "am going to be." More than a century earlier Lord Palmerston, explaining a drastic British intervention in Greece, mostly for the sake of a (somewhat dubious) claim for redress by a Portuguese Jew born in Gibraltar, and thus the holder of a British passport, declared in the famous Don Pacifico debate in Parliament that the principle of *civis Britannicus sum* should assure the protection of every British citizen by the full might of Great Britain—akin to the erstwhile privilege and pride of the *civis Romanus* of that great world empire nearly two thousand years before.

† "The challenge before the British was to create an open society in the order of the mind. Their opportunity was to make India an extension of the Western world. But they failed as completely in using their opportunity as they did in meeting the challenge. Compared with this failure, which was a betrayal of the West in India, their bad manners were mere peccadillos." Nirad C. Chaudhuri (a great Indian writer and thinker) in "Passage To and From India," *Encounter*, June 1954.

narrow. The minds of the American imperialists were different, but the sources of their ultimate failure were essentially the same. Had they combined with the British, the world wars could have been avoided and Western civilization would have entered a long rich afternoon for at least a century, similar to the Antonine Ages. This was the vision of Winston Churchill, a noble vision and not an unrealistic one. But perhaps the very vision—and not merely the possibility of its materialization—had come too late. All of their then prestige and power notwithstanding, during the twentieth century the Anglo-American peoples would not, and therefore could not, rule the world.

7

THE ELECTIVE MONARCHY
The Degeneration of Popular Democracy to a Publicity Contest

How the propagation of popular democracy resulted in an American political system that is monarchical and bureaucratic at the same time.

(1)

During the twentieth century the President of the United States became the prince of the world. Much of this was due to American prosperity and power; even more of it was due to mass communications. Abraham Lincoln was probably unknown to the vast majority of mankind during his lifetime. People in the British Isles may have recognized his name; most of the people on the continent of Europe probably did not. Forty years and one generation later the name of Theodore Roosevelt was far more widely known than that of Abraham Lincoln. During those forty years the greatest extension of popular literacy, of newspaper reading and printing had occurred throughout the world. Another twenty years later Woodrow Wilson appeared as a new world apostle: when he landed in England and France in 1918 little girls in white dresses threw rose petals at his feet; in unpronounceable and unspellable new republics such as Czechoslovakia, hotels, boulevards, and railroad stations were given the name of Wilson. The veneration of this particular President was transitory; the worldwide interest in the American presidency was not. In 1940, another twenty years later, during the most dramatic phase of the Second World War, the

United States was not yet a belligerent: but the American presidential election, for the first time in the history of the world, played an important part in the calculations of the rulers of the greatest powers. When Hitler's invitation to receive Molotov in Berlin finally arrived in Moscow, Stalin chose to set the date of that long-desired meeting in Berlin after the American election. (In November 1940 Hitler, too, wrote Mussolini that Italy's attack on Greece ought to have been postponed at least until after the American presidential election.) Another twenty years later, a President such as John Kennedy could have been elected as first President of the World, including President of Europe, had elections throughout the world been popularity contests. To hundreds of millions everywhere Kennedy and his family represented the image of the successful New World: youthful, powerful, suntanned, and rich. This marked something that went beyond the nineteenth-century image of America: it marked the Californization of the dreams of people everywhere. During the second half of the twentieth century the peoples of the world followed the American presidential elections with an interest that, on occasion, would surpass their interest in elections of their own. The most celebrated journalists and television people of many nations crowded into Washington and New York to signal the early omens and to report the results (for the first time in 1948). There remained now two elective monarchs in the world: the President of the United States of America and the Pope of the Holy Roman Catholic Apostolic Church. The occasional elections of the second may have been, in the long run, more consequential than the regular quadrennial elections of the first; however, few people thought that way, and the interest in the first far exceeded the interest in the second among all kinds of people, including the Catholic population and clergy in the United States.

This is an interpretation of the history of the United States, not a history of the world and not even a history of the American image before the world, topics that are so huge and so amorphous that no decent historian ought to attempt to write them. Yet there is a correspondence between this development and the developing problems of American historiography. The tremendous increase in the projection and reception of the image of American presidents in the twentieth century corresponded with the enormous increase in the quantity of records that Americans amassed about their presidents and that the latter amassed about themselves. The canons of scientific and professional historiography, laid down in the nineteenth century, required that the historical reconstruction of the life of a person, of a certain place, of a certain period exhaust all of the written and printed sources related to the topic. Yet by 1900 at the latest this requirement became impossible to fulfill. Theodore Roosevelt may have been the first President about whom so much was written and published that even the most assiduous biographer or team of biographers could not read or even find most of the "material." This did not mean that a first-rate biography of Roosevelt, or a history of the Roosevelt years, could not be written. It meant that a change in the historian's perennial problem had occurred. The problem was no longer the insufficient quantity, it was the overwhelming quantity of "materials"—an increase that involved a decrease in quality, that is, a decrease in the authenticity of presidential "documents."

The increase in the number of documents was involved with the enormous increase of the executive bureaucracy. The consequences of this bureaucratic growth around the presidency were increasingly strange, and at times ludicrous. Herbert Hoover was the first President to establish a library bearing his name. Every President since that time followed with this practice, depositing the papers of his presidency in a presidential library building somewhere in the United States. The largest and the most opulent of these is the Lyndon B. Johnson Library in Austin, Texas, housing the papers of a President who almost never wrote letters on his own, and whose principal means of communication was that of multiple telephoning, including his occasional reliance on a telephone set installed within easy reach of his toilet seat. But, then, this development corresponded with the general development during the passing of the Modern Age: the increase in the holdings of libraries developing apace with the decrease in the habit of reading.

The list of presidents of the United States during the second century of the Republic does not compare favorably with those who led the nation during the first century of its existence. Of course there was a devolution from the generation of the Founding Fathers (this term was, oddly enough, coined by Harding) to such mediocrities as Pierce or Buchanan or Arthur—a decline about which Henry Adams said that the evolution of the presidency from Washington to Grant was alone sufficient to disprove the theory of Darwin. Adams's acidulous witticism in the 1870s may have been premature. One hundred years later the comparison of Grant, Hayes, Garfield with Nixon, Ford, Carter suggests a difference not of degree but almost of kind—not to speak of the devolution from the literacy of a President such as Ulysses S. Grant, whose own memoirs, composed and handwritten during his painful illness, are an American classic, to the movie and television personality of Ronald Reagan, who preferred to be briefed by film clips. During the last one hundred years the names of the two Roosevelts stand out; perhaps Cleveland, perhaps Truman. The development of the reputation of the latter is significant. Truman was not an especially popular President; had he chosen to run against Eisenhower in

1952 he surely would have been defeated. Yet there is hardly any relationship between the temporary popularity of a President and his eventual reputation; as a matter of fact, the relationship is often obverse. (The most popular President during the twentieth century was Calvin Coolidge.) Truman's reputation began to rise several years after he left the White House. During the 1960s and the 1970s it reached nearly unprecedented and sentimental heights. The reason for this was not so much (or perhaps not at all) a retrospective judgment of his achievements: it was a retrospective judgment of his character. It was the national appreciation for a man of the older American type: outspoken, courageous, loyal to his friends, solidly rooted in his mid-American past, and *real*—a self-crafted piece of solid wood, not a molded plastic piece. In his private notes Truman once wrote, "I wonder how far Moses would have gone if he'd taken a poll of Egypt? What would Jesus Christ have preached if he'd taken a poll in Israel? . . . It isn't polls or public opinion of the moment that counts. It is right and wrong."[1] Less than a decade after Truman had quit the presidency there was an appreciable rise of national nostalgia for this kind of old-fashioned President, an authentic relic of Americana compared to his successors.*

Perhaps this was not only a matter of retrospect. In 1948 the American people, surprisingly and contrary to the projections of all of their polsters, voted for Truman against Dewey, surely for all kinds of reasons, but perhaps because they sensed that the character of the former was stronger, that he was more of a traditional political person than the latter. In any event, during the last hundred years the majority of American voters seldom chose wrongly on the first Tuesday of every fourth November. This, of course, is a personal estimate—but it may be shared by responsible historians. There was only one presidential election during the last one hundred years whose outcome was surely deleterious for the nation and for the world in the long run. This was the election in 1912, when Woodrow Wilson was chosen instead of Theodore Roosevelt. But, then, it was not really the American people who denied Roosevelt the presidency. Had he been nominated he would have won over Wilson. His nomination was denied him by the Republican politicians.

During the twentieth century the voters were, generally speaking, wrong less often than were their self-styled political representatives. What went wrong were not elections but the procedures of nomination. From 1840 to 1900 in every presidential election more than two thirds of the eligible voters voted. Since then there has not been a single presidential

* Hoover was the last President who composed most of his speeches; Truman was the last President who wrote at least some of them.

election when more than two thirds of the eligible voters voted. From 1840 to 1900 there was only one election (in 1852) when less than 70 percent of those entitled to vote did so, whereas twice in the twentieth century less than half of those entitled voted. After 1960 the trend became definite: 62.8 percent in 1960; 61.9 in 1964; 60.9 in 1968; 55.5 in 1972; 54.4 in 1976; 52.3 in 1980. Perhaps this meant a decrease of civic responsibility among the American people. But other factors contributed to the decrease of voting, ranging from the increasing complexities of voter registration, through the broadening of the electorate, to the decrease of the nineteenth-century custom of politics as grand entertainment. Still, this decrease happened during the century when voting rights, the education of voters, the length, extent, and cost of the campaigns were increased, the latter astronomically so.† Since World War II in the democracies of Europe 80 to 95 percent of those eligible voted in national elections, in the United States barely half. After 1970 federal laws provided for the public financing of the campaigns of presidential candidates and they also lowered the requirements of voting age to eighteen. Yet the portion of actual voters dropped significantly and steadily.

All of this happened as the transformation of the Republic to a mass democracy was completed—and when the measurement and the production of popularity had become a scientific practice and an accepted fundament of the electoral process. Those chastened observers and conservative critics who attributed this to popular irresponsibility and to the inevitable shortcomings of egalitarian populism may have been right on occasion, but I believe that we must go beyond their ideas. During the twentieth century American politics in general, and the politics of the presidency in particular, passed beyond the stage where democracy devolved into a popularity contest. Note the title of this chapter: the elective monarchy of the United States has come to mean the degeneration of popular democracy to a contest of *publicity,* which is not identical with *popularity*—a difference that their connections must not obscure.

† During the crucial election campaign of 1932 less was spent than in 1928. The reported (that is, very much underestimated) expenditures on presidential campaigns rose eightfold in twenty years, from $5 million in 1948 to more than $40 million in 1968. In 1980 the major candidates reported that they had spent $73 million on the campaign, whereof more than $63 million was covered by the public financing provisions of the Federal Election Campaign Act as amended in 1974.

(2)

More than two hundred years ago Americans became a republican people. "Republic," in the eighteenth century, did not mean quite what it would later. The word was not necessarily connected with democracy. During the eighteenth century most of the few existing republics in Europe, such as Venice, were aristocratic republics, not democratic ones. In England, too, a considerable segment of the Whig party was composed of noblemen whose inclinations were aristocratic and antimonarchical. In the Declaration of Independence and in the Constitution the word "democracy" did not figure once. When Jefferson established his political party, he gave it the name "Democratic-Republican," of which two adjectives the first was the qualifying and the indicative one, emphasizing what kind of a republic he and his friends wished to see. The other party were the Federalists, the more conservative of the two (relatively and imprecisely speaking: the adjective "conservative" was not yet applied to politics then). At any rate, the Federalists went out of business after 1816, and during the next fifteen years the ideological transition of the United States from a republic to a democracy was completed. The political transition to democracy was completed by the time of the election of Andrew Jackson, who defeated the patrician John Quincy Adams in 1828; there was that famous scene the day of Jackson's inauguration, with his partisans, many of them rough people and farmers from the then West, crowding into the White House with their muddy boots. What followed Jackson's election was even more important: the first convention of political parties nominating a President—in his case in 1832. By 1836 the Whigs, the party opposing the Democrats (who had by then dropped the adjective "Republican" from their name) resorted to the same kind of electoral practices as had their opponents.

It was then that American campaigns, including the election of the President, became full-fledged popularity contests. This development was regarded bitterly and skeptically by the few remaining conservatives in this country, and by some of the liberals in England (Macaulay, who said, "Your constitution is all sail and no anchor"). Their criticism was often judicious, yet it mattered little. In one important sense most critics of popular democracy‡ missed an essential point. What loomed ahead was not the rule of the mob; it was the manipulation of the masses by the politicians. A brilliant description of what happened may be found in three obscure papers (one an honors' thesis at Harvard) written by the young Boies Penrose in the 1880s. Penrose wrote that with the election of Jackson the sovereign people had "asserted their power. But in reality Jackson, the man of the people, was but a puppet in the hands of the politicians. In reality, the majesty of the politicians, not of the people, was asserted. . . ." It was Martin Van Buren, not Jackson, who "marks the transition in American politics from statesmen like Adams and Webster to the great political bosses and managers of today. . . . Adams was the last statesman of the old school who was to occupy the White House, Van Buren was the first politician president . . . the first of that class of statesmen who owe their success not so much to their opinions or characters, as to their skill in managing the machinery of party. . . ." And this was "the inevitable outcome of the development of the country. . . . In the rivalries of parties the mechanical arts of electioneering were soon reduced to a system. . . . Political opinions, in fact, were a secondary consideration. All the statesmanship that the times required was the artful adaptation of general propositions to the existing temper . . . of the masses."[2] The mechanization of politics, in other words, developed apace with the cult of the people. Penrose's career exemplified his vision: after a few years of a dull life as a young lawyer, this Philadelphia patrician abandoned his early support of reform and chose the low life of politics, not for financial reasons, but because of his disabused and stoical recognition of what American politics were all about. Even more trenchant than Penrose's analysis of the transformation of American politics in the 1830s was his criticism of the reformers of his time.* He had a contempt for them. They were "watery-eyed," "pious fools," hypocrites from the so-called better classes, priding themselves on having opinions higher than those of the common man.

Yet Penrose's public career, from 1885 to 1920, coincided with the American Age of Reform. The proponents and the movers of reform were the Progressives and the Populists. They were different in their back-

‡ Except for Tocqueville, who foresaw that the result of popular rule would not be extremism but conformism with long periods of intellectual stagnation.

* "The reformers' attacks on the politicians of today are peculiarly unjust. By management and not by statesmanship are questions generally decided in the Legislatures. . . . When management is all that is essential, have we a right to be disappointed if Van Buren is not Webster?" cited in John Lukacs, *Philadelphia 1900–1950: Patricians and Philistines* (New York, 1981), pp. 57–58.

grounds and in their social and political aims. The one thing they had in common was their belief that democracy ought to be improved through its extension—through education and by increasing political participation—since political corruption meant that the just desires of the people were being thwarted. They did not understand that "the people" were (as indeed they are) an abstraction. For who are the people? A statement by a king is a statement by a king; a statement by a group of nobles is a statement by a group of nobles; a statement by Napoleon is a statement by Napoleon. Yet a statement by the people is a statement by one remove, it is a statement made *in the name of the people.* That such a statement may, on occasion, be in accord with the sentiments of the majority of the people may be true; yet its potential truthfulness does not alter its indirect nature. This is, too, why the historian of democratic times faces problems different from those of the past: "the people wanted," "the people thought," "the people resisted" are vague phrases. They may not be entirely untrue. Yet the historian of democratic times must be very careful, aware, as he ought to be, of the difficulties inherent in his task of reconstructing who the people really were,† and what they thought and believed at a certain time —problems which are less statistical than they are structural.

One of these problems is the difference between public opinion and popular sentiment. Like "the people," "public opinion" has a history of its own. Its classic age was the nineteenth century. The first generation of American statesmen was still keenly aware of the difference between "public" and "popular." "Popularity" for John Adams was not an approbatory term. "The form of popular government," the *Federalist No. 10* stated, "enables it to sacrifice to its ruling passion or interest both the public good and the rights of other citizens." In the United States before the 1830s, in England before the 1880s public opinion meant the opinion of the more-or-less educated classes,‡ while popular sentiment belonged to the masses. With the extension of democracy and public education the two categories began to overlap. "The public" was no longer synonymous with an educated class; it was less and less separable from "the people." More and more people were entitled to vote; more and more people read newspapers; more and more people had opinions on more and more subjects. Whether

† Dickens, in *Hard Times,* attacked the "national dustmen," that is, members of Parliament, for their "abstraction called a People."

‡ Walter Bagehot (1869): "The middle-classes—the ordinary majority of educated men, are in the present day the despotic power in England. 'Public opinion,' nowadays, is the opinion of the bald-headed men at the back of the omnibus." There was a corresponding American linguistic usage. Before 1918 the phrase "men in the cars" (that is, in the streetcars) was the equivalent of the later "man in the street."

these opinions were ready-made or not mattered little. What mattered was the preoccupation with popularity, to which the entire electoral process was being subordinated.

"Public opinion is strong," Samuel Butler wrote toward the end of the nineteenth century, "while it is in its prime. In its childhood and old age it is as weak as any other organism." In Europe, too, the great historian Jakob Burckhardt saw as early as 1870 that the prime of public opinion was passing.* Earlier it was still taken for granted that the public was the more articulate portion of the population; that it was almost always a minority;† that public opinion was, simply, opinion made public; that it was articulate, active, actual, while popular sentiment was potential rather than actual, its expressions often dependent on the ideas presented to it by public opinion. By the end of the century suffrage and literacy were being exploited by manufacturers and distributors of publicity. They were making a living out of what people still called public opinion, but which they tried to transform into something that was inseparable and, on occasion, indistinguishable from popular sentiment.

In the 1830s John C. Spencer, an American lawyer, impressed Tocqueville when he said that certain "leaders" of public opinion in the United States should be reproached not so much because they flatter the people but because they "do not struggle with enough courage against an opinion believed to be shared by the people." "You can't be a leader," said Governor Meyner of New Jersey in 1957, "unless you know where the people want to go." That this was something different from the tyranny of the majority had been noticed by James Fenimore Cooper as early as 1838: "In a democracy, as a matter of course, every effort is made to seize upon and create publick opinion, which is, substantially, securing power," he wrote in *The American Democrat.* "One of the commonest arts practiced, in connection with this means of effecting objects, is *to simulate* the existence of a general feeling in favor, or against, any particular man, or measure; so great being the deference paid to publick opinion, in a country

* By 1789, he said, the ruling people had learned "that opinion makes and changes the world—as the traditional authorities had become too feeble to put obstacles in its ways, and as they themselves had begun trafficking with some of its features. . . . But today the success of the press lies more in the general levelling of views than in its direct function . . . often the press shrieks so loud *because* people no longer listen. . . ."

† "So far as their extent goes, we may venture to say that public opinion is usually smaller than the majority which, in turn, is smaller than popular sentiment; but, so far as their articulateness goes, public opinion is often more important than either the majority or than popular sentiment." John Lukacs, *Historical Consciousness* (New York, 1968 and 1984), p. 82.

like this, that men actually yield their own sentiments to that which *they believe to be* the sentiment of the majority." The italics are mine. Note that this thoughtful American writer was concerned less with the tyranny of the majority or with the deference paid to public opinion than with its simulation.

During the nineteenth century, and for some time thereafter, the main instrument of the mechanization of politics, with its subsequent creation of electoral majorities, was the political party. Party loyalties were near-sacred, unbreakable, they often ran in families through generations; party affiliation, among Americans, was often not altogether different from religious affiliation. In this respect there was something medieval‡ in the American process of nominating and electing presidents, especially in the unanimity with which the temporarily and bitterly divided nominating convention closed. "The shout is the test": whereafter, as during the Middle Ages, the unanimity was taken for granted, it could not be broken. In the Middle Ages as well as in the United States people would deny the existence of divided opinions for a long time,* in political parties as well as in small-town life. Yet it was a mistake to attribute the occasional wrong-headedness of majorities to mere partisanship, as it was attributed by the progressive reformers. An editorial in the first issue of *The New Republic,* the then quintessential intellectual voice of modern progressivism, in 1914 bewailed that the new practice—recently established by a constitutional amendment—of the direct election of senators made little or no change to the better. A "severe blow to non-partisan progressivism" had occurred, said the editorial. Machine politicians with unsavory records were elected, even though they were opposed by the progressive elements in their parties. "Yet they were all nominated and elected by popular vote, and no adherent of popular government can question their title to their offices. The meaning of the lesson is unmistakeable. Direct primaries and the direct popular election of Senators will not contribute much to the triumph of genuine political and social democracy as long as partisan allegiance remains the dominant fact in the voter's mind. . . ." But the problem was no longer the domination of partisan allegiance. It was the

‡ There was also the Indian element of war slogans. George Bancroft, in his *History of the United States* (New York, 1880), vol. II, p. 113, about Indians: "Anyone who, on chanting the war-song, could obtain volunteer followers, became a war-chief." (The caucus was another Indian term and practice in American politics; so was Tammany.)

* The English historian Maitland in 1898: "One of the great books that remains to be written is the History of the Majority. Our habit of treating the voice of a majority as equivalent to the voice of an all is so deeply engrained that we hardly think that it has a history."

domination of publicity.† For by 1914 the second transformation of the American political system, that from a contest in popularity to a contest in publicity, had begun.

(3)

The word "publicity," in its present sense: "the business of making goods or persons publicly known" appeared as late as 1904, the Oxford English Dictionary tells us. This was different from the first English usage of the word (1791): "The quality of being public; the condition or fact of being open to public observation or knowledge." "Publicity agent," "public relations," "public relations expert," "the public relations industry" (or "business") are Americanisms of the twentieth century. Some of these words were coined by Edward L. Bernays, an American publicity magnate, in 1919. Forty years later the abbreviation "P.R." had entered the American popular vocabulary; it was recognized by everyone.

The American respect and attention paid to publicity was older than that.‡ Benjamin Franklin was an early public relations man. His famous asseveration that all that an American had to do was to build a better mousetrap was nonsense. What he had to do was to *advert* people—often at the cost of frequent and incessant repetition—of the existence of this or that mousetrap, the prerequisite of people's acquaintance with the quality (and even with the price) of aforesaid mousetrap. During the nineteenth century the effort to direct the minds of people to the availability of something or of somebody began to merge with the effort of adverting them of the particular quality of the thing or of the person—especially when the effort was directed at large numbers of people. This was happening, too, with advertisements in the press. The press was beginning to depend more and more on advertising; but, unlike in the earlier newspapers, the language, and later the pictorial content, of the advertisements changed. The

† George Kennan: "I . . . suspect that what purports to be public opinion in most countries that consider themselves to have popular government is often not really the consensus of the feelings of the mass of people at all but rather the expression of the interests of special highly vocal minorities—politicians, commentators, and publicity-seekers of all sorts: people who live by their ability to draw attention to themselves. . . ."

‡ In 1893 a huge Department of Publicity at the Chicago Columbian Exposition was in charge of editing all of the printed material; its approval was required for every pamphlet, no matter of what organization.

earliest newspapers, during the eighteenth century, merely published notices about the availability of certain goods. During the nineteenth century the emphasis shifted to their qualities and prices. This corresponded to the entire history of newspapers during the centuries of the Modern Age. In the beginning they printed snippets of news among their advertisements which indeed had been their principal profit-making function. Later their dependence on advertisements became predominant again.

During the nineteenth century the space occupied by advertisements in American newspapers and on American streets, walls, and roads was growing very large. In this field American practices were well ahead of those of Europe. The pictorial appearance of advertisements became more perfected and more startling. Their language was, at times, strikingly modern, having acquired early the often surrealistic tone of twentieth-century advertising, with the purpose of attracting attention rather than of emphasizing the unique (and specific) qualities of a product or a store—in other words, with the purpose of creating a general image rather than concentrating on a particular reality.

The electoral campaigns adopted these developments. At the time of their first transformation, in the 1830s, the change of the verb was telling: it was then that candidates began to "run," and no longer "stand," for office. But there was more to it than that. In the crude presidential campaigns of 1836 and 1840, which disheartened James Fenimore Cooper and other Americans of the older political persuasions, the Whigs had unearthed the old General Harrison because of his potential popular appeal: the slogans of "Old Tip," and then "Tippecanoe and Tyler too," the exaggeration of the contrast between the rough and ready frontier hero and "silver-spoon" Van Buren was manufactured by the Whig politicians. It is significant, and telling, that the Whigs were, relatively (but only relatively), the more conservative party of the two.

Yet publicity, as a business, was still in its infancy. Except here and there, the politicians were the publicity agents. Besides the newspapermen it was the politicians themselves who labored mightily in the creation of popular men and of popular slogans. During the first decades of the twentieth century came a subtle change. This involved the transition from verbal to pictorial images; the invention and production of photography, of movies, of pictorial reproduction in the newspapers greatly contributed to it. Warren Harding was the first presidential candidate in whose selection his solid good-looking appearance played an important part.* It is sense-

* Harding's majority was impressive; yet the politicians' expectations for the feminine vote (in 1920, for the first time, all American women had been enfranchised) may have been

less to speculate whether Abraham Lincoln—who, no matter how impressive, was an ugly man—could have been nominated in the age of the pictorial newspaper or in the age of television. It is not senseless to argue that, had television existed in 1932, Franklin Roosevelt's crippled condition would have been a serious, and perhaps insurmountable, obstacle to his nomination. However, he was the President who made the best use of the radio, where the tone of his voice was inspiring, even as the content of his speeches reads somewhat less inspiring in retrospect.

During the first decades of the twentieth century the effectiveness of verbal politics was weakening. This was noticed by Van Wyck Brooks in 1915: "The most striking American spectacle today is a fumbling about after new issues which no one as yet has been able to throw into relief. We have seen one president advocating a 'New Nationalism,' another president advocating a 'New Freedom' . . . phrases that illustrate just this vague fumbling, this acute consciousness of the inadequacy of habitual issues, this total inability to divine and formulate new issues that really are issues. With us the recognized way of pinning down something that is felt to be in the air is to adopt some cast-off phrase and tack the word 'New' before it."[3] When Theodore Roosevelt said that the presidency is "a bully pulpit" he was only restating forcefully what had become obvious in his lifetime (the presidency had not been a bully pulpit one or two generations earlier). Yet it was the pale professorial Wilson, not the sanguine and impatient Roosevelt, who instituted new practices in the presidency. Wilson was the first President to hold "news conferences" (about which wags were wont to say that they contained no news and were not conferences). In 1917 he created the Creel Committee on Public Information. That this committee perpetrated many a fraud in the service of wartime propaganda is not our concern here; what is significant is the President's creation of the first official American government agency dedicated to large-scale national opinion-making. Wilson was also the first President to encourage the investigative function of congressional committees. These functions tended to become publicity stunts. Like so many other progressive "reforms," their functions often developed at the cost of American civil liberties. Harding, who was chosen because of his image, was a limited man; he sought popularity in his artless ways while he kept private some of his beliefs, not to speak of habits.

An interesting case was the complex character of Calvin Coolidge. The accepted image of Coolidge was, and still is, that of a tight-lipped New

---

exaggerated. The total number of voters among the eligible was less than 50 percent in 1920 (it was 61 percent in 1916).

Englander, a kind of Last Puritan in the presidency, a taciturn Yankee with certain private convictions. In reality Coolidge was an unsure man, rarely at ease; and when "Coolidge was at ease and not on public display, he was the most garrulous occupant that the White House has ever had."[4] He was constantly concerned with his public image, which he cultivated endlessly. He delivered more speeches in four years than any other President before or after him; he also held more press conferences than any American President before him. His press secretary, C. Bascom Slemp (a name which would have been dear to Anthony Trollope or to Artemus Ward), was very much aware of the importance of the Coolidge image, including the pictorial representations thereof—whence the famous photographs of Coolidge wearing Indian headdresses and the one of Coolidge in a New England farmer's overalls (over gleaming city shoes), from which picture the photographers failed to crop out in the upper corner the presidential Pierce-Arrow limousine and the presidential chauffeur, cap in hand, respectfully waiting for the august subject of this kind of iconography.†

I am again referring to pictorialization, since the twenties was the last decade of the Golden Age of the Press. By the 1930s their monopoly on the "news," on informing the people, had been cracked by radio, newsreels, newsmagazines. During the interlude between the Golden Age of the Newspaper and the Silver(?) Age of Television much of public opinion was made, and reflected, in the newsmagazines. In the newsmagazines such as *Time* many of the proper distinctions between information and opinion were washed away. The newspapers were still influential, but the character of their influence was changing. Apart from the important condition that they were now increasingly dependent on advertising, in most of the newspapers, too, the previous attempts of at least a half-decent separation of information from opinion, of reporting from editorial content, were progressively obliterated. "This era," Douglas Cater wrote, in an article in *The Reporter* magazine in 1959,

> illustrates the degree to which the reporting of events can itself be a major political event. Publicity is a force that has become uniquely essential to the American system of government. . . . Within the

† There's still another fine Coolidge portrait: in it he holds up—without discernible enthusiasm—a distinctly antiquated fish which he has supposedly just landed; it is bent at an alarming angle, *rigor mortis* having long since set in. (Told me by Geoffrey C. Ward.) This was the Coolidge who said in 1926 in a speech to the American Association of Advertising Agencies, "There can be no permanent basis for advertising except the representation of the exact truth."

> Executive branch itself, grown large and infinitely compartmentalized, the publicity competition often takes on the character of a life-or-death struggle. . . .‡ This tendency for the development of news to influence reactively the development of events* is a force that cannot be precisely charted. The interaction can be a result of pure chance. It can, as modern practitioners of the art of public relations appreciate, be made the object of manipulation. It can even be a product of conscious cooperation, or lack of it, between the politician and the press.

Twenty years later this analysis is still valid, but with two exceptions. The influence of the press became limited to the few remaining national newspapers, to the Washington *Post* perhaps even more than to the New York *Times.* Meanwhile the influence of the newsmagazines decreased, while the influence of television grew.

About ten years before the advent of television another phenomenon appeared: that of the pollsters. (Again the development of the language is telling. Before about 1940 the word "poll" was associated with elections; after that, with public-opinion research.) Sporadic attempts to "measure" public opinion were made earlier, here and there; but it was during the thirties public-opinion research institutes came into being, the most celebrated among them that of Dr. Gallup in Princeton. Soon political figures and organizations became interested in their findings. This included Franklin Roosevelt, who, all of his patrician self-assurance notwithstanding, was fairly well aware of the existence of certain undercurrents of popular sentiment. Twice, in 1936 and in 1948, the pollsters' predictions of presidential elections were wrong. Yet the public interest in their findings continued, and their techniques of sampling improved until, in the 1950s, the sampling of popularity, on every conceivable issue, became an accepted practice for most politicians and especially for presidential candidates and presidents.

‡ *The Reporter,* 19 March 1959: "When an Army colonel was court-martialed in 1957 for leaking to the press information about the Army missile Jupiter, Dr. Wernher von Braun, head of the Army Missile Program, testified in his defense: 'The Jupiter involves several million dollars of the taxpayers' money. One hundred per cent security would mean no information for the public, no money for the Army, no Jupiter. . . .' "

* One example of this is the "hurrying on" of an event (often desired by the reporter himself) by publicizing it, as in the case of a presidential appointment or decision, with the hope that this kind of publicity will tilt the balance and make it difficult for the President to withhold or to change the appointment or the decision in question. In other words, the "reporting" of an event sometimes precedes, and not follows, the "event" itself.

This seemed as if it were the ultimate extension of popular democracy.† Yet the pollsters' pretensions were essentially fraudulent. They pretended to be in the business of "researching," that is, of ascertaining, public opinion. In reality they were making soundings of popular sentiment—by means of primitive and crude questions about precooked alternatives, and by cooking the results into percentages. Whatever the difference between public opinion and popular sentiment, they have this in common: neither opinion nor sentiment can be enumerated, quantified, and therefore measured, since they involve broadly and profoundly varying elements of quality, of intensity, and authenticity. It is therefore that almost any numerical representation of "opinion" is, by necessity and by definition, false.

How, then, have the pollsters and their rapidly growing research organizations become accepted, necessary, successful? That their influence grew was not surprising: modern democracy has a dumb kind of respect—even though not unmixed with resentment—for all kinds of experts. Despite the frequent failures of their performances, it seems as if modern democracy cannot do without them. But the pollsters have gone one better than most other experts. After a decade or so of trial and not infrequent error they improved their technique of samplings to the extent that their predictions of elections became less inaccurate. Their margin of error was diminishing, even though as late as in 1980 their predictions of the popular vote were fairly wide of the mark. This happened because their work had little to do with opinion or with sentiment. They were dealing with choosing, not with thinking. Now choosing and thinking are different things—especially when the choosing involves predetermined and unalterable alternatives, whether in presidential elections or in market research. Which box of soap powder a tired housewife will choose from the shelves of a supermarket depends, of course, on many things: on her memory (ranging from definite consciousness to subliminal reactions) of the incessant, or at least frequent, repetitions of the name or of the image of the product in all kinds of advertisements; on the color and the shape of its packaging; on its positioning on the shelves; and, of course, on its quality and price—but the last two matters are not always the determinant factors. This kind of choice, involving usually a low-level kind of consciousness and a low level of personal and private commitment, is fairly predictable, especially when it comes to large numbers of people. When it comes to electoral choice, the

† During the Kennedy presidency there was some talk about the establishment of a simple electronic device in every American home whereby a President could, in a matter of seconds, ascertain the preferences of the American people of a single alternative or question.

level of commitment is to some extent different (after all, voting requires some kind of personal effort, including that of registering); but the difference is often that of degree, not of kind; and the prediction of the pollster is made easier by the fact that the choice involves only two predetermined alternatives.‡ Hence the approximate accuracy of the pollsters' predictions when it comes to electoral choices—a rather low level of achievement at that. (This is probably why the pollsters, with all of their extensive efforts and sophisticated equipment, were seldom able to predict the total number of voters—or, conversely, the number of voters who did not bother to vote.)

There was worse to come. We have seen that the choice, or at times even the voice, of the people has often been an abstraction, one remove away from reality. We have seen that more than one hundred and forty years ago James Fenimore Cooper was exercised not so much by the prevalence of political popularity-seeking as by the simulation of popularity. In the twentieth century this meant that popularity could be manufactured by publicity—amounting to a distortion of the political process to which the pollsters then contributed. This was the political and social phenomenon corresponding to the so-called Heisenberg principle (which in the world of matter was a discovery more fundamental than the relativity theory of Einstein): that the observation of a certain matter may influence and change the matter itself. By repeating and repeating that someone is popular he may become popular. (This, too, may have been one of the reasons for the immense increase of the national interest in athletic achievement, which, after all, *is* measurable and real. By repeating that this or that artist or record is popular, he or she or it may become popular; but by repeating that this tennis player or that sprinter is the best is not enough; he has to beat all his opponents or run faster than anyone else.)

During the 1950s the Department of State got involved in the manufacture of popularity, in assisting politicians allegedly friendly to the

‡ This essential condition of predetermined alternatives governs, of course, the most extensive and "sophisticated" public-opinion questionnaire as much as the choice of two soap cartons or of two presidential candidates—because the questions to which the answers are being solicited have been determined and asked by the researchers themselves and because the answers have been formulated by them, usually in the form of two or more alternatives that can be mechanically counted and computed. They have, thus, nothing to do with either the intensity or authenticity or with the possible range of choices (not to speak of opinions) by the person who does the "answering." One may ascertain the number of certain limited, and preformulated, choices: one cannot really "measure" opinions and sentiments. It is wrong to coax people in order to elicit preformulated opinions and fictitious choices, just as it is wrong to berate a child with questions that he never asked himself: the more the child is forced to answer prematurely, the less he will know himself.

United States in all parts of the world. In Washington arrangements were made to the effect that the motorcades of foreign dignitaries arriving in Washington should move through Constitution Avenue around 12:30 "just as Government buildings will be discharging lunch-bound workers. This will give the visitor the impression of a spontaneous demonstration in his honor." (From a government pamphlet of the Dulles period.) In New York, worried lest some of the distinguished foreign visitors receive an unduly small share of ticker tape descending on their motorcade, the agents of the Department of State got together with those of the New York City Department of Sanitation and with the president of the New York Stock Exchange. They agreed that the Exchange would save ticker tape for a week or ten days before the arrival of prominent visitors from abroad, after which assiduous preservation the leftover tape would be gathered and delivered to the Department of Sanitation, whose workers then would ascend to the lofty offices of stockbroking firms and help to toss down the mounds of tape which thereafter they would sweep up from the street again.

By the middle of the century all principal political candidates had their own pollsters, whose multiple tasks included not only the selection of popular programs or issues or phrases but the public pronouncement (often "a news release") that their candidate or client was doing well in the polls, that he had become a popular choice. (A consequence of this was the increasing practice of announcing that a candidate was "ahead"—ahead, that is, days, weeks, months before people were actually to enter the voting booths to register their choice.) In this way the functions of the pollster and of the publicity agent overlapped, often to the extent of their inseparability. The same thing happened to the lobbyists of special interests who, in the past, had attempted to influence legislators by emphasizing the material interests of the latter, tempting them with financial advantages. After 1950 this kind of corruption became less material, more intellectual, and therefore more insidious. The job of the lobbyist, and of the jobber, was to simulate and to produce expressions and "evidences" of popularity.

This corresponded with certain mutations in the American political process. The old-fashioned ward-leader, whose principal task and purpose was to bring out the vote, gave way to the newer kind of publicity expert, whose principal concern was the public image of his candidate. At the same time partisanship and party membership among the voting public at large declined until it became a secondary, at times even a nugatory, factor. By the 1970s the traditional Democratic and the traditional Republican voter were disappearing from many a political scene. Certain thoughtful conservative observers of the American scene said that what happened in the 1830s was a transition on the part of the elected legislator from delegation to representation. One hundred and twenty years later there was another transition, from representation to "presentation." This was what "public opinion" was all about: publicness, rather than opinion. Through publicity an enormous overhead to American industry and business had been created, allowing them to spend huge amounts on advertisements that could be deducted through Byzantine tax laws, as if they were production expenses, eventually at the cost of the efficiency of production itself. It was through publicity, too, that the function of what had gone under "society" in older America was transformed: old society in America was rather private, the newer society determinedly, anxiously public. To be well-known—or, more accurately, to be widely known—was what counted, in political as well as in social, business, and intellectual life.*

(4)

During the twentieth century the American President became an elective monarch. In the history of Western civilization the hereditary (as well as the so-called absolute) monarchy was more typical of the early Modern Age than of the Middle Ages. In many instances and in some ways the medieval king was an elective monarch, dependent on the nobles. The principle of elective monarchy had been, of course, established in the constitution of the Republic from the beginning. In accord with their preferences for the English concept of "balanced government," the founders of the American state invested the President with certain monarchical prerogatives, yet dependent on the other two, relatively aristocratic and relatively democratic, branches of the government, as well as on the electoral process. During the nineteenth century the presidential powers were not especially strong. Tocqueville thought that with the further extension of democracy the President would be more and more dependent on Congress. About 1900 the congressional domination began to weaken. Because of the complexities of an industrialized country, executive orders were needed in

* We can see its effects not only in literary but also in academic life where the chances of promotion of the most popular (for whatever reasons) teacher had become decidedly secondary to those of his colleagues who were "publishing" (no matter what) *and* who were publicly visible through their publicized attendances at meetings, conferences, committees, conventions. The ideal of privacy in the ivory tower was gone—together with its no less illusory successor, the Democratic Teacher.

an increasing variety of instances in order to regulate matters that could not be left to the slow and cumbrous and often inadequate process of congressional or state legislation. Even more important was the growth of the publicity machinery. "The people" wanted a leader, a father, a husband. This was a worldwide phenomenon. The revolutions of the eighteenth century, whether in France or in America, were antimonarchical. The mass movements of the first half of the twentieth century were not. I am using the word "monarchy" in its original Aristotelian sense of one-man rule, and not in the sense of hereditary, that is, aristocratic, royalty. The examples of Mussolini, Hitler, Perón, or of many others, showed that democracy and monarchy were even more compatible than aristocracy and monarchy had been.

During the twentieth century, and especially after 1920, popular participation in presidential voting fluctuated and actually decreased. Yet popular interest in the person of the President did not. With the advent of mass publicity, increasing amounts of information (mostly tawdry) about successive presidents were produced, much of which were false. Because of publicity the distance between image and reality was widening. There have been few revelations about presidents of the nineteenth century that contrast sharply with their contemporary image, or that are really surprising in retrospect. In the twentieth century this began to change for the worse. Conscious as he was of the effects of publicity and the press, Theodore Roosevelt was too much of a piece, whence there is no sharp contrast between his real (and historic) personality and that of his contemporary public image. The same thing may be true, *mutatis mutandis,* of his successor, Taft. But when it came to Wilson the contrast between the public and the private President was indeed very large, in some instances strikingly so. Without going into a character analysis of that most complex of presidents let us note only an indubitable fact: that the physical and mental condition of Wilson, incapacitated as he was after his stroke in September 1919, was kept from the American people for more than a year, in spite—or, perhaps, because—of the enormous influence of the press and of the publicity machinery at large. There was the startling contrast between the public image of the tight-lipped and determined Coolidge and the garrulous and insecure private Coolidge. Millions knew all kinds of details about Franklin Roosevelt's private life—the name of his dog, the fact that he served hot dogs to the King and Queen of England when they visited him in 1939. Often the very same millions were unaware that this President was crippled and dependent on a wheelchair. They were unaware, too, that during the last year of his life he had weakened drastically, indeed, that he was a dying man. During Franklin Roosevelt's presidency the hereditary impulse began to influence the elective monarchy of the American presidency. Roosevelt was elected four times in a row; perhaps he could have been elected again, had he so wished and had Providence allowed. Theodore Roosevelt was the first President in whose family life the American people took excessive interest; Franklin Roosevelt's wife was an important public figure, perhaps for the first time in the history of the presidency. Yet the Roosevelts, patrician Americans as they were, still guarded their private lives from undue publicity (with more than one reason). Eventually this kind of separation of public from private lives was further eroded by the machinery of publicity.

For a while the hereditary tendency ran strong. Had John Kennedy not been assassinated there is reason to believe that he would have been reelected triumphantly and that four years later his brother Robert would have been elected, had he not been killed in turn by a deranged Arab. The public image of John Kennedy, that of the prototype of the ideal young American husband, gloriously and happily married, seems to have been very different from the realities of his private life; but very few people knew that at the time. Americans now took more and more interest in presidential wives. That President Nixon's daughter married President Eisenhower's grandson was not surprising; their alliance was reminiscent of the hereditary inclination as well as of the intermingling of the new bureaucratic and state aristocracies, as happens frequently within leading families in the Soviet Union. The kind of American populism that during the nineteenth century had been often suspicious and hostile to rich people in high political offices was vanishing. Before 1920 the name of Rockefeller or Vanderbilt would have been a decided obstacle, if not anathema, to candidacies to public office, though that of a Ford would not. A generation later Rockefellers were elected to governorships of states. One of them went on to become a presidential candidate and Vice-President, without appreciable popular hostility. What counted in his favor was not his philanthropic record but his political celebrity, the public recognition of his name. An unknown brother or relative of a President did not stand a chance; a well-known brother did. Celebrity in the 1950s and 1960s made movie actors into senators and governors, until eventually one of them became President.

Let me insist again that the increasing influence of publicity did not mean the increasing democratization of American politics. Critics of populism or of democracy, whether in the nineteenth century or in the twentieth, have feared or castigated "the common man," believing that the further democratization and popularization of any process, of any institution, would necessarily lead to anarchy and/or extremism. In many ways the opposite has been happening. The American people, overwhelmed by the oceanic tides of daily (and nightly) publicity, have been surprisingly docile. Many of them may not have liked this or that President; yet their fear of not having a President was very great—this in spite of the fact that, beginning with Eisenhower, presidents have often absented themselves from the White House for unconscionably long periods of time. An evidence of this has been the enormous sense of national relief in the swift and smooth resumption of the presidency after a President in office had been suddenly eliminated by death (or, in Nixon's case, by abdication). During the nineteenth century, presidents died in office, other presidents were murdered, but there seemed to have been none of the fretful anxiety to have their successor sworn in within hours, if not minutes. As late as in 1901 the news of McKinley's death reached Theodore Roosevelt in the more-or-less normal way, when he was vacationing in the Adirondacks. (It is true that when Roosevelt arrived in Buffalo to take his presidential oath he made sure that plenty of newspapermen were present.) The first dramatic innovation in this instance involved Calvin Coolidge, a man whom most people still regard as a nineteenth-century survival in the America of the twenties, whereas he was, in more than one way, a prototypical man of his times, excessively aware of the advantages of publicity. When Harding died on a hot August night his Vice-President, Coolidge, was in Vermont. A congressman friend (Porter H. Dale) rushed up to him. "The United States has no President!" he shouted. "Mr. Coolidge, the country should never be without a President!" (All of this happened before the age of cold wars and intercontinental rockets.) So Coolidge, known to the nation as a businesslike President who went to bed early and slept soundly, stayed up in the night and was sworn in by his father, a local official, at 2:47 A.M., after which his swearing-in was restaged for the photographers.† When President Kennedy was assassinated, his successor was sworn in even before the presidential plane took off for Washington. When President Nixon resigned, his successor was sworn in in a matter of minutes; when President Reagan was wounded by an assassin's attempt, his Secretary of State rushed to the White House to announce to the nation with trembling lips that according to the Constitution he was in charge. (He was wrong.) In

† A few days later Coolidge's Attorney General, Harry M. Daugherty, told him that Coolidge's father had no authority to swear in a federal official. Several days later Coolidge took a new oath in the White House, administered by Justice Hoehling of the Supreme Court of the District of Columbia. This was not told to the nation. That Daugherty turned out to be a crook is telling. His cramped insistence on constitutional exactness reminds one of the gamblers and mobsters who put their hands on their hearts and whose eyes are filmed over by tears when the national anthem is played before the—sometimes fixed—prizefight.

each of these instances there was an immediate feeling of national relief; the senators, public figures, newspapermen, and television commentators gave vent to their immense satisfaction that the Constitution "worked," there *was* a President, after all. . . . But in the Middle Ages, too, people could not *imagine* not having a king.

"The emergence of the physical and symbolic defining characteristics of the modern presidency is evident in the several city blocks surrounding 1600 Pennsylvania Avenue," Professor Fred Greenstein wrote:

> William Hopkins, who began working as the White House stenographer under Hoover in 1931, went on to become executive clerk, and held his White House position until his retirement in the Nixon years, remembers that he had shaken hands with President Hoover the year before going to work in the White House. Hoover still found it possible to carry on the leisurely nineteenth-century New Year's Day tradition of personally greeting any person who cared to join the reception line leading into the White House.
>
> In Hoover's time, the presidency had not become so central a symbol for public emotions and perceptions about the state of the nation that elaborate procedures for protecting the White House from potentially dangerous intruders were deemed necessary. The White House of our time is surrounded by a high, electronically sensitized fence; its gates are locked and carefully guarded; and the fence extends across West Executive Avenue to the ornate Old Executive Office Building, creating a two-block "presidential compound." In Hoover's time, the lower, unelectrified fence surrounded only the White House grounds and had open gates. Anyone walking east of the White House from what then was not a presidential office building, but rather the site of the State, Navy and War Departments, customarily did so by strolling across the White House grounds.[5]

The 1950s represent another turning point, including a mutation in presidential character. General Eisenhower, who was elected by a large majority in 1952 and again in 1956, was not a mere creation of publicity. Nor was he the first example of a presidential candidate who was chosen by the politicians because of his reputation as a victorious general. Yet already in 1942 General Marshall and President Roosevelt had chosen Eisenhower as the commander of the Allied forces in the European theater partly because he was the kind of American general—democratic, agreeable, accommodating and well-equipped with a photogenic smile—who would be acclaimed by the press and who, in the difficult position of having to command all kinds of allies, would be a good chairman of the board. Eisenhower's favorable publicity potential as well as his bureaucratic capacities decided in his favor. These qualities propelled this general after the war to the presidency of Columbia University, to the command of NATO, and eventually to the White House. He was well aware of the importance of publicity. If Truman was the last old-fashioned President in the White House, Eisenhower was the first bureaucratic one. Eisenhower campaigned on a Republican platform against Big Government and Big Bureaucracy, but the bureaucracy of the White House during the Eisenhower years grew very fast. By 1960 the full-time staff was nearly three times as large as that of the Roosevelt period and nearly twice as large as that of the Truman years. Eisenhower delegated all kinds of authority to his staff. The most important task of this staff was to choose who could see and talk to the President, a dubious practice that restricted his reception to information, people, policies, and ideas of which certain influential men on his staff approved. He wrote none of his speeches. In the 1950s the number of speechwriters in the White House began to abound; eventually dozens of them would snip and paste and assemble the text of a presidential speech.

Eisenhower was not the first President who found his task onerous. From John Adams to Truman, presidents had complained about the presidency being a kind of gilded prison. Still Eisenhower was the first President who regarded his occupation as that of a chairman of the board, on a nine-to-five schedule, absenting himself from the White House on golfing vacations as often as he deemed possible. He was also the first television President. In 1948 Truman appeared on television only for a short, three-minute appearance, urging the citizenry to vote; in 1952 Eisenhower hired the actor Robert Montgomery to prepare his television grooming and appearances; this actor remained on the staff of the White House for some time. In 1956 another actor, George Murphy (eventually to become a senator from California) took his place. Eisenhower's countenance was photogenic and reassuring, more impressive than his voice. The shift to the pictorialization of American imagination as well as the bureaucratization of American life was now amply represented by the very functioning of the American presidency—that elective monarchy which in more than one way contained elements of neo-medievalization. The great historian Huizinga had described how imagination and life in the late Middle Ages were excessively public and pictorial. Like the medieval monarch, the American President now depended on a court of advisers who planned his public appearance and who presented not only the various options but the very selection and the formulation of those problems which, in their opinion, and always with an eye on immediate publicity, the elective monarch had to address.

In the 1950s another transformation of the American procedure of presidential elections was developing fast. This was the increasing influence of presidential primaries. It was yet another example of the shortcomings of the populist and progressive ideas propagated half a century earlier. (The first presidential primary took place in 1905, in the prototypically populist-progressive state of Wisconsin, the same state whose voters supported the demagogue Joseph R. McCarthy with enormous majorities in the 1950s; in 1952 he received 72 percent of the vote in the Republican primary.) At first sight the introduction of primaries seemed to be a further extension of the democratization of the American political process—another move in the direction of making the election the equivalent of a popularity contest. A closer look ought to reveal that, instead of an extension of popularity, the hullabaloo of the presidential primaries resulted in the achievement of popularity through publicity. In 1954 the state of Oregon enacted a primary law, according to which "the names of those persons who the Secretary of State of Oregon determines in his sole discretion to be 'generally advocated or recognized in national news media throughout the United States' as presidential candidates are placed on the ballot." In other words, the nominators were the "national news media," not the people.

In 1960 the first televised "debate" of presidential candidates took place. As with all subsequent ones, this was a debate only in the broadest (and flattest) possible meaning of the word. It consisted of a few selected and alternating statements by the two candidates who had not only been prompted and trained for these decisive sixty minutes and who had also been combed, primped, dressed, and face-smoothed for many hours and after interminable consultations with advertisers, movie people, hairdressers, and other assorted beauticians. Since in 1960 John Kennedy won the election by a narrow margin, there is at least reason to believe that his attractive appearance on the screen was an important contribution to his victory over the less attractive Nixon. These television "debates" subsequently became prime events in the presidential contests. Their most absurd example occurred in 1976. The scene was a theater in Philadelphia, chosen by the respective staffs of the two candidates after months of assiduous consultation, carefully apportioning the audience, who served as theatrical props, mechanically applauding now one candidate and then the other. An electrical failure cut off the sound toward the end of the "debate." The President of the United States, Gerald Ford, and his eventual successor, Jimmy Carter, stood for fifteen minutes numb and dumb, facing the nation (and the world) without saying a word, not daring to turn toward or to talk to each other, standing uneasily behind their lecterns, with their eyes downcast. Consumed by fear and embarrassment, they looked as if they were unable to move because their trousers had fallen down.

Their predecessor, Richard Nixon, was the only President in the history of the Republic who had to resign, threatened as he was with the prospect of impeachment. Nixon was an extremely complex character, not devoid of certain talents and even of vision, yet in many ways deeply unsure of himself. He was not especially successful with the publicity media. Thus it would not be accurate to say that Nixon, like other presidents and presidential candidates of his era, was the creature of publicity. There was also an appreciable difference between the public and the private Nixon; as a matter of fact, the frequent, and unconsciously revealing, occasionally startling, expressions of the private Nixon greatly contributed to the dislike, ranging from disdain to outright hatred, that many people felt for him. Yet this unusual man was as much, if not more, obsessed with publicity than were any of his immediate predecessors or successors. In this respect Nixon, too, was an example—and perhaps an extreme example—of the *homo americanus* of a new breed, in regarding and treating his image as if it were not a reflection of reality but reality itself. His first successful election campaign in 1968 was criticized in a best-selling book as *The Selling of the President,* even though this campaign differed from others of that period by degree, not in kind. What was incontestable was that by the 1960s many of the principal agents and aides of presidential candidates were publicity men, whose main experience and achievement was not in the field of industry or business but in public relations. They, too, were a new breed: neither political partisans nor even ideologues, for the most part. Such people, for the first time in the history of the presidency, became the most trusted aides of Richard Nixon. Since Nixon was the first elected President in the history of the United States who openly avowed that he was a "conservative," supporters as well as opponents of Nixon thought that he would depend on people with such an ideological persuasion. Yet the principal liegemen and barons of his staff were California public relations men such as Haldeman and Ehrlichman, uninterested in ideological persuasions, which is perhaps the reason they felt surprisingly at ease with the police bureaucrats whom they met in Moscow or Peking. Their principal preoccupation was to shield the President from people and influences opposed to their own vocation, which was the maintenance of their President's power through every conceivable kind of publicity and practice justifiable in the name of "national security." In this, mostly because of their own shortsightedness, they failed. Still the President himself attributed the rising wave of his popular opposition to the power of the public "media,"‡ obsessed as he was with his image.

The superficial good looks of both Spiro Agnew and Gerald Ford were the main elements in Nixon's choosing them for his vice-presidents. He was also confident that these men of mediocre talents would not overshadow him in his office, which was indeed the case. The public relations men and the pollsters had become the important people in the White House. By 1970 the very selection of a presidential press secretary (previously a former journalist giving handouts to reporters) had become an event that was analyzed with more assiduity than the selection of a cabinet member. In 1976 the main element in the election of Jimmy Carter was a wave of national empathy for the picture of an unassuming person emerging from the rural America of the South. In reality the character of this self-styled simple and frugal person was as complex as that of Nixon or Wilson. It may be at least arguable that Carter was the first American President whose purpose in becoming President consisted entirely of his wish to win the presidential race, and who gave little, if any, thought to what he would do once that race was won. Having won the governorship of Georgia once, he decided to try for the big one, somewhat like a TV contestant trusting his luck (and the sympathy of the producers) in a quiz show. He depended on pollsters and public relations experts even more than had his predecessors. The insubstantiality of his character defeated him in the long run. (Napoleon once said that he who fears his reputation is sure to lose it; Maurice Baring wrote, "Nothing in the world is more insuperable than the obstinacy of the weak.") Finally, in 1980—in part due to the disillusionment with the utter incompetence of Carter's administration, in part because of a conservative surge, the American people, for the first time in the history of their Republic and in the history of modern Western civilization, chose a former movie actor for President.

Of course Ronald Reagan was not only a movie actor; he had been governor of California. Still, his emergence as a public statesman was due in part to the pictorialization of the American imagination. When in 1956 the U.S. Air Force Academy came into existence, Eisenhower's Secretary of the Air Force announced that the uniforms of the Air Force cadets were being designed by the movie producer Cecil B. De Mille and his associates.

‡ In Nixon's memoirs *(RN: the Memoirs of Richard Nixon,* New York, 1978), p. 1017, June 1974: "We must have gotten some lift from the trip [to the Middle East] although it seems almost impossible to break through the polls"—whatever that meant.

In 1971 President Nixon had the entire White House guard dressed up in movie-parade uniforms. (This was not a success: eventually the costumes were sold off piecemeal, some of them going to high school bands in the West, some to Bolivia.) In the 1970s, the movie actor John Wayne became an American kind of national hero because he represented in his films—in contrast to most other films of the period—traditional American virtues (traditional, that is, since the movies and *The Virginian)* that seemed to be incarnate in the western cowboy or sheriff. In 1979, when the United States was humiliated by a Persian mob in Teheran, students of San Jose University in California marched around the streets holding up pictures of John Wayne. What counted even more than the stereotyped roles that Wayne played was his well-publicized personal image, whereby in the minds of millions the political opinions and the social preferences of this virile actor corresponded exactly with his roles on the screen. His death was mourned by a congressional proclamation; in California airports and high schools were named after him. About Ronald Reagan we may say, even at this time of writing (1983), that few of his predecessors depended on pollsters and public relations "experts" as much as he has. His cabinet and his advisers included certain "neoconservatives" or even "conservatives": but power in the White House was exercised by three of his advisers, every one of them involved in public relations previous to their appointment, one of them the previous owner of a public relations firm in California. "In the middle of this enterprise," reported an article about the Reagan administration in the New York *Times Magazine,* "stands David Gergen, whose official title is Assistant to the President for Communications. . . . Gergen now serves as the chief White House spokesman, oversees the operations of the press and communications offices and plays a highly influential role in setting strategy and policy."[6] In other words, the packaging, presentation, and advertising of the "product"—that is, the deliberations of the highest statecraft—not only influenced the product but were part and parcel of its creation.

Ronald Reagan's election was not the result of a publicity hoax. He was, and for some time remained, a popular President, popular with the American people at large. Yet it was evident from the beginning that most of the decisions and statements of this amiable and benevolent President were made with the immediate impact of publicity in mind; a disturbing and potentially disastrous practice, especially when it comes to foreign policy. When, for example, a few months after the election, the pollsters in the White House began to worry about the popularity of the President slipping because of proposed policies involving El Salvador, Richard S. Beal, one of the President's speechwriters and publicity analysts, admitted to the reporter, "What was wrong with El Salvador was the packaging of the activity, in terms of policy and presentation to the public. It wasn't well staged or sequenced." (His very language was telling; "sequencing"—the timing and order of a series of actions—"voter cohort targets," "resistance ratios," "opportunity windows," "and the need to be 'proactive' rather than reactive.") At the time of this interview this pollster was engaged in writing the President's State of the Union speech. Of his work he told the reporter, "We lay out the scenarios of winning and losing. Our work concerns the identification of issues, goals and principles at the macro level. . . ." "By analyzing polling results," the reporter added, "[Beal] believes he can tell what public views on what question are likely to prevail at a given time. . . . This helps the President [or, rather, the President's men] decide how to proceed."* That this was something very different from presidential leadership in the past—or, perhaps from any kind of leadership in the traditional sense—should be obvious. The transformation of the political process from a popularity contest to a publicity contest did not begin in 1980, but it was now nearly complete. The very word "popular" was fading in political usage, while "image" and "publicity" became more frequent.†

One of the main themes of Ronald Reagan's presidential campaign was the reduction of governmental bureaucracy. Yet with all of the reductions ordered in government, the staffing of the White House diminished not at all. When the New Deal came in in 1933 the White House staff

* Ibid. "The President's strategists are at the center of the new political age. At the end of the day, they become spectators, seeing their performance tested by the contents of the television news program. For the Reagan White House, every night is election night on television. How an Administration action is placed and portrayed in the network news often determines what initiatives the President will take the next day.

"Gergen's office desk faces a television set, on top of which are stacked a dozen newspapers, mostly unread. Like other important White House officials, Gergen has a special hookup, so that he receives a broadcast of the CBS Evening News from Baltimore a half-hour earlier than it is shown in Washington. On a recent occasion, he turned the set on by remote control, saying, 'Let's see how Casey's playing.' Allegations of financial wrongdoing on the part of William J. Casey, the new Director of Central Intelligence, had not been good news for the Administration. That night, the lead news item was about Britain. 'Good!' Gergen exclaimed."

† As late as 1941 Admiral Leahy reported from Vichy to President Roosevelt, "The radical de Gaullists whom I have met do not seem to have the stability, intelligence, and *popular standing* [my italics] in their communities that should be necessary to succeed in their announced purpose." This writer remembers a sign in 1958 on the Nantucket beaches put there by the Yankee selectmen of that community concerning local regulations of bathing suits: "On Nantucket Island bikini-style suits are not popular." This usage of "popular" has disappeared since that time.

numbered less than fifty. Fifty years later it consisted of six hundred or more—and this includes only full-time White House employees.‡

> Something more than Parkinson's law has been at work in the growth of the White House staff. . . . The shift from exclusive use by Roosevelt of behind-the-scenes advisors to use of a staff authorized by statute is recorded in the *United States Government Manual* released in October 1939. Listed immediately following the page identifying the President of the United States is what continues to be the umbrella heading under which presidential agencies are grouped—the Executive Office of the President (EOP). The White House Office (WHO) is listed next. (In October 1939 only three WHO aides had been selected. In the 1970–1971 *Manual,* about the peak year for size of WHO staff, over fifty were listed.)[7]

That the transformation of the American presidency to a publicity enterprise is inseparable from the existence of such a vast "executive" bureaucracy should now be obvious. In the Middle Ages, indeed, until about the seventeenth century, kings had no cabinets; they depended on councils of advisers. In the second half of the twentieth century the elective monarchy of the American presidency assumed more and more of the characteristics of medieval kingship, with the liege lords having the power of determining access to the monarch, to the extent that even cabinet officers could no longer see the President on their own, that is, without the consent of the aforementioned liege lords who determined not only what and whom the President should see but also what he should hear—and perhaps, subsequently, think. That such a near-absolute preoccupation with publicity involves an underestimation of the character (and, implicitly, of the necessary intelligence) of the elected President—as well as of the American people—should be obvious too.

For a long time American democracy has been criticized by many a skeptical conservative for proceeding on the basis of overestimating the intelligence of the democratic masses, of the people at large. This may have been true on occasion. Yet, after everything is said, idealism is preferable to cynicism, and even gullibility to distrust. The habitual overestimation of

‡ 1941: 62; 1954: 250; 1960: 355. Even more White House employees are statistically concealed under other headings of bureaus. The six hundred mark was first reached by the Nixon White House in 1970. Jimmy Carter tried to cut back the number of full-time employees, yet the staff of Rosalynn Carter *alone* was one half as large as Roosevelt's at the height of the Second World War.

popular or public, private or personal intelligence, too, is infinitely preferable to its habitual underestimation. The traditional, and often thoughtless, strain of generosity in the American character prevailed, by and large, through two centuries: this was what F. Scott Fitzgerald, in a memorable sentimental phrase, called the American "willingness of the heart." But underneath its superficial symptoms grew a dark countercurrent: the unwillingness of the managerial mind. Thus the paradox: the very people who professed their faith in the reality of "public opinion" now depended on a cynical estimate of it.

In American education, too, the fatal decline of its institutions and purposes in the twentieth century was the result of a corroding kind of cynicism within a vast educational bureaucracy, increasingly dependent on their assumption that of American youth not much should be, because not much could be, demanded. As with the presidency, the material costs and the administrations of the schools grew monstrously expensive; yet the duties and the learning and the very imagination of the youth declined. There was more than a parallel, there was a connection between these devolutions. With the pictorialization of instruction and of imagination, to which television contributed, the American cult of youth extended the period of confused adolescence rather than that of youthfulness. An increasing number of public figures gave the impression of immature men. A kind of puerilism marked many American attitudes—an unnaturally extended puerilism which tended to transmute itself into senility alarmingly and swiftly. As Johan Huizinga wrote, "Puerilism we shall call the attitude of a community whose behavior is more immature than the state of its intellectual and critical faculties would warrant, which instead of making the boy into the man adapts the conduct to that of the adolescent age. The term has nothing to do with that of infantilism in psychoanalysis." In 1851 Tocqueville wrote about the first democratically elected national assembly in France in 1848, "I am sure that nine hundred English or American peasants chosen at random would have had much more the look of a great political body." A century later this was no longer true.

Yet this condition can no longer be blamed exclusively on the people themselves, true though the old adage—every people has the government it deserves—remains. By the 1970s the dangers of the Revolt of the Masses, of the Mass Man, of the Tyranny of the Majority faded; they had an unreal sound. The danger of the tyranny of the majority belonged to that phase of American and democratic history when politics and presidential elections *were* popularity contests. Now the wishes of the people and the inclinations even of majorities could be submerged, while the influence and the very existence of certain minorities could (and would) be exaggerated by publicity, beyond proportion and reason.

During and after the two world wars of the twentieth century the power and prestige of the American presidency became enormous. Some of this prestige was the result of American power; much of it was due to the flooding of the world with "communications," that is, with publicity.* But this kind of democratic Caesarism was different from the past, and even different from what Tocqueville had feared. (He had seen it come to pass during his lifetime, in 1849, when the first democratic presidential election in France brought Louis Napoleon to power, clear evidence that the progress of Liberty and Equality were not the same, or not even necessarily parallel.) Yet some time during the twentieth century it began to appear that the danger to democracy was no longer the tyranny of the majority but that of certain insistent, influential, and powerful minorities. Their pursuit of popularity through the commercialization of politics, of entertainment, of education, of art obscured this. The taste of the public may have become debased, but it was not vicious by nature. It was not the people who decided what was being shown on television; it was not the students who decided what was being taught and required in their colleges; it was not the choice of the public that governed the reputation of artists—it was the television producers, the faculty committees, the art critics, and the foundation executives. And so we cannot really speak of the Tyranny of the Majority, except in an indirect sense: for the majority has been often silent, passive, acquiescent, and in certain instances long-suffering.

This relationship of "hard" minorities and "soft" majorities has not only compromised the democratic process of legislation and government, including the knowledge of what really happens. It has also compromised the chances of the reconstruction of what happened: the task of the historian who—unless he is equipped with a great deal of independent probity and insight—will be easily misled in his "research" of majority opinion and sentiment that may have been simulated by minorities but that, in reality, represented the true state of opinions and sentiments current among the people hardly or not at all.

The great historian Burckhardt wrote that during the Renaissance, in

* We have seen that in 1972 President Nixon found it proper to divide his State of the Union address into two parts, the second called "The State of the World"—at a time when American influence in the world was declining. In December 1981, after the Polish military coup d'état, President Reagan announced that he had called the Pope on the telephone—this at a time when the American ability to actively influence the situation in Poland existed not at all.

the beginning of the Modern Age, an important mutation occurred in the Italian attitude toward leadership:

> The highly gifted man of that day thought to find it in the sentiment of honour. This is that enigmatic mixture of conscience and egotism which often survives in the modern man after he has lost, whether by his own fault or not, faith, love, hope. This sense of honour is compatible with much selfishness and great vices, and may be the victim of astonishing illusions; yet, nevertheless, all the noble elements that are left in the wreck of a character may gather around it, and from this fountain may draw new strength. . . . It is certainly not easy, in treating of the Italian of this period, to distinguish this sense of honour from the passion for fame, into which, indeed, it may easily pass. Yet the two sentiments are essentially different.[8]

In our times, toward the end of the Modern Age, the difference—indeed, the discrepancy—between fame and honor has become so great that in the character of presidents, and in those of public figures in all kinds of endeavor, the passion for fame has well-nigh obliterated the now remote and ancient sense of honor.

There remained, too, a discrepancy between those who still believed in original sin and those who believed in secular progress, a discrepancy between two articles of belief: according to orthodox Christian doctrine the prince of this world is Satan; according to the kind of American doctrine that became a kind of American orthodoxy in the twentieth century, the prince of this world is the President of the United States.

8

MUTATIONS OF MINDS AND MORALS

The Transformations of American Thinking

How, contrary to the lamentations of intellectuals, vast portions of American life became intellectualized.

(1)

"The American is a new man who acts on new principles," wrote J. Hector St. John de Crèvecoeur in the eighteenth century; "he must therefore entertain new ideas and form new opinions." "A new order of the ages," Jefferson said. One hundred and fifty years later Chesterton visited the United States. He liked it: it was a country based upon a creed. This creed—which some people have since called, with an ungainly phrase, the American "civic religion"—was, of course, democratic equality. A creed is not a philosophy; but all philosophy depends on the philosopher's belief of human nature. What has happened with the American view of human nature is inescapably a main theme of this chapter, as it must be a theme of this book, as it is the main theme of American history.

There are—in addition to its potentially enormous scope—all kinds of problems with such a theme. There is the problem of the subtle discrepancy between the powerful and categorical American belief in the perfectibility of society and the much less powerful and much less clear American trust in the improvability of man. There is the allied problem of the compound of two essential factors in the American mind, optimism and materialism; of the national unwillingness, rather than inability, to recognize their contradictions; and of the curious and perhaps basic American condition that it is American materialism, even more than American optimism, which is essentially idealistic. There is, last but not least, the overall problem of the evolving relationship of mind and matter. When such a problem has been the main intellectual and existential preoccupation of a writer and historian during most of his lifetime it is impossible, and perhaps even unreasonable, for him to avoid it, even at the risk of the superficiality of its summation, which is that the historical evolution of consciousness is something quite different from biological evolution. What happens is inseparable from—though, of course, not identical with—what people think happens. But this relationship of what happens with what people think happens is not constant. During the last two hundred years the mental intrusion into the structure of events increased. During the last one hundred years Americans were no longer immune to this condition.

During the nineteenth century the United States often led the rest of the world in material inventions and innovations, but only in part because of the mechanical bent of the American mind. That mechanical bent was also instantly practical, because institutional and bureaucratic obstacles in the way of such innovations were fewer in America than they were in Europe; they had not yet hampered the introduction of private innovations into public practice.

Charmed as he was by the pervasiveness and the endurance of what he saw as the American creed, Chesterton did not pay attention to its allied component, to the American belief that the New World represented the opposite of the Old World. During the last one hundred years this American belief—sometimes gradually, sometimes in fits and starts—began to wane. With it waned the institutional differences between the Old World and the New. That the history of a nation, at least in the long run, depends even more on its character than on its institutions is a theme of this book; but while character subtly influences and profoundly changes the development of institutions, institutions have their effects on character too, especially in a country where the crystallization of the national character has been delayed and confused by a variety of influences, including successive waves of immigration. It is difficult, and perhaps useless, to separate the influence of institutions from those of character—when, for example, it comes to certain American practices such as waste, the wastefulness of American material as well as of American intellectual resources. In this chapter I must attempt to say something about the historical development, the evolution and the devolution, of American education, of the American intelligentsia, of the movements of intellectual life and art, of political and religious thought, in that order, ending with what is perhaps a central problem of the modern American character: the confusion between what is public and what is private.

(2)

In the history of nations the history of their educational institutions often mattered little. During the Golden Age of Spanish literature, art, and philosophy, the schools and the universities of Spain were wretched. During the century of the Enlightenment the university of France played virtually no role at all. But two hundred years ago this began to change. The causes of human equality and the cause of education became allied in many minds, and not only in Rousseau's, whose forerunners were the Puritans. In Massachusetts they established public schools as early as the 1630s. The Massachusetts and the Pennsylvania constitutions included provisions for education. "To instruct youth at low prices": in 1776 Franklin wrote this typically Franklinian phrase into the latter. Belief in education, of all kinds and forms, has been an enduring and abiding American prejudice, amounting to a creed. The pursuit of education and the forms of schooling were different in the South and the North, but the belief in the powers of formal education was not wanting anywhere among the people, at any time. The institution of universal education grew apace with the full acceptance of the democratic principle, as in the states of New York and Massachusetts around 1840. Illiteracy receded, even among the poorest and the most deprived of the black populations in the South. In 1900 less than 11 percent of the American population was illiterate.* Since there are reasons to fear that by the year 2000 the proportion of functional illiterates among the American people will be higher than in 1900 and also higher than in most civilized countries of the world, a survey of what happened to American education during the last one hundred years may be of some interest.

That the progress of universal education has proceeded together with the decline of culture and even with the decline of literate civilization during the twentieth century is a sorry fact at the time of the passing of the Modern Age. But this has been happening in many nations. We must separate the particular from the general: what has been specifically Ameri-

* Comparable percentages in 1900: Austria-Hungary: 23.8 percent; Belgium: 21 percent; Italy: 48.5 percent; Spain: 64 percent; Russia: 72 percent (where it was dropping fast). That to many Americans literacy was a mark of character is perhaps suggested by the fact that the first laws restricting immigration called for a literacy test.

can about this? We must also be careful to avoid those distortions of retrospect which are particularly tempting when it comes to cultural matters: illusions of nostalgia as well as dissatisfactions with the present will distort and exaggerate the virtues and the standards of the education of previous generations. Still, at the cost of inevitable imprecision, we may state that a century ago American schooling was fairly in harmony with the democratic character and the democratic expectations of the American people. In primary education American schools were among the best in the world —in spite (or perhaps because) of the condition that many of the teachers in the public and private and church-related elementary and grammar schools, were unmarried women without degrees or diplomas. The democratization of American education developed rapidly. In 1890 more than 78 percent of American children between five and seventeen years of age attended some kind of school; this proportion rose only slowly, to 83.2 percent in 1920 and to 97.8 percent in 1970. As late as 1920, 90 percent of these children were enrolled in public schools. Impressive, in retrospect, is the rise in numbers of black children in schools: less than 10 percent attended schools in 1870, but ten years later 33.8 percent of them did (in 1930, 60 percent, in 1970 more than 85 percent). As early as 1880 more than 56 percent of American girls attended a school of some kind.

As the age requirements of compulsory education rose state by state, so did the numbers of the secondary school population. In 1890 less than 4 percent of the American people had completed senior high school, in 1920 more than 16 percent, in 1941 half of the population, in 1965 more than three quarters. (It is interesting to note that among these girls outnumbered boys as late as 1920—in 1890 they had outnumbered them by more than 30 percent—a discrepancy that after 1950 diminishes to insignificance.) From 1880 to 1920 the population doubled; but public school expenditures rose nearly tenfold. (In the six years between 1910 and 1916 alone they increased by 60 percent.) Even more enormous was the rise in "administrative costs": from $0.5 million in 1880 to $79 million in 1930 (a 160-fold increase); and from $220 million to more than $1.6 billion, a nearly eightfold increase from 1950 to 1970.

Before the turn of the century the character of the American school system was already changing. On the elementary level the beginning of the school years was gradually pushed back; the kindergarten and the nursery school, mostly of German origin, began to appear. By 1900 continental European—again, mostly German—influences and practices appeared on the high school level. The then novel interests in pedagogical methodology and educational psychology had a few salutary results; yet their main contribution was the growth of a vast administrational bureaucracy. The other change was the propagation of civic functions, especially within the public high schools, in the service of "Americanization." This was especially so in the large cities, with thousands of immigrants' children pouring in; but it was, as we have seen before, a national phenomenon. Alone among the great nations of the world, in the United States the principal purpose of public education had shifted from the preparation of the life of the mind, or even for a career; the main purpose was now to establish the national fundaments for good citizenship. Still, in the half century from 1890 to 1940—the height of the American bourgeois interlude—the level of requirements in a good American high school (mostly in the great cities of the Republic) was at least comparable to that of the middle years of a Central European gymnasium; and the instructional levels of certain private preparatory schools in America were only partly different from the average run of the English private schools of the period.

The differences in standards were greatest in the colleges and universities. At one end of the scale the standards of American colleges and universities, including medical and law schools, were so uneven and unqualifiable that, unlike in Europe, the substance and the meaning of American diplomas varied alarmingly: what counted—unlike in England, not only socially but in every sense—was not the degree but its issuant. About 1910 these worrisome discrepancies began to be corrected by the self-policing efforts of American higher education itself, first in the medical schools, then in other graduate schools. This was altogether an admirable endeavor, achieved by serious private initiative. At the high end of the scale, in the most prestigious American colleges and universities, the English (or, to be more exact, the Anglo-Celtic) ideal of education remained prevalent for a long time, concentrating on the formation of character rather than on intellect. Unlike in England, the young men and women of the upper classes were accepted in the best colleges with few entrance requirements; as in England, their college years were dedicated to the perfection of their social selves. What was different from England was the, more or less unspoken, requirement of social conformity not only among the college students but among the college faculty. There was a great deal of timidity among the professorate, including timidity of mind. The pettiness and the backbiting, characteristic of a professional intellectual class, now appeared in the United States. Because of the separation of the professorate from the general population these anomalies festered within their close airless circles. Yet this separation was often self-chosen. There was a world of difference between Emerson's democratic proclamation in his famous "The American Scholar" of the function of such a scholar, in 1837, and his view expressed in his Phi Beta Kappa address at Harvard thirty years later, in

1867. The latter address, "The Progress of Culture" was unabashedly minoritarian, elitist, self-consciously aristocratic in its pretensions. The progress of culture, Emerson proclaimed, depended on small "minorities," on "the few superior and attractive men," forming "a knighthood" of learning and of virtue.† This was exactly what most of the professorate wanted to hear. Fifty years after the democratic vistas of "The American Scholar" the alienation of American scholars was in full development. The Shavian aphorism ("Those who can't do, teach") and the wittier, less brutal Wildean paradox ("Everybody who is incapable of learning has taken to teaching—that is really what our enthusiasm for education has come to") were now applicable to the United States. Still the harm to college education was relatively limited, precisely because the function of college education was not predominantly intellectual.

What happened to the high schools was more important. There the educational bureaucracy assumed its powers already before World War I. Outside his classroom the American college professor had no control over his institutions—not until the 1960s did a bureaucracy of departments and of professorial committees achieve its stifling controls over the hiring of their colleagues and over the entire curriculum—while the presidents and the administrators of the colleges and universities showed little interest in and exercised little control over the contents and the methods of classroom teaching. But in the public high schools the entire business of the classroom was more and more rigidly determined by a large administrative bureaucracy that emphasized educational method over content of learning. This was beginning to constrain the learning of American youth within patterns and standards that contributed to a protracted puerilism or, at best, to protracted attitudes of adolescence among large masses of the national population, a condition which the momentous deterioration of learning during the television age merely extended further. To believe, as so many people do, that all of this began in the 1960s is wrong. The emphasis on "social sciences" at the expense of history, on qualifying degrees in education at the expense of degrees in the humanities or in the sciences, on "communications" at the expense of English, on "civic" and "relevant" subjects at the expense of the "dead past," on the custodial function of the schools (including their time-consuming athletic and social programs) at the expense of mental formation and training, the profitable sentimentalism in favor of "minorities" (mostly immigrants then), the scal-

† This was Emerson's progress from 1837 to 1867, from the Open Workshop to the Ivory Tower. That it was not much of a progress toward refinement should be obvious to those of us who recognize that life in an ivory tower may be as unsanitary as it is stifling.

ing down of requirements and of the level of textbooks, the increasing dependence on pictorial materials, were all there sixty or even more years ago, promoted and applied, if not altogether enforced, by an educational bureaucracy which was eager to adapt its public image to any idea that was (or which seemed) popular and progressive. There were exceptions to this national devolution; but the very reputation that certain public high schools with high standards maintained reflected the fact that they were exceptional, different from a pattern that had become general.

The 1910s was the progressive decade. The nation had, for the first time, a professor-President. The condition that Wilson was a typical, and successful, academic bureaucrat contributed to this; but in this transition he was by no means out of step with the ideology of the nation at large, an ideology that included the older puritanistic tendency to legislate morality. This was evident in the development of American politics and American law, and in the investigative and in the propaganda activities assumed by the government. It was even more evident in education. Between 1911 and 1916 school enrollment rose by 5 percent, but public school expenditures rose by 50 percent. Between 1912 and 1920 instructional expenditures doubled, while administration expenses rose more than fourfold. The National Educational Association came into existence, a giant lobby of administrators marking the transformation of education in America into an enormous industry. The belief that the extent and value of democratic citizenship—indeed, of the national character—depended on education and public schooling was held, as we have seen, by Progressives and Populists alike. A naïve and engagingly primitive lyrical expression of the populist creed may be heard through the music of these lines by Vachel Lindsay:

A ballot-box in each apple,
A state capital in each apple,
Great high schools, great colleges,
All America in each apple.

There was hardly any limit to what Americans were willing to spend on their schools; hardly any limit to what they thought their schools could do for their children; hardly any limit when it came to the buildings, the staffing, the equipment, and the administrations of what soon became the most gigantic school system in the world. In the 1920s, in small and even middle-sized American towns, especially in the Midwest, the most impressive public building was the high school—not city hall, not a church, not even a bank. The most important cultural and social events of the town took place in the high school. Events involving the high school were (and still are) reported on the first page of American small-town newspapers—with the possible exception of Canada, nowhere else in the world.

Yet the deterioration of the American secondary school began at this time—not a century earlier when these schools had been relatively austere and primitive when compared to their European counterparts. This was only partly the result of universal compulsory education, whereby millions of children were forced to follow a so-called academic curriculum for which they had little preparation and little use—yet another example of the endemic tendency of democracy to inflation, including the inflation of high school diplomas. Nor was this deterioration simply attributable to the extension of the school programs, whereby the traditional disciplines were compounded, and therefore weakened, by the inclusion of all kinds of athletic and social activities—often with the enthusiastic support of parents, who were transferring their own educational responsibilities to the schools. These inclinations allowed the educational bureaucracy to flourish. About 1920 the bureaucracy of the educational industry was already such that most of the teaching staff had to possess degrees in education, intellectually almost worthless, yet professionally indispensable. Besides being self-serving, this bureaucracy was also opportunistic. When in the 1920s provincial nationalists tried to force their ideologies on the high schools, few school administrators put up an opposition. Like the police bureaucracy within the totalitarian dictatorships of the twentieth century, the educational bureaucracy, surely in the secondary schools, was indifferent to ideology while it was by no means indifferent to power.

By the 1920s the national mania for education had become part of the American creed. There was hardly any difference in the way it was espoused by Republicans or by Democrats, by capitalist materialists or socialist determinists, by nationalists or internationalists. Education meant Progress—and progress, for many Americans, called for the expenditure of money, since money and energy would solve problems and create innovations, and discard obsolete traditions along the way. When Henry Ford (and we have seen that he was not alone) proclaimed that history and tradition were bunk, Thomas Edison in 1915 proclaimed that books would be soon eliminated from public schools because movies would soon be the prime instruments of education. (His argument was favorably treated by *The Nation.* Thirty years later famous scientists, such as Vannevar Bush, said the same thing about television.) Progress in education meant the progress of democracy. In 1916 two populist senators threatened to investigate the University of Chicago to determine "whether the University is to educate an aristocratic few to destroy the government or whether it will educate the democratic many."[1] *The Saturday Evening Post,* reflecting, or at least pretending to reflect, the values of middle-class America, in 1912 wondered whether the colleges were "encouraging . . . that most un-American thing called class and culture. . . ." The editorial asked how long high schools would be "dominated by the believers in that snobbish, useless, indefinable conception, 'culture.' When would they start teaching men how to get jobs and women how to keep house?" Nonetheless, *The Saturday Evening Post* was more confident about the universities than were the Populists:

> We are pleased to hear that out of a Harvard class in comparative literature, containing about a hundred students, not one could tell when Aristotle lived, though half a dozen guessed that the period was subsequent to 1840! Knowing when Aristotle lived—or anything else about him—is one of the least profitable uses to which lay human brains can be put. . . .[2]

Whatever college professors may have thought about such sentiments, they did not conflict with the sentiments of the public school bureaucracy. Intellectually speaking, the golden age of American secondary schools was the fifty years from 1870 to 1920, after which the golden age of their extensive buildings and administrations began.

After 1920 the proportion of the college population was increasing fast. Intellectually speaking, the golden age of American higher education was the fifty years from about 1910 to 1960; financially speaking, its golden age (the height of the financial emoluments of its funding and of the status of its professors) was the 1960s, the decade of precipitous intellectual decay. (During those ten years the instructional staff in American higher education doubled, from 280,000 to 551,000.)

Yet the deterioration in the character of the professorate was there well before 1910—another example of the time lag in American life, especially in that of ideas and institutions. Santayana noticed this as early as 1893 at Harvard, where "a gentleman had begun to be an anomaly."

> The growth of the community and of the college in wealth had made an increasing force of professors and instructors necessary. These men, generally students of high standing who after graduation have seen something of German universities, cannot conceive their function as did the worthy teacher of a hundred years ago, whose ambition was, while gaining heaven for himself, to infuse Euclid and virtue into the souls of his pupils. Some teachers of the old school naturally

> remain—teachers in whom the moral and personal relation to their pupils is still predominant, but the main concern of our typical young professor is not his pupils at all. It is his science. His vocation is to follow and promote the development of his branch of learning by reading the new books and magazine articles on his subject and contributing himself to its "literature."[3]

Henry Seidel Canby, who was a student in Yale at the time, wrote a generation later that the new American professorate "were not interested in the American youth who was not going to be a specialist. . . . It was as if St. Paul had spent his energies upon raising theologians and let the Gentiles go hang. . . ."[4] The results were similar, though of course not identical, to that deterioration in the character of the German professorate which led to the melancholy absence of moral and civic courage among its members during the era of the world wars and of the Third Reich. Intellectual courage was rare. Canby wrote:

> We lived in a cautious society and caution bred timidity. . . . That is why there was so much that was feminine in academic life, so much jealousy, so much vanity, so much petty intrigue. The faculty seethed with gossip. Some of our best professors were so vain that it was impossible to argue with them over any opinion they had made their own. . . . Not only were individuals jealous of each other, but whole departments. The anthropologists told terrible stories of the vagaries of the geographers, and every scientist believed that the English professors filled their lecture rooms by easy marking. A woman who knows she has no vocation but marriage and the home, and is lost if she loses them, will best understand the timidities, the inhibitions, and the lack of social courage of the professor. . . .[5]

We should not dwell too long on these relatively early observations about the decline of the professorial qualities. At least in the first half of the twentieth century the characteristics of American colleges were such that what professors did or did not do made little difference. The principal function of college life was still the social, rather than the intellectual, preparation of students. More important was the condition that during the half century from about 1900 to 1960, American colleges and universities profited as much, if not more, from the growth of national wealth and prosperity than other institutions of the nation. During this golden age the plants, buildings, dormitories, libraries, laboratories, observatories, and the material opportunities of American colleges and universities became spacious and opulent. The quantity and the quality of their material equipment and holdings became unequaled in the history of the world. The quality of instruction, too, rose, especially on the graduate level and in the sciences. There was no longer any need for the best students and aspirant professors to accustom themselves to the high rarefied peaks of professional preparation in German universities or in England. After Hitler took over Germany several hundred thousand Central European refugees arrived in the United States, including a considerable proportion of intellectuals, would-be intellectuals, professional scholars, and potential professors, many of whom broadened the extent and enriched the quality of American higher learning. This was an intellectual migration unique in the history of the United States—even though its effects may not have been as universally beneficial as some of its admirers put it, comparing it to the influx of Greek refugees to the Italy of the Renaissance at the time of the fall of Byzantium.‡

The rest of the story is well known: the drastic and, in many ways, precipitous decline (and in some instances, the collapse) of educational standards in the United States during the last twenty years, a fact not contradicted by the other fact that during these twenty years American professors and scientists began to accumulate Nobel prizes by the dozen. Actually the troubles began not in the mid-1960s but at least a decade earlier. They were latent within the discrepancy between two views about education, between the cult of progress and that of tradition, between the concentration on quantity rather than on quality. This discrepancy was exemplified by the contrasting statements by two men whom American conservatives even now regard as representatives of the same humane tradition, whereas they could not have been more different. In *Notes Towards the Definition of Culture,* T. S. Eliot wrote in 1951 that we must "combat the delusion that the maladies of the modern world can be put right by a system of instruction. A measure which is desirable as a palliative, may be injurious if presented as a cure. . . . There is also the danger that education—which indeed comes under the influence of politics—will take upon itself the reformation and direction of culture, instead of keeping to its place as one of the activities through which culture realizes itself." This was very different from the self-congratulatory progressive optimism of

‡ Alfred North Whitehead, addressing the American Academy of Arts and Sciences in 1942: "In so far as the world of learning today possesses a capital city, Boston with its various neighbouring institutions approximates to the position that Paris occupied in the Middle Ages." Cited by Walter Muir Whitehill, *Boston in the Age of John Fitzgerald Kennedy* (Boston, 1966), p. xii. Hmm.

Herbert Hoover, who wrote in 1955, "With only about six per cent of the world's population we have almost as many youth in our institutions of higher learning as the rest of the world put together. We could probably enumerate more libraries and more printed serious works than the other 94 per cent of the people of the earth."[6] When Hoover said this the public schools in the cities had already deteriorated into custodial institutions within whose enclaves hordes of adolescents, including adolescent gangsters, were kept imprisoned for a few hours each day by administrators and teachers whose self-serving cynicism was tempered only by their lassitude. By 1960 the disorder in the schools spilled out into the streets. In cities such as Chicago and Philadelphia the police requested the school administrators to notify them of early dismissals, because soon after school was out gangs of youth were roaming the streets and the subways, occasionally robbing passengers and passersby. The last great wave of government-induced enthusiasm for education, coming after the Russians had preceded Americans in firing the first satellite into space, produced silly statements, such as that by Edward Teller, the "Father of the Hydrogen Bomb," one of the most celebrated but least appealing members of the Central European migration of refugee scientists, who said in 1957 that American teen-agers would soon be "as enthusiastic about science as they are about baseball." Twenty-five years later the national dissatisfaction with public schools was such that, for the first time in the history of the Republic, federal legislation that would provide tax credits for people whose children were sent to *non*-public schools was seriously being considered by the Congress.

Meanwhile—again in line with its transformation into a bureaucracy—something else was happening in higher education. This was the development of an American educational elite. Distinctions of education—to be more precise, distinctions by diploma—were replacing earlier distinctions of birth and even wealth, something that seemed, and still may seem, a propitious and democratic development, although its results may be the very opposite of what is salutary, there being no appreciable relationship between cleverness and character. We may observe an early example of this devolution from democracy to bureaucracy occurring within a few years. After World War II the GI Bill of Rights provided the opportunity for millions of young Americans who had served in the armed forces to rely on governmental assistance in pursuing a college education after their demobilization. Consequently American college ranks were flooded; new colleges sprang up all over the Republic. With all of its costs and excrescences, this was a salutary development. The professors of the period were impressed with these millions of young students who, after their experiences of military service, were both more serious and more mature than many of the fledgling adolescents to whom college was a lark, the social institution where they could enjoy themselves after high school. But as early as 1951, during the Korean War, something very different happened. Enrolled college and graduate students were exempted from military service, as they would also be during the Vietnam War. For the first time in the history of the Republic its legislators and administrators had come to regard the potential recipients of college degrees as precious assets for the nation whose lives had to be preserved to the extent of their being exempt from the dangers of military duty. It was a long step away from populism, indeed, from democracy itself.

During the 1950s and most of the 1960s the prosperity of American colleges and universities and of their professors and administrators increased, sometimes beyond their dreams of avarice. Between 1958 and 1965 the salaries paid to college professors rose more steeply than the incomes of most other professional groups. This, of course, corresponded to the influx of college and graduate students, the result not only of a then great increase in the number of Americans of college age but of the reputation and of the desirability of college education. Not only the absolute numbers but also the proportion of Americans who were going to college and to graduate schools had risen sharply. Many universities—and not only state institutions—grew to a size that dwarfed that of most giant corporations. When we include students, teachers, and administrators (as in industry we must include workers, salaried employees, and administrators) there were, and still are, but a handful of American corporations larger than such universities as the University of California in Los Angeles, the universities of Michigan, Texas, and even Yale (57,000, 47,000, 37,000, and 14,000 at this time of writing). These material developments proceeded apace with the increased fame and status of professors and of intellectuals in general. The evidences of the latter were so protean—and at times ludicrous—that one or two examples ought to suffice. In 1957 the Sons of Indiana, the leading citizens of a state which in the 1920s had been a stronghold of the Ku Klux Klan, and was for a long time a prototypical provincial state upholding the ideal of a fundamentalist morality, awarded their Hoosier of the Year award to Professor Alfred C. Kinsey, the nationally celebrated archivist of pornography and head of the Institute for Sex Research in their state university. In the same year a professor (Harold E. Gray) at Michigan State University established an Idea Factory, supported energetically by business executives, whereof the prospectus stated, "The class meets for two hours a week and thinks." Yet it was then that Professor Richard Hofstadter, perhaps the most famous American historian at the time, wrote his *Anti-Intellectualism in American Life,* an intellectual best seller which received unanimous approbation, of course principally from intellectuals.

It was not the businessman or the legislator but the occasional lonely thinker from within the academy itself who was painfully aware of the critical state of intellectual life in the country, including its universities. Yet serious books such as Jacques Barzun's *The House of Intellect* (1959) or Geoffrey Wagner's *The End of Education* (1976) (perhaps it is significant that Barzun and Wagner were not American natives) were statements with hardly any effect among the professional intelligentsia. During the 1960s professional intellectuals rose higher in American society than they had ever risen before. The professorate now attracted people who before would have scorned academic life with its relative isolation and low pay, people whose natural bent was that of jobbers; now they could make their careers as jobbers not of fashionable garments but of fashionable ideas. That there is a difference between these two aspirations—"I want to be able to follow the interests of my mind" and "I want to make my career as a professional intellectual"—they did not know, perhaps because they did not want to think of it.

Dependence on experts and intellectuals had existed before, especially during the closing years of the Wilson and during the beginning of the Roosevelt administrations. Yet foreign-born theorists of "international relations" such as professors Kissinger and Brzezinski, who could not have risen much beyond the level of second-rank consultants during the First World War or beyond a job within the Office of War Information during the Second, in the 1970s were in charge of spinning the globe for presidents and explaining the world to them. At the same time higher education, as Eliot had feared, began to absorb a large portion of the cultural life of the nation. Not only research but entertainment, theaters, films, entire musical productions were now under the aegis of certain universities, while professorships and academic positions were being awarded to poets, ballet dancers, and idea-mongers of all kinds. This false prosperity grew like a cancer; it began to devour American culture; and it progressed apace with the deterioration of the traditional functions of the universities. The student riots of the 1960s have been often ascribed to the national malaise due to the Vietnam War: wrongly so, since at the same time, similar riots were wrecking, or nearly wrecking, the universities of European nations, whose problems—overcrowding in the classrooms, the rule by ministries of education, the remoteness of their professors—were entirely different from those of American universities, not to speak of the fact that Europeans were not at war in Vietnam. The abdications of the administrators and of much of the professorate before the senseless, primitive, and often dishonest demands of the student spokesmen were appalling. Yet this hardly affected their emoluments and the continuation of the uncertain respect with which the nation regarded its institutions of higher learning.

By the middle of the 1970s the student population was dropping, enrollments were down, as were moneys from the state and federal and municipal governments on which educational administrators had come to depend. The inflated prosperity of the education industry came to an end before the recession, about 1980, began to affect other areas of business and American life in general. The American educational system had weathered the Depression of the 1930s better than had many other structures of the nation; but now, especially in higher education, the end of prosperity had come. However, when it came to trimming, this involved the lean as well as the fat. This was mainly the result of the democratization of authority in the colleges and universities, of the dissemination of authority among departments, a democratization that had quickly degenerated into bureaucratization in its worst form, that is, to the self-perpetuation of the pettiest and most mediocre of interests.

Extreme democratization led to free enrollment in many colleges and universities. In some city and municipal universities qualifications for admission were dropped. Near the end of the 1970s some of these practices were abandoned, but the general decline of levels was now omnipresent in every institution of the nation. In 1978 many of the students in Harvard Law School could write English only with considerable difficulty; a remedial English course was then offered to them. In 1963 only 10 percent of all grades in the courses of Yale University were A's; in 1977, 80 percent of all Yale grades were A's or B's. Perhaps the century of literacy in America was coming to its end.

Yet the American belief in education continued, sometimes in novel forms. For one thing, the average age of students was increasing; more and more people of middle age were taking college courses, more people were entering college in their late twenties or thirties. And the commercialization of academic life was a mirror image of the intellectualization of commercial life: universities granting advanced degrees in Management and Business were doing well in those "fields." Their enviable graduates would enter the corporate bureaucratic life with little education and culture but with the prospect of the best money that diplomas could buy.

(3)

One hundred years ago there were no intellectuals in the United States. The usage of "intellectual" as a noun, designating a certain kind of person, did not exist. "Intellectual" was an adjective (as in "intellectual ability," "intellectual courage," "intellectual application"), not yet a noun. In George Gissing's *New Grub Street* (1884) "intellectual" was still an adjective ("She is intellectual and very rich."). As late as 1916 John Buchan (in *The Power House)* still wrote of (Russian) *intellectuels* as if the word was French, and in italics. Yet it was between these two dates, 1884 and 1916, that the English and American usage of "the intelligentsia" was established. The phenomenon had become recognizable.

It is significant that this was one of the handful of words and usages that the English language took from the Russian.* (The very word and spelling of "intelligentsia" immigrated from Russia to America, the "ts" being a transliteration of a single letter in the Cyrillic alphabet.) The nouns "intellectual" and "intelligentsia" were introduced into English and American usage mostly by Marxist and Jewish immigrants who began to arrive in the United States after 1882; but the fact that the usage of these words spread rapidly and began to be ascribed by considerable numbers of men and women to themselves suggests that these terms corresponded to an emerging reality. These were people whose principal source of pride was that they possessed a "culture" different from and superior to that of the common run of men—in other words, a class resting not on standards of birth or of wealth or even of education but of opinion. That this emergence of a class of opinion illustrates the intellectualization of American life is obvious. Less obvious, and certainly paradoxical, is that the evolving presence and influence of an intelligentsia in the United States, the most democratic nation of the world, should have had so many similarities with the intelligentsia of Russia, the most autocratic and repressive of nations—but

* "Above all, it is in Russia that we can study in its purest form the phenomenon of an intelligentsia—that is to say, an educated class—that is entirely detached from social responsibilities and provides a seed-bed for the propagation of revolutionary ideas," Christopher Dawson, *Dynamics of World History* (New York, 1956), p. 225. Richard Hare (1951): "intelligentsia" is a word that the Concise Oxford Dictionary "with a touch of possibly unconscious irony defines as 'that part of a nation (especially Russian) which aspires to independent thinking.' "

this has been but one of those odd similarities of Russia and America which appear at unexpected times and on unexpected levels.

A class of opinion prides itself on its intellectual originality. Yet their eager embracing of modern ideas and of modern art did not mean that the intellectuals were very original. They moved in the progressive direction, but they also wanted to move faster than the progressive mainstream. They were wont to reassure themselves, again and again, that they were indeed ahead of it, which was a nugatory condition, and mattered seldom. What mattered was that by the 1910s it was no longer possible to exclude the influence of the American intelligentsia from the main currents of American thought. The peak period of American urban civilization contributed to this. It was in the cities that intellectuals found each other, and here their excitement rose as they swarmed together. As Henry F. May wrote about Sherwood Anderson in Chicago, "Literary conversation and the excitement of belonging to a movement complemented his yearnings and discontents." By 1912 the New York rebel sometimes was called, and sometimes called himself, "a Young Intellectual."

> The noun was new in America. Its origins were partly socialist; the intellectual to the Marxists was the bourgeois who repudiated his class. . . . Exactly for the same reason that Henry James shuddered and conventional middle-class progressives shook their heads, the Young Intellectuals exulted: New York, whatever else it was, was not Anglo-Saxon. This meant more than cheap and good French and Italian restaurants; it meant a serious invitation to attack the dominant conception of culture exactly where it was weakest, in its narrow exclusiveness. The Young Intellectuals went further than mere tolerance: they turned the conventional hierarchy upside down. Anglo-Saxons, repressed and bigoted, were at the bottom of the scale; at the top were the Italians, and Slavs, and above all, the Eastern European Jews of the East Side.[7]

Forty years later the aspirations of a young American writer from the Midwest, Elizabeth Hardwick, were essentially the same, as she recorded in her memoirs, "I wanted to be a New York Jewish intellectual."

When the United States entered the First World War President Wilson established a Committee on Public Information, a propaganda machine staffed by intellectuals and journalists, people who suddenly discovered the pleasures of government positions. Their performance was sometimes marked by dishonesties worthy of a staff recruited by Joseph Goebbels. It included the crudest kind of propaganda, and the occasional perpetration of forgeries of German documents. There were, of course, intellectuals who opposed the war and its propaganda, individual thinkers such as the thoughtful radical critic Randolph Bourne: their brave strictures on the propaganda of their colleagues shine in retrospect. But our principal subject here is not politics: it is the existence of intellectuals as a class. During the 1910s this had become a fact. A symptom thereof was the appearance of a new type of magazine, a magazine of opinion as well as of literature and the arts. *The New Republic* began in 1914, a new colleague to the older *The Nation.* Its advocacy of political progressivism had little influence on most of the politicians and voters of the nation; but its presentation of certain opinions and ideas had an influence that was considerable. The fatal split-mindedness of American liberalism was there in its pages from the beginning. On the one hand *The New Republic* advocated the further extension of democracy and of education. On the other hand its more thoughtful contributors (Walter Lippmann, for example) articulated their skepticism of the wisdom of the popular mind.

By 1917 the intellectual landscape was no longer the same. The breakthrough to "modernism" had come before the recognition of Joyce and Eliot *circa* 1922. Mencken wrote approvingly of the Flapper as early as 1915, when New York was "a city gone mad over the fox trot and the white lights."[8] By the end of the First World War the designation "highbrow" (to many people synonymous with "intellectual") had become part of the American vocabulary. This cultural distinction between highbrow, middlebrow, and lowbrow was proposed by Van Wyck Brooks in a famous essay in 1915, the main purpose of which was to point out the moral and intellectual shortcomings of the kind of "culture" purveyed by magazines such as *The Saturday Evening Post* or *The Ladies' Home Journal.* Yet Van Wyck Brooks, who still stood with one leg on the ground of the older culture, was also critical of the New Intellectuality, of the "meticulous technique of our contemporary 'high-class' magazines, a technique which, as we know, can be acquired as a trick and which, artistic as it appears, is really the mark of a complex spiritual conventionality and deceives no sensible person into supposing that our general cleverness is the index of a really civilized society."[9] It may not have deceived him; but it deceived plenty of the aspirant men and women during the high phase of the American bourgeois era, the twenties. During the 1920s modern art, the defiance of conventions, the respect for such iconoclasts as Mencken, were not uncommon among the people of the American upper classes, especially (though not exclusively) in the East. For the first time in the history of the nation young sons and daughters of the rich wished, at least on occasion, to be associated with what was "intellectual," "highbrow," "avant-garde."

For the first time in the nation's history certain people found it publicly† fashionable to regard not only politics but democracy as vulgar, while they wished to assert the superiority of their opinions and tastes by being hospitable to radical ideas.

The "exiles" of the 1920s—those American writers, artists, and intellectuals who went to Paris, ostensibly escaping from American commercialism and provinciality (their "exile" was highly convenient because of the favorable exchange rate of the American dollar)—were not as daring or unique as many of them thought. Their self-conscious separation from America was but part of the self-conscious separation that highbrows and aspiring highbrows were practicing at home. It took a foreigner to recognize that this did not make much difference. "It struck me from the beginning as a remarkable fact," wrote Hermann Keyserling in 1927, "that American radicals—the word taken in its European sense—do not seem to feel responsible: neither do they seem to take their criticism very seriously. . . . The reason is that their position in life is very much the same as that of the court jester in the Middle Ages. The significance of the court jester was not that he was a fool—usually he was even the wisest man at the court—but that his wisdom was without any power or influence."[10] (To me the title of a little literary and artistic magazine of the period, striking and un-English, shiny and brummagem at the same time, sums up the avant-gardism of the American twenties: *Pagany.)*

The intellectuals did not recognize the widespread (and, sometimes unwarranted) respect for intellectuality in the minds of their countrymen. Seldom, if ever, in the history of mankind could a savant or a scientist have expected anything like the outpouring of curiosity and expectation that greeted Einstein when he first visited the United States in 1921. The publicity from which Einstein profited was that of a perfect rendition of a visual and mental prototype: the rumpled genius, fumbling for his pipe, his head crowned by astral hair and by the aura of knowing something so wondrously complicated that it could not be put into everyday language. The newspaper headline "Einstein Idea Puzzles Harding, He Admits as Scientist Calls" expressed exactly the good-natured American reception of Einstein and of Einsteinism, and the fact that a President such as Harding found it politic and useful to receive him was equally significant. After Einstein finally settled in America (in 1932) he had nothing more to offer

† I am constrained to use this limping adverb, for there is plenty of evidence (among others, from Tocqueville's notes) that in the 1830s, too, many of the cultured and older (and richer) American families were unsure and critical of popular democracy, but that they were very careful not to voice these anxieties in public.

in physical theory (indeed, his own theories were already outdated and proven partially wrong), but this did nothing to halt the further inflation of his reputation during the rest of his lifetime or thereafter. Streets, buildings, and hospitals were named after him; a postage stamp carried his picture; in sum, respect for him and his reputation among Americans has not abated during the sixty years since 1921. So much for anti-intellectualism in American life.

As the title of Malcolm Cowley's *Exile's Return* reveals, after 1929–30 came a change. Elitism among intellectuals was now, at least partially, submerged. They sought common causes with the American masses. They were returning home. This impression, too, was fairly misleading. It was true that by 1932 most American intellectuals, having abandoned their artistic elitism, became political again; many took up a radical and Marxist ideology, pretending to recognize the bankruptcy of "capitalism" and the consequent desirability of transforming the American system into a popular democracy without privileges—except for intellectual privileges, that is. Yet the separation between intellectuals and the masses was as great as ever. In 1932 a large number of well-known American intellectuals supported the Communist ticket in a manifesto published in *The New Masses;* yet the Communist Party garnered but 0.25 percent of all votes cast in November 1932, at the deepest point in the crisis of American capitalism. (The Socialist Party vote was lower in 1932 than in 1920.) It could be argued, and it was so argued, that this was not the fault of the intellectuals; the American masses were too docile, too steeped in their nationalist traditions to respond to the passionate diagnoses of their intellectuals. It could also be argued that the masses, if less clever, were also less shortsighted than were many of the intellectuals.

In the 1930s, for the second time in the nation's history, the government began to invite more and more intellectuals into its administrative ranks. It was then, too, that governmental support to arts and letters began, a development which has continued, in one way or another, ever since. Some of the intellectuals in the Administration were clandestine Marxists, a fact that fifteen years later would jolt the consciousness of a nation, obsessed as it then was with the danger of international communism. Within the government Marxists were hidden, a small and often unimportant minority. Outside of the government Marxist intellectuals were numerous and influential. Why was it that in the United States (and, somewhat differently, in England) so many intellectuals espoused some kind of Marxism during the 1930s when Marxism proved itself bankrupt for the second time (the first time was 1914 when nationalism everywhere proved much more powerful than socialism) and when in the United States as well as in Europe the Depression led to the rise of radical nationalists, not of internationalists? Intellectuals, no less and no more than other people, believe what they want to believe. The profession of some kind of Marxism was in harmony with the aspirations of people whose ambitions were intellectual as well as bureaucratic. They believed that Marxism, unlike capitalism and fascism (two imprecise terms) was "progressive," not "reactionary"; that it was modern, not traditional; that it was in harmony with the great general ideas of evolution and material reason that had replaced superstition and religion; that it could be brought into harmony not only with Darwin but even with Freud; that it was an intellectual system, forever applicable for dialectical explanations. Most important, Marxism allowed its intellectual representatives and proponents (wasn't the very noun "intellectual" a Marxist term?) to take pride, pleasure, and eventual profit from the fact that they were ahead of the rest of the people, and ahead of the few remnant bourgeois intellectuals, and that therefore they would eventually land on top of the heap.‡

Those ambitious Marxist intellectuals who eventually would perform clandestine (and often amateur) services for the Soviet Union were relatively few, and the harm they did was relatively limited. A minority of American intellectuals—especially in New York—recognized, finally by 1937–38, the monstrous cruelties of Stalin, whereafter they split off from the Communists. The self-willed blindness of the remaining Communists thereafter deserves not more than a footnote in a history of American intellectuals, even though their self-deception is worthy of human interest: flagrant examples of the frequent unwillingness—unwillingness rather than inability—of men and women, no matter how clever, to change their minds even in the face of accumulated evidence contrary to their beliefs. The slowness and the inability of many of the Marxists to recognize reali-

‡ As Edmund Wilson wrote in retrospect, in 1953, in his foreword to a paperback edition of his 1929 novel, *I Thought of Daisy*, "Some time in the late thirties, at the time when [the Soviets were] . . . coming to seem respectable and Communism a passport to power in an impending international bureaucracy, I thought of doing a brief sequel to *Daisy*, in which . . . some Washington official . . . would be giving himself a sense of importance and enjoying a good deal of excitement through an underground connection with the Communists. . . . [Their] set would go on drinking, playing bridge and making passes at one another's girls with the conviction that these activities had been given a new dignity by being used to cover up operations which would eventually prove world-shaking and land them somehow at the top of the heap. . . ." I consider this passage to be the best, and the most concise, description of a certain kind of American Communist. To this I must add that as late as 1935 Wilson, returning from a Russia in the grip of Stalin's purges, wrote that in Russia he had been "at the moral top of the world." *Travels in Two Democracies*, p. 321. William Barrett (1982) properly called Wilson's famous, and non-Communist, "history" of communism, *To the Finland Station*, "a romance."

ties was the consequence, too, of the unhistorical nature of their social-scientific thinking. So many intellectuals regarded Russia as a society instead of a nation, a social instead of a cultural prototype. Their preoccupation with the social institutions of the Soviets blinded them from recognizing the national and historical character of Russia, a category which they refused (and which many people still refuse) to recognize as a reality; in sum, that the Russian people, and that their government, remained very Russian indeed.

In any event the overwhelming majority of American intellectuals, virtually all of the influential ones among them, were well to the Left of the mainstream of American politics, and modernists to a man (and to a woman). That modernism was not compatible with Stalinism dawned on some of them sooner or later; but the rejection of both modernism and Marxism was too strong a diet for most of them. Those few who were skeptical of both modernism and Marxism were scattered and ineffectual for a long time. As Philip Rahv said (as late as the 1950s), not to be "liberal" in American intellectual circles meant "suicide," by which he meant the self-condemnation of being an outcast, unrecognized, unheard, perhaps even unpublished, a failure. He may have exaggerated the importance of the liberal consensus in national life at large; he did not exaggerate its intellectual influence.* Liberals and Marxists (though no longer necessarily pro-Soviet) did not merely dominate American intellectual commerce, they monopolized it. The first cracks in this monopoly did not develop until the 1950s, and it was not until the 1970s that the post-liberal chapter of American intellectual history opened—another evidence of the slowness with which ideas move in the twentieth century.†

As in many other places in the world, the verbal warfare that the

* So did his friend William Barrett in his memoir, *The Truants* (1982), where he wrote of "a large segment of the American public," and Marxism having been "an important chapter in our national and intellectual history." Intellectual, yes. National, no. On another level, the only quarrel I have with this very honest writer is Barrett's diagnosis of the fault of the liberal mind. "The Liberals" were pro-Soviet for a long time, because they "find it hard to believe in the reality of evil" (p. 94)—something that was perhaps true of liberal Anglo-Saxons, surely not true of liberal Jews.

† That this slowness is not necessarily identical with slowness of mind is obvious. On occasion, and in certain situations, the mental reactions of intellectuals could be very quick. Here is a vignette of New York Trotskyists in the 1930s, from Dwight Macdonald's memoirs: "When a fire broke out in our headquarters, one of the top leaders elbowed aside lesser comrades, male and female, and clattered to safety down the rickety wooden stairs. Later, he explained that he felt it necessary to 'save the cadres'—that is, the cadres *of* the cadres. The fire, incidentally, was promptly put out by the efficient if capitalist New York Fire Department." ("The average citizen of the classless Society" Trotsky once wrote, "will be raised to the level of an Aristotle, a Goethe, a Marx.")

avant-garde intelligentsia waged against the hypocrisies of governments and of the bourgeoisie, often in the name of justice, and at the expense of truth, frequently blinded them to their own intellectual dishonesties, to the condition that the pursuit of truth is of a higher order than the pursuit of justice, and that intellectual dishonesty is even more deplorable than hypocrisy. In 1945 George Orwell wrote, "I do not think it an exaggeration to say that if the [English] intellectuals had done their work a little more thoroughly, Britain would have surrendered in 1940." I do not think it an exaggeration to say that if intellectuals in America had been more influential in 1945, the United States would have surrendered all of Europe to the Soviet Union.‡ Fortunately their influence was limited. The revelations of the pro-Soviet activities of certain bureaucrats and intellectuals led to the distressing, and often dishonest, excesses of the Second Red Scare, and to the temporary semblance of anti-intellectualism among the politicians and people at large. Around 1952 the word "egghead" became a national designation of ridicule. Yet all of this was temporary: underneath all of the uneasy anti-intellectualism, the respect—not unmixed with fear—for intellectual endeavor was as strong as ever. (One evidence of this may appear from the language used by Joseph McCarthy when he kept referring to some of their opponents and victims as "pseudo-intellectuals.")

There was one important exception to the often deadening uniformity of liberal domination in American intellectual life. This was provided by the writers of the South. The inclinations of the so-called Fugitives and Agrarians, beginning as early as around 1930, were truly reactionary, but in the best sense of that much misused word: patriotic rather than nationalist, demophile rather than populist, regional rather than cosmopolitan, traditionalist rather than bourgeois, romantic rather than sentimental, and classicist rather than rationalist—representing thereby a vein of fineness of heart and mind. The fame of certain southern writers and poets (William Faulkner and Allen Tate) notwithstanding, it was not until the 1950s that Flannery O'Connor, a Catholic southern writer (in itself an unusual combination), became a quiet and glowing new incarnation of this philosophical and cultural tradition. The general explanation for the unusual maturity of these southern (to be more precise, southeastern) writers has been that, unlike other Americans, they had been born in a country that, through its defeat in the Civil War, had once experienced the Fall, among people who were more chastened in their human expectations and more

‡ See in this respect the chapter "A Sketch of the National Mind: American Public Opinion (and Popular Sentiment) in 1945" in John Lukacs, *1945: Year Zero* (New York, 1978).

imbued with the understanding of original sin than were people and intellectuals in other parts of the Republic. To this we may add that the Southeast continued to be the most homogeneous Anglo-Saxon region of the nation, devoid of much cosmopolitanism, a condition that in cultural matters in the twentieth century may be an advantage rather than a handicap.

In the year of Flannery O'Connor's early death, 1964, the nomination of the two presidential candidates showed that the center of gravity of American politics and perhaps of American dynamism had shifted to the Southwest, to a part of the nation that was even more western than southern. The nomination of Barry Goldwater proved that the once principal influence of eastern and financial interests in the Republican Party was gone. Yet the concentration of intellectual commerce in New York continued. Except for two old Boston firms (Houghton Mifflin and Little, Brown) all of the large publishing houses of the nation were now in New York. That the reading of reviews had replaced the reading of books was shown by the transnational influence of *The New York Review of Books,* founded in 1963, edited by a coterie of editorial entrepreneurs in New York. During "that disturbed decade of the 1960s, with its squalid atmosphere of permissiveness . . . the spirit of 'Anything goes!' was in the air. The notion of good taste itself appeared suspect. . . ." (William Barrett.) Yet the 1960s were revolutionary only on a superficial level. Their governing ideas and fashions were but extreme continuations and projections of ideas and tastes and fashions that had appeared in the 1920s, during what had been perhaps the only "modern" decade. Then there came a change. Soon after 1970 the post-liberal era was opening: the monopoly of liberal ideas and influences on American intellectualism was broken.

(4)

In the United States, unlike in prerevolutionary Russia, the intellectual life of the nation was not preempted by formal education or by the intelligentsia, neither by professors nor by critics. The trouble with the Genteel Intellectual Tradition, Santayana said, existed not only because it was thin but also because it was narrow: irrelevant to the nation's main interests, entirely different from the aggressive spirit of enterprise of the period. During the twentieth century these conditions began to change. Large portions of national life became intellectualized, in one way or another. The gradual change from a productive to an administrative society meant the corresponding decrease of manual and the increase of intellectual occupations, eventually for the majority of American men and women. The rising preoccupation of Americans with themselves was manifest in the national mania for psychology, in every possible form. (Who, in 1900, would have predicted that seventy years later *Psychology Today* would outsell *Popular Mechanics* in the United States?) Such mental preoccupations—preoccupations in the literal sense of this word—were bound to affect what I have often called "the structure of events," that is, how certain things have been happening, in public as well as in private life. They also affected the images Americans had of themselves and of each other. The necessity to represent—and, even more, to incarnate—not only a certain kind of breeding, a certain kind of taste, but certain sets of opinions gradually affected many Americans, including segments of the population that had been previously indifferent to such considerations.* More and more people found it necessary to suggest their opinions by their very appearance. The minute attention that Americans paid to each other's clothes (something as prevalent, if not more so, among men than among women, and something that was less common during the preceding century) reflected their interest in the detection of mental attitudes from outward evidences. An extreme example of this necessity of actually wearing opinions was the widespread habit of wearing T-shirts and buttons emblazoned with all kinds of opinions or cultural symbols and slogans. By 1970 an American girl, no matter what her education or social class, would sometimes give as much (if not more) thought to her choice of phrase or picture printed on a T-shirt or of a button she would wear at a party than to the color and suitability of her costume jewelry. The triviality of this illustration should not obscure the significance of this development: the necessity to demonstrate in public the inclinations of one's mind.

In 1914 magazines such as *The Nation* or *The New Republic* had fewer than 6,000 subscribers. Ten years later *The American Mercury* or *Vanity Fair* or *The Smart Set* influenced the opinions and the tastes of considerable segments of the upper and upper-middle classes. *The New Yorker* came into existence at the very time (1925) when certain kinds of opinions about literature and art were no longer restricted to men of letters and aesthetes. During the 1930s and 1940s the success of newsmagazines

* Another phenomenon was the appearance in the 1920s of that Anglo-Saxon archetype, the liberal snob. (His occasional antecedents may be found among the Bostonian mugwumps a generation earlier; but the prototype of the genus had not yet crystallized.) Since snobbery has a natural inclination for aristocracy and tradition, the liberal snob is often less attractive, because less natural, than the conservative one.

such as *Time* or *Newsweek* was due to their breezily informative style, in which every word was carefully shaped through editing, providing opinion disguised as information. At the same time people were assuring themselves that intellectuality could be as American as anything. In 1925 *The Independent* reported a convention of scientists. "The fact is that in America . . . a convention of scientists, such as the American Association for the Advancement of Science annually brings together, is as clean-shaven, as youthful, as jazzy as a foregathering of Rotarians."[11] In the 1930s a writer such as Hemingway became recognized through his public personality as an all-American asset, a feature of modern American civilization. "Writing the great American novel" had become an American cliché. By 1935 the news that a young man was working on it reduced his social reputation in a small town not at all, rather the contrary. What few people saw is that such a confluence of public and private aspirations is often fatal: for there is a difference between wanting to write a great American novel and wanting to be a great American novelist.

The growing intellectualization of life had not speeded up the movement of ideas. In 1900 Mark Twain and around 1920 Vachel Lindsay, independent of each other, noticed the same thing: people were much more talkative than they used to be. The taciturn Yankee of Tocqueville's time had become a relative rarity. The rhythm of American speech changed too: increasing communications, and perhaps also the changing national composition of the people, contributed to the fact that Americans were talking faster than before. Yet sociologists as well as novelists like Sinclair Lewis described the curious, unwritten, and unspoken rules of rhetoric in American small towns of the twenties: the near-automatic repetition of a large number of standard phrases, the ritual dependence on certain patterns of speech, the tacit understanding of what could be talked about and what could not, the virtual taboo of discussing anything deleterious to the public image of the town and of its people. In the 1930s the Oxford scholar Maurice Bowra visited his sister in San Francisco and wrote about the conversational habits of the Californian upper class: "The only ideas which interested them were those which they had in common and repeated like incantations to another in the hope that this would make them feel good." What Bowra wrote about Republican bankers at that time was depressingly true of liberal intellectuals a decade later. "In the loose modern style, by which everybody is John and Henry," Jacques Barzun wrote about the Harvard report, *General Education in a Free Society*, "the goal seems to be not so much to transact business as to stagnate in friendly feelings." Anyone who has attended symposia or faculty meetings or academic conferences ought to attest to the condition that what is being said and how it is being said (not to mention why it is being said) often have very little to do with the matter at hand.

This brings us to the essential paradox of the twentieth century: the tremendous increase of external and technical communications throughout the world occurring together with increasing breakdowns of communications between people. The latter condition harbors another paradox: the development of increasing self-centeredness, together with the decrease in the conscious cultivation of private integrity, in the ability to live with oneself. Symptoms of this were the shortening of the attention span and the related inability to listen. Seventy years ago Oswald Spengler wrote that in the twentieth century the newspaper would expel the book from the mental lives of entire peoples. This became worse with the advent of television. Yet Spengler's prediction to the effect that people would believe what they read in the newspapers has not really happened. (Whether they believe what they see on television this writer cannot tell.)

In the 1920s the serious American classicist and critic Irving Babbitt wrote of the Sunday newspapers, "Whole forests are being ground into pulp daily to minister to our triviality." An increasing amount of this triviality consisted of advertisements, eventually occupying as much as 80 percent of the Sunday newspapers. In 1940 the average American daily newspaper had twenty-four pages, of which ten were advertisements; by 1960 it had thirty-seven pages, of which twenty-four were advertisements. Advertising, during the twentieth century, became a veritable institution, affecting not only the daily lives but the very imagery (and at times the vocabulary) of peoples. Advertising may have affected Americans differently from other people—in part because of the American respect (and, at times, awe) for publicness, in part also because of certain tendencies of American rhetoric. American advertisements often had a surrealist and abstract bent, as did the tendencies of American poetry. A telling illustration of this, going back as early as 1859, was provided by Professor Marshall McLuhan in his earliest book, *The Mechanical Bride:* "Just about the time when the classical program of studies collapsed, Macy's was experimenting with the hypnotic power of words. In the New York *Herald* for 5 January 1859, it carried a long Gertrude Stein sort of dry-goods poem which in part ran as follows:

Come, come, time, time
Come, come, time, time
The time has come

What is to be done? Is the question
What is to be done? Is the question

What shall be done?
What shall be done?
Mark every article
Mark every article
Way
Way
Way down
To some price which will make it
To some price which will make it
Sell and go quick,
Sell and go quick,
Sell and go quick,
LADIES
Ladies, all this has been done in a most thorough manner.
OUR GOODS SHALL BE SOLD CHEAP!
OUR GOODS SHALL BE SOLD CHEAP!
IN THIS GREAT SELL OUT.
IN THIS GREAT SELL OUT.[12]

That advertising and publicity powerfully contributed to the inflation of words and that the inflation of words affected the mental habits of people in the democratic age ought to be obvious. The inflation of words affected intellectual life on all levels. The inflation of intellectual communications increased the momentum and the time lag in the movement of ideas, not merely encumbering the latter but making it predictable. Whereas the misery and the glory of intellectual life is latent within its unpredictability, meaning that the originality and the novelty of its creations and of its subjects spring from the authentic interests of its creators, one of the most damaging results of the bureaucratization of intellectual life was this decrease of authenticity, whereby not only the treatment but the very selection of certain subjects became predictable. This happened not only because of the increasing influence of middlemen in the commerce of ideas. It was the result of the development of generations of intellectuals whose unceasing concern with public success or academic career led them to the exemplification or representation or incarnation of ideas that had already become current—at the expense of authenticity and originality and often of personal probity itself. The development of intellectual movements of the 1960s and their involvement with publicity at least suggest the question whether able men and women knew any longer how to think for themselves or how to make up their own minds. Ezra Pound's phrase of fifty years before, that "the artist is the antennae of the race," and Victor Hugo's phrase of more than one hundred years before about ideas "whose time has come," were no longer very telling, publicity having compromised the movement of ideas to the extent that most ideas whose "time had come" were no longer any good. Evelyn Waugh stated this clearly in the 1950s. "In a democracy," he wrote, "men do not seek authority so that they may impose a policy. They seek a policy so that they may achieve authority." It may be significant that the Oxford English Dictionary registered the first appearance of the word "opportunism" only around 1870—almost at the same time when the noun "intellectual" became current in English.

This slowing down of movements was reminiscent of what Burckhardt had seen in the decline of culture during the third century A.D., when "the natural capacities and talents for art and literature were as great as ever, but society was such that the artist or writer who worked out of inner necessity and with a strict conscience would be swamped by all the clever little talents who could adapt themselves to a vulgar taste and make a good business of it." Unlike in the late Roman Empire, political freedom and freedom of expression in the United States during the second half of the twentieth century were broader than ever before. That pressure of public opinion whereof Tocqueville spoke when he wrote about the tyranny of majorities became transformed to the extent that in the United States all kinds of things could be represented or published without impunity, censorship—political and social—having virtually ceased to exist. There remained, however, the kind of censorship—unspoken but rigid and fearful—exercised by the intellectuals. Again there was a parallel with prerevolutionary Russia where, in addition to the clumsy and often unthinking official and narrowly political censorship of the Tsarist regime, the intelligentsia exercised a censorship that in many ways was more efficient than was the official one. It allowed no recognition, no space, no discussion of the works of conservative Russian writers and thinkers, works often of considerable worth.

Another result of this slowing down of the movement of ideas was the failure of intellectuals and of "experts" of all kinds to give useful guidance to American political and administrative institutions that were asking for it. In 1929 the projections of nearly every eminent economist were proven wrong—with little or no deleterious effects on their careers. During the last fifty years there have been protean manifestations of wrong predictions by "experts" in almost every field. They had acquired the habit of projecting the continuation of whatever seemed to be going on.†

Such intellectual habits occurred on the conscious not on the unconscious levels of thinking. This was true of the American habit of split-mindedness—something quite different from the modern and Freudian accepted idea of the structure of mental functions. Unlike the division of consciousness from subconsciousness, split-mindedness is a phenomenon that exists on the same level, within the same mind. As George Orwell wrote about doublethink, it "means the power of holding two contradictory beliefs in one's mind simultaneously and accepting both of them." Whatever Emerson said about consistency being "the hobgoblin of little minds," it was surely not characteristic of his own. "This same man," the young Knut Hamsun wrote about Emerson, "who in one essay is ecstatic over this two-sidedness of Plato, declares just as ecstatically in another essay: 'I love facts. An actually existent fly is more important than a possibly existent angel!' "[13] In *Alma Mater* Henry Seidel Canby remem-

† From time to time articles appeared in popular magazines featuring predictions of How Americans Will Live Ten (or Twenty, or Fifty) Years From Now. Since they consisted of nothing but projections of already existing ideas and technologies they were almost always wrong. Giants of American enterprise and industry, public intellectuals with the greatest of reputations did much the same thing—without the least harm to those reputations. The liberal Professor John Kenneth Galbraith, who took justified pleasure in pointing out the follies of economists before and during 1929 (in his *1929: The Great Crash)* achieved his fame around 1960 with his book *The Affluent Society,* published but a few years before affluence in America began to decline. The conservative Professor Milton Friedman predicted in 1972 that the Law of Supply and Demand (whatever that is) meant that the price of a barrel of oil could not rise over $9 per barrel; within one year it rose to $25, whereafter he was awarded the Nobel Prize. Hannah Arendt, the popess of the New York intelligentsia, established her enduring reputation with *The Origins of Totalitarianism* in 1949, in which work she explained that the essence of totalitarianism meant that such governments were bound to become more and more totalitarian as time went on; within a few years came the relaxation of terror in Russia under Khrushchev. The dean of American demographers, Professor Frank Notestein, wrote in 1945 in *The Atlantic Monthly* (the article bore the title "The Facts of Life") that "in the next five years the birthrate will almost certainly fall below its wartime level"; within a few months it rose to its highest level in the century. The director of the Bureau of the United States Census proclaimed in 1946 that the population of the nation would not reach 163 million until the year 2000. He was forty-five years off. The panel of prime experts summoned by the National Association of Manufacturers declared in 1954, "Guided by electronics, powered by atomic energy, geared to smooth, effortless workings of automation, the magic carpet of our free economy heads for distant and undreamed horizons." David Sarnoff, the chairman of RCA, predicted in 1956 "5000 mile-an-hour rocket planes, controlled weather and push-button homes by 1976." He also forecast "the collapse of Soviet communism, the outlawing of war and a worldwide rise in living standards . . . impressive as the developments of the last century had been, I am convinced that they will be eclipsed by the events of the next twenty years." (The New York *Times,* 1 October 1956.) In 1955 Admiral Lewis Strauss, chairman of the Atomic Energy Commission, predicted that nuclear energy would be so cheap that by the 1970s electricity would no longer have to be metered.

bered the atmosphere of New England university life around the turn of the century: "There was bluff among the students, but bluff in the faculty also; and what was worse, for the older men an intrinsic self-deception from which few escaped. Students and faculty alike learned to salute idealism with one hand while doing what they pleased with the other."[14]

The danger to the American mind, at least for a long time, was not materialism but a false idealism. Woodrow Wilson was a prototype of the resultant split-mindedness. "Sometimes people call me an idealist," Wilson said. "Well, that is why I know I am an American. America is the only idealistic nation in the world."[15] ("American idealism," said Herbert Hoover, "is wholly unfitted to Europe.") One of the results of this kind of split-mindedness was the coexistence of conservatism and radicalism within the same intellect. "No man that I know and trust, no man that I will consent to consort with, is trying to change anything fundamental in America," Wilson said in 1912.[16] This from a man whose mind entertained a host of ideas whose revolutionary portents he himself would occasionally recognize, indeed, proclaim—for example, that America stands for "the conquest of the world by the ideals of internationalism and democracy . . . which mark the coming of universal peace."

This kind of split-mindedness encompassed an unwillingness, rather than an inability, to think things through. It contained elements of intellectual dishonesty as well as of the kind of cowardice of which Charles Péguy wrote *(circa* 1910) that it is the result of the fear of being insufficiently progressive. In other ways this kind of split-mindedness contributed to the substitution of vocabulary for thought, and to the taking for real of what is merely conceptual. Together with pictorialization, this deterioration of verbal habits (and of thinking) led to a weakening of American imagination itself. When we look at the vicious surrealism of much of American popular music, popular poetry, literature, and art during the last quarter century we ought to recognize that not only the human intellect but human imagination must have a fairly healthy diet if it is not to feed on poisons.

By the 1970s the lamentations of the intelligentsia proved unwarranted. In spite of the shrinking marketplace for professors, intellectuals and intellectuality were not less influential than before. Their potential emoluments from governments, foundations, and corporations were still munificent, while government and business became intellectualized to an extent unforeseen by their critics earlier. At the same time there were developments of promise. One was the dispersion of American intellectuality across the nation. Americans with independent minds, considerable learning, and serious concerns existed now in the oddest places, even though usually isolated from each other: a geographical, social, and civilizational phenomenon which was as different from the urban coagulation of the conventicles of a self-conscious intelligentsia as from the unsure egocentricity of an unduly self-conscious individualism. Many of these people were older men and women, serious readers of books; but an important element, too, was the existence of young academics with first-rate minds in small institutions of little reputation in the least expected places and circumstances—a salutary and unforeseen by-product of the depression of the professorial marketplace. Whether the existence of such men and women was sufficient to counteract their isolation we cannot tell. Intellectually at least their existence suggested that the very opposite of Tolstoy's sentimental first sentence in *Anna Karenina* was true: at least in the twentieth century it is unhappy families who are all alike, while happy families are inspiringly different.

The other development involved the perils and the defenders of the American language. As late as the 1940s it was arguable that the language of the American businessman was more direct and less abstract than the language of American academics and that of the intelligentsia. By 1960 this was no longer the case. Most American businessmen had come to express themselves in a language that was not only more complicated and abstract and often imprecise than that of other businessmen across the world (whose national languages, too, were bureaucratizing and Americanizing themselves) but even than that of many American academics. By the 1970s a small but significant reaction set in. The number of Americans who had become not only interested but concerned with their native language grew. To maintain and, on occasion, to defend the decencies and the proper use of the American language‡ became a matter of intellectual refinement and of cultural, indeed, of patriotic, import for certain people. Some of the more serious academics and intellectuals, too, have shifted their linguistic interests and aspirations from the inflation of the language to its deflation, from avant-garde to rearguard tasks, from being the purveyors and managers of recondite vocabularies to being the serious guardians of the English language. A breed of men and women existed now athwart the Republic, truly patriotic intellects because of their anxious and watchful concern for the preservation and the care of the greatest patrimony of their nation, the ever-living treasure of the English language—a widely scattered class of men and women whose mark of general culture

‡ An evidence of this is the relative success of such American publications as *The Underground Grammarian* and *Verbatim*—American examples of "samizdat," the underground literature provided by deeply concerned people in the Soviet Union.

and of personal probity was their concern with language and therefore with thinking. "We are not divided now into those who know and those who do not know. We are divided into those who care and those who do not care." What Chesterton said seventy years ago was as applicable to the older intelligentsia as it was to this newer one, probably even to the people of the Republic at large.

(5)

During the early nineteenth century American artists, with few exceptions, had not yet begun to consider themselves as a separate class of people. An American painter was a craftsman, as was an American cabinetmaker, or an American architect. Aesthetic and revolutionary theories had little to do with their minds. The self-conscious separation of artists from the bourgeoisie, beginning in Western Europe around 1830, hardly existed in the United States. During the second century of the United States this, too, began to change. Eventually the perception of art and the aspirations of many American artists became not very different from that of their European counterparts. In the United States, as in Europe, intellectualization began to devour the world of art itself.

There was one particularly American inclination which continued to exist: the democratic belief that aspiration was the equivalent or at least the near equivalent of talent. If few people recognized the difference between the aspirations of writing the great American novel and of becoming a great American novelist, the same thing was true of the popular American attitude toward art. In the 1880s the young Knut Hamsun was enraged by an exhibition of children's art in a midwestern city. "Such an American jury has so little shame artistically that as a matter of course it also accepts the works of children *because* they are the works of children, giving them space anywhere, preferably in a spot which catches the eye. A card is hung on these childish scribblings indicating that the artist is twelve years old and an orphan. The card on a black-chalk drawing depicting two hens calls attention to the fact that the artist is fifteen, deaf, dumb, and lame. What has aesthetics to do with pity? As an artist I would not hesitate to take the cripple's two hens off the wall. This drawing brazenly makes a fool of the viewer, and it besmirches the pictures in its vicinity. . . ."[17] Such inclinations changed not at all during the century that followed. Ronald Berman noted that according to the Bureau of the Census "by 1976 about a million people described themselves as artists by occupation. The self-ascription does not mean that anything was created or sold. It only means that their hopes were artistic."[18] People in American cities and suburbs took pleasure in saying that this man or that woman was "an artist." It is interesting, and perhaps disturbing, to notice that while many of these artists knew little about the highbrow world of avant-garde art, they were equally uninterested and undisturbed by traditional art: I have met young American painters (and fairly good craftsmen at that) who have never heard the names of Bellini or Vermeer, and who have seldom, if ever, set foot in a museum. (And since in the second half of the twentieth century there is a definite tendency for art, very much including painting, to return to its original, primary function of decoration—the function which began on the walls of cavemen—it is entirely possible that this democratic tendency of art may survive the intellectualization of it.)

By the 1890s American bohemias were coming into existence. Thereafter the bohemian artist became as recognizable a phenomenon as had the American intellectual. This happened not only in New York but also in Chicago and in cities of the West Coast, suggesting that these social developments cannot be ascribed mainly to the influence of immigrants. The tendency of bohemia to separate itself from philistinism may have been even more inevitable than the tendency of the intelligentsia to pronounce its separation from the bourgeoisie. The gathering of American bohemias was not restricted to cosmopolitan places such as Greenwich Village in New York. What had happened in certain English artistic and intellectual circles in the 1890s repeated itself in America after a time lag of ten or fifteen years at the most. There were ephemeral communities such as Arden, Delaware, "where in 1912 men and women worked in wrought iron and leather, danced dutifully on the village green, and listened to lectures on socialism, anarchism, *and* the culture of the future."[19] In 1913 Mabel Dodge said that the Armory Show in New York City was "the most important event in America since 1776." The common denominator of these events and of their attendant pronouncements was the belief that artistic avant-gardism was an inevitable factor of political and social salvation.* Their promoters and participants failed to understand that what young artists in America needed was not more freedom but more discipline.

While inadequate discipline could be an obstacle in the full develop-

* Henry F. May, *The End of American Innocence* (Chicago, 1959), p. 375: "To Susan Glaspell and George Cram Cook, their mission was 'to keep alive in the world the light of imagination' and they could fulfill this mission best through the Provincetown Players"—a testimony to the want of imagination bedeviling Miss Glaspell and Mr. Cook.

ment of art, it was surely not an obstacle to its collection. The American bourgeois interlude led to the great American collections of art, with the transportation of great works and even of artists and performers from the Old World to the New. We have also seen that a first-rate American tradition, especially in painting, was developing even before the flourishing of the high bourgeois period. When painters such as Thomas Eakins, Mary Cassatt, John Singer Sargent, Childe Hassam, not to speak of Whistler and Homer, had come into their own, they had little to do with the already forming conventicles of an American bohemia, even though they had their occasional troubles with American philistinism.

Between 1915 and 1955, during the high period of American prosperity and power, America was coming of age in what could be called the secondary arts: in graphics, illustration, industrial design, photography, the movies. In literature, too, the intellectual quality of American criticism rose even higher than that of American poetry, prose, or drama. Between 1900 and 1950 American popular music reached a level of sophistication and occasional fineness, unequalled perhaps in the entire history of popular music of the world. But after 1950 a curious duality came about. On the one hand the appreciation of American art, artists, and literature had reached unprecedented heights both within the United States and in Europe. French intellectuals, for example, despite all of their political (and often fraudulent) anti-Americanism, convinced themselves (wrongly) that American writers such as Ernest Hemingway or Nelson Algren represented a style and a vision of the world that were very fresh and new. By 1955 the art capital of the world had moved from Paris to New York, which was now the center of art dealing and commerce: and American painters such as Jackson Pollock, Mark Rothko, Willem De Kooning were searched out by European critics and dealers. On the other hand the commercialization and intellectualization of art—two influences that were often parallel, sometimes divergent—produced the kind of instant damage that was well-nigh irreparable. The "Abstract Expressionism" produced by the painters, proclaimed as "The American Style" by the leading New York critics and reviewers and art dealers, soon thereafter completed the processes of intellectualization and of commercialization. Such phenomena, signifying the decay of art, were happening in Europe, too; but in America they were a living denial of the much-touted promise of the uniqueness of American art at what seemed to be the zenith of American power and influence, the starry American hour in the history of the world. The previously interesting detail and imaginative features of American movies, too, were declining; so, alas, were the unique harmonious charms and beauties of American popular music—the latter due to commercialization even more than to intellectualization, as the purveyors of the record companies discovered that most purchasers of records were adolescents who had no appreciation or feeling for those sophisticated harmonies. During the 1950s American popular music decayed very fast, descending to a level where rock and roll, no longer an isolated or regional aberration, became a national and worldwide phenomenon after 1955—that ominous milestone and turning point, again. It was reminiscent of what the Greek Aristoxenus, the first historian of music, wrote during the late Hellenistic age: "Since audiences have degenerated into barbarians and the popular music has greatly deteriorated, too few of us remember what music once was." In an article, "The Taste of the Age," in 1958 Randall Jarrell wrote that "if we have the patience (or are given the opportunity) to wait until the West has declined a little longer, we shall all see the advertisements of Merrill Lynch, Pierce, Fenner, and Smith illustrated by Jean Dubuffet."[20] Well we have.

The pictorialization of American imagination, at the expense of its verbal component, has been furthered immensely by television, leading to such habits of mind as inattention and passivity, the opposites of concentration and contemplation. Pictorialization influenced not only publishing but writing: the recurrent ambition of American writers to produce certain verbal effects, rather than precise descriptions, had something to do with it. The purpose in using certain words or phrases was not really that of conveying a picture; the purpose was to produce a startling impact through the picturesque management—more than often an unusual juxtaposition—of words.

Meanwhile the prevalence of pictures in all kinds of American printed material increased steadily. The printed pages of magazines and journals were interrupted by irrelevant pictorial material. These were no longer even remotely illustrations of the text: often they were taken from existing albums of nineteenth-century engravings of monstrous caricatures or steel cuts, with no relationship to the printed text of the article which they were interrupting. The care and the expense lavished on the selection and on the technical exactitude of pictorial matter in magazines and books was great, while editorial preoccupation with the accuracy of their text had become increasingly careless and haphazard. Such inclinations were also evident in the primers and textbooks. College textbooks were stuffed with expensive pictures, often in color. First readers for six-year-old children in the 1920s contained on the average 645 new words; in the 1950s, 330 new words; in 1960–63 this was down to 150. During these years the number of pictures in the primers doubled.

Among all American forms of art the promise of American architecture was exceptional, mainly because of the inseparable relationship of architecture with engineering. After the 1870s the image of the United States not only was that of a land of unlimited opportunities but also that of technical wonders. Before the 1870s the inventions of Fulton or Morse or Whitney were occasional achievements; but the 1870s was the decade of Pullman, McCormick, Singer, Edison, of the sewing machine, barbed wire, the mechanical thresher, the reaper, the telephone, the sleeping car, the electric bulb. During the 1880s and 1890s American architecture began to impress the world. In 1883 the Brooklyn Bridge was a magnificent construction, celebrated and discussed by American writers as a monument not only in the history of American engineering but of American culture. Still the purpose of the Brooklyn Bridge was that of transportation; ten years later the purpose of the Columbian Exposition was ideological. By 1900 the reputation of American architecture was worldwide. Architects such as Louis Sullivan were achieving an American style, the principal mark of which was the harmonization of technology with tradition, of American monumentality with a specifically American version of the Beaux-Arts. Lesser architects failed to achieve such harmonizations. Skyscrapers such as the Flatiron and the Woolworth buildings in New York, wonders of the world then, have not stood the test of time: their very shapes, not to speak of their opulent stony decorations, soon acquired at best a strangely antiquated, at worst a deadly look: the one a monstrous high-button shoe, the other a turriferous wedding cake. Yet the sum total of the New York skyline, no matter how largely unplanned or impractically situated, became a symbolic landmark not only of the United States but of the entire twentieth century: dynamic, powerful, and characteristically American. On a more mundane level of development American domestic architecture also achieved standards of considerable excellence during the high bourgeois period.

But American architecture, too, was not immune from the influences of intellectualization and abstraction. These influences, originally European, appeared in the United States relatively early. Even before the First World War modern architecture broke out in places in Scandinavia, Austria, on occasion in Germany and even in England. The American exemplar of modern architects, Frank Lloyd Wright, soon acquired a reputation greater even than his influence. Yet the intellectual, as well as the aesthetic, grounds of his vision were astonishingly feeble. With his (mostly verbal) "total" rejection of tradition (and particularly of the European tradition) and his concept of a functional (in theory, rather than in practice) architecture, which was to be wholly in accord with a "liberating" technology, Wright revealed—or, rather, ought to have revealed—that he was entirely the product of his time, the architectural equivalent not of Whitman or even of Lindsay but of the gassy populism of Carl Sandburg, holding ideas identical with those of Edison or Ford. Despite his midwestern origins, Wright was a perfect complement of the American bohemian movement *circa* 1912, extremely conscious of his public persona.

By the 1930s Wright's buildings had become more and more grotesque and less and less functional. At that time the best of American federal architecture was neoclassical, transforming the cityscape of Washington, D.C., with buildings whose European equivalents were the monumental (and not always unattractive) designs of Albert Speer. In sum, "modern" American architecture, like much of "modern" American painting, turned out to have been a period creation. And, as in other fields of American intellectual life, after the 1930s the influence of European refugees became an important element. The influences, while widespread, were seldom salutary. The pronouncements of the Bauhaus School, of which Walter Gropius was an example (he wrote that "the art of building is contingent on the co-ordinated teamwork of a band of active collaborators whose orchestral cooperation symbolizes the co-operative organism we call society") was yet another example of a heavy intellectual vocabulary cloaking the near-absence of creative thought—unfortunately in the case of architecture, with visible and tangible results. It was not until the 1970s that certain American architects, belatedly chastened by their own experiences, began to grope toward a return of the old-fashioned belief that architecture is indeed an art.

It is too early to assess the potential, let alone the actual, effects of this kind of reaction, the eventual development of which will be inevitably slowed by accumulated institutional and technical, by intellectual and financial obstacles. Yet it may have a certain significance. Sometime during the 1970s the American mind and American art began to enter their post-progressive and post-modern phase. Historically speaking, "pre-" and "post-," "before" and "after," are more telling and more meaningful qualifying prefixes than are "pro-" or "anti-." In this respect it was interesting and perhaps encouraging that, at least on certain levels, this American post-liberal and post-progressive reaction in some ways preceded corresponding developments in Europe and elsewhere. To the origins and the development of this new chapter in the political and intellectual history of the Republic we must now turn.

(6)

Of the three political adjectives, "conservative," "liberal," "radical," only the last one is ancient and English. The political usage of "conservative" and "liberal" derives from France and from Spain. They were not applied to politics in the English-speaking nations before about 1825—that is, fifty years after the American Revolution. Of course there were conservatively inclined people within the new nation, including not only Loyalists but men among the Founding Fathers; but while we must recognize their existence, it would be wrong to invest them with the categorical label of "conservative." After all, even Burke was a Whig, not a Tory; and there were enough radical elements in John Adams's vision of the world to keep us from designating him as a conservative, *pur et simple.* But it remained for Tocqueville to recognize, and explain, that many of the institutions and the character of society and public opinion in the American democracy were neither radical nor revolutionary—which was what conservatives and even certain liberals in Europe at the time had feared.

This does not mean that American institutions or the American national temper is altogether conservative. It means that conservative tendencies of American democracy existed from its very beginning. It also means that American conservatism differed even more from European conservatism than American radicalism differed from European radicalism, something that went back to the very psychic origins of American consciousness.† Scratch the American conservative and you'll often find a radical of sorts. That the South was more conservative than was the North is fairly obvious; but the conservatism of its few political theorists had a radical tinge. (Fifteen years before the publication of the first volume of *Das Kapital* in 1867, George Fitzhugh, one of the few southern political theorists, wrote that slavery was "the only political alternative to world-wide communism.") The radical strain was there within the Federalists, who around 1800 ranted and raved in favor of "real Americanism" (by

† Example: an American of older native stock will usually prefer to assert that this or that ancestor of his was a radical, since somehow this will sound better (and even socially preferable) than to say that his ancestor had been a conservative. The same thing holds for the reputation of an occasional American Indian ancestor (except perhaps among the lower class of white people in the South). It is the immigrant who—sometimes fraudulently—will claim that this or that of his European ancestors was an aristocrat.

which, of course, they meant federalism). That component of radicalism was there within the conservatism of the otherwise humble Abraham Lincoln, who spoke in Cincinnati shortly before his election in 1860: "The good old maxims of the Bible are applicable, and truly applicable, to human affairs, and in this, as in other things, we may say here that he who is not for us is against us; he who gathereth not with us scattereth"—an argument identical with that employed by Joseph McCarthy a century later, arrogating to himself the power and the glory of Christ. Still, Richard Weaver, an early intellectual apostle of the American conservative movement in the mid-twentieth century, called Lincoln "a Conservative in the legitimate sense of the word. It is no accident that Lincoln became the founder of the greatest American conservative party, even if that party was debauched soon after his career ended. He did so because his method was that of the conservative." Yet the Republicans began as a radical party, "an assemblage of Whigs, Abolitionists, Know-Nothings, Sore-heads and fag-ends."[21] The English conservative historian Lord Acton called the New England Republicans, and particularly their chief, William Henry Seward, dangerous radicals. Wendell Phillips, the prophet of Republican abolitionism, said in 1871 that "there is no hope for France but in the Reds," since the Communards were "the foremost, purest, and the noblest patriots of France." Yet during the presidency of Benjamin Harrison the American ambassador to France joined the British ambassador in disassociating himself from the one hundredth anniversary celebrations of the French Revolution, in 1889. There was a conservative strain within the Republicans' populist opponents too: a man such as William Jennings Bryan may have been radical in his domestic politics while he was a religious conservative. A parochial conservatism and a populist radicalism coexisted in Henry Ford's mind. The Populist Ignatius Donnelly in *The Golden Bottle* foretold the coming of universal peace through the establishment of literacy in Russia and through world government—a forerunner of Woodrow Wilson's beliefs.

My purpose in this scatteration of paradoxical examples was to illustrate the frequent coexistence of conservatism with radicalism in the same minds. Yet thirty years ago Professor Louis B. Hartz of Harvard, in *The Liberal Tradition in America* (1955), argued that the liberal tradition *was* the American tradition. This was one of those bland Harvardian works which, to paraphrase Wilde, pursue the obvious with the enthusiasm of a shortsighted detective: but in one important sense Hartz was right. Even though the political meaning of "liberal" came in the 1820s, the liberal vision of the world came from the eighteenth century. That vision was *the* dominant vision of the modern age: the vision that society was perfectible, that there was no such thing as original sin, that it was within the power of man (and especially of the New Man) to transform the world: a vision which, with all of its then merits and with its optimistic progressivism was essentially antihistorical, or at least a-historical. Against it arose the recognition of history by a thinker such as Burke, who was not behind but ahead of Paine, just as fifty years later Tocqueville was not behind but ahead of Marx. For Burke was not merely a defender of tradition: he recognized and expressed the inevitability of the historical dimension of human nature, something that not many Americans were willing to accept. In a broad sense, the liberal vision was the dominant American vision, propounded by Jefferson as well as by Paine. Until now—because the most important event in the recent history of the American people is that the liberal dogma of linear and evolutionary progress is no longer shared by many Americans.

It is noteworthy that Hartz's book was published at the very time when the American conservative movement had begun to crystallize. Hartz composed his book during the McCarthy era, when a powerful wave of antiliberalism seemed to overwhelm, at least temporarily, American popular sentiment. Yet as late as 1955 few Americans would accept the designation "conservative," while twenty-three years later opinion polls (whatever their limitations) showed that more Americans preferred to designate themselves as conservatives rather than as liberals. But perhaps even more important than these semantic preferences is the condition that most of the principal figures of that American conservative movement, which from 1955 to 1980 had grown to the extent that it helped to propel Ronald Reagan into the White House, have not only shared but espoused the originally Jeffersonian and Painean ideas of progress and modernism and American exceptionalism—at the expense of the kind of historical understanding that had been enunciated by Burke.

In any event, it is historical development, rather than abstract ideological analysis, that tells us something of the character of a political movement, as indeed of the character of a man.

The antithesis between liberalism and conservatism was typical not of America but of Europe; and it was typical not of the twentieth century but of the century before 1870. Thereafter this antithesis was superseded by the newer, and more universal, relationship of nationalism and socialism. I write "more universal" because during the twentieth century these realities have applied to American politics too, the difference between Republicans and Democrats being that Republicans, by and large, have been more nationalistic than socialistic, whereas Democrats have been, by and large, more socialistic than nationalistic—a difference which is also applicable to the modern American "conservative" and to the American twentieth-century "liberal." Because of the general acceptance of the practice of the welfare state during the twentieth century (in this the differences between Republicans and Democrats, and between "conservatives" and "liberals" were differences of degree, not of kind), the development of various nationalisms have been generally more interesting and significant than the development of various socialisms—a worldwide phenomenon from which the United States was not exempt.

In the United States during the first half of this century a division, at times amounting to a chasm, came into visible existence, a division which temporarily corresponded to that between conservatives and liberals. This was the division between American isolationists (who could be more accurately called American nationalists) and American internationalists. The differences between them went deeper than disagreement about domestic politics, deeper even than arguments about foreign policies. They involved different ideas and different sentiments about the destiny and the character of American nationhood and of American civilization.

There was, in this division, a great and perhaps even profound similarity between Americans and Russians. The American division between internationalists and isolationists corresponded to the Russian division between their "Westernizers" and "Slavophiles." The Russian Westernizers were those who believed that Russia had to come closer to Europe, that she had to become more progressive, more cosmopolitan, more liberal, less Asian, and more European. The Russian Slavophiles were orthodox nationalists, often isolationist and expansionist, conservative and messianic at the same time: Europe was decadent, while Russia had her unique destiny, she was the greatest and most Christlike nation in the world. Thus the difference between Westernizers and Slavophiles involved more than advocacies of different domestic and even foreign policies; it was ideological and cultural. Among Americans, too, the division was less political than it was geographical and ideological and cultural, with religious undertones. It was a division between two different geographical and historical views of American destiny, between those who believed that the advance of American civilization should bring the New and the Old World closer together, and those who believed that American civilization was meant to represent the opposite of that of the Old World. The national rhetoric of American exceptionalism produced plenty of believers who were suspicious of Europe: the United States had little to gain from a closer contact with Europe, and not much to learn from it.

The existence of a duality in the emotional relationships of Americans with the Old World was evident from the beginning, but we ought not indulge here in its psychoanalysis. Our interest must be directed to the pedigree of ideas. Most of the ideas that led to the first conscious appearance of a "conservative" political movement after 1950 were inseparable from the development of American isolationism—that is, from a peculiarly American form of nationalism—during the first half of this century.

American isolationism was a powerful factor during all of the twenties and most of the thirties, at the very time when in many ways—physically, financially, culturally—America and Europe were closer than they had been before. This division had existed for some time among American writers and artists too: between those who believed in American exceptionalism, moving away from and ahead of Europe, and those who believed that Americans should and finally could not avoid the realization that they shared the traditions of Europe, essentially the same problems and conundrums of human nature—the difference, say, between Mark Twain and Henry James. Somewhat later this division was dubbed, fairly successfully, as one between Redskins and Palefaces. That the formulator of these labels was an American intellectual of Russian birth (Philip Rahv) was perhaps not an accident.

Isolationists, nationalists, Redskins; internationalists, cosmopolitans, Palefaces: these categories are simple and often telling; but, as always in historical life, the human realities were more complex. Consistent isolationists and consistent internationalists were few. Many, if not most, of the isolationists were so only in regard to Europe; when it came to foreign policy they were often Asia-Firsters. The adoption and the advocacy of isolationism or of internationalism depended on the particular object, on the particular foreign nation. Many of the isolationists who were opposed to the American commitment to Britain and to the liberation of Western Europe from Hitler's Germany very soon became advocates of military commitments against Russia and of the liberation of Eastern Europe from communism. The reverse was also true: many liberal internationalists and enthusiastic advocates of the wartime American alliances after 1945 were opponents of American commitments restraining communism and Russia. Most American isolationists who believed in America for Americans also believed that what was good for America was good for the world: but wasn't that, in reality, a broad American version of internationalism? Most American internationalists believed that it was America's destiny to Make the World Safe for Democracy: but wasn't that, in reality, Americanism broadly applied unto the world? Scratch the American nationalist and you may find an American internationalist: scratch the American internationalist and you may find an American isolationist underneath—but then, as we have seen, much of the same thing applies, too, to American conservatives and American radicals.‡

In sum, these terms of isolationist and internationalist are telling only inasmuch as they refer not to constant categories but to tendencies of American minds. A statement of human paradox may be entertaining: but, after all is said, human paradox is the result of the often inevitable primacy of life over theory. Here lie the roots of yet another similarity in Russian and American developments. In 1917 in Russia the triumph of the Westernizers over the Slavophiles seemed complete. Orthodoxy and Tsarism had collapsed; and the inheritors of the collapse were the Bolsheviks, who claimed to represent that most radical of Western ideas, Marxist communism. Yet within a few years it became apparent—apparent, that is, except to Western intellectuals—that Stalin and his Soviet Union incarnated in many ways the inclinations of Slavophilism, which were then institutionalized in a police state that was reminiscent not of Marx or Engels but of Ivan the Terrible. In 1945 in the United States the triumph of Internationalism over Isolationism seemed complete. Some of the most influential isolationists in Congress announced their adoption of internationalism, which, to them, had become inevitable. American internationalism—the externalization of a liberal and progressive ideology—was now in full development. Yet less than a generation later the appeals of liberalism and of progressivism were melting away. As late as 1970 the principal proponents of an American internationalism, of an Americanized world order, were the conservatives, descendants of isolationists, representing an antiliberalism that corresponded to the sentiments of many Americans, as indeed Stalin's neo-Slavophilism had corresponded with the sentiments of many Russians.

In this respect there was yet another similarity of Russian and American nationalism, and perhaps especially of Russian Slavophiles and American conservatives of a certain kind. Their inclinations, and their propaganda, were conservative at home and revolutionary abroad. During the second half of the nineteenth century the Russian Slavophiles propagated revolutions and Russian intervention in the Balkans against the Turkish and, on occasion, the Austro-Hungarian Empire. During the second half of the twentieth century American conservatives propagated American interventions everywhere in the world against the vague monster of Inter-

‡ And to Redskins and Palefaces. Hemingway was a modern American Redskin of sorts: but he enjoyed that image especially against a European background. In this respect he was but a successor of that other public relations American, Benjamin Franklin, who wore his coonskin cap not in Philadelphia but in Paris.

national Communism—unaware of John Adams's warning in 1821 that the United States will and should not go "abroad in search of monsters to destroy."

In tracing the pedigree of the ideology of the American conservative movement we must note that from, say, 1935 to 1955 (more precisely from the rise of Father Coughlin to the demise of Joseph McCarthy) the emergence of a powerful radical Right in America was a possibility. This, too, followed a development in Europe, though with the usual time lag. In the history of Europe the twenty-five years from 1920 to 1945 were a quarter century during which radicalism was no longer the monopoly of the Left, when neither communism nor capitalism but what is—inadequately and imprecisely—called "fascism" was the rising and dynamic political phenomenon, eventually leading to the Second World War, when such men as Hitler and Mussolini proved to be the dynamic world leaders after Wilson and Lenin were gone. In the United States, too, the Depression was followed by the rise of the popular appeal of radical nationalists. There was a mass potential for a radical Right in the United States even after the death of Huey Long and the episcopal (and partial) silencing of Father Coughlin. This was evident in 1940–41 and again after 1950. Anne Morrow Lindbergh described this potential, having witnessed it at the Madison Square Garden rally of the America First Committee in May 1941. Her description is especially telling not only because of her sensitive intelligence but because she was the wife and supporter of Charles Lindbergh, the popular hero of that movement. There, she wrote, she felt "the animal quality of the crowd," she sensed "for the first time in my life—the rumbles of revolution. Would it break now? Or was this only one of those instants when a grain of the future has by accident fallen in among the grains of the present? But one knows in a flash of insight: of such will the future be."[22] In some ways this was so. When in 1941 Senator Taft said that the danger to America was not Hitlerism but communism—"for fascism appeals but to a few, and communism to the many"—his diagnosis was entirely wrong; yet less than a decade later the majority of Americans would agree with him, having convinced themselves that communism—outside as well as within the United States—was a far greater danger than fascism had ever been.

It was then, shortly after 1950, that the American conservative movement made its appearance; and the great majority of its early proponents and supporters shared these sentiments. During the late 1940s the designation "conservative" was still shunned by every American politician, as if it had pejorative and unpopular connotations. Yet by 1950 the opposition to liberalism and to the Democratic Party and even to the philosophy of the

New Deal was not restricted to wealthy Republicans; it had broad popular support, including masses of people who had been the beneficiaries of the reforms of the New Deal. The development of the cold war with the Soviet Union and the successive revelations about domestic Communists seemed to have vindicated Franklin Roosevelt's nationalist opponents in the minds of many people. The consequent opinion that the American alliance with Britain and Russia against Germany had not only been wrongly handled but that it may have been a mistake altogether was held by a minority within that majority, mostly by German-Americans and midwestern Populists; but the realignment of American politics that took shape twenty-five years later was already in the making. Still in the 1950s the radical Right—the potential mass movement behind Joseph McCarthy notwithstanding—did not carry the day, for many reasons: Joe McCarthy, despite all of his demagogic instincts, did not have the political savvy of a Hitler (or even of a Perón); Eisenhower, in spite of all of his procrastinating opportunism, was not really a Hindenburg; and all of the several similarities between modern Americans and Germans notwithstanding, the United States was not really like Germany.

The first national magazine of the conscious conservative movement, William F. Buckley's *National Review,* appeared in 1955, a few months after McCarthy's meteoric fall from political grace had begun. Many of its subscribers were isolationists, resentful of the American participation in the Second World War. When in November 1956 *National Review* approved the Israeli-British-French attack on Suez/Egypt (only because Egypt seemed to have had the support of the Soviet Union) the magazine lost thousands of, presumably anti-Jewish, subscribers. But thereafter a dual development was taking place. On the one hand most of the isolationism, a fair amount of the Anglophobe nationalism, and a considerable portion of the religious conservatism among Irish-Americans and many other American Catholics melted away.* On the other hand the American conservative movement was widening. Its ranks were no longer composed

* In 1940–41 John F. Kennedy was a secret contributor to America First; in 1950 he gave financial support to Richard Nixon against the latter's liberal opponent in California; as late as 1955 he chose not to take a stand, and preferred not to vote against McCarthy; but in 1960 he ran, and won, his campaign for the American presidency as an internationalist; and by the time of his death the entire Kennedy clan had associated themselves with certain liberal causes while they incurred the opposition and the occasional wrath of conservatives. Much of this was due to the Kennedys' political opportunism and to the then still prevalent American phenomenon of becoming more liberal as one moves up with the social and intellectual and institutional establishment. (This liberalization was taking place among the Irish-American population at large: with their rise in American society many of their bitter memories and old animosities were vanishing from their minds.)

mainly of the isolationist remnant but of all kinds of people: disillusioned old radicals,† ex-liberals, individualist libertarians, and ideological anti-Communists—the latter being the common denominator of the conservative movement till this day.

As late as 1950 the isolationist Robert A. Taft—Eisenhower's opponent within the Republican Party—refused the label "conservative." By 1960 Eisenhower, the broad-smiling democratic soldier handpicked by Roosevelt for the command of the crusade against "fascism" said that he was a conservative. In 1941 Charles A. Lindbergh, the leading figure of American isolationism, said that his principal opponents were "intellectuals, Anglophiles, and Jews."[23] Less than thirty-five years later a fair number of American intellectuals and American Jews opted for neoconservatism.‡ This was a revolution in American intellectual history that still awaits its judicious historian.

One of the main elements in this revolution was the changed image of Soviet Russia. In the 1950s the American conservative movement came into existence at the time when anti-communism was being equated with American patriotism. That equation was as wrong as it was shallow. In the minds of many people it was but another manifestation of their belief in American sinlessness. God had given America a monopoly of virtue, and communism a monopoly of sin. Communism represented the exact opposite of what America stood for; conversely there were few evils in the world that were not the creation of Communists and their sympathizers. Apparently as late as 1983 this was still the essence of President Ronald Reagan's beliefs. In 1982 Mrs. Phyllis Schlafly, the heroine of many Amer-

† Between 1935 and 1945 a host of such intellectuals: Max Eastman, John Dos Passos, Charles A. Beard, Harry Elmer Barnes, H. L. Mencken—this list is not at all complete—had become post-liberals. In this respect they were "antennae of the race," forerunners of a national development, in some cases in extreme forms. Harry Elmer Barnes, an intellectual debunker in the twenties, Darwinist and bitter enemy of religion *(The Twilight of Christianity,* 1929) became a defender of Hitler; the Nietzscheite Mencken became an acrid opponent of Roosevelt; Beard became a nationalist isolationist and saw Roosevelt's foreign policy as a conspiracy, etc. All of this had a significance beyond mundane politics, a significance that went beyond the usual appeal of conspiracy theories to embittered intellectuals whose cause does not prevail. This significance resides in the fact that for at least fifty years most conversions among American intellectuals went from Left to Right—as in Russia during the nineteenth century, where despite the overall (and, as I wrote above, ultimately deceptive) triumph of the Westernizers, the few significant conversions (e.g., Dostoevski) had gone in one direction, from Westernizer to Slavophile, from liberal to conservative, from cosmopolitan to nationalist.

‡ In an article in the New York *Times Magazine* (28 December 1980) about the American neoconservative movement all of the six intellectuals described therein (Kristol, Lipset, Podhoretz, Gershman, Decter, Hook) were Jews, and at least two of them former Trotskyites.

ican conservatives, said that "God gave America the atom bomb." No: the atom bomb was made in America by Central European refugee scientists whose ideas of morality could not have been more different from those espoused by Mrs. Schlafly. Yet concerning the Soviet Union the ideas of the conservatives and of the ex-liberal neoconservatives had now become largely the same, while many Americans (and not only liberals) had grown uneasy with the nuclear prospects of an American global strategy of anti-communism.

The other element was the decay of liberalism. During the 1950s American liberals became fearful of democracy itself. Persons accused of Communist associations were not only hiding behind the antique constitutional barrier of the Fifth Amendment; in almost every instance they preferred to avoid their trial by jury, since they were afraid of the American people. The liberal interpreters of the McCarthy phenomenon were the prisoners of their own outdated intellectual categories. In 1954 Edward R. Murrow said that Joseph McCarthy was "to the Right of Louis the Fourteenth"; in 1955 Bernard De Voto called the Reece Committee of the House of Representatives "reactionary: they hate and defy the twentieth century."[24] These images defied reason. (Imagine Joe McCarthy at Versailles, or Carroll Reece from Tennessee in the company of Metternich.) In 1953 McCarthy was investigating a former Broadway Communist. This former disciple of Lenin and Stalin now invoked Tacitus and Suetonius. "On his part," the New York *Times* reported, "Senator McCarthy quoted former President Woodrow Wilson as writing that 'the informing function of Congress should be preferred to its legislative functions.' "[25] In 1958 a gang in Harlem called themselves "Conservatives." (They would no more call themselves "The Liberals" than would children play at being pacifists* rather than soldiers.) Meanwhile the number of adherents to the conservative movement grew. The civil rights movement, its legislation, the extension of welfare, the reaction to the Vietnam War did show that the generous impulse of the American character was not yet spent. What was bankrupt were the institutionalized ideas of liberalism, very much including the modern liberal view of human nature. The realization that the liberals had contributed to—indeed, that they had vested interests in the maintenance of—the bureaucracies and the institutionalized legalism that were choking free choice, obstructing freedom, and creating disorder in so many American places was swimming up to the surface of consciousness in many minds.

* As late as the 1950s the New York *Times* was sponsoring an annual mock-United Nations Assembly composed of ten- to twelve-year old American children.

The conservatives contributed to this recognition. By 1970 the constituency of the conservative movement had changed. It was no longer overwhelmingly Irish, German, Catholic, Western Republican—indeed, it had become internationalist. The number of conservative journals and the intellectual quality of their contents increased. Even in the universities and colleges the presence of conservative professors began to make itself felt. The Republican Party now openly avowed its conservatism.† Republicans and conservatives together survived the shattering defeat of Barry Goldwater (the first avowedly "conservative" candidate) in 1964 as well as the shameful resignations of their erstwhile heroes Agnew and Nixon ten years later. In 1980 the landslide triumph of Ronald Reagan coincided with the twenty-fifth anniversary of the founding of Buckley's *National Review.* A glittering celebration took place in the Plaza Hotel in New York; and the very names of those present showed that in the realm of intellectual as well as in that of political celebrity the monopoly of the once liberal establishment was gone.

Less than two years after that auspicious celebration it was evident that the conservatives had not fulfilled their own expectations. Here was a peculiarly American paradox: *the liberals had become senile, while the conservatives were immature.* Their intellectual—and moral—substance was not sufficient to fill the post-liberal vacuum. The reason for this was not the cultural inferiority of American conservatives when compared to American liberals: that was a condition that the conservative intellectual movement had, by and large, outgrown. The reason for this was the conservatives' split-mindedness—suggesting that split-mindedness, too, was not a monopoly of American liberals. The conservatives argued against big government: yet they favored the most monstrous of government projects, laser warfare, biological warfare, nuclear superbombs. They were against the police state: yet they were eager to extend the powers of the FBI and the CIA.‡ They were against government regulations of "free" enterprise: yet they supported at times the government shoring up or bailing out large corporations. They stood for the conservation of America's heritage: yet they were indifferent to the conservation of the American land. They pro-

† For about three decades before 1965 the Liberal Party in New York was an important municipal political force, whose endorsement was eagerly sought by candidates. By 1970 the Conservative Party replaced it to such an extent that no Republican (and, on occasion, not even a Democratic) candidate in New York City could hope to be successful wtihout Conservative support.

‡ Bill Buckley started out as an isolationist: as late as 1950 he was suspicious of the Yalie types who made up the CIA and its forerunner, the OSS. Twenty years later the hero of his ideological thrillers was a CIA agent out of Yale, an amoral American James Bond.

claimed themselves to be the prime defenders of Western civilization: yet many of them had a narrowly nationalist, and broadly Californian, view of the world—narrow enough to be ignorant, broad enough to be flat. "I was a nationalist," Hitler wrote in *Mein Kampf* about his youth, "but I was not a patriot." So were, unfortunately, most American conservatives, unaware of the crucial difference (George Orwell described it in one of his prime essays) between the ideological nationalist and the true patriot: the former is moved by the desire to extend the power of his nation, the latter is moved by the love of his country. They were nationalist rather than patriotic: they put their nationalism above their religion, their nationalism *was* their religion. Thus American conservatives welcomed (at worst) or were indifferent (at best) to the dangers of excessive American commitments to all kinds of foreign governments or—what was more important—to the flooding of the United States by countless immigrants from the south who would provide cheap labor but whose increasing presence could only exacerbate deep national problems. There were many Catholics among the conservatives; but their publications would criticize popes and bishops when the allocutions of the latter did not coincide with the desiderata of their ideological nationalism. The true patriot and the true conservative is suspicious of ideology, of any ideology: yet the American conservatives were, more than often, ideologues, disregarding John Adams's pithy statement that *ideology* amounted to *idiocy*. Their view of the world and their consequent advocacies of foreign policies were lamentable, since their view of the Soviet Union as the focus of a gigantic atheistic conspiracy and the source of every possible evil in the world was as unrealistic, unhistorical, ideological, and illusionary as the pro-Soviet illusions of the former liberals and progressives had been. Even though intellectuals of the American conservative movement were often more generous and less narrow-minded than were liberal intellectuals, they seldom hesitated to ally themselves with, and to seek the support of, some of the most uncouth and slovenly-minded people and politicians. That was just the trouble. As Jonathan Swift said, certain people "have just enough religion to hate but not enough to love." Many American conservatives, alas, gave ample evidence that they were just conservative enough to hate liberals but not enough to love liberty.

As a matter of fact, they were not really conservative. Their insubstantial heroes were Coolidge, Hoover, Taft. Their very advocacy of a materialist capitalism was merely a negative reaction to socialism—they have overlooked, among other things, that capitalism and industrialism were the great anticonservative and antitraditional forces of the nineteenth century and after.* The wanting appreciation of tradition among American conservatives was evident not only among some of their politicians but also among their star intellectuals. Bill Buckley was an unquestioning admirer of Secret Agents, of computerism and nuclear technology; Tom Wolfe of fast-flying and fast-living pilots; the two twentieth-century heroes of Hugh Kenner were Ezra Pound and Buckminster Fuller. Jeffrey Hart, the chief editor of *National Review,* wrote in 1982 that American conservatism amounted to American modernism: that the progress of technology, the breaking away of modern literature and modern art from all traditional forms, and the new loosening of the family and sexual mores were matters that American conservatives should welcome, indeed, that they should espouse. In another article in *National Review* in 1983 Hart advocated not only the public listing of those Russian cities that American nuclear missiles would pulverize in the event of an atomic war but that this novel kind of diplomacy (he called it a "new conceptualization of atomic strategy") "has numerous connections elsewhere. In one area after another, we appear to be entering an epoch in which reality will be defined increasingly in terms of abstract analysis . . . abstract analysis becomes the only knowable reality . . . we now appear to be entering a distinctively new phase, in which abstract thought will again become [as in the Middle Ages] a decisive part of our sense of the real." For at least two hundred years, beginning with Burke and Dr. Johnson, the commonsense argument against abstract reasoning has been the strongest and the best intellectual weapon of conservative thinkers against the celebration of modernism. Yet the admiration of the mechanical and the abstract, in the age of computerization and of nuclear international relations, seems to have had a strange and particular appeal to many American conservatives.

Not to all of them, of course: but then the conservatives have not been really united. The marriage—more properly, the cohabitation—of conservatives and neoconservatives has been uneasy. There has not been much compatibility in an alliance of nationalist Redskins with worried intellectuals who thought that their neoconservatism completed their acculturation in America. One need not be a prophet to see that in an event of a danger-

* "Tradition is the enemy of progress." This was not a statement by a liberal or an intellectual. It was stated in 1928 by Julius A. Klein, Herbert Hoover's Assistant Secretary of Commerce, with enthusiastic approval by the Great Engineer (who was himself a Wilsonian and a progressive). In 1960 the neoconservative Seymour Martin Lipset wrote: "The growth of large organizations may actually have the more important consequences of providing new sources of continued freedom and more opportunity to innovate." *Political Man* (New York, 1960), p. 414, cited by Samuel P. Huntington, *American Politics: the promise of disharmony,* (Cambridge, Mass., 1981), p. 170.

ous crisis the nationalists would prevail. Their radical and populist strain was there from the beginning of the conservative movement, within the ideas of the otherwise thoughtful Richard Weaver, who said that Tom Paine, "philosopher of a starker principle," was preferable to Burke, or within those of Willmoore Kendall, who advocated a populist majoritarianism that was a half-mad expostulation of what Tocqueville had called the tyranny of the majority into a virtue.

Fifty years ago the greatest conservative thinker of the twentieth century, the Spanish José Ortega y Gasset, wrote in *The Revolt of the Masses,* "Liberalism—it is well to recall this today—is the supreme form of generosity; it is the right which the majority concedes to minorities and hence it is the noblest. . . . It announces the determination to share existence with the enemy; more than that, with an enemy which is weak. It was incredible that the human species should have arrived at so noble an attitude, so paradoxical, so refined, so acrobatic, so antinatural. Hence, it is not to be wondered at that this same humanity should soon appear anxious to get rid of it. It is a discipline too difficult and complex to take firm root on earth." He was right. Forty years ago the English Christopher Hollis, representative of the Burkean and Chestertonian tradition, wrote that "the phrase 'conservative mind' is today almost a tautology. There are no minds but 'conservative minds.' " He was right. By 1980 these concordant—meaning, only superficially contradictory—statements became applicable to the United States. They reflected a certain kind of American reality. American life was still multiform and protean. On the one hand the dissolution of religion, the loosening of families, the deterioration of older beliefs and customs and manners went on, together with the growth of the political appeal of conservatism: by 1980 millions of *Playboy* readers voted for Reagan.† On the other hand for the first time in their history large numbers of Americans had become conscious of their essential conservatism—a movement of ideas in which the conservatives played but the role of a minor catalyst. For the first time the unquestioned belief in progress, in the beneficial results of man's increasing management of nature was no longer held as an article of faith by many Americans. Their growing oppo-

† The belief that the United States is not only the greatest country in the world but that it represents the culmination of the entire history of mankind was still dearly held by millions of Americans, including (from all evidence) Ronald Reagan: but this did not mean that they, or he, were old-fashioned or conservative, except in a very limited and unhistorical sense. This kind of shortsighted and self-congratulatory inclination was, alas, only too evident among conservative intellectuals, too—as, for example, in the incredible statement of Michael Novak *(National Review,* 16 September 1983): ". . . the American people are, by every test of fact, the most religious on this planet."

sition to the pollution of nature or to genetic engineering or to atomic plants or to nuclear weapons could not be simply attributed to liberalism, the impulses of which were still alive, but the attraction of whose ideas was fairly gone. In sum, conservatism and neoconservatism have been but a partial phenomenon of the larger, post-liberal and post-progressive, development of the American mind.

One indication of this maturation existed among the young. For almost a century before 1970 one could take it for granted that most of the brightest American students would be more liberal than were their fellow students. After 1970 this was no longer so: often its opposite was true. On the stock exchange of American words, too, the adjective "conservative" has risen. Perhaps even more significant the increasing approbation and respect granted to adjectives such as "old-fashioned" and "traditional" at the time when the connotations of "modern" or "progressive" are no longer very approbatory. We must at least essay the supposition that these are marks of a profound sea change, of an ebbing away not only of the rhetoric of a superficial public optimism but of the erstwhile dogmatic American belief in the inevitable benefits of Progress. Such post-progressive realizations, opening around the end of the second American century, may have meant the painful but evident maturation of the American mind, rising toward its acceptance and comprehension of the tragic sense of life, and perhaps even toward a new synthesis.

That was one possibility. The other was the floundering of the majority of the American people between two hard (and, on occasion, increasingly vicious) minorities: the so-called conservatives, enthusiastic advocates of technological "progress," indifferent to the poisoning of the land, propagating the American (and nuclear) domination of the world; and the so-called liberals, opposed to nuclear technology while tolerant of the poisons of pornography, propagating the public and legalized abolition of personal moral restraints in every possible form, indifferent to the killing of millions unborn by abortions. This was the danger: that without a more mature conservatism the American political alternatives would be dominated by the thoughtless proponents of atomic war or by those of the suicide of the race.

(7)

The history of religion transcends the history of the churches as well as the history of ideas. It is difficult enough for the historian to ascertain what people did; it is even more difficult for him to find out what people thought; it is very difficult for him to know what they believed. To some extent people reveal their religious dispositions by their behavior. But together with the perennial human problem of the discrepancy between belief and behavior another discrepancy arises during the democratic age, perhaps especially during the last one hundred years when the desire to believe and the capacity to believe were no longer equally strong: the discrepancy between what people believe and what they say (and sometimes think) they believe. How authentic, and how profound, are their religious beliefs? About such matters the penetrating eye of the novelist is sometimes better than that of the historian: but the latter at least ought to try.

Here was the amazing prevalence of churches and the avowal of religious belief in a nation whose origins and whose very idea came from the rationalistic eighteenth century. The first Americans Tocqueville met told him that religion was most useful, since no free or civilized society could exist without religion. "At the same time," Tocqueville noted, "there is no other country in the world where the most extreme *[les plus hardies]* political doctrines of the *philosophes* of the eighteenth century were as institutionalized as in America; only their antireligious doctrines never come to the surface, not even through the unlimited liberty of the press." In France, he wrote, people told him every day "that religion is not compatible with democracy. . . . I have nothing to say to this, save to answer that those who maintain this have never been in America and have never seen either a religious people or a free people."[26] Half a century later Lord Bryce wrote in *The American Commonwealth,* "Half of the wars of Europe, half of the internal troubles that have vexed European states, from the Monophysite controversies in the Roman Empire of the fifth century down to the *Kulturkampf* in the German Empire in the nineteenth, have arisen from theological differences or from the rival claims of church and state. This whole vast chapter of debate and strife has remained virtually unopened in the United States."[27] Bryce attributed this to the American idea of the church as a spiritual body existing only for spiritual purposes. Another forty years later Santayana wrote:

> Consider, for instance, the American Catholics, of whom there are nominally many millions, and who often seem to retain their ancestral faith sincerely and affectionately. This faith took shape during the decline of the Roman empire; it is full of large disillusions about this world and minute illusions about the other. It is ancient, metaphysical, poetic, elaborate, ascetic, autocratic, and intolerant. It confronts the boastful natural man, such as the American is, with a thousand denials and menaces. Everything in American life is at the antipodes to such a system. Yet the American Catholic is entirely at peace. His tone in everything, even in religion, is cheerfully American. It is wonderful how silently, amicably, and happily he lives in a community whose spirit is profoundly hostile to that of his religion. He seems to take stock in his church as he might in a gold mine—sure it is a grand, dazzling, unique thing; and perhaps he masks, even to himself, his purely imaginative ardour about it, with the pretext that it is sure to make his fortune both in this life and in the next. His church, he will tell you, is a first-rate church to belong to; the priests are fine fellows, like the policemen; the Sisters are dear noble women, like his own sisters; his parish is flourishing, and always rebuilding its church and founding new schools, orphan asylums, sodalities, confraternities, perpetual adoration societies. No parish can raise so much money for any object, or if there are temporary troubles, the fact still remains that America has three Cardinals and that the Catholic religion is the biggest religion on earth. Attachment to his church in such a temper brings him into no serious conflict with his Protestant neighbours. They live and meet on common ground. Their respective religions pass among them for family matters private and sacred, with no political implications.[28]

One hundred years ago (and for a long time afterward) Americans seemed more religious than were most Europeans. They surely were more churchgoing. No matter how strong were the legal barriers separating church and state (as early as 1842 a state law in New York forbade religious instruction in the public schools) the element of respectability, that great force of the nineteenth century, played its role. Contrary to the fears of priests and pastors, most of the immigrants coming to America were not losing their faith; they were gaining or regaining it. Millions of immigrants who had not been churchgoing in the Old World joined churches or even formed new ones in the New World. Church building and church membership rose steeply during the twenties, that otherwise most modern of decades. As in England and Ireland, there was a religious element within American radical movements: it was there among the Populists, it was deeply rooted in the work of a poet such as Vachel Lindsay, it was discernible in the rhetoric of the American Socialist Norman Thomas. Some of this was due to the survival of the medieval strain in American thinking (something which, as we have seen, contributed to the national inclination to split-mindedness). Much of this was due to the social function of churches and of churchgoing in the United States. To belong to a church, to attend a church or a synagogue regularly was not at all old-fashioned, it was essentially American: respectable and beneficial—socially at least as much as (if not more than) spiritually.‡

If and when the historian considers statistics: the number of Americans affiliated with religious congregations, the number of regular churchgoers, the number of churches, the money spent on and in them (or even statistics registering belief: how many Americans believe in God?, etc.) he will find all kinds of astonishing information—indicating that Americans were (and perhaps even now are) among the most religious, if not *the* most religious, people of the world; that the erosion of religious belief, so widespread in the twentieth century, affected them less than any other people in the formerly Christian nations of the West. Yet when it comes to religion, statistics are largely useless. How can one measure the extent of inner convictions? How can one quantify quality? The above-mentioned statistics are not entirely meaningless, they are surely indicative of something: but they indicate not so much the religiosity of Americans as the Americanness of their religion. That, of course, is a general phenomenon, at least during the Modern Age: German Catholics have been different from French Catholics, Danish Lutherans from German Lutherans, etc. But this prevalence of the national (and social) ideology within a particular religion has been particularly apparent in the United States and full of meaning. When an overwhelming majority of American Catholic college

‡ As late as 1956 a feature article in the *Ladies' Home Journal:* "Church is a safe place to meet a man too. A smart girl will sometimes wait near the door until some unattached young man comes along, then walk into church just ahead of him and sit down in a pew where there is still plenty of room for him. Don't wear gloves in such a case, even if they are fashionable. Keep your left hand in sight so that he can see you are not wearing a ring on the third finger. Investigate the young people's society of any church before you stay with it. Maybe it's a small one broken up into little cliques of old-timers, or with the few eligible men already spoken for. It may pay you to go two or three times as far to a church equally satisfactory for you in other ways but with a larger and more active group of young people."

students in the 1950s said that they were Americans who happened to be Catholics what they were really saying was something like this: "Even though we are Catholics we are Americans."

The devolution of the old Puritan dispensation to the modern, liberal, and progressive Protestantism of the early twentieth century was not a devolution from a stern religion to a compromise with materialism. To the contrary, it was a devolution from practice to philosophy, a gradual acceptance not of materialism but of certain materialist ideas. When Emerson resigned as a Unitarian minister in 1832 because, as he said, he could not in conscience administer Communion in bread and wine, since his religion must be a purely spiritual and commemorative observance, free of material elements, he only exemplified a devolution which eventually led to the acceptance of the very idea of evolution among liberal Protestants, whether implicitly or explicitly, two or three generations later. This development, in the long run, was far more important than the influence of Social Darwinism posited, among others, by Professor Hofstadter. It was not Social Darwinism but liberal Protestantism that funneled straight into the mainstream of American progressivism. (An interesting list could be made of Americans who were the sons or daughters of Protestant ministers and who became socialists and radicals during or after the 1910s.) The very Social Gospel, exemplified by popular ministers, pronounced that the salvation of mankind was a progressive and evolving process, in which America was probably ahead of the world. By 1930 the carved figures on the portals of the Riverside Church in New York (founded by John D. Rockefeller, Jr.) included those of Charles Darwin and Albert Einstein. This kind of religious progressivism lasted much longer than had the Social Darwinist period; it led directly to the 1960s when theologians, ministers, and bishops chose not merely to defend the spiritual rights of homosexuals but to extend the sacramental privileges of the latter, including their right to become pastors and ministers governing their congregations. Thereafter the weird customs and eclectic liturgical innovations of such ministers would sometimes fester in the pulpits and around the altars of those splendid and beautiful American replicas of English chapels and European churches, interrupted only by the hallowing music and the fragmentary sonorities of what still remained of the magical archaic English of the King James Bible.

What was particularly American about this devolution? One condition, of course, was the universal (and inhibiting) American belief in progress. The thought that religious beliefs and practices were immune, if not contrary, to progress was alien to the American mind, at least for a long time.* Another element was latent in the condition that in the religious attitudes of millions of Americans seventeenth-century, pre-modern and pre-scientific factors survived for a very long time, well into the twentieth century. Consequently many Americans finally came to regard the movement from religion to science as a step ahead—unready to recognize that a belief in science could be even more superstitious than a belief in religion. Many others avoided this problem through a characteristic split-mindedness: hence the curious coexistence of seventeenth-century and twentieth-century elements in their minds. "Enoch's brain," Flannery O'Connor wrote in *Wise Blood,* "was divided into two parts. The part in communication with his blood did the figuring but it never said anything in words. The other part was stocked up with all kinds of words and phrases."

Last but not least there was the religious—in the broadest sense of the word—element of the American civic religion, allied with the trust in the uniqueness of America in the history of the world, something which by the 1950s became synonymous with a religious tolerance but which, in reality, amounted to little more than indifference. Its evidence included the acceptance of the repeated ritual of Protestant-Catholic-Jew[29] at public functions, the presence of the American flag in every church, the frequent singing of the national anthem in place of religious hymns. Recall President Eisenhower's statement: "Our government makes no sense unless it is founded on a deeply felt religious faith—and I don't care what it is." This kind of belief was not altogether new. "At the beginning of his career," D. H. Lawrence wrote about Benjamin Franklin, "he drew up for himself a creed that should 'satisfy the professors of every religion but shock none.' Now wasn't that a real American thing to do?" The prevalence of the mythical element within American history was exemplified by the professor from the West who wrote Thomas Beer around 1918, "You are like all these other Bolsheviki who are trying to degrade the character of Abraham Lincoln and make him appear an ordinary man. Lincoln was the greatest man born in the world since our Savior, *if it is fair to call him a man at all.*"[30] In Woodrow Wilson's mind we can recognize his nonconformist and southern Presbyterian origins. But, again, the question should be properly phrased: was Wilson's Americanism essentially of religious

* Tocqueville in one of his letters: "A religion is either true or false. How can it make progress?" In another letter he wrote that the adjective *progressif* was ungrammatical and repellent. Santayana: "Of all words in the modern lexicon, to me the most odious was progress." Benny Goodman: "That word 'progressive' kind of makes me ill. That's a political word. If it's good, it can be reactionary."

origin? Or was his religion essentially American?—the answer, I think, must be the second.

This was not a matter of sociology or of anthropology.† It was a matter lodged within the national mind, resulting in the national desire to assert that the otherworldliness of the Christian religion and the secular salvation of which the United States was the representative in this world were compatible, indeed, harmonizable within one mind, one kind of belief. In 1917 an article in *The Practical Magazine of Efficient Management* stated that Christ, "The Perfect Man of Nazareth . . . embodied in life and character 'One Hundred Per Cent Efficiency.' " Less than ten years later Bruce Barton, the most successful and celebrated advertising magnate of that era, composed *The Man Nobody Knows* in which he wrote that Christ was "a masterly executive and salesman who had taken twelve men from the bottom ranks and forged them into an efficient organization." When in 1956 the American Institute of Management reported that its survey of the Roman Catholic Church showed "A-1 Management" and a "90-plus efficiency," this imbecilic statement was welcomed by many American Catholic journals in a spirit of self-congratulatory satisfaction. That the religious doctrines of Catholicism were irreconcilable with those held by liberal Protestants, that the beliefs and the religious practices of American Jews in 1840 were very different from those of most of their descendants in 1940 mattered little. What mattered was the universal acceptance of Americanism (or what they thought was Americanism) by the great majority of American churchgoers and their religious spokesmen.

But what mattered too—beneath and apart from this American universalism—was the astonishing separateness of Americans of different religions, the existence of what sociologists are wont to call "subcultures." In this respect there was a significant change after 1870, and again after 1960. The country was very large; different people did not rub uncomfortably against each other; there was a place for every kind of church, for every kind of religion, without much competition. There was very little evidence of proselytism among various churches and their congregations. After 1880 the geographical patterns of settlement and the increasing social function of the various churches meant that people belonging to different congregations were becoming more and more separate from each other.

† The notion that religion is a kind of old-fashioned liniment, by the then dean of American anthropologists, Carleton S. Coon, *The Story of Man* (New York, 1954): "Religion is the sum-total of behavior concerned with restoring equilibrium to the individual or to the group after disturbance. Every person is disturbed at one time or another . . . and this disturbance must be reduced to its lowest possible level for the well-being of the group."

Because of the peculiarly American coexistence of perplexity with incuriousness, the ignorance of churchgoing people about other churchgoing people, sometimes within their very neighborhoods, was extraordinary. During the last hundred years, when otherwise the democratization and standardization of American society grew in leaps and bounds, this separateness hardly decreased at all. There were relatively few intermarriages between Protestants and Catholics and Jews during the century before 1960. American nationalism held this vast population together; but there were subcultural—meaning ethnic as well as religious—differences in the quality, character, and perception of that nationalism. External manifestations existed, here and there—revivalist meetings under huge tents, radio preachers, plastic madonnas on the automobile dashboard—but they had little to do with the Catholics' ignorance of Protestants, or of Protestants' ignorance of Catholics, or of their ignorance of Jews (who for a long time older Americans would still regard as a biblical people). The suspicions were ethnic rather than religious: anti-Irish, anti-English, anti-Polish, anti-Semitic (the latter appearing only after 1880).

Still it is a tribute to American goodwill that the greatest change in the religious composition of the American people—a change which, for a moment, seemed to have transformed the nature of American patriotism—led to relatively little strife or open hostility in spite of all evidences to the contrary (the anti-Catholicism of the 1928 election was one). This was the great rise in the numbers and in the power of American Catholics. By the early twentieth century Catholics were by far the largest denomination. This was a long-range development. They had been a small minority in the beginning, fearing—with every reason—the potential tyranny of the majority. ("A mere democracy is but a mob" said the aristocratic Archbishop Charles Carroll of Baltimore to Tocqueville in 1831.) Two significant turning points were 1884 and 1960: the first marked the election of the first Irish Catholic mayor in the hub of Puritanism, in anti-Irish and anti-Catholic Boston, the second was the election of the first Irish Catholic President of the Republic.‡ In 1884 the number of Catholics in the United States was about eight million; in 1960 it was more than forty million. Well before 1884 the Irish had demonstrated their passionate allegiance to the United States as well as their national genius for petty politics. The passive

‡ In 1884, too, a presidential election was decided by the Catholic Irish vote in New York, where a last-hour surge of Catholic voters to the polls had taken place. They were reacting to the deranged sermon of an anti-Catholic and anti-Democratic preacher on the Sunday before the election, who accused the Democratic Party of being that of "Rum, Romanism, and Rebellion."

church of the gentle early archbishops had gradually given way to the militant church governed by its Irish hierarchs. The truly heroic efforts of the nuns and priests who were establishing the parochial schools, out of concern for the immigrants who might lose their faith in the public schools, produced two parallel school systems in many places in the country. The influence of the Catholic masses made itself felt on the national scene. In 1919 Woodrow Wilson, in Rome, still refused to call on the Pope, but twenty years later Franklin Roosevelt found it politic and necessary to establish relations with the Vatican; during the 1940s and 1950s Cardinal Spellman of New York often played the role of an American Mazarin in international affairs.

Notwithstanding the essentially conservative and traditionalist Roman Catholic doctrines, during the nineteenth century American Catholics as well as their hierarchy were generally less conservative than were most American Protestants, especially in the field of social justice where the Church condemned extreme individualism and materialism and untrammeled capitalism. During the thirty years of the two world wars most Catholics were Democrats. Many of them were isolationists rather than internationalists, unhappy with the American alliance with Great Britain and of course with Soviet Russia. After 1960 came another change, away from isolationism and conservatism. Until that time American Catholics—whether liberal or conservative, Republican or Democratic—were at least as much, if not more, nationalist than were most of their fellow countrymen. They tried not only to align but to equate their religion with their Americanism—at least within their own minds, and increasingly within the perception of their fellow countrymen, with remarkable success. During the First Vatican Council in 1870 American bishops were among the few who voted against the promulgation of the doctrine of papal infallibility. Less than a century later they were in the forefront of the movement for putting the Mass into the vernacular, that is, national, languages. During the 1890s the so-called Americanism controversy developed among the American hierarchy. This was a conflict not so much between "modernists" and "conservatives" but rather between Irish-Americans and German-Americans: a phantom heresy, ending with a papal condemnation of "Americanism" as being tainted with "modernism." The controversy was still running its course when it came to the war with Spain in 1898; but about that there was no division among American Catholics at all. A letter from Archbishop O'Connell to Archbishop Ireland is telling:

> For me, this is not simply a question of Cuba. If it were, it were no question or a poor question. Then let the 'greasers' eat one another up

> and save the lives of our dear boys. But for me it is a question of much more moment—it is the question of two civilizations. It is the question of all that is old and vile & mean & rotten & cruel . . . in Europe against all that is free & noble & open & true & humane in America. When Spain is swept of *[sic]* the seas much of the meanness & narrowness of old Europe goes with it to be replaced by the freedom and openness of America. This is God's way of developing the world. . . .

Then he spoke of "the nonsense of trying to govern the universal church from a purely European standpoint," that is, from Rome. "America must do for her products what England has done for her manufactures and that implies navies, and that implies coaling stations and that means ports of her own at every favorable point all over the world. . . . The time is gone by when America can live in a state of domestic isolation. . . . Now God passes the banner to the hands of America, to bear it. . . . America is God's Apostle in modern times, a new civilization. . . . War is often God's way of moving things onward. The whole history of Providence is the history of the war; survival of the fittest."[31] No Anglo-Saxon imperialist, no Protestant warrior could have improved upon this battle hymn of a "liberal" Irish archbishop.

During the First World War the fighting spirit of the Irish-Americans became part of the national imagery, including New York's Fighting Sixty-Ninth and George M. Cohan. During the Second World War the Fighting Marine Chaplain was a standard cartoon strip in Catholic newspapers. During the 1950s American patriotism seemed not only to be represented but actually incarnated in the combative Irish-American. In 1955 John McCarten (himself an Irishman) wrote about a popular movie in *The New Yorker:* " 'The Long Gray Line' is a Gaelic interpretation of life at West Point, and in the course of the film there are many occasions when the institution on the Hudson seems to be a colonial outpost of the Irish Republic." In the 1950s it seemed that the rise of Catholics within the society of the United States corresponded to the then equation of anti-communism with American patriotism, an equation which was repeatedly and vocally proclaimed by religious Catholics, ranging from simple nuns in its schools to its highest hierarchs. Joseph McCarthy had the enthusiastic support of most Catholics, especially of German-American ones. There was a fair minority of Irish-Americans who detested McCarthy but their representation in the Catholic press and among the hierarchy was remarkably limited. Certain pronouncements by priests and bishops ran counter to the very essence of the Catholic religion (when in 1954, for example, diocesan newspapers criticized the State Department for having turned back a Soviet adolescent, obviously a juvenile delinquent, to his father, a Soviet officer, in Berlin; or when the influential editor of *The Catholic World,* Father James Gillis, reprimanded an Irish diplomat for having said a prayer for the soul of a deceased Soviet colleague).[32] The rhetoric of the official diocesan press was not merely anti-Communist: it showed an extreme nationalism that had all kinds of—fortunately ephemeral—consequences, internal as well as external ones, detecting and proclaiming the existence of anti-American conspiracies everywhere.

For the first time in the history of the nation, being a Catholic had become a political and occupational advantage. During the cold war against communism, Catholics were being regarded as naturally and automatically the most reliable of Americans. This was not only the policy of governmental and other employers. Before 1950 the most suspicious and extreme anti-Catholic opinions and prejudices had been held by Protestant fundamentalists and their churchmen, often in the Midwest, Southwest, and West. Having discovered the common ground of extreme nationalism, many of these fundamentalists now aligned themselves with Catholics, with states such as Texas becoming the bastions of right-wing Catholicism.*

During the 1950s it often seemed that a virtual marriage of Americanism and Catholicism had taken place, at least on the popular level. The most famous television personality was Bishop Fulton J. Sheen, rising beyond the ratings of Milton Berle, the most celebrated television comedian. *Time* and *Life* editorialized that while McCarthyism was a venial sin, communism was a carnal sin. As in every marriage the influences were reciprocal; but sooner or later one could detect which of the two partners was the more influential, and that was Americanism. Articles with titles such as "Ireland Belongs to U.S. Orbit, Not British" coexisted within the same issue of Catholic magazines with "Let's Put the Mass Into American."[33] The article "The American Catholic" by Father John L. Murphy in March 1956 proclaimed that the Church was adapting itself "to the needs of modern"—that is, American—life. "American Catholicism has come of age, and it must take its proper place in the . . . life of the universal Church. . . . The American Church must take a more active part in this work of adapting the Church to modern life." (Note the phrase "the *American* Church.") Out of this popular Americanism came all kinds of popu-

* In 1956 Kevin was one of the three most popular names for boys in Texas. That year I saw in a mail-order catalog from the state of Ohio (a predominantly Protestant state) two printed T-shirts for children: the names were Patty and Mike.

lar, and even vulgar, excrescences: a liturgical exhibition in Philadelphia named the Catholic Vistarama; episcopal blessings of motorcycles, footballs and basketballs; basketball players crossing themselves before a foul shot; advertisements for religious vocations with all of the flavor of cheap salesmanship: "Do You Want to Become a Priest? Duties Are Few . . ." When, in 1957, Father John Tracy Ellis wrote that American Catholics paid insufficient attention and respect to intellectual life he was roundly refuted by the diocesan newspapers: American Catholics did not need the kind of intellectuality Ellis was proposing.†

The election of John Fitzgerald Kennedy to the American presidency in 1960 was a turning point in the history of American Catholics, especially in the history of Irish-Americans. It marked the end of a long period —more than a century—when Irish people in the United States were subjects of a long series of discriminations. It marked the end of their tribal period in the United States, the last vestiges of their separateness within the American mainstream. They were now wholly secure, unvexed by the need to demonstrate their assertive Americanness, on political, social, or even intellectual grounds. This was the generational difference, too, between John Kennedy and his father ("How long do you have to live in this country to be called an American?" the latter is said to have asked two decades before). During his strenuous campaign for the presidency, Kennedy assured a convention of Baptist ministers in Texas that his Catholic religion would not conflict with, indeed, that it was decidedly secondary to his Americanism. Kennedy, as we have seen, had abandoned his isolationism for internationalism, and for a judicious social liberalism. Indeed, the style of his tenancy in the White House made an extremely favorable impression precisely on those portions of the American upper classes to whom the political ideology and the social aspirations of *nouveau riche* Irish-Americans had been anathema not so long before. (A Boston Brahmin such as Samuel Eliot Morison concluded his *Oxford History of the American People* with the statement that the presidency of John Fitzgerald Kennedy was the shining zenith of American history; on the last page of that book Morison decided to reproduce the music of that most sentimental of songs, "Camelot"—staves, notes, silly syllables and all.) A decade or

† In the 1950s the great English Catholic historian and thinker Christopher Dawson proposed that the curricula of Catholic colleges and universities ought to be integrated along the lines of "Christian culture." In almost every instance American Catholic educators rejected his proposals: in the United States there was no need for them. The Reverend Robert Hartnett, editor-in-chief of the most influential American Catholic weekly, *America,* wrote that secularization and the cult of modernity were European diseases; they did not apply to the United States.

so after Kennedy's death, Americans reluctantly learned that his personal morality, very much including his years in the White House, was far from salutary; and the aura of martyrdom and adulation that had followed his untimely death began to dissipate. Kennedy died on the same day (22 November 1963) as the profound English Christian C. S. Lewis. Lewis had written of himself that he was "a converted pagan living among apostate Puritans." Kennedy had lived the life of a paganized Catholic at the very time when many of the apostate American Puritans might have been ready for conversion: but this was not to be.

Yet the early 1960s—a time span fairly corresponding to the Kennedy era—*were* a turning point in the history of Roman Catholicism. The papacy of John XXIII (1958–63) was marked by a spirit very different from that of his predecessor Pius XII (1939–58), who came to regard the fate of the Church as closely allied with the power of the United States.‡ Besides his charitable ecumenism, John XXIII began to improve the relationship of the Vatican with the East, including the Soviet Union. Certain American anti-Communist Catholics were disturbed by this (Buckley's *National Review* criticized the Pope). This made little difference, at least in the long run. The greater difference was the beginning of the erosion of Christian practice among large portions of the American population, including considerable numbers of Catholics—despite all of the charitable or fashionable manifestations of ecumenism. During the early 1960s American Catholic churches were still overflowing; Catholic institutions, schools, and colleges prospered. The fervor, discipline, and prosperity of the American Catholic Church amazed visiting Europeans. In the Soviet Union Lenin had turned churches into movie theaters; in the New Jersey and New England shore resorts Sunday masses were celebrated in movie theaters for the overflowing crowds. But after 1963 it became evident that the erosion of religious practice which during the previous century had affected entire classes and even the majority of certain European populations was now occurring in the United States. In this, as in other matters, the New World was catching up with the Old. Among American Protestants this development was the continuation of a tendency for at least two decades. Among American Catholics this devolution was novel and its results were startling. In 1965 Pope Paul VI, and in 1979 John Paul II, visited the United States. Between

‡ His funeral in 1958 was a global spectacle. Among the dignitaries of the world attending was John Foster Dulles, who arrived early and stayed late, inquiring into the chances of certain candidates for the papacy among the cardinals whose election would have been particularly agreeable for the American Government, a task from which his harsh Presbyterian ancestors would have recoiled in horror.

these dates the number of priests and nuns in America fell so precipitously that entire parishes and schools had to be closed—even though it was then that the remnants of discipline still observed in Catholic schools began to attract considerable numbers of non-Catholic children (or, rather, their parents). The appeal of religious vocations declined so much that in 1980 the number of seminarists and postulants in many dioceses was one tenth of that of 1960. This was happening in Europe, too; but the contrast was greatest in the United States, where as late as 1960 it seemed that the Catholic Church was immune to this kind of erosion. After 1965 entire orders of priests and nuns were abandoning their religious habits, shedding the last vestiges of their otherworldliness, wishing to demonstrate that they were not at all apart from the world. The substitution of the vernacular for Latin and for the traditional English in the Mass, enthusiastically pushed by the American clergy, meant the substitution of something that was at least traditional and mysterious in favor of patches of a vulgar and smarmy pap, as deadening as it was meaningless.* In order to curry popularity, the most rigid of pastors introduced guitar masses in their churches; many of the hymns of American Catholics now included the worst kind of sentimental doggerel. It is interesting to note that many of the priests and nuns who were "liberals" in the 1970s had supported McCarthy in the 1950s—another example of how people may adjust their beliefs to circumstances rather than adjust circumstances to their beliefs—but then, the 1950s and the 1970s were not that different: the principal aim, the adjustment of religion to popular Americanism, remained the same.

Such were the results of the "acculturation" of American Catholicism. How this affected the deeper beliefs of the laity is difficult to tell. In 1950 it seemed that American Catholics were the most vigorous element within the nation. There was plenty of material evidence for this. Among other things, they were taking over some of the institutions and buildings of the former upper classes. In 1950 it seemed that the end of the Protestant bourgeois epoch in American history came together with a Catholic populist renaissance; but this proved to be ephemeral, it did not last. Around 1900 the then new rich had built their estates on the outskirts of the great American cities,

* Examples: in the wedding of Cana the chief steward was now "headwaiter," the unjust steward was "a devious employee" who got "credit for being enterprising." John the Baptist became a "herald" in the wilderness. Entire phrases of the Gospels and of the Mass were put into television language.

palatial mansions with turrets and Norman roofs and parterred parks, erected on foundations twenty feet deep and two feet thick, impressive monuments to the founders of family fortunes, to the glory of themselves and to that of their wives and children. Yet their glory lasted nary beyond a generation, and sometimes not even that. By 1950 [most] of these estates and magnificent houses were empty; they could no longer be kept up. The reasons for this were taxes and the dearth of servants. Their owners could no longer afford them—this is what they said; it seemed reasonable enough then, it seems even more reasonable now. Yet there was another reason, on a deeper, more personal level: for when people say that they cannot afford something, this usually means that they don't really want to afford it. . . . But then they, and their fathers, had not had these houses for long.

I saw some of the houses in 1950 and, again, twenty years later. Most of them were sold to institutions, often to Catholic religious orders. There was something sadly telling in the aspect of these estates, but there was also something in their prospect that was very American and perhaps even inspiring. Here were these palatial houses, these merchants' castles, erected at a time when Protestant financiers and men of business had gathered much wealth and began to live as if they were the Borgias and Medicis of the rising twentieth century, the richest and most powerful representatives of American civilization in the world. Well, it did not happen. After thirty or forty years of opulent (and often uneasy) living, they sold their houses to the grandchildren (and sometimes to the children) of their Irish gardeners and handymen and chauffeurs. And so, around 1950, their estates became the novitiates and the scholasticates and the convents, the training schools of nuns, brothers, priests of the children of the common Catholic people of America, full of vitality. In occupying these houses the latter would sometimes change things around with a kind of thoughtless vulgarity; still, they brought a new kind of life into these abandoned premises, tending their gardens where elegant thin-stemmed flowers had leaned against the walls, growing thick-stemmed vegetables for their own plastic-sheeted tables, keeping the rose beds, and pointing out to their visitors the rich mullioned windows, the carved moldings, the Renaissance mantels over the fireplaces, with respect and with pride. There was, after all, a strange kind of historical justice in the fact that some of these objects of the old European civilization now reverted to the possession of a new, American, and Catholic people; that the mantel carved by a French *ébéniste* four hundred years before, that the old stained-glass window set by an Irish glazier sixty years before, that the stucco swirls and crenellations on a ceiling kneaded into place by an Italian immigrant plasterer fifty years before now looked down on a crowd of some of *their* descendants, who came to occupy these buildings after the cold men and women who had ordered them to be built had left them for good. The smell of hot dogs, of sweet popcorn, and the sound of television now wafted across these baronial halls—and also the occasional scent of incense, the communal murmurs of the rosary, plainchant, and lusty caroling.

It did not last. Twenty years later many of these houses were abandoned again by their occupants. I have seen some of them, with the grass growing rank, the mansions shut down, except perhaps for a gatehouse or a modern refectory and, once more, the wrought-iron gates locked save for a few hours of the day. By 1970 there were few young Catholics who had chosen the life of a religious; the number of vocations dropped precipitously, and the various orders chose to close down large portions of their novitiates or scholasticates. They, too, decided that they could no longer afford this kind of upkeep. With their increasing worldliness, bureaucracy had penetrated deeply into their thinking; they were ready to listen to management "experts" and to consider the offers of "developers." And so, in many instances, the occupation of these once-grand premises by the new Catholic peoples was transitory; the latter, with all of their demonstrable vitality, were not impervious to that strange atrophy of the will, to the fatalism and the impermanence that may be the eternal Indian curse on the American land.†

In science it is the rule that counts; in history—and surely in religious history—it is the exception. One exception to the decline of religion in the

† John Lukacs, *Philadelphia: Patricians and Philistines, 1900–1950* (New York, 1981), pp. 335–37. To this let me add that this kind of melancholy contemplation may be typical of a native European; it is surely not typical of Americans—which is an evidence of their perhaps thoughtless, but surely cheerful, vitality. Here is an earlier example. One of the myriads of small ambitious enterprises that soon folded around the turn of the century was St. John's Polish College in Philadelphia, lasting but five years. Its historian, however, took comfort from the fact that while this college "contained all the necessary accommodations required for such an enterprise, it was so solidly built that when its existence as a college was no longer feasible, it was readily put to use by the Atlas Casket Company." Sister M. Theodorette Lewandowska, "The Polish Immigrant in Philadelphia Before 1914," *Records of the American Catholic Historical Society of Philadelphia,* 1955, pp. 74–75.

1960s was the change in the self-ascribed loyalties of American Jews. In American social, intellectual, and political life the presence of American Jews was increasing (in 1982 there were three times as many Jewish congressmen and senators as in 1962). We have also seen that the Protestant-Catholic-Jewish trinity in American civic celebrations became a frequent practice in the 1950s, although the American Jews were a small minority when compared to Protestants and Catholics. Until the 1960s, the majority of American Jews were not avowed Zionists. Many of them would emphasize their Americanness, if need be at the expense of their identification with the cause of the state of Israel. In 1967, after Israel fought and won its war alone against its Arab neighbors, this began to change fast. By 1970 the non-Zionists among American Jews were an insignificant minority. What was more important, a considerable number of agnostic Jews rediscovered their attachment to their ancestral religion, something that cannot be ascribed as a mere consequence of the increased power and prestige of Jewishness and of Israel in the world.

During the 1970s diverse phenomena signifying a movement from an Age of Reason to an Age of Faith were discernible among the American population. Their qualities and manifestations differed widely, from the congregations of mindless and rootless youngsters following Indian gurus and Korean businessmen-preachers to the astonishing revivals of radical Christian groups. The widespread antiabortion movement after 1973 showed that the convictions of some of the laity may have been stronger than that of some of the hierarchy. The appearance of the so-called Moral Majority in the late 1970s was less significant, since its pronouncements as well as its composition were reminiscent of the fundamentalism of the twenties. What the Republic needed was a moral minority, not a Moral Majority; but, then, a moral minority is always small in numbers, though it may be the leaven of greater developments in the long run. And there was such a moral minority in the country, men and women often separated by great distances, hardly aware of each other's existences, yet more and more reminiscent of the functions of early Christians during the age of the Catacombs. The most remarkable among them were the Catholic Workers, established by Dorothy Day fifty years ago, surviving the death of their founder in 1980, breathing charity into the catacombs of New York.

After about 1975 the empty churches began to fill up, here and there. The first cautious, but later more outspoken, condemnations of nuclear weapons by the American Catholic hierarchy (suggested to them by a Polish Pope) were significant, since they could not be merely ascribed to conformity. Rather the contrary: people were now being told—true, not by every priest, and often uneasily—that in certain crises of conscience their

Catholic faith and doctrine must take precedence over their Americanism. If liberalism was outdated, so was superpatriotism. In 1945 General Patton spoke to the youngsters of the Church of Our Saviour in San Gabriel, California: "You are the soldiers and the nurses of the next war. There will be another war. There always has been. Sunday school will make you good soldiers." Thirty years later this kind of talk no longer made much sense. The old conservative vs. liberal dichotomy was not only imprecise; it had become outdated, and perhaps nowhere more so than in religion. The nationalist conservatives got less and less support from the churches. This was all to the good, since the—superficially—"realistic" view of the world held by certain conservatives could easily slip into cynicism. Taylor Caldwell, the writer of religious novels, and chosen Catholic Woman of the Year, wrote in 1956, "Let us be honest and confess that we do not like each other, that we hate universally, and love only a few, and that even those few we love we do not like." The contrast between this kind of post-liberalism and the other kind may be glimpsed from what Flannery O'Connor wrote in 1955: "It is easy to see that the moral sense had been bred out of certain sections of the population, like the wings have been bred off certain chickens to produce more white meat on them. This is a generation of wingless chickens, which I suppose is what Nietzsche meant when he said God was dead."[34]

That the decay of liberalism and materialism would eventually lead to new religious commitments and perhaps to a new age of faith had become at least a plausibility; of the proverbial American willingness of the heart still much could be expected. What was yet to be overcome was the mental unwillingness to recognize the contradictions between two sets of unexamined beliefs. Too often it seemed that the bitter remark of someone, uttered twenty years ago, when 96 percent of Americans polled had said that they believed in God, was true: yes, Americans believed in God except that they did not believe in His existence. Or, as the English Catholic writer Magdalen Goffin put it, "If God does not exist, the best, most unselfish, most gifted man in the world is no more than a bundle of chemicals. . . . Good works were never the justification of our Lord's life. He believed that evil was in the first place not environmental but in men's hearts. It is men's hearts that have to be purified—filled with God, not self." The roots of the American predicament may have always lain in the American unwillingness to recognize, let alone believe in, the existence of original sin—and perhaps even of free will. Contrary to the accepted idea, the Puritans themselves did not really believe in original sin. They were preoccupied with sinful behavior, obstructing those Good Works which they believed could mean the perfectability of society, in sum, with Progress. As Milton had written, "They are not skilful considerers of human things who imagine to remove sin by removing the matter of sin." By Emerson's time, as Santayana put it, "the second and native-born American mentality began to take shape. The sense of sin totally evaporated." The Puritans' fundamentalist successors believed (and still believe) that through conversion Man Can Be Born Again, cleansing himself of all sinfulness—but isn't that a denial of original sin? Their progressive successors came to think, as the Reverend Shailer Matthews, the dean of the Divinity School at the University of Chicago said in 1930, that "the doctrine of Original Sin was a theory of human behavior adequate to the scientific knowledge of Saint Augustine's time, but overthrown by more recent research." The Catholic hierarchy and Catholic teaching in the United States, too—all superficial and wildly inaccurate references to Irish "Jansenism" (a seventeenth-century French tendency that was characterized by excessive intellectual scrupulosity) notwithstanding—seldom emphasized original sin in its teaching. Nor did it sufficiently emphasize the doctrine of free will, with all of its liberating sense of responsibility. But then free will, too, has been ignored or at least diluted within the American ethos, all superficial appearances to the contrary, free will being implicitly denied by scientific determinism as well as by religious fatalism, two inclinations which for a long time have suited the American mind and which—when you think of it—have much in common. Bryce thought of it, in his *American Commonwealth* (1888) when he mentioned "the mass fatalism of the American people." In 1957 John F. Kennedy took Hemingway's definition of courage, "grace under pressure," for the motto of his book, *Profiles in Courage,* a phrase suggesting a compound of bullfighter and airplane pilot, baroque-Spanish and modern-American, religious and mechanical, fatalistic and deterministic at the same time, both grace and pressure being external. He was wrong. Courage comes from the inside; it is the willingness to overcome our own fear.

(8)

In *The Civilization of the Renaissance in Italy* Jakob Burckhardt began Part VI, "Morality and Religion," with a subchapter, "Morality and Judgment":

> The relation of the various peoples of the earth to the supreme interests of life, to God, virtue, and immortality may be investigated up to a certain point, but can never be compared to one another with absolute strictness and certainty. The more plainly in these matters our evidence seems to speak, the more carefully must we refrain from unqualified assumptions and rash generalizations.
>
> This remark is especially true with regard to our judgment on questions of morality. It may be possible to indicate many contrasts and shades of difference among different nations, but to strike the balance of the whole is not given to human insight. . . . A great nation, interwoven by its civilization, its achievement, and its fortunes with the whole life of the modern world, can afford to ignore both its advocates and its accusers. It lives on with or without the approval of theorists.

"Accordingly," Burckhardt went on, "what here follows is no judgment, but rather a string of marginal notes, suggested by a study of the Italian Renaissance extending over some years." This warning, and this statement of a modest caveat by a great historian, is applicable to my following pages, ending this chapter on the mutations of minds and morals.

Whatever may be said about the medieval (or neo-medieval) characteristics of American doublethink, it transcends ethnic differences. Whatever its origins, it is inseparable from the American inclination for publicity.

In Tocqueville's notes for *Democracy in America* he wrote that "American manners are grave, deliberate, reserved"—something that has surely changed since the 1830s. That change was not only the result of the shifting ethnic composition of the nation, even though that contributed to it. Tocqueville, who wrote at length and with great insight about the effects of public opinion, did not—and could not yet—say anything about the pervasive effects of publicity. The deliberate and reserved character of American manners and conversation was due to the condition that privacy was a jealously guarded possession among Americans. But during the last century and a half, privacy in America declined, publicity having penetrated within the private sphere of American life to an astonishing extent.

At the beginning of the Modern Age, La Rochefoucauld wrote that the world has always recognized appearances of merit rather than merit itself. During the twentieth century, near the end of the Modern Age, a mutation has taken place, publicized recognitions of merit having become more important (and lucrative) than appearances of personal merit. The influence of publicity became more pervasive than the tyranny of the majority. It invaded the spheres of private thinking, private tastes, and private judgment.

During the last decades of the nineteenth century this influence changed the nature of advertising. The success of a man such as Edward W. Bok *circa* 1900 was different from, say, P. T. Barnum's success *circa* 1870. Bok was not merely the Barnum of magazine publishing. He was a *homo americanus* of a newer breed: a man who was not only, like Barnum, successful in making and raking in the profits of the publicity of his enterprises but in the enterprise of having made a public success of himself. He would have understood—though perhaps not sympathized with—the wag who, later in this century, would say that a celebrity is someone who is famous for being well known.

The transition from "society" to "café society," from being a member of "society" (something that, despite the society pages, is a private matter) to someone whose "belonging" consists of the condition that his membership in a group receives publicity, occurred after 1900. About the influence of publicity on politics we need say little at this point, having dealt with it in the previous chapter, except to notice that the publicity with which political figures were invested in the 1920s was different, too, from that of a generation before. When in 1925 James Walker was selected as the Democratic candidate for mayor of New York this happened because some people thought that the leading Irish politician, the incumbent John F. Hylan, was too stuffy. These influential people included the actor George M. Cohan and the Broadway comedian George Jessel, who made Walker's nominating speech. Irving Berlin wrote a song, "We'll Walk in With Walker." Jimmy Walker was the show-business candidate, the Broadway candidate, at a time when this kind of celebrity had become more important than a political record. That this was not a phenomenon peculiar to New York may be seen in what happened to Coolidge during his vacation in the Black Hills the following year. It was to be a very private vacation, devoted to fishing, but when upon his arrival at backwater North Dakota stations he and his minions found large crowds and bands of Boy Scouts serenading him (with the song "Cal, Our Pal!") Coolidge immediately convinced himself (or was convinced by his friends) to change his entire attire. Thereafter he bedecked himself in cowboy regalia, red shirt, bandanna, ten-gallon hat and was so photographed and reported during his entire vacation. The image became the reality—paradoxically because of the practical shrewdness whereof the managers of publicity pride themselves, unaware of its illusory nature, which is the very opposite of pragmatism.‡

At the beginning of the Modern Age the passion for honor, as Burckhardt recognized, began to transcend the passion for fame, even though the two were not always easy to separate. At the end of the Modern Age the passion for fame has well-nigh obliterated aspirations for honor. In 1924 a murderer apprehended in Los Angeles immediately asked the detectives, "Will I get as much publicity as Leopold and Loeb did?" In 1981 the principal, and self-avowed, purpose of John Hinckley, who attempted to murder the President, was celebrity, public notice, as he repeated before, during, and after his trial. This kind of desire for publicity was not merely a mental liniment after one was caught; publicity was the purpose of the very act itself, another example of the mental confusion of our times. But we need not look for extreme and criminal examples of this condition. The kind of loneliness which is consequent to the inadequacy of inner resources and which therefore seeks consolation not in privacy but from publicity was often represented by a plethora of peculiar American practices. Men hired billboards or put advertisements in newspapers in order to proclaim their love for a woman. Others were impelled to express their gratitude for the most private and spiritual causes by inserting notices in the press.* There was the astonishing phenomenon of radio talk shows (the word "show" is in itself telling), where lonely people told a cheerfully vulgar radio "personality" the most intimate of their concerns or troubles, involving their husbands or wives, in-laws or neighbors, taking a peculiar kind of comfort from the fact that their voices were broadcast and heard by millions "on the air,"† while strangely oblivious of the condition (and

‡ Philosophers interested in such matters may consider this American penchant for nominalism. "I can imagine the spontaneous pragmatism of some president of a State University, if obliged to defend the study of Sanskrit before a committee of senators," Santayana once wrote. " 'You have been told,' he would say, 'that Sanskrit is a dead language. Not at all: Sanskrit is Professor Smith's department, and growing. The cost is trifling, and several of our sister universities are making it a fresh requirement for the Ph. D. in classics. That, gentlemen, is what Sanskrit *is.*' " Fifty years later during a faculty meeting discussing the validity of certain grades, I heard a colleague (and a philosopher at that) say that the condition that a student who deserves an A is usually given an A is irrelevant: a student who is given an A *is* an A student. On another occasion I recall arguing that Joe McCarthy was not a conservative. "Well, perhaps," I was told, "but he is what people call a conservative." There are now people in this country who think it is cold because the radio says it is—not the opposite.

* Example from my local newspaper (not a religious one): "I wish to thank St. Jude, St. Ann, and St. John Neumann for answering my prayers." The ad was signed.

† Interestingly enough, the callers were often taking less satisfaction from getting free advice than from some kind of confirmation of what they were saying out loud: that is, from talking rather than from listening.

of the risk) that their frustrations and complaints might be overheard by the very people of whom they were complaining.

It was because of publicity that sometimes Americans tended to be caricatures of themselves, when their obsession with their image became powerful enough to obscure the distinction between image and reality. This condition involved the very shape of things: buildings, ceremonies, clothes, uniforms, phrases, gestures could become caricatures of themselves (e.g., the ritualistic gestures of cheerleaders, or the man who dons the cap of a locomotive engineer when he sets up his model trains in the basement). This tendency toward the perfection of images could result in self-caricature, sometimes amounting to absurdity. The mental confusion of what is public and what is private often involved a curious mixture—or, again, a curious split-mindedness—of insensitivity and oversensitivity,‡ with the further consequence of the confusion of public and private communications: effects as well as causes of doublethink.

Because of this confusion many Americans, during the second half of the twentieth century, found it difficult to listen to each other even in private conversation—a habit of inattention which, surely furthered by the pervasive noise of radio and television, was also due to the ritual standardization or routinization of discourse, that is, to the ritual exchange of publicly acceptable phrases. In a remarkable little book (1958) the American sociologists Bensman and Vidich described how in American small communities "the code of the proper conversational level is as proper as the code of formalities among the Japanese. . . . The public life is always more 'normal' than the private. Since this is the case [individuals are forced to repress their private anxieties] in order to be able to express the public image which is created by similar expressions on the part of others. . . . The sharpness of the conflict between illusion and reality is avoided, it appears, by the unconscious altering and falsification of memories. . . . Public life is dominated by the system of illusion."[35]

This was written during the bland and "conformist" 1950s, the Eisenhower years. Yet in this respect, too, the claims of the "revolutionary" changes, of the "consciousness-raising" of the 1960s were false. The erosion of the line separating what is public from what is private went on—with a vengeance. It was the source of evils: consider but the legal justifica-

‡ A good description of this in Vladimir Nabokov's *Lolita* (New York, 1957), p. 88: "Charlotte, who did not notice the falsity of all the everyday conventions and rules of behavior, and foods, and books, and people she doted upon, would distinguish at once a false intonation in anything I might say with a view of keeping Lo near. She was like a musician who may be an odious vulgarian in ordinary life, devoid of tact and taste: but who will hear a false note in music with diabolical accuracy of judgment."

tion of unnatural acts, with the pretext of the toleration of "private acts between consenting adults" when, in reality, the gross increase in the frequency of such acts was the result not of an increasing respect for privacy but of the increasing prevalence of their publicity. The extreme individualism touted in the 1960s was often conformism of the worst sort—at the expense not only of self-discipline but of independent, that is, private, thought.

During the twentieth century intellectual dishonesty replaced hypocrisy to such an extent that we may look back with a fair amount of nostalgia to the hypocrisies of the previous century. Hypocrisy was, after all, the tribute that vice did pay to virtue. Hypocrisy, therefore, could flourish only in a world and at a time when people knew how to distinguish between virtue and vice. (The cult of publicity compromised and obscured this to the extent that during the second half of the twentieth century in the United States there were plenty of examples of would-be virtue paying tribute to vice.) Like the bourgeois way of life, hypocrisy had certain salutary by-products, whereas intellectual dishonesty had none. To do the right thing for the wrong reason is, after all, preferable to doing the wrong thing for the right "reason." (The quotation marks are not accidental: they refer to the pestilential intellectual habit of the attribution of motives.) In the end the historian must note this distinction: the hypocrite wears a mask in public, while he pursues his inclinations in private. During the twentieth century we have seen many American public figures to whom the metaphor (and the practice) of wearing a mask in public no longer applied. Their public personality (something that was not at all identical with the Jungian term of persona) largely or wholly preempted their private selves. The mask became the face; they became unknown to themselves, caricatures of themselves—something that will make the task of their biographers more difficult, not less.

That the world tends to recognize appearances of merit rather than merit itself is an old story, a part of human nature; but during the twentieth century it was not merely the appearance of merit but publicity given to merit that influenced the bureaucratic meritocracy. If a celebrity was someone who was famous for being well-known, not being well-known often meant being ignored by one's peers. (Indeed, not being well-known suggests the literal meaning of the word "infamous.") Examples of this kind of intellectual corruption were many. They involved not only the publicly current ideas but the very methods and language of books.* Even-

* Bruce Catton wrote in his review-essay of Fogel and Engerman, "Time on the Cross: The Economics of American Negro Slavery" in *American Heritage* (November 1974): "A

tually these corruptive influences obstructed not only the commerce of ideas but the spirit of artists. In 1960 Norman Rockwell, of all people, writing in *The Saturday Evening Post* about himself, described the governing idea of one of his most famous paintings: "In 1951, for the Thanksgiving issue of *The Post,* I painted a cover showing an old woman and a small boy saying grace in a shabby railroad restaurant. The people around them were staring, some surprised, some puzzled, some remembering their own childhood; but all were respectful. *If you actually saw such a scene, some of the staring people would have been indifferent, some insulting and rude, and perhaps a few would have been angry. . . .*" The italics are mine. How could Rockwell be sure of that? Here was another sad revelation of how the publicly expressed optimism of certain Americans was the result not of naïveté but of a corroding and perhaps even despairing cynicism.

During the Middle Ages much of life was inescapably public: privacy hardly existed at all.† The cult of privacy came in with the Modern Age, three centuries ago: it was a bourgeois aspiration. A return to these aspirations, in the absence of their then original sources, is impossible. In our mass democratic age a mere reaction against what is public is not enough. A contempt for what is public may be the expression of private disorder. It is private disorder that lies at the roots of the person who steals from the public or who besmirches public property. Pervasive publicity and increasing bureaucratization led to the diminution of whatever was (or ought to be) private: they also led to the increasing disrespect for many things that are (or ought to be) public. In 1950 an American city park, an American airport, an American railroad or bus or comfort station, an American schoolroom or building was cleaner than an Italian one. By 1980 the opposite was true. One would think that in a mass democracy public services would be preferred, wherefore they would be meticulously maintained, extended, improved. Yet during the twentieth century in the United States public transportation deteriorated, public schools deteriorated, public health services deteriorated. More and more people preferred private schools, private transportation, private medical attention.‡

Those who can afford them are not necessarily the carriers of new

---

great breakthrough in history cliometrics is not; but it *is* a breakthrough in the field of publicity."

† Here, too, we may observe the neo-medieval tendency: in the significance which Americans attribute to the appearance of things and people (their clothing, for example) at the very time when "informality" is supposed to reign. The *internal* influence of publicity occurs together with the *external* emblematization of the person.

‡ The exception was "public" television and certain public hospitals. And now we ought to take another step. Since private schools and private transportation are not so private either

hope. The carriers of hope are those—and there are many such people in this country now, tucked away in the oddest places—who have discovered privacy in ways of life (and of thinking) hardly current before, people whose very respect for and use of language reveals that they have their own private conditions, that they are *making up their own minds.* They are the true inheritors of Western civilization, Americans who reject the illusion of "the new man."* Concerned with the awful prospects of genetic engineering, Charles Frankel wrote in 1974, "What united the Puritan radicals, the Jacobins, the Bolsheviks, the Nazis, the Maoists is the deliberate intention to create a 'new man,' to redo the human creature by design. . . . The partisans of large-scale eugenics planning, the Nazis aside, have usually been people of notable humanitarian sentiments. They seem not to hear themselves. It is that other music they hear, the music that says that there shall be nothing random in the world, nothing independent, nothing moved by its own vitality, nothing out of keeping with some idea. . . ." How different this is from the New Man posited by Crèvecoeur! How different—indeed, how wholly contrary—are our dangers from those that were posed by the ideas of the eighteenth century—about the nature of the world, including human nature.†

The above passage, written by a Jewish scholar, was cited by a Jesuit who posed the question of whether administering American society "raw judicial power" will not finally yield to "raw biological power" one day.[36] But that is not yet certain—in any event, no more certain than the possibility that more than a moral majority among Americans will change their minds, outgrowing the illusions of "progress." Let me conclude with

(dependent as they are on public funds and public regulations) the most enviable citizens of the Republic in this age of a bureaucratic meritocracy are those who can assure for themselves bureaucratic transportation (official cars at their disposal), bureaucratic medical care (paid not by themselves but by their corporations or by the government), and bureaucratic educational privileges for their children (frequently now it is the sons and daughters of the intellectual establishment and of public celebrities, even more than those of rich alumni, who gain preferred admissions to prestigious colleges and universities).

* *Novus homo* was the Roman phrase for an "outsider," about the same as the heretic in the eyes of early Christians. *Tabulae novae* meant a repudiation of debt. Delisle Burns, *The First Europe* (London, 1949), p. 665.

† Eugenic planning and eugenic human breeding was an idea dear to many American conservatives, including John Adams. In Ezra Pound's "expression of agreement with Hitler, in his [radio] talk of 18 May 1942, on the application of eugenic theory to humans as well as cattle Pound incidentally did not get this idea from Germany but from John Adams . . . and other earlier sources." Noel Stock, *The Life of Ezra Pound* (New York, 1982), p. 394. Randall Jarrell in the New York *Times Book Review*, 23 August 1953: "Most of us know, now, that Rousseau was wrong: that man, when you knock his chains off, sets up the death camps. Soon we shall know everything the eighteenth century didn't know, and nothing it did, and it will be hard to live with us."

Burckhardt's words from the same paragraph with which I began this subchapter: "What eye can pierce the depths in which the character and fate of nations are determined? In which that which is inborn and that which has been experienced combine to form a new whole and a fresh nature?" Burckhardt wrote of the evolution of the Italian mind from the twelfth century to the sixteenth; but his wisdom is applicable to Americans in the twentieth, and to civilization in general: "How can we possibly judge of the infinite and infinitely intricate channels through which character and intellect are incessantly pouring their influence one upon the other. A tribunal there is for each one of us, whose voice is our conscience; but let us have done with these generalities about nations. For the people that seems to be the most sick the cure may be at hand; and one that appears to be healthy may bear within it the ripening germs of death, which the hour of danger will bring forth from their hiding-place."[37]

9

INHERITANCES AND PROSPECTS

The Passage from a Democratic Order to a Bureaucratic State

How and why a new science of politics, a new economics, and a new kind of history are necessary for a new world.

(1)

Early in this book I wrote that for a long time, and in many ways—perhaps even in the most important of ways—the great good fortune of the United States consisted in the condition that it was behind Europe. The great American spaces, the emptiness of much of the country, the unhampered possibilities of enterprises of all sorts, the ungoverned riches of its flora and fauna, the absence of many governmental and bureaucratic regulations, the trust in law, and even the structure—structure, rather than content—of many American beliefs, that protomedieval fideism, including even the naïve American materialism that refused to recognize the intrusion of mind into matter or the split-mindedness of American idealism: these were features of the country and of its society that had faded away in Europe long ago. But around 1955 the United States moved definitely ahead of Europe. The United States was passing out of the Modern (that is, the Bourgeois) Age faster than was Europe. Before that time, life in the United States was simpler than in Europe. To get a job, to buy a house, to receive credit, to transmit money, to send a telegram, to bequeath or to inherit, to achieve a college education or a professional degree, to participate in politics and in elections was simpler and easier in the

United States than in Europe or South America or the Far East. Before and during World War II the complications and the hypocrisies of their bureaucratic states and societies led to the anger and despair of the masses in many a European nation, some of which sought a solution in post-parliamentary dictatorships and authoritarian regimes of national unity, accepting the principle of the complete supremacy of the national state. Among the American people there was little inclination to exalt the state thus, not even among the nationalists who opposed Roosevelt. Indeed, there was something nicely outdated in the entire American view of someone like Hitler: he was simply and squarely seen as a reactionary (which of course he wasn't). Within this misreading there survived, among other things, an element of old-fashioned American decency: Americans, still clinging to their broad-minded optimism, refused to recognize the democratic element in the Hitler phenomenon. In any event, Europeans arriving in the United States during the 1930s and 1940s were charmed and occasionally exhilarated (as was this writer) by the living presence here of nineteenth-century institutions and nineteenth-century characteristics, representative survivals from an older and better world: a great deal of freedom and spaciousness, little or nothing of a police state, the rule of law, a bland kind of decency, a skittish respect for cultural and intellectual achievements—in sum, a world that was more advanced technically but also less bureaucratic than the world from which these Europeans had escaped. During the 1950s this changed. American life, on many levels, became more complicated than life in some of the democracies of Western Europe. The transformation of a democratic society to a bureaucratic one ran at full tide. William H. Whyte's *The Organization Man,* published in 1957, described what was happening within the large corporations and contrasted these practices to the older American habits of individual enterprise, relating this transformation to business; but its effects were there in many fields of American life, ranging from the military to education, culture, and art.

In the *Federalist No. 14* Madison warned against "the confounding of a republic with a democracy. . . . In a democracy, the people meet and exercise the government in person; in a republic, they assemble and administer it by their representatives. . . . A democracy, consequently, will be confined to a small spot. A republic may be extended over a large region."* By 1830 the United States became a wholly democratic republic,

* In 1783 the Free, or Fighting, Quakers of Philadelphia (that group among the Quakers who had chosen to relinquish their pacific principles and fight in the Continental Army) erected their own meetinghouse, in which a tablet was imbedded marking the year 1783 as

proving that its democracy could indeed be extended over a large region. By 1950, another one hundred and twenty years later, the American democracy was changing into something else, a bureaucracy of a novel kind.

Around 1900 Henry Adams wrote about "the new science of dynamic sociology"; American organization had left European organization behind. Europe was declining because it was too old-fashioned, too restricted. His near-contemporary Theodore Roosevelt worried about the corruption of American political and social institutions and the dilution of the character of the American people. He lived to see some of the reforms of some of those institutions; he did not live to see the consequences. What he would have thought of the changing composition of American society we do not know, even though we know that he was less despairing of mass democracy than Henry Adams had been. The few conservative Americans of the 1920s, men such as Irving Babbitt or Albert Jay Nock, echoed the Federalists' fears of an enormous, uniform, unruly democracy of millions. They were American articulators of the thesis of the mass man that Ortega y Gasset was to propound in 1930 in *The Revolt of the Masses.* "Democracy in its degenerative form," Ortega wrote, "leads to a general lowering of values, since the mass man does not seek excellence but more comfort, and to intolerance of individual differences, since the mass man feels comfortable when everyone behaves as he does. Such is not the true European spirit; Europe has always respected a plurality of cultures and a diversity of opinion. The abuses of democracy now threaten that old but vital spirit." Yet it was in Europe that masses of people proved insensitive to these values: they supported, or at least they did not really resist, a Mussolini or a Hitler. Another intelligent summary was offered by the voluble Hermann Keyserling toward the end of the 1920s:

> The majority principle leads to a tyranny more powerful than any which has ever existed before. For it is this tyranny which makes for the happiness of the man in the street, all the more as it enforces a sort of optimism which, however it may fail to represent the true state of affairs, is for that reason more effective—like prohibited alcohol. . . . Sooner or later, those social strata which today have no power, will some day acquire it. The tension between the old colonial culture and that of a young life becoming conscious of itself must become more and more accentuated, for the first already bears the aspects of senility. . . . The period between the *Mayflower* and the World War,

"year of the Empire 8." "Why Empire?" they were asked. Because "we are destined to become the greatest empire in the world."

> with Washington, a Constitution, will some day be regarded as the equivalent of what the Golden Age meant for Greece. But what is good for America may be ruinous for the rest of the world. America has now seized the material power, which under all circumstances brings with it the greatest prestige. Thus America's primitiveness, healthy as it is in itself, may so long be mistaken for progress as to mean the beginning of a great night of spiritual darkness for the whole of this planet. . . .[1]

There was much truth in what Ortega and Keyserling wrote; but they were mistaken about the essential issue. They attributed the dangers of Western civilization and the degeneration of its nations to the extreme extension of democracy, to the mass man. Yet what happened was something else, of which the institutional outgrowth of democracy was but a part. What was developing and institutionalized further was bureaucracy, not democracy; and it was incarnated not by the mass man but by the organization man.

(2)

It would be wrong to attribute the development of bureaucracy in America to European influences, even though the German-type mind-set of many immigrants from Central and Eastern Europe contributed to it. The mechanical way of perceiving the world was there among the Puritans, in spite of their—verbal—emphasis on faith rather than on works, an emphasis which in any event was Calvinist rather than American. Even in England the Puritan democracy of 1649 was already influenced by the New England example. The cult of progress, the belief in the possibility of a perfect (or at least perfectible) society, the categorization of human actions, including intellectual beliefs, and the consequent tendency to regulate morality through legislation were surely the American legacy of the New England Puritans. Benjamin Franklin was not a Puritan, but this was exactly what he and the Puritans had in common. As D. H. Lawrence wrote feverishly in the early 1920s, Franklin in Philadelphia set up his "little idea, or automaton, of a pattern American . . . this dry, moral, utilitarian little democrat . . . Americanizing and mechanizing . . . [leading to] millions of squirrels running in millions of cages . . . this dummy of a perfect citizen as a pattern of America. . . . From Benjamin

Franklin to Woodrow Wilson may be a long stride, but it is a stride along the same road. . . . Theoretic and materialistic."[2]

Eventually this emphasis on what is mechanical over what is organic became embedded in the American consciousness and in the language. Twentieth-century American embodiments of Noble Savages exemplified it as much as did professors of sociology, and the American tramp as much as the corporate executive. Here is a phrase from *To Build a Fire,* one of Jack London's most dramatic short stories of the wilderness, with machines a thousand miles away, in which a lonely man faces Nature, the primal experience of freezing. It is cold; his fingers are numbed; he cannot hold the few sticks. And how does London put it: "The wires were pretty well down between him and his finger-ends." What a metaphor! It is in line with what had become an American tradition of taking the mechanical for the real, as in Hemingway's "grace under pressure."†

In 1891 Joseph Chamberlain, the English politician who more than anyone else tried to Americanize British politics, declared in the House of Commons that the state was entitled to pass any law which may "increase the sum total of human happiness." "Underlying the technical and political advance of the nineteenth century," Ortega y Gasset wrote forty years later, "was the belief that progress in all of its positive manifestations was inevitable. . . . The security of periods of 'plenitude'—such as the last century—is an optical illusion which leads to neglect of the future, all direction of which is handed over to the mechanism of the universe. Both progressive Liberalism and Marxist Socialism presume that what is desired by them as the best of possible futures will be necessarily realized, with a necessity similar to astronomy."[3] Ortega probably did not know that Woodrow Wilson had described the American Constitution as "Newtonian."

The American entry into World War I in 1917, as Professor Noble was to write, "brought to logical fulfilment the major patterns of the progressive outlook as it had been developed since 1890. To escape the disintegrating identity of the nation established by the Founding Fathers—a perfect agrarian republic of saintly citizens isolated in the western hemisphere from European corruption—the progressives had postulated a new perfection based on industrialism."‡ (The—superficially—antimechanical atti-

† No wonder that London and Hemingway have been favorites in Soviet Russia (just as the mechanical and utilitarian philosophy of the English Henry Thomas Buckle had been the favorite of the Russian intelligentsia in the nineteenth century).

‡ *The Progressive Mind: 1890–1917* (Chicago, 1971), p. 179. "All of the major developments in the progressive mind between 1890 and 1917 were preparing Americans to define

tudes of the environmentalists [their history, too, begins with the conservationists among the Progressives] were no exception to this. Ever since the beginning of the century they failed to recognize that the pollution of "the environment" was the result of the pollution of minds, rather than the reverse; that their reverence for "Nature"—a reverence that has been mechanical and animistic at the same time—was essentially Darwinian, unwilling to accept that there is a fundamental difference between human life and all other forms of life. Consequently their, often necessary, defense of "the environment" depended on their extension of extremely bureaucratic regulations. It was perhaps not accidental that Gifford Pinchot, one of the founders and principal figures of American conservationism and environmentalism, was a convinced prohibitionist and a proponent of administrative government.) The Progressives contributed heavily to the transition to the American administrative state, a process during which the legislative establishment of Interstate Commerce Commissions and Federal Trade Commissions were milestones rather than turning points.

It is wrong to believe that the Republican presidents and their administrations in the 1920s were truly "conservative," and that they wished to reverse this progression to the administrative state. Herbert Hoover was a Wilsonian, a Progressive, an engineer. Calvin Coolidge was not a self-styled Progressive, but he wholly accepted the mechanical concept of life as well as the desirability of the production of consumption. "After all, the chief business of the American people is business . . . buying, selling, investing . . . are the moving impulses of our life."* The pronouncements of this sour apostle of New England probity and thrift ought to reveal that he was, in reality, a prophet and proponent of inflation. He said that he believed in budgets: "I regard a good budget as among the noblest monuments of virtue." Yet he also said, "The uncivilized make little progress because they have few desires. The inhabitants of our country are stimulated to new wants in all directions."[4] The road of the essentially inflationary idea of advertising and public relations ran from Franklin not only to Wilson but to Coolidge and beyond.

The main phase of the transition from the legislative to the administrative state was then completed by Roosevelt and the New Deal. That many of its reforms and regulations were necessary and probably inevita-

---

their participation in World War I as that Armageddon in which the victory of the forces of light would usher in the millenium of God's kingdom on earth."

* To the American Society of Newspaper Editors, January 1924. To the New York Chamber of Commerce in 1925: American business "rests squarely on the law of service . . . reliance on truth and faith and justice . . . it is one of the great contributing forces to the moral and spiritual advancement of the human race."

ble is now a truism. Yet it was then that the bureaucratization of intellectual life—more precisely, the attraction that their bureaucratic positions have for intellectuals—jumped ahead. We saw how Edmund Wilson regarded the ambitions of the Communists and proto-Communists of the 1930s: their aspirations were not revolutionary but bureaucratic (as indeed is the case of most intellectuals in Communist states). "Communism," to them, was "a passport to power in an impending international bureaucracy . . . [which would] land them somehow at the top of the heap." Malcolm Cowley recalled much of the same thing. The intellectual generation of the thirties, he wrote, "was more affected than its elders by the Depression and by the lack of opportunities, after the crash, for success achieved by private initiative. Its members were more inclined to attach themselves to thriving institutions that could promise them a step-by-step rise to positions of affluence or honor. . . . In general, security was their ideal, rather than glory [?] or independence, and many of them pictured a future in which everyone would be made secure by collective planning and social discipline: that explains the special appeal to them of the Russian experiment."† After 1940 the rising influence of Central European refugees, many of whose cultural baggage was shaped by German intellectual inclinations, contributed to the bureaucratization of their disciplines. In 1944 a competition for ideas for the political reorganization of Boston (governed by a committee that was chaired by one of the direct descendants of the Adamses) was won by a Harvard group led by Professor Carl Friedrich, a then recent German refugee political scientist, thoroughly at home at Harvard (and Harvard at home with him), who advocated that sixty-six cities of the Boston area be amalgamated into one metropolitan authority.

As early as 1920 R. H. Tawney in England, as early as in the 1930s intelligent American observers of the development of corporate life, such as Adolf A. Berle, noted that a new phenomenon had arisen: the large corporations and industries were no longer governed by their owners but by their managers. In 1940 James Burnham proclaimed this phenomenon as if it were the principal reality of world politics: the era of *The Manage-*

† Not that this was limited to admirers of the "Russian experiment." As late as 1953 Professor James L. McCamy, a respected political scientist and former Washington official, wrote in the *Annals of the American Academy of Political and Social Sciences,* "If we are dependent upon human nature for responsiveness and efficiency, we need, of course, to examine traits of personality and attitude, as well as traits of technical competence, to admit people to the bureaucracy and to measure them while in service. I have often thought that we need a layman's catalogue of personality types so that we could sum up a person quickly by placing him in one of the categories that all of us recognize in common. Think what a saving of time this would mean in writing letters of recommendation! 'Mr. Smith is Type 325. Sincerely yours.' "

rial Revolution (the title of his book) was upon us. Yet in a most important sense Burnham was mistaken. He believed that he was the proponent of a new realism; that the "managers" of the new politics and of the new society were tough men, replacing political idealists and ideologues and dreamers, somewhat like Spengler who had predicted that engineers (preferably German ones) would be the last heroic figures in the last iron age during the decline of the West. Burnham did not see that the managerial type—whether the executive of a corporation or the dean of a university or the campaign director of a political party—was not at all "tough." He was not a manager but a bureaucrat. The new aristocracy that Burnham saw emerging was nothing more than a meritocracy, the difference between an aristocrat and a meritocrat corresponding to that between a man of conviction and an organization man (an aristocrat assumes his high social position with an authority that does not come to him from any organization; the meritocrat assumes his authority from the office that is given to him by the organization or by the state). But, then, much of this was stated by Burke two hundred years ago, when he said that he stood for Parliament "to support his opinion of the public good, and does not form his opinion in order to get into Parliament or to continue in it."[5]

While the main phase of the transition from the American legislative to the American administrative state may have occurred in the 1930s, the main phase of the transition from an American democratic to an American bureaucratic state took place in the 1950s. Of course this was not an exclusively American phenomenon. Twenty years after Burnham's *The Managerial Revolution* its corrective was provided by the English C. Northcote Parkinson, who, along with other witty observations, in his book *Parkinson's Law,* illustrated his argument with such examples as that of the British Admiralty: during the very time when the number of ships and the tonnage of the Royal Navy became a fraction of what it had been twenty years before, the administrative personnel of the Admiralty increased four- or fivefold. In the United States between 1948 (which was the crisis year of the Berlin blockade) and 1958, during a decade in which the Russians did not conquer a single square mile of new territory (they actually retreated from Austria), the American military budget grew from $14 billion to $45 billion, the federal bureaucracy doubled in size, and the staff of the State Department multiplied five- or sixfold. Most of this increase took place during the Eisenhower administration but it was not a particularity of the executive branch of the government. The staffs of congressional committees, supposedly serving legislative purposes, increased by 250 percent during the 1950s (and by more than 600 percent from 1950 to

1980). To illustrate further this protean increase of administration would serve no further purpose here, where we are concerned with the spirit that produced it. A poignant example of this spirit was the letter, signed by President Eisenhower, which every American received with his passport in 1956, admonishing Americans to behave well when going abroad, "to help to mold the reputation of our country"—the free traveling of a free people having become an experiment in public relations.

> As the holder of this passport, you will be the guest of our neighbors and friends in the world family of nations. . . . To all the varied people of these many countries, you the bearer of an American passport, represent the United States of America. . . . Thus, you represent us all in bringing assurance to the people you meet that the United States is a friendly nation and one dedicated to the search for world peace and to the promotion of well-being and security of the community of nations. Sincerely, Dwight D. Eisenhower.

But the phenomena of bureaucracy were not restricted to government. The mutation from legislative to administrative government corresponded to the mutation from a productive to an administrative "economy" (the quotation marks are not accidental: they suggest the historical phase when the very meaning of "economy" was wrenched out of its original meaning, a point to which I shall return). For the last thirty years American conservatives have been campaigning against Big Government. Leaving aside their inconsistency (and, at times, their intellectual dishonesty) in supporting tremendous military expenditures and bureaucracies, we must criticize them, too, for failing to recognize that the same phenomenon of unproductive and deadening bureaucratic habits that encumbered and corrupted the operations of government became ubiquitous, visible, and extant within what is—more and more euphemistically—called "the private sector." By the 1950s the mental attitudes, the inclinations, procedures, aspirations, and the very language of a government bureaucrat was not one whit different from that of a college administrator or foundation official or corporation executive. Here, side by side, are two ludicrous examples from the late 1950s, one a memorandum from the Air Force, the other a directive of a top national corporation—fact having, indeed, become more strange than fiction in an increasing number of instances, and the prose and the mental processes of bureaucracies inadvertently more comical than the boffo jokes of comedians:

From an Air Force reserve squadron (1956)

Gentlemen:

We would like to request the presence of Miss Jayne Mansfield on the evening of Wednesday, April 11, 1956 during the period 6:30 to 7:05 P.M.

Our desire is to take one or two publicity stills from 6:30 to 7:00 following which Miss Mansfield will be taken into the training room and introduced to the officers. It would be appreciated if she would take two or three minutes to make a few comments to the group.

One photograph we have in mind will be presented as follows:

Research and Development

Photograph of a Major using a tape measure to get Miss Mansfield's chest measurement.

A little research on a large development. Miss Jayne Mansfield has been selected as the "Research project they would like most to develop" by the Air Force Reserve Research and Development Squadron. The Major performing the desirable research is Adjutant of the squadron which trains at the N. Y. Air Reserve Center.

Thank you for your cooperation.

Very truly yours,

From a corporation in New York

CHRISTMAS PARTY

RECEPTION AND DISMISSAL OF CHILDREN

1. Two persons at door, preferably two who can speak Spanish.
2. All female sponsors to wait in hospital area to be assigned to children (two or three sponsors per 10–12 children).
3. Two persons to register the children and each is to have a male assistant.

4. Numbers assigned to the children are to be worn around the neck. Cardboard tags with nylon cord will be used.
5. As children are registered, the parents are given the card stub taken from the card worn by the child. This stub will indicate the child's number and sponsor's number.
6. Two or three female sponsors (all to have same sponsor number) assigned to each group of 10–12 children will take them *by way of the elevator* to the cafeteria where their clothes will be given a number corresponding to the number on the tag and stored in shopping bags. At the end of the party the children can use these bags to take home their presents. *Sponsors* are also to record the child's *first name* on the tag for Santa Claus' use. Some male sponsors will be on duty to handle the unpredictable needs of the male children.
7. All sponsors will see to it that the children do not rush Santa Claus, but keep their seats.
8. Presents should be distributed according to numbers starting with child number 1 etc. In other words the sponsors in charge of children 1–10 inclusive will take their children for gifts and when this has been done, group 11–20 will receive theirs, etc. Santa Claus will be stationed in Conference Room A.
9. The parents calling for their children are to be escorted by male sponsors to the cafeteria and are to be seated in order on the Flushing Avenue side near Conference Room A. This will avoid confusion between incoming parents and outgoing personnel who clock out at 4:30 P.M. All parents will be told the approximate time to call for their children. This time will be set at definite intervals starting at 3:00 P.M. No parents will be allowed to stay throughout the party.
10. When the children are ready to leave, additional sponsors will escort the parents (one at a time) to the child or children whose numbers correspond with the number held by parent and then escort them to the stairway. This procedure is repeated until all the children are claimed.
11. All children who come unescorted will be permitted to leave whenever they wish. An unescorted child will be registered with a number and designated *unescorted.* Unescorted will be written on their number tag.

When around 1955 the number of Americans employed in production slipped beneath the number of those employed in nonproductive occupations, the era of the organization man had already replaced that of the mass man. When Stefan Zweig visited the United States in the early 1910s he found it exhilarating to learn how easy it was for anyone to walk into an office or a factory in quest of a job. Forty years later, during the otherwise booming "economy" of the 1950s, this was hardly possible: not only would he have had to fill out endless application forms, but he would have been "interviewed" by a personnel officer in the office of the personnel director, a man undoubtedly equipped by a degree in business administration or in personnel management who would have seen right then and there that this applicant did not fit, presumably because he was "overqualified."‡

And we have to take yet another step: we must recognize that this overwhelming bureaucratization of life involved not only government and the "private sector" of the economy and industry but the private lives of people, not only what they were doing from nine to five in the office buildings but what they were doing after five in their homes in their suburbs. The "togetherness" of the 1950s rested on very insubstantial foundations. The social life, entertainments, leisure time and leisure activities of an increasing number of people were shaped by their corporate affiliations. In one sense American society was becoming increasingly classless; but in another sense the homes, the entertainments, the travels, the social aspirations, and the snobberies of many people depended more and more on the standards of what they saw and thought were the standards of their peers: standards and activities and mannerisms and fashions and clothes whose selections were public rather than private. The cult of their families, including their appearance and the activities and the schools their children were attending, were geared and calculated accordingly, even during that

‡ Russell Baker in 1969: "It is not surprising that modern children tend to look blank and dispirited when informed that they will someday have to 'go to work and make a living.' The problem, of course, is that they cannot visualize what work is in corporate America. . . . Not so long ago . . . when a child asked, 'What kind of work do you do, Daddy?' his father could answer in terms that a child could come to grips with. 'I fix steam engines.' 'I make horse collars.' Well, a few fathers still fix steam engines and build tables, but most do not. Nowadays, most fathers sit in glass buildings doing things that are absolutely incomprehensible to children. The answers they give when asked, 'What kind of work do you do, Daddy?' are likely to be utterly mystifying for a child. 'I sell space.' 'I do market research.' 'I am a data processor.' 'I am in public relations.' 'I am a systems analyst.' Such explanations must seem nonsense to a child. How can he possibly envision anyone analyzing a system or processing a datum? Even grown men who do market research have trouble visualizing what a public relations man does with his day, and it is a safe bet that the average systems analyst is as baffled about what a space salesman does at the shop as the average space salesman is about the tools needed to analyze a system. . . ." The New York *Times,* 16 October 1969. In the rest of this column Baker expounds what took me a chapter to describe: that the American "economy" in the second half of the twentieth century is built on paper.

last decade of the 1950s when the image of a well-adjusted couple and of a well-adjusted family were important and recognizable assets in the corporate reputation of a man. This publicization of private family life meant a fatal weakening of what a family should have meant: for it is in the nature of human society that a family is a private and an exclusive element, whereas corporate institutions and the state are forces of inclusion.

(3)

Between 1950 and 1980 the conditions of private enterprise in the United States were contracting. So were the conditions of a free market and of free competition. I wrote earlier that the new science of politics that Tocqueville wished to see ("a new science of politics is necessary for a new world") has not been forthcoming, since during the last hundred and fifty years the vocabulary and categories of political thought have remained largely the same. Even worse was the condition of the so-called science of economics, whereof American developments of the last few decades should furnish abundant examples. A new kind of economics was needed for the understanding of the post-modern world: but there was not the slightest sign that it was forthcoming. The economic and financial development of the United States (and also of much of the world) since 1945 was alone sufficient to disprove all of the theorists of economics about "the business cycle," that is, of alternating cycles of inflation and deflation. Now we have to take up the thread of the development of inflation for the last time, since this includes phenomena intricately involved with the very fabric of American life—and therefore of American thinking—during the second half of the twentieth century.

We must, once more, recognize how certain eighteenth-century concepts—concepts that had developed at the zenith of the Modern Age—became outdated and useless two hundred years later, during the passing of the Modern Age, mortgaging the function of American institutions, and encumbering the further development of American thought. That almost everything Marx had predicted has proven false is, or ought to be, obvious; his thinking was a typical product of nineteenth-century materialism, a cast-iron "system" of history, of economics, of human nature, a piece of mechanical junk, corroded and broken. Unlike Marx in the nineteenth century, Adam Smith in the eighteenth century represented some of the better elements in the mind-set of his times; but his precepts of economics have become outdated too. His view of human nature rested entirely on the eighteenth-century category of Reason, wherefrom sprang his view of economics, to the effect that men will naturally maximize their profits. This may have been too simple an explanation of human motives then; it surely has proven too simple now. That vanity is much more complicated than greed is something that Dr. Johnson knew and expressed very well, while Adam Smith did not. Moreover, while material needs *were* elemental in the lives of millions two hundred years ago, during the development of a modern democracy such as the United States, these "old poor" have largely (though of course never completely) vanished, while about the same time vanity (unlike pride) ceased to be a phenomenon typical of aristocratic ages. The desires and aspirations of all kinds of people, including their possession and consumption of things, have become increasingly complicated, and "materialistic" merely on a superficial level: as I wrote earlier, because of the increasing mental intrusion into the very structure of events. Economists were of course unable to admit or even to recognize matters such as vanity, this having no place in their mathematic calculations or even, in spite of themselves, in their own minds. The Marxists and the liberals and the conservatives among them had different ideas about the supposed benefits or damages of "competition"; yet all of them based their calculations on Adam Smith's assumption to the effect that people and corporations always try to make the most profits they can.

Some time during the 1950s most American corporations and an increasing number of American businessmen discovered that profits, and the volume of their sales, no longer depended on competitive prices. Every study of top-level executives that W. David Slawson reported in his *The New Inflation* (1982) "concluded that profit is not their primary motivation, still less their sole motivation, as the profit-maximization principle would require."* This had something to do with the increasing near-monopoly of corporations providing certain products. It had more to do with the enormous influence of advertising (essentially a nonproductive endeavor), whereby competition in prices and in quality (that is, in the private recognitions of people) was being overwhelmed by competition in publicity. It had much to do with the spending habits of people, habits which were now far more dependent on publicity than before. The very perceptions of money and of durable possessions had changed. For one

* P. 124. "I am aware of no case prior to the 1950s in which an industry was able to raise prices in face of low or falling demand, except through explicit and therefore illegal price-fixing [although] there were many situations prior to the Fifties in which industries were able to prevent their prices from falling. . . ." *The New Inflation,* pp. 77–78.

thing, large numbers of people began to assume not only that a product must be better because it was widely advertised. Many people also assumed that a product must be better because its price was higher—an obvious example of how publicity and vanity complicate and dilute rational calculations of spending, not to speak of old-fashioned thrift or even greed. Moreover, the habit of instant gratification and the allied unwillingness to think or plan ahead contributed tremendously to the endemic inflationary condition. Increasing numbers of people (and perhaps especially the young) allowed themselves to be influenced by convenience and by instant availability rather than by price differences unless the latter were exceptionally large and obvious. Another example of this condition was the fact, curiously prevalent in the United States after 1960, that the prices of many consumer goods were actually higher in the poorer sections of cities and suburbs, including slum areas, than elsewhere, and not merely because of higher insurance rates due to the local prevalence of vandalism and crime: because of a lower level of self-discipline on the part of the consumers, the providers of the products charged such prices as the traffic would bear. Yet another example was the practice of retailers, especially in supermarkets, to advertise "specials," offering and selling them for *more* than their usual price, knowing that among thousands of customers few people were able to recognize this kind of attenuated fraud.† In these supermarkets the persistently advertised brands of foods and beverages often sold at higher prices than the less advertised or unadvertised brands.

In 1973 and 1974 the fourfold rise of gasoline and oil prices reduced their sales only marginally. At the same time a drastic drop in coffee prices increased coffee sales only marginally too. People now tended to accept steeply rising prices of goods and services at the very time when the durability of such goods (clothes, for example) and the extent of services (checking the oil levels or wiping the windshields of cars at the filling stations, for example) decreased—evidence to the effect that money adjusts to social conditions, rather than the reverse. In 1979 *The Wall Street Journal* reported that the domestic liquor industry, "after having 'vainly tried to stimulate demand through price discounts,' became the *last* major con-

† "All the executives whom I interviewed who worked for firms that manufactured consumer products took it for granted that the people who bought their firms' products did not understand them. Unless they were engineers, they generally did not understand them themselves. All but one of these executives also told me that in their opinion relatively small price differences had, or would have, no significant effects on sales. Research by others indicates that the usual response of a manufacturer of consumer products to a perceived need for lower prices is to redesign the product so that it costs less to produce, after which the price is reduced. Such a 'price reduction' is really not one, of course." Ibid., p. 60.

sumer-products industry to abandon price competition in favor of what the *Journal* called the new form of 'planning, budgeting and marketing' designed to raise prices and increase sales. Sometime in 1979, it seems, an era of competition that had existed in the United States since the nation began came to an end."[6]

By that time an entire generation of Americans had grown up who took the unceasing increase of prices and of wages as the normal state of things. They had never known the opposite of inflation, whether of words or of money. Together with the credit-card practice (another form of the insubstantialization of matter) this meant not only a reduction of the value of American money but a transformation of people's attitudes to it. Neither reductions of the rate of inflation (first in 1976 during the Ford, then in 1981–83 during the Reagan administration) nor the increase of unemployment after 1980 changed these attitudes. Corporations and business people knew that a reduction of prices was almost always less profitable than a creeping inflation of these prices.‡ At any rate, inflation was far from being eliminated or reversed—and this at a time of rising unemployment—its rate of increase was merely slowed down somewhat. Yet a "creeping" inflation may be even worse than a "runaway" one, in the long run: for the public demand for draconian measures in order to eliminate the ravages of a runaway inflation will not be forthcoming during a creeping inflation to which entire generations become accustomed.

Slawson wrote that "for the most part this condition is incurable. Price competition will never work very well on most products in a modern economy." Yet it was Edmund Burke who said that "the people must never be seen as incurable." In any event, the people became the victims of the outgrowth of democracy, of the new bureaucratic order, a development which was intrinsically involved with inflation. That they have been accomplices to it cannot, alas, be doubted. (As I write this I read in the New York *Times* business section, "The TV advertising that pleases the public most is non-rational and generally more visual than verbal.")[7] They were victims as well as accomplices to the inflation of communications—whereof, let me repeat, the inflation of money was but a consequence. In October 1982 unemployment in the United States reached 10.4 percent, the highest rate in more than four decades. Significantly enough, unemployment was highest in the productive industries, less in the service in-

‡ *The Wall Street Journal,* 7 October 1980: "Slump Forces Auto Renters to Raise Rates." An example—unquestioned by the pro-capitalist editors of that newspaper—of how corporations and industries tend (note the verb "forces") to raise prices at the time of falling demand, completely contrary to the postulates of *all* economists.

dustries, and lowest in the administrative ones: more than 21 percent of construction workers, more than 15 percent of steel and automobile workers, but only 2.1 percent of people in the "communications industry" were unemployed.* There are few clearer illustrations of the transformation of the United States from a democratic to a bureaucratic society, and from a productive to an administrative one.

But the roots of these developments—not only intellectual and administrative but financial and economic ones—reached back many decades. American capitalists (if that is the word) were seldom so committed to "free enterprise" as they would publicly state. Even before the Civil War, and surely thereafter, the builders and the financiers of the railroads depended on all kinds of governmental assistance, while most industrialists (and definitely the Republican Party) demanded, and got, tariffs and protection. Between 1888 (the establishment of the Interstate Commerce Commission) and 1935 (the federal regulation of trucking and bus rates) the entire transportation network of the nation became regulated and protected. Much of this was probably unavoidable, but what is significant is how railroads and truckers kept on fighting to maintain (and on many occasions to extend) the protection provided by the bureaucratic regulations of these commissions. Long before the extension of the American welfare state labor and the farmers wanted more governmental protection, not less. When in 1979 some of the trucking rates were deregulated, the trucking lobby (one of the most corrupt lobbies of the nation, consisting of both owners and unions) fought against deregulation, as a matter of course. By that time the very function of lobbies had changed. (The nature of *their* competition, too, had become nonmaterial: it was no longer the fabrication of money grants squeezed out from the government but the fabrication of images of public and popular support.) But already in 1900 Senator Boies Penrose, the unreconstructed boss of the Senate, and the Republican archopponent of Progressives and reformers, advised Henry Clay Frick not to fight the strikers: "Give 'em a little extra gravy till they settle down, then raise prices of the tariff to pay for it"—an inflationary

* Contrary to general belief, this had little to do with automation, automation having pervaded the routine of offices and of paper work and "communication" as much as (if not more than) the production in factories and on farms.

Another example: during the financial depression which, beginning about 1970, befell American educational institutions before other institutions of the nation, the hiring of new teaching personnel stopped, in some cases the faculties shrank, in almost all cases the quality and the content of the "product" (i.e., the standards of teaching provided to students and the performance expected of them) decreased, while tuition fees kept on rising steeply, and while there was no reduction—rather the contrary—in the numbers of administrative personnel.

philosophy which Richard Nixon, seventy years later, would have approved. After 1935, and increasingly after 1950, the collusion of contractors and unions became endemic, since the former found that higher wages often cost them little or nothing, and they would often resist the unions' demands only for public show.

This was the phenomenon of the "new inflation," involving a novel kind of competition not of prices but of public images. The producers of goods and of services (and, of course, their lobbyists) found that they could increase their sales without lowering their prices. Much of this increase has been due to "promotion," that is, to advertising, which was now simply added to production costs.† Advertising, promotion, packaging are, of course, expensive. No matter: while driving prices up, managers found that a clever advertising campaign could increase sales for some time. These sales would be matched only by similarly extensive promotion efforts by competitors, while price reductions could be watched instantly: but the latter would have little or no effect unless they were impressed on the minds of the masses of consumers. It was thus that price competition declined, sometimes to the extent of disappearing entirely.‡

Thus the "new inflation" had little to do with demand. Small, or creeping, increases in the prices of appliances, medical services, or tuition costs did not really diminish their sales, since vast numbers of people had become accustomed to such increases and because they were not inclined to forgo such essentials at the cost of changing their ways of living. This unwillingness (and often the inability) of large numbers of people to shop around allowed the producers of goods and the providers of services to keep increasing their prices by small amounts (or to reduce the size and quality of their products or services, again by small amounts). The "causes" of this kind of inflation were not too few goods or too much

† I wrote in *The Passing of the Modern Age* (1970), "In the early 1950s I was amazed to read how the president of a large American cigarette manufacturing company explained to a congressional committee that the rise in the price of cigarettes was due to 'increasing production *and advertising costs'* [my italics]. No one questioned this argument which would have made our grandfathers turn purple with rage."

‡ Slawson, op. cit., p. 36: "In the course of my interviews with businessmen I never met one whose firm sold consumer products who did not express a preference for non-price forms of competition. One told me proudly that his firm had *never* engaged in price competition during his entire tenure as vice-president in charge of sales, some twenty years." P. 80: For retailers, too, "the dollar amounts of their markups generally *increase* more rapidly than the dollar amounts of their costs. . . . As a result, retailers do not as a rule resist price increases initiated at the wholesale level. On the contrary, they generally welcome them. This too is contrary to the teaching of traditional economics, which assumes that everyone resists a price increase that would increase his costs."

money. The "causes" were inflationary expectations—and the inability of many people to exercise financial discipline or monetary discrimination. Thus this writer, who is neither an economist nor a prophet, makes bold to say that the reduction of the rate of inflation at the time of this writing (1983) is bound to be temporary, and also fairly unimportant. We have now seen, at best, a reduction of the rate of inflation but not a reversal of it. Also, this reduction of the rate has been very uneven, many of the prices (especially those of services) having continued to rise as steeply as before. It is also bound to be temporary, because of the prevalence of inflationary habits and expectations in the spending patterns of many people, and because it is still sellers, rather than buyers, who set the prices. Because of the "recession" the government has expanded its efforts to stimulate demands, instead of reforming or reducing them. Of course nothing lasts forever. At some future time the "new inflation" will come to its end, as all other inflations came to their end in the history of mankind. Probably this will happen neither gradually nor in a more-or-less orderly manner. It will happen when the confidence of large masses of people in the paper economy erodes suddenly, because of some kind of unpredictable external shock, occurring well beyond the sphere of economic institutions and practices.

The beginning of the "new" or "creeping" inflation was the result of creeping bureaucratization. The welfare, or provider, state of course contributed to this; but it did not alone cause it. (In 1950 37.6 percent of all American government expenditures involved social welfare, in 1980 nearly 60 percent did. Yet in 1935 the percentage was higher than in 1950: 48.6 percent. In 1980 nearly 40 percent of the welfare budget was destined for older people; yet only 12 percent of the population was over sixty-five.) And long before a public bureaucracy was administering "welfare" the bureaucratization of private charity had been in full development, in the form of foundations or bequests to institutions, probably less because of tax advantages than because of the decreasing impulses of personal charity, including the weakening fabric of the family, and of the kind of personal certainty of judgment that results in individual patronage on the part of the testators. After all, private property is justified because it provides a man or a woman with something to give to people he cares about, for which organized "charity" is no real substitute. A century ago Samuel Butler accused people who gave or left their money to institutions "because they did not see merit where they should have seen it, people, to express their regret, will go and give a lot of money to the very people who will be the first to throw stones at the next person who has anything to say and finds a difficulty in getting a hearing. These foundations of colleges and scholarships are just as bad as the foundations of monasteries and religious houses in the middle ages. . . . What a beast a man must be too who leaves his money in this way. I wonder he is not ashamed to tell the world that he has died without having seen one person whom he has loved well enough to let him have his money when he can no longer use it himself. . . ."[8] Such practices, evident already in Butler's late-Victorian England one hundred years ago, became widespread in the United States then and thereafter—and it does not require especial imagination to recognize therein but another example of what I am wont to call the insubstantialization of matter.*

That this kind of insubstantialization is full of dangers should be obvious. Already during the 1940s the exact ascertainment of a man's income or of his assets became as inaccurate as it was difficult, since the very figures had become dependent on methods of computation and categories of accounting (in part because of their public presentation in the tax declarations). This became even more difficult, inaccurate, and complicated in the case of businesses and corporations: their income and assets and profits being the results of confections and constructions of accountants that were, again, "fictitious" in the original meaning of that word, meaning mental constructions, at times bordering on the metaphysical. By 1980 the nation had come close to a situation where such practices could corrupt government in hitherto almost unprecedented ways. The economic temperature, diagnosis, and prognosis of the nation had become dependent on statistics periodically issued after their computation in government offices. It has become at least conceivable that in a certain situation an administration may attempt to improve matters by producing economic statistics favorable to its image, by announcing statistical figures that are, after all, largely unverifiable, except for the specialists and the bureaucratic administrators who concoct them. (The latter, if found out—which is by no means certain—could defend themselves through abstruse arguments involving alternative methods of computation.) By 1980 there were numerous examples of falsifications of "scientific" data by respected researchers in the most prestigious universities of the nation, surprisingly and regrettably with only ephemeral damage to their careers and with hardly any

* When a man gives his money to his daughter this transaction is private, material, and direct. When he gives his money to an institution (say, his alma mater) this transaction is public and indirect. Consider only the gradual dissipation of a rich man's bequests to a university; the gradual, and often nonmaterial, transformation of the original purpose through its administrators with the passing of years. They, and the recipient professorate, are "laundering" the bequest with a detergent effect worthy of the most accomplished international swindlers.

damage to the reputations of the university administrators who had employed and protected them. Such cookings of "data" depend, of course, on the very verbal categories which are provided for their "definitions." In the Beginning Was the Word; and in the end too. In the beginning of inflation was the inflation of words; near its end the inflation of words includes the cooking of numbers.

"In this stage," wrote Robert Cluett in 1965,

> the inflated style, like Newspeak, is a means not only of expressing bureaucratic orthodoxy but of making all other modes of thought impossible. For example, consider the testimony [in 1963] of a prominent industrial executive before a Senate committee. This man testified that the truest competition exists when differing companies put identical price tags on similar products. In other words, this man *said* that true competition will exist in, say, the toothpaste business when all manufacturers charge 50 cents for a seven-ounce tube, 89 cents for a ten-ounce tube, and so forth. And this was an impeccably honest man who believed what he said. The significance of this testimony is that it could be given only by a man who lives in a culture the linguistic habits of which have been designated to conceal or distort reality rather than to express it. . . .[9]

(4)

To regard matters of rhetoric as if they were the "packaging" of the substantial matters of everyday life seems to be commonsensical and pragmatic. Surely what people do and how they do it are more important than what they say and how they say it. Yet acts as well as speech depend on thought, which in turn inevitably depends on language. If language is false or largely incorrect, then what is said is not meant; and when what is said is not what is meant, then what ought to be done remains undone, and the result is widespread confusion. The Greeks knew this, Christ said it, and Montaigne restated it at the beginning of the Modern Age. ("The generalization of lying could, by itself, dissolve human society.") That the source of every inflationary phenomenon is the inflation of words is not a "law" of history; but it is a historical phenomenon, and particularly relevant to the democratic age. Four of the great nations of the world attempted democratic revolutions during the last two hundred years: Americans in 1776, the French in 1789, the Germans in 1848, the Russians in 1917. The American "revolution" was more successful than the French one, the German attempt failed, and the Russian one dissolved in bloody disorder. They have been described and studied by countless historians, attempting to ascertain the causes of their respective achievements and failures, more or less convincingly. Among these causes someone ought to have made a study of their respective records of rhetoric. The mere quantity of verbiage itself may indicate that the French in Versailles outtalked the Americans in Philadelphia, that another sixty years later the Germans assembled at Frankfurt outtalked the French, that another sixty or seventy years later the Russians outtalked everybody else, in descending order of efficiency. Whatever the ratio of words per capita, the Americans who met in Philadelphia had an experience of public discussion and of politic procedure which they had inherited from their largely English traditions—traditions whereof the members of the French National Assembly, with all of their intellectual brilliance and occasional lucidity, were largely bereft and of which the hapless German professors in Frankfurt were completely bereft. I am not saying that habits of rhetoric and the experience of knowing how to run a meeting alone determines important decisions and great historical developments. I am saying that whoever ignores the development, and the devolution, of rhetoric overlooks a very important element in the structure of events, and that perhaps especially in the age of democracy it is imperative to recognize that element.

Two generations ago H. L. Mencken, who chastised the mass man while he exalted the manly virtues of the American democratic language, failed to recognize that just as the organization man was about to succeed the mass man, the American language would soon become more, and not less, bureaucratic than the English one. In 1958, a generation later (the year after the publication of *The Organization Man),* Randall Jarrell wrote, "If the young Queen Victoria had said to the Duke of Wellington: 'Sir, the Bureau of Public Relations of Our army is in a deplorable state,' he would have answered: 'What is a Bureau of Public Relations, ma'am?' When he and his generals wanted to tell lies, they had to tell them themselves; there was no organized institution set up to do it for them. . . . Queen Victoria—think of it!—had never heard a singing commercial, never seen an advertisement beginning: SCIENCE SAYS. . . ." At the end of the Middle Ages Francis Bacon discussed the legal survival of military tenures which had entirely ceased to fulfill their original function. *Vocabula manent,* he wrote, *res fugiunt.*[10] "Words remain; the things themselves have disappeared"—another example of the corrupt and corrupting insubstantialization of matter.

We have seen that during the twentieth century one of the sources of this devolution has been the mutation from a largely verbal to increasingly pictorial communications,† involving the imagination of people in the United States, something that began as early as one hundred years ago. Somewhat like in the late Middle Ages, the sense of sight has again become predominant: a tendency "closely connected with the atrophy of thought," as Huizinga wrote in *The Waning of the Middle Ages.* ("Thought takes the form of visual images. Really to impress the mind a concept has first to take a visible shape. The insipidity of the allegory could be borne, because the satisfaction of the mind lay in the vision.")

Another, related, source of the bureaucratic society was latent in the devolution of American law, and of lawyers. One of the reasons (and probably the main reason) why Americans succeeded in their revolution two hundred years ago was their experience with and respect for the English tradition of the law. Throughout this book I have suggested that what was, and what has for long remained, the rather unique American achievement of a prosperous and relatively orderly democracy was greatly due to this Anglo-American tradition of respect for the law. American lawyers and judges had won significant small victories for American freedom even before 1776. For many generations after 1776 judicious observers recognized the importance of lawyers within the American democracy. Tocqueville saw them as representatives of a generally conservative force, as an implicit and typically American aristocracy of a kind. But he knew, too (as had Burke), that often the law may sharpen the mind only to narrow it,‡ and that, as he would later write in the *Ancien Régime,* "even a mediocre usurper will easily find legal advisers to prove that Terror is Law, that Tyranny equals Order, that Servitude means Progress." "Lawyers," he wrote elsewhere, "are rarely able to escape from one of two habits: they

† Note, however, that verbal and oral are not quite the same thing. Verbal language depends on a wide acquaintance with written, and not merely with spoken, language, the advantage of the former being that language cannot be written (though it can be spoken) without a measure of forethought; it requires a more or less rational kind of consideration of its effects. In an oral culture (as well as in a pictorial one, molded by movies and television) it is habits of speech that serve as models of writing rather than the reverse—something that has become increasingly evident in the habits of certain American writers, especially those with pretensions to comedy.

‡ Especially in his chapter "On the Legal Mind and How It Serves as a Counterweight to Democracy" but also throughout his book. It is significant that Tocqueville used the term *légistes* rather than *avocats,* legal scholars rather than lawyers. See about this, in respect to the devolution of "the Philadelphia lawyer," in my *Philadelphia 1900–1950: Patricians and Philistines* (New York, 1981), pp. 35–38 and 312–18.

accustom themselves either to plead what they do not believe or persuade themselves very easily of what they wish to plead."

During the twentieth century, increasingly after 1910, American law and American legalism became extensive rather than intensive. The legal authorities saw their principal function in the extension of democratization and of its bureaucratic applications rather than in the preservation of traditional liberties from the encroachments of regulations, of public opinion, and of the state. The proliferation of regulations transformed the functions of hordes of lawyers into tax accountants of one sort or another. Six hundred years ago in England, Trinity College in Cambridge had been founded by a bishop who wanted to make sure that after the Black Death there would be no possible shortage of theologians and of lawyers. He need not have fretted himself. In 1980 Irving Younger, a professor of law himself, said in his Charles Evans Hughes Memorial Lecture, "American democracy has fallen upon hard times. A chief symptom of its travail is the inflation of the laws. . . . Our generation has thirty times more law than our great-grandparents' generation, most of that increase attributable to legislation. Inflation indeed! Will anyone venture to contend that with thirty times more law we are thirty times happier or wiser or better governed or more contented"—I may add, or more secure—"than our great-grandparents were!"[11]

In the beginning of the United States the best legal minds contributed to the strengthening of the walls of those vital vessels within which the blood of the new democratic society was to course. Two hundred years later their descendants contributed mightily to the encrustation of these vessels, increasing and not reducing the condition of the arteriosclerosis of American institutions. In the beginning American law provided the defense against the rigidities and occasional excesses of legislation; two hundred years later laws and regulations became the substance on which bureaucracy came to depend. In many ways and instances the lawyers became the prime bureaucrats. *Vocabula manent, res fugiunt:* when the abstract spiritualization of matter is pushed to its corrupt extremes, it degenerates into its opposite, into the intellectual materialization of substances that do not exist. This happens at the end of an age; it happened at the end of the Middle Ages when theologians discussed seriously (and came up with formulae and data) how many angels could stand on the head of a pin or how much the soul of a man weighed.

For once (and only once in this book) this historian is compelled to make a proposal. Since inflation has become endemic and since, as we have seen, monetary inflation is a consequence of the inflation of society and of the inflation of words, a drastic corrective must include a corrective of the latter condition, and not merely of its consequences. Such a correction would include the strengthening of laws of libel, including restraints on all excessive claims in advertising, the elimination of the acceptance of advertising and promotion costs as if they were production costs, and a consequent drastic simplification of accounting procedures and tax laws, on the basis of gross income—whereafter the solidification of the currency would follow. This would, of course, go against the present practice of the courts, which, by providing more and more "constitutional" protection to libelous speech, are saying in effect that words really matter very little. Yet the entire future of civilization in America may well depend on a renewed respect for the word—inseparable as that is from a renewed respect for the person.

(5)

During the second half of the twentieth century American institutions changed together with the composition of the American people. A substantial change in the composition of the American population had taken place before, largely due to the mass immigration from 1840 to 1920; yet during that time, as we have seen, the older principal elements of the population maintained their leadership; therefore the slow mutation of the American national character was gradual. The second great change in the composition of the American people, which began with the new immigration after 1965, developed apace with the changing character of traditional American institutions, and with the change in the mental and occupational habits of the American people, including such matters as the influence of television, the decline of functional literacy, and the growth of the corporate and provider state, involving the increasing prevalence of bureaucratic occupations and of bureaucratic habits of mind. By 1980 one out of six Americans worked for the government. The income of one out of three Americans depended entirely on the government. About half of the population depended directly or indirectly on the government. One out of eight Americans had an annual income over $25,000—at the same time that the Department of Health, Education and Welfare spent $16,000 a year bringing up (or, rather, keeping) a delinquent or an abandoned child, whose numbers were legion. By 1961 the five hundred largest corporations accounted for 52 percent of the gross national product, while various levels of government accounted for 26 percent. This kind of corporate bureaucracy, as Robert Cluett wrote in 1964, was "whether we like it or not, the key feature of our lives. As the key feature, it may well have the most profound and far-reaching influence on our mode of expression. . . ."

> The effects are all around us . . . a softening of diction, a turning of the concrete into the abstract, a general muting of all that is frank, harsh, anthropomorphic, or indeed true in our thoughts. It is impossible for us to consider the modern corporation without focusing our study on the new and dominant species that the post-World War II era has given us in the field of management. It is the career manipulator, a man with no experience on the production line, no direct and personal knowledge of what he is making, no feel for the people under him who are doing the actual producing. . . . The distinguishing feature of the career manipulator is that he is a man with no marketable productive skills. Probably he is a graduate of one of the better business schools, where he spent two years taking courses in human relations, in management organization, in varied and elaborate kinds of bookkeeping, and in what is euphemistically called "personnel management." His gifts . . . have little or nothing to do with the article or service that his company produces. They lie in other areas. This man can juggle books, convene committees, listen to subordinates. . . . Tempted by "the skills of human relations," he finds himself both the master and slave of "a tyranny more subtle and pervasive" than that which he has come to supplant. . . .[12]

An ominous phenomenon was the sudden emergence, and the assumption of influence, of the so-called military intellectuals after 1956, in most instances men who had never held either a shotgun or a rifle and knew not the difference between them. By 1957 they were supported by public figures such as Nelson Rockefeller. Among other things, they invented the—in retrospect, nonexistent—Missile Gap. By 1960 the London *Times Literary Supplement* wrote that the American military intellectuals "move freely through the corridors of the Pentagon and the State Department rather as the Jesuits through the courts of Madrid and Vienna three centuries ago"—with less spiritual purpose, we may add. In 1961 Robert Strange McNamara, a graduate of the Harvard Business School and then a top executive of the Ford Motor Company, became the Secretary of Defense, an august position that he occupied for more than seven years. Impressed with Systems' Analysis (whatever that was) he announced, among other things, "the consolidation of eighteen different types and sizes of butcher smocks, four kinds of belt buckles, and six kinds of women's exercise bloomers" in warehouses of the American Army. In addition to such jejune matters, it was the systems' analysts, their methods, and their language that in 1963 helped to grease the skids whereon the elephantine machinery of the Pentagon slid down into the Vietnam War. Yet compared to the absurd enormities proposed at the time of this writing by his successor, Caspar Weinberger, according to whom American nuclear rockets were "defensive," Soviet ones "offensive"—a corporate executive (Harvard-California) of the Bechtel Corporation who was appointed by President Reagan to the Secretaryship of Defense—McNamara looked like a modest businessman of bygone days. (Already in the 1960s Eugene Rostow, one of McNamara's advisers, another legalist intellectual whose ambitions led him from the Yale Law School to the Pentagon, declared that American nuclear weapons served purposes of "deterrence," whereas Russian ones served the purposes of "intimidation.")

"Some day," Henry Adams wrote in 1900, "science may have the existence of mankind in its power and the human race commit suicide by blowing up the world." During the 1940s few men among the band of scientists (most of them recent refugees from Central Europe) who worked on the first atom bomb, devotees of chamber music and of all kinds of liberal causes, felt much compunction for their endeavors. When the first atomic bomb exploded in the New Mexico desert in July 1945 one of those scientists jumped and shouted with glee, slapping the chief scientist on the back, as the first hot atom bomb burst and darkened the sun. Twenty years after the Cuban missile crisis the reminiscences and the analyses of the American participants of the then deliberations in the White House, published in the New York *Times,** revealed that they had still misread what had actually happened in 1962, including the Russians' intentions. So these members of the meritocracy have learned nothing and forgotten nothing.

During the last twenty-five years the American military corporations (there, too, the once meaningful line separating public and private enterprises was eroding) were increasingly influenced by people, many of them military intellectuals who were unaware of the abstract and soulless character of their "nuclear scenarios"—as well as of the often equally fraudulent ephemeral "system" of International Relations in the terms of which the world was being explained to the highest officials of the United States, including presidents. Here, too, the institutions of bureaucracy and the promises of status corrupted character. Abstractions obscured realities,

* 22 October 1982. As I wrote earlier, the Soviet Union in 1962, with all of its maleficent inclinations, had no more intention of risking a nuclear war for the sake of Cuba than had the United States for the sake of Hungary in 1956.

ideology succeeded old-fashioned patriotism, the most abstruse technological projections replaced the most elementary knowledge of history and of the character of nations, as if considerations of the latter belonged to a now outdated past—whereas almost every way the opposite was true.

"Utilitarian economists," Dickens wrote in *Hard Times* one hundred and forty years ago,

> skeletons of schoolmasters, Commissioners of Fact, genteel and used-up infidels, gabblers of many little dog's-eared creeds, the poor you will have always with you. Cultivate in them, while there is yet time, the utmost graces of the fancies and affections, to adorn their lives so much in need of ornament; or, in the day of your triumph, when romance is utterly driven out of their souls, and they and a bare existence stand face to face, Reality will take a wolfish turn, and make an end of you.

This has not happened. Reality has not—yet—taken a wolfish turn. There was no revolution of the masses in Britain or in the United States. Romance was not driven out of their souls: the movies and television saw to that. What arose were new masses of the new poor, unforced to stand face to face with a bare existence. How long this kind of surrogate romance and the soulless bureaucracy of the provider state will satisfy them we cannot tell. What we can tell is that Reality has become dependent less on those who cry "Wolf!" than on those who see that the emperor has no clothes, indeed, that he is not a human figure at all; and that the inevitable element in the reality of that kind of seeing is a knowledge—or at least a consciousness—of history.

(6)

This book began with the observation that in 1876, at the time of the nation's one hundredth birthday, few Americans were interested in history. They believed in progress and in evolution, whether they were conscious Darwinists or not. At the great Centennial Exhibition in Philadelphia, dedicated to machinery, there were a few plaster casts of Washington and of the Firsts of the Republic. The contents of the customary patriotic orations and the sepulchral whiteness of the monuments showed that the Founders and the founding of the United States were solidly embedded in mental and sentimental substances that were legendary rather than historical. They were mythical figures, semideities, revered, unquestioned, accepted in the public mind and in popular imagination somewhat like the Romans who had repeated to themselves the pristine legends of the early heroes of their republic. But during the last one hundred years the American interest in history began to grow. The unexamined condition of American history, part and parcel of the insufficiency of American self-knowledge, furthered by the unquestioned belief in endless progress as well as by the self-made amnesia with which millions of first- and second-generation Americans turned their minds away from their own past, began to dissipate. This development of the American people's interest in history, this evolution of their historical consciousness, is a broad and complex story,† of which the growth of professional history in the United States has been but a part; but it is with a survey of the latter that I must begin the last portion of this book, leading to its conclusion.

The "scientific" study of history, with its methods taken mostly from German universities, began in the United States one hundred years ago. The first American Ph.D. in history was granted in 1881; a little more than a decade later the American Historical Association (and the *American Historical Review)* came into existence. By that time the first magisterial historian had arisen among Americans. This was Henry Adams, whose principal and abiding interest was the philosophy of history, even more than history writing (in spite of which he was a better historian than philosopher: but, then, the ultimate aims and the actual accomplishments of men of genius are so often different). In the 1890s the teaching of history, and its systematic inclusion in the requirements of schools and colleges and universities, spread across the nation.

This professionalization of history in the United States was, of course, inextricably involved with the emergence of a professional intelligentsia as well as with the progressive ideology of the time. The progressive and democratic historians saw and declared that their task was eminently practical (even though, as so often with the Progressives, they sometimes mistook for practical what was merely utilitarian). History "should be consistently subordinated" to the needs and interests of the present, James Harvey Robinson and Charles A. Beard wrote in the preface of their book *The Development of Modern Europe* in 1907. In 1912 Robinson wrote, "Society is today engaged in a tremendous and unprecedented effort to

† I have written about this often, but most recently in the new and concluding chapter of the new edition of my *Historical Consciousness,* published around the same time as this book (1984).

better itself in manifold ways. . . . We must develop history-mindedness . . . for this will add a still deficient element in our intellectual equipment and will promote rational progress as nothing else can do. The present has hitherto been the willing victim of the past; the time has now come when it should turn to the past and exploit it in the interest of advance." This was surely the voice of American progressivism *par excellence:* democratic as well as progressive, populist as well as intellectual. Yet soon it became evident that these purposes (and their representatives) were often contradictory. The Populists were not necessarily progressive, and the democratic process was not necessarily intellectual. We have seen that after 1920 the legislatures of some of the most progressive states such as Wisconsin and of populist states such as Texas or Illinois enacted laws which amounted to the worst kind of censorship.‡ Populist democracy preferred the legendary over the historical, and tried its best (or, rather, worst) to perpetuate and enforce the dissemination of the former. In the first issue of *The American Mercury* (1924; "The Drool Method in History") Harry Elmer Barnes described "the recent and still continuing war of the accountants, plumbers, druggists, blacksmiths and lawyers who constitute our school committees upon feeble and helpless historians who have been making some faint beginnings in the way of telling some small fraction of the truth with respect to our national development. . . ."

All of this was but a piece of period controversy, like Mencken vs. Guest or Darrow vs. Bryan. Yet already in 1912, at the height of the progressive wave, "a large number of young historians," as Henry F. May wrote, "had ceased to think of themselves either as moral instructors or as transmitters of tradition. They were, instead, scientific specialists, looking for detailed answers to limited questions. A smaller group, radically progressive, were making history itself into a tool to attack all kinds of traditionalism."[13] "Feeble and helpless" the historians, as Harry Elmer Barnes wrote, may have been; yet their cause was bound to prevail. Populist fundamentalism was no match for "scientific" progressivism in the 1920s (as indeed sixty years later the so-called Moral Majority in the 1980s was no match against the orthodoxy of Darwinism). Within the circles of professional historians the progressive and scientific ideology remained dominant. Around 1930 the principal interpreters of American history were

‡ The Wisconsin law stated, "No history or other textbook shall be adopted for use or to be used in any district school, city school, vocational school, or high school which falsifies the facts regarding the War of Independence, or the War of 1812, or defames our nation's founders or misrepresents the ideals and causes for which they struggled and sacrificed, or which contains propaganda favorable to any foreign government."

Frederick Jackson Turner, Vernon Parrington, Charles A. Beard, Merle Curti (the first at the end, the last at the beginning of his career). With the partial exception of Beard, who was beginning to veer away from a rigid determinism and objectivism, they were exponents of a radical progressivism that was not unsimilar to nineteenth-century Marxism, albeit in an American version. Turner wrote that "today the questions that are uppermost, and that will become increasingly important, are not so much political as economic questions. The age of machinery, of the factory system, is also the age of socialistic inquiry." ("History," wrote the Soviet historian Pokrovski in 1930, "is the concrete investigation of social questions. . . . Most importantly we must unite the historical work we are carrying out with the proletariat's fight against wage slavery.") In his encyclopedic American intellectual history Parrington dismissed writers such as F. Scott Fitzgerald as insignificant. The views of the younger Merle Curti about the history of the American mind were very narrow. And even Beard, the most independent-minded American historian before World War II, who came around to reject socialistic determinism, continued to believe in the 1930s that "the expanded role of government" would increase and not reduce "the freedom of the individual."

Whether they admitted this or not, most of these historians were considering history as nothing less but also nothing more than a social science—perhaps the principal social science but a social science nonetheless. A ludicrous outgrowth of this tendency was the methodical attempt at making history more scientific, produced by Sidney Hook, whom a committee of American historians had commissioned in his capacity as a philosopher in 1942–46 for the purpose of establishing Historical Definitions—these, together with other staggeringly obtuse matters, were then published in a monstrosity entitled *Bulletin 54 of the Social Science Research Council,* a prototypical confection representing American nominalism at its worst.

Yet during the same time, important and salutary developments were taking place. The libraries of American colleges and universities grew to an extent that the quantity and the quality of their holdings began to surpass the accumulated riches of many European universities and libraries. This increase of research facilities corresponded with an increase of the standards of research and of teaching. After 1920 the works of several American historians not only approximated but matched and in several instances surpassed the achievements of their European colleagues. Again it may be significant that most of these admirable American teachers and writers of history (the names of Charles Homer Haskins, Garrett Mattingly, Carlton Hayes, Jacques Barzun, James H. Breasted come to mind) chose to work in Egyptian, Medieval, Renaissance, and Modern European fields rather than in the history of their own country—an exception in the history of historianship. The transatlantic migration of Central and Eastern European historians in the 1930s and 1940s then contributed further to the progress and extension of historical research in many fields.

Until about 1960 it seemed that the professional study of history was largely unaffected by the philosophical crisis that had undermined the basic concepts (and pretensions) of professional intellectuals in a variety of disciplines, ranging from psychology to physics and through all of the so-called social sciences. Then it became apparent that this impression was misleading. The reactions (if they could be called that) of most professional historians to the upheavals of the 1960s revealed that their characters as well as their concepts of their profession were, save for many lonely exceptions, not different from that of other intellectuals. Thereby they contributed to the decline of the standards and, on occasion, to the near demise of the prevalence of the teaching of history. Because of its narrow professional interests, the university and the college professorate proved largely indifferent to the virtual elimination and to the watering down of history from the curricula of many American public and secondary schools. Then it allowed the elimination or the dilution of history requirements in their own colleges and universities. By 1980 undergraduate history majors in American colleges and universities had fallen to one fourth or one fifth of their numbers twenty years earlier. In the graduate schools their numbers declined even further. Less important but more significant than this decline of history students and history courses was the devolution of the very standards of the profession. Insubstantial fads such as Quantification and Psychohistory, together with the preoccupation with "timely"—that is, ephemeral and politic and predictable—subjects became prevalent.* This is not the place to attack such ephemeral fads; in any event, they may be fading now, though not after having done a great deal of harm to the study of history in the United States. Such fads have been symptoms and not causes of the degeneration of the historical profession. They have been symptomatic of the still prevalent concept of professional history as a kind of social science, with its professionals taking comfort in the belief that they are practitioners of complex methods and the posses-

* In 1972 the American Historical Association officially recognized the existence of a Caucus of Gay Historians. In 1981–82 the Guide to Departments of History, published by the same association, listing the specialized fields of scholarship of faculty members in the academic institutions of the nation (for example: "Medieval; Tudor England") found it proper to list "sadomasochism" as the specialized field of a tenured professor in a respectable university in Philadelphia.

sors of arcane subjects of knowledge that are unavailable to and unreachable by common men and women. That such a belief is essentially undemocratic is obvious; that it is essentially bureaucratic should be obvious too.

The endurance of the professional pretense of "scientific" history, as well as the lip-service (lip-service, rather than strict observance) of the methods and formalities of historical presentation originating in the nineteenth century when history had been first regarded as a "science," was especially regrettable because history, instead of being a social science, is both more and less than a science: history is an essential form of thought which has no method or jargon or language of its own, since it is written and spoken and thought in words, in the everyday language of men and women. During the nineteenth century its professional methods were largely taken from Germany, at a time when they contributed immensely to the improvement of historical research and to the creation of a vast body of historical literature. Yet during the twentieth century these methods—and perhaps especially for American history, with its vast and inchoate body of records that are the history of a people rather than the history of a state—have become more and more outdated. For example, that prime canon of historical research that calls on a rigorous and principal dependence on primary materials made less and less sense during this century when often the private letters of presidents and political figures were not written by their authors; often they were not even personally dictated or signed by them. Another example was the increasing difficulty of the older monographic tradition, according to which the historian must exhaust the entire body of records and materials relating to his subject: yet by 1900 the quantity of records and materials (another by-product of bureaucratization) became such that for many subjects this requirement has become virtually impossible. In the past the historian was handicapped by the relative scarcity of records and materials: in the twentieth century by their depressing multiplication. In an increasing number of instances—fortunately not in all of them—the so-called apparatus of scholarship became, in reality, a hypocritical appendage, cloaking the poverty of the historian's ideas and of his imagination.

"Because the civilization of ancient Rome perished in consequence of the invasion of the Barbarians," Tocqueville wrote in his chapter on the Americans' addiction to practical science in the second volume of *Democracy in America,* "we are perhaps too apt to think that civilization cannot perish in any other manner. If the light by which we are guided is ever extinguished, it will dwindle by degrees and expire of itself. By dint of close adherence to mere applications, principles would be lost sight of; and when the principles were wholly forgotten, the methods derived from them would be ill pursued. New methods could no longer be invented, and men would continue, without intelligence and without art, to apply scientific processes no longer understood."

In more than one way new kinds of history have become necessary for the New World, and perhaps especially for the history of the American people. This will be a difficult task. Consider only the intrusion of bureaucracy into the very structure of events; its presence at the very origin of developments. This is a relatively new phenomenon. How did the United States become involved in the Vietnam War? Or: how did history become eliminated from the required courses in X. University? (Notice the emphasis on process in the syntax: not "how *was,*" but "how did it *become.*") The historical answers to such questions will be very difficult to trace. In both of the above-mentioned instances the momentum of a bureaucracy produced the decision that after a while became irreversible, at least for a time. Notice again the verb "produced." In the past bureaucracies responded to decisions made higher; they had not produced anything except their narrow applications of those decisions. This is happening in the second half of the twentieth century too. But there is this other phenomenon, whereby the bureaucracy is the virtual originator of certain ideas and of the consequent decisions. It is no longer a ukase of the Tsar that tells the bureaucracy what to do; it is the bureaucracy that presents the Chief Executive (whether of the United States or of a university) with a decision, often wrapped in reams of cloudy verbiage, that the latter may accept. Now the historical problem is this: the bureaucracy (and its language) are anonymous and impersonal. The first mention of the decision may be in the minutes of a National Security Council Task Force or of a Curriculum Steering Committee of the Faculty. But who pushed the decision? Sometimes we may find out—through confidential and personal information issuing from personal likes or dislikes, that is, usually not gatherable from these minutes and memoranda. For here the anonymity and the hypocrisies of the bureaucratic process, disguised by democratic trappings, go hand in hand. The proponents of an idea or of a decision—whether within a government or a faculty—know how to efface themselves. Their propositions are politic and impersonal. They are likely to ease them, rather than push them, through the dull maze of pseudoparliamentary procedures and of committee verbiage that leave their potential opponents insufficiently engaged or even interested, boredom and lassitude having contributed to their lack of awareness of what is really going on.

For the history of the American people the older academic methods of archival research are still unavoidable; but they are also insufficient. Contrary to previous expectations, the history of a democracy is more difficult to write than the history of an aristocratic society or age: the surface, with all of its accumulated and manufactured debris, is often deceiving. The quantity of documents is overwhelming, while their quality decreases—yet another example of inflation. When there is more and more of something, it is worth less and less, not only because of its volume and its availability but because of the decrease in its authentic, that is, inherent, value. The need, however, is less for new methods than for new insights; not for new "tools" of research but for new recognitions of historical consciousness, including, first of all, the relationship of the historian to the history of his own people. There are signs, here and there, that this new kind of relationship already exists, even though its participants may not be aware of the philosophical meaning of it. A conscious and participant (as distinct from "objective" and "detached") interest in history (as distinct from a widespread but vague appetite for it) is already manifest in the efforts of all kinds of people, often coming forth from the remotest places of the nation, in a great variety of books (some of them privately published) that tell us about the American past, *their* past, with a mature kind of affection.

For at the same time something else has been happening—a development that may be summed up by the quip that history is too important to be left to professional historians. Until the 1950s, as we have seen, the development of professional history in America reflected the national mental climate, by and large. It corresponded to the nationalist rhetoric in the nineteenth century, and to the progressive ideals and illusions in the first part of the twentieth century. But during the last twenty or thirty years a duality, a contrary development, took place. At the very time of the narrowing and of the actual shrinking of the historical profession the popular appetite for history, perhaps for the first time in the United States, was rising. In 1980 there were in the United States more than 3,000 local historical societies, most of them in small towns, nearly twice as many as thirty years before. After 1950 in hard-cover commercial publishing popular histories outsold fiction. Historical best sellers of all kinds were published. Television and the movies corresponded to the same popular inclination, manifest in the increasing frequency of cinematic "documentaries" or social-historical soap operas. Of course many of these presentations of history were insufficient, superficial, often twisted and falsified. In 1976 the Bicentennial was entirely consumed by history—by history on all kinds of levels, to be sure, including "historical" junk and souvenirs—but by history nonetheless. In sum, there exists now in the United States a widespread appetite for history—more exactly, for physical and mental reminders of the past—that in the history of this country had no precedent, an appetite which developed at the time when much of the teaching of history was thoughtlessly and shamefully abandoned by those responsible for it. During the last thirty years nonprofessional historians—that is, men and women without doctorates, and unaffiliated with the history departments of colleges and universities (examples: David McCullough, Margaret Leech, George Kennan)—were writing and publishing works, the narrative excellence, the insight, and the standards of research of which were superior to those of most professionals, and at least equal to those produced by the best of American professional historians of theii own country (examples: William Leuchtenburg, Henry F. May, C. Vann Woodward). The best historians of the American nation and of the American people have often been amateurs—in the best and original sense of that word.

Sometimes I believe that a new kind of historical classic may be soon created by an American, a new form of history, perhaps even the kind of classic of which history has been hitherto bereft. (After all, history has not yet had its Dante or its Shakespeare.) But I have written about this elsewhere; these speculations do not belong here. In any event, I think that the growth—often unrecognized but a growth nonetheless—of historical consciousness among the American people is the most promising sign of a painful maturation at the beginning of the third century of American independence, and at a time of great dangers, not the least of which are certain self-annihilating inclinations festering within the American soul.

Outside the airport of Orlando, Florida, the road sign has two arrows. One points to Disneyworld, the other to the Kennedy Space Flight Center. Under the latter arrow are these words: THIS WAY TO REALITY.† No: the way to reality lies within us, within and not outside the bounds of our mother earth; within our historical consciousness, which is nothing else but our consciousness of ourselves, potentially drawing on inexhaustible essences, including the inexhaustible wisdom of the past. "Life itself," as the Canadian writer Robertson Davies put it, "in which man moves from confident inexperience through the bitterness of experience, toward the rueful wisdom of self-knowledge"—at the end of the second American century, the American task.

† In 1960 I ended *A History of the Cold War* with this footnote: "Joseph Conrad, in *Under Western Eyes:* 'I suppose one must be a Russian to understand Russian simplicity, a terrible corroding simplicity in which mystic phrases clothe a naïve and hopeless cynicism. I think sometimes that the psychological secret of the profound difference of that people consists in this, that they detest life, the irremediable life of the earth as it is, whereas we westerners cherish it with perhaps an equal exaggeration of its sentimental value.'

"The American tragedy, then, is that to some extent—and only to some extent—this is true of Americans, too: but that is another book."

This nation was created two hundred years ago, at the peak of the Modern Age. One hundred years ago many of its people thought that its destiny was to escape from the history of the past. Another hundred years later the best Americans may be beginning to recognize that toward the end of the Modern Age they are the representatives and the guardians of the heritage of what remained, and of what still remains, of Western civilization.

For more than one hundred years after the establishment of the United States most Americans saw themselves as representing something that was the opposite of the Old World and its sins. After about one hundred years this vision gradually transformed: the United States was the advanced model of the Old World . . . and perhaps of the entire world. Neither of these visions is meaningful any longer. Will the American people have the inner strength to consolidate, and to sustain, the belief that their civilization is different not from the so-called Old but from the so-called Third World, and not merely its advanced model? At the beginning of the third century of American independence this is—or, rather, this ought to be—the question.

REFERENCES

NOTES TO CHAPTER 1

1 In *The Nation,* 29 December 1951. 2 José Ortega y Gasset, *Obras completas* (Madrid, 1961–63), vol. VI, p. 37. 3 John A. S. Grenville and George Berkeley Young, *Politics, Strategy and American Diplomacy: Studies in Foreign Policy 1873–1917* (New Haven, Conn., 1966), p. 290. 4 George F. Kennan, *Soviet-American Relations 1917–1920, I. Russia Leaves the War* (Princeton, 1957), p. 22. 5 *The Ladies' Home Journal,* August 1923. 6 Paul A. Carter, *Another Part of the Twenties* (New York, 1973), p. 2. 7 Cited in Carter, op. cit., p. 137.

NOTES TO CHAPTER 3

1 W. T. Stead, *The Americanization of the World* (London, 1902), pp. 354–55.

NOTES TO CHAPTER 4

1 F. J. Warne, *The Immigrant Invasion* (New York, 1913), p. 176. 2 Gerald Shaughnessy, *Has the Immigrant Kept the Faith?* (New York, 1926), p. 104. 3 Ibid., p. 167. 4 John Higham, *Strangers in the Land* (New Brunswick, 1955), p. 311. 5 Cited in Henry S. Commager, ed., *America in Perspective* (New York, 1947), p. 191. 6 Henry F. May, *The New Era of American Innocence* (Chicago, 1959), pp. 39, 58. 7 Robert Pastor, article in *The Atlantic Monthly,* July 1982. 8 Herbert Agar, *The Price of Power* (New York, 1952), p. 102. 9 Betty Flanders Thomson, *From the Changing Face of New England* (New York, 1958).

NOTES TO CHAPTER 5

1 *Maud* (Isabelle Maud Rittenhouse), Strout, ed. (New York, 1939), p. 22. 2 *Small Town America: A Narrative History, 1620 to the Present* (New York, 1980), p. 382. 3 *Harper's,* December 1948. 4 *America and Cosmic Man* (New York, 1948), pp. 166–67. 5 *Tennyson* (London,

1927), p. 242. 6 *The Age of Confidence* (New York, 1934), p. 22. 7 *The American Scholar,* Autumn, 1957. 8 James Mark Baldwin, *Between Two Wars: Being Memoirs, Opinions and Letters Received* (Boston, 1926), vol. I, p. 35. 9 Higham, *Strangers in the Land,* p. 196. The sociologist was Frederick A. Bushee *(Ethnic Factors in the Population of Boston,* New York, 1903); H. B. Wollston, "Rating the Nations," *American Journal of Sociology,* 1916, pp. 381–90, cited by Higham, p. 372. 10 Henry F. May, *The End of American Innocence* (New York, 1964), p. 372. 11 Harold Nicolson, *Small Talk* (London, 1937). 12 A. Edward Newton, *A Tourist in Spite of Himself* (Boston, 1930), p. 217. 13 "The Evolution of a Cow-Puncher," *Harper's,* July 1895. 14 *The First Europe* (London, 1947), p. 667. 15 *The Waning of the Middle Ages* (New York, 1956), pp. 215–16, 218. 16 *The Shuttle* (New York, 1906), p. 5. 17 *Pilgrim's Way* (London, 1940), pp. 289–90. 18 *The Revolt of the Masses* (New York,1932), p. 52.

NOTES TO CHAPTER 6

1 Cited in W. T. Stead, *The Americanization of the World* (New York, 1901), p. 14. 2 Cited in Walter LaFeber, *The New Empire: An Interpretation of American Expansion, 1860–1898* (Cornell University Press, 1963), pp. 123, 127. 3 Ibid., pp. 255–56. 4 Cited in Norman Foerster, ed., *American Poetry and Prose* (Boston, 1947), p. 100. 5 Cited in James Morris, *Pax Britannica* (London, 1978), vol. III, p. 28. 6 *Burke* (London, 1897), p. 87. 7 Stead, op. cit., pp. 4, 12, 13, 15. 8 Stead, op. cit., p. 396. 9 *The Country of the Pointed Firs* (New York, 1957), p. 134. 10 *The Shuttle,* p. 95. 11 These quotes cited in LaFeber, op. cit., pp. 26, 345, 378. 12 Henry F. May, *The End of American Innocence* (Chicago, 1964), pp. 30–31. 13 Statement by Admiral Huse, USN, 22 February 1921. 14 *Dominations and Powers* (New York, 1950), pp. 278–79. 15 Winston Churchill, *The Grand Alliance,* p. 431. 16 Joseph M. Jones, *The Fifteen Weeks* (New York, 1964), p. 140. 17 Robert Strausz-Hupé in the first issue of the International Relations periodical *Orbis,* 1957.

NOTES TO CHAPTER 7

1 Robert H. Ferrell, ed., *Off the Record: The Private Papers of Harry S. Truman* (New York, 1980). 2 These quotes are from my chapter on Penrose in *Philadelphia 1900–1950: Patricians and Philistines* (New York, 1981), pp. 56–60. 3 Van Wyck Brooks, *America's Coming-of-Age* (New York, 1915), pp. 79–80. 4 Jules Abels, *In the Time of Silent Cal* (New

York, 1969), p. 29. 5 Fred I. Greenstein, "Change and Continuity in the Presidency," in *The New American Political System,* A. King, ed. (Washington, D.C., 1975), pp. 46–47. 6 Sidney Blumenthal, "Marketing the President" in New York *Times Magazine,* 13 September 1981. 7 Greenstein, op. cit., p. 51. 8 *The Civilization of the Renaissance in Italy* (New York, 1954), p. 321.

NOTES TO CHAPTER 8

1 Reinhard H. Luthin, *American Demagogues* (Boston, 1954), p. 161. 2 Cited in Henry F. May, *The End of American Innocence* (Chicago, 1959), p. 137. 3 George Santayana, "The Spirit and Ideals of Harvard University" in *The Education Review,* April 1894. 4 Henry Seidel Canby, *Alma Mater* (New York, 1934), pp. 88–89. 5 Ibid., p. 161. 6 Address at Newberg, Oregon, reprinted in the *Reader's Digest,* February 1956. 7 May, op. cit., p. 282. 8 *The Nation,* 3 June 1915, quoted by May, op. cit., p. 338. 9 In "Old America" (1918), reprinted in *America-Coming-of-Age* (New York, 1958), p. 107. 10 *America Set Free* (New York, 1929), p. 77. 11 Cited by Paul A. Carter, *Another Part of the Twenties* (New York, 1972), p. 66. 12 *The Mechanical Bride* (New York, 1951), p. 42. 13 Hamsun, *The Cultural Life of Modern America,* Morgridge, ed. (Cambridge, Mass., 1969), p. 74. 14 Canby, op. cit., p. 98. 15 Cited in David W. Noble, *The Progressive Mind 1890–1917* (Chicago, 1971), p. 167. 16 Speech in Richmond, 2 February 1912, cited by May, op. cit., p. 116. 17 Hamsun, op. cit., pp. 80–81. 18 Ronald Berman, *Advertising and Social Change* (Beverly Hills, 1981), p. 97. 19 May, op. cit., p. 32. 20 *The Saturday Evening Post,* 26 July 1958. 21 An Illinois newspaper in 1859, cited in Edgar Lee Masters, *Lincoln, the Man* (New York, 1931), p. 215. 22 Anne Morrow Lindbergh, *War Within and Without: Diaries and Letters of Anne Morrow Lindbergh 1939–1944* (New York, 1980), pp. 189–90. 23 Speech in Des Moines, Iowa, October 1941. 24 *Harper's,* April 1955. 25 15 December 1953. 26 *De la démocratie en Amérique* (Paris, 1951), vol. I, p. 307. 27 *The American Commonwealth* (London, 1888), vol. II, p. 554. 28 *Character and Opinion in the United States* (New York, 1919), pp. 47–48. 29 Will Herberg, *Protestant-Catholic-Jew: An Essay in American Religious Sociology* (New York, 1955). 30 My italics. Thomas Beer, *Hanna* (New York, 1929), p. 34, note 2. 31 24 May 1898. Cited in Thomas T. McAvoy, *The Great Crisis in American Catholic History, 1895–1900* (Chicago, 1957), p. 207. 32 10 December 1954. 33 *The Catholic World,* April 1957. 34 *The Habit of Being* (New York,

1979), p. 90. 35 Arthur Vidich and Joseph Bensman, *Small Town in Mass Society* (New York, 1958), pp. 303–6. 36 Robert Brungs, S.J., "Human Life vs. Human Personhood" in *Human Life Review,* Summer 1982. 37 Jakob Burckhardt, *The Civilization of the Renaissance in Italy* (New York, 1954), p. 319.

NOTES TO CHAPTER 9

1 *Europe* (New York, 1928), pp. 384–85. 2 *Selected Essays* (London, 1950), pp. 241–42. 3 *The Revolt of the Masses,* pp. 116–17, 45–46. 4 Paul A. Carter, *Another Part of the Twenties* (New York, 1973), p. 177. 5 *Two Letters to Gentlemen in Bristol,* 1778. 6 W. David Slawson, *The New Inflation* (Princeton, 1982), pp. 44–45. 7 8 August 1982. 8 Samuel Butler, *Notebooks* (London, 1912), p. 18. 9 Robert Cluett, "Our Linguistic Inflation" in *Teacher's College Record,* March 1965. 10 Alfred Cobban, "The Vocabulary of Social History" in *Political Science Quarterly,* March 1956. 11 Reprinted in *Commentary,* February 1981. 12 Cluett, op. cit., pp. 541–42. 13 *The End of American Innocence* (New York, 1959), p. 42.

ACKNOWLEDGMENTS

My first duty is to acknowledge my debt to the Lehrman Institute and to the President and Board of Directors of Chestnut Hill College for a sabbatical semester in 1981–82, during which I wrote the first drafts of three chapters of this book and without which I should still be years away from its completion. Thus I record my thanks to Nicholas X. Rizopoulos, Director of the Lehrman Institute, with whom what had been a sympathetic association from the very beginning matured into a precious friendship. During the writing of no other book have I depended on and profited from the close reading of my manuscript by so many friends and associates. The fact that this, necessarily alphabetical, list begins with the name of my editor, Sally Arteseros, is just and proper—another of those coincidences (Chesterton: "coincidences are spiritual puns") which logicians loathe and poets love. So here I go, with this Spiritual Bouquet of thanks: to Sally Arteseros, Donald Atkins, Jacques Barzun, Reid Boates, Lee Congdon, Lester Conner, David Contosta, Kevin Delmasse, Steven Englund, Eugene Genovese, Fred L. Greenstein, Brooks Kelley, Thomas S. W. Lewis, Robert Lilienfeld, Michael Mandelbaum, Michael von Moschzisker, John Rossi, David Slawson, Griffin Smith, Jr., James F. Sullivan, Robert Tucker, Geoffrey C. Ward, and Linda Wrigley.

Because of the wide scope of this book and because of the fact that most of its illustrations come from so-called secondary sources the addition of even a selective bibliography would be senseless as well as hypocritical.

I must express my gratitude to Dr. Helen Hayes, Director of the Library of Chestnut Hill College, for her assiduous help in many instances and on many levels, ranging from Decipherer of Cacography to Comptroller of Research.

"Old Pickering School House,"
Williams' Corner, near Phoenixville, Pennsylvania
1980–83

INDEX

Abbott, Lyman, 185
Abdication crisis of 1936 (England), 227–28
Abels, Jules, 105n
Abolitionism, 328
Abortion, 80, 81, 173
Abstract Expressionism, 323
Abstraction, 10, 150, 182, 325, 394–95
Acheson, Dean, 61–62, 241, 242, 243, 244–45, 246
Acronyms, 86–87n
Acton, Lord, 12n, 328
Adams, Brooks, 213
Adams, Henry, 167, 185, 186, 203n, 213, 258, 344, 370, 396
Adams, John, 5–6, 7, 21, 33n, 180, 262, 263, 279, 327, 333, 338, 366n
Adams, John Quincy, 261
Adultery, 80
Affluent Society, The (Galbraith), 318n
Africa, 102, 118
Agar, Herbert, 157
Agnew, Spiro, 282, 337
Agriculture, 93, 117, 118, 162
Airlines, 105
Alcott, Louisa M., 180
Algren, Nelson, 323
Allen, Woody, 147, 147n, 154n
Alma Mater (Canby), 229n, 318–19
America (weekly), 352n
America First Committee, 333
American Academy of Arts and Sciences, 299n
American Association for the Advancement of Science, 314
American Association of Advertising Agencies, 269n
American-British relationship, 201–55; affinities and differences (American empire and British imperial idea), 212–18; between the wars (1918–39), 227–33; British Empire (1895–98), 201–5; elements of, 205–11; post-World War II, 239–49; turning point (1956), 249–55; World War I, 209, 211, 216, 218–27; World War II, 233–38
American Commonwealth, The (Bryce), 342–43, 359
American democracy: Eisenhower years, 64–68; Kennedy era, 68–71; in 1960s to 1970s, 68–86; in 1980s, 86–87; post-World War II, 59–64; production of consumption (1950s), 64–68; second century, 3–58. *See also* United States
American Democrat, The (Cooper), 177, 196–97, 264–65
"American Gothic" (Wood), 169, 181, 183
American Heritage (publication), 364–65n
American Historical Association, 396, 399n
American Historical Review, 396
American Image of the Old World, The (Strout), 203n
American Indians, 157, 265n, 327n; influence of, 187–88
American Institute of Management, 347
Americanization of Edward W. Bok, The (Bok), 33, 142, 175n
Americanization of the World or The Trend of the Twentieth Century, The (Stead), 93–94, 207–8, 210, 212
American language, 182n, 320. *See also* English language
American Language and Its Supplements, The (Mencken), 146
American Legion, 34–35, 143
American Mercury, The, 313, 397
American Mind, The (Perry), 150
American Politics: the promise of disharmony (Huntington), 339n
American Renaissance, 167–68
American Revolution, 4, 159, 197, 205, 327, 388, 389, 390
American Society of Newspaper Editors, 373n
American Tragedy (Dreiser), 151
America's Conquest of Europe (Jordan), 224
America Set Free (Keyserling), 112n
Anderson, Sherwood, 305
Andropov, Yuri, 119
Andy Hardy movies, 106
Anglo-American alliance. *See* American-British relationship
Anna Karenina (Tolstoy), 320
Another Chance: Postwar America (Gilbert), 66n, 105n
Anti-Catholicism, 35, 69, 348, 348n
Anti-communism, 60, 64, 70, 82, 120, 237, 244–45, 247, 251, 335–36; equated with patriotism, 335

Anti-Intellectualism in American Life (Hofstadter), 302
Antin, Mary, 150, 150n
Anti-Semitism, 33, 35, 42, 69, 128, 348
Arab-Israeli War of 1973, 110
Arabs, 79, 120, 121
Arden, Delaware, 322
Arendt, Hannah, 318n
Argentina, 148
Aristocracy, 166–67, 147, 215, 216, 230, 275, 313n, 390; difference between meritocracy and, 375
Aristoxenus, 324
Arizona (battleship), 49n
Arlen, Harold, 145
Armament program, 47, 82
Armory Show of 1913 (New York City), 322
Armstrong, Neil, 76
Arthur, Chester, 258
Arts, the, 321–26; architecture, 324–26; bohemias, 322; collections of art, 322; commercialization and intellectualization, 323, 324; popular music, 323–24
Asia and Western Dominance (Panikkar), 231n
Astaire, Fred, 145–46
Atlantic, The (magazine), 53
Atlantic Charter, 235
Atlantic Monthly, The, 155, 237, 318n
Atom bomb, 55, 57, 57n, 122, 242, 394
Australia, 18, 96, 139, 216, 245
Austria, 19, 47, 63, 203, 375; emigration, 124, 130, 136
Austro-Hungarian Empire, 14, 220, 291n, 332
Automation, 384n
Automobiles and automobilization, 66, 101–11, 112–13, 114, 117; dependency, 110–11; Depression years, 106–7; design and quality, 109–10; in Europe, 121n; installment buying, 108; mass production, 25–26, 103–4, 105–6, 111; number of cars, 102, 105, 107–8; public transportation and, 113–14; traffic jams, 109, 109n; World War II, 107

Babbitt, Irving, 315, 370
Baby boom, 188–89
Bacon, Francis, 389
Bagehot, Walter, 263n
Baker, Russell, 379n
Balfour, Arthur, 206
Balfour Declaration, 144, 222n
Bancroft, George, 180, 265n
Bani-Sadr, Abolhassan, 119
Baptist Church, 352
Bardèche, Maurice, 119n
Baring, Maurice, 282
Barnes, Harry Elmer, 335n, 397
Barnum, P. T., 185, 361
Barrett, William, 309n, 310n, 312
Barton, Bruce, 151, 347
Baruch, Bernard, 223
Barzun, Jacques, 302, 314–15, 398
Bauhaus School, 326
Bay of Pigs, 70–71, 253
Beal, Richard S., 283
Beard, Charles A., 7, 142, 164, 169, 335n, 396–97, 398
Beasley, Norman, 106n
Beatles, 253
Beaumont, 147–48n
Beaverbrook, Lord, 208
Bechtel Corporation, 394
Beer, Thomas, 346
Belgium, 130, 234, 291n
Bellini, Giovanni, 322
Belloc, Hilaire, 111n
Bellotti, Francis X., 138n
Benavides, Sergeant Roy P., 145
Bennett, Arnold, 22, 217
Bensman, Joseph, 363
Bergson, Henri, 25
Berle, Adolf A., 374
Berle, Milton, 351
Berlin, Irving, 31, 361
Berlin blockade, 375
Berman, Ronald, 98n, 321
Bermuda, 233
Bernanos, Georges, 69n, 191
Bernays, Edward L., 266
Bernstein, Leonard, 147n
"Better off" concept, 91
Beveridge, Albert J., 210, 213
Bible, 9, 328, 345
Biddle, Francis, 50
Bierce, Ambrose, 22
Big Navy program, 232
Birth control, 173
Birthrate, 66, 80, 318n
Bismarck, Otto von, 26, 35, 212
Blacks, 15, 16, 73, 74, 84–86, 108, 146n, 173n, 291; civil rights of, 85–86; education, 292; lynchings of, 135; migration, 85; slavery, 84–85, 85n
Blaine, James G., 204
Boas, Franz, 137–38
Boer War, 207, 210, 215, 217, 253
Bohemias, 322
Bok, Edward W., 33, 175–76, 184–85, 361
Bookstores and book readers, 191
Borah, William, 226
"Born Again" fundamentalism, 140n
Boston in the Age of John F. Kennedy (Whitehill), 113n, 150, 299n
Bourgeois interlude, 159–200, 221, 293; dissolution of, 171–79; distinction between middle class and bourgeoisie, 164–65; *embourgeoisement* of society, 164–70; German, medieval tendencies, and Indian influences, 179–88; meaning of, 159–60; paradoxical dualities, 191–97; passing of, 188–91; prospects of civilization, 197–200; zenith of, 168. *See also* Materialism and material development
Bourne, Randolph, 306

Bowra, Maurice, 314
Boy Scouts, 217, 361
Brasillach, Robert, 119n
Braun, Dr. Wernher von, 143, 182, 270n
Breasted, James H., 398
Brezhnev, Leonid, 119, 122
British Empire, 18, 46, 65, 161, 201–5. *See also* American-British relationship; Great Britain
Brogan, D. W., 107
Brooklyn Bridge, 325
Brooks, Van Wyck, 22, 193, 194, 268, 306
Brownsville, Texas, race riot of 1917, 74
Bruckberger, Father Raymond, 103n
Bryan, William Jennings, 39, 92, 183, 184, 186, 328, 397
Bryce, Lord, 342–43, 359
Brzezinski, Zbigniew, 302
Buchan, John, 198, 304
Buchanan, James, 258
Buckle, Henry Thomas, 372n
Buckley, William F., 334, 337, 337n, 339, 353
Bulgaria, 148
Bulletin 54 of the Social Science Research Council, 398
Burckhardt, Jakob, 11, 20, 24n, 264, 264n, 287–88, 317, 358–60, 362, 367
Bureaucratization, 7, 65–66, 74, 82, 100, 116, 118; of the American language, 182n; development of, 371–80; education and, 290, 292, 294, 296, 297; inflation, 380–88, 402; of intellectuals, 316, 320; provider state, 392–95; study of history, 395–404; transformation of democratic society to bureaucracy, 368–404; of words, 388–92
Bureau of the Census, 318n, 321–22
Burke, Edmund, 178, 327, 329, 339, 383, 390
Burmese Days (Orwell), 230n
Burnett, Frances Hodgson, 193–94, 210
Burnham, James, 374–75
Burns, C. Delisle, 187, 366n
Burns, John, 206
Bush, Vannevar, 296
Butler, Samuel, 264

Café society, 361
Cahan, Abraham, 142
Cajuns, 15
Caldwell, Taylor, 358
California (battleship), 49n
Californization, 83, 257
Cambodian refugees, 124
Canada, 18, 61, 132, 139, 154, 169n, 205, 216, 234, 296
Canby, Henry Seidel, 177, 229, 229n, 298, 318–19
Capitalism, 18, 19, 39–40, 41, 152, 165, 177, 179, 296, 308, 309, 338, 349
Capote, Truman, 73
Carnegie, Andrew, 210
Carroll, Archbishop Charles, 348
Carter, Jimmy, 72, 79, 140, 155, 156, 223, 244; popular democracy and, 258, 281, 282, 285n
Carter, Paul A., 35–36
Carter, Rosalynn, 285n
Casey, William J., 284n
Cassatt, Mary, 323
Castlereagh, Lord, 32
Castro, Fidel, 63, 71, 155, 252, 253
Cater, Douglas, 269–70, 270n
Cather, Willa, 142, 194
Catholic Workers, 357
Catholic World, The (newspaper), 351
Catton, Bruce, 364–65n
Caucus of Gay Historians, 399n
CBS Evening News, 284n
Censorship, 317
Centennial Exhibition (Philadelphia), 3, 395
Central Intelligence Agency (CIA), 63, 70, 71, 75, 242, 249, 250, 252–53, 337, 337n
Chamberlain, Joseph, 207, 372
Chamberlain, Neville, 232
"Changes in Bodily Form of Descendants of Immigrants" (Boas), 137–38
Chaplin, Charlie, 23, 190n
Chapman, John Jay, 134–35
Chaudhuri, Nirad C., 230n, 254n
Chayefsky, Paddy, 138
Chesterton, Lord, 84, 146n, 289, 290, 321
Chiang Kai-shek, 61
China, 15, 44, 45, 46, 55, 61, 62, 119, 121, 154, 161, 231, 244n; emigration, 125, 132; Nixon visit (1971), 78, 79
Chrysler, Walter P., 105
Churchill, Winston, 47–48, 51, 52, 60, 205, 207n, 216, 226, 227–28, 232, 233, 234–38, 239, 240, 244, 246, 246n, 247–49, 253, 255
Church of England, 131
Cincinnati *Commercial Tribune,* 213
Cities, growth of, 161–62, 163
Civilization of the Renaissance in Italy, The (Burckhardt), 359–60
Civil rights movement, 336
Civil War, 19, 29, 85, 147, 160, 311
Clemenceau, Georges, 32
Cleveland, Grover, 258
Cluett, Robert, 388, 393
Coatesville, Pennsylvania, lynching of 1912, 135
Coca-Cola, 120, 121
Cockburn, Claud, 187
Cohabitation, 173
Cohan, George M., 23, 350
College, English (and Scots) influence on, 17. *See also* Education
College textbooks, 324
Columbia Broadcasting System (CBS), 120
Columbian Exposition (Chicago), 6, 266n, 325
Columbia University, 279
Columbus, Christopher, 29
Committee of Foreign Affairs, 134
Committee on Public Information, 305
Common Market, 254
Communism, 40, 42, 42n, 54, 56, 57, 59, 60–61, 62, 71, 119, 120, 122, 143, 227n, 237, 245,

245n, 246n, 248, 309, 309n, 331, 333, 336, 351, 374
Communist Party (U.S.A.), 136n, 308
Concentration camps, 50
Congregationalist, The, 213n
Congress of Vienna, 32, 252
Connell, Evan, 164n, 229–30, 230n
Conservationism, 373
Conservatism, 18, 82, 137, 157, 174, 242, 245n, 282, 327–41; antithesis between liberalism and, 329–30; campaign against Big Government, 376; Republican Party, 337, 337n
Conservative Party (New York), 337n
Containment, policy of, 60, 243
Contriving Brain and the Skillful Hand, The (Malin), 85
Coolidge, Calvin, 34, 36, 111, 133, 151, 152, 338, 361, 373; popular democracy and, 259, 268–69, 269n, 275, 277, 277n
Cool Million, A (West), 138
Coon, Carleton S., 347n
Cooper, James Fenimore, 177, 193, 196–97, 264, 267, 272
Copernicus, Nicolaus, 20
Coral Sea, Battle of, 51
Cosmopolitanism, 17
Coughlin, Rev. Charles, 42, 333
Coughlinites, 49
Counter-Currents (publication), 150n
Country of the Pointed Firs, The (Jewett), 194
Coward, Noel, 187
Cowboys, 185–86
Cowley, Malcolm, 308, 374
Cram, Ralph Adams, 167
Creel Committee on Public Information, 268
Crèvecoeur, J. Hector St. John de, 289, 366
Crime, 74, 81, 86, 190; increase in, 191–92
Croce, Benedetto, 206n
Cromer, Lord, 217
Cuba, 44, 394n; Bay of Pigs invasion, 70–71, 253; emigration, 124, 126, 154–55; Spanish-American War, 202, 203, 204
Cuban missile crisis, 71, 394
Cultural Life of Modern America, The (Hamsun), 22n
Curti, Merle, 398
Curzon, Lord, 220
Cyprus, 250
Czechoslovakia, 47, 60–61, 256

Dale, Porter H., 277
Darrow, Clarence, 39, 166, 397
Darwin, Charles, 9, 25, 137, 258, 309, 345
Darwinism, 9, 39, 137, 345, 373, 397
Daugherty, Harry M., 277n
Davies, Robertson, 403
Dawson, Christopher, 304n, 352n
Day, Dorothy, 357
Declaration of Independence, 3, 5, 35, 83, 103n, 148, 261
Decter, Midge, 335n
De Gaulle, Charles, 53, 107, 238
De Kooning, Willem, 323
De Mille, Cecil B., 282
Democracy in America (Tocqueville), 3–4, 67, 83–84, 95, 147–48, 197, 360, 400
Democratic Party, 58, 61, 78, 242, 296, 329, 348n; liberalism, 333–34
Democratic-Republican Party, 261
Denmark, 28n, 36n
Depew, Chauncey M., 6
Depression of the 1930s, 8, 27, 40–43, 73, 81, 105, 130, 152, 303, 309, 333, 374; automobile ownership, 106–7; material development, 98–100, 106–7; unemployment, 43, 47
Deregulation, 384
Descartes, René, 9
Detroit race riot of 1943, 74
Development of Modern Europe, The (Robinson and Beard), 396–97
De Voto, Bernard, 105n, 336
Dewey, Admiral George, 20
Dewey, Thomas, 259
Dickens, Charles, 16, 263n, 395
Diem, Ngo Dinh, 75
Dilke, Sir Charles, 205–6
Displaced Persons' Act, 124
Disraeli, Benjamin, 26, 215
"Divorce Is Going Out of Style" (Maisel), 176
Divorce rate, 59, 80, 173, 174, 176, 189, 193
Doctorow, E. L., 141n
Dodge, Mabel, 322
Dodsworth (Lewis), 105
Donnelly, Ignatius, 328
Dos Passos, John, 335n
Dostoevski, Feodor, 25, 335n
Dreiser, Theodore, 151
Drieu la Rochelle, Pierre-Eugène, 119n
Drivers' licenses, 108n
Drugs, 80
Dubuffet, Jean, 324
Dulles, Allen, 63, 70, 252–53
Dulles, John Foster, 22, 63, 182, 353n
Dynamics of World History (Dawson), 304n

Eakins, Thomas, 164, 323
East Berlin, 63, 250
Eastman, Max, 335n
Eaton, Charles A., 36
Economics of Divine Unity (Bani-Sadr), 119
Ecuador, 148
Eden, Anthony, 249–50, 251
Edison, Thomas A., 38, 296, 325, 326
Education, 147, 263, 368; bureaucratization, 290, 292, 294, 296, 297; college and university, 293, 294, 298–99, 301–2; decline in, 296, 299–300; democratization of, 292, 303; differences in standards, 293; expenditures, 292, 295; German influences, 146, 292, 396, 400; high school, 292, 294–97; historical development, 291–303; intellectuals and, 302; literacy rate, 291, 303; student population, 303

Edward VII, King, 215
Edward VIII, King, 227
Egypt, 59n, 249–50, 334
Ehrlichman, John, 281
Einstein, Albert, 9, 272, 307, 345
Eisenhower, Dwight D., 51, 54, 54n, 62–68, 69, 70, 72, 74, 100, 108, 111, 117, 124, 171, 174, 179, 237, 247–48, 247n, 250–51, 253, 335, 346, 363, 375–76; popular democracy and, 258–59, 276, 277, 278–79
Eliot, T. S., 228, 299, 302, 306
Ellis, Father John Tracy, 352
El Salvador, 155, 283–84
Emerson, Ralph Waldo, 150, 293–94, 294n, 318, 345, 359
Encounter (publication), 254n
End of American Innocence, The (May), 222, 322n
End of Education, The (Wagner), 302
Engels, Friedrich, 332
England. *See* Great Britain
English language, 35, 127, 137n, 145n, 227, 228, 320
English People, The (Orwell), 246n
Enlightenment, 6, 7, 131, 159, 291
Episcopal Church, 131n
Eugenic planning, 366n
Exile's Return (Cowley), 308
Exports, 93

Fairlie, Henry, 253
Falklands War, 254
Farewell Address (Washington), 204
Fascism, 42, 119n, 206n, 309
Faulkner, William, 311
Federal Aid Road Act of 1916, 104
Federal Bureau of Investigation (FBI), 337
Federal Council of Churches of Christ of America, 151
Federal Election Campaign Act, 260n
Federal Highway Act of 1921, 104
Federal income tax, 24
Federalist No. 10, 263
Federalist No. 14, 469
Federal Trade Commission, 373
Feminism, 194–96
Ferrero, Guglielmo, 206n
Fetuses, 81n
Fiedler, Leslie, 181
Fifth Amendment, 336
First Europe, The (Burns), 187, 366n
First Vatican Council, 349
Fisher, Lord, 216
Fitzgerald, F. Scott, 37, 166, 188, 286
Fitzgerald, John F., 113n
Fitzhugh, George, 327
Flatiron Building (New York City), 325
Florida, Caribization of, 155
Ford, Gerald, 78–79, 83, 244, 383; popular democracy and, 258, 276, 280–81, 282
Ford, Henry, 25–26, 28, 37–38, 103–4, 103n, 106, 111, 112, 183, 221, 296, 326, 328
Ford, Patrick, 143
Fordism, 119
Foreign Affairs (publication), 243
Foreign trade, 93–94
Forster, E. M., 230n
Fort Knox, 51
Fortune (magazine), 53, 95, 169, 247
Fourastié, Jean, 8
Fourteen Points, 28, 31, 53, 224, 235
France, 4, 5, 8, 32, 45, 47, 67, 99, 105, 118, 129, 148, 165, 167, 203n, 245, 256, 275, 286, 327, 328; automobilization, 121n; emigration, 130, 149; Suez War, 249–50, 334; World War I, 30–31, 218, 219, 220, 225; World War II, 48, 49, 51, 52, 233, 234
Franco-Prussian War, 180
Frankel, Charles, 366
Frankfurter, Felix, 237
Franklin, Benjamin, 112, 174, 225n, 266, 291, 332n, 346, 371–72, 373
Free Love advocates, 175–76
French Indochina, 63
French language, 118
French Revolution, 215, 389
Freud, Sigmund, 9, 25, 309
Freudianism, 139, 318
Frick, Henry Clay, 384
Friedman, Milton, 318n
Friedrich, Carl, 374
Frost Advertising Agency (Harry M.), 58n
Fuller, Buckminster, 339
Fulton, Robert, 325
Fundamentalism, 140n, 168, 183–84, 351, 357
Furcolo, Foster, 138

Gabriel over the White House (motion picture), 40–41
Galbraith, John Kenneth, 318n
Gallup, Dr. George, 270
Gandhi, Mohandas K., 231
Garden Party, The (Belloc), 111n
Gardner, Mrs. "Jack," 194
Garfield, James A., 258
General Education in a Free Society (Barzun), 314–15
General Electric Company, 100, 114n
General Motors Corporation, 11, 114n
"Generation Gap," 189
Genio latino, Il (Ferrero), 206n
Gergen, David, 283, 284n
German-Americans, 32, 49, 228, 334, 349
German Jews, 47
Germany, 27, 40, 46, 47, 59, 92, 105, 119, 143n, 203, 206, 207, 208, 216, 231, 232–33, 299, 331, 334, 342; Depression of 1930s, 41, 42; division of (post-World War II), 242–43; emigration, 124, 136, 149, 154, 180; influence on U.S.A., 146, 179–83, 292, 396, 400; World War I, 30–

31, 214, 218–27; World War II, 48, 49, 50–53, 55, 57, 94, 107, 171, 233–38, 239
Gershman, Carl S., 335n
Gershwin, George, 145, 163
GI Bill of Rights, 300
Gibson, Charles Dana, 152
Gilbert, James, 66n, 105n
Gillis, Father James, 351
Gissing, George, 199, 304
Gladstone, William, 25
Glasgow, Ellen, 194
Goebbels, Joseph, 119n, 305
Goffin, Magdalen, 358
Gold, 65, 100, 117
Golden Bottle, The (Donnelly), 328
Goldwater, Barry, 74, 312, 337
Goodman, Benny, 346n
Goodyear Tire & Rubber Company, 114n
Grant, Ulysses S., 258
Grapes of Wrath, The (motion picture), 107
Gray, Harold E., 301
Gray, Thomas, 129
Great Britain, 4, 14, 19–20, 27, 32, 42, 45, 47, 54, 56, 67, 81, 92, 102, 105, 117, 118, 144, 148n, 165, 166, 167, 169n, 171, 182, 256, 261, 263, 293, 311, 331, 334, 344, 349, 391; Americanization of, 216, 227–28, 253; emigration, 124, 130, 149, 154, 180, 183; Falklands War, 254; prestige of, 122; relationship with U.S.A., 201–55; Suez War, 249–50, 334; urbanization, 96; Venezuela dispute, 202, 213; World War I, 30, 31, 211, 214, 217, 218–27; World War II, 48, 51, 233–38
Great Crash, The (Galbraith), 318n
Greater Britain (Dilke), 205
Great Gatsby, The (Fitzgerald), 105, 151
"Great Society," 73, 75
Greece, 60, 245, 257; Communist intervention, 240–41; emigration, 124, 128, 129, 154
Greece (ancient), 20
Greeley, Horace, 185
Greenland, 48, 234
Greenstein, Fred, 278
Greenwich Village, 176, 332
Grey, Lord, 222n
Gropius, Walter, 326
Guedalla, Philip, 119
Guest, Edgar A., 397

Haiti, 28n, 36, 148
Haldeman, H. R., 281
Hammerstein, Oscar, 181
Hamsun, Knut, 22n, 37, 318, 321
Handbook of Heraldry (Cussans), 216–17n
Handguns, 81
Hardie, Keir, 206
Harding, Warren G., 307; popular democracy and, 267, 268, 267–68n, 277
Hard Times (Dickens), 263n, 395
Hardwick, Elizabeth, 305
Hardy, Thomas, 22
Hare, Richard, 304n
Harnett, Rev. Robert, 352n
Harrison, Benjamin, 203, 328
Harrison, William Henry, 267
Hart, Jeffrey, 339
Hartz, Louis B., 328, 329
Harvard University, 151, 193, 229, 262, 293–94, 303, 374, 393
Haskins, Charles Homer, 398
Hassam, Childe, 323
Hawaii, 132, 203, 204
Hawthorne, Nathaniel, 16, 166
Hay, John, 204–5
Hayes, Carlton, 398
Hayes, Rutherford B., 258
Headland, Rev. Isaac Taylor, 213–14n
Hearst, William Randolph, 40
Heisenberg, Werner, 11
Heisenberg principle, 272
Hemingway, Ernest, 120, 166, 228, 314, 323, 332n, 359, 372, 372n
Herbert, Victor, 181
Higham, John, 133
Highways, 107, 108, 108n, 110, 113n
Hinckley, John, 362
Hindenburg, Paul von, 334
Hiroshima, atomic bombing of, 55
Hiss, Alger, 246
Historical Consciousness (Lukacs), 264n, 396n
Historical development (transformation of American thinking), 289–367; the arts, 321–26; confusion of public and private, 359–67; education, 291–303; intellectuals, 304–21; religion and religious beliefs, 342–59
History of the Cold War, A (Lukacs), 403n
History of the English-Speaking Nations (Churchill), 248–49
History of the United States (Bancroft), 265n
Hitler, Adolf, 14, 26, 35, 43, 46, 47, 48, 49, 58, 59, 100, 106, 106n, 107, 117, 124, 143, 143n, 182, 219, 223, 226, 231, 232, 233, 237, 245n, 257, 275, 299, 331, 333, 334, 335n, 338, 366n, 369, 370
Hoehling, Justice Adolph A., 277n
Hofstadter, Richard, 301–2, 345
Hollis, Christopher, 340
Hollywood, 38, 79, 152
Holmes, Justice Oliver Wendell, 41
Homer, Winslow, 164, 323
Homosexuality, 80
Hook, Sidney, 335n, 398
Hoover, Herbert, 38, 43, 53, 83, 105, 179, 180, 223, 300, 319, 338, 339n, 373; popular democracy and, 258, 259n
Hoover, J. Edgar, 42, 70
Hopkins, Harry, 237
House of Intellect, The (Barzun), 302
House Un-American Activities Committee, 139
Houston race riot of 1917, 74
Howells, William Dean, 16

Hughes, Charles Evans, 45
Hugo, Victor, 317
Huizinga, Johan, 112, 187, 279, 286, 390
Humphrey, Hubert, 76
Hungarian Revolution of 1956, 63, 65, 124, 250, 251, 394n
Hungary, 14, 105, 245; emigration, 124, 130, 136
Huntington, Samuel P., 339n
Hylan, John F., 361
Hyphenated-Americans, 138–40

Iceland, 48, 234
Illegal immigrants, 125, 155
Illiteracy, 291, 303
Immigrant Invasion, The (Warne), 135
Immigrants and immigration, 13, 14, 21, 30, 33, 37, 101, 123–58, 180, 183, 322, 392; Americanization of, 136–42; characteristics of, 123–25, 147; departures (return to homeland), 130; in the 1880s, 15–16; financial gains from, 130–31; hyphenated-Americans, 138–40; illegal aliens, 125, 155; influence of, 144–47; literacy test, 291; mortality rate, 127; name changes, 138; native Anglo-Americans and, 147–53; naturalization requirements, 137; in 1960s, 153–58; opposition to, 134–36; patriotism and nationalism, 142–44; population and, 126–28; purposes and motives, 129–31; quota system, 154; religion and religious beliefs, 343–44, 349; religious and racial composition, 131–32; restrictions, 15, 44, 124, 132–34; statistics, 125–28, 131n; World War I, 136, 143; World War II, 136
Immigration Act of 1921, 228
Immigration Act of 1965, 156, 156n
Immigration and Naturalization Service, 155
Imperialism, 6, 19, 92–93, 121, 203, 204, 212–15, 224–25n, 230; role of missionaries, 213n
Imports, 93, 110
Independent, The (magazine), 314
India, 240
Individualism, 177, 179, 197, 320, 349
Infant mortality, 160
Inflation, 9, 64, 172, 173, 296; bureaucratization of, 380–88, 402; dollar decline, 116–17; essence of, 95–96; runaway, 97
Installment buying, 116
Institute of Sex Research, 301
Intellectuals, 25, 68, 69, 72, 147, 165n, 169, 175, 191, 214, 332, 335n, 337; advertising and publicity, 315–17; bureaucratization of, 316, 320; censorship, 317; dishonesty, 364–65; education and, 302; emergence of, 168; French, 323; highbrow designation, 306; historical development, 304–21; Marxist, 304, 308–10; military, 393–95; Russian, 304–5, 304n, 372n; snobs, 313n; split-mindedness, 318–19
Internationalism, 29, 34, 43, 53, 197, 214, 236, 247, 337, 352; American concept of, 56; division between isolationists and, 330–32; World War I, 221
Interstate Commerce Commission, 373, 384
In the Time of Silent Cal (Abels), 105n
Inventions, 160, 290
Iran, 119–20; hostage crisis, 79, 120, 252, 283
Iran, Shah of, 79
Iraqi revolutionaries, 120
Ireland, 148n, 206, 218, 314; civil wars, 226; emigration, 124, 127, 128, 130, 138, 140, 143, 183
Ireland, Archbishop John, 349–50
Irish-Americans, 32, 228, 334, 334n, 349, 350, 352
Isolationism, 32–40, 42, 43, 47, 49, 52, 60, 64, 73, 74, 93, 132, 181, 242, 252, 334, 335, 349, 352; division between internationalists and, 330–32; World War I, 221–22, 225, 229; World War II, 233
Israel, 79, 249–50, 334, 357
Italy, 14, 47, 67, 168, 245, 291n, 299; emigration, 124, 127, 128, 129, 130, 138–39, 140, 154; World War I, 220; World War II, 51
I Thought of Daisy (Wilson), 309n
Ivan the Terrible, 332

Jackson, Andrew, 56, 261, 262
Jackson, C. D., 247n
Jacob, H. E., 146n
James, Henry, 17, 164, 210, 331
Jamestown colony, 29
Jansenism, 359
Japan, 14, 15, 20, 47, 61, 62, 67, 111, 117, 161, 226, 231, 231n, 232, 242, 243; Americanization of, 44–45; automobilization of, 121n; emigration, 125, 132; parliamentary democracy, 101; World War I, 45, 220; World War II, 46, 49–53, 54, 55, 57, 94, 235, 238, 240
Jarrell, Randall, 6, 324, 366n, 389
Jazz, 35–36, 38, 145, 192–93
Jeffers, Robinson, 36
Jefferson, Thomas, 5, 9, 83, 178, 203, 261, 289, 329
Jessel, George, 361
Jewett, Sarah Orne, 194, 209
Jews, 15, 23, 47, 128, 133, 135, 138, 143n, 144, 145, 181, 222, 304, 310, 335, 335n, 348, 357; emigration to U.S.A., 124, 126, 128, 130, 131, 150, 154
Johann Strauss, Father and Son: A Century of Light Music (Jacob), 146n
John Paul II, Pope, 353, 357
Johnson, Hiram, 226
Johnson, Ladybird, 76
Johnson, Lyndon B., 73–76, 156, 253
Johnson, Samuel, 72, 85, 142, 178, 339, 381
Johnson Act of 1921, 133
Johnson-Reed Act of 1924, 133
John XXIII, Pope, 353
Jonestown massacre of 1978, 81–82
Jordan, David Starr, 224
Juárez, Benito, 156n
Juvenile gangs, 185

"K," cult of the letter, 185
Kaiser, Henry J., 51
Kapital, Das (Marx), 327
Kemble, Fanny, 144
Kendall, Willmoore, 340
Kennan, George F., 60, 243, 266n, 403
Kennedy, John F., 68–71, 72, 74, 151, 252, 253, 334n, 352–53, 359; popular democracy and, 257, 271n, 276, 277, 280
Kennedy, Robert, 76, 188, 276
Kenner, Hugh, 339
Kern, Jerome, 145, 163, 181
Keyserling, Hermann A., 37, 112, 112n, 187, 307, 370–71
Khrushchev, Nikita, 63, 66, 119, 121, 244n, 250, 251, 318n
Kinsey, Alfred C., 176, 301
Kipling, Rudyard, 16, 20, 205, 206n, 208, 213, 217
Kirk, Russell, 186
Kissinger, Henry, 76, 79, 122, 183, 244, 252, 302
Klein, Julius A., 38, 339n
Know-Nothings, 328
Korea, 45, 61–62, 154, 244
Korean War, 62, 64, 75, 145, 244, 244n, 301
Kristol, Irving, 335n
Krupp Industries, 100
Ku Klux Klan, 35, 151, 185, 228, 301
Kulturkampf, 342

Labour Party (Great Britain), 216, 239, 240
Ladies' Home Journal, The, 169, 175–77, 306, 344n
La Follette, Robert M., 33n
Lamarck, Jean Baptiste, 137
La Rochefoucauld, François de, 360
Las Vegas, first casino-hotel, 57n
Lawrence, D. H., 22, 187, 346, 371
Lazarus, Emma, 128, 129
League of Nations, 28, 34, 56
Leahy, Admiral William D., 284n
Leech, Margaret, 403
Lend-Lease program, 48, 60, 234
Lenin, Vladimir Ilyich, 26, 118–19, 219, 223, 248, 333, 336, 353
Leuchtenburg, William, 403
Lewandowska, Sister M. Theodorette, 356n
Lewis, C. S., 353
Lewis, Sinclair, 33–34, 105, 166
Lewis, Wyndham, 119n, 172–73, 187
Liberalism, 327, 328–30, 332, 334n, 341, 352, 358, 372, 381; antithesis between conservatism and, 329–30; decay of, 336; Democratic Party, 333–34
Liberal Party (Great Britain), 215–16
Liberal Party (New York), 337n
Liberal Tradition in America, The (Hartz), 328
Life (magazine), 53, 190, 247–48, 351
Life expectancy, 8, 18, 174
Life of Ezra Pound, The (Stock), 366n
"Lifestyle," 80
Life-style of 1960s, 192
Lilburne, John, 183–84
Lilienfeld, Robert, 147n
Lincoln, Abraham, 74, 144, 145, 156n, 212, 256, 328, 346
Lindbergh, Anne Morrow, 333
Lindbergh, Charles A., 48–49, 76, 122, 333, 335
Lindsay, Vachel, 295, 314, 326, 344
Lingeman, Richard, 169
Lippmann, Walter, 241n, 306
Lipset, Seymour Martin, 335n, 339n
Little Women (Alcott), 180
Lloyd George, David, 32, 216, 220
Lodge, Henry Cabot, 20, 150
Lolita (Nabokov), 363n
London, Jack, 372, 372n
London *Times Literary Supplement,* 393
Long, Huey, 42, 333
Los Angeles Electric Tramway Company, 114n
Lowell, Abbott Lawrence, 151
Luce, Clare Boothe, 247n
Luce, Henry, 53, 105, 213n, 247n
Luciano, Charles "Lucky," 253n
Lukacs, John, 262n, 264n, 311n, 356n
Lumumba, Patrice, 253
Lutheran Church, 131n, 344
Lynd, Robert S. and Helen, 104
Lyndon B. Johnson Library, 258

MacArthur, General Douglas, 50, 53, 55, 62, 119, 237, 242, 246
Macaulay, Thomas B., 261
McCamy, James L., 374n
McCarten, John, 350
McCarthy, Joseph R., 63–64, 143, 182, 245, 245n, 248, 280, 311, 328, 329, 333, 334, 350, 351, 354, 362n
McCarthy, Mary, 120n
McCormick, Cyrus, 325
McCullough, David, 403
Macdonald, Dwight, 310n
McGinley, Phyllis, 170
Machine politics, 265
Mackenzie (journalist), 94
McKinley, William, 20, 136n, 277
McLuhan, Marshall, 189, 315
McNamara, Robert S., 393–94
Madariaga, Salvador de, 187
Madison, James, 369
Maeztu, Ramiro de, 206n
Mahan, Albert Thayer, 210
Mailer, Norman, 72, 138, 154n
Maine (battleship), 213
Maisel, Albert Q., 176
Maitland, Frederic, 265n
Malin, James C., 85
Managerial Revolution, The (Burnham), 374–75
Manchuria, 45, 62
Manifest destiny, 212. *See also* Imperialism
Mann, Thomas, 37
Man Nobody Knows, The (Barton), 151, 347

Mao Tse-tung, 119, 244
Marriage rate, 59, 66, 80, 174, 174n, 189
Marshall, George, 237, 278
Marshall Plan, 60, 67, 241, 242
Marx, Groucho, 147n
Marx, Karl, 9, 18, 26, 69, 137, 329, 332, 380
Marxism, 165, 308, 309, 332, 372, 381, 398; intellectuals, 304, 308–10
Masters and Johnson, 176–77n
Materialism and material development, 10, 87, 91–122, 177, 191, 227n, 289, 290, 345, 349, 358, 368, 380; advance in (1895–1955), 160; automobile, 101–11, 112–13, 114, 117, 121; "better off" concept, 91; change in the 1890s, 92–93; decline in, 8; Depression of 1930s, 98–100, 106–7; home ownership, 115–16; inflation of society, 95–98, 98n, 103, 114, 116–17; influence of, 118–22; "making money," 92; overall decline, 111–18; production of consumption, 95, 100, 115–16, 121; urbanization, 96. *See also* Bourgeois interlude
Mather, Cotton, 174
Matin, Le (newspaper), 184
Matthews, Rev. Shailer, 359
Mattingly, Garrett, 398
Max, Peter, 183
Maxwell, Elsa, 53, 53n
May, Henry F., 25, 222, 222n, 305, 322n, 397, 403
Mayer, Louis B., 152
Mead, Margaret, 177
Mechanical Bride, The (McLuhan), 315
"Mechanization and Standardization of American Life, The" (Mueller-Freienfels), 138
Mein Kampf (Hitler), 143n, 338
Mellon, Andrew, 166
Melville, Herman, 16, 166
Mencken, H. L., 37, 146, 168–69, 228, 306, 335, 389, 397
Merchant Marine (American), 19
Merrill Lynch, Pierce, Fenner, and Smith, 324
Metternich, Prince Klemens von, 32
Mexico, 120, 132, 154, 161, 224; illegal aliens, 125, 155
Meyner, Governor Robert B., 264
Michener, James, 145
Michigan State University, 301
Middle Ages, 159, 162, 183, 185, 187, 189, 190, 265, 279, 285, 307, 365, 390, 391
Middletown (Lynds), 104, 169
Midway, Battle of, 51
Mill, John Stuart, 25
Milner, Alfred, 209
Milton, John, 358–59
Missile Gap, 393
Missionaries, 36, 213n
Missouri (battleship), 55
Mrs. Bridge (Connell), 164n, 229–30, 230n
Mitford, Nancy, 119
Modern Age (publication), 142n
Modernity, cult of, 38
Molotov, Vyacheslav M., 257
Monroe, James, 203
Montaigne, Michel de, 388
Montgomery, Robert, 279
Moral Majority, 357, 397
Morgan, J. P., 114
Morison, Samuel Eliot, 150–51n, 352
Morley, Felix, 142, 142n
Morley, John, 205
Mormons, 175, 175n
Morrow, Dwight, 98n
Morse, Samuel F. B., 325
Mother's Day, 173, 173n
Motion picture industry, 152–53
Motor (publication), 106n
Moynihan, Daniel P., 82n
Mueller-Freienfels, Richard, 138
Multinational corporations, 121
Municipal corruption, 18
Murphy, George, 279
Murphy, Father John L., 351
Murrow, Edward R., 336
Music, 323–24. *See also* Jazz
Mussolini, Benito, 47, 52, 106, 231, 232, 234, 257, 275, 333, 370
My Ántonia (Cather), 142

Nabokov, Vladimir, 363n
Nagasaki, atomic bombing of, 55
Napoleon I, 41, 45, 117, 202, 263, 282
Napoleon III, 287
Nation, Carry, 194
Nation, The (magazine), 296, 306, 313
National Abortional Rights, 142n
National Academy of Broadcasting, 142
National Association of Manufacturers, 318n
National Educational Association, 295
Nationalism, 20–21, 24, 35, 42, 55, 58, 60, 67–68, 142–44, 143n, 197, 210, 216, 226, 296, 308, 329, 331, 333, 334, 338
National Review (magazine), 334, 337, 339, 340n, 353
National Women's Political Caucus, 142n
National Wrecking Company, 142
Nava, Julian, 156n
Nazi Party, 40, 58, 60, 143n, 240, 366
Negroes. *See* Blacks
Netherlands, 49, 234
Neutrality Act, 44, 234
New American Review, The, 147n
New Deal, 41, 42, 49, 58, 60, 73, 76, 245, 284, 334, 373–74
New Grub Street (Gissing), 304
New Inflation, The (Slawson), 381, 381n, 383
New Masses, The (publication), 308
New Republic, The (magazine), 82n, 104, 165n, 221, 265, 306, 313
Newsmagazines, 269–70, 313–14
Newspapers, 189–90, 296; advertisements, 315; popular democracy and, 267, 269–70
Newsweek (magazine), 314

New Yorker, The (magazine), 168, 313, 350
New York *Herald,* 315–16
New York Review of Books, The, 312
New York *Times,* 54n, 104, 115n, 189, 204, 247–48, 270, 283, 318, 335n, 336, 336n, 366n, 379n, 383, 394
New Zealand, 105n, 139, 216
Nicaragua, 36, 155, 227
Nichols, Mike, 183
Nicolson, Harold, 163, 175, 181, 235
Nietzsche, Friedrich, 25
1945: Year Zero (Lukacs), 311n
Nixon, Richard, 31, 68, 76–78, 81, 83, 156, 157, 233, 244, 244n, 246, 252, 334n, 337, 385; China visit, 78, 79; popular democracy and, 258, 276, 277, 280, 281–82, 282n, 283, 287n; resignation of, 277, 281; slogan of, 254
Noble, Professor David, 372–73
Nock, Albert Jay, 370
North Atlantic Alliance, 60
North Atlantic Treaty Organization (NATO), 61, 241, 252, 279
North Korea, 244, 244n
North Vietnam, 75, 76, 244n
Notestein, Frank, 318n
Notes Towards the Definition of Culture (Eliot), 299
Notre Dame University, 143, 182
Novak, Kim, 153n
Novak, Michael, 340n
Nuclear energy, 318n
Nuclear power industry, 66

O'Connell, Archbishop Dennis, 349–50
O'Connor, Charles, 172
O'Connor, Flannery, 311, 312, 346, 358
Office of War Information, 302
Oil, 110, 116, 121, 318n, 382
Okies, 107
Oklahoma (battleship), 49n
O'Konski, Alvin, 138
"Old America" (Brooks), 193
Olney, Richard, 204
One World (Willkie), 52
Open Door policy, 44
Organization Man, The (Whyte), 369, 389
Oriental Exclusion Act, 15
Origins of Totalitarianism, The (Arendt), 318n
Orlando, Vittorio Emanuele, 32
Ormandy, Eugene, 140
Ortega y Gasset, José, 7, 199, 340, 370, 371, 372
Orwell, George, 192, 230n, 246n, 311, 318, 338
Oxford History of the American People (Morison), 352

Pacifism, 221, 336
Paine, Thomas, 329, 340
Palestine, 144, 240
Palmerston, Lord, 254n
Panama Canal, 25
Panama Canal Zone, 20
Pan American Airways, 105
Panic of 1907, 96
Panikkar, L. M., 231n
Paris Peace Conference, 31–32
Parkinson, C. Northcote, 375
Parkinson's Law, 375
Parrington, Vernon, 398
Pascal, Blaise, 56
Passage to India, A (Forster), 230n
Passing of the Modern Age, The (Lukacs), 385n
Patton, General George, 107, 358
Paul VI, Pope, 353
Peace Ship (World War I), 28, 221
Pearl Harbor, 50, 51; bombing of, 235, 237; warships sunk at, 49n
Pearl Harbor Day, 55
Péguy, Charles, 319
Pennsylvania Turnpike, 106
Penrose, Boies, 139n, 262, 384
Pepsi-Cola, 120–21
Perón, Juan, 275, 334
Perry, Bliss, 150
Perry, Commodore Matthew C., 55
Philadelphia 1900–1950: Patricians and Philistines (Lukacs), 262n, 356n, 390n
Philippines, 44, 50, 93, 154, 205
Phillips, Wendell, 328
Pierce, Franklin, 258
Pinchot, Gifford, 373
Pius XII, Pope, 353
Plato, 318
Plato's American Republic (Woodruff), 112n
Plattsburg training encampment, 28
Playboy (magazine), 72, 80, 340
Pledge of allegiance, 35
Podhoretz, Norman, 138, 335n
Poe, Edgar Allan, 16, 166
Pokrovski, Mikhail, 398
Poland, 63, 126, 140, 287n; anti-Russian rising (1956), 250; invasion of (1939), 47
Polish-Americans, 144n
"Polish Immigrant in Philadelphia Before 1914, The" (Lewandowska), 356n
Political beliefs, historical development, 327–41
Political Man (Lipset), 339n
Pollock, Jackson, 323
Pollsters, 270–73, 282, 283
Pollution, 10
Popular democracy, degeneration and, 256–88; elective monarchy, 260, 274–88; eligible voters, 259–60, 275; machine politics, 265; meaning of, 256–60; newsmagazines, 269–70; newspapers, 267, 269–70; pollsters, 270–73, 282, 283; popularity contests, 261–66; public opinion, 263–65, 263n, 271, 272n, 274, 286; television, 265, 269, 270, 280–81
Popular Mechanics (magazine), 313
Popular music, 323–24
Populism, 18–19, 25, 32, 35, 42, 49, 92, 166, 181, 182, 237, 244, 245, 262–63, 276, 295, 297, 301,

326, 334, 344, 397; divorce from progressivism, 39; medieval elements, 184
Pornography, 72–73, 80, 301, 341
Porter, Cole, 163
Portnoy's Complaint (Roth), 154n
Portugal, 148
Potsdam Conference, 55
Pound, Ezra, 103n, 317, 339, 366n
Poverty, 38, 81
Power House, The (Buchan), 304
Practical Magazine of Efficient Management, The, 347
Pravda (newspaper), 237
Preminger, Otto, 183
Preppy Handbook, 154n
Present at the Creation (Acheson), 241
Prince of Wales (battleship), 235
Princeton University, 229
Production of consumption: material development and, 95, 100, 115–16, 121; in 1950s, 64–68
Profiles in Courage (Kennedy), 359
Progressive Mind, The: 1890–1917 (Noble), 372–73n
Progressive Party, 24
Progressivism, 22, 24–25, 28, 32, 39, 42n, 44, 49, 92, 174, 224, 226, 262–63, 265, 268, 295, 305, 306, 329, 342, 345, 372, 384, 397, 398, 402
"Progress of Culture, The" (Emerson), 294
Prohibition, 38, 41, 194–95, 228
Protestantism, 183, 207, 343, 344, 348, 349, 351, 355, 356
Proust, Marcel, 167
Psychohistory, 399
Psychology Today (magazine), 313
Public Broadcasting System (PBS), 120
Public opinion: American democracy and, 263–65, 263n, 271, 272n, 274, 286; pollsters and, 271. *See also* Popular democracy
Public transportation, 113–14, 365, 365–66n
Puddinhead Wilson (Twain), 166
Puerto Rico, 203, 204
Pullman, George M., 325
Puritanism, 92, 174, 180, 183, 186, 187, 291, 345, 353, 358, 359, 366, 371

Quakers, 17, 150, 369n
Quantification, 399
Quota system, 154

Race riots, 74, 85
Radicalism, 33, 173, 307, 327, 328, 333
Radio, 268; talk shows, 362–63
Ragtime (motion picture), 141n
Rahv, Philip, 310, 331
Railroads, 101, 104, 113, 384
Rainbow 5 (World War II), 238
Reader's Digest, 176
Reagan, Ronald, 79, 80, 82–83, 84, 145, 152, 156, 156n, 157, 188, 223, 254, 329, 335, 340, 341n, 383, 394; popular democracy and, 258, 277, 282, 283–85, 284n, 287n
Real estate prices, 172, 172n
Recessional (Kipling), 208
Red scares, 61, 143, 311
Reece, Carroll, 336
Reece Committee, 336
Reeve, Henry, 215
Religion and religious beliefs, 342–59; decline in 1960s, 356–57; immigrants and, 343–44, 349. *See also* names of religions
Remington, Frederic, 186
Renaissance, 168, 183, 287–88, 299
Reporter, The (magazine), 269–70, 270n
Repplier, Agnes, 97, 188, 194
Republican National Committee, 58n
Republican Party, 19, 20, 23, 31, 35, 44, 58, 61, 62, 64, 65, 78, 83, 111, 139n, 182, 242, 247, 296, 312, 328, 329, 335, 384; conservatism, 68, 337, 337n
Revolt of the Masses (Ortega y Gasset), 199, 340, 372
Revolution of 1848, 389
Reynaud, Paul, 107
Rickover, Admiral Hyman, 140
Rise of David Levinsky, The (Cahan), 142
Riverside Church (New York City), 345
RN: the Memoirs of Richard Nixon, 282n
Robinson, James Harvey, 7, 396–97
Rockefeller, John D., 112
Rockefeller, John D., Jr., 345
Rockefeller, Nelson, 252, 393
Rockefeller family, 56, 242, 276
Rockwell, Norman, 365
Rodgers, Richard, 145
Roman Catholic Church, 35, 69–70, 127, 131, 184, 209–10, 257, 334, 338, 343, 344–45, 347, 348–56, 357–58
Roman law, 180
Rooney, Mickey, 106
Roosevelt, Eleanor, 188, 223, 240, 276
Roosevelt, Franklin D., 41, 42–50, 56, 59, 61, 62, 69–70, 107, 124, 144n, 223, 226, 232, 244, 302, 334, 335, 349, 369, 373–74; attempted assassination of, 136n; death of, 54, 238; foreign policy, 43–50, 335n; Lend-Lease program, 48, 60; popular democracy and, 258, 268, 270, 275–76, 279, 284n; "quarantine" speech (1937), 46–47; Teheran Conference, 52; World War II, 46, 50–53, 233–38, 240, 253n; Yalta Conference, 53, 54–55, 57, 244n
Roosevelt, Theodore, 21–23, 24, 28, 29, 45, 135–36, 179n, 204, 210, 210n, 211, 214, 224, 370; popular democracy and, 256, 257–58, 268, 275, 276, 277, 278
Root, Elihu, 29
Rosebery, Lord, 215
Rostow, Eugene, 394
Roth, Philip, 154n
Rothko, Mark, 323
Rough Riders, 204
Rousseau, Jean-Jacques, 291
Rumania, 126

Rusk, Dean, 74, 223, 253
Russia, 13, 29, 44, 45, 291n, 317, 330; emigration, 127, 131, intelligentsia, 304–5, 304n, 372n; World War I, 30, 219, 220, 226. *See also* Union of Soviet Socialist Republics (after 1917)
Russian Revolution, 29, 30, 31n, 389
Russian Struggle for Power, 1914–1917, The (Smith), 222n
Russo-Japanese War of 1904–5, 20, 45, 53

St. John's Polish College, 356n
Saki (Hector Hugh Munro), 217
Salisbury, Lord, 207n
Sandburg, Carl, 37, 326
Sanger, Margaret, 173
San Jose University, 283
Santayana, George, 8, 25, 136, 178, 230, 231, 254, 297–98, 312, 343, 346n, 359, 362n
Santo Domingo, U.S. intervention in (1916), 28n
Sargent, John Singer, 323
Sarnoff, David, 318n
Saturday Evening Post, The, 189–90, 297, 306, 365
Saturday Review, 53
Scandinavian-Americans, 32, 228
Schlafly, Phyllis, 335–36
Schlesinger, Arthur M., Jr., 56
Scopes trial, 38–39, 183, 184
Security Council (United Nations), 62
Segregation, 86
Selling of the President, 1968, The (McGinniss), 281
Seward, William H., 212, 213, 328
Sex education, 174–77
Shakers (religious sect), 175, 175n
Sheen, Bishop Fulton J., 351
Shine, Perishing Republic (Jeffers), 36
Shuttle, The (Burnett), 193–94, 210
Siegel, Benjamin "Bugsy," 57n
Silver, 116
Singapore, 50, 51, 231n, 240
Singer, Isaac M., 325
Sinn Fein, 226
Slavery, 84–85, 85n, 135, 327
Slavophilism, 330, 332, 335n
Slawson, W. David, 381, 381n, 383, 385
Slemp, C. Bascom, 269
Slovakia, 140
Smart Set, The (magazine), 168, 313
Smith, Adam, 380–81
Smith, C. Jay, 222n
Sneakers, wearing of, 80n
Snobs, 313n
Socialism, 33, 35, 42, 58, 68, 100, 197, 308, 329, 338, 372; capitalistic element (in U.S.A.), 41
Socialist Party, 308
Sokolsky, George, 245n
Some By-Products of Missions (Headland), 213–14n
Sons of Indians, 301
Sousa, John Philip, 20
South Africa, 216
South America, illegal aliens, 125
South Korea, 62
South Vietnam, 75, 76
Space program, 76
Spain, 102, 118, 148, 206, 207, 327
Spanish-American War, 19–20, 202, 203, 204, 210, 213
Speer, Albert, 326
Spellman, Francis Cardinal, 349
Spencer, John C., 264
Spengler, Oswald, 315, 375
Spiritualization of matter, 11–12
Split-mindedness, 318–19, 344, 368
Sputnik, 64
Stalin, Joseph, 45, 46, 52, 53, 57, 60, 61–63, 119, 144n, 219, 226, 231, 236, 240, 243, 245, 246, 247, 250, 257, 309, 309n, 331, 336
Stalingrad, Battle of, 51, 220n
Standard Oil of Ohio, 114
Stanford University, 224
"Star-Spangled Banner, The," 35
Star Wars (motion picture), 185
Statute of Westminster, 230–31
Stead, W. T., 93–94, 207–8, 210, 212
Stein, Gertrude, 315–16
Stephenson, George, 102
Stettinius, Edward R., 237
Stimson, Henry L., 45, 237
Stock, Noel, 366n
Stock-market crash of 1929, 36, 40
Story of Man, The (Coon), 347n
Strauss, Admiral Lewis, 318n
Strong, Josiah, 213
Strout, Cushing, 203n
Student Volunteers for Foreign Missions, 213n
Study of History, A (Toynbee), 199–200
Suburbs and suburbanization, 17, 113, 114, 161, 162, 172
Suez Canal, 65, 249–50
Suez War of 1956, 249–50, 334
Sullivan, Louis, 325
Sullivan brothers, 145
Sun Yat-sen, 119
Surrealism, 25
Swift, Jonathan, 338
Switzerland, 117, 118–19, 129

Taft, Robert A., 59, 246, 333, 338
Taft, William Howard, 24, 275
Talleyrand, Charles-Maurice de, 32
Tate, Allen, 311
Tattnall, Josiah, 209
Tawney, R. H., 374
Teamsters Union, 108
Technology, 10–11, 55
Teheran Conference, 52
Television, 66, 76, 80, 153n, 190, 315, 392, 395; education and, 294; popular democracy and, 268, 269, 270, 280–81

Teller, Edward, 200
"Tet" offensive (Vietnam War), 75
Thomas, Norman, 344
Time (magazine), 53, 189, 247, 248, 248n, 269, 314, 351
Titanic (liner), 218
To Build a Fire (London), 372
Tocqueville, Alexis de, 3–4, 7, 41, 43, 67, 68, 83–84, 95, 144, 147–48, 177, 183n, 193, 197, 198, 200, 215, 262n, 264, 274, 286, 287, 307n, 317, 327, 329, 340, 346n, 360, 380, 390, 390n, 400
Tolstoy, Leo, 25, 320
To the Finland Station (Wilson), 309n
Tower, John, 156n
Toynbee, Arnold, 199–200
Tracy, Benjamin F., 203
Trade balance, 117
Travels in Two Democracies (Wilson), 309n
Trente glorieuses, Les (Fourastié), 8
"Trickle-down" theory, 84
Triumph and Tragedy (Churchill), 235–36, 238, 247
Trollope, Anthony, 269
Trotsky, Leon, 310n
Trotskyists, 310n, 335n
Truants, The (Barrett), 310n
Truck drivers, 108–9n, 384
Truman, Harry S, 54, 55, 62, 136n, 244, 246; character of, 59–60; popular democracy and, 258, 259n, 279; reputation of, 259; speeches of, 259n
Truman Doctrine, 60, 241, 242
T-shirts, 313, 351n
Turkey, 60, 71, 129
Turner, Frederick Jackson, 22, 398
Twain, Mark, 120, 166, 314, 331
Twilight of Christianity, The (Barnes), 335n
Two-party system, 67

Ulster, 218. *See also* Ireland
Unconditional surrender, policy of, 31
Underground Grammarian, The (publication), 320n
Unemployment, 8, 40–41, 116, 383–84; Depression of 1930s, 43, 47
Union of Soviet Socialist Republics (Soviet Union), 4, 30, 42, 54, 56, 63, 65, 66, 67, 71, 78, 79, 84, 101, 105, 118, 126, 161, 227n, 243, 244n, 246n, 257, 276, 309–10, 311, 318, 320, 330, 331, 334, 335, 338, 349, 353, 372, 375, 394, 394n; automobilization, 212–22; deteriorating prestige of, 86–87; emigration, 124; Suez War proposal, 250; U.S. relations (1930s), 45–46; World War II, 46, 48, 51, 52–53, 55, 57, 60, 107, 220, 234, 236–37. *See also* Russia (before 1917)
Unitarians, 17
United Garment Workers of America, 128
United Nations, 28, 32, 53, 56, 62, 236, 242, 251
United States: bourgeois interlude, 159–200; degeneration of popular democracy, 256–88; democracy (historical background), 3–87; historical development (transformation of American thinking), 289–367; immigrants and immigration, 123–58; materialism and material development, 91–122; relationship with Great Britain, 201–55; reversal of Tocqueville, 59–87; second century, 3–58; transformation to bureaucratic society, 368–404. *See also* American democracy
U.S. Air Force Academy, 282
U.S. Army, 34, 54
U.S. Constitution, 5, 24, 81, 142, 194–95, 261, 372
U.S. Department of Health, Education, and Welfare, 392
U.S. Department of State, 63, 237, 240, 241, 272–73, 351, 375
U.S. Foreign Policy (Lippmann), 241n
U.S. Naval Air Corps, 51
U.S. Navy, 19, 20, 34, 51, 54, 203, 209
U.S. News and World Report, 182n, 241n
U.S. Supreme Court, 35, 73, 80, 86
United World Federalists, 143
University of California in Los Angeles, 301
University of Chicago, 151, 296–97, 359
University of Michigan, 301
University of Texas, 301
University of Wisconsin, 35
Updike, John, 72
Upper classes, 17, 21, 27, 113, 122, 166, 168, 192, 204, 209, 217, 228n, 229n, 238, 314; anti-American prejudices (in England), 227, 227n; education of, 293
Urban growth, 161–62, 163
Utah (battleship), 49n

Valentino, Rudolph, 153
Van Buren, Martin, 262, 262n, 267
Vanderbilt family, 276
Vanity Fair (magazine), 168, 313
Vatican, 353
Veblen, Thorstein, 115, 177
Venezuela dispute of 1895, 202, 213
Verbatim (publication), 320n
Vermeer, Jan, 322
Victoria, Queen, 201, 209, 389
Victorianism 16, 33, 39–40, 171, 194
Vidich, Arthur, 363
Viereck, Peter, 69
Vietnamese refugees, 124
Vietnam War, 74–75, 145, 192, 244n, 252, 253, 254, 301, 302, 336; opposition to, 75–76, 77
Villa, Francisco "Pancho," 120
Violence, 191
Virginian, The (Wister), 21, 22, 23, 134, 186, 283
Virgin Islands, 28n, 36n
Vodka, 86n
Volk and *völkisch*, 181
Volpe, John A., 138n
Voltaire, 114, 122

Wagner, Geoffrey, 302
Walker, James J., 361
Wallace, Henry A., 52, 59, 246
Wall Street Journal, The, 382–83, 383n
Waning of the Middle Ages, The (Huizinga), 187, 390
Ward, Artemus, 269
Ward, Geoffrey C., 269n
Warne, Frank Julian, 135
War of 1812, 202
Washington, George, 5, 6, 144, 204, 258
Washington Conference of 1922, 45, 232
Washington *Post,* 204, 270
WASP, 153
Watergate scandal, 78
Waugh, Evelyn, 119, 230, 253, 317
Wayne, John, 283
Weaver, Richard, 340
Webster, Daniel, 262, 262n
Webster, Noah, 146
Weimar Republic, 119
Weinberger, Caspar, 394
Weitz, John, 183
Wellington, Duke of, 75, 171, 389
Wells, H. G., 135, 135n
"We'll Walk in With Walker" (Berlin), 361
Wendell, Barrett, 150, 222n
West, Nathanael, 138
West Berlin, 61
West Germany, 67, 81, 117, 182; automobilization, 121n; parliamentary democracy, 101
Westmoreland, General William C., 75
Wharton, Edith, 164, 194
Whistler, James McNeill, 323
White, William Allen, 210
Whitehead, Alfred North, 299n
Whitehill, Walter Muir, 113n, 150, 299n
White House staff, 285, 285n
Whitman, Walt, 12n, 326
Whitney, Eli, 325
Whyte, William H., 369
Wilde, Oscar, 22
Wilder, Billy, 183
Wilhelm I, Kaiser, 47, 226
Williams, Talcott, 139n
Willkie, Wendell, 49, 52
Wilson, Charles E., 111
Wilson, Edmund, 165n, 309n, 374
Wilson (motion picture), 28
Wilson, Woodrow, 23, 24–25, 36n, 43, 54, 56, 295, 302, 328, 336, 346–47, 349, 372, 373; internationalism of, 29; Paris Peace Conference, 31–33; popular democracy and, 256, 259, 268, 275; reputation of, 28–29; on Russian Revolution, 31n; split-mindedness of, 224, 319; World War I, 223–26, 232, 305
Wilsonianism, 28, 29, 31, 45, 251
Wise Blood (O'Connor), 346
Wister, Owen, 21, 22, 23, 134, 185–86, 194
Witherspoon, John, 139
Wolfe, Tom, 339
Women, 18, 51, 119; employment of, 73; liberation movement of 1960s to 1970s, 195–96; life expectancy, 174; 1920 election vote, 267n; right to have an abortion, 81; rise in status of, 193–97
Women's Party, 175, 175n
Wood, Grant, 181, 183
Woodberry, George Edward, 222n
Woodruff, Douglas, 112n
Woodstock festival, 75
Woodward, C. Vann, 403
Woolworth Building (New York City), 325
World War I, 24, 26–29, 37, 44, 45, 51, 94, 97, 135, 160, 161, 171, 209, 211, 214, 217, 218–27, 230, 231, 237, 302, 350, 372; anti-Germanism, 181–82, 228; internationalism, 221; isolationism, 221–22, 225, 229; national sentiment of pride, 28; propaganda, 305–6; public opinion, 27–28; soldier-heroes, 145; stalemate, 219; turning point, 29–32
World War II, 26–27, 30, 31, 43, 48–53, 57, 58, 75, 85, 94, 95, 97, 101, 106, 152, 171, 233–38, 248, 256–57, 302, 333, 350, 369; anti-Germanism, 181–82; automobilization, 107; bombing of Pearl Harbor, 235, 237; food shortages and price controls, 51–52; isolationism, 233; Lend-Lease, 48, 60, 234; military expenditures, 64; personal income savings, 114n; Rainbow 5 plan, 238; Sicily landing, 253n; soldier-heroes, 145
Wright, Frank Lloyd, 188, 325–26
Wurlitzer era, 23

Yale University, 229, 298, 301, 303, 337n, 394
Yalta Conference, 53, 54–55, 57, 244n
Yeats, John Butler, 23n
Yiddish language, 126, 136n, 181
York, Sergeant Alvin, 145
Younger, Irving, 391
Young Europe, The (Ferrero), 206n
Young Men's Christian Association, 29

Zangwill, Israel, 21
Zhukov, Marshal Georgi, 63
Zionism, 222n, 357
Zola, Émile, 25
Zweig, Stefan, 379